Baseball Prospectus Futures Guide 2017

The top prospects for every MLB team and more

by The Baseball Prospectus Team of Experts

Martin Alonso, Mark Barry, David Brown, Lance Brozdowski, Tim Finnegan, Aaron Gleeman, Scooter Hotz, Joshua Howsam, Wilson Karaman, Domenic Lanza, Jesse Lippin-Foster, Eric Garcia McKinley, Rob McQuown, Andrew Mearns, Harry Pavlidis, Dave Pease, Stephen Reichert, Eric Roseberry, Andrew Salzman, Bret Sayre, Jarrett Seidler, Gideon Turk, Collin Whitchurch, Jared Wyllys, and Austin Yamada

Front Cover Photo: J.P. Crawford, by Scott Martin Photography

Back Cover Photos: Dansby Swanson & Yoan Moncada by Bill Mitchell; Andrew Benintendi by Scott Martin Photography

Headshots courtesy milb.com

Cover Design: Karen Siatras

Design and layout: Bryan Davidson,
Misty Horten, and Colleen Cunningham

TABLE OF CONTENTS

ARIZONA DIAMONDBACKS

The State of the System: *"I shivered in those solitudes when I heard the voice of the saltin the desert"*
— Pablo Neruda, "Ode to Salt"

THE TOP TEN

1. LHP Anthony Banda	6. RHP Brad Keller
2. SS/2B Domingo Leyba	7. RHP Taylor Clarke
3. 3B/SS Dawel Lugo	8. LHP Alex Young
4. OF Anfernee Grier	9. OF Victor Reyes
5. SS Jasrado Chisholm	10. RHP Jon Duplantier

The Big Question: Where Has All The Talent Gone?

Headlined by a trio of promising starters and flanked by high-floor position players, the 2015 Diamondbacks had one of the best farm systems in baseball. Arizona had talent in both the upper and lower levels, and three players—Archie Bradley, Braden Shipley, and Aaron Blair—in the first half of our top 101 prospect list. With the first pick of the upcoming draft on the horizon, and all the bonus pool money that comes with it, the D-Backs seemed destined to add even more talent to their already healthy farm, one that we ranked as the seventh best in all of baseball.

Fast forward two years, and the Diamondbacks now have one of the worst systems in the league. There are precious few starting pitchers who throw hard, no power hitters with a chance to anchor the middle of a lineup, and no big-money teenagers steadily translating stickball protoplasm into baseball stardom. You can find a few crafty lefties and future utility players, and if you squint, even a couple of guys with big tools and miles of developmental work ahead.

Ultimately though, Arizona's system is almost entirely devoid of impact talent. Very few players in the upper levels have a chance to be Role 50 types, much less future stars, and after a spate of free agent signings, poor trades, and almost criminal mismanagement of Latin American money, the low minors are nearly as barren. Last year, Arizona's minor league rosters were often populated with players who would likely have been cast aside by other organizations. That trend will continue in 2017.

The unraveling of Arizona's once-promising farm system sprang from several directions, some preventable, some not. What is clear is that the lack of young talent stems from an organization-wide failure that will hamstring the Diamondbacks for years to come. To briefly recap, the D-Backs were hurt by…

Graduations

The most innocuous development was that many of the players from the 2015 list are now in the big leagues. Brandon Drury and Jake Lamb are both developmental wins. They could both be strong offensive contributors who could help the D-Backs lineup throughout the rest of the decade. Bradley and Shipley have also exhausted their prospect eligibility, though with less major league success.

Trades

A series of deals designed to help Arizona win now have instead devastated Arizona's minor league depth without translating into big league success. The Diamondbacks shipped Dansby Swanson, the top pick in the 2015 draft, to Atlanta in a trade for Shelby Miller. Many evaluators would have considered a straight-up Swanson-for-Miller swap unwise; adding Blair to the outgoing package was foolish. It was the second time in less than a year that the Braves had picked Arizona's pocket: Earlier in the year, the D-Backs traded Touki Toussaint, their fourth-best prospect, to Atlanta for salary relief and Phil Gosselin. Arizona also dealt its top remaining positional farmhand, Isan Diaz, to the Brewers last January, only to see him blossom in Milwaukee.

To be fair, the D-Backs have added a few added a few players through trades, most notably Jack Reinheimer and Dawel Lugo. Unfortunately, this is a case where the subtractions were much more damaging than the additions were beneficial.

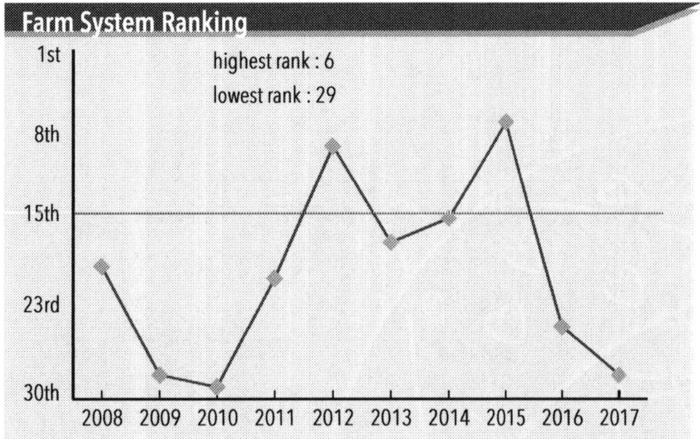

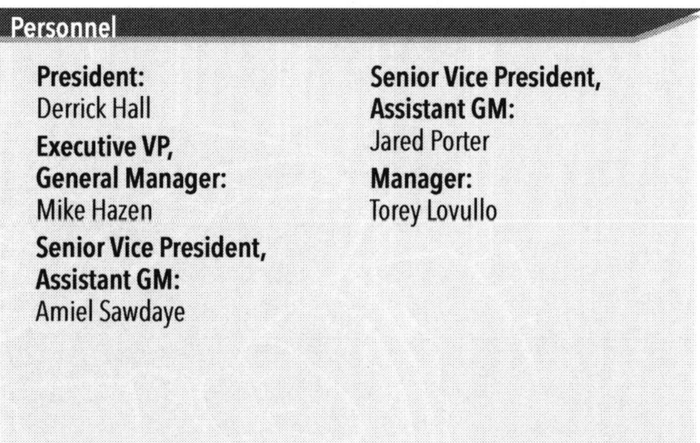

Personnel

President:
Derrick Hall

Executive VP, General Manager:
Mike Hazen

Senior Vice President, Assistant GM:
Amiel Sawdaye

Senior Vice President, Assistant GM:
Jared Porter

Manager:
Torey Lovullo

Draft

Conventional wisdom suggests that a No. 1 overall pick can alter a franchise's long-term trajectory, and the principle perniciously applies to Arizona in Swanson's case. Deprived of Swanson and a first-round pick last season (thanks to the Zack Greinke signing), the Diamondbacks haven't been able to add impact talent to their farm system through the draft. Last year's supplemental round pick, Anfernee Grier, is a project. Second-rounder Andrew Yerzy was picked ahead of where most evaluators had him. Third-rounder Jon Duplantier is an upside gamble, but he's already had arm trouble and a heavy college workload. It's still early, but last year's draft looks like a punt.

International Spending

The international market is a complex arena and one that Arizona's inexperienced front office was unprepared to navigate. The Diamondbacks blew $8 million on mercurial right-hander Yoan Lopez in 2013, which was seen as a massive overpay before his stuff went backward. Even worse, Arizona's brass reportedly didn't realize that the size of Lopez's bonus precluded them from spending in Latin America over the next two seasons. Needless to say, Arizona hasn't injected much talent from this pipeline since, though adding Jasrado Chisholm from the Bahamas was a nice bit of scouting.

Development

It's unfair to attribute every stagnant prospect to organizational ineptitude; sometimes players just don't get better. Nonetheless, the story isn't much happier on the developmental front. Most of the non-big-league-ready prospects from the 2015 list have either regressed or failed to improve significantly. Reliever Jimmie Sherfy still oscillates between unhittable and uncatchable. Wei-Chieh Huang was sitting in the low-to-mid 80s last summer. Marcus Wilson was always going to be a slow burn, but he hasn't hit for any power in the two and a half years he's been in the system. Gabby Guerrero, one the prizes in the Mark Trumbo trade, was deemed surplus to requirements 16 months after the deal. Bradley and Shipley are both young and have flashed the ability that made them such valuable commodities in Arizona, but neither has approached their ceiling either.

This is not to ignore Arizona's developmental successes, like Lamb, Drury, or Jake Barrett: The developmental machine hasn't been entirely out of order. It's impossible to look at the state of the farm, however, without noting that the lower minors haven't born much fruit lately.

Diamondbacks fans looking for some solace should be comforted by the idea that the farm system will probably be better twelve months from now. With a new front office, and another high draft pick, the D-Backs should get a much-needed injection of talent a few months from now. It's also plausible that a guys like Duplantier or Chisholm takes a step forward. The bottom line is, as the White Sox demonstrated this winter, that it doesn't take a long time to turn a farm system around. Given Arizona's relative standing around the league, that's a good thing.

—Brendan Gawlowski

1. Anthony Banda, LHP

DOB: 08/10/1993

Height/Weight: 6'2" 190 lbs.

Bats/Throws: L/L

Drafted/Acquired: Drafted in the 10th round of the 2012 MLB Draft by Milwaukee; San Jacinto College (Pasadena, TX); signed for $125,000; traded to Arizona from Milwaukee for Gerardo Parra

Previous Ranking(s): #10 (Org.)2016

2016 Stats: 2.12 ERA, 1.78 DRA, 76.1 IP, 70 H, 28 BB, 84 K in 13 games at Double-A Mobile, 3.67 ERA, 3.41 DRA, 73.2 IP, 73 H, 27 BB, 68 K in 13 games at Triple-A Reno

The Role: OFP 55—A healthy Patrick Corbin, maybe?
Likely 45—A healthy Brian Anderson

YEAR	TEAM	LVL	AGE	W	L	SV	G	GS	IP	H	HR	BB/9	K/9	K	GB%	BABIP	WHIP	ERA	FIP	DRA	VORP	WARP	cFIP	MPH
2014	WIS	A	20	6	6	2	20	14	83^{2}	84	4	4.1	8.9	83	50%	.339	1.46	3.66	3.52	3.86	14.20	1.5	94	
2014	SBN	A	20	3	0	0	6	6	35	32	2	1.8	8.7	34	45%	.303	1.11	1.54	2.97	4.51	3.40	0.4	94	
2015	VIS	A+	21	8	8	0	28	27	151^{2}	150	8	2.3	9.0	152	48%	.336	1.25	3.32	3.31	2.62	41.40	4.5	86	
2016	MOB	AA	22	6	2	0	13	13	76^{1}	70	4	3.3	9.9	84	50%	.317	1.28	2.12	2.94	1.78	28.10	3.0	75	
2016	RNO	AAA	22	4	4	0	13	13	73^{2}	73	6	3.3	8.3	68	46%	.313	1.36	3.67	4.11	3.41	15.80	1.6	86	
2017	*ARI*	*MLB*	*23*	*1*	*1*	*0*	*14*	*0*	*14*	*14*	*1*	*3.9*	*7.9*	*13*	*42%*	*.303*	*1.47*	*4.15*	*3.72*	*4.28*	*1.1*	*0.1*	*98*	
2018	*ARI*	*MLB*	*24*	*3*	*1*	*0*	*49*	*0*	*52^{1}*	*43*	*5*	*4.9*	*10.5*	*61*	*42%*	*.322*	*1.37*	*3.93*	*4.08*	*4.35*	*4.4*	*0.5*	*97*	

Breakout: 27% Improve: 39% Collapse: 16% Attrition: 41% MLB: 59% *Comparables: Wily Peralta, Matt Magill, Nick Tropeano*

The Good: Hey guys, do you want to hear about another potential mid-rotation starter? Wait, where are you going? Yes there have been a lot of them so far—though they usually don't sit at number one on a team's prospect list—but Banda is...uh...well, like most of them. He works off a plus fastball that sits in the mid-90s after a velocity bump in 2016. The pitch also showed more arm-side life than in the past. He also features a low-80s curve that...anyone...that's right! It flashes plus with good depth. Banda has a starter's frame and delivery and a clean arm action. There's no physical concerns about his ability to start...

The Bad: ...but get this: he needs to improve both his changeup and command. Banda lacks feel for the cambio and it's not much more than a show-me offering at present—and a "show-me the seats" offering when he hangs it. The control outpaces the command at present and the overall arsenal isn't good enough to make much of an impact with merely average command.

The Irrelevant: Unsurprisingly, Randy Johnson has six of the 10 best ERA+ seasons by a left-handed pitcher in Diamondbacks history. Slightly more surprising is the only other name with multiple entries in the top ten: Omar Daal.

The Risks:I think someone once wrote that there is no such thing as a mid-rotation starter. The command and change will get there, or they won't, but the fastball is good enough he will get chances to start. Unless he gets hurt, which he might, because he's a pitcher.

Major league ETA: 2017, as needed

Ben Carsley's Fantasy Take: Yikes. There's nothing inherently wrong with Banda, but he's not a top 100 name and we're leading off the article with him, so, yeah ... this isn't going to be a terribly useful piece of internet content for dynasty league owners. Banda might have value as a decent all-around backend starter once he's firmly entrenched in the rotation, but frankly, you can often find that type of value on the waiver wire. Take the plunge if your league rosters 200 prospects because of Banda's proximity, but otherwise, yawn.

2. Domingo Leyba, SS/2B

DOB: 9/11/1995

Height/Weight: 5'11" 160 lbs.

Bats/Throws: S/R

Drafted/Acquired: Signed in July 2012 out of the Dominican Republic for $400,000; traded to Arizona from Detroit in three team trade

Previous Ranking(s): N/A

2016 Stats: .294/.346/.426, 6 HR, 5 SB in 86 games at High-A Visalia, .301/.374/.436, 4 HR, 4 SB in 44 games at Double-A Mobile

The Role: OFP 50—Average regular at second
Likely 45—Second-division starter or quality utility infielder

YEAR	TEAM	LVL	AGE	PA	R	2B	3B	HR	RBI	BB	K	SB	CS	AVG/OBP/SLG	TAv	VORP	BABIP	BRR	FRAA	WARP
2014	ONE	A-	18	154	20	11	1	1	17	8	17	1	2	.264/.303/.375	.252	4.8	.294	1.9	2B(35): -5.3, SS(3): -0.6	-0.1
2014	WMI	A	18	124	20	7	0	1	7	6	13	1	2	.397/.431/.483	.346	16.8	.441	1.0	SS(17): 0.4, 2B(13): 2.1	2.0
2015	VIS	A+	19	562	60	21	5	2	43	26	90	10	6	.237/.277/.309	.239	14.2	.278	4.2	SS(123): 0.5	1.6
2016	VIS	A+	20	374	48	25	1	6	40	29	62	5	1	.294/.346/.426	.285	26.5	.341	2.1	SS(66): -3.0, 2B(17): -1.9	2.2
2016	MOB	AA	20	174	21	7	1	4	20	17	22	4	2	.301/.374/.436	.302	14.7	.331	0.8	SS(39): -2.8, 2B(5): 0.1	1.3
2017	*ARI*	*MLB*	*21*	*250*	*27*	*12*	*1*	*5*	*24*	*14*	*51*	*1*	*1*	*.253/.296/.385*	*.221*	*0.9*	*.298*	*-0.2*	*SS -1, 2B -0*	*0.0*
2018	*ARI*	*MLB*	*22*	*347*	*38*	*18*	*2*	*8*	*38*	*18*	*68*	*2*	*1*	*.261/.302/.401*	*.244*	*5.7*	*.303*	*-0.4*	*SS -1, 2B -1*	*0.4*

Breakout: 4% Improve: 9% Collapse: 2% Attrition: 6% MLB: 14% *Comparables: Tyler Pastornicky, Gavin Cecchini, Jose Pirela*

The Good: Leyba's compact stroke and strong hand-eye coordination combine to generate quality bat-to-ball skills that are advanced for a twenty-one-year-old, having already proven capable of translating against Double-A pitching. He demonstrated significant gains with his approach in a second tour of the California League to start the year, exhibiting greater selectivity and staying inside the strike zone more consistently. There's a potentially above-average hit tool at maturity if last year's gains continue to hold against advanced pitching. He's a technically sound defender up the middle, with solid hands and fundamentals that allow him to convert grounders he can reach into outs. The arm can scrape average from short, while playing to solid-average on the other side of the bag.

The Bad: His body is already pretty maxed out, and there's some lower-half density that limits both his foot speed and range to fringe-average. He lacks the kind of explosiveness or fluidity in his lateral movements that an ideal shortstop possesses and fits more naturally at second. The swing is relatively flat, and he lacks for strength or leverage to drive pitches over the fence with much regularity. Coupled with the unremarkable run tool, his secondary offensive skills aren't particularly exciting.

The Irrelevant: The first man to sport a "Domingo" moniker in Major League Baseball was Adolfo Domingo de Guzman Luque, better known as "Dolf" Luque. "The Pride of Havana" made his debut for the Boston Braves in 1914, and went on to win 194 big-league games across a 20-year career en route to enshrinement in the Cincinnati Reds Hall of Fame in 1967.

The Risks: Leyba has made steady and impressive gains at the plate, while his instincts and feel on the dirt have kept him in the running for shortstop reps despite less than ideal physicality. While he lacks for a standout tool, his solid skill set on both sides of the ball makes him a higher-probability big-league contributor.

Major league ETA: 2018 —Wilson Karaman

Ben Carsley's Fantasy Take: If you've ever watched Joe Panik play and thought, "damn, I wish he had less power," Leyba is the prospect for you.

3. Dawel Lugo, 3B/SS

DOB: 12/31/1994

Height/Weight: 6'0" 190 lbs.

Bats/Throws: R/R

Drafted/Acquired: Signed July 2011 out of the Dominican Republic for $1.3 million; traded to Arizona from Toronto for Cliff Pennington

Previous Ranking(s): N/A

2016 Stats: .314/.348/.514, 13 HR, 2 SB in 79 games at High-A Visalia, .306/.322/.451, 4 HR, 1 SB in 48 games at Double-A Mobile

The Role: OFP 50—Borderline average regular
Likely 45—Second-division starter

YEAR	TEAM	LVL	AGE	PA	R	2B	3B	HR	RBI	BB	K	SB	CS	AVG/OBP/SLG	TAv	VORP	BABIP	BRR	FRAA	WARP
2014	LNS	A	19	498	40	17	2	4	53	18	72	3	3	.259/.286/.329	.224	-4.8	.296	-5.6	SS(110): -17.3	-2.3
2015	KNC	A	20	86	12	1	1	0	3	4	13	2	2	.333/.372/.370	.272	2.2	.397	-1.5	SS(14): -0.7, 2B(2): -0.4	0.1
2015	DUN	A+	20	276	16	9	2	2	21	9	49	1	3	.219/.258/.292	.207	-7.5	.262	-3.8	SS(67): 2.0	-0.6
2015	LNS	A	20	132	15	6	1	2	23	5	24	3	1	.336/.348/.451	.284	8.4	.386	0.1	SS(29): 2.0	1.1
2016	VIS	A+	21	333	61	14	5	13	42	15	41	2	1	.314/.348/.514	.303	28.6	.328	2.5	3B(60): -3.2, SS(14): 2.0	2.8
2016	MOB	AA	21	177	24	9	2	4	20	4	15	1	1	.306/.322/.451	.287	13.3	.318	2.7	3B(41): 4.6, SS(10): 0.4	2.0
2017	*ARI*	*MLB*	*22*	*250*	*23*	*11*	*2*	*7*	*29*	*6*	*53*	*0*	*0*	*.252/.274/.400*	*.218*	*-2.6*	*.294*	*-0.2*	*3B 2, SS -0*	*-0.1*
2018	*ARI*	*MLB*	*23*	*293*	*32*	*12*	*2*	*9*	*35*	*10*	*65*	*0*	*0*	*.250/.280/.407*	*.240*	*0.7*	*.294*	*-0.4*	*3B 3, SS 0*	*0.4*

Breakout: 1% Improve: 9% Collapse: 2% Attrition: 14% MLB: 18% *Comparables: Giovanny Urshela, Josh Harrison, Josh Vitters*

The Good: The stroke is quick and direct to the ball, with good early rhythm that puts him in position to adjust within swings and make consistent contact with pitches all around (and beyond) the zone. He has strong wrists and produces solid-average bat speed, ingredients that portend above-average raw power at his peak. A former shortstop, he moves well laterally and shows soft hands on receipt. The arm strength pushes plus at third, with throws that hold their plane from line to line.

The Bad: Lugo is a wildly aggressive hitter who has shown little in the way of development over the past year in refining his approach. He frequently chases pitches outside the zone, and his lack of selectivity threatens to deflate his game power against quality arms. The glove is okay, though not an asset at third, with range limitations keeping the defensive projection in check. He's a below-average runner already, and a thick, higher-maintenance frame means he'll have to work hard to keep his speed from declining further.

The Irrelevant: Lugo is the one and only known "Dawel" to have ever laced 'em up for a professional baseball team.

The Risks: There is ostensibly a path for Lugo to develop into something resembling an average regular if he can make some inroads with the approach to become a more patient hitter who draws out the majority of his power in games, but as a bat-first prospect with a fairly long track record of significant aggressiveness at this point it is a lower probability that he makes those necessary adjustments and reaches his ceiling.

Major league ETA: Late 2018/Early 2019 —Wilson Karaman

Ben Carsley's Fantasy Take: You know that scene in Interstellar where Matt Damon's Dr. Mann attempts to dock with the Endurance but he can't do it and everything blows up? Dr. Mann still had a better approach than Lugo. Yeah, that was a long way to go but reading this system makes me want to die.

4. Anfernee Grier, OF

DOB: 10/13/1995

Height/Weight: 6'1" 180 lbs.

Bats/Throws: R/R

Drafted/Acquired: Drafted 39th overall in 2016 MLB Draft, Auburn University (Auburn, AL); signed for $1.5 million

Previous Ranking(s): N/A

2016 Stats: .214/.267/.500, 1 HR, 0 SB in 4 games at short-season Missoula, .240/.278/.307, 1 HR, 9 SB in 20 games at short-season Hillsboro

The Role: OFP 50—Second-division outfielder
Likely 40—Bench outfielder

YEAR	TEAM	LVL	AGE	PA	R	2B	3B	HR	RBI	BB	K	SB	CS	AVG/OBP/SLG	TAv	VORP	BABIP	BRR	FRAA	WARP
2016	MSO	Rk	20	15	2	1	0	1	2	0	5	0	0	.214/.267/.500	.252	0.0	.250	0.0		
2016	YAK	A-	20	79	8	2	0	1	6	3	21	9	2	.240/.278/.307	.221	-2.8	.321	-0.6		
2017	*ARI*	*MLB*	*21*	*250*	*32*	*10*	*1*	*6*	*21*	*12*	*81*	*11*	*4*	*.208/.251/.342*	*.193*	*-9.7*	*.284*	*1.0*	*CF 0*	*-1.1*
2018	*ARI*	*MLB*	*22*	*223*	*23*	*10*	*1*	*6*	*24*	*11*	*72*	*10*	*4*	*.216/.261/.360*	*.216*	*-2.7*	*.294*	*1.3*	*CF 0*	*-0.3*

Breakout: 0% Improve: 0% Collapse: 0% Attrition: 0% MLB: 0% *Comparables: Destin Hood, Kyle Waldrop, Tyler Goeddel*

The Good: Grier always had tools to dream on during his time at Auburn, but he finally started putting them on the field his junior season. He's a plus runner with potentially average power in center field. That's a nice start. His above-average arm will play in right if he loses speed or if he struggles to refine his jumps and routes in the pros.

The Bad: It's going to be a long road to major-league contribution considering he is a college outfielder that went in the first 50 picks. He can sell out for power at times and get a little one-gear with his swing. A below-average hit tool might limit how much his power plays. His glove is carried by his premium athleticism at this point. Potential tweener profile.

The Irrelevant: Russell County High School has produced three major leaguers: Billy Moran and the Rasmus brothers.

The Risks: Grier has a limited amateur track record of getting his tools into games. He may not hit enough to get the power into games or be on base enough to have the speed be more than a useful weapon in the late innings.

Major league ETA: 2019

Ben Carsley's Fantasy Take: The power/speed combo makes Grier a potential top-200 name, but that's about as high as we can go until we see some of the tools translate to MiLB production. He's arguably the second-best dynasty prospect in this system. I wish I lived a fuller life.

5. Jasrado Chisholm, SS

DOB: 2/1/1998

Height/Weight: 5'11" 165 lbs.

Bats/Throws: L/R

Drafted/Acquired: Signed July 2015 out of the Bahamas for $200,000

Previous Ranking(s): N/A

2016 Stats: .281/.333/.446, 9 HR, 13 SB in 62 games at short-season Missoula

The Role: OFP 50—Glove-first everyday shortstop
Likely 40—Glove-first utility infielder

YEAR	TEAM	LVL	AGE	PA	R	2B	3B	HR	RBI	BB	K	SB	CS	AVG/OBP/SLG	TAv	VORP	BABIP	BRR	FRAA	WARP
2016	MSO	Rk	18	270	42	12	1	9	37	19	73	13	4	.281/.333/.446	.264	12.2	.363	1.0	SS(60): 2.8, 2B(1): -0.0	1.1
2017	*ARI*	*MLB*	*19*	*250*	*26*	*9*	*1*	*7*	*22*	*12*	*93*	*3*	*1*	*.196/.235/.327*	*.183*	*-8.3*	*.286*	*0.0*	*SS -0, 2B 0*	*-0.9*
2018	*ARI*	*MLB*	*20*	*328*	*35*	*12*	*2*	*10*	*36*	*18*	*117*	*5*	*2*	*.210/.255/.359*	*.214*	*-4.0*	*.299*	*0.2*	*SS 0, 2B 0*	*-0.5*

Breakout: 0% Improve: 4% Collapse: 1% Attrition: 5% MLB: 9% *Comparables: Raul Mondesi, Elvis Andrus, Nomar Mazara*

The Good: Chisholm is a potential plus glove at shortstop despite only average athletic tools. He makes hard contact when he makes contact and could grow into more power and better barrel control as he adds strength.

The Bad: Despite his power performance in the Pioneer League air, Chisholm's power plays more to gap, but the swing-and-miss potential might limit even that. He's very busy pre-swing and can struggle to control the bat. He's an aggressive hitter that will expand the zone even against short-season arms.

The Irrelevant: Six Bahamians have played in the major leagues, the most recent of which was Antoan Richardson, who got cups of coffee with the Yankees and Braves in 2011 and 2014.

The Risks: Hey, another good athlete that might not hit enough to be a regular in the majors. I guess betting on athleticism beats betting the farm—literally—on Shelby Miller.

Major league ETA: 2020

Ben Carsley's Fantasy Take: A glove-first everyday shortstop who's three-plus seasons away from the majors? Just cut the line and pick up Deven Marrero or something.

6. Brad Keller, RHP

DOB: 7/27/1995

Height/Weight: 6'5" 230 lbs.

Bats/Throws: R/R

Drafted/Acquired: Drafted in the eighth round in 2013 MLB Draft, Flowery Branch HS (Flowery Branch, GA); signed for $125,000

Previous Ranking(s): N/A

2016 Stats: 4.47 ERA, 3.22 DRA, 135 IP, 147 H, 26 BB, 99 K in 24 games at High-A Visalia

The Role: OFP 50—No. 4 Starter
Likely 40—No. 5 Starter/Swingman

YEAR	TEAM	LVL	AGE	W	L	SV	G	GS	IP	H	HR	BB/9	K/9	K	GB%	BABIP	WHIP	ERA	FIP	DRA	VORP	WARP	cFIP	MPH
2014	MSO	Rk	18	1	4	0	8	8	33^{2}	50	6	4.8	8.0	30	0%	.404	2.02	6.95	6.44	4.33			102	
2014	DIA	Rk	18	4	0	0	6	3	31^{1}	30	2	2.6	5.7	20	0%	.301	1.24	2.30	4.73	5.66			108	
2014	YAK	A-	18	1	0	0	1	1	6	1	0	1.5	12.0	8	73%	.091	0.33	0.00	1.65	2.57	1.90	0.2	81	
2015	KNC	A	19	8	9	0	26	25	142	128	3	2.3	6.9	109	58%	.293	1.16	2.60	3.13	3.19	32.00	3.4	92	
2016	VIS	A+	20	9	7	0	24	24	135	147	13	1.7	6.6	99	56%	.321	1.28	4.47	4.12	3.22	33.80	3.5	89	
2017	*ARI*	*MLB*	*21*	*7*	*8*	*0*	*21*	*21*	112^{1}	*140*	*16*	*3.4*	*4.6*	*57*	*48%*	*.337*	*1.63*	*5.26*	*5.21*	*5.80*	*-3.0*	*-0.3*	*138*	
2018	*ARI*	*MLB*	*22*	*5*	*8*	*0*	*20*	*20*	119^{1}	*126*	*18*	*4.6*	*7.3*	*97*	*48%*	*.327*	*1.56*	*5.28*	*5.45*	*5.82*	*-3.0*	*-0.3*	*137*	

Breakout: 7% Improve: 10% Collapse: 6% Attrition: 19% MLB: 23% *Comparables: Manny Banuelos, Michael Bowden, David Holmberg*

The Good: Keller has a good kind of big-donkey body, a hulking John Lackey frame that can wear innings for days. He manipulates a low-90s fastball with two-way action, controlling it effectively down in the zone to create copious amounts of rolled-over contact. He sells a firm change with quality arm speed, and while the pitch doesn't miss a ton of bats it does induce additional worm-burners on the regular. He made some strides with his slider this year as well. He doesn't beat himself with walks, and his mound intelligence and feel for managing a game allow him to compete for multiple runs through a lineup.

The Bad: The stuff has its limits, and he can't really claim a pitch that projects to miss bats consistently. While he made progress with the slider, he doesn't have a ton of natural feel for spinning the ball. The delivery lacks for fluidity and great athleticism, and his fine command in the zone lags behind his control, making for a sometimes-dangerously hittable combination.

The Irrelevant: As of this writing Keller has tweeted 17 times in the new year, and save for a retweet confirming the tragic passings of Yordano Ventura and Andy Marte, all of his tweets have been about football, with the Atlanta Falcons (nine) edging out Clemson University (seven) as the chief beneficiaries of his fandom.

The Risks: Keller spent much of the year as one of the youngest pitchers in the Cal League and held his own, posting his second-consecutive season with more than 130 innings of sub-3.25 DRA pitching. He'll need to continue developing his slider and miss a few more bats in order to reach his ceiling as a fourth-starter, but even without an above-average third pitch the innings-and-ground-balls profile can still be enough to round out a rotation.

Major league ETA: Late 2018 —Wilson Karaman

Ben Carsley's Fantasy Take: He who fights with back-end starters should be careful.

7. Taylor Clarke, RHP

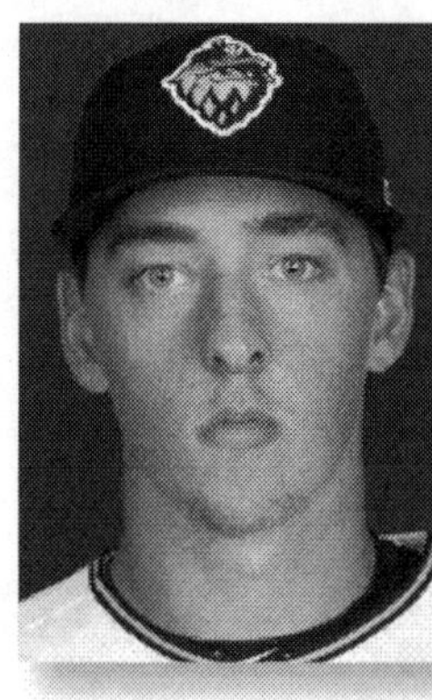

DOB: 5/13/1993

Height/Weight: 6'4" 200 lbs.

Bats/Throws: R/R

Drafted/Acquired: Drafted 76th overall in 2015 MLB Draft, College of Charleston (Charleston, SC); signed for $801,900

Previous Ranking(s): N/A

2016 Stats: 2.83 ERA, 3.96 DRA, 28.2 IP, 24 H, 5 BB, 24 K in 6 starts at Single-A Kane County, 2.74 ERA, 6.32 DRA, 23 IP, 19 H, 7 BB, 22 K in 4 starts at High-A Visalia, 3.59 ERA, 5.66 DRA, 97.2 IP, 99 H, 21 BB, 72 K in 17 starts at Double-A Mobile

The Role: OFP 50—No. 4 starter
Likely 40—No. 5 starter

YEAR	TEAM	LVL	AGE	W	L	SV	G	GS	IP	H	HR	BB/9	K/9	K	GB%	BABIP	WHIP	ERA	FIP	DRA	VORP	WARP	cFIP	MPH
2015	YAK	A-	22	0	0	3	13	0	21	8	0	1.7	11.6	27	51%	.186	0.57	0.00	1.74	1.70	7.50	0.8	73	
2016	KNC	A	23	3	2	0	6	6	28^2	24	1	1.6	7.5	24	32%	.277	1.01	2.83	2.78	3.96	3.40	0.4	97	
2016	VIS	A+	23	1	1	0	4	4	23	19	3	2.7	8.6	22	31%	.262	1.13	2.74	4.80	6.32	-2.20	-0.2	115	
2016	MOB	AA	23	8	6	0	17	17	97^2	99	9	1.9	6.6	72	38%	.297	1.23	3.59	3.84	5.66	-6.10	-0.7	106	
2017	*ARI*	*MLB*	*24*	*5*	*6*	*0*	*28*	*16*	*100^2*	*123*	*19*	*3.1*	*5.8*	*65*	*31%*	*.332*	*1.57*	*5.53*	*5.47*	*6.19*	*-7.9*	*-0.8*	*147*	
2018	*ARI*	*MLB*	*25*	*6*	*9*	*0*	*31*	*20*	*135^2*	*135*	*26*	*4.2*	*8.5*	*128*	*31%*	*.312*	*1.46*	*5.48*	*5.69*	*6.13*	*-8.4*	*-0.9*	*145*	

Breakout: 8% Improve: 9% Collapse: 4% Attrition: 11% MLB: 16% *Comparables: Tony Watson, Asher Wojciechowski, Jimmy Nelson*

The Good: Clarke shot up the organizational ranks in 2016 on the back of a low-90s fastball with some deception that he can command to either side of the plate. Both secondaries have a chance to be average. That counts as good, really. I'm taking what I can get at this point. We have a ways to go. He spots the curve down in the zone well.

The Bad: The stuff is average-ish across the board. He may lack an out pitch at higher levels—or even at Double-A, where he struggled some against better-quality hitters.

The Irrelevant: Per Google Maps, the trip from Kane County to Visalia to Mobile is 4,189 miles and will take around 60 hours to complete. Please note, this route has tolls.

The Risks: The risk is when I took this job I'd eventually have to write the Diamondbacks list. Oh, you mean for Clarke? Lacks a swing-and-miss offering, hasn't really passed the Double-A test. He's not an obvious bullpen candidate, though the fastball has touched significantly higher in the past. And yes, he's a pitcher.

Major league ETA: Early 2018

Ben Carsley's Fantasy Take: Lest he thereby become a back-end starter.

8. Alex Young, LHP

DOB: 09/09/1993

Height/Weight: 6'2" 205 lbs.

Bats/Throws: L/L

Drafted/Acquired: Drafted 43rd overall in the 2015 MLB Draft, Texas Christian University; signed for $1.4314 million

Previous Ranking(s): #5 (Org.)

2016 Stats: 2.16 ERA, 4.71 DRA, 50 IP, 39 H, 16 BB, 37 K in 9 games at Single-A Kane County, 4.59 ERA, 6.10 DRA, 68.2 IP, 79 H, 21 BB, 56 K in 12 games at High-A Visalia

The Role: OFP 50—Back-end starter or lefty setup man
Likely 40—Middle reliever with platoon issues

YEAR	TEAM	LVL	AGE	W	L	SV	G	GS	IP	H	HR	BB/9	K/9	K	GB%	BABIP	WHIP	ERA	FIP	DRA	VORP	WARP	cFIP	MPH
2015	DIA	Rk	21	0	0	0	1	1	1	0	0	0.0	9.0	1	100%	.000	0.00	0.00	1.82	3.79	0.20	0.0	93	
2015	YAK	A-	21	0	0	1	6	1	6	5	0	1.5	7.5	5	44%	.312	1.00	1.50	2.43	3.80	0.80	0.1	96	
2016	KNC	A	22	3	1	0	9	9	50	39	1	2.9	6.7	37	44%	.268	1.10	2.16	3.34	4.71	1.70	0.2	106	
2016	VIS	A+	22	2	7	0	12	11	68^2	79	10	2.8	7.3	56	36%	.324	1.46	4.59	4.98	6.10	-4.90	-0.5	119	
2017	*ARI*	*MLB*	*23*	*4*	*6*	*0*	*15*	*15*	*79^1*	*106*	*18*	*4.1*	*4.8*	*42*	*30%*	*.339*	*1.79*	*6.55*	*6.49*	*7.22*	*-14.6*	*-1.5*	*174*	
2018	*ARI*	*MLB*	*24*	*4*	*7*	*0*	*16*	*16*	*94^2*	*103*	*20*	*5.0*	*7.7*	*81*	*30%*	*.323*	*1.65*	*6.19*	*6.44*	*6.82*	*-11.8*	*-1.2*	*162*	

Breakout: 3% Improve: 3% Collapse: 1% Attrition: 2% MLB: 4% *Comparables: Jake Brigham, Ross Detwiler, Colin Rea*

The Good: Young has a really advanced slider. It flashes plus, and he can get ugly swings from both righties and lefties with it. He has an easy, repeatable delivery. The two-seam fastball moves a bit with both arm-side run and some sink.

The Bad: Despite the sink and run, the fastball sits in the upper 80s and can be quite hittable. The changeup has some fade, but not enough velocity separation to be an effective major league offering. This feels like it could just be a LOOGY profile at the end of the day.

The Irrelevant: Kevin Costner spent a semester in high school in Visalia, which may be why it gets a mention in Bull Durham.

The Risks: Below-average fastball velocity and the lack of a third pitch really limits the ceiling, although the slider is good enough, and Young is left-handed enough that their should be a bullpen spot for him in the majors eventually. He's still a pitcher, so maybe that doesn't even happen. I don't know man. This is only #7. We got a ways to go still.

Major league ETA: Early 2018

Ben Carsley's Fantasy Take: And if thou gaze long into an abyss.

9. Victor Reyes, OF

DOB: 10/5/1994

Height/Weight: 6'3" 170 lbs.

Bats/Throws: S/R

Drafted/Acquired: Signed in July 2011 out of Venezuela for $365,000; traded to Arizona from Atlanta for 2015 supplemental second-round pick

Previous Ranking(s): N/A

2016 Stats: .303/.349/.416, 6 HR, 20 SB in 124 games at High-A Visalia

The Role: OFP 45—Second-division left-fielder
Likely 40—Up-and-down fourth outfielder

YEAR	TEAM	LVL	AGE	PA	R	2B	3B	HR	RBI	BB	K	SB	CS	AVG/OBP/SLG	TAv	VORP	BABIP	BRR	FRAA	WARP
2014	ROM	A	19	361	32	13	0	0	34	24	58	12	7	.259/.309/.298	.230	-8.6	.312	-3.3	RF(79): 2.7	-0.5
2015	KNC	A	20	458	57	17	5	2	59	22	58	13	4	.311/.343/.389	.269	18.1	.352	4.4	LF(60): 4.9, RF(52): 3.2	3.2
2016	VIS	A+	21	509	62	11	12	6	54	33	78	20	8	.303/.349/.416	.284	24.6	.352	1.3	RF(89): -8.5, LF(20): -2.7	1.5
2017	*ARI*	*MLB*	*22*	*250*	*24*	*10*	*3*	*4*	*24*	*11*	*56*	*3*	*2*	*.251/.284/.372*	*.213*	*-4.5*	*.307*	*0.2*	*RF 1, LF 0*	*-0.3*
2018	*ARI*	*MLB*	*23*	*298*	*31*	*11*	*3*	*6*	*31*	*13*	*67*	*4*	*2*	*.248/.282/.376*	*.230*	*-2.7*	*.300*	*0.4*	*RF 1, LF 0*	*-0.1*

Breakout: 2% Improve: 7% Collapse: 0% Attrition: 5% MLB: 7% *Comparables: Lorenzo Cain, Socrates Brito, Rafael Ortega*

The Good: Reyes is a natural hitter, with strong wrists, quickness into the zone, and good balance to track pitches deep and put quality contact on the ball. A switch-hitter, he recognizes spin well and manages to put decent swings on bad balls with some consistency. The frame has some room to project strength, and he'll flash occasional leverage from the left side.

The Bad: In order to put decent swings on bad balls he has to chase those pitches, and chase he will do. He's a highly aggressive hitter, and while his high-caliber bat-to-ball skills have won the day thus far in the low minors, it's unclear if they'll be enough to continue doing so. It's an especially valid concern in his case, as the frame is beanpole skinny, and his narrow shoulders aren't built for much bulk even at max capacity. He's a fringy runner, as his long strides lack explosiveness, and the arm is a bit light for right field, so he may wind up relegated to left field.

The Irrelevant: Reyes was traded straight-up for a draft pick in 2015, and the Braves used the pick to select injury-riddled left-hander A.J. Minter, who would probably crack this top 10 list himself.

The Risks: Reyes' raw hitting talent lends some optimism for a big-league future, but the whole package is just a really weird profile without a ton of precedent for sustained success at the highest level.

Major league ETA: 2019 —Wilson Karaman

Ben Carsley's Fantasy Take: You should have little interest in the low-budget remake of Raimel Tapia. Now, where were we ...

10. Jon Duplantier, RHP

DOB: 7/11/1994

Height/Weight: 6'4" 225 lbs.

Bats/Throws: L/R

Drafted/Acquired: Drafted 89th overall in 2016 MLB Draft, Rice University (Houston, TX); signed for $686,600

Previous Ranking(s): N/A

2016 Stats: 0.00 ERA, 0.00 DRA, 1 IP, 0 H, 2 BB, 3 K in 1 game at short-season Hillsboro

The Role: OFP 50—I guess he could be a no. 4 starter, but we are probably talking about a setup man
Likely 40—Or just a good middle reliever

The Good: In 2016, a healthy Duplantier showed off a lively fastball he could run up into the mid-90s and a potentially plus power curve. He's a good athlete with the frame to start.

The Bad: Duplantier already missed an entire season—his sophomore one—with shoulder issues. The changeup lags well behind the other two offerings. The delivery has some effort and can be a bit torquey, causing him to lose his line to the plate and negatively impact his command. Between that and the durability concerns, it is hard to project a starter here, and the stuff isn't special in the bullpen.

The Irrelevant: The track record of Rice pitchers in the majors is...well, if you are reading Baseball Prospectus, you are probably aware. The best of the lot was Norm Charlton, who picked up 11.2 WARP across a 14-year career as an itinerant bullpen arm.

The Risks: Command and change concerns plus a shoulder issue. Sigh. And he's a pitcher.

Major league ETA: 2019

Ben Carsley's Fantasy Take: The abyss will also gaze into thee.

OTHERS OF NOTE:

One of These Days He's Going to Start Throwing Strikes, and You'll See! You'll All See!

Jimmie Sherfy, RHP

Sherfy's raw stuff is of the premium variety, led by a potential 70-grade heater that explodes late at 96–97. He pairs it with a nasty two-plane slider that dives late and can miss all of the bats when properly located. He'll also work in an occasional split-like change in the upper-80s that has hard vertical action and flashes the potential for sporadic utility. The delivery is violent; it's a max-effort affair with a long arm action, backside collapse, and some crossfire to boot. He doesn't repeat well, and the command spends more time going than it does coming as a result. It looked like things were finally starting to come together enough for the stuff to play this year, as he destroyed everything in his path between High A and Double A. But the control hit a wall in Reno, where he was bled for walks and battered by homers. If he's able to shake off the season's end and keep the ball around the zone, he's got the kind of stuff that can miss big-league bats and add homegrown value to the middle innings of games this summer. *—Wilson Karaman*

"Well, we did five more guys for every other organization"

Wei-Chieh Huang, RHP

Huang boasts one of the best secondaries in the system, a plus changeup in which he has the utmost confidence. He'll double it up to righties, work backwards off it, and generally deploy it in any situation. It's a tough pitch to read, with a good tunnel off his fastball and above-average movement. He'll show flashes of average fastball command, but the velocity at its best is fringe-average for a right-hander, and both of his breaking pitches are below-average offerings. Huang's frame is wiry and elastic, with obligatory durability questions that consecutive seasons with chunks lost to injury have done little to quell—he was reportedly struggling to find the mid-80s during late-season rehab in the Northwest League. If he can stay healthy, his elastic frame and fluid delivery suggest above-average command potential that could drag the profile into a big-league swing role. *—Wilson Karaman*

Matt Koch, RHP

I liked Matt Koch as a prospect—in the way you love a Double-A long reliever—but the Diamondbacks moving him back to the rotation is as concise an indictment of the depth of their system as I can think of (other than the preceding Top 10 list). Koch was miscast as a minor-league starter after sharing closing duties at Louisville, but once he moved to the pen in Binghamton, his heavy fastball ticked up into the mid-90s and his slider tightened up. It wasn't an impact profile in the pen, but it was a major-league arm. He was never going to be a big K guy, but you can hide that for an inning in the pen, because he throws strikes and gets ground balls. I guess you'd have to consider the move back to the rotation a success for Koch though. He made seven appearances in the majors, including two starts, and he's hanging around the fringes of major league depth charts. He gets 40-man money—the Mets were unlikely to add him, one of the reasons he ended up in the deal for Addison Reed—and given the Diamondbacks current bullpen depth chart, fans at Chase Field likely haven't seen the last of him.

Colin Bray, OF

Bray is a borderline plus-plus runner and the speed plays well in center field. Despite the Cal League numbers, he has well-below-average power (and we're only talking about a .137 ISO anyway). But it's not like the Top 10 lacked for potential bench pieces, and Bray has the speed and glove to be one. Well, he'll still need to hit a little, and he has a noisy, hitchy setup, and a stiff, slashing swing. That means a lot of bad contact and maybe less contact against upper minors arms. You can't steal first base after all (and Bray hasn't been all that efficient at stealing second in his career, despite his speed). The speed and glove still may be enough to have an up-and-down major league career, assuming the offensive profile doesn't completely collapse in Double-A. But even in the Diamondbacks Top 10, we have to draw the line at fifth outfielders. We're also drawing it at four others.

TOP 10 TALENTS 25 AND UNDER (BORN 4/1/91 OR LATER)

1. **Robbie Ray**
2. **Taijuan Walker**
3. **Archie Bradley**
4. **Anthony Banda**
5. **Brandon Drury**
6. **Ketel Marte**
7. **Braden Shipley**
8. **Domingo Leyba**
9. **Dawel Lugo**
10. **Jake Barrett**

The Diamondbacks have long sought cost-controlled pitching as a way to stay relevant in a division with more deeply-pocketed peers. Zack Greinke aside, the team has stuck by that mantra, and it should come as no surprise to see the top of this list deep with young, cheap arms that are under team control for 2017 and beyond. The problem is, they all come with their flaws.

Robbie Ray can bring the gas from the left side and finished fourth in the NL in strikeout rate last season, sandwiched between Noah Syndergaard's flowing locks and Madison Bumgarner's country manners. That's good company, but he also struggled to retire batters efficiently (again) and hasn't made much progress with his secondaries. Taijuan Walker is a welcome addition to the D-Backs' rotation, but he's not exactly found consistent footing in the majors despite his undeniable talent. Archie Bradley is the much of the same with big raw stuff that can give hitters fits, but his lack of command leaves much to be desired. While Walker appears the safer bet to remain in the rotation long-term, it wouldn't be a shock to see Bradley in the back of the bullpen one day, pairing his fastball with that hammer curve. Of course, either or both could iron out a kink or two and become stars. It's just a matter of development, a common thread applicable to most young hurlers.

Brandon Drury and Ketel Marte have their warts too. Drury has been a stalwart of prospect lists for a few years now and his rookie season came with its peaks and valleys. He played five different defensive positions in 2016 and didn't rate well at any of them. After a white-hot start, he fell off in a big way over the summer, only to make a few swing adjustments late and soar yet again. Meanwhile, Marte was imported along with Walker and adds another name to their middle infield mixture. His offensive struggles down the stretch, paired with Jerry Dipoto's desire to make all the trades, resulted in a new lease on life in the desert where the thin air helps everybody hit. Both have positional question marks and their viability depends on their capacity to make meaningful contact with regularity.

Braden Shipley was the top prospect in this system just a year ago, though he's taken a big hit as he was routinely punished by big-league hitters in his debut season. The fastball velocity was deliberately lacking, and while the changeup and curveball have their moments, Shipley's inconsistent command brought the whole arsenal down, and the results suffered. Jake Barrett was once considered the closer-in-waiting and that time came last season once Brad Ziegler and Tyler Clippard were traded and Daniel Hudson tanked. The results were okay, but "okay" means he'll now be superseded by Fernando Rodney's broke-off ball cap, which provides some helpful context. He remains the team's best young reliever, however, with a strong fastball/slider combination that's tailored for a high-leverage role.

If this seems underwhelming, it's because it is. Ray's position is secure, but Walker and Bradley are wearing out the word "upside" like it's going out of style. Both Drury and Marte have questions to answer about their long-term viability but have flashed an ability to make useful big-league contributions. Shipley's a pitch-to-contact back-end starter and Barrett is, well, a reliever. If more than a few of these bets can pay off for Mike Hazen, things could start looking up. If they don't, well, it's never too soon to start tanking.

—Jeff Wiser

ATLANTA BRAVES

The State of the System: *The Braves system had a strong case as the best in baseball, and that was before Dansby Swanson retained his prospect eligibility by one at-bat. This organization is flooded with potential above-average arms up-and-down the system, and has a ready-to-contribute up-the-middle combo near the top. It's almost an embarrassment of riches.*

THE TOP TEN

1. SS Dansby Swanson	6. LHP Kolby Allard
2. CF Ronald Acuna	7. RHP Ian Anderson
3. SS Ozhaino Albies	8. SS Kevin Maitan
4. LHP Sean Newcomb	9. LHP Luiz Gohara
5. RHP Mike Soroka	10. RHP Touki Toussaint

The Big Question: Shouldn't you be introducing these lists?

Probably. Although they won't look all that different from last year's with the exception of a short essay in front. Like this one...

This is the first of 30 prospect lists that that the Baseball Prospectus prospect team will roll out over the next three months. All told, that will mean reports on 450ish baseball players. A lot of them will play in the majors in the coming years. The eighth-best prospect on one team's list might have a better career than the fourth-best one. Heck, the eighth-best prospect might be the fourth-best prospect next year and might have been the third-best prospect last year. As one of my predecessors once opined, this is just a snapshot in time. And it's one that exists primarily for you, the reader, to yell at me in a couple years on Peach about how I was too low on that eighth-best prospect in 2017. But introductions, right:

Hello, I'm Jeffrey Paternostro, senior prospect writer at Baseball Prospectus, and I hate prospect lists. Inconveniently, I am also in charge of 30 of them to be rolled out in the next three months. Literally the only things I have to do to discharge my professional duties is complete these lists, a national Top 101, 2017 org rankings, and a 2017 midseason list. I should have just asked the Monkey's Paw for a turkey sandwich.

There's a false precision implied when you throw an ordinal ranking on a player. And the whole process hews too closely to lines of thinking that lead to referring to minor leaguers as "assets" or "property of." Maybe use "farmhands" (although agricultural workers can at least be assured of minimum wage). But this time of year our job is to make a call in bold print, so here you go.

The Braves are are a good place to start, as they have one of the deepest, best systems in baseball, one worthy of agog adulation (and if you prefer Myötähäpeä, don't worry, the Marlins will be along shortly). They are also useful for illustrating another important point about prospect lists.

As imprecise as a simple ordinal rankings can be, they are a judgment on what we as evaluators value. They are not meant to be a comprehensive accounting of who might eventually play in the majors.

The earliest my name will pop up in the *Baseball Prospectus* archives is an appearance on Effectively Wild to talk about Jacob deGrom. As we chatted, Sam mentioned that Jacob deGrom had never appeared in a single BP Annual, even as a lineout. He never made a Mets Top 10 list on this site (or any of mine for the record). He's now an all-star, an elite top-of-the-rotation starter. This was unusual, a 99th percentile outcome, but it wasn't a surprise that he pitched in the majors *at some point*.

The circumstances of his debut aren't all that unusual either. He was an older prospect who had some success in the upper minors, was capable of starting, though it was probable that he would be best-suited to the bullpen. The 2014 Mets were not a good baseball team, and had two starters hit the DL at the same time. deGrom was a logical choice for one of the spots.

The 2016 Braves were a significantly worse team than the

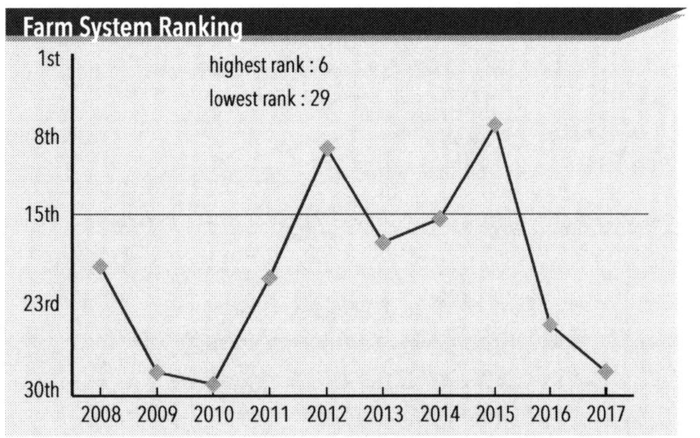

Personnel

President:
John Schuerholz

President, Baseball Operations:
John Hart

General Manager:
John Coppolella

Manager:
Brian Snitker

BP Alumni:
Kiley McDaniel
Noah Woodward

2014 Mets. If you will pardon a bit of tautology, a second-division team employs second-division starters. And the Braves were on the bottom rung of even that designation. Whether by design or misfortune, the 2016 Braves used many players you wouldn't have found on recent prospect lists.

John Gant was on Atlanta's Opening Day roster. He made 20 appearances, seven of which were starts. He essentially skipped Triple A a season after being skipped over Advanced-A. I saw a fair amount of Gant in the minors, and I always liked him as a prospect. As it turns out, I wasn't his number one fan or anything, but I thought he had a good shot to pitch in the majors in a role not unlike the one he found himself in 2016, an up-and-down swingman/spot starter type. Gant was optioned on five separate occasions over the course of the season. In between he pitched 50 innings within a shout either way or replacement level depending on your metric of choice.

Adonis Garcia was signed as a 27-year-old out of Cuba. He wasn't bonus-pool-eligible, but no one would have had to blow out their budget to find the 400k he signed for. He hit a bit in the minors, but didn't show enough power to profile in a corner infield spot. He was eventually released by the Yankees and found his way to Gwinnett in 2015, where he hit a bit more before finding himself pressed into service after the Braves dealt Juan Uribe and Kelly Johnson at the deadline. He hit enough to get himself an everyday job on a team in 2016 actively not looking for upgrades. Like Gant, he was generally in the vicinity of replacement level.

Rob Whalen and Ryan Weber are the guys you call up when John Gant gets hurt or you just need a few September starts. They both got six figures once upon a time, the cost of doing business. They have 90ish mph fastballs and pitched well enough in the upper minors to be an option on a 60-win team. It didn't go well for either in the majors.

The above may feel almost casually cruel, but Gant and Garcia, Whalen and Weber, they are all player development wins. The signing scout brags about them behind the backstop, lists them as a bold-type accomplishment on their C.V. when they get promoted to crosschecker. They are not "easy scouts," but they are also not really what we are looking for when we write prospect lists.

And for the players themselves, and this is not an original observation, even the worst major leaguers are among the 1000 or so best at their craft in the world. And they are major leaguers, unlike our 17-year-old prospects du jour, but they are also not really what we are looking for when we write prospect lists.

As a group, prospect writers often get accused of obsessing too much over "upside," of composing Keatsian odes to as-of-yet-unrealized tools. Our model is based loosely on normal distribution, but baseball talent is not normally distributed. The gap between the best prospect in baseball and the fiftieth is usually larger than the chasm between 50 and 200. By the time you get down to 500 or so, you may find some major leaguers, but they aren't that much better than the Adonis Garcias you find as minor league free agents. Major league value is not linear, and the possibility of elite talent is what gets us to the stadium three hours early.

Finally, these lists are a collaborative effort by the entire prospect team. I am one person with ten or so minor league stadiums across four leagues within driving distance. Although I am responsible for the final rankings and roles, whenever possible the reports on players are authored by the writers that have had eyes on them and know them the best.

As I said at the outset, the format is very similar to last year. We've split out the individual reports a bit more, although the lines between good, bad, and risk will be a bit fuzzy at times.

"Others of note" are not the 11th to 15th best prospects in the system unless noted. It's an opportunity to write about players in the system we find interesting for whatever reason, like they were traded recently or their name allows us to make labored references to early 1990s noise rock band The Jesus Lizard (this applies to two different prospects!).

And now, "here they come, the young thousands."

Or alternatively:

"But I've inched my way down the Eastern seaboard, I am coming to Atlanta again."

—Jeffrey Paternostro

1. Dansby Swanson, SS

DOB: 02/11/1994

Height/Weight: 6'1" 190 lbs.

Bats/Throws: R/R

Drafted/Acquired: Drafted first overall by Arizona in the 2015 MLB Draft, Vanderbilt University, signed for $6.5 million; acquired by Atlanta from Arizona in deal for Shelby Miller

Previous Ranking(s): #27 (Top 101), #1 (Org) 2016

2016 Stats: .302/.361/.442, 3 HR, 3 SB in 38 games at the major league level, .261/.342/.402, 8 HR, 6 SB in 84 games at Double-A Mississippi, .333/.441/.526, 1 HR, 7 SB in 21 games at High-A Carolina

The Role: OFP 70—All-star shortstop
Likely 60—First division shortstop

YEAR	TEAM	LVL	AGE	PA	R	2B	3B	HR	RBI	BB	K	SB	CS	AVG/OBP/SLG	TAv	VORP	BABIP	BRR	FRAA	WARP
2015	YAK	A-	21	99	19	7	3	1	11	14	14	0	0	.289/.394/.482	.372	17.9	.333	2.5	SS(22): 1.7	2.1
2016	CAR	A+	22	93	14	12	0	1	10	15	13	7	1	.333/.441/.526	.361	14.9	.391	1.0	SS(21): 1.6	1.7
2016	MIS	AA	22	377	54	13	5	8	45	35	71	6	2	.261/.342/.402	.295	29.9	.309	2.0	SS(83): 16.0	5.0
2016	ATL	MLB	22	145	20	7	1	3	17	13	34	3	0	.302/.361/.442	.303	13.1	.383	0.8	SS(37): -2.2	1.1
2017	*ATL*	*MLB*	*23*	*615*	*75*	*27*	*4*	*16*	*63*	*54*	*141*	*6*	*2*	*.253/.324/.406*	*.265*	*25.3*	*.308*	*-0.1*	*SS 10*	*3.8*
2018	*ATL*	*MLB*	*24*	*512*	*64*	*22*	*3*	*16*	*62*	*46*	*118*	*5*	*1*	*.257/.330/.424*	*.281*	*28.7*	*.311*	*0.1*	*SS 10*	*4.2*

Breakout: 6% Improve: 43% Collapse: 9% Attrition: 18% MLB: 77% *Comparables: Marcus Semien, Eugenio Suarez, Wilmer Flores*

The Good: Dansby Swanson is eligible for this list by one-at-bat, in what was totally not part of a plan to make him the presumptive favorite for the 2017 Rookie of the Year award. In those 129 at-bats he posted an .800 OPS despite only a half season of experience in the high minors. And it sure looked sustainable. The swing is simple, and he uses the big part of the park. He can go the other way naturally with a bit of inside-out. Overall, it's a plus hit tool, and he could have some full seasons where he hits .300. The approach is already solid considering his dearth of experience against upper level arms. He's a polished shortstop who will stick at the position.

The Bad: We're mostly nitpicking here. He's quick enough inside to yank a few bombs, but power won't be a significant part of his offensive game. He's just average at shortstop, with good instincts and actions, but not enough athletic tools to make plays on all the balls he gets to. His plus speed plays better on the bases than in the infield. He tracks pitches east/west well, but major-league arms could generate swings and misses working him north/south out of the zone.

The Irrelevant: Fourteen other players took exactly 129 at-bats in their first major league season. None of them won the Rookie of the Year, although Bob Elliott, who posted the best OPS of the group, eventually bagged an MVP.

The Risks: Swanson's done it for 129 major league at-bats, and while there is the possibility of growing pains second time through the league in 2017, his initial success and overall broad base of skills make him the lowest-risk prospect in the minors.

Major league ETA: Debuted in 2016

Ben Carsley's Fantasy Take: Thanks to the wave of young shortstop talent in the majors, it's easy to forget that this is still a relatively shallow fantasy position, even if it's much better than it used to be. Thankfully, Swanson will make it deeper still. He's a cut below the Lindor/Seager/Correa/Bogaerts class for our purposes, but Swanson's high floor, impact AVG/SB combo and MLB readiness make him mighty attractive, as does his hair. A .300-plus average with 20-plus steals (and 100-plus runs in time) should be in play on the reg. We've learned many times over that calling any fantasy prospect "safe" is a fool's errand, and yet...

2. Ronald Acuna, CF

DOB: 12/18/1997

Height/Weight: 6'0" 180 lbs.

Bats/Throws: R/R

Drafted/Acquired: Signed out of Venezuela in 2014 for $100,000

Previous Ranking(s): N/A

2016 Stats: .311/.387/.432, 4 HR, 14 SB in 40 games at Low-A Rome

The Role: OFP 70—All-star center fielder
Likely 55—Above-average outfielder

YEAR	TEAM	LVL	AGE	PA	R	2B	3B	HR	RBI	BB	K	SB	CS	AVG/OBP/SLG	TAv	VORP	BABIP	BRR	FRAA	WARP
2015	BRA	Rk	17	157	31	9	2	3	11	18	23	11	3	.258/.376/.424	.273	8.2	.292	1.1	CF(33): -2.1	0.7
2015	DNV	Rk	17	80	10	5	2	1	7	10	19	5	1	.290/.388/.464	.318	8.8	.388	1.2	CF(12): -2.1, RF(6): -0.8	0.6
2016	BRA	Rk	18	8	1	0	0	0	1	1	1	0	0	.333/.500/.333	.342	0.9	.400	0.0	CF(1): -0.3	0.1
2016	ROM	A	18	171	27	2	2	4	18	18	28	14	7	.311/.387/.432	.326	18.4	.359	2.9	CF(34): 0.6	2.2
2017	*ATL*	*MLB*	*19*	*250*	*32*	*8*	*1*	*6*	*22*	*20*	*69*	*8*	*4*	*.221/.290/.350*	*.229*	*1.0*	*.284*	*0.0*	*CF 0, RF -0*	*0.1*
2018	*ATL*	*MLB*	*20*	*397*	*48*	*14*	*3*	*12*	*46*	*35*	*104*	*14*	*8*	*.241/.315/.399*	*.267*	*14.1*	*.300*	*1.0*	*CF 0, RF 0*	*1.6*

Breakout: 0% Improve: 22% Collapse: 2% Attrition: 9% MLB: 31% *Comparables: Mike Trout, Carlos Correa, Jurickson Profar*

The Good: Flashes all five tools with quick-twitch ability at an up-the-middle position. Despite average size, there's plus power and even more raw because of explosive hands and lower half. Also shows advanced tracking and pitch recognition for age and above-average to plus speed.

The Bad: Center field defense remains more projection than results, and his future in center isn't guaranteed. Swing can get slightly long from high hands and long stride that affects his bat plane at times and leaves the future hit tool around a low 50. Could be a moment-of-truth period with his swing in the upper levels that requires an adjustment.

The Irrelevant: Acuna Matata, roughly translated, means "no worries, I'm going to hit 10 straight bombs in batting practice."

The Risks: Acuna suffered a torn thumb ligament but recovered well late in the season, so the injury appears to be past him. The main question is his future defensive home. His value could take a slight hit with a move off center, but many believe he'll be able to stick up the middle. His swing could also be exposed a little against advanced pitching, but his tracking skills should serve him well. *—David Lee*

Major league ETA: 2019

Ben Carsley's Fantasy Take: We're two players in and I'm already pouring cold water all over your prospect flames. Look, I get it. Acuna's power/speed/athleticism combo gives him an OF1 ceiling, and OF1s win leagues. Plus, you have to get in early on players like Acuna or you're not going to get in on them at all. Just be mindful of how long it's going to take Acuna to get to the majors, how little playing time he has under his belt, and how far his hit tool has to go. The ceiling here makes Acuna a very good fantasy prospect, but his value is capped by a long lead time and a low floor.

3. Ozzie Albies, SS

DOB: 01/07/1997

Height/Weight: 5'9" 160 lbs.

Bats/Throws: S/R

Drafted/Acquired: Signed out of Curacao July 2013 for $350,000

Previous Ranking(s): #37 (Top 101), #3 (Org)

2016 Stats: .248/.307/.351, 2 HR, 9 SB at in 56 games at Triple-A Gwinnett, .321/.391/.467, 4 HR, 21 SB in 82 games at Double-A Mississippi

The Role: OFP 60—First-division second baseman, assuming the Braves ever qualify there
Likely 55—Solid-average second baseman

YEAR	TEAM	LVL	AGE	PA	R	2B	3B	HR	RBI	BB	K	SB	CS	AVG/OBP/SLG	TAv	VORP	BABIP	BRR	FRAA	WARP
2014	BRA	Rk	17	78	16	3	0	0	5	11	6	7	2	.381/.481/.429	.212	0.3	.414	0.0		0.0
2014	DNV	Rk	17	161	25	4	3	1	14	17	17	15	3	.356/.429/.452	.331	20.6	.395	2.8		2.1
2015	ROM	A	18	439	64	21	8	0	37	36	56	29	8	.310/.368/.404	.304	41.5	.358	4.7	SS(93): 5.8	5.0
2016	GWN	AAA	19	247	27	11	3	2	20	19	39	9	4	.248/.307/.351	.242	4.9	.290	1.1	SS(33): 1.5, 2B(23): 2.1	0.9
2016	MIS	AA	19	371	56	22	7	4	33	33	57	21	9	.321/.391/.467	.339	44.7	.376	4.5	2B(60): 3.2, SS(22): 2.9	5.5
2017	*ATL*	*MLB*	*20*	*250*	*31*	*12*	*2*	*5*	*23*	*18*	*53*	*9*	*4*	*.258/.318/.393*	*.251*	*8.5*	*.311*	*0.4*	*2B 3, SS 2*	*1.4*
2018	*ATL*	*MLB*	*21*	*427*	*50*	*20*	*4*	*9*	*48*	*32*	*86*	*15*	*6*	*.269/.331/.418*	*.277*	*22.9*	*.319*	*1.5*	*2B 5, SS 3*	*3.3*

Breakout: 6% Improve: 22% Collapse: 0% Attrition: 7% MLB: 24% *Comparables: Jonathan Schoop, Rougned Odor, Jurickson Profar*

The Good: The 19-year-old Albies was jumped over Advanced-A, and then pushed further to Triple-A after a month in the Southern League. He held his own at both stops before settling back in as Dansby Swanson's double-play partner in Mississippi. He's a solid defender with good hands and actions that can handle shortstop, although his arm is stretched there. His swing is unorthodox. It's a very open stance and he remains upright throughout, but he controls the barrel well. He's a plus-plus runner with 30-plus SB potential in the majors.

The Bad: Albies' slash-and-dash approach will severely limit his over-the-fence power, although he will be able to run into some extra bases. The swing is funky enough to make me question the ultimate hit tool projection in the majors, and he already has issues pulling off pitches down or away. He lacks a standout tool aside from his speed. He's a better fit at second base even on a team not currently employing Dansby Swanson.

The Irrelevant: You'd be forgiven for thinking the primary Curaçaoan export was Atlanta Braves baseball players, but they also are responsible for the liqueur, made from the laraha, a type of valencia orange. I recommend the Pierre Ferrand Dry as the best expression of the style.

The Risks: Albies is only 19 and already has a half-season at Triple-A under his belt. There is still some risk in the hit tool until we see it succeed against major-league pitching, but his present polish, overall athleticism, and up-the-middle defensive profile gives him a pretty high floor for a teenager.

Major league ETA: 2017, post super-two

Ben Carsley's Fantasy Take: Josh Harrison hit .283 with four homers and 19 steals this season and was *still* a top-20 option at the keystone, per ESPN's Player Rater. That's not to say Albies has a Harrison-like future in store, but be mindful of just how useful a second baseman who can nab 30-plus bags with a decent average can be. Albies may enjoy relatively few top-10 2B finishes, but he's in line for plenty of top-15 and top-20 placements. You can target him for your MI slot as soon as 2018. I still like Jose Peraza better..

4. Sean Newcomb, LHP

DOB: 06/12/1993

Height/Weight: 6'5" 240 lbs.

Bats/Throws: L/L

Drafted/Acquired: Drafted 15th overall in the 2014 MLB Draft, University of Hartford; signed for $2.5184 million; acquired by Atlanta in deal for Andrelton Simmons

Previous Ranking(s): #41 (Midseason Top 50), #32 (Top 101), #2 (Org)

2016 Stats: 3.86 ERA, 4.33 DRA, 140 IP, 113 H, 71 BB, 152 K at Double-A Mississippi

The Role: OFP 60—No. 3 starter
Likely 55—There isn't really a lefty reliever with this profile other than Andrew Miller...so less good Andrew Miller.

YEAR	TEAM	LVL	AGE	W	L	SV	G	GS	IP	H	HR	BB/9	K/9	K	GB%	BABIP	WHIP	ERA	FIP	DRA	VORP	WARP	cFIP	MPH
2014	ANG	Rk	21	0	0	0	2	2	3	3	1	3.0	9.0	3	0%	.286	1.33	3.00	7.36	3.56			99	
2014	BUR	A	21	0	1	0	4	4	11^2	13	1	3.9	11.6	15	28%	.387	1.54	6.94	3.31	4.36	1.40	0.1	100	
2015	BUR	A	22	1	0	0	7	7	34^1	25	1	5.0	11.8	45	66%	.308	1.28	1.83	2.90	1.97	12.40	1.3	82	
2015	INL	A+	22	6	1	0	13	13	65^2	50	2	4.5	11.5	84	49%	.300	1.26	2.47	3.17	2.49	18.90	2.0	86	
2015	ARK	AA	22	2	2	0	7	7	36	22	2	6.0	9.8	39	47%	.235	1.28	2.75	3.94	4.06	4.10	0.4	100	
2016	MIS	AA	23	8	7	0	27	27	140	113	4	4.6	9.8	152	46%	.302	1.31	3.86	3.19	4.04	16.40	1.8	93	
2017	*ATL*	*MLB*	*24*	*1*	*1*	*0*	*3*	*3*	*15*	*14*	*1*	*4.8*	*8.1*	*13*	*41%*	*.295*	*1.47*	*4.25*	*4.10*	*4.77*	*0.7*	*0.1*	*100*	
2018	*ATL*	*MLB*	*25*	*8*	*9*	*0*	*28*	*28*	*173^2*	*129*	*15*	*5.7*	*10.7*	*206*	*41%*	*.298*	*1.37*	*3.79*	*4.23*	*4.53*	*16.3*	*1.7*	*103*	

Breakout: 12% Improve: 27% Collapse: 15% Attrition: 28% MLB: 48% *Comparables: Trevor May, Charles Brewer, Chris Withrow*

The Good: He's a lefty that touches the upper 90s, sits near 95, and the velocity comes easy from his simple mechanics. The fastball is heavy down in the zone, and pops when he elevates it. He pairs the heater with a big curve that flashes plus with sharp 1-7 break at its best. Newcomb's got a frame built to log innings and elicit equine homologies from prospect writers. There still may be some room for development despite his frame and time in Double-A as there were very few miles put on his arm as an amateur.

The Bad: The mechanics are simple, but he doesn't repeat them well. His upper and lower halves end up out of sync and he loses his release point, especially on the fastball. The overall command profile is below-average even when he is throwing strikes, which isn't as often as you'd like for a guy already in Double-A. He can get on the side of the curve at times and it will lose some depth. The change is okay, but a clear third pitch and doesn't project as more than average.

The Irrelevant: Newcomb would be the fourth University of Hartford graduate to play in the majors and the first since Jeff Bagwell retired in 2005. It is also one of two schools the author can claim as an alma mater (since they both hit him up for money). Unfortunately it is unlikely we will see a Hampshire College major leaguer any time soon (although Bill Lee was known to show up there on occasion to toe the rubber)

The Risks: Newcomb is a good test case for what we mean by "risk." Does risk speak to the range of outcomes, or is it the risk of "actualization of the likely?" Ninety-five percent of the prospects we'll write about over the coming months don't have a major-league "floor," or at least not one of "meaningful contributor." I also might underestimate Newcomb's OFP. Lefties especially tend to put it together late, and Newcomb still has the cold-weather amateur profile as a reason for why he hasn't progressed as much as you might like since he was drafted. Still, once you get to Double-A, you are only a phone call away, and the continuing command/change issues make it hard for me to throw a top-of-the-rotation OFP on Newcomb. Conversely, the half-grade spread makes him seem less risky than he is, but there just aren't that many lefties with that fastball/breaking ball combo, and some of them do turn into Andrew Miller...or at least Brad Hand. Sometimes the 20/80 scale can feel overly prescriptive rather than descriptive. This is one of those times. Of course a lot of this could be mitigated if I was willing to use 65. I'm not, so instead you get another short(er) essay.

Also, he's a pitcher.

Major league ETA: September 2017

Ben Carsley's Fantasy Take: Ben Carsley's Fantasy Take: Enjoy this incredibly topical reference: If you start Newcomb, will you want to watch your team's WHIP? Nay, nay. Newcomb is attractive to us chiefly for his ability to miss bats, but he's as capable of murdering your ratios as he is grabbing you some cheap Ks. His best path to fantasy value might be as a high-strikeout closer, though that sells short his The Good Matt Moore upside if it does click for Newcomb in the rotation. Don't sell low on him if you've already got him, but I wouldn't be gunning to acquire him right now, either.

5. Mike Soroka, RHP

DOB: 08/04/1997

Height/Weight: 6'4" 195 lbs.

Bats/Throws: R/R

Drafted/Acquired: Drafted 28th overall in the 2015 MLB Draft, Bishop Carroll HS (Calgary, AB); signed for $1.9747 million

Previous Ranking(s): #7 (Org)

2016 Stats: 3.02 ERA, 3.25 DRA, 143 IP, 130 H, 32 BB, 125 K at Low-A Rome

The Role: OFP 60—High No. 3 starter
Likely 55—Mid-rotation starter

YEAR	TEAM	LVL	AGE	W	L	SV	G	GS	IP	H	HR	BB/9	K/9	K	GB%	BABIP	WHIP	ERA	FIP	DRA	VORP	WARP	cFIP	MPH
2015	BRA	Rk	17	0	0	0	4	3	10	5	0	0.9	9.9	11	54%	.208	0.60	1.80	2.00	2.38	3.90	0.4	81	
2015	DNV	Rk	17	0	2	0	6	6	24	28	0	1.5	9.8	26	53%	.384	1.33	3.75	2.10	2.22	9.70	1.0	79	
2016	ROM	A	18	9	9	0	25	24	143	130	3	2.0	7.9	125	52%	.305	1.13	3.02	2.78	2.76	35.60	3.9	88	
2017	*ATL*	*MLB*	*19*	*5*	*7*	*0*	*19*	*19*	*96^{2}*	*96*	*12*	*3.8*	*7.1*	*76*	*47%*	*.313*	*1.42*	*4.52*	*4.60*	*5.45*	*1.2*	*0.1*	*127*	
2018	*ATL*	*MLB*	*20*	*9*	*10*	*0*	*30*	*30*	*185^{1}*	*162*	*21*	*4.2*	*9.3*	*191*		*.311*	*1.35*	*3.96*	*4.42*	*4.77*	*13.4*	*1.4*	*109*	

Breakout: 1% Improve: 1% Collapse: 0% Attrition: 0% MLB: 1% *Comparables: Taijuan Walker, Manny Banuelos, Tyler Skaggs*

The Good: Soroka shows the potential for two plus pitches and a third average offering along with average command for the makings of a mid-rotation starter. His fastball has plus potential in the low-90s with above-average run and sink, and his curveball has silly late movement with two-plane ability. He has a strong, durable body with the makings of an innings-eating arm, and he's a very smart kid.

The Bad: He struggled getting a feel for his curve and changeup on the same day, but that improved as the season progressed. He's still adjusting to his developing body and learning to repeat his mechanics.

The Irrelevant: Soroka is from Canada. He chose baseball over hockey pretty early in life. We're all better for it.

The Risks: The risk is pretty minimal with Soroka, relative to teenagers who throw baseballs for a living. He has the aptitude to adjust, he has the body to log innings, and he has the stuff to turn over a lineup multiple times. But it is worth keeping in mind that he is a pitcher. *—David Lee*

Major league ETA: Late 2018

Ben Carsley's Fantasy Take: Soroka is slightly more interesting than most SP5/6 prospects in the low minors, but that's like being the flashiest pre-owned Hyundai Elantra on the lot. He's worth monitoring as he ascends through the ranks, but the ETA and relatively modest ceiling should conspire to relegate him to the deepest of dynasty leagues only.

6. Kolby Allard, LHP

DOB: 08/13/1997

Height/Weight: 6'1" 180 lbs.

Bats/Throws: L/L

Drafted/Acquired: Drafted 14th overall in the 2015 MLB Draft, San Clemente HS (San Clemente, CA); signed for $3.0424 million

Previous Ranking(s): #82 (Top 101), #5 (Org)

2016 Stats: 3.73 ERA, 3.23 DRA, 60.1 IP, 54 H, 20 BB, 62 K at low-A Rome, 1.32 ERA, 1.59 DRA, 27.1 IP, 18 H, 5 BB, 33 K at short-season Danville

The Role: OFP 60—Mid-Rotation Starter
Likely 50—Back-end rotation starter

YEAR	TEAM	LVL	AGE	W	L	SV	G	GS	IP	H	HR	BB/9	K/9	K	GB%	BABIP	WHIP	ERA	FIP	DRA	VORP	WARP	cFIP	MPH
2015	BRA	Rk	17	0	0	0	3	3	6	1	0	0.0	18.0	12	43%	.143	0.17	0.00	-0.20	1.99	2.60	0.3	74	
2016	DNV	Rk	18	3	0	0	5	5	27^{1}	18	0	1.6	10.9	33	53%	.281	0.84	1.32	2.01	1.53	12.70	1.3	71	
2016	ROM	A	18	5	3	0	11	11	60^{1}	54	5	3.0	9.2	62	38%	.312	1.23	3.73	3.51	4.97	0.30	0.0	102	
2017	*ATL*	*MLB*	*19*	*3*	*4*	*0*	*12*	*12*	*59^{2}*	*60*	*8*	*3.8*	*7.3*	*49*	*47%*	*.314*	*1.42*	*4.57*	*4.64*	*5.51*	*0.4*	*0.0*	*129*	
2018	*ATL*	*MLB*	*20*	*8*	*10*	*0*	*29*	*29*	*181^{2}*	*158*	*22*	*3.9*	*9.2*	*185*		*.307*	*1.31*	*3.93*	*4.39*	*4.74*	*13.2*	*1.4*	*109*	

Breakout: 0% Improve: 0% Collapse: 0% Attrition: 0% MLB: 0% *Comparables: Manny Banuelos, Noah Syndergaard, Vicente Campos*

The Good: Flashes a plus curveball, potential for plus control and command. Added physicality should push a fastball that already sinks to plus. The delivery and arm action are easy. More than held his own as one of the youngest players in the South Atlantic League despite a late start due to offseason back surgery.

The Bad: Back concerns impacted his draft stock and required offseason surgery, though the severity was later downplayed. Promising pitchers physically breaking down is nothing new to anyone reading this, so Allard starting his professional career with a physical question mark will be a red flag to some.

The Irrelevant: Like many of his baseball colleagues, Allard sees dollar signs in a potential Head & Shoulders endorsement deal.

The Risks: Single A is a long way from las grandes ligas for any pitcher. Allard possesses an advanced feel that certainly softens some of that risk. That said, the curveball has some consistency issues to be ironed out, the fastball is unlikely to add much more velocity, and the changeup might not progress beyond average. All in all, there is a future in a big-league rotation for Allard; it's more a question of the extent of his impact. Also, he's a pitcher. *—Adam Hayes*

Major league ETA: 2020

Ben Carsley's Fantasy Take: If you want to gamble on a Braves starter from their last two drafts, Allard is your guy. The risk is higher for sure, but when you're dealing with arms this far away from the Majors, you're forfeiting safety from the start. Allard may lack true top-of-the-rotation upside, but he has the stuff to miss bats, and as a left-hander he'll be given 400 chances to make it as a starter. A future as an SP3/4 with 200 strikeouts is within the realm of possibility here.

7. Ian Anderson, RHP

DOB: 05/02/1998

Height/Weight: 6'3" 170 lbs

Bats/Throws: R/R

Drafted/Acquired: Drafted 3rd overall in the 2016 MLB Draft, Shenendehowa HS (Clifton Park, New York); signed for $4 million.

Previous Ranking(s): N/A

2016 Stats: 3.74 ERA, 4.40 DRA, 21.2 IP, 19 H, 8 BB, 18 SO at Advanced Rookie level Danville, 0.00 ERA, 2.60 DRA, 18 IP, 14 H, 4 BB. 18 K at the Gulf Coast League Braves

The Role: OFP 60—No. 3 Starter
Likely 50—You know the drill by now

YEAR	TEAM	LVL	AGE	W	L	SV	G	GS	IP	H	HR	BB/9	K/9	K	GB%	BABIP	WHIP	ERA	FIP	DRA	VORP	WARP	cFIP	MPH
2016	BRA	Rk	18	1	0	0	5	5	18	14	0	2.0	9.0	18	59%	.304	1.00	0.00	1.98	2.24	7.00	0.7	82	
2016	DNV	Rk	18	0	2	0	5	5	21^{2}	19	1	3.3	7.5	18	60%	.290	1.25	3.74	3.71	4.29	3.40	0.3	99	
2017	*ATL*	*MLB*	*19*	*2*	*3*	*0*	*8*	*8*	35^{2}	*36*	*5*	*3.9*	*7.7*	*31*	*47%*	*.321*	*1.44*	*4.62*	*4.64*	*5.56*	*0.0*	*0.0*	*130*	
2018	*ATL*	*MLB*	*20*	*7*	*8*	*0*	*28*	*28*	*168*	*151*	*21*	*3.7*	*9.4*	*175*		*.317*	*1.31*	*3.88*	*4.33*	*4.67*	*11.8*	*1.2*	*107*	

Breakout: 0% Improve: 0% Collapse: 0% Attrition: 0% MLB: 0% *Comparables: Tyler Glasnow, Jake Thompson, Luis Severino*

The Good: Anderson has the prototypical starter's frame, an easy delivery and a fastball that can bump 95 with arm-side run. His curve is inconsistent at present but flashes plus, and I'd expect it to sit more in the upper-70s once as he both tightens the pitch up and fills out his frame. He's projectable generally, and there may be additional added growth given his background.

The Bad: With added growth potential comes the need for more growth than even your average prep pitcher. The stuff doesn't project as more than plus and it's got a ways to go to get there. The curve can tend to have a bit of a hump out of the hand. The changeup is crude at present.

The Irrelevant: I will not make a Jethro Tull reference... I will not make a Jethro Tull reference... I will not make a Jethro Tull reference...

[deadline approaches]

Ian Anderson shares a name with the lead singer of British progressive rock band Jethro Tull, although he will need to fill out a bit more to be Thick as a Brick.

The Risks: In addition to the usual risks posed by any prep pitcher with just a summer of rookie ball experience, Anderson didn't pitch much this spring between an injury and bad weather. The arm strength isn't in question, but the rest of the profile is quite raw, and he may move more slowly than his 2016 prep class peers. Also, he's a pitcher.

Major league ETA: 2021

Ben Carsley's Fantasy Take: Like Mike Soroka, for our purposes, but the used Elantra has 10,000 more miles on it and is a model year older.

8. Kevin Maitan, SS

DOB: 02/12/2000

Height/Weight: 6'2" 190 lbs

Bats/Throws: S/R

Drafted/Acquired: Signed out of Venezuela in 2016 for $4.25 million

Previous Ranking(s): N/A

2016 Stats: N/A

The Role: OFP 60—Above-average regular.

YEAR	TEAM	LVL	AGE	PA	R	2B	3B	HR	RBI	BB	K	SB	CS	AVG/OBP/SLG	TAv	VORP	BABIP	BRR	FRAA	WARP
2017	*ATL*	*MLB*	*17*	*250*	*19*	*9*	*1*	*2*	*18*	*13*	*68*	*3*	*1*	*.191/.235/.262*	*.177*	*-10.0*	*.250*	*-0.1*	*SS 0*	*-1.1*

Breakout: 0% Improve: 0% Collapse: 0% Attrition: 0% MLB: 0% *Comparables: Wilmer Flores, Raul Mondesi*

The Good and the Bad are mostly Irrelevant: Even in a system as deep as the Braves, you could throw a dart at a board and have a good chance at landing on a reasonable ranking for Maitan, as long as you avoided the double and triple rings. He has only made a cameo in American instructs and was born a day after The Beach was released, which was the first movie date I went on with my high school girlfriend. The possibilities for Maitan now are a little more open-ended than they were for me at the time.

He maybe won't go on to be as big a star as DiCaprio in his chosen field, but the switch-hitting shortstop was the consensus best prospect in this year's J2 class, and has a huge offensive ceiling. He has above-average bat speed with some natural whip and could be a plus hit/plus power bat that plays on the left side of the infield, somewhere. Even the people scouting him can't agree on what the shape of that ceiling is, or where his ultimate defensive home will be, so I find it difficult to put an OFP and a Likely grade on him. We'll stick with one for now, rather than try to hedge with three.

The Risks: Maitan has yet to take a swing in an official game. This could go an awful lot of different ways even in just the next three years. But at least he's not a pitcher.

Major league ETA: 2022

Ben Carsley's Fantasy Take: If you met someone tomorrow, you could begin to date them, get engaged, get married and have children in a traditional, linear fashion before Maitan makes his MLB debut. The timeline adds tremendous risk to his fantasy profile—you're probably punting a roster spot for at least a half-decade if you acquire him—but the ceiling justifies the probable wait. I cannot in good faith give you any stat estimates at this point in the game, but be patient with Maitan, because potential plus-average/plus-power infielders don't come along very often.

9. Luiz Gohara, LHP

DOB: 07/31/1996

Height/Weight: 6'3" 240 lbs.

Bats/Throws: L/L

Drafted/Acquired: Signed in August 2012 out of Brazil for $880,000; acquired by Atlanta in the Mallex Smith trade.

Previous Ranking(s): #3 (Org.)

2016 Stats: 1.76 ERA, 1.65 DRA, 15.3 IP, 13 H, 3 BB, 21 K in 3 games at short-season Everett, 1.82 ERA, 2.61 DRA, 54.3 IP, 44 H, 20 BB, 60 K in 10 games at Low-A Clinton

The Role: OFP 60—Mid-rotation starter
Likely 50—Late-inning reliever. If you think it's just as likely that he never reaches the majors, you'd have a case.

YEAR	TEAM	LVL	AGE	W	L	SV	G	GS	IP	H	HR	BB/9	K/9	K	GB%	BABIP	WHIP	ERA	FIP	DRA	VORP	WARP	cFIP	MPH
2014	MRN	Rk	17	1	1	0	2	2	12^2	11	0	1.4	11.4	16	0%	.333	1.03	2.13	1.98	2.02			75	
2014	EVE	A-	17	0	6	0	11	11	37^1	46	6	5.8	8.9	37	60%	.348	1.88	8.20	6.25	6.78	-5.90	-0.6	110	
2015	CLN	A	18	0	1	0	2	2	9^2	10	0	5.6	4.7	5	60%	.333	1.66	1.86	4.22	5.25	0.00	0.0	110	
2015	EVE	A-	18	3	7	0	14	14	53^2	67	4	5.4	10.4	62	53%	.404	1.84	6.20	4.27	3.70	9.40	1.0	97	
2016	EVE	A-	19	2	0	0	3	3	15^1	13	1	1.8	12.3	21	68%	.333	1.04	1.76	2.47	1.50	6.40	0.7	68	
2016	CLN	A	19	5	2	0	10	10	54^1	44	1	3.3	9.9	60	52%	.314	1.18	1.82	2.61	2.04	17.90	2.0	84	
2017	*SEA*	*MLB*	*20*	*3*	*4*	*0*	*12*	*12*	51^2	*61*	*8*	*5.2*	*6.2*	*36*	*42%*	*.314*	*1.76*	*5.61*	*5.65*	*5.99*	*-3.0*	*-0.3*	*142*	
2018	*SEA*	*MLB*	*21*	*6*	*9*	*0*	*25*	*25*	*146*	*147*	*22*	*5.6*	*8.5*	*138*	*42%*	*.303*	*1.63*	*5.19*	*5.26*	*5.54*	*-0.8*	*-0.1*	*132*	

Breakout: 3% Improve: 3% Collapse: 0% Attrition: 3% MLB: 3% *Comparables: Tyrell Jenkins, Randall Delgado, Jose Berrios*

The Good: Gohara's fastball regularly reaches the upper-90s and comfortably sits in the 94-96 mph range throughout games. He's strong and has a quick arm; the velocity isn't the product of an overly-aggressive delivery. His curve flashes plus, but just as promisingly, it looked competent far more often than it had in years past. It feels like Gohara has been a prospect for a long time, but he's still just 20 years old, and after struggling in short-season ball for a couple of years, he posted his best statistical campaign of his career down the stretch in Low-A last year.

The Bad: The Brazilian lefty has a boom-or-bust profile, and unfortunately, the deficiencies in his game are still quite apparent. His changeup is a clear third pitch, and while both of his offspeed offerings are much-improved, each requires considerable refinement. Gohara's command comes and goes, and his delivery often falls apart in games. Part of that stems from his weight—he's huge, especially for his age—and it's fair to question how well his body will hold up in the long run. The cumulative weight of these concerns may eventually push him to the bullpen. Some evaluators have also questioned his effort level and commitment to his craft.

The Irrelevant: Billy Hamilton and Luiz Gohara are the only two baseball players I've ever seen drinking Mountain Dew in the middle of a game (to be fair, Gohara was charting that night).

The Risks: Where should we start?

Major league ETA: 2019 —*Brendan Gawlowski*

Ben Carsley's Fantasy Take: I've beat it into your heads by now that pitchers with upside are the only pitchers worth gambling on, but Gohara is too risky for me to recommend that you take the plunge. I get that he could be a high-strikeout starter in a (usually) good park, but it doesn't seem like the odds of him reaching those heights are very good. Unless your league rosters in excess of 150 prospects, you can pass for now.

10. Touki Toussaint, RHP

DOB: 06/20/1996

Height/Weight: R/R

Bats/Throws: 6'3" 185 lbs.

Drafted/Acquired: Drafted 16th overall by Arizona in the 2014 MLB Draft, Coral Springs Christian Academy (Coral Springs, FL); signed for $2.7 million; acquired by Atlanta in deal for Phil Gosselin

Previous Ranking(s): #6 (Org)

2016 Stats: 3.88 ERA, 5.15 DRA, 132.1 IP, 105 H, 71 BB, 128 K at low-A Rome.

The Role: OFP 60—No. 3 starter or quality major league closer
Likely 50—No. 4 starter/high-leverage reliever

YEAR	TEAM	LVL	AGE	W	L	SV	G	GS	IP	H	HR	BB/9	K/9	K	GB%	BABIP	WHIP	ERA	FIP	DRA	VORP	WARP	cFIP	MPH
2014	DIA	Rk	18	1	1	0	7	5	15	14	0	7.2	10.2	17	0%	.326	1.73	4.80	4.56	5.78			115	
2014	MSO	Rk	18	1	3	0	5	5	13^{2}	24	5	4.0	9.9	15	0%	.422	2.20	12.51	8.35	5.30			106	
2015	KNC	A	19	2	2	0	7	7	39	31	4	3.5	6.7	29	38%	.243	1.18	3.69	4.55	5.77	-2.40	-0.3	113	
2015	ROM	A	19	3	5	0	10	10	48^{2}	40	6	6.1	7.0	38	41%	.252	1.50	5.73	5.74	7.22	-10.80	-1.1	123	
2016	ROM	A	20	4	8	0	27	24	132^{1}	105	13	4.8	8.7	128	40%	.263	1.33	3.88	4.56	5.68	-10.00	-1.1	116	
2017	*ATL*	*MLB*	*21*	*4*	*9*	*0*	*20*	*20*	91^{2}	*100*	*17*	*6.1*	*5.2*	*53*	*29%*	*.299*	*1.77*	*6.56*	*6.60*	*7.75*	*-22.2*	*-2.3*	*184*	
2018	*ATL*	*MLB*	*22*	*4*	*10*	*0*	*22*	*22*	130^{2}	*128*	*25*	*7.7*	*8.2*	*118*	*29%*	*.306*	*1.83*	*6.29*	*7.04*	*7.43*	*-21.4*	*-2.2*	*174*	

Breakout: 3% Improve: 4% Collapse: 0% Attrition: 3% MLB: 5% *Comparables: Timothy Melville, Tyler Matzek, Alex Cobb*

The Good: Toussaint's combination of stuff and athleticism makes you want to cry tears of joy. He has a plus fastball and double-plus-potential curveball and enough feel to project an above-average changeup. His fastball sits low-90s but can bump 97 and hit 95 when he wants, while his curveball is a 12-6 hammer that can make a heart race. Toussaint is an elite athlete, with plus arm speed, and a great teammate.

The Bad: Command remains well behind the stuff, so much so that it's uncertain whether he sticks in a rotation despite the three-pitch mix. He made strides to improve his delivery's timing and sync his halves better, but he needs to maintain it over a full season.

The Irrelevant: Toussaint has quite the humor, from playfully jabbing at teammates on Twitter to asking for teammate Austin Riley's autograph during an interview.

The Risks: Toussaint's gap between present and ceiling remains large because of feel and command. He worked to close it slightly this season and did so, but he needs to prove it further over a full season. He remains a prospect with one of the highest ceilings in the system but lacks a guaranteed floor. Also, he's a pitcher. —David Lee

Major league ETA: Late 2018

Ben Carsley's Fantasy Take: You'll get a sense for this as these top-10 lists roll out, but I'm a firm believer that fantasy starting pitcher prospects are only worth investing in if they come with upside. That's why I'd prefer to gamble on Toussaint than Soroka, Allard or Anderson—he's got better fantasy impact potential than the rest, even if his floor is lower. I get the sense there's some prospect fatigue here, but if Toussaint is available in a league that rosters 150-plus prospects, he's worth a look as someone who could fan more than a batter per inning, and who could possibly collect some saves as a fallback option.

OTHERS OF NOTE:

#11

Max Fried, LHP

The second-best arm on his high school team at Harvard-Westlake, Fried is a very good prospect in his own right. His best pitch is a knee-buckling curveball that could get big leaguers chasing now. The fastball sits plus and can touch the mid- to upper-90s. Most importantly, he put in a full healthy season returning from **Tommy John**. He spent the season repeating Low A, albeit recovering from surgery, and the results were simply okay until the late season push, when he struck out 10-plus in each of his last four starts. His changeup features a noticeable mechanical issue that should be exploited by more advanced hitters if left uncorrected, and there's enough effort to the delivery and shortness to the arm action that long-term viability in the rotation could be called into question. With the potential for two plus, even plus-plus pitches, there will always be a bullpen cushion to land on. But do keep in mind that he is a pitcher. —Adam Hayes.

#12

Patrick Weigel, RHP

Weigel came out of nowhere as a seventh-round pick in 2015 and immediately started throwing gas with a lively arsenal. He has plus arm speed and comes from a tough angle to throw low-90s while touching 97 with above-average run and sink, and he can reach back for 95 when he wants. He adds a hard-biting slider with three-quarters tilt in the low-80s that projects average or better, while he occasionally tosses a slower curveball and changeup to change the pace. The arsenal's depth varies by day, but it's enough to start in the upper levels on a good day. The fastball and slider tick up in short bursts to offer high-leverage relief potential, but the ceiling is closer to a back-end type. *—David Lee*

And because there haven't been enough pitchers on this list

Joey Wentz, LHP

The Braves paid Wentz like a top-15 pick in this year's draft, and it isn't hard to find people to sign off on him as possessing that level of talent. To wit, the projectable prep lefty out of Kansas would be a top ten prospect in most systems in baseball. He touched 95 this spring and should grow into more consistent mid-90s velocity as he fills out. Wentz also showed feel and command for his curveball and change. The stuff did tick down later in the high school season, so he is a riskier proposition than the group of pitchers that made Atlanta's top ten. Still, there's three potential plus pitches here, and I wouldn't be surprised if he has a breakout season in 2017 that rockets him up the Atlanta list and into our 2018 Top 101. And if I had to bet on a ranking I will look back on next year and regret, it's not putting Wentz in the top ten *this year*.

Lucas Sims, RHP

Sims approached the 2016 season with some helium following a promising showing in the Arizona Fall League. After a brief stint in double-A Mississippi, he was called up to Gwinnett where he struggled mightily, seeing his walk and home run rates reach alarmingly high levels. The walk rate remained high after returning to Mississippi, but the results smoothed out otherwise. He features a straight fastball that sits plus and a curveball that is above-average, arguably plus. His changeup is fringy and his arm action short, pushing the needle on this former first-round pick towards a future in a relief role. *—Adam Hayes*

Who's that guy? (who's that guy) It's Travis

Travis Demeritte, 2B

A solid upside play as the return for two pitchers the rebuilding Braves are unlikely to miss, Demeritte boasts an impressive pile of tools suffocating under one of the bigger question marks in his hometown team's system. *How much will he actually hit?* A 34-percent career strikeout rate in the low minors tends to suggest an unplesant answer. His production in the high-octane Mojave environs of his season's first half proved cause for cautious optimism, and it held reasonably after his journey to the less-enticing Carolina League. But at the higher levels? Unclear. He has the bat speed and loft to damage mistakes regardless of where he plays, but he struggles to track breaking balls and stay in the zone, and he frequently loses his mechanics to over-swings. Outside the box, there are notable instincts to help average speed play with utility on the bases. And he's an athletic, rangy defender at second, with enough arm strength to test the left-side waters in a utility role if the ultimate answer to that central query comes back "not enough." *—Wilson Karaman*

The guy we like less than others

Austin Riley, 3B

There's quite a bit of division over Riley's future. Some aren't able to fully pull the trigger and project a major leaguer, while others see the tantalizing plus power and want a corner power hitter. There will always be miss in his game and that's the main concern regarding his future. He made tweaks to his hands to shorten his path to the zone, but his swing remains stiff and muscled, and upper-level pitchers will force him to get the barrel to inside fastballs. If he can surpass a 40 hit tool, the 60 power will carry him to that valuable corner power profile. But below-average is the safe bet on his hitting ability. We haven't even mentioned the division regarding his defense. He lacks the lateral range and quickness to profile well at third base despite a plus arm, and that could ultimately push him to first base, which will put even more pressure on his bat. There's plenty intrigue as a potential 30-homer corner guy, but there are major questions that will need to be answered as he progresses. *—David Lee*

TOP 10 TALENTS 25 AND UNDER (BORN 4/1/91 OR LATER)

1. Dansby Swanson	6. Matt Wisler
2. Ronald Acuna	7. Aaron Blair
3. Ozzie Albies	8. Mike Soroka
4. Sean Newcomb	9. Kolby Allard
5. Mike Foltynewicz	10. Ian Anderson

It's telling that the overwhelming majority of Atlanta's top 25-under talent comes from the farm system. Sure, a lot of the 25-under talent in organizations is still prospect-eligible, but the Braves are different. This is done on purpose, for a reason.

In case you haven't heard, the Braves are rebuilding. They restocked their dwindling farm system at a lightning-quick pace, so much so that they've flipped their system from one of the most depleted to one of the strongest in the span of a couple years. They sacrificed winning during that span and that's still felt, which means the major-league 25-and-under talent is tough to find here, but it's all part of a plan.

See all those prospects on this list? The Braves are really good at developing talent. They're banking on that ability and expect these names to soon fill the 25-man roster. As that happens, the roster is expected to be complemented with acquired talent. It's all meant to come together and mold into a perennial winner.

Not all prospects pan out. That's okay. You could add an additional five spots to this list and the talent level wouldn't decrease by the end of it. In addition to their development knowledge, they're pretty smart at scouting. The Braves are deep.

Swanson at No. 1 signifies more than just holding the top spot on this list. He's seen as the future face of the franchise alongside Freddie Freeman. He might not have eye-popping tools, but he'll do everything well at the major-league level while giving the Braves a strong clubhouse presence.

After the first four prospects, you have the three major leaguers stuck together. Foltynewicz has the highest ceiling and the most major-league success, but none of the three have done enough so far to lock down a long-term spot. All three have the potential to log innings in a mid-rotation role, and the Braves are in a position to patiently let them work on things in the majors. If one works out as a back-end starter, one is a decent reliever, and one flames out, that's a net win.

As mentioned earlier, you could expand this list to 15 or so and the talent wouldn't decrease much. When you're leaving out players like Kevin Maitan (inexperience keeps him off), Mauricio Cabrera, Tyrell Jenkins, Max Fried, Touki Toussaint, Patrick Weigel and their plethora of recent high-upside draft picks, you're doing something right in your organization. The Braves are on the right track.

—David Lee

BALTIMORE ORIOLES

The State of the System: *Thin and lacks impact profiles at the top, but a bevy of young, intriguing arms keeps the Orioles out of the bottom tier of systems at least.*

THE TOP TEN

1. C Chance Sisco	6. LHP Keegan Akin
2. SS Ryan Mountcastle	7. RHP Ofelky Peralta
3. RHP Cody Sedlock	8. LHP Garrett Cleavinger
4. 1B Trey Mancini	9. RHP Gabriel Ynoa
5. 3B Jomar Reyes	10. LHP Alex Wells

The Big Question: Why are we so bad at projecting future roles for catchers?

Here's a list of catchers to make the Top 101 in recent seasons (highest rankings in parentheses):

Blake Swihart (17)

Despite having a reputation as a solid two-way catching prospect, got moved to left field on a team using Sandy Leon and Christian Vazquez as their primary catchers. Then he got hurt.

Jorge Alfaro (31)

Still very much Jorge Alfaro, for good and for ill.

Reese McGuire (59)

Still a very good defender, but has never hit in the minors.

Kevin Plawecki (80)

Hit in the minors, had a fringy defensive profile, is now a 20-hit framing god.

Francisco Mejia (84)

Good catching prospect.

Andrew Susac (91)

Got beat out for the Giants backup job by Trevor Brown.

Chance Sisco (101)

Oh we'll get there.

Austin Hedges (18)

Great defender, hasn't hit outside of El Paso.

Josmil Pinto (56)

Turned out he wasn't actually a catcher.

Travis d'Arnaud (15)

Good when healthy, wasn't healthy enough. Now isn't that good when healthy. Another bat-first profile that "turned into" a good defender once we had framing metrics.

Gary Sanchez (47)

Was a good catching prospect, then a less good catching prospect, now may be Babe Ruth.

Christian Bethancourt (93)

Decent backup catcher, may be a middle reliever next year.

—

So that's not a great hit rate. A quick scan of our 2013 Top 101 third baseman for example includes Miguel Sano, Anthony Rendon, Nick Castellanos, Nolan Arenado, and Jedd Gyorko (also Matt Davidson, Kaleb Cowart, and Mike Olt, mind you). That's more solid major leaguers than three years of catchers. We also got the shape of the production far closer than we did for catchers. Arenado turning into an 80 glove at third notwithstanding, Miguel Sano is a TTO bopper that maybe wasn't really a third baseman, Nick Castellanos is a bat-first profile that has to battle at the hot corner, Rendon is injury-plagued, but brilliant when healthy. This is all in line with their prospect profiles. The catchers above, busts, Babe

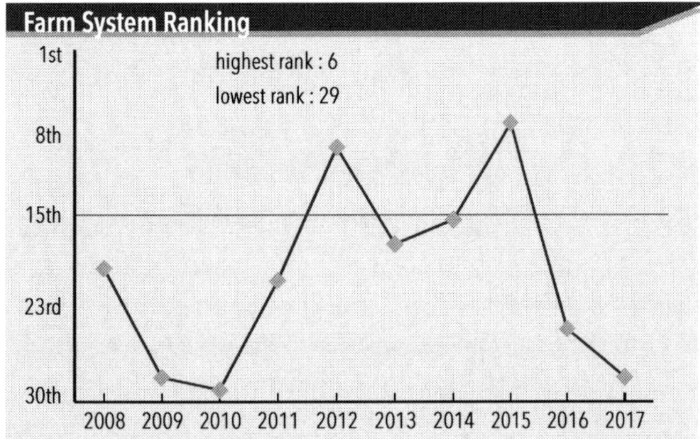

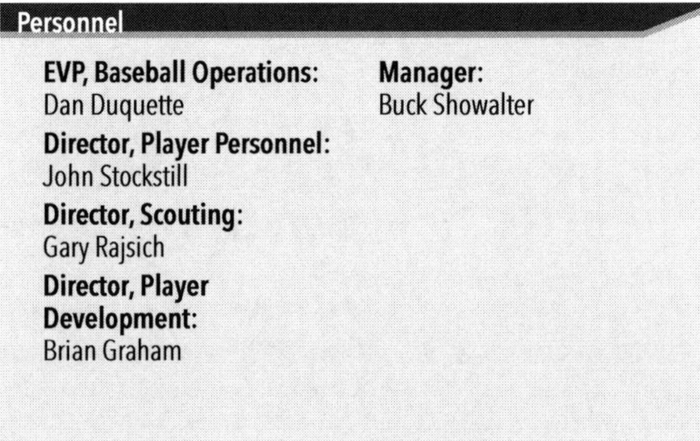

Ruth, and everything in between often look like completely different players than their minor-league reports.

The most common underlying issue here is "they didn't hit." This is true of most minor leaguers, but not true of most prospects. This is more art than science—see Kaleb Cowart—but generally we are pretty good at figuring out who we think will hit in the majors. If you had seen Rendon and Arenado in the minors, for example, they wouldn't have been hard scouts on the offensive end. With catchers though, we are more willing to accept risk in the offensive tools, because (A) catching is so damn hard and (B) thus the bar for offense at catcher is much lower. If Kevin Plawecki even had a 40 hit tool, he'd be a much easier sell as a role 5 starter. But those guys that you hope get to a 40 hit tool, McGuire, Hedges, and Bethancourt jump to mind, have very little room to fall short until the bat is completely unplayable even with the defensive tools. A prospect at any other position with McGuire's offensive projection would just be an org guy at best.

On the flip side, does it even matter if they can't hit? In 2016, Russell Martin hit .231/.335/.398. He was a three-win player by WARP. Jason Castro hit .210/.307/.377; WARP sees him as a perfectly cromulent starter. Rene Rivera and the aforementioned d'Arnaud both posted .630 OPS. They were each worth a 1.5 WARP in 70 games of playing time.

At SaberSeminar this year during their presentation on catcher game calling metrics, BP Stats maven Jonathan Judge said—I'll paraphrase—that he didn't care if his catcher hit at all. I've long been a bit of a James Randi when it comes to catcher defensive metrics, but even I've come around in the last year or so. This leaves me with a bit of a quandary.

All public prospect writing suffers from information asymmetry. The Orioles are going to have a whole heck of a lot more information on the ten names to follow than we are. Other teams have more looks going back further. In most cases though, we are at least looking at the same things. It's less true with catchers. Pitching prospect X might be a bit of a jerk, a bad tipper, a little lazy in PFP drills, but if he is 94-96 with a plus slider, we'd probably overlook that even if we knew it. With catchers, the important stuff is almost completely hidden from view. It's been a meme at times in sabermetric circles, Nichols Law of Catcher Defense. Turns out there might actually be a quantifiable reason that old no-hit backup catcher is around (see Rene Rivera again).

It's pretty clear teams have known this longer than us. Consider Juan Centeno—yes, bear with me—occasional third catcher for the Mets, Brewers, and Twins. The Twins were bad enough this year that Centeno got longer run as a back up and hit .260 with an average OBP and some doubles. That's not out of line with his mino-league scouting reports. He was usually backing up "better" catching prospects in the Mets system, like Francisco Peña and Blake Forsythe, but there was some bat-to-ball from the left side of the plate, and he was a good catch-and-throw type. You may remember him as the first catcher to throw out Billy Hamilton in the bigs, back when we thought that was going to be an event as frequent as a sighting of the Leonid Meteor storms.

Centeno hasn't turned out to be a great catch-and-throw guy in limited major-league opportunities—his minor-league caught-stealing rate is still 40 percent—but that kind of profile should get more opportunities as a backup. There's a reason three teams have passed on his services for the most part, one that's become clearer with the research that the BP Stats team has done—*he's not a good receiver*. We used to scoff at "pitchers don't like throwing to him" as an excuse to keep our favorite catching prospect on the fringes, but if I'm taking nothing else away from the research BP has done as catcher defense in the last couple years, it's that my stopwatch gives me much less useful information about a catcher's major-league future than a blind org quote of "pitchers don't like throwing to him."

Receiving/framing can be an observable physical skill. The problem is we're usually in the wrong place to see it. The scout's vantage point is great for evaluating pitching mechanics and pitches in general. It's pretty good for swing stuff. And it's fine for catch-and-throw actions. It's not great for receiving. The actions are hidden from view. This seems like an appropriate metaphor to conclude with.

Oh, well I suppose at this point you might still be wondering why this is the big question for the Orioles system. About that...

1. Chance Sisco, C

DOB: 02/24/1995

Height/Weight: 6'2" 193 lbs

Bats/Throws: L/R

Drafted/Acquired: Drafted 61st overall in the 2013 draft, Santiago HS (Corona, CA); signed for $785,000

Previous Ranking(s): #3 (Org)

2016 Stats: .320/.406/.422, 4 HR, 2 SB in 112 games at double-A Bowie

The Role: OFP 60—Above-average, two-way catcher
Likely 50—Bat-first backstop, whose defensive tools keep him closer to average

YEAR	TEAM	LVL	AGE	PA	R	2B	3B	HR	RBI	BB	K	SB	CS	AVG/OBP/SLG	TAv	VORP	BABIP	BRR	FRAA	WARP
2014	DEL	A	19	478	56	27	2	5	63	42	79	1	2	.340/.406/.448	.312	41.1	.406	-1.2	C(74): -6.4	3.6
2015	FRD	A+	20	300	30	12	3	4	26	33	41	8	1	.308/.387/.422	.299	21.3	.350	-0.7	C(57): -1.3	2.2
2015	BOW	AA	20	84	9	4	0	2	8	9	14	0	1	.257/.337/.392	.268	2.0	.293	-1.9	C(17): -0.1	0.2
2016	BOW	AA	21	479	53	28	1	4	44	59	83	2	2	.320/.406/.422	.297	28.8	.387	-5.7	C(83): -10.9	1.9
2016	NOR	AAA	21	18	4	0	0	2	7	2	5	0	0	.250/.333/.625	.313	2.2	.222	0.4	C(4): -0.4	0.2
2017	*BAL*	*MLB*	*22*	*60*	*6*	*3*	*0*	*1*	*6*	*6*	*13*	*0*	*0*	*.259/.331/.382*	*.251*	*2.1*	*.322*	*-0.1*	*C -3*	*-0.2*
2018	*BAL*	*MLB*	*23*	*299*	*38*	*14*	*1*	*8*	*34*	*30*	*66*	*0*	*0*	*.267/.345/.414*	*.258*	*9.5*	*.325*	*-0.7*	*C -14*	*-0.5*

Breakout: 10% Improve: 24% Collapse: 8% Attrition: 29% MLB: 45% *Comparables: Travis d'Arnaud, Gary Sanchez, Hank Conger*

The Good: Sisco will hit. He ticks all the boxes you look for when projecting a plus major-league hit tool: Good zone control, short to the ball, quick wrists with barrel control. He's comfortable deep in counts and should add a shiny OBP to the profile as well. He's improved his defense behind the plate to the point where you're more confident he sticks at catcher. The arm is average, and his catch/throw and receiving actions have improved in 2016.

The Bad: Sisco is still rough behind the plate. He's improved, but he's not a slam dunk to be an average defender there. The hit tool should still carry the profile, but it will have to as there is well-below-average game power here due to a swing geared for contact over loft.

The Irrelevant: Sisqo the performer grew up in Baltimore and worked at the Fudgery in the Inner Harbor.

The Risks: Catchers are weird, man. I wrote an essay about it and everything.

Major league ETA: Early 2018

Ben Carsley's Fantasy Take: The great thing about me is that I read that entire essay about catching prospects and thought "yeah, but Sisco will be different." Hell, I wrote this two-plus years ago and still think "yeah, but Sisco will be different." I know Sisco might not be a catcher, but I'll sell out for a hit tool faster than Craig will sell out for retweets. There's a good chance I'll have Sisco as my No. 2 or 3 dynasty catching prospect in the game. If (big if, yes) he can stick behind the plate, I think Sisco can be a high-average top-10 catcher in his prime, sort of like what Yadier Molina did from 2011-2015 (minus that 22-homer year). And so ends the first and last time you'll ever see Sisco comp'd to Yadier Molina.

2. Ryan Mountcastle, SS

DOB: 02/18/1997

Height/Weight: 6'3" 185 lbs

Bats/Throws: R/R

Drafted/Acquired: Drafted 36th overall in the 2015 draft, Paul J. Hagerty HS (Oviedo, FL); signed for $1.3 million

Previous Ranking(s): #7 (Org)

2016 Stats: .281/.319/.426, 10 HR, 5 SB in 115 games at Low-A Delmarva

The Role: OFP 60— Above-average middle infielder
Likely 50— Bat-first regular further down the defensive spectrum

YEAR	TEAM	LVL	AGE	PA	R	2B	3B	HR	RBI	BB	K	SB	CS	AVG/OBP/SLG	TAv	VORP	BABIP	BRR	FRAA	WARP
2015	ORI	Rk	18	175	21	7	0	3	14	9	36	10	4	.313/.349/.411	.287	10.9	.381	-1.3	SS(33): 0.0, 3B(3): 0.7	1.1
2015	ABE	A-	18	34	2	0	0	1	5	0	10	0	1	.212/.206/.303	.193	-2.0	.261	-0.5	SS(6): -1.0	-0.3
2016	DEL	A	19	489	53	28	4	10	51	25	95	5	4	.281/.319/.426	.287	28.5	.331	-1.7	SS(105): -21.3	0.8
2017	*BAL*	*MLB*	*20*	*250*	*27*	*11*	*1*	*8*	*26*	*10*	*68*	*0*	*0*	*.231/.265/.378*	*.215*	*-0.8*	*.288*	*-0.4*	*SS -6*	*-0.7*
2018	*BAL*	*MLB*	*21*	*364*	*41*	*16*	*1*	*12*	*44*	*16*	*95*	*0*	*0*	*.241/.277/.400*	*.229*	*0.3*	*.295*	*-0.8*	*SS -8*	*-0.9*

Breakout: 2% Improve: 10% Collapse: 0% Attrition: 4% MLB: 16% *Comparables: Raul Mondesi, Tim Beckham, Alen Hanson*

The Good: Mountcastle jumps up the Orioles list this year on the back of a strong campaign in the Sally as a 19-year-old. Although he's a bit of a free-swinger, there's the potential for above-average game power as he grows into his 6-foot-3 frame. He was better than expected at the 6 as well, although it is hard to find 6-foot-3 shortstops nowadays.

The Bad: Mountcastle is a bit of a free swinger, and it wouldn't be shocking if upper level arms exploit that. There aren't many 6-foot-3 shortstops and it's still likely he ends up sliding over to third. His below-average arm could mean a move to left field rather than third. The bat should handle the move to the hot corner, but it is a less exciting offensive profile the further down the defensive spectrum he goes.

The Irrelevant: Mouncastle's alma mater, Paul J. Hagerty High School, ranked first among Seminole County high schools the year he graduated.

The Risks: High. Mountcastle is still years off from major-league contributions, and the approach may limit his ability to get the potential power into games. Corner profile wouldn't put more pressure on the bat.

Major league ETA: 2019

Ben Carsley's Fantasy Take: Mountcastle is a bit too far away and a bit too unlikely to stick at shortstop to garner serious top-100 consideration yet, but he's definitely one to watch as 2017 progresses. If he keeps hitting well at higher levels and/or starts getting improved defensive reports, Mountcastle could jump up these rankings quickly. He is Lysa Arryn's least favorite prospect..

3. Cody Sedlock, RHP

DOB: 06/19/95

Height/Weight: 6'3" 190 lbs

Bats/Throws: R/R

Drafted/Acquired: Drafted 27th overall in 2016 draft, University of Illinois (Champaign, IL), signed for $2,097,200

Previous Ranking(s): N/A

2016 Stats: 3.00 ERA, 4.51 DRA, 27 IP, 16 H, 13 BB, 25 K at short-season Aberdeen

The Role: OFP 55—Good setup guy, occasional closer.
Likely 50—Your standard issue 6/6 two-pitch eighth-inning arm

YEAR	TEAM	LVL	AGE	W	L	SV	G	GS	IP	H	HR	BB/9	K/9	K	GB%	BABIP	WHIP	ERA	FIP	DRA	VORP	WARP	cFIP	MPH
2016	ABE	A-	21	0	1	0	9	9	27	16	1	4.3	8.3	25	60%	.200	1.07	3.00	3.35	3.57	5.00	0.5	99	
2017	*BAL*	*MLB*	*22*	*2*	*3*	*0*	*8*	*8*	*30²*	*38*	*6*	*6.0*	*5.1*	*18*	*44%*	*.309*	*1.90*	*6.51*	*6.64*	*6.62*	*-3.9*	*-0.4*	*157*	
2018	*BAL*	*MLB*	*23*	*4*	*8*	*0*	*26*	*26*	*153*	*163*	*24*	*5.9*	*7.0*	*119*	*44%*	*.298*	*1.72*	*6.01*	*5.80*	*6.11*	*-7.1*	*-0.7*	*146*	

Breakout: 1% Improve: 1% Collapse: 0% Attrition: 1% MLB: 1% *Comparables: Chi Chi Gonzalez, Mike Mayers, Adam Morgan*

The Good: Big arm speed and big fastball from a long, lean frame. Sedlock sits in the mid-90s and touched higher in his pro debut, although he had issues holding that velocity in even three-inning stints after a full college season. The pitch can be a bowling ball at times, making up for his lack of a true swing-and-miss offering elsewhere at present. Breaking ball is slurvy but will show good, hard tilt at times. Should be solid-average or even better in the end.

The Bad: Mechanical profile points toward the bullpen. Effort, crossfire, and a full pause before foot strike to let his arm accelerate all negatively effect the command profile and ability to repeat his release point. Fastball can be wild in the zone as a result. Changeup is used sparingly and is firm and well-below average at present.

The Irrelevant: In Sedlock's only year as a starter at the University of Illinois, he threw 22% of his team's innings.

The Risks: Post-college-season pro looks at pitchers are always a bit fuzzy, and Sedlock was worked hard at Illinois in his first season as a starter. That can work in either direction. The fastball is good enough at present that he shouldn't encounter too much resistance through the minors. Secondaries/command development will be the biggest risks to the profile. Could move very quickly as a reliever, but likely to stay stretched out for a while.

Major league ETA: 2018

Ben Carsley's Fantasy Take: As impressive as Sedlock's fastball and first-round pedigree may be, he's either years and years away from starting in the majors or a reliever. He's also in a system that's struggled to develop meaningful fantasy arms, Kevin Gausman's turnaround aside. That's not going to cut it for our purposes, even in a relatively down year overall for fantasy prospects.

4. Trey Mancini, 1B

DOB: 03/18/1992

Height/Weight: 6'4" 215 lbs

Bats/Throws: R/R

Drafted/Acquired: Drafted in the eighth round of the 2013 draft, University of Notre Dame; signed for $151,900

Previous Ranking(s): #6 (Org)

2016 Stats: .357/.400/1.071, 3 HR in five games at the major-league level, .280/.349/.427, 13 HR, 2 SB in 125 games at triple-A Norfolk, .302/.413/.698, 7 HR in 17 games at double-A Bowie

The Role: OFP 55—Solid-average major-league first baseman with pop carrying the offensive profile
Likely 45—Fringe starter at first base

YEAR	TEAM	LVL	AGE	PA	R	2B	3B	HR	RBI	BB	K	SB	CS	AVG/OBP/SLG	TAv	VORP	BABIP	BRR	FRAA	WARP
2014	DEL	A	22	291	30	13	3	3	42	14	52	1	1	.317/.357/.422	.292	11.7	.378	-1.1	1B(66): 1.8	1.4
2014	FRD	A+	22	295	37	19	0	7	41	14	43	0	1	.251/.295/.396	.243	-2.8	.273	-0.4	1B(69): -6.7	-1.0
2015	FRD	A+	23	217	28	14	3	8	32	9	35	4	2	.314/.341/.527	.299	10.6	.345	-0.1	1B(51): 2.8	1.4
2015	BOW	AA	23	354	60	29	3	13	57	22	58	2	1	.359/.395/.586	.340	32.5	.400	0.2	1B(75): -0.8	3.4
2016	BOW	AA	24	75	18	4	0	7	14	10	17	0	0	.302/.413/.698	.346	7.8	.308	0.6	1B(15): 0.4	0.9
2016	NOR	AAA	24	536	60	22	5	13	54	48	123	2	2	.280/.349/.427	.281	15.4	.351	-1.9	1B(121): 6.4	2.2
2016	BAL	MLB	24	15	3	1	0	3	5	0	4	0	0	.357/.400/1.071	.435	2.7	.286	-0.1		0.3
2017	*BAL*	*MLB*	*25*	*204*	*23*	*9*	*1*	*8*	*27*	*13*	*49*	*0*	*0*	*.262/.315/.445*	*.263*	*3.8*	*.314*	*-0.4*	*1B 0*	*0.4*
2018	*BAL*	*MLB*	*26*	*407*	*51*	*19*	*2*	*15*	*54*	*28*	*103*	*0*	*0*	*.256/.312/.443*	*.255*	*5.8*	*.311*	*-0.8*	*1B 1*	*0.7*

Breakout: 6% Improve: 25% Collapse: 8% Attrition: 25% MLB: 45% *Comparables: Mark Trumbo, Christian Walker, Steve Pearce*

The Good: Mancini hit in Double A. He hit in Triple A. He hit in the majors (okay it was 15 PA). It's in no way an exciting profile. He's a big, brutish, right-handed, bat-first first baseman. The pop is above-average, though not prodigious. This sounds sarcastic placed in this section, but it isn't? There isn't that much right-handed power around, and Mancini has it and is ready to deploy it in the majors.

The Bad: You'd be forgiven for thinking this did sound like a potential Quad-A profile. The power comes from a long swing with a near armbar, and while the K-rates have been high but manageable so far, major-league arms may exploit the holes. He's first base (and DH) only. If he isn't starting there, he's not an ideal bench piece.

The Irrelevant: Mancini's first major-league hit was, unsurprisingly, a dinger.

The Risks: Mancini is low risk, but your reward might only be something in the vein of C.J. Cron. It's tough to carry a Role 45 right-handed 1B/DH nowadays, even if they add a 26th roster spot.

Major league ETA: Debuted in 2016

Ben Carsley's Fantasy Take: I used C.J. Cron as a comp to disparage Dom Smith, and here I'm using it to compliment (sort of) Mancini. Really, this is all about managing expectations. If you want to take the plunge with Mancini in TDGX-sized leagues that roster 200-plus prospects, sure, why not? He's MLB-ready and has good contextual factors. You could do worse than to bet on him as a bench bat/backup CI. But you couldn't really do worse than to bet on him as a starting fantasy 1B. Just take it slow and keep your hopes modest.

5. Jomar Reyes, 3B

DOB: 02/20/1997

Height/Weight: 6'3" 220 lbs

Bats/Throws: R/R

Drafted/Acquired: Signed in January 2014 out of the Dominican Republic for $350,000

Previous Ranking(s): #5 (Org)

2016 Stats: .228/.271/.336, 10 HR, 3 SB in 126 games at high-A Frederick

The Role: OFP 55—See Trey Mancini
Likely 45—See, uh, Trey Mancini (I guess there's a bit better bench profile if someone stands him at third)

YEAR	TEAM	LVL	AGE	PA	R	2B	3B	HR	RBI	BB	K	SB	CS	AVG/OBP/SLG	TAv	VORP	BABIP	BRR	FRAA	WARP
2014	ORI	Rk	17	207	23	10	2	4	29	15	38	1	0	.285/.333/.425	.346	12.5	.329	0.7		1.1
2015	ORI	Rk	18	19	2	2	0	0	4	2	5	1	0	.250/.368/.375	.283	0.8	.364	-0.1	3B(2): -0.1	0.1
2015	DEL	A	18	335	36	27	4	5	44	18	73	1	0	.278/.334/.440	.309	23.1	.351	-3.4	3B(74): -6.5	1.8
2016	FRD	A+	19	498	53	16	2	10	51	25	102	3	0	.228/.271/.336	.214	-7.8	.269	0.8	3B(122): -4.0	-1.2
2017	*BAL*	*MLB*	*20*	*250*	*22*	*10*	*1*	*7*	*27*	*10*	*69*	*0*	*0*	*.219/.258/.353*	*.208*	*-5.8*	*.278*	*-0.3*	*3B -3*	*-1.0*
2018	*BAL*	*MLB*	*21*	*412*	*44*	*18*	*1*	*12*	*46*	*18*	*107*	*0*	*0*	*.226/.269/.371*	*.222*	*-7.6*	*.279*	*-0.8*	*3B -5*	*-1.4*

Breakout: 1% Improve: 3% Collapse: 0% Attrition: 1% MLB: 4% *Comparables: Jefry Marte, Maikel Franco, Alex Liddi*

The Good: Reyes is a massive human being and he has the massive raw power to match. Potential 25-home-run hitter at maturity. More than enough arm for third base, if he ever improves his actions and footwork enough to play at third. While the swing has some length to it, there's some feel for hitting as well.

The Bad: After holding his own as an 18-year-old in the Sally, it didn't go quite as well as a 19-year-old in the Carolina League. The big frame means big swings, and big swing-and-miss. It's not as bad as the stat line, but he does struggle with spin, and the overall hit tool issues mean the raw power hasn't really shown up in games yet. He's rough at third even considering the body type, and the body type will eventually move him to first regardless.

The Irrelevant: Reyes ended up a third baseman because his father noticed the catcher throws to third after every strikeout. (No, really)

The Risks: High. We are banking on some projection, a lot more hit tool utility, and an eventual first base profile. As we mentioned earlier, that fringy right-handed first base profile is tough as a bench bat, so it limits his major-league impact if he isn't a starter of some sort.

Major league ETA: 2019

Ben Carsley's Fantasy Take: The fantasy third base prospect scene is pretty barren right now once you get past the first few names. It's so bad that Reyes is probably still a top-15 (and maybe a top-10) dynasty prospect at the position, but please don't confuse that with making him anything close to a top-100 prospect overall. The power is intriguing and he might not be super far away if it clicks, but you can say that about lots of CI prospects. Pray he turns into 2016 Maikel Franco (.255, 25 homers) but be prepared to settle for 2015 Luis Valbuena (.224, 22 homers). Or, you know, worse.

6. Keegan Akin, LHP

DOB: 04/01/1995

Height/Weight: 6'0" 225 lbs

Bats/Throws: L/L

Drafted/Acquired: Drafted 54th overall in 2016 draft, Western Michigan University (Kalamazoo, MI), signed for $1,177,200

Previous Ranking(s): N/A

2016 Stats: 1.04 ERA, 2.96 DRA, 26 IP, 15 H, 7 BB, 29 K at short-season Aberdeen

The Role: OFP 50— No. 4 starter or set-up man
Likely 45— Set-up man

YEAR	TEAM	LVL	AGE	W	L	SV	G	GS	IP	H	HR	BB/9	K/9	K	GB%	BABIP	WHIP	ERA	FIP	DRA	VORP	WARP	cFIP	MPH
2016	ABE	A-	21	0	1	0	9	9	26	15	0	2.4	10.0	29	51%	.231	0.85	1.04	1.85	2.60	7.60	0.8	80	
2017	*BAL*	*MLB*	*22*	*2*	*3*	*0*	*9*	*9*	*32^{2}*	*38*	*6*	*4.5*	*6.8*	*24*	*35%*	*.311*	*1.65*	*5.64*	*5.69*	*5.77*	*-1.1*	*-0.1*	*137*	
2018	*BAL*	*MLB*	*23*	*5*	*8*	*0*	*29*	*29*	*178^{1}*	*178*	*29*	*4.2*	*8.3*	*164*	*35%*	*.295*	*1.47*	*5.18*	*4.99*	*5.30*	*2.1*	*0.2*	*127*	

Breakout: 3% Improve: 3% Collapse: 1% Attrition: 2% MLB: 4% *Comparables: Tyler Wilson, Andrew Heaney, Wilking Rodriguez*

The Good: If you caught Akin on the right day you would see a pitcher with a much more quiet delivery than before, with three potentially average or better pitches. His fastball has been as high as 96, with sink, which will be his bread and butter. His secondary pitches need to find consistency but his slider has flashed above average on occasion, and late in the year with Western Michigan he found feel for his changeup.

The Bad: The odds you caught Akin on that day are not good. In my viewings of Akin I saw all of that, but never all at once. He needs to gain consistency and while the reduction in effort is attractive, he will need to show that he can consistently use his three pitches.

The Irrelevant: In the championship game of the MAC tournament Akin pitched on three days of rest against Kent State, who refused to throw future first-rounder Eric Lauer on three days of rest.

The Risks: The risk on Akin is that he never can put together the whole package that he has flashed, and is relegated to the bullpen. Even if this happens, Akin will be successful in the role.

Major league ETA: 2020, possibly faster in the pen —Grant Jones

Ben Carsley's Fantasy Take: Because Akin possesses the ability to be something more than a back-end starter, he's slightly more interesting for our purposes than you might think. I only mean, like, maybe a top-300 prospect interesting, though. Wait to see if it clicks for Akin, or if more positive reports start flowing in before you take the leap. Or, given Baltimore's track record of producing viable fantasy starters, spend your time focused on literally anyone else.

7. Ofelky Peralta, RHP

DOB: 04/20/1997

Height/Weight: 6'5" 195 lbs

Bats/Throws: R/R

Drafted/Acquired: Signed in September 2013 out of the Dominican Republic for $325,000

Previous Ranking(s): N/A

2016 Stats: 4.01 ERA, 7.98 DRA, 103.1 IP, 87 H, 60 BB, 101 K at low-A Delmarva

The Role: OFP 50— Effectively wild setup man
Likely 40— Middle reliever that drives his manager and fans nuts with leadoff walks

YEAR	TEAM	LVL	AGE	W	L	SV	G	GS	IP	H	HR	BB/9	K/9	K	GB%	BABIP	WHIP	ERA	FIP	DRA	VORP	WARP	cFIP	MPH
2014	DBA	Rk	17	0	4	0	11	11	43^{1}	28	0	7.7	6.9	33	0%	.231	1.50	3.12	4.71	9.53			130	
2015	ORI	Rk	18	0	2	0	11	10	25^{2}	20	0	6.7	10.9	31	47%	.294	1.52	5.61	3.57	5.22	1.80	0.2	111	
2016	DEL	A	19	8	5	0	23	23	103^{1}	87	3	5.2	8.8	101	39%	.301	1.42	4.01	3.77	8.64	-41.60	-4.6	127	
2017	*BAL*	*MLB*	*20*	*2*	*7*	*0*	*16*	*16*	*61^{2}*	*83*	*15*	*7.9*	*4.3*	*29*	*28%*	*.309*	*2.22*	*8.24*	*8.16*	*8.49*	*-20.7*	*-2.1*	*195*	
2018	*BAL*	*MLB*	*21*	*2*	*8*	*0*	*18*	*18*	*104^{1}*	*125*	*23*	*8.9*	*6.8*	*79*	*28%*	*.307*	*2.18*	*8.00*	*7.75*	*8.24*	*-21.6*	*-2.2*	*189*	

Breakout: 0% Improve: 0% Collapse: 0% Attrition: 0% MLB: 0% *Comparables: Shawn Morimando, Tyler Matzek, Brett Marshall*

The Good: Peralta is a big kid with a big arm. I'm going to guess that 195 is his signing weight at this point, because even at 19, he has developed a bit of the vaunted "Chad Billingsley ass." Fastball touched 98 this year, although he will work more in the low-90s. Even at 92-93, it appears to get on you in a hurry and is a lively pitch. Change is ahead of the breaking ball. It isn't a big fader at present, but the arm speed is good and lends it some additional deception. I really, really like the arm, but...

The Bad: ...if Sedlock's mechanics point to the pen, Peralta screams "reliever!" like it's the first lyric of a Brutal Truth song. And the brutal truth is the command profile will probably never allow him to start at the major-league level. The delivery is all arm speed over lower-body usage. His upper and lower halves are rarely in sync. Release point may be governed by the Heisenberg Uncertainty Principle. Okay, we think you get the picture. Oh, breaking ball is slurvy and lacks depth, but it's more projectable than the command/control profile.

The Irrelevant: You've probably read enough of these by now to know that I am about to tell you he is the only Ofelky pitching in organized baseball. Only 243 more of these to go!

The Risks: Peralta is raw. Really raw. First-course-of-a-three-michelin-starred-omakase-menu-with-one-eight-person-seating raw. He may never throw enough strikes to satisfy anyone. And he's a pitcher.

Major league ETA: 2019

Ben Carsley's Fantasy Take: I maintain that someday Mauricio Rubio will invent a fantasy league with "ass" as a category. Until that day, Ofelky can remain on waivers in your league.

8. Garrett Cleavinger, LHP

DOB: 04/23/1994

Height/Weight: 6'1" 210 lbs

Bats/Throws: R/L

Drafted/Acquired: Drafted in the third round of the 2015 draft, University of Oregon (Eugene, OR), signed for $500,000

Previous Ranking(s): N/A

2016 Stats: 4.82 ERA, 3.25 DRA, 37.1 IP, 35 H, 23 BB, 49 K at High-A Frederick, 1.38 ERA, 1.60 DRA, 25 H, 11 BB, 53 K at Low-A Delmarva

The Role: OFP 50—Power lefty set-up man with 4-plus out possibilities
Likely 40—Generic lefty middle reliever with enough stuff to crossover

YEAR	TEAM	LVL	AGE	W	L	SV	G	GS	IP	H	HR	BB/9	K/9	K	GB%	BABIP	WHIP	ERA	FIP	DRA	VORP	WARP	cFIP	MPH
2015	ABE	A-	21	6	1	1	19	0	25	14	2	6.5	11.5	32	44%	.231	1.28	2.16	4.39	5.13	-0.60	-0.1	112	
2016	DEL	A	22	5	0	4	17	0	39	25	3	2.5	12.2	53	51%	.278	0.92	1.38	2.60	1.92	11.90	1.3	74	
2016	FRD	A+	22	2	3	0	20	0	37¹	35	2	5.5	11.8	49	37%	.367	1.55	4.82	3.71	3.33	7.30	0.7	100	
2017	*BAL*	*MLB*	*23*	*2*	*1*	*2*	*48*	*0*	*51*	*57*	*9*	*5.5*	*7.2*	*41*	*33%*	*.310*	*1.73*	*5.78*	*5.80*	*5.87*	*-7.3*	*-0.8*	*140*	
2018	*BAL*	*MLB*	*24*	*1*	*0*	*1*	*18*	*0*	*32*	*30*	*5*	*6.2*	*10.0*	*36*	*33%*	*.306*	*1.63*	*5.40*	*5.20*	*5.48*	*-1.4*	*-0.1*	*130*	

Breakout: 5% Improve: 5% Collapse: 0% Attrition: 2% MLB: 5% *Comparables: Carson Smith, Joe Paterson, Lester Oliveros*

The Good: He's a lefty with a fastball that gets up into the mid-90s and a potential plus power curve. That's a pretty good start.

The Bad: But there's not much more there. He's a college closer who's now a minor-league reliever and will eventually be a major-league reliever. The curve can be inconsistent at times, and even at its best it can be a tick below 1-7 and more effective against lefties than righties. The command is below-average, but acceptable for a reliever.

The Irrelevant: No, he's not that Clevenger.

The Risks: Cleavinger's command profile might be limiting in roles other than where he needs to come in for an inning or two and blow a power fastball/curve combo by guys. Fortunately we aren't projecting him for that role, so he should be a major-league arm and potentially quickly. But he is a pitcher, so...

Major league ETA: Early 2018

Ben Carsley's Fantasy Take: I don't miss Felix Doubront, to be honest.

9. Gabriel Ynoa, RHP

DOB: 5/26/93

Height/Weight: 6'2" 205 lbs

Bats/Throws: R/R

Drafted/Acquired: Signed out of the Dominican Republic by the New York Mets in November 2009. Acquired from New York for cash considerations.

Previous Ranking(s): N/A

2016 Stats: 3.97 ERA, 4.57 DRA, 154.1 IP, 170 H, 40 BB, 78 K at Triple-A Las Vegas, 6.38 ERA, 4.86 DRA, 18.1 IP, 26 H, 7 BB, 17 K at the major-league level

The Role: OFP 50—No. 4 starter or seventh inning arm
Likely 40—Up and down fifth starter/pen arm with a shorter commute

YEAR	TEAM	LVL	AGE	W	L	SV	G	GS	IP	H	HR	BB/9	K/9	K	GB%	BABIP	WHIP	ERA	FIP	DRA	VORP	WARP	cFIP	MPH
2014	SLU	A+	21	8	2	0	14	14	152[1]	95	7	1.4	7.0	64	44%	.330	1.32	3.95	3.44	2.43	28.9	2.9	88	
2014	BIN	AA	21	3	2	0	11	11	154[1]	74	9	1.6	5.7	42	40%	.304	1.30	4.21	4.52	6.47	-9.2	-1.0	108	
2015	BIN	AA	22	9	9	0	25	24	18[1]	157	14	1.8	4.8	82	47%	.283	1.23	3.90	4.11	4.41	11.5	1.2	103	
2016	LVG	AAA	23	12	5	0	25	25	1	170	15	2.3	4.5	78	48%	.300	1.36	3.97	4.86	4.57	13.4	1.4	103	
2016	NYN	MLB	23	1	0	0	10	3	5	26	0	3.4	8.3	17	51%	.413	1.80	6.38	2.63	5.36	-0.3	0.0	100	95.4
2017	*BAL*	*MLB*	*24*	*2*	*2*	*0*	*13*	*5*	*33*	*38*	*4*	*3.2*	*4.1*	*15*	*43%*	*.292*	*1.48*	*5.07*	*5.04*	*5.13*	*1.2*	*0.1*	*100*	
2018	*BAL*	*MLB*	*25*	*3*	*4*	*0*	*27*	*9*	*71*	*70*	*9*	*5.0*	*7.1*	*56*	*43%*	*.288*	*1.54*	*4.63*	*4.99*	*5.40*	*-0.1*	*0.0*	*125*	

Breakout: 18% Improve: 25% Collapse: 21% Attrition: 38% MLB: 53% *Comparables: Adam Wilk, Kendry Flores, Chaz Roe*

The Good: Ynoa has shuffled along for years, going level-by-level, always on the fringes of a team top ten list. He makes it now in part because he moved to a much shallower farm system, but he also made some real gains in 2016. His fastball ticked up and now sits 93-96 with hard sink at times. His slider flashes solid-average now, with late cut and some tilt in the upper-80s. His change is now his third pitch, and never really improved much from his projectable, short-season days, but it's still an average offering

The Bad: Ynoa has been searching for an outpitch for five years in the minors and never really found one. The slider did jump in 2016 with some help from Dan Warthen, but is still fringy overall. The velocity jump has flattened out his fastball's natural armside run and firmed up his changeup. The heater is still too hittable even at 95 due to his long arm action and low slot. His curve is used more to steal a strike than miss a bat. Ynoa can throw all four of his pitches for strikes, but the command profile is has regressed a little with the added velocity and is now fringy.

The Irrelevant: Ynoa has won two minor-league championships in his career, spraying champagne with Savannah in 2013 and Binghamton in 2014.

The Risks: Ynoa is major-league ready, but it isn't clear what major-league role he should have. He's always relied on keeping the ball in the park and minimizing free passes, which may no longer be a workable strategy against major-league bats. He's been as healthy as you could possibly ask a pitching prospect to be over the last half-decade, but he is still a pitcher.

Major league ETA: Debuted in 2016

Ben Carsley's Fantasy Take: Ah, an Orioles pitcher without an outpitch. Tempting ...

10. Alex Wells, LHP

DOB: 02/27/1997

Height/Weight: 6'1" 190 lbs

Bats/Throws: L/L

Drafted/Acquired: Signed in September 2015 out of Australia for $300,000

Previous Ranking(s): N/A

2016 Stats: 2.15 ERA, 2.50 DRA, 62.2 IP, 48 H, 9 BB, 50 K at short-season Aberdeen

The Role: OFP 50— Command and pitchability No. 4 starter
Likely 40—No. 5 starter/swingman/middle-reliever roulette

YEAR	TEAM	LVL	AGE	W	L	SV	G	GS	IP	H	HR	BB/9	K/9	K	GB%	BABIP	WHIP	ERA	FIP	DRA	VORP	WARP	cFIP	MPH
2016	ABE	A-	19	4	5	0	13	13	62[2]	48	1	1.3	7.2	50	46%	.269	0.91	2.15	2.36	2.46	19.40	2.0	83	
2017	*BAL*	*MLB*	*20*	*2*	*3*	*0*	*7*	*7*	*36[1]*	*45*	*8*	*3.6*	*5.4*	*22*	*31%*	*.309*	*1.65*	*6.11*	*6.09*	*6.20*	*-2.9*	*-0.3*	*151*	
2018	*BAL*	*MLB*	*21*	*6*	*9*	*0*	*23*	*23*	*136[2]*	*151*	*28*	*3.8*	*7.2*	*110*	*31%*	*.298*	*1.53*	*5.89*	*5.68*	*5.98*	*-6.4*	*-0.7*	*146*	

Breakout: 1% Improve: 1% Collapse: 0% Attrition: 0% MLB: 1% *Comparables: Kyle Lobstein, Robert Stephenson, Cesar Vargas*

The Good: Wells is a young lefty with precocious command of a fastball/change combo that kept Penn League hitters off balance in 2016. The fastball only touches 90 at present, but he commands it well to both sides of the plate, and there is some boring action against righties. The fastball plays up past the 87-90 radar readings due to some deception in the mechanics and arm action. The change is very advanced for his age, and a potential plus pitch with further refinement. It features good sinking action. Like the fastball, he can command it to both sides of the plate. He will spot it for a strike, even first pitch, and throws it left-on-left as well.

The Bad: The breaking ball is a soft downer curve in the low-70s that is just a chase pitch at present. I wonder if he doesn't try a slider at some point (though betting on the Orioles improving an internal pitching prospect…) from that high-three-quarters slot. The fastball velocity is always likely to be fringy as there isn't much projection left and there is already some effort in the delivery.

The Irrelevant: Alex's identical twin brother, Lachlan, who pitches in the Twins organization, is listed as five inches shorter than him.

The Risks: Wells only has a short-season resume, needs a significant grade jump on the breaking ball, and will be working off fringy fastball velocity. I think that about covers it. Oh yeah, and he's a pitcher.

Major league ETA: 2020

Ben Carsley's Fantasy Take: If you enjoyed Wade Miley's 2016 work in Baltimore but want to wait three or four seasons to relive it, go all-in on Wells.

OTHERS OF NOTE:

#11

Chris Lee, LHP

Lee could rank as high as seventh on this list, as our seven through eleven here are all pretty similar. Lee is left-handed (which is good) and you could very well see him in 2017 at some point (also good). But he has a little less stuff that some of the names ahead of him (that's bad). He works off a 90-mph fastball that is deceptively fast and shows good arm-side life at times. He'll take a little off and cut it to righties as well. Lee will cast his slider at times, but it's a weapon against left-handed bats, and there is an average change in here with continued refinement, and even if it is more of a 40 or 45 pitch, that's enough to crossover in a bullpen role. There's not a real swing-and-miss offering in the arsenal yet. Lee has to ramp up the effort to get the fastball to the top end of this range, and he has reliever mechanics to begin with. The delivery is herky-jerky even when he isn't maxing out for the low 90s, and he throws across his body with a slight crossfire. The stuff and command is fringy enough that it's unlikely he could go through a major-league lineup multiple times anyway, but funky lefties rarely want for work.

#12 #1 #DamnedIfIKnow

Hunter Harvey, RHP

On talent/stuff/OFP/whatever, Harvey is the best prospect in the system. I wrote a whole introduction to these lists justifying the need to chase "upside" in prospect rankings. Harvey will miss most of, if not all, of the 2017 season recovering from Tommy John surgery. This happens to pitching prospects of course. We ranked Tyler Kolek No. 3 in a bad Marlins system. The Orioles system isn't that bad, but it's below-average, and Harvey is better than Kolek. Harvey's injury history is more checkered than just this UCL sprain, but hey, we ranked Jameson Taillon as the 51st best prospect in baseball, and he hadn't thrown a pitch in two seasons. Harvey was 58th, despite his comment focusing on the forearm soreness that plagued him in 2015 and kept him off the mound entirely. He threw 12 innings this year before finally going under the knife. He's never thrown more than 87 innings in a pro season. He has thrown 125 innings total in a four-year pro career. He still may have top-of-the-rotation upside, but at what point do you say: "I have no idea if this guy will ever be able to physically pitch?"

Also not the 90s-noise-rock band but this one does go to #11

Jesus Liranzo, RHP

The Yankees system is up next so "future reliever week" will not be stretching into a fortnight at least. Liranzo comes with a fun backstory at least. Released out of Braves camp before throwing a single pro pitch for them, he was signed by the Orioles who stuck a pin in his elbow to repair a fracture (well it's not Tommy John?). Liranzo has a quick, loose arm, and he gets some good sink and run on his mid-90s fastball. He can also elevate it to get K's, or turn to his mid-80s downer slider. It's another middle reliever with a chance for more, but the O's did think enough of him to add him to the 40-man, and he could be a factor in the 2017 bullpen.

Mammas, don't let your babies grow up to be right-handed

Tanner Scott, LHP

At this point it has gone unnoticed by no one that there is a lot more velocity in the minors than there was even a few years ago. But lefties that can throw 100, well that's still worthy of note. You pair it with a slider that flashes plus, and you start dreaming of a late-inning monster. It could be an embarrassment of riches in the Orioles pen in 2017. Just one small problem: Scott can't throw strikes. He pitches like a guy who finds the idea of having even the bare minimum of a wind-up to be a giant inconvenience to just chucking the ball as hard as he can. Despite a potential 80/60 two-pitch mix, Scott has yet to post an ERA under 4.00 at any full-season stop. That said, he is a lefty that throws 100. He will never want for work as long as there are triple-digits in his left arm. Some pitching coach will always think they can unlock enough control and command to make him a major-league reliever. And if one is right about that, look out.

The still-not-that-inspiring

D.J. Stewart, LF

After a wildly underwhelming stint in the South Atlantic League in the first half of the season, Stewart showed some signs of life in the Carolina League this summer. That still isn't what you want to hear about your first round college pick from the previous Summer, but it beats not having him in this section at all. He's still likely a first baseman long term, and lacks the plus power potential of Mancini and Reyes. The mechanical swing leaves me with the same concerns about his future hit tool, so they are up there, and he is down here.

TOP 10 TALENTS 25 AND UNDER (BORN 4/1/91 OR LATER)

1. Manny Machado	6. Cody Sedlock
2. Dylan Bundy	7. Trey Mancini
3. Jonathan Schoop	8. Jomar Reyes
4. Chance Sisco	9. Keegan Akin
5. Ryan Mountcastle	10. Ofelky Peralta

The Orioles' list of top players 25-and-under has all the hallmarks of being the makings of a really good organization. There's serious star power at the top in the form of young major-league talent. There's a glut of prospects following that which includes some premium position players (catcher, shortstop, etc.) and plenty of intriguing arms.

The trouble is the presence of serious question marks in the major-league talent and general lack of quality in the group of prospects. The Orioles' system is less a function of having a lot of high-quality prospects, and more the result of having little-to-no young talent on the major-league roster that profiles as anything more than a bench guy.

There is one massive caveat that I'd be remiss without noting, and that is Manny Machado. He's a top-10 player in the American League, and arguably all of baseball. I'm not going to waste time talking about Machado, because at this point we all probably know how good he is.

After Machado there are Dylan Bundy and Jonathan Schoop. Bundy is/was remarkably talented, but his injury history is lengthy to put it mildly. The team likely overworked him in 2016—asking him to throw 110 innings despite not even reaching the 25-inning mark the previous season. For a player with an injury history like Bundy's, that approach was surely bold. In terms of performance, Bundy flashed the promise that he once held as a prospect, although he wasn't able to pitch that well consistently. The big question is whether he'll be able to improve and stay healthy in his sophomore season.

Schoop is another interesting player in that slick-fielding second baseman who hit 25 home runs aren't exactly the Pidgey of the baseball world. Schoop suffers a bit from the Adam Jones issue where the eye test says he's a pretty great defender, but the stats don't seem to agree. That and his inability to get on base stunt his value, making him just a 1-win player in 2016. There's room for improvement, especially in approach, but Schoop has already proved to be a dynamic player that can hold down a major-league job for now.

Overall the young talent in the Orioles' organization—beyond centerpiece Manny Machado—is filled with big question marks. Health has been a major question throughout the organization, so it'll be important for the club's future that this new batch of young pitchers stays relatively healthy. There's not a lot of position player depth either, so O's fans should be crossing their fingers that guys like Sisco and Mountcastle continue to develop.

All in all, the system and overall young talent leaves a lot to be desired. As a result, the O's should be feeling the pressure to make a deep playoff run over the next year or two or else there might be some big changes leading up to Machado's impending free agency after the 2018 season.

—Jeff Long

BOSTON RED SOX

The State of the System: *I could just C&P the Nats lines here. Incredible top five, falls off quickly after that, and past the top ten, even fewer intriguing names than the Nats.*

THE TOP TEN

1. OF Andrew Benintendi	6. 1B Josh Ockimey
2. 3B Rafael Devers	7. 3B Bobby Dalbec
3. LHP Jason Groome	8. 3B Michael Chavis
4. 1B Sam Travis	9. RHP Michael Shawaryn
5. LHP Brian Johnson	10. OF Lorenzo Cedrola

The Big Question: Why don't we give out 80 hit tools?

Andrew Benintendi is about as sure a bet to hit for a good batting average as a prospect can be. He was a top-ten overall draft pick as a small, late-blooming, moderately bat-first player. The bat has to be really good for that to happen. His minor-league performance record is absolutely flawless, outside of a rough first couple weeks in Double A that got drowned out in the season line quickly when he started crushing the ball. He is essentially already established as a major-league regular, only eligible for this list because a minor injury kept him just a touch under the rookie-eligibility requirements. He hit .295 for a month-and-a-half in the majors in a pennant race. He's got one of those picture-perfect beautiful lefty swings. He makes a short, aggressive move on the ball. His wrists are great, his bat speed is excellent, and he has a really good idea of what he wants to do. The ball jumps off his bat in a way it does for the truly special ones. There's basically nothing to nitpick here. This is the total hit package.

We've had a lot of eyes on Benintendi as a prospect, and even after he made the majors. Nobody has come away less than enthused by his hitting ability. We may not get a still-eligible prospect with this combination of raw hitting ability, polish, and statistical foundation for years to come.

We're not giving Andrew Benintendi a future 80 hit tool. We're giving him a 70.

Future 80 tools are and should be rare, but a lot of them are honestly pretty obvious too. If a hitter can consistently be clocked 3.9 seconds down the line as a lefty or 4.0 down the line as a righty, he's an 80 runner. If a pitcher can consistently sit around 97-98 with appropriate movement and command, it's an 80-grade fastball. Future 80s in power, field, and arm are loud grades you can see quickly and easily, and are easily calibrated against major-league equivalents. For example, Giancarlo Stanton is an 80 power player, and Joey Gallo's batting practice sessions and dingers sure look right compared to Stanton's, so it's easy to throw 80 raw power on Gallo. I can go watch what Francisco Lindor looks like in the field if I need a reminder what an 80 defender at shortstop is.

The hit tool is never as easy to spot. It depends on hitting mechanics and hand-eye coordination; natural bat speed and subtle physical abilities; approach and pitch recognition; and the ability to recognize pitch sequencing, along with a dozen other things that are hard for even the very best scouts to pick out. (Kiley McDaniel, currently the Assistant Director of Baseball Operations for the Atlanta Braves, once wrote a six-part series on evaluating hit tools, and if you're really interested in a deep dive on how to try and piece this all together, that's a good place to start.) The hardest evaluation to make on nearly every young position player worth talking about is, "Will this dude hit legitimate major-league stuff?" When we miss on position players bigly, it's usually the hit tool where we miss worst. This is, of course, why we keep mentioning how important it is that players like Benintendi and Dansby Swanson have performed well and looked the part against MLB pitching—we've got actual information that they can hit major-league stuff. It's early, incomplete information that you can only somewhat rely on, but it is information that we don't have for, say, J.P. Crawford and Amed Rosario.

The explanation of an 80 hit tool in our internal BP handbook, which tracks closely enough with the

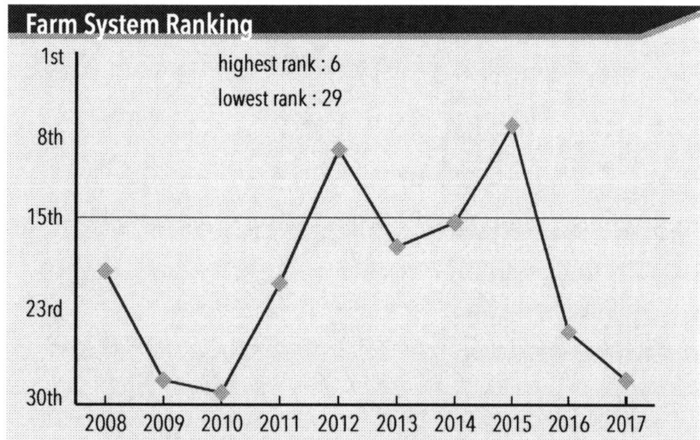

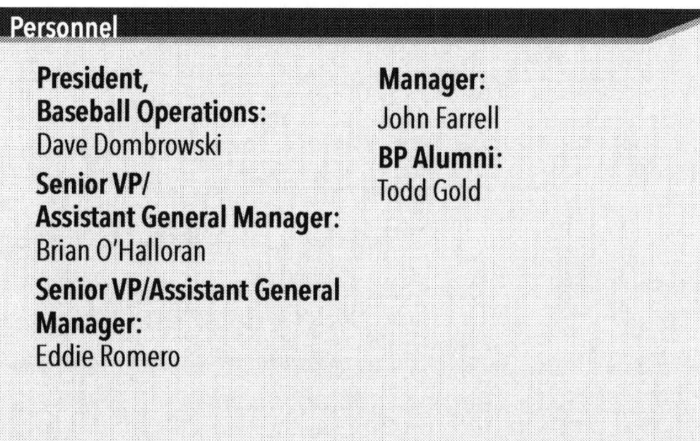

explanation in McDaniel's public 20/80 scale translation, and also give or take the vernacular most teams use, is that an 80 hit tool is a .320 hitter. But what does that actually mean? Andrew Benintendi is probably going to hit .320 in some random season at some point, so isn't he a future 80 hit? Not quite. Take a few players from the recent past. DJ Lemahieu hit .348 last year, but nobody is out here touting DJ Lemahieu as an 80 hit tool player. Why? It was a.) only over a one-season sample, b.) in a favorable hitting environment, and c.) sure looks like an outlier when taken in context of his whole career. If you want to go for someone not in Coors, pick Jean Segura. He hit .319 in 2016, and I'm not sure you could get everyone here to agree he has an above-average hit tool, let alone an 80. You can go back through the years and see the same thing. Dee Gordon hit .333 in 2015. An otherwise-rapidly declining Justin Morneau hit .319 in 2014. Michael Cuddyer and Chris Johnson both cleared .320 in 2013. None of these guys are or were close to an 80 hit, even though they all hit close to or over .320 in a season.

I would suggest that a real 80 hit tool player is a guy who, with roughly average luck and variance in his peak seasons, often hits around .320 or higher. Given that definition, I'd posit Miguel Cabrera, Mike Trout, and Jose Altuve as no-doubt present 80 hit players, with Joey Votto, Adrian Beltre, and Buster Posey right on the edge. Perhaps Daniel Murphy now too, and maybe Bryce Harper when healthy, you get the point. These are all the guys you think of when you think of the best hitters in the majors, right?

We feel reasonably confident that Andrew Benintendi has good potential to be a regular .300 hitter in The Show. We think he might be a future batting champion. We don't feel reasonably confident that he's going to be a better hitter for average than guys like Joey Votto or Adrian Beltre. Now, if you want to start talking about Mookie Betts having a future 80 hit…

—Jarrett Seidler

1. Andrew Benintendi, OF

DOB: 07/06/1994

Height/Weight: 5'10" 185 lbs.

Bats/Throws: L/L

Drafted/Acquired: Drafted 7th overall in the 2015 Draft, University of Arkansas (AR); signed for $3.5904 million

Previous Ranking(s): #4 (Org.), #46 (Overall)

2016 Stats: .295/.359/.476, 2 HR, 1 SB in 34 games at the major-league level, .295/.357/.515, 8 HR, 8 SB in 63 games at double-A Portland, .341/.413/.563, 1 HR, 8 SB in 34 games at high-A Salem

The Role: OFP 70—All-Star outfielder
Likely 60—First-division outfielder

YEAR	TEAM	LVL	AGE	PA	R	2B	3B	HR	RBI	BB	K	SB	CS	AVG/OBP/SLG	TAv	VORP	BABIP	BRR	FRAA	WARP
2015	LOW	A-	20	153	19	2	4	7	15	25	15	7	1	.290/.408/.540	.317	15.0	.279	1.6	CF(31): 8.1	2.5
2015	GRN	A	20	86	17	5	0	4	16	10	9	3	2	.351/.430/.581	.374	13.5	.355	1.0	CF(18): -2.9	1.2
2016	SLM	A+	21	155	30	13	7	1	32	15	9	8	2	.341/.413/.563	.343	18.0	.354	-0.2	CF(30): 4.9	2.3
2016	PME	AA	21	263	40	18	5	8	44	24	30	8	7	.295/.357/.515	.304	19.4	.308	0.7	CF(53): -1.0, LF(4): 1.8	2.2
2016	BOS	MLB	21	118	16	11	1	2	14	10	25	1	0	.295/.359/.476	.284	5.0	.367	-0.6	LF(29): 0.4, CF(5): -0.2	0.6
2017	*BOS*	*MLB*	*22*	*583*	*79*	*33*	*6*	*18*	*66*	*49*	*103*	*12*	*7*	*.273/.338/.464*	*.272*	*25.6*	*.307*	*-0.1*	*LF 17, CF 1*	*4.3*
2018	*BOS*	*MLB*	*23*	*560*	*73*	*33*	*6*	*19*	*75*	*48*	*100*	*12*	*6*	*.278/.345/.481*	*.270*	*20.5*	*.311*	*0.5*	*LF 16, CF 1*	*4.1*

Breakout: 6% Improve: 43% Collapse: 2% Attrition: 13% MLB: 71% *Comparables: Mookie Betts, Joc Pederson, Colby Rasmus*

The Good: As first reported, oh up ↑ there a bit, Benintendi can really hit. Despite a compact and at times violent swing, he controls the barrel well and generates way more 'oomph' than you would expect from a hitter his size. The ball just carries. This was true in the minors, and it was true even against major-league pitching. Benintendi may not have more than average over-the-fence power, but he should be a doubles machine, and a potential .300 hitter to boot. He also controls the zone incredibly well and may end up an ideal no. 2 hitter in the Red Sox lineup.

The Bad: Benintendi probably *could* play center field if you needed him to—the Red Sox don't need him to—but he's not a burner out there, and his instincts and routes aren't quite good enough to make up for it. Put another way, he just doesn't make quite enough plays in the Inside Edge 40-60 bucket. He should be an asset in left where his range and arm will be adequate or better, but the over-the-fence power will not be special for a corner, even with the friendly home park.

The Irrelevant: Benintendi barely kept his eligibility with his 105 at-bats. We expect him to get a lot more, but he has a ways to go to catch Kevin McReynolds, whose 5,423 at-bats is the most for a Razorback.

The Risks: Benintendi has arrived in the majors and has hit in the majors. He'll start 2017 in the majors and I imagine he will continue to hit. If Dansby Swanson isn't the lowest risk prospect of the 300, it's Benintendi.

Major league ETA: Debuted in 2016

Ben Carsley's Fantasy Take: If you're reading these fantasy blurbs with the hopes of finding help for 2017, Benintendi is your best bet. He could flirt with a .300 average even as a rookie, and while he doesn't have explosive power/speed he could challenge for 15 homers and steals apiece. Put that type of baseline production in the Red Sox's high-powered offense, and you're looking at a potential OF3 who could contribute across the board and score a ton of runs, a la 2016 Adam Eaton but without the bad tweets. The Red Sox have plenty of other reasonable OF options, though, so beware that Benintendi's leash probably isn't as long as you think it is.

2. Rafael Devers, 3B

DOB: 10/24/1996

Height/Weight: 6'0" 195 lbs

Bats/Throws: L/R

Drafted/Acquired: Signed August 2013 out of Dominican Republic for $1.5 million

Previous Ranking(s): #3 (Org.), #35 (Overall)

2016 Stats: .282/.335/.443, 11 HR, 18 SB in 128 games at high-A Salem

The Role: OFP 70—All-Star third baseman who battles the position, but hits so much you don't care
Likely 55—Solid first baseman

YEAR	TEAM	LVL	AGE	PA	R	2B	3B	HR	RBI	BB	K	SB	CS	AVG/OBP/SLG	TAv	VORP	BABIP	BRR	FRAA	WARP
2014	DRS	Rk	17	128	26	6	3	3	21	21	20	4	1	.337/.445/.538	.345	0.0	.386	0.0		0.0
2014	RSX	Rk	17	174	21	11	2	4	36	14	30	1	0	.312/.374/.484	.270	2.6	.363	-0.2		0.4
2015	GRN	A	18	508	71	38	1	11	70	24	84	3	2	.288/.329/.443	.282	25.1	.326	1.6	3B(72): -9.0	1.7
2016	SLM	A+	19	546	64	32	8	11	71	40	94	18	6	.282/.335/.443	.276	25.1	.328	-1.2	3B(117): 21.1	4.7
2017	*BOS*	*MLB*	*20*	*250*	*26*	*13*	*1*	*7*	*30*	*11*	*61*	*3*	*1*	*.245/.283/.405*	*.227*	*-1.0*	*.298*	*-0.1*	*3B 4*	*0.3*
2018	*BOS*	*MLB*	*21*	*435*	*51*	*25*	*2*	*15*	*54*	*20*	*101*	*5*	*2*	*.254/.293/.429*	*.240*	*0.8*	*.302*	*-0.2*	*3B 7*	*0.8*

Breakout: 2% Improve: 10% Collapse: 0% Attrition: 5% MLB: 12% *Comparables: Josh Vitters, Matt Dominguez, Maikel Franco*

The Good: Devers has big bat speed from the left side with leverage. There's 70 raw power in the frame, and it should end up plus in games. It's not boom-or-bust at the plate either, he's a potential plus hitter who shows off good balance and bat control in the box. Devers is a well below-average runner, but better on the bases than you'd expect just off the tool grade. If judged just on his hands and above-average arm, you could project a decent everyday third baseman.

The Bad: His listed weight of 195 is, uh, optimistic, and a very thick lower half at 19 may portend a move across the diamond to first base. The athleticism and footwork are already stretched at the hot corner. There's potentially more swing-and-miss in here at higher levels—especially once he starts seeing better soft stuff— than you'd expect from a 19-year-old who posted that line in High A. The approach is currently very aggressive and will need refinement as he moves up the organizational ladder.

The Irrelevant: 19-year-olds in Salem aren't as uncommon as you'd think. In addition to Devers teammate, Luis Alexander Basabe, Anthony Rizzo and Xander Bogaerts both spent time in the Carolina League in their Age-19 season. That might actually be relevant, so we should mention that Wendell Rijo and Heiker Meneses did too.

The Risks: You get the best of both high-risk worlds here. A 19-year-old who needs some hit-tool refinement and a potential first-base profile when it's all said and done.

Major league ETA: Late 2018

Ben Carsley's Fantasy Take: Devers gets lost a bit in this system, and I think dynasty leaguers will be surprised by how highly he ranks heading into this season. The potential for plus hit and plus power from third is a beautiful thing, and Devers is good enough at the plate that he won't be a complete wash as a prospect if he has to move to first base. He might not hit the ground running in the majors because of his youth, but Devers has upside as a Kyle Seager-esque fantasy third baseman who can hit .280 with 25-plus homers and plenty of RBI. If he settles in as more of a 2016 Adrian Gonzalez-type option at first (.285, 18 homers), that'd still make him a valuable CI option.

3. Jason Groome, LHP

DOB: 8/23/98

Height/Weight: 6'6" 220 lbs.

Bats/Throws: L/L

Drafted/Acquired: Selected 12th overall in the 2016 MLB Draft, Barnegat HS (Barnegat, NJ); signed for $3.65 million

Previous Ranking(s): N/A

2016 Stats: 2.25 ERA, 4 IP, 3 H, 0 BB, 8 K in 2 games at Gulf Coast League, 3.38 ERA, 2.2 IP, 4 BB, 2 K in one game at short-season Lowell

The Role: OFP 70—Top of the rotation starter
Likely 55—Mid-rotation starter

YEAR	TEAM	LVL	AGE	W	L	SV	G	GS	IP	H	HR	BB/9	K/9	K	GB%	BABIP	WHIP	ERA	FIP	DRA	VORP	WARP	cFIP	MPH
2016	RSX	Rk	17	0	0	0	2	2	16	3	0	0.0	18.0	8	50%	.375	0.75	2.25	-0.70	2.21	1.6	0.2	81	
2016	LOW	A-	17	0	0	0	1	1	16	0	0	13.5	6.8	2	57%	.000	1.50	3.38	6.26	6.58	-0.4	0.0	114	
2017	*BOS*	*MLB*	*18*	*2*	*2*	*0*	*8*	*8*	*32²*	*38*	*6*	*4.2*	*7.3*	*27*	*47%*	*.320*	*1.63*	*5.30*	*5.41*	*5.74*	*-1.0*	*-0.1*	*135*	

Breakout: 0% Improve: 0% Collapse: 0% Attrition: 0% MLB: 0% *Comparables: J.C. Ramirez, Chris Archer, Roberto Osuna*

The Good: Think of the most beautiful left-handed curveball you've ever seen. You're probably thinking of Clayton Kershaw right now, maybe Sandy Koufax if you're a little older, Rich Hill if you're Sam Miller. Groome can sometimes snap off two-plane curves that look like that. It's not there with consistency yet, and Lucas Giolito—whose curveball had every bit this much potential and more—is a cautionary tale that the road from a raw awesome curve to an effective major-league offering can be bumpy. But Jason Groome has certified feel for spin, and you can't teach that. He's also 6-foot-6 and touches the mid-90s from the left side, and you can't even teach that, either.

The Bad: He didn't always have his best fastball in the spring, pitching more at 91-94 early in games. He struggled with in-game fatigue at times, which is certainly common for a 17-year-old pitcher but worth following. The change is still a work in progress. Highly publicized but vague makeup concerns have followed him ever since his one year stint at the IMG Academy in Florida, and along with rumors about a sky-high bonus demand likely caused him to slip much further in the draft than he should've on talent. Lord knows it wasn't on talent, because he was the realest guy in the room.

The Irrelevant: Groome was suspended for nearly a month of his senior season because the New Jersey State Interscholastic Athletic Association ruled that his moving back from Bradenton, Florida to Barnegat, New Jersey did not constitute a "bona fide change of residence."

The Risks: I know we've been doing "and he's a pitcher" in all of these, but seriously, he's a pitcher who just turned 18. What it looks like now and what it looks like in four years could be dramatically different things. Good command for your age at 17 doesn't mean you have good command at 21. A promising change at 17 doesn't mean you're even throwing a change at 21. The fastball could settle in literally anywhere in the 90s and it wouldn't surprise me, which is both positive and negative risk.

And, of course, he's a pitcher.

Major league ETA: 2019 —Jarrett Seidler

Ben Carsley's Fantasy Take: I've generally addressed pitching prospects with the enthusiasm of a call center employee so far in this series, but Groome is the type of dynasty arm I advocate going all-in on. There's a good argument that he's already the best southpaw fantasy SP prospect depending on how you feel about Sean Newcomb, and he's certainly on the short list of fantasy arms with the highest upsides. He'll take a while to get there and you can expect plenty of ups and downs as he progresses through the minors, but he's a legit potential SP1/2 in the mold of ... wait for it ... Jon Lester. Take the plunge.

4. Sam Travis, 1B

DOB: 08/27/1993

Height/Weight: 6'0" 195 lbs.

Bats/Throws: R/R

Drafted/Acquired: Drafted 67th overall in the 2014 MLB Draft, University of Indiana (IN); signed for $846,800

Previous Ranking(s): #7 (Org.)

2016 Stats: .272/.332/.434, 6 HR, 1 SB in 47 games at triple-A Pawtucket

The Role: OFP 50—Avg/OBP-driven everyday first baseman
Likely 40—We've been here before, it's tough to carry a right-handed first-base-only dude

YEAR	TEAM	LVL	AGE	PA	R	2B	3B	HR	RBI	BB	K	SB	CS	AVG/OBP/SLG	TAv	VORP	BABIP	BRR	FRAA	WARP
2014	LOW	A-	20	174	28	5	1	4	30	4	18	5	1	.333/.364/.448	.291	6.7	.357	-0.7	1B(33): -1.7	0.5
2014	GRN	A	20	115	12	11	1	3	14	7	14	0	1	.290/.330/.495	.276	1.8	.308	-1.3	1B(23): 0.3	0.2
2015	SLM	A+	21	278	35	15	4	5	40	26	43	10	6	.313/.378/.467	.306	17.6	.356	2.0	1B(46): 2.3	2.2
2015	PME	AA	21	281	35	17	2	4	38	33	34	9	6	.300/.384/.436	.297	15.9	.332	2.7	1B(63): 8.7	2.7
2016	PAW	AAA	22	190	26	10	0	6	29	15	40	1	0	.272/.332/.434	.283	7.8	.320	1.4	1B(34): 2.0	1.0
2017	*BOS*	*MLB*	*23*	*32*	*4*	*2*	*0*	*1*	*4*	*2*	*7*	*0*	*0*	*.264/.325/.422*	*.256*	*0.4*	*.314*	*0.0*		*0.0*
2018	*BOS*	*MLB*	*24*	*279*	*35*	*15*	*1*	*9*	*35*	*23*	*60*	*3*	*2*	*.269/.332/.446*	*.259*	*3.9*	*.317*	*-0.3*	-	*0.4*

Breakout: 10% Improve: 26% Collapse: 6% Attrition: 19% MLB: 37% *Comparables: Max Kepler, Mike Carp, Josh Bell*

The Good: Before his ACL injury, Sam Travis was very Sam Travisy in 2016. You know what you are getting here; a plus hitter who offers some doubles, a good approach at the plate, and a little more athleticism than your average first-base prospect.

The Bad: Even before the ACL injury, Sam Travis was going to be a first baseman. Now he is going to be a first baseman who lost more than half of a triple-A season to an ACL injury. He never had a prototypical power tool for the far right side of the infield, but it may not even be acceptably fringy.

The Irrelevant: Travis wasn't the only Hoosier from the 2014 draft class to suffer an ACL injury early in 2016. College teammate Kyle Schwarber suffered the same fate (you may have heard about that).

The Risks: Well, the ACL injury is less concerning for a player who was going to be limited to first base anyway, but we still have to see how he recovers from it. After he recovers from it he is still a first baseman with below-average power, so that hit tool will really have to play up.

Major league ETA: Post-Super-2, 2017

Ben Carsley's Fantasy Take: Travis could be an okay option in deeper leagues when he's starting every day for the Athletics in 2019 (*I seriously almost comp'd him as righty Daric Barton- jp*). That's especially true in OBP leagues. But for now Travis lacks the power we want from a fantasy first baseman, and despite the fact that the position isn't as deep as it once was (as you can read here and here and here), Travis doesn't profile as a guy you'd want to start in a 16-team league.

5. Brian Johnson, LHP

DOB: 12/07/1990

Height/Weight: 6'4" 235 lbs.

Bats/Throws: L/L

Drafted/Acquired: Drafted 31st overall in the 2012 MLB Draft, University of Florida (FL); signed for $1.575 million

Previous Ranking(s): #8 (Org.)

2016 Stats: 3.86 ERA, 3.06 DRA, 7 IP, 7 H, 2 BB, 9 K in 2 games at the Gulf Coast League, 0.00 ERA, 2.39 DRA, 11 IP, 7 H, 2 BB, 11 K in 2 games at short-season Lowell, 4.09 ERA, 7.25 DRA, 77 IP, 38 H, 36 BB, 54 K in 15 games at triple-A Pawtucket

The Role: OFP 50—no. 4 starter
Likely 40—no. 5 starter/swingman/lefty middle reliever type, deploy as needed

YEAR	TEAM	LVL	AGE	W	L	SV	G	GS	IP	H	HR	BB/9	K/9	K	GB%	BABIP	WHIP	ERA	FIP	DRA	VORP	WARP	cFIP	MPH
2014	SLM	A+	23	3	1	0	5	5	25²	23	0	2.5	11.6	33	41%	.333	1.17	3.86	1.76	2.48	8.90	0.9	79	
2014	PME	AA	23	10	2	0	20	20	118	78	6	2.4	7.6	99	48%	.229	0.93	1.75	3.15	1.96	42.90	4.6	86	
2015	BOS	MLB	24	0	1	0	1	1	4¹	3	0	8.3	6.2	3	33%	.250	1.62	8.31	4.49	5.43	-0.20	0.0	118	91.7
2015	PAW	AAA	24	9	6	0	18	18	96	74	6	3.0	8.4	90	47%	.264	1.10	2.53	3.22	2.24	32.70	3.3	86	
2016	RSX	Rk	25	0	1	0	2	2	7	7	0	2.6	11.6	9	33%	.389	1.29	3.86	1.60	3.54	1.70	0.2	93	
2016	LOW	A-	25	0	0	0	2	2	11	7	0	1.6	9.0	11	37%	.259	0.82	0.00	1.82	2.55	3.30	0.3	88	
2016	PAW	AAA	25	5	6	0	15	15	77	74	9	4.2	6.3	54	36%	.284	1.43	4.09	4.73	5.27	0.60	0.1	117	
2017	*BOS*	*MLB*	*26*	*2*	*2*	*0*	*20*	*3*	*33*	*33*	*4*	*4.0*	*6.6*	*25*	*38%*	*.290*	*1.43*	*4.69*	*4.68*	*4.92*	*0.8*	*0.1*	*100*	
2018	*BOS*	*MLB*	*27*	*3*	*3*	*0*	*39*	*5*	*68*	*59*	*9*	*5.8*	*9.2*	*70*	*38%*	*.281*	*1.51*	*4.89*	*4.92*	*5.34*	*-0.7*	*-0.1*	*122*	

Breakout: 7% Improve: 19% Collapse: 15% Attrition: 29% MLB: 41% *Comparables: Tyler Anderson, Rudy Owens, Charles Brewer*

The Good: He's a tall lefty with a good curveball. The change is pretty good too. Did we mention he's tall? Starter's build. That's important. He's pretty much a finished product and major-league ready so that saves you on...I don't know, roving pitching instructor Delta miles. Okay, it's not the most exciting profile but it's a major-league arm.

The Bad: It's Brian Johnson, man. You know what this is. The upper-80s fastball is fringy even with his ability to cut and run the offering. There may not be enough stuff here to start. And it's an awkward relief profile although he has been able to find more velocity in short bursts.

The Irrelevant: The pitching market has been sparse recently, and lefties usually pitch forever, but Johnson may have to in order to make more money than the AC/DC frontman, whose net worth is estimated at 90 million dollars. That buys a lot of Yorkshire flat caps. Like most minor-league pitchers, I assume this Johnson prefers Nike Golf snapbacks though.

Major league ETA: Debuted in 2015, will probably get back there in 2017

Ben Carsley's Fantasy Take: Everyone knows that back-end lefties have great success in Fenway, right? Wrong. Johnson might be a streamer if he gets shipped to a team with a big ballpark or in certain super-favorable matchups, but that's his ceiling. Hard pass.

6. Josh Ockimey, 1B

DOB: 10/18/95

Height/Weight: 6'1" 215 lbs.

Bats/Throws: L/R

Drafted/Acquired: Drafted in the fifth round of the 2014 MLB Draft, Sts. Neumann and Goretti HS (Philadelphia, PA); signed for $450,000

Previous Ranking(s): N/A

2016 Stats: .226/.367/.425, 18 HR, 3 SB in 117 games at low-A Greenville

The Role: OFP 50—TTO First baseman
Likely 40—Lefty pop off the bench is better than righty on-base off the bench, but...

YEAR	TEAM	LVL	AGE	PA	R	2B	3B	HR	RBI	BB	K	SB	CS	AVG/OBP/SLG	TAv	VORP	BABIP	BRR	FRAA	WARP
2014	RSX	Rk	18	130	17	3	1	0	10	14	37	1	0	.188/.292/.232	.186	-3.4	.276	0.4		-0.5
2015	LOW	A-	19	229	30	13	3	4	38	25	78	2	2	.266/.349/.422	.277	4.9	.408	-1.6	1B(47): -3.8	0.1
2016	GRN	A	20	499	60	25	1	18	62	88	129	3	1	.226/.367/.425	.287	18.9	.284	1.8	1B(101): -3.3	1.7
2017	*BOS*	*MLB*	*21*	*250*	*27*	*10*	*0*	*8*	*30*	*32*	*83*	*0*	*0*	*.204/.310/.369*	*.231*	*-3.1*	*.283*	*-0.4*	*1B -2*	*-0.5*
2018	*BOS*	*MLB*	*22*	*394*	*51*	*17*	*1*	*13*	*46*	*53*	*126*	*0*	*0*	*.212/.323/.386*	*.241*	*-3.7*	*.292*	*-0.9*	*1B -3*	*-0.7*

Breakout: 2% Improve: 8% Collapse: 1% Attrition: 4% MLB: 14% *Comparables: Chris Parmelee, Chris Carter, Matt Olson*

The Good: If you are going to be a first base prospect, mashing dingers is a good way to stay on the major-league radar, and Ockimey has the ability to do that. There's plus raw power here and it is already showing up in games due to an advanced approach and the loft and extension to do damage in the zone.

The Bad: Somewhere Ben Carsley twitches involuntarily as he prepares to write about another first base prospect (it feels like it has been a lot to me so far too). At least Ockimey is left-handed so he can't comp him to C.J. Cron again. And unlike Sam Travis there is some real power potential here. He is also a first base prospect in A-ball with some swing-and-miss issues so...

The Irrelevant: Ockimey finished fifth in the South Atlantic League in home runs, six behind league leader Jose Pujols.

The Risks: I T ' S A F I R S T B A S E P R O S P E C T. In addition to that, Ockimey faded in the second half of his first full professional season, and the prodigious power comes with similarly prodigious strikeouts. There may be additional development time here if he ever even figures out upper level pitching at all.

Major league ETA: 2020

Ben Carsley's Fantasy Take: Ockimey's ceiling is as a left-handed C.J. Cron and I want to die.

7. Bobby Dalbec, 3B

DOB: 6/29/1996

Height/Weight: 6'4" 225 lbs

Bats/Throws: R/R

Drafted/Acquired: Drafted in the 4th round (118th overall) in the 2016 MLB draft, University of Arizona (Tucson, AZ), signed for $650,000.

Previous Ranking(s): N/A

2016 Stats: .386/.427/.674, 7 HR, 2 SB in 34 games at short-season Lowell

The Role: OFP 55 — 30-to-40 homer corner guy, but a decade too late to be considered a superstar
Likely 30 — What role would you put on the modern Brooks Kieschnick or Micah Owings, exactly?

YEAR	TEAM	LVL	AGE	PA	R	2B	3B	HR	RBI	BB	K	SB	CS	AVG/OBP/SLG	TAv	VORP	BABIP	BRR	FRAA	WARP
2016	LOW	A-	21	143	25	13	2	7	33	9	33	2	2	.386/.427/.674	.357	19.0	.473	1.3	3B(22): 2.5	2.3
2017	*BOS*	*MLB*	*22*	*450*	*45*	*19*	*1*	*13*	*49*	*22*	*139*	*1*	*0*	*.219/.262/.367*	*.215*	*-5.3*	*.290*	*-0.9*	*3B 1*	*-0.4*
2018	*BOS*	*MLB*	*23*	*243*	*28*	*11*	*1*	*9*	*30*	*13*	*74*	*0*	*0*	*.231/.277/.402*	*.227*	*-2.7*	*.298*	*-0.5*	*3B 1*	*-0.1*

Breakout: 4% Improve: 7% Collapse: 4% Attrition: 13% MLB: 13% *Comparables: Will Middlebrooks, Renato Nunez, Mat Gamel*

The Good: Coming soon to your local A-ball home run derby! Dalbec is something of a righty, lesser version of Joey Gallo as a prospect, with mammoth raw power that convinced the Red Sox to start him out as a position player despite a fastball he could run up into the mid-90s. Regardless of the horrible swing-and-miss problems, he's absolutely mashed with wood bats so far both on the Cape in the summer of 2015 and in the New York-Penn League this past summer after the draft. As a pitcher, he flashed legitimate pro-quality stuff with, ironically, strong polish, moving from closing into Arizona's rotation in time to be one of the best pitchers in 2016's College World Series. So he definitely has a pitching fallback if the hitting thing doesn't work out. With shorter benches and longer bullpens, one wonders if teams will be more amenable to trying guys in Christian Bethancourt-type hybrid roles; Dalbec could certainly be a candidate for that.

The Bad: He has two minus tools: hit and field. Dalbec is a huge human with a long, out-of-control swing. His plate approach is "tries to hit everything thrown in the direction of the plate past Mars all the way to Jupiter." He struggled mightily to control his strikeouts at times in college, and still struck out over 23 percent of the time even while crushing it in his short-season A pro debut. Like Gallo, he will likely end up at first despite a very strong arm, although in Dalbec's case this is due to glove reliability problems at third and not Adrian Beltre's existence. Even if things work out pretty well, and Dalbec remains a hitter capable of fielding some position, the ultimate upside might look something like Chris Carter—a huge power bat able to be hidden in a corner. And Chris Carter has been non-tendered and then picked up cheaply in consecutive seasons, the last one after hitting 41 homers. So it's a tough profile, to say the least.

The Irrelevant: Dalbec's roommates in college included Scott Kingery and Kevin Newman. I'm not sure you could find two real position player prospects more different than Bobby Dalbec.

The Risks: I'm going to be honest, I have utterly no idea what the role grades are here, because he could be a good hitter, a bad hitter, a pitcher, or some combination thereof. He's a legitimately unique prospect. As a hitter, he's very, very raw, with as much grade variation as could be possible for a college hitting prospect. With swing-and-miss issues like these, there's a very real chance that upper-minors pitching eats him for lunch.

Also, he might be a pitcher. If he's a 40, it's probably as a pitcher.

Major league ETA: 2020 — Jarrett Seidler

Ben Carsley's Fantasy Take: Dalbec is probably a top-200 dynasty prospect because of the power upside, but they don't make 'em with lower probabilities. Watch list only.

8. Michael Chavis, 3B

DOB: 8/11/1995

Height/Weight: 5'10" 190 lbs

Bats/Throws: R/R

Drafted/Acquired: Drafted 26th overall in the 2014 MLB draft, Sprayberry HS (Marietta, GA), signed for $1,870,500.

Previous Ranking(s): N/A

2016 Stats: .160/.222/.160, 0 HR, 1 SB in 7 games at high-A Salem, .244/.321/.391, 8 HR, 3 SB in 74 games at low-A Greenville.

The Role: OFP 50—Average major-league third baseman
Likely 40—Right-handed bench bat with some pop and maybe some outfield utility

YEAR	TEAM	LVL	AGE	PA	R	2B	3B	HR	RBI	BB	K	SB	CS	AVG/OBP/SLG	TAv	VORP	BABIP	BRR	FRAA	WARP
2014	RSX	Rk	18	150	21	12	3	1	16	15	38	5	3	.269/.347/.425	.365	10.2	.368	-1.4		1.0
2015	GRN	A	19	471	56	29	1	16	58	29	144	8	5	.223/.277/.405	.244	2.2	.293	-1.2	3B(68): 3.7, SS(1): -0.1	0.6
2016	GRN	A	20	312	30	11	3	8	35	22	74	3	1	.244/.321/.391	.270	13.2	.303	1.3	3B(68): -0.4	1.4
2016	SLM	A+	20	27	5	0	0	0	1	2	7	1	0	.160/.222/.160	.180	-0.8	.222	1.1	3B(2): -0.7	-0.2
2017	*BOS*	*MLB*	*21*	*450*	*44*	*18*	*1*	*14*	*48*	*22*	*154*	*2*	*1*	*.203/.251/.350*	*.208*	*-6.7*	*.280*	*-0.8*	*3B 2*	*-0.8*
2018	*BOS*	*MLB*	*22*	*364*	*41*	*16*	*1*	*12*	*42*	*21*	*122*	*1*	*1*	*.210/.265/.374*	*.218*	*-7.2*	*.286*	*-0.6*	*3B 3*	*-0.5*

The Good: Chavis was considered to be one of the best hitting prospects in the 2014 draft class. The primary developmental question was if he would develop enough power to carry an eventual corner-infield profile (he was technically drafted as a shortstop). So, of course he came out in his first pro season and bashed 16 home runs in a little over 100 games for Greeneville. The raw power is above-average, and although the swing can get long, he has enough barrel control to get most of the power into play for now. He's not gonna light up a scouting report, but he's a solid third baseman with a strong arm, and potential average hit and power grades.

The Bad: Chavis cut his strikeout rate down to a more manageable level in his second pass at the South Atlantic League, but there is still a fair bit of swing-and-miss here. The culprit is the aforementioned length in the swing from occasional bat wrap. Chavis is fine at third base at present, but he is built a bit like a fire hydrant, so it's not impossible that changes in his twenties. A hand injury cost him a chunk of 2016, and the big K-rates returned after he got back on the field.

The Irrelevant: Sprayberry High School feels like an appropriate alma mater for a hitting prospect, but the only other alum to make the majors as a hitter is Marlon Byrd.

The Risks: Upper level arms might exploit the swing. Hand injuries can linger. Two years into his pro career I don't know that we have a great handle on what he is, which makes him feel even riskier.

Major league ETA: 2019

Ben Carsley's Fantasy Take: Guilty until proven innocent at this point. Watch to see if he starts hitting, but don't expect anything.

9. Michael Shawaryn, RHP

DOB: 09/17/1994

Height/Weight: 6'2" 200 lbs

Bats/Throws: R/R

Drafted/Acquired: Drafted in the 5th round of the 2016 MLB draft, University of Maryland (College Park, MD), signed for $637,500.
Previous Ranking(s): N/A
2016 Stats: 2.87 ERA, 15.2 IP, 15 H, 7 BB, 22 K at short-season Lowell.

The Role: OFP 50—no. 4 starter or set-up
Likely 40—Middle reliever

The Good: Shawaryn is a bulldog who goes right after opponents with a low-90s, riding fastball that gets on batters quicker than you'd think due to some deception in his mechanics. He can cut or run the pitch from his low three-quarters slot and shows advanced fastball command for an arm with little pro experience. He'll also feature a low 80s change with good sink.

The Bad: This was a better system before the Moncada trade, and while I like Shawaryn as a prospect, I did not expect him to be making this top ten list. The low arm slot and somewhat stiff mechanics make Shawaryn a pretty good bet to end up in the pen long term even if the breaking ball improves. That's a tough projection too as the arm slot makes it difficult for him to consistently get on top of the pitch, and it tends to be sweepy.

The Irrelevant: Shawaryn holds the University of Maryland record for wins, strikeouts, and innings pitched.

The Risks: The body is a little soft, the slot a little low, and the delivery a little violent. So yes, he ticks all the boxes as a future pen arm, and there isn't really late inning stuff here. But for whatever reason something—perhaps there was an alchemy of sorts when watching him pitch live—leaves me with the nagging suspicion that he outpaces that modest projection.

He is a pitcher though.

Major league ETA: Late 2018/Early 2019
Ben Carsley's Fantasy Take: Dear god this was a better system before the Moncada trade.

10. Lorenzo Cedrola, OF

DOB: 1/12/1998

Height/Weight: 5'11" 170 lbs

Bats/Throws: R/R

Drafted/Acquired: Signed February 2015 out of Venezuela for $35,000.

Previous Ranking(s): N/A

2016 Stats: .290/.350/.393, 2 HR, 9 SB in 53 games at rookie ball in the GCL.

The Role: OFP 50—Average major-league center fielder, albeit one that bats ninth
Likely 40—Useful bench outfielder

YEAR	TEAM	LVL	AGE	PA	R	2B	3B	HR	RBI	BB	K	SB	CS	AVG/OBP/SLG	TAv	VORP	BABIP	BRR	FRAA	WARP
2015	DRX	Rk	17	312	61	8	7	1	31	23	33	27	7	.321/.420/.415	.324	38.7	.362	5.9	CF(63): -0.2	3.8
2016	RSX	Rk	18	238	33	14	1	2	21	11	28	9	4	.290/.350/.393	.288	13.7	.323	-1.1	CF(48): 4.0, RF(3): -0.3	1.7
2017	*BOS*	*MLB*	*19*	*450*	*44*	*19*	*2*	*8*	*41*	*15*	*119*	*7*	*3*	*.221/.265/.334*	*.207*	*-5.0*	*.285*	*0.0*	*CF 1, RF -0*	*-0.6*
2018	*BOS*	*MLB*	*20*	*377*	*41*	*16*	*2*	*9*	*40*	*16*	*94*	*6*	*3*	*.241/.291/.379*	*.227*	*-2.4*	*.300*	*0.3*	*CF 2, RF 0*	*0.0*

The Good: The back-end of these top-10 lists are dotted with potential slap and dash center fielders, and Cedrola is certainly one of them. He's a well-above average runner and already has enough present-day outfield instincts to project as a plus centerfielder. He has a contact-oriented swing, and should beat out enough infield singles and run into enough extra bases to fit in comfortably toward the bottom of an American League lineup.

The Bad: This was a better system before the Moncada trade, and while I like Cedrola as a prospect, I did not expect him to be making this top ten list. He's going to have to hit his way up, because there is no power projection here, and the listed height and weight might be a bit generous. The overall offensive approach is raw.

The Irrelevant: The Academy-Award-nominated Lorenzo's Oil was released five years before Cedrola was born.

The Risks: He hasn't played outside of the complex yet. Upper level—or even full-season—arms might eat him up with better velocity.

Major league ETA: 2022
Ben Carsley's Fantasy Take: Good for those of you in 30-team AL-only leagues with 10-man MiLB rosters.

OTHERS OF NOTE:

The ex-Top-Ten Prospect
Austin Rei, C

I wrote a whole essay about how we (I) struggle to evaluate catchers as prospects. Well, the nice thing about Rei is everyone seems to agree that he's a really good defender behind the plate. Neat! That saves me a lot of time. Potential plus defensive backstops are thoroughly my shit. I don't even really care if they hit much. And as this isn't a particularly deep system, I might normally be inclined to sneak him into the back of the top ten over the uninspiring backend arm and the A-ball first baseman with hit tool questions. Well, in the interest of time, let me just indulge in a little C&P from my Ali Sanchez entry on the Mets list. I will edit as needed.

"In the end, ranking the dude with a .649 OPS in A-ball is something that can make you look really bad in 2019, so let's just call Rei a sleeper and move on."

(I am still holding out some hope for Reese McGuire though.)

Jeffrey's guy?
Tzu-Wei Lin, IF

One of my favorite things Jason Parks ever wrote was about Julian Hilario, the sixth starter in a New York Penn League rotation. He didn't even show well for Jason. Politely, his outing was a disaster. I spoke to him about the piece shortly after and he made the point to me that you should be able to see a major leaguer—or at least major-league tools—even when the performance is dire. As evaluators, I think we more intuitively know the opposite is true. You need to be able to see through good on-field performance, the A-ball lefty that sits 88-90 with a 45 change, the big, strong college mistake hitter in short-season. You are going to see future stars struggle and org guys have the best series of their lives.

Now Tzu-Wei Lin is not Julian Hilario. Lin got two million dollars as an IFA. Expectations were going to be loftier here. And politely, he hasn't hit. Now that said, I can't really sit here and claim that I saw the best game of his career. He went 2-4 with a triple and made a few very nice plays in the field. He went 2-4 with a triple on two separate occasions the week before I saw him. But there was hard contact to the opposite field. The ball jumped. He looked like an easy plus shortstop. And I must again admit my biases: I am a sucker for a double-A shortstop with a slick glove and a paucity of actual offensive tools. The somehow acid and tragic undercurrent of it enhances the aesthetic appeal.

I saw Julian Hilario a few times in A-ball bullpens. He never did develop a better breaking ball, or really any breaking ball. The fastball looked good in the Sally, touching 96, with good arm action on the change. It all went backward in the Florida State League, and the last time I saw him he almost started a fight with the Hammerhead bench from the bullpen chairs. He was released at the end of the season and disappeared into the ether.

I don't know if you can glean any useful lessons from one-game looks. They are maybe even inherently misleading, but there's another game tomorrow for everyone from the elite prospect to the org guy.

TOP 10 TALENTS 25 AND UNDER (BORN 4/1/91 OR LATER)

1. Mookie Betts	6. Eduardo Rodriguez
2. Xander Bogaerts	7. Jason Groome
3. Andrew Benintendi	8. Marco Hernandez
4. Rafael Devers	9. Sam Travis
5. Blake Swihart	10. Josh Ockimey

Look, this is an incredibly talented list of players, even if it's not quite as talented as it was six months ago. There are probably 25 other teams that would trade their 25-and-Under lists for this group without hesitation. And yet compared to some Red Sox lists of recent years past, it ... feels a little thin? Maybe we're just getting greedy.

For several seasons, we were able to debate the merits of Betts or Bogaerts topping this list. Mookie put an end to that (at least temporarily) in 2016, finishing second in AL MVP voting and producing 6.9 WARP while blossoming into Boston's best overall player. Bogaerts had a fine season in his own right, but a second-half swoon and his merely average defense at short conspire to place him firmly behind Betts here. He has the upside to make this close again, but right now, it's not close (I love you Xander I'm sorry).

Benintendi was an easy choice for the next two spot on this list. He is an easy role-6 with some star potential who's ready now. Plus, the hair. Have you seen his hair?

The next four spots engender more debate. Devers has looked good enough while staying super young for his level that he gets the nod at four, but you can make an argument for the young MLBers Swihart and E-Rod over him. Unfortunately, Swihart's 2016 was a disaster thanks mostly to elements that were out of his control—the Sox forced him to learn the outfield on the fly after prematurely yanking him from behind the plate, and he promptly broke his ankle. He still has the potential to be a bat-first everyday catcher, but Boston did him no favors last year. Rodriguez was hurt, terrible and finally very good in 2016. He still carries some risk, but he's close to an actualized mid-rotation MLB starter, and he's basically the first one of those who Boston has developed since Clay Buchholz.

Groome is a flashier name, but he's just too far away to outrank current major-leaguers, even if he does possess top-of-the-rotation upside. Groome is left-handed and has Great Stuff (TM), but is far enough away that the edge goes to players who can produce some value right now. He could rank much, much higher next season, though.

Marco Hernandez is a backup, but he's contributing now and he slides in at eight due to the newfound lack of depth among the organization's prospects. Brian Johnson would have slotted in in the final spot if he weren't already 26, which highlights just how exciting his potential is. Jackie Bradley Jr. has aged out as well. So too have Matt Barnes and Christian Vazquez, though neither of them would've cracked this list based on their 2016s. Henry Owens has fallen apart. So yes, despite the big four names at the top, this list might strike you as a bit thinner than you would've imagined. Such is life when you trade away Yoan Moncada, Michael Kopech, Manny Margot, Anderson Espinoza, Javier Guerra and others. But the silver lining? This entire 25-and-Under list will be eligible when we do this exercise again next season. That provides the Red Sox with an incredible nucleus of talent that can help both now and a little ways down the line.

If we know Dave Dombrowski, not all of these players will reach the majors wearing Red Sox uniforms. But if we know Dombrowski, the value those who do get traded will return should help the Sox stay in contention for the foreseeable future all the same. With the new Killer Bs at the top of this list, Boston's ceiling and floor are both pretty damn high.

—Ben Carsley

CHICAGO CUBS

The State of the System: *Flags fly forever, baby! (It's not very strong at the top, but there's a lot of interesting young upside plays further down the list)*

THE TOP TEN

1. OF Eloy Jimenez	6. RHP Jose Albertos
2. 2B/OF Ian Happ	7. RHP Dylan Cease
3. OF Albert Almora Jr.	8. OF Eddy Julio Martinez
4. RHP Trevor Clifton	9. RHP Oscar De La Cruz
5. 3B Jeimer Candelario	10. RHP Thomas Hatch

The Big Question: How might it all go wrong for the Cubs?

A popular technique in project management or consultation is the premortem. For those of you not as well-versed in behavioral economics—or at least those who have spent fewer hours of your life teching corporate conferences than I did—we'll take a page out of Adam McKay's book and let Richard Thaler sum it up:

"Assume we are at some time in the future when the plan has been implemented, and the outcome was a disaster. Write a brief history of that disaster."

There has already been a whole lot of ink spilled on how the Cubs got to the point where they could fly a World Series pennant on Waveland Ave. Even here at BP we gushed about how well Theo Epstein and company's plan worked.

So let's let the air out of the party balloons briefly. The Cubs dealt some pretty premium prospects to the Yankees for a few months of Aroldis Chapman, but the system is still pretty healthy. At the top, one of the best prospects in baseball. And past that, some close-to-the-majors bats and high upside arms. There's the spoils from a huge 2015 IFA class yet to even come stateside and begin to make their mark (more on them later). But if there is one thing you take away from composing prospect lists, it's that there are oh so many ways it can go wrong (and people will remind you about all of them on Twitter three years from now).

So how might it go wrong from the Cubs 2017 Top Ten Prospects?.

Eloy Jimenez is an elite prospect bat. Those tend to have relatively low bust rates, but there's a lot of hype around him—and more about to come courtesy of the author of this essay. He's a teenager in A-ball with some swing-and-miss. Those sometimes grow into a 22-year-old in Double A with more swing-and-miss. That causes the power to play down to 55 or 60, and suddenly—or I guess gradually—we end up with a major leaguer that doesn't look all that different from 2016 Corey Dickerson. Those left field profiles are risky.

Ian Happ may be a left fielder and...well, those left field profiles are risky. Happ doesn't have Jimenez's offensive tools either. He's a fine hitter, but if he can't play a plurality of his games at second base, it's very possible he's just another bench bat.

Albert Almora already has a month of major-league time under his belt. I guess more like two if you count the playoffs. He's also a pretty safe bet to be a major-league contributor. However, it's possible that he keeps hacking, and major-league arms start expanding the zone, and now he's hitting an empty .250, and okay, he's not THAT good a center fielder. Good enough to caddy there in late innings though, which is what ends up happening.

Trevor Clifton is a pitcher. Need we say more? Well at times we haven't said more. But maybe he's just a middle reliever with a fastball he struggles to command and a curve that still only flashes in 2019.

Jeimer Candelario made defensive strides at third base this year, but if he bleeds a little more athleticism in his twenties...well, he's already playing about once a week at first base. And on the right side of the infield he's not even interesting enough offensively to be one of those dudes that Ben comps to C.J. Cron in the Fantasy blurb.

Jose Albertos is an 18-year-old pitcher. He's a heckuva prospect. We might even end up a year late by having him this low. He might end up a double-A reliever too. It's plausible, if not likely, but absolutely a disaster.

Dylan Cease...okay, I set out to try and come up with something for all the arms that wasn't just "he gets hurt," but given Cease's track record of health (or lack thereof),

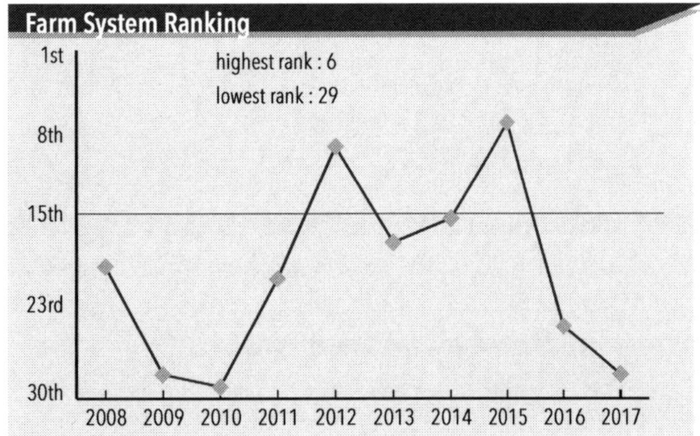

Personnel

President:
Theo Epstein

General Manager:
Jed Hoyer

Senior Vice President:
Jason McLeod

Manager:
Joe Maddon

BP Alumni:
Jeremy Greenhouse
Jason Karegeannes
Jason Parks

let's just say "second Tommy John" and move on to the next disaster.

Eddy Julio Martinez gets eaten alive by swing and miss and doesn't have Jimenez's light tower raw power to fall back on. He ends up an up-and-down bench outfielder.

Oscar De La Cruz dominates younger competition in the Midwest League with his advanced command of the fastball and breaker. Double-A bats aren't as kind and eventually force a move to the pen where the velocity doesn't play up enough to be more than an Iowa shuttle candidate.

Thomas Hatch gets hypnotized as part of a preseason team-building exercise and now thinks he's a chicken.

On the final ledger we end up with one second division starter, a troika of bench bats, a middle reliever, a couple of triple-A shuttle guys, one injury bust, and a forced *Simpsons* reference. That won't all happen of course, but none of it individually is too wild an outcome. It's *The Apple* from a player development standpoint. I've just turned a top-half system in baseball into roughly the likely outcomes for the Marlins Top Ten. But the Cubs are well-positioned to weather this storm. As it is, they don't have places for the close-to-ready guys to play even if they hit their OFP. Theo Epstein could truly say he's a victim of his own success here, but it falls into the good problem to have category. Of course, after you've won your first World Series in over a century, there won't be many bad problems to find.

And anyway, they award as many Prospect List Pennants as they do $/WAR Trophies.

1. Eloy Jimenez, OF

DOB: 11/27/1996

Height/Weight: 6'4" 205 lbs.

Bats/Throws: R/R

Drafted/Acquired: Signed August 2013 out of the Dominican Republic by Chicago for $2.8 million

Previous Ranking(s): #8 (Org)

2016 Stats: .329/.369/.532, 14 HR, 8 SB in 112 games at low-A South Bend

The Role: OFP 70—All-star corner outfielder
Likely 60—First-division corner outfielder

YEAR	TEAM	LVL	AGE	PA	R	2B	3B	HR	RBI	BB	K	SB	CS	AVG/OBP/SLG	TAv	VORP	BABIP	BRR	FRAA	WARP
2014	CUB	Rk	17	164	13	8	2	3	27	10	32	3	1	.227/.268/.367	.231	-0.3	.261	-0.1		-0.1
2015	EUG	A-	18	250	36	10	0	7	33	15	43	3	2	.284/.328/.418	.300	15.1	.321	-0.2	LF(46): -5.4, RF(8): 3.0	1.4
2016	SBN	A	19	464	65	40	3	14	81	25	94	8	3	.329/.369/.532	.320	35.4	.391	-0.3	LF(86): -5.3, RF(11): 0.2	3.5
2017	*CHN*	*MLB*	*20*	*250*	*26*	*12*	*1*	*9*	*32*	*10*	*66*	*0*	*0*	*.241/.274/.415*	*.234*	*1.2*	*.291*	*-0.4*	*LF -1, RF 0*	*0.1*
2018	*CHN*	*MLB*	*21*	*398*	*47*	*19*	*1*	*15*	*52*	*17*	*101*	*1*	*0*	*.250/.286/.427*	*.255*	*6.9*	*.300*	*-0.8*	*LF -1, RF 1*	*0.7*

Breakout: 5% Improve: 15% Collapse: 0% Attrition: 6% MLB: 18% *Comparables: Chris Marrero, Nomar Mazara, Gary Sanchez*

The Good: Jimenez progressed from a raw, toolsy, but exciting corner outfield prospect in April to one of the best offensive prospects in baseball by the end of the year. He has plus-plus raw power and enough barrel control to get almost all of it into games. There's leverage and bat speed, and all those good scouty words, but cutting to the chase, we are talking a potential 30-home-run hitter, and even with the ball a bit more juiced—allegedly—that is no common feat. He's no mere corner masher either—although there would be enough mashing for a corner—he's an advanced hitter for a teenager, and his approach improved throughout the season against the more experienced arms of the Midwest League.

The Bad: He's a below-average runner already limited to a corner spot in A-ball. That will likely be left field in the majors as his arm is only average. He projects as an average defender there, which is more neutral than bad, but it isn't moving the needle. While he doesn't need to "grip it and rip it" to tap into his power, the swing does get long at times, and we'll need to see him against upper minors arms before we're completely confident in an above-average hit tool here.

The Irrelevant: You might remember Jimenez from such exhibition games as the 2016 Futures Game.

The Risks: Man that performance in A-ball was great. But it was still only A-ball. Also, blah blah blah corner profile, blah blah blah hit tool. We've done twenty of these lists, you know the drill.

Major league ETA: 2019

Ben Carsley's Fantasy Take: Frankly, you already missed the boat on Jimenez if you don't own him. But if you're starting a dynasty league, it's safe to say Jimenez is a top-25 prospect. He's got dreamy tools. He's in a great org. He's got MiLB production on his side. Drool. There's a potential OF1 here, and I want him.

2. Ian Happ, 2B/OF

DOB: 08/12/1994

Height/Weight: 6'0" 205 lbs.

Bats/Throws: S/R

Drafted/Acquired: Drafted ninth overall by Chicago in the 2015 MLB Draft, University of Cincinnati (OH); signed for $3 million

Previous Ranking(s): #3 (Org), #67 (Top 101)

2016 Stats: .262/.318/.415, 8 HR, 6 SB in 65 games at double-A Tennessee, .296/.410/.475, 7 HR, 10 SB in 69 games at high-A Myrtle Beach

The Role: OFP 55—Joe Maddon's new favorite swiss army toy
Likely 50—Another dude who isn't as good at this role as Ben Zobrist

YEAR	TEAM	LVL	AGE	PA	R	2B	3B	HR	RBI	BB	K	SB	CS	AVG/OBP/SLG	TAv	VORP	BABIP	BRR	FRAA	WARP
2015	EUG	A-	20	130	26	8	1	4	11	23	28	9	0	.283/.408/.491	.355	19.4	.347	2.7	CF(28): -5.3	1.5
2015	SBN	A	20	165	24	9	3	5	22	17	39	1	1	.241/.315/.448	.277	6.1	.288	-0.1	LF(14): 0.4, RF(12): -1.4	0.7
2016	MYR	A+	21	293	37	16	3	7	42	48	69	10	3	.296/.410/.475	.320	26.1	.381	0.2	2B(50): -3.1, LF(6): -0.0	2.4
2016	TEN	AA	21	274	35	14	0	8	31	20	60	6	2	.262/.318/.415	.271	9.8	.310	0.4	2B(42): -0.7, RF(7): -1.9	0.9
2017	*CHN*	*MLB*	*22*	*250*	*28*	*10*	*1*	*9*	*31*	*24*	*71*	*3*	*1*	*.227/.303/.397*	*.242*	*4.9*	*.287*	*0.0*	*2B -1, LF 0*	*0.4*
2018	*CHN*	*MLB*	*23*	*347*	*43*	*14*	*2*	*12*	*43*	*32*	*100*	*4*	*1*	*.225/.300/.401*	*.256*	*8.8*	*.287*	*0.0*	*2B -2, LF 1*	*0.8*

Breakout: 2% Improve: 23% Collapse: 4% Attrition: 19% MLB: 43% *Comparables: Matt Davidson, Eddie Rosario, Dilson Herrera*

The Good: Happ is a polished hitter from both sides of the plate with an excellent approach and feel for the barrel. There is a balanced offensive profile here with a potential above-average hit tool and enough power to make the advanced approach translate into good on-base skills against major-league arms. Enough leverage in the swing and strength in the body to be a doubles machine even if the over-the-fence power won't be all that notable. There is real defensive flexibility here, even if he's just fringy or below-average at multiple positions, that has value. We don't broadly consider this for the purposes of projecting him, but Happ is in a good organization to get the most out of this skillset.

The Bad: He's not the most athletic of second baseman. His range isn't ideal and his footwork can be choppy. He's a below-average runner so is limited to a corner—probably left—in the outfield. There's some bat drag at times which can give his swing some length, and he's vulnerable to good velocity above the hands. The ultimate game power will end up as a 40 or 45, which is good for a second baseman, not so good for a corner outfielder.

The Irrelevant: Happ ranks third all-time at the University of Cincinnati in both walks and on-base percentage.

The Risks: Happ should hit, but it is yet to be clear if he hits enough to be more than a fringy corner outfielder, which is where he might end up.

Major league ETA: Late 2017

Ben Carsley's Fantasy Take: The hit tool is nice, as is the potential for multi-position eligibility, but there's nothing about Happ that's particularly special. If he remains 2B eligible for the longrun, there's top-12 potential at his position, sure. But he's not gonna get a lot of time there if he remains in this org, and even if he changes hands I'm not convinced he'll be a middle infielder for a long time. He's a top-100 fantasy prospect, yes, but despite what Bret Sayre tells you, he should be closer to 100 than to 1.

3. Albert Almora, OF

DOB: 04/16/1994

Height/Weight: 6'2" 180 lbs.

Bats/Throws: R/R

Drafted/Acquired: Drafted sixth overall in the 2012 MLB Draft, Mater Academy (Hialeah Gardens, FL); signed for $3.9 million

Previous Ranking(s): #7 (Org), #83 (Top 101)

2016 Stats: .277/.308/.455, 3 HR, 0 SB in 47 games at the major league level, .303/.317/.416, 4 HR, 10 SB in 80 games at triple-A Iowa

The Role: OFP 55—Batting-average-driven everyday center fielder
Likely 50—Second-division starter + first division team = good fourth outfielder

YEAR	TEAM	LVL	AGE	PA	R	2B	3B	HR	RBI	BB	K	SB	CS	AVG/OBP/SLG	TAv	VORP	BABIP	BRR	FRAA	WARP
2014	DAY	A+	20	385	55	20	2	7	50	12	46	6	3	.283/.306/.406	.254	10.5	.305	0.9	CF(87): 4.6	1.7
2014	TEN	AA	20	144	20	7	2	2	10	2	23	0	1	.234/.250/.355	.212	-3.0	.267	-0.1	CF(32): -2.3	-0.5
2015	TEN	AA	21	452	69	26	4	6	46	32	47	8	4	.272/.327/.400	.271	17.8	.291	1.2	CF(69): 2.1, LF(18): -0.7	2.3
2016	IOW	AAA	22	336	46	18	3	4	43	9	44	10	3	.303/.317/.416	.285	22.5	.336	3.8	CF(69): -1.5, LF(6): 1.5	1.8
2016	CHN	MLB	22	117	14	9	1	3	14	5	20	0	0	.277/.308/.455	.267	5.1	.315	0.9	CF(33): -0.3, LF(8): 1.6	0.5
2017	*CHN*	*MLB*	*23*	*207*	*20*	*10*	*1*	*5*	*21*	*7*	*35*	*2*	*1*	*.250/.277/.386*	*.239*	*3.0*	*.279*	*-0.1*	*CF 1*	*0.2*
2018	*CHN*	*MLB*	*24*	*417*	*45*	*21*	*2*	*11*	*47*	*15*	*70*	*4*	*2*	*.253/.283/.400*	*.250*	*7.6*	*.278*	*-0.1*	*CF 3*	*1.1*

Breakout: 5% Improve: 16% Collapse: 3% Attrition: 13% MLB: 33% *Comparables: Logan Schafer, Charlie Blackmon, Matt Szczur*

The Good: Almora has some of the best outfield instincts you will see, and it helps make the glove play as potentially plus in center, despite his not lighting up a stopwatch home-to-first. The defense would be a weapon in a corner spot. At the plate, Almora likes to swing, but has a simple swing and outstanding feel for contact, so he hasn't seen good enough arms to exploit that approach yet. He's a heady baserunner and—like in the outfield—the skills play up past the straight-line speed, something Cleveland is now well aware of.

The Bad: Almora is a bit of a hacker, and while he has the hand-eye to make contact, it isn't always good contact. The power is average at 5 o'clock, but plays more to 40 in games. He's only an average runner, which may limit his defensive ceiling in center-field. It's not a tweener profile—he could comfortably play center field everyday—but it does lack some impact potential.

The Irrelevant: Fun Fact: Almora scored a go-ahead run in extra innings in the 2016 World Series. Not a bad thing to have on your C.V. before you lose prospect eligibility.

The Risks: He's a pretty safe major-league contributor, but unless he is Juan Lagares w/r/t being a 70 CF with only average speed, he's more solid regular than star, and that approach will really have to work against major-league pitching to even reach that.

Major league ETA: Debuted in 2016

Ben Carsley's Fantasy Take: Simply put, Almora is a better MLB prospect than a fantasy one because his profile doesn't scream "I need to play every day." If he does end up in an everyday role, he could ride a good average and relevant HR/SB totals to OF5 status. If not, well, how many backup outfielders do you roster in your league?

4. Trevor Clifton, RHP

DOB: 05/11/1995

Height/Weight: 6'1" 170 lbs

Bats/Throws: R/R

Drafted/Acquired: Drafted in the 12th round of the 2013 MLB draft, Heritage High School (Maryville, TN); signed for $375,000

Previous Ranking(s): N/A

2016 Stats: 2.72 ERA, 4.27 DRA, 119 IP, 97 H, 41 BB, 129 K at High-A Myrtle Beach

The Role: OFP 55—Mid-rotation starter
Likely 50—No. 4 starter or set-up man

YEAR	TEAM	LVL	AGE	W	L	SV	G	GS	IP	H	HR	BB/9	K/9	K	GB%	BABIP	WHIP	ERA	FIP	DRA	VORP	WARP	cFIP	MPH
2014	BOI	A-	19	4	2	0	13	13	61	59	3	4.4	8.0	54	54%	.316	1.46	3.69	4.31	4.82	3.60	0.4	103	
2015	SBN	A	20	8	10	0	23	22	108[2]	91	7	3.9	8.5	103	39%	.287	1.27	3.98	3.94	4.41	9.80	1.0	105	
2016	MYR	A+	21	7	7	0	23	23	119	97	4	3.1	9.8	129	37%	.300	1.16	2.72	3.05	4.27	15.90	1.6	93	
2017	*CHN*	*MLB*	*22*	*6*	*7*	*0*	*20*	*20*	*100[1]*	*94*	*17*	*4.5*	*6.8*	*76*	*30%*	*.283*	*1.43*	*5.39*	*5.48*	*6.10*	*-6.0*	*-0.6*	*147*	
2018	*CHN*	*MLB*	*23*	*6*	*11*	*0*	*26*	*26*	*154[1]*	*140*	*27*	*5.9*	*9.2*	*157*	*30%*	*.304*	*1.57*	*5.53*	*5.95*	*6.26*	*-9.9*	*-1.0*	*151*	

Breakout: 3% Improve: 10% Collapse: 3% Attrition: 12% MLB: 19% *Comparables: Gabriel Ynoa, Daryl Thompson, Robert Stephenson*

The Good: I am a sucker for a fastball with hard arm-side run down in the zone, and Clifton's ticks all my buttons. His best feature above-average velocity and wiffle ball late action. He can get swing-and-misses with it in the zone due to the movement. His curve flashes plus with hard, late 10-5 break and was a bat-misser by the end of the season.

The Bad: Both of Clifton's secondaries need further improvement. Velocity worked more around 90 in some outings. The arm slot can drift down and he'll get on the side of the curveball at times, causing the pitch to flatten out. His command of the curve is still fringy. The change is a non-factor currently. The fact that he works out of the stretch, the slot, his less-than-ideal size and the slingy arm action all point to a potential bullpen future.

The Irrelevant: Maryville, TN had a strong abolitionist presence in the early 1800s due to its large Quaker population.

The Risks: The changeup and command need refinement, might be a reliever. Oh, yeah, he's a pitcher too.

Major league ETA: Late 2018

Ben Carsley's Fantasy Take: You probably haven't heard of Clifton—and even if you have, most of your league mates probably haven't. That makes him a good value buy if your league rosters, like 200 prospects, but he lacks the upside or immediate impact potential to flirt with a ranking closer to the top-100. If we're being honest, his name is boring.

Please note a previous version of this article referred to Clifton as "undersized" in The Risks based on prior 2016 internal reports. He has since been confirmed to be 6-foot-4, 220 pounds, rather than closer to his listed height and weight. We regret the error.

5. Jeimer Candelario, 3B

DOB: 11/24/1993

Height/Weight: 6'1" 210 lbs

Bats/Throws: S/R

Drafted/Acquired: Signed September 2010 by the Cubs out of the Dominican Republic for $500,000.

Previous Ranking(s): N/A

2016 Stats: .091/.286/.091, 0 HR, 0 SB in 5 games at the major league level, .333/.417/.542, 9 HR, 0 SB in 76 games at triple-A Iowa, .219/.324/.367, 4 HR, 0 SB in 56 games at double-A Tennessee

The Role: OFP 55— Late-career-Martin-Pradoish third baseman
Likely 50—Average major leaguer at the hot corner

YEAR	TEAM	LVL	AGE	PA	R	2B	3B	HR	RBI	BB	K	SB	CS	AVG/OBP/SLG	TAv	VORP	BABIP	BRR	FRAA	WARP
2014	DAY	A+	20	244	24	10	2	5	26	23	44	0	3	.193/.275/.326	.224	-4.0	.218	-2.1	3B(57): 8.1	0.4
2014	KNC	A	20	263	32	19	3	6	37	18	45	0	1	.250/.300/.426	.264	8.9	.284	-0.6	3B(62): 5.7	1.5
2015	MYR	A+	21	343	42	25	3	5	39	20	62	0	1	.270/.318/.415	.270	13.2	.320	-0.5	3B(77): -8.3	0.5
2015	TEN	AA	21	182	21	10	1	5	25	22	21	0	0	.291/.379/.462	.306	14.1	.308	0.2	3B(44): -3.6	1.1
2016	TEN	AA	22	244	30	17	1	4	23	32	46	0	0	.219/.324/.367	.247	4.2	.261	0.0	3B(54): 2.7, 1B(2): -0.3	0.7
2016	CHN	MLB	22	14	0	0	0	0	0	2	5	0	0	.091/.286/.091	.178	-0.5	.167	0.2	3B(3): -0.4	-0.1
2016	IOW	AAA	22	309	44	22	3	9	54	38	53	0	2	.333/.417/.542	.353	40.9	.383	1.7	3B(67): -0.8, 1B(10): 1.1	4.2
2017	*CHN*	*MLB*	*23*	*123*	*13*	*6*	*1*	*3*	*14*	*10*	*27*	*0*	*0*	*.232/.301/.391*	*.248*	*1.6*	*.275*	*-0.3*	*3B -0, 1B 0*	*0.1*
2018	*CHN*	*MLB*	*24*	*367*	*44*	*19*	*2*	*12*	*44*	*32*	*82*	*0*	*0*	*.239/.310/.412*	*.263*	*7.9*	*.281*	*-0.9*	*3B 0, 1B 1*	*0.9*

Breakout: 5% Improve: 25% Collapse: 8% Attrition: 20% MLB: 38% *Comparables: Colin Moran, Taylor Green, Jedd Gyorko*

The Good: It's tempting, in the interest of time—still ten more of these lists to go—to just C+P the Happ entry here, but we'll try to wordsmith it a bit so it's not too obvious. Candelario is an...uh... "advanced" hitter from both sides of the plate. The swing is simple, short, and geared for contact, but he is strong enough to make it loud if he gets a pitch to drive. And like most Cubs prospects not named Albert Almora, Candelario has a keen eye and strong approach at the plate. So he knows which pitches to drive. All things considered, it's a plus hit tool, and a plus arm that plays well at third base.

The Bad: Hey it's another polished Cubs hitter with a fringy defensive profile and maybe-not enough power to carry the day. Candelario improved at third base this past season, but you will see the phrase "he battles there" a bit too much for my liking. The bat will be doing the heavy lifting here, and his swing lacks the loft to project more than low-double-digit bombs, though he'll bop his fair share of doubles.

The Irrelevant: Candelario grew up in San Pedro de Macoris and signed out of the Dominican Republic but he was born in New York, NY.

The Risks: At the risk of repeating myself some more, Candelario is another polished, major-league ready—or close to it—prospect without a ton of upside. If he doesn't hit quite as much as we project, there isn't much else to carry the profile.

Major league ETA: Debuted in 2016

Ben Carsley's Fantasy Take: A change of scenery would be nice (sense a theme?), because if Candelario plays every day as a second-division 3B I do think he could flirt with many top-20 finishes at the position. But we can't really factor "he might get traded" into these rankings, and as such, Candelario has very little present-day value. That sucks, because if he was on, say, the Angels, he might be a back-of-the-top-100 fantasy prospect. (*How dare you suggest he would play over My Main Main Jefry Marte-j.p.*)

6. Jose Albertos, RHP

DOB: 11/07/1998

Height/Weight: 6'1" 185 lbs

Bats/Throws: R/R

Drafted/Acquired: Signed July 2015 by the Cubs out of Mexico for $1,500,000.

Previous Ranking(s): N/A

2016 Stats: 0.00 ERA, 2.57 DRA, 4 IP, 1 H, 1 BB, 7 K at complex-level AZL

The Role: OFP 60—No. 3 starter
Likely 45—Back-end starter or good middle reliever

YEAR	TEAM	LVL	AGE	W	L	SV	G	GS	IP	H	HR	BB/9	K/9	K	GB%	BABIP	WHIP	ERA	FIP	DRA	VORP	WARP	cFIP	MPH
2016	CUB	Rk	17	0	0	0	1	1	4	1	0	2.2	15.8	7	50%	.167	0.50	0.00	1.38	2.57	1.40	0.1	82	
2017	*CHN*	*MLB*	*18*	*2*	*3*	*0*	*8*	*8*	*36^1*	*32*	*6*	*3.8*	*7.4*	*30*	*47%*	*.267*	*1.29*	*4.90*	*5.02*	*5.66*	*-0.4*	*0.0*	*133*	
2018	*CHN*	*MLB*	*19*	*4*	*5*	*0*	*17*	*17*	*99*	*90*	*15*	*3.5*	*8.5*	*93*		*.292*	*1.30*	*4.56*	*4.88*	*5.27*	*2.6*	*0.3*	*124*	

Breakout: 0% Improve: 0% Collapse: 0% Attrition: 0% MLB: 0% *Comparables: Roberto Osuna, Jordan Lyles, Yohander Mendez*

The Good: So if you are going to rank a 17-year-old arm with very limited pro experience this highly—even one who just got a seven-figure bonus, he needs to pass our rigorous questionnaire:

Big arm? *Yep, potential plus-plus fastball here*

Any advanced secondary of note? *Oh yeah. Unusually it's the change, not the breaking ball, and it could be a very good one.*

Okay, but is he really going to be a starter? *Look, he's a teenager in the complex, but he's got about the best chance of that general profile to stick in a rotation as you'll find.*

The Bad: Well, he's still seventeen and a long ways from the majors. You would need "two gymnasium-sized super computers" to calculate and enumerate the baseball version of everything that could go wrong for Albertos between now and that shiny OFP below.

The Irrelevant: If you are hustling for an irrelevant late at night and, say, just search for Albertos' birthdate, you get a whoooooooole bunch of Phish setlists from that night's show at the UIC Pavillion. It featured an encore of "While My Guitar Gently Weeps" which I am going to guess was roughly 23 minutes long.

The Risks: All of them. He has all of the risks. And he's a pitcher.

Major league ETA: 2021

Ben Carsley's Fantasy Take: I mean, I get it. There's a little bit of an Anderson Espinoza vibe here. But Albertos is too far away and too much of a pitcher to go nuts about. If your league rosters 200 prospects and you love upside, go for it. Otherwise, meh. The profile isn't that unique, even if he has a better shot of making the profile work than most. But still, probably don't.

7. Dylan Cease, RHP

DOB: 12/28/1995

Height/Weight: 6'1" 175 lbs.

Bats/Throws: R/R

Drafted/Acquired: Drafted in the sixth round of the 2014 MLB Draft, Milton HS (Milton, GA); signed for $1.5 million

Previous Ranking(s): #6 (Org)

2016 Stats: 2.22 ERA, 1.69 DRA, 44.2 IP, 27 H, 25 BB, 66 K in short-season Eugene

The Role: OFP 60—Major-league closer
Likely 45—7th-inning guy that misses bats but struggles to throw strikes

YEAR	TEAM	LVL	AGE	W	L	SV	G	GS	IP	H	HR	BB/9	K/9	K	GB%	BABIP	WHIP	ERA	FIP	DRA	VORP	WARP	cFIP	MPH
2015	CUB	Rk	19	1	2	0	11	8	24	12	0	6.0	9.4	25	66%	.207	1.17	2.62	3.98	4.91	2.40	0.2	107	
2016	EUG	A-	20	2	0	0	12	12	44^2	27	1	5.0	13.3	66	55%	.295	1.16	2.22	2.92	1.69	17.60	1.9	78	
2017	*CHN*	*MLB*	*21*	*2*	*3*	*0*	*10*	*10*	*35^2*	*29*	*3*	*5.6*	*8.2*	*33*	*42%*	*.291*	*1.45*	*4.42*	*4.39*	*4.98*	*2.3*	*0.2*	*116*	
2018	*CHN*	*MLB*	*22*	*6*	*8*	*0*	*28*	*28*	*171*	*136*	*14*	*6.1*	*9.9*	*189*	*42%*	*.309*	*1.48*	*4.22*	*4.52*	*4.76*	*9.2*	*0.9*	*112*	

Breakout: 2% Improve: 2% Collapse: 0% Attrition: 1% MLB: 2% *Comparables: Wilking Rodriguez, Nick Tropeano, Carl Edwards Jr*

The Good: Cease has a big fastball. Of that there can be no doubt. It's a high-90s howitzer and a potential plus-plus pitch with command refinement. His 12-6 hammer curve will flash plus, and it did that more often as the season went on. He was healthy. That's good in this case! The delivery doesn't have any obvious red flags, unless you count elite arm speed as a red flag, which, well...

The Bad: His durability is going to be a question mark until he gets through a full season of full-season ball as a starter. And even if that happens, you question if he's a starter in the long term. He's undersized—although a good athlete—for a starting pitcher. The command is below-average. The changeup is firm and needs grade jumps to be a major-league third pitch. The fastball doesn't move a ton (for as much as that matters when it can touch 100).

The Irrelevant: Do not be alarmed if you see Cease in the cockpit of your private jet. That's actually his twin brother, Alec.

The Risks: I love Cease, but the fact that this came up as a question before he's even made full season ball tells you quite a lot:

Major league ETA: 2020

Ben Carsley's Fantasy Take: There's a lot to like with Cease, but as alluring as his potential is, the red flags outweigh the potential ceiling at this point. Sure, if he proves he can hold up and he can hold up without his stuff suffering, you've got a pretty nice pitcher on your hands. But the odds of both of those things happening, well, Vegas wouldn't take 'em. So basically, when it comes to Cease as a fantasy prospect ... not yet. If he proves more durable, sure. But not yet.

8. Eddy Julio Martinez, OF

DOB: 01/18/1995

Height/Weight: 6'1" 195 lbs.

Bats/Throws: R/R

Drafted/Acquired: Signed October 2015 by the Cubs out of Cuba for $3 million

Previous Ranking(s): #5 (Org), #97 (Top 101)

The Role: OFP 55—Above-average outfielder
Likely 45—Fourth outfielder

2016 Stats: .254/.331/.380, 10 HR, 8 SB in 126 games for low-A South Bend

YEAR	TEAM	LVL	AGE	PA	R	2B	3B	HR	RBI	BB	K	SB	CS	AVG/OBP/SLG	TAv	VORP	BABIP	BRR	FRAA	WARP
2016	SBN	A	21	517	72	24	2	10	67	50	113	8	5	.254/.331/.380	.272	11.9	.315	-1.3	RF(106): -1.2, CF(9): -0.2	1.5
2017	*CHN*	*MLB*	*22*	*250*	*24*	*9*	*1*	*7*	*28*	*19*	*70*	*0*	*0*	*.212/.275/.355*	*.220*	*-3.6*	*.268*	*-0.4*	*RF 0, CF -0*	*-0.4*
2018	*CHN*	*MLB*	*23*	*200*	*22*	*7*	*0*	*6*	*21*	*15*	*58*	*0*	*0*	*.204/.270/.340*	*.226*	*-3.6*	*.263*	*-0.4*	*RF 0, CF 0*	*-0.4*

Breakout: 0% Improve: 5% Collapse: 0% Attrition: 5% MLB: 7% *Comparables: Destin Hood, Zoilo Almonte, James Jones*

The Good: Martinez has a broad base of tools and improved throughout his first stateside season in the Midwest League. He has premium bat speed and will flash plus raw power. The hit tool is raw at present, and he tinkered with his timing mechanisms in 2016, but it projects as at least average. He's an above-average defender in a corner with a plus arm that plays well in right field, and he has enough present day footspeed to take some reps in center field as well.

The Bad: He lacks a carrying offensive tool, especially if he ends up in right field. The plus raw power plays down in games currently because of his line-drive approach, and there's swing and miss in the profile as well. Some of that could be chalked up to rust and lost game reps, but you can get him to expand on stuff running down and away. He's an above-average runner at present, but if he loses speed as he ages, center field even once a week may be a bit of a stretch.

The Irrelevant: Martinez's Cuban team was Leñadores de las Tunas. This translates (per Google) to "the Woodcutters" (shame he didn't somehow end up in Williamsport). Their logo features a cactus, so...you tell us.

The Risks: Martinez hasn't played above A-ball, and the offensive tools will have to play all the way top projection for him to be a viable starter in a corner outfield spot.

Ben Carsley's Fantasy Take: I definitely suggest keeping an eye on Martinez, because there are enough pieces of offensive tools here that he could be a good fantasy player. But they're just pieces right now, so Martinez is mostly just an idea at this point, despite the hype that surrounded him last year. If it starts click, don't be afraid to jump on board.

9. Oscar De La Cruz, RHP

DOB: 03/04/1995

Height/Weight: 6'4" 200 lbs

Bats/Throws: R/R

Drafted/Acquired: Signed October 2012 by the Cubs out of the Dominican Republic for $85,000.

Previous Ranking(s): N/A

2016 Stats: 3.25 ERA, 2.07 DRA, 27.2 IP, 22 H, 8 BB, 35 K in low-A South Bend, 1.08 ERA, 1.76 DRA, 8.1 IP, 5 H, 2 BB, 14 K in short-season Eugene

The Role: OFP 50—No. 4 starter
Likely 40—No. 5 starter or middle reliever

YEAR	TEAM	LVL	AGE	W	L	SV	G	GS	IP	H	HR	BB/9	K/9	K	GB%	BABIP	WHIP	ERA	FIP	DRA	VORP	WARP	cFIP	MPH
2014	DCU	Rk	19	8	1	0	14	14	75	56	2	2.3	7.7	64	0%	.249	1.00	1.80	2.92	2.48			83	
2015	EUG	A-	20	6	3	0	13	13	73	56	4	2.1	9.0	73	41%	.271	1.00	2.84	3.18	2.52	22.40	2.3	92	
2016	CUB	Rk	21	0	1	0	1	1	3	3	1	3.0	6.0	2	60%	.222	1.33	6.00	8.13	4.02	0.60	0.1	99	
2016	EUG	A-	21	0	0	0	2	2	8¹	5	1	2.2	15.1	14	31%	.267	0.84	1.08	3.41	1.76	3.20	0.3	81	
2016	SBN	A	21	1	2	0	6	6	27²	22	0	2.6	11.4	35	43%	.328	1.08	3.25	2.14	2.07	9.10	1.0	80	
2017	*CHN*	*MLB*	*22*	*2*	*3*	*0*	*7*	*7*	*38*	*37*	*6*	*4.2*	*6.5*	*27*	*29%*	*.288*	*1.44*	*5.36*	*5.30*	*6.08*	*-2.4*	*-0.2*	*146*	
2018	*CHN*	*MLB*	*23*	*6*	*8*	*0*	*21*	*21*	*125≤*	*114*	*20*	*4.8*	*8.9*	*124*	*29%*	*.302*	*1.44*	*4.97*	*5.36*	*5.64*	*-1.5*	*-0.2*	*136*	

Breakout: 4% Improve: 6% Collapse: 4% Attrition: 6% MLB: 10% *Comparables: Adam Wilk, David Paulino, Bruce Billings*

The Good: De La Cruz is a big, athletic arm, a converted infielder that has taken to life on the mound well, if not all that quickly. He features a heavy fastball that sits primarily in the low-90s at present, although it has ticked higher at times. He commands the pitch well down in the zone, and it's a potential plus offering if he can find those extra ticks more often. His mid-70s curveball projects as above-average, and he can already spot it for a strike to both sides of the plate or bury it as needed.

The Bad: The stuff—while it projects as major-league quality— doesn't jump off the scouting report, and there isn't much projection left here. Injury issues have left De La Cruz over-age for the leagues he's pitched in and...well, that means there are injury issues. The curveball's shape and velocity can be inconsistent. It will flatten out when he tries to find an extra few mph. The change is still rough and he's shown limited feel for it.

The Irrelevant: Ervin Santana leads all players from De La Cruz's birthplace of La Romana with 26.5 WARP, narrowly edging out Edwin Encarnacion. *(at least until Jefry Marte overtakes both of them - j.p.)*

The Risks: He's an older Midwest League arm with a crude changeup. There's a very good chance he's just a solid relief arm. On the other hand, he's got limited enough miles on his arm, that there might be some positive risk here as well, and two advanced pitches give him a better base than most Midwest League arms regardless of age.

Major league ETA: 2019

Ben Carsley's Fantasy Take: You already know how I feel about back-end starters. Spend your time elsewhere.

10. Thomas Hatch, RHP

DOB: 09/22/1994

Height/Weight: 6'1" 190 lbs

Bats/Throws: R/R

Drafted/Acquired: Drafted in the third round of the 2016 MLB draft, Oklahoma State (Stillwater, OK); signed for $573,900

Previous Ranking(s): N/A

2016 Stats: N/A

The Role: OFP 50—No. 4 Starter
Likely 40—Swingman/7th-inning arm

The Good: Hatch bounced back after missing 2015 because of elbow injury, winning the conference pitcher of the year award and leading Oklahoma State to the College World Series. His fastball has a lot of life from his low-three-quarters slot, which caused a fair amount of weak contact and awkward swings. Working 91-94 in college, his velocity did bump into the mid-90s in instructs in short outings. His slider is a potential above-average offering with depth and late movement. His changeup works and is an effective enough offering against left-handers.

The Bad: While no surgery was performed, Hatch did miss the 2015 season with a sprained elbow ligament. He isn't a bat-misser, relying more on weak contact and pitchability. The changeup is usable but is still somewhat raw as he didn't use it that often in college. There isn't much projection left given his age and his filled out body.

The Irrelevant: Other winners of the Big 12 Pitcher of the year include Max Scherzer, Aaron Crow, Andrew Heaney, and Taylor Jungmann

The Risks: Elbow injury in 2015, he's a pitcher, pitchability over stuff. The arm slot could create difficulties against left-handers in pro ball.

Major league ETA: 2019

Ben Carsley's Fantasy Take: You already know how I feel about back-end starters. Spend your time elsewhere.

OTHERS OF NOTE:

#11

Mark Zagunis, OF

The differences between Zagunis and the more highly-ranked Happ and Candelario are of degree rather than kind. Of course when making a list like this, it's all about those degrees. A move from catcher to the corner outfield can often be the death knell for any prospect's status, but Zagunis' bat has survived the move due to that vaunted Cubs-hitter approach. The swing is more than a little stiff and lacks much lift, so once again, if you are looking for a traditional corner offensive profile, you won't find it here. He also lacks the ability to play on the dirt, so his defensive flexibility is limited to right field and left field. But while it isn't the prettiest profile, Zagunis keeps hitting enough and getting on base enough that he merited consideration for the back of this list, and he might end up with too many major league at-bats to make next year's.

The stand-in

Isaac Paredes, SS

Sierra here. Or any other of the big six-figure signings from the Cubs 2015 IFA class. It feels a bit like that international splurge went a little under the radar compared to the Yankees and Padres recent attempts to blow out the bonus pool. Maybe because the Cubs had been quiet in the market previously, due to the time they blew out their pool. There also weren't any huge names at the time—though Albertos has quickly established himself as a top tier prospect—but it's a reminder that the Cubs have the resources to be major players in the amateur market and a front office willing to leverage them.

I could have just as easily mentioned Aramis Ademan, Kwang-Min Kwon, or Jonathan

Another Cubs approach dude

Alec Mills, RHP

When we write that Skoglund throws strikes, we don't mean to imply that he throws nearly as many strikes as Alec Mills. Mills looks rather unassuming on the mound, a bit of an Anthony Edwards in sports goggles, but he has an above-average sinker and changeup that work well off each other. He offers a couple of breaking balls as well, but both are below-average. He's in the same range as Skoglund, but has already pitched in the majors. So there's that.

Not eligible for the 25U, but worth a mench here

Jose Rosario, RHP

Rosario debuted with the Cubs Dominican Summer League team in 2008. He spent a second summer there, then three years in short-season ball. In 2014 his results in Advanced-A as a 23-year-old would have had him on the verge of release in many orgs. Then, he lost all of the 2015 season to Tommy John. The Cubs moved him to the pen this year, and now he touches 100 with a razor blade slider. He carved up three levels in 2016 and got added to Chicago's 40-man five years after his first year of Rule 5 eligibility. The backstory here will make for great color when beat writers are struggling for material to fill out the PFP days in camp. The stuff here makes Rosario a real factor on the farm for a team that could use another power arm in the pen.

The former future breakout guy

Duane Underwood, RHP

We pegged Underwood as a riser for 2016, but it didn't quite work out that way. An elbow injury cost him some time, but even when he was on the mound, the stuff and command went in the wrong direction this year. He didn't consistently show the mid-90s fastball of the past, and the curve continued to just flash. He still struggles to throw strikes, and coupled with the recent arm woes, the Cubs might be best off moving the former second-round pick to the bullpen sooner rather than later.

TOP 10 TALENTS 25 AND UNDER (BORN 4/1/91 OR LATER)

1. Kris Bryant	6. Eloy Jimenez
2. Addison Russell	7. Carl Edwards, Jr
3. Kyle Schwarber	8. Ian Happ
4. Javier Baez	9. Albert Almora, Jr.
5. Willson Contreras	10. Trevor Clifton

When the future of a franchise is also its present, as is the case in Chicago, lists like these are a little beside the point. Ordinality doesn't do a great job representing the yawning gulf between someone like Kris Bryant—first on this list, and one of the three or four most valuable players in baseball—and the man ranked at number ten, Trevor Clifton. There's more than nine degrees of separation there. But The Lord looked upon such statements with displeasure and said, "Thou shalt write ranked lists, for they art both easy to read and easy to write." And it was Good.

Since I wrote last year's version of this list, three of its members—Jorge Soler (4), Gleyber Torres (6), and Billy McKinney (9)—have been traded for AL relievers. Net those debits against their replacements in the ranking—Jimenez (6), Edwards, Jr. (7), and Almora, Jr. (9)—and replace Eddy Julio Martinez at 10 with Clifton, by virtue of each's performance, and you get a list with not much movement at the top and quite a bit less upside toward the bottom, if a hair more certainty.

A few questions remain: Is Russell's future more of what he is now—a light-hit, good-field shortstop with a little more pop than you'd expect—or a .280/.370/.485 MVP type in the mold of Miguel Tejada? That promise, overexcited though it is, has always been hanging in the air around this kid, and we're now getting into the stretch of seasons where either it or something like it is going to actually materialize on paper, or we're going to have to accept that he's the Edgar Renteria of this era's loaded shortstop class.

Schwarber, meanwhile, will have to prove that his bat can hold up to the increased demands that his new position—left field—places upon it, and that his surgically reconstructed knee doesn't fall apart at the first sign of a fly ball to the position. His dominant turn in the World Series went a long way towards allaying the first concern, and his extraordinary work ethic will mean rehab that'll limit risk related to the second, but 2017 will still be Schwarber's first ever chance to prove himself over the full 162.

Jimenez, the one potential star on the list not already mashing at Wrigley, is ranked sixth. Seven through ten are a collection of guys hovering at the back-end of the 25-man and guys still a few months away. Happ and Clifton, the entrants in the latter category, could both be big-league contributors as soon as the end of the year, but have unfinished business in the minors. The Juniors, Edwards and Almora, are already playing at Wrigley but still trying to find out where and how much. This will be a pivotal year for each.

Looked at in totality, this isn't a list you can dream on in quite the way last year's was. But does that really matter? For the guys in the top half of the list, last year's dreams have already become this year's reality.

—Rian Watt

CHICAGO WHITE SOX

The State of the System: *"We're just happy the White Sox got all those deals done before we submitted the org rankings for the Annual."*

THE TOP TEN

1. 2B Yoan Moncada	6. RHP Alec Hansen
2. RHP Lucas Giolito	7. RHP Carson Fulmer
3. RHP Reynaldo Lopez	8. OF Luis Alexander Basabe
4. RHP Michael Kopech	9. RHP Zack Burdi
5. C Zack Collins	10. RHP Dane Dunning

The Big Question: Is the White Sox pitching development team magical?

We could have copy-pasted "Not sure if all these guys can hit their ceilings" for the sole analysis of every system and been technically correct, and probably would not even lose our entire subscription base in the process. But in pulling off two of the biggest trades of the entire offseason for a surfeit of high-ceiling prospects, surely the White Sox have achieved some small measure of uniqueness in the raft of arms they have acquired; whose ability to utilize their potentially electric stuff out of the starting rotation is dependent on how they respond to the next one or two years of instruction under the helm of Don Cooper & Co.

The Sox are not flush with natural competitive advantages, but what they have is well defined: they can develop homegrown arms and they can keep them healthy. Cooper and newly named pitching coordinator Richard Dotson (entering his 16th year in the organization), have a well-worn formula for cleaning up deliveries, keeping pitchers upright through their throwing motion and emphasizing extension. The results are not universal—Jeff Samardzija certainly wasn't much for the tweaks—but they have fueled the strength of the organization for more than a decade. Given the accomplishment of the White Sox during that span, this has proven to not be quite enough of an organizational hallmark to cover for other warts, but there's no point in abandoning the well now, as they try to build a larger, deeper core.

But even for a franchise that rode to the 2005 World Series title on the shoulders of a dominant starting rotation, never has the pitching development staff been responsible for overseeing such a collection of young, high-octane arms. Moreover, never have they been staked with fortifying the foundation of a rebuild of this scale and scope. Turn Lopez, Kopech, Hansen and Fulmer into reliable major-league starters and they have the most enviable slate of young arms in the league, already in their organization less than a year after beginning their harrowing sell-off. Yet a more realistic scenario is where all four of them are relievers, and the White Sox rebuild becomes one of those five-year slogs built slowly from the draft.

Lopez, the highest-rated of this group, even Cooper has readily acknowledged could end up in the pen, Kopech has a head whack to rival the early days of Carlos Rodon, Hansen was acknowledged as a reclamation project on the day he was drafted after a disastrous final season at Oklahoma, and his forward momentum with the Sox has brought him just to the height of "major conference college pitcher dominating Low-A." Fulmer is at the back of this group after a difficult first-full season in the organization, where he struggled to adapt the Sox' adjustments to his game on their typical accelerated timeline for advanced college arms. In this high-wire act, Giolito, the former future ace coming off a down year, becomes the most predictable pitching prospect of the bunch, with the Sox only having to complete the reasonable goal of tossing aside his mechanical adjustments from 2016 and overcoming early indications that his fastball lacks the life and spin rate to be a swing-and-miss offering. There's a ton of talent here, but the White Sox have staked the first step of their future on the idea that they can conquer the risk and difficulties present.

And they very much have to. The White Sox are not the team that will look to win the Bryce Harper sweepstakes in the future, they would not even dream of incurring a penalty for an aggressive international amateur free agency spending spree to stack their talent coffers, if they even could, given

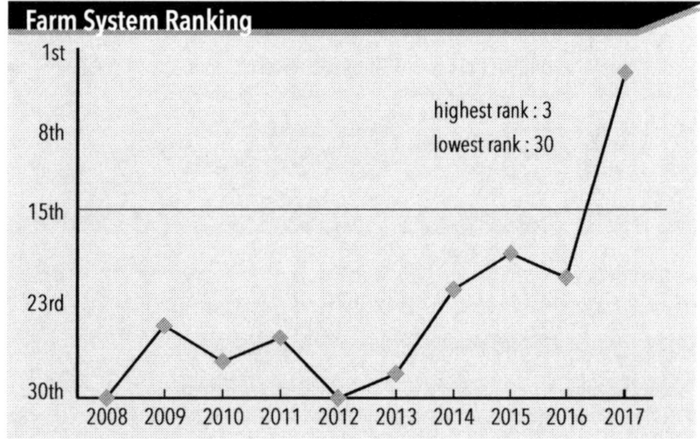

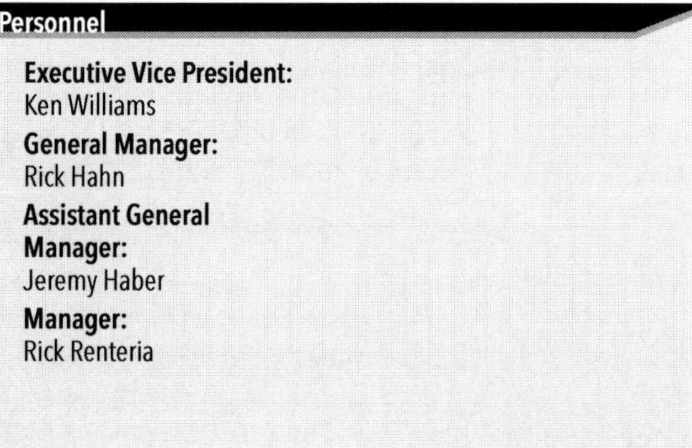
Personnel

Executive Vice President:
Ken Williams

General Manager:
Rick Hahn

Assistant General Manager:
Jeremy Haber

Manager:
Rick Renteria

the David Wilder-shaped crater their international scouts have been dutifully climbing out of for a decade.

This is their path, this is the strength the Sox will rest their fate on 100 times out of 100. The big question is whether it's merely good, or whether its franchise-altering, and whether it's franchise should change how we conceive of the pitchers on this list while they remain in the Sox' tow. That's probably not the case, since we're pretty good at this prospect analysis thing after all, but those are the stakes on which the Sox are testing their pitching development. If they are wrong, they are just another rebuilding club.

—James Fegan

1. Yoan Moncada, 2B

DOB: 05/27/1995

Height/Weight: 6'2" 205 lbs

Bats/Throws: S/R

Drafted/Acquired: Signed March 2015 out of Cuba for $31.5 million

Previous Ranking(s): #1 (Org.), #7 (Overall)

2016 Stats: .211/.250/.263, 0 HR, 0 SB in 8 games at the major league level, .277/.379/..531, 11 HR, 9 SB in 45 games at Double-A Portland, .307/.427/.496, 4 HR, 36 SB in 61 games at High-A Salem. Acquired from Boston in the Chris Sale deal.

The Role: OFP 70—Perennial All-Star 2B or 3B
Likely 60—First-division regular...somewhere

YEAR	TEAM	LVL	AGE	PA	R	2B	3B	HR	RBI	BB	K	SB	CS	AVG/OBP/SLG	TAv	VORP	BABIP	BRR	FRAA	WARP
2015	GRN	A	20	363	61	19	3	8	38	42	83	49	3	.278/.380/.438	.312	35.7	.353	7.6	2B(71): -5.6	3.2
2015	GRN	A	20	363	61	19	3	8	38	42	83	49	3	.278/.380/.438	.312	35.7	.353	7.6	2B(71): -5.6	3.2
2016	SLM	A+	21	284	57	25	3	4	34	45	60	36	8	.307/.427/.496	.320	31.9	.395	6.2	2B(58): -1.7	3.1
2016	SLM	A+	21	284	57	25	3	4	34	45	60	36	8	.307/.427/.496	.320	31.9	.395	6.2	2B(58): -1.7	3.1
2016	PME	AA	21	207	37	6	3	11	28	27	64	9	4	.277/.379/.531	.309	16.4	.373	0.6	2B(34): -4.6, 3B(10): 0.7	1.3
2016	PME	AA	21	207	37	6	3	11	28	27	64	9	4	.277/.379/.531	.309	16.4	.373	0.6	2B(34): -4.6, 3B(10): 0.7	1.3
2016	BOS	MLB	21	20	3	1	0	0	1	1	12	0	0	.211/.250/.263	.189	-0.5	.571	0.3	3B(5): 0.2	0.0
2016	BOS	MLB	21	20	3	1	0	0	1	1	12	0	0	.211/.250/.263	.189	-0.5	.571	0.3	3B(5): 0.2	0.0
2017	*CHA*	*MLB*	*22*	*130*	*17*	*5*	*1*	*4*	*14*	*14*	*42*	*7*	*2*	*.223/.312/.387*	*.250*	*2.8*	*.310*	*0.9*	*3B 1, 2B -1*	*0.3*
2018	*CHA*	*MLB*	*23*	*361*	*46*	*14*	*2*	*13*	*44*	*39*	*119*	*20*	*5*	*.224/.317/.402*	*.250*	*8.6*	*.308*	*2.9*	*3B 2, 2B -2*	*1.0*

Breakout: 2% Improve: 24% Collapse: 4% Attrition: 14% MLB: 47% *Comparables: Chris Carter, Matt Davidson, Andy Marte*

The Good: He might have the best body in baseball. He is one of the best overall athletes in baseball. He's got a good idea of what he wants to do at the plate and recognizes pitches very well for his age/level. He swings the bat quite hard from both sides of the plate. He has at least plus raw power from both sides of the plate. He's a 70 runner. He has a strong arm.

The Bad: I thought Moncada was capable of being an average second baseman, but he wasn't there yet and it's irrelevant unless he's traded, because he's never playing the keystone in the organization already employing the services of Dustin Pedroia and Mookie Betts. Reports on his defense at third—a position that should've suited his defensive strengths better—were mixed, and it's far from a lock that his arm accuracy and hands will play long-term at the hot corner. Is he really beating out Benintendi or Betts for a corner outfield spot? Could he end up sliding all the way to first? If you want some offensive concerns, Moncada looked badly overmatched in his one-week MLB trial in early-September, and there's always been just a little more swing-and-miss here than there should be given the rest of the profile.

The Irrelevant: With the new Collective Bargaining Agreement capping bonuses at a small fraction of his, Moncada's record $31.5 million bonus for a July 2nd international free agent is going to stand for a very, very, very long time.

The Risks: Is Moncada destined to be traded to a team that can develop him as a second baseman? [ed. Note: yes] If he stays in Boston [ed. Note: nope], he could end up much further right on the defensive spectrum than anyone thinks, and with those positions comes greater offensive responsibility [ed. Note: probably'll be fine]. There's some downside potential for the takes too many borderline strikes/swings through too many hittable pitches profile combination that can lead to an inordinate number of strikeouts at the major-league level.

Major league ETA: Debuted in 2016 —Jarrett Seidler

Ben Carsley's Fantasy Take: Sure, Moncada has some warts, but he's still the top overall dynasty prospect in the game. His eventual upside is as a five-category monster and potential top-10 pick, but when he gets to the Majors he'll be interesting right away thanks to his speed and ability to hit for average. Factor in the likelihood that he'll play in the infield and his relatively short lead time and there's quite a bit to like. A future with a .280-plus average, 30-plus steals and 15-20 homers from 2B is very much in play. His floor might look something like Ian Kinsler's career, which has been plenty rewarding to fantasy players. His ceiling might be something closer to Starling Marte, but on the dirt. He's extra valuable in leagues that count Tom Verducci meltdowns as a stat.

2. Lucas Giolito, RHP

DOB: 07/14/1994

Height/Weight: 6'6" 255 lbs

Bats/Throws: R/R

Drafted/Acquired: Drafted 16th overall in the 2012 MLB draft, Harvard-Westlake HS (Los Angeles, CA); signed for $2.925 million. Acquired from Washington in the Adam Eaton deal.

Previous Ranking(s): #3 (Top 101), #1 (Org) 2016

2016 Stats: 6.75 ERA, 7.87 DRA, 21.1 IP, 26 H, 12 BB, 11 K at the major league level, 2.17 ERA, 2.42 DRA, 37.1 IP, 31 H, 10 BB, 40 K at Triple-A Syracuse, 3.17 ERA, 3.71 DRA, 71 IP, 67 H, 34 BB, 72 K at Double-A Harrisburg

The Role: OFP 70—Possible top-of-the-rotation starter
Likely 60—Mid-rotation starter or closer

YEAR	TEAM	LVL	AGE	W	L	SV	G	GS	IP	H	HR	BB/9	K/9	K	GB%	BABIP	WHIP	ERA	FIP	DRA	VORP	WARP	cFIP	MPH
2014	HAG	A	19	10	2	0	20	20	98	70	7	2.6	10.1	110	51%	.262	1.00	2.20	3.16	1.68	40.90	4.2	73	
2015	POT	A+	20	3	5	0	13	11	69^{2}	65	1	2.6	11.1	86	54%	.352	1.22	2.71	1.96	1.17	29.70	3.2	64	
2015	HAR	AA	20	4	2	0	8	8	47^{1}	48	2	3.2	8.6	45	56%	.341	1.37	3.80	3.18	3.00	11.00	1.2	87	
2016	HAR	AA	21	5	3	0	14	14	71	67	2	4.3	9.1	72	53%	.323	1.42	3.17	3.30	3.69	11.10	1.2	90	
2016	HAG	A	21	0	0	0	1	1	7	6	2	0.0	5.1	4	36%	.200	0.86	5.14	5.97	5.12	-0.10	0.0	104	
2016	SYR	AAA	21	1	2	0	7	7	37^{1}	31	3	2.4	9.6	40	56%	.298	1.10	2.17	2.95	2.36	12.40	1.3	68	
2016	WAS	MLB	21	0	1	0	6	4	21^{1}	26	7	5.1	4.6	11	42%	.271	1.78	6.75	8.25	7.87	-6.20	-0.6	136	96.1
2017	*CHA*	*MLB*	*22*	*5*	*6*	*0*	*16*	*16*	*91*	*96*	*11*	*4.0*	*7.1*	*72*	*47%*	*.302*	*1.53*	*4.75*	*4.61*	*5.05*	*2.2*	*0.2*	*100*	
2018	*CHA*	*MLB*	*23*	*9*	*10*	*0*	*27*	*27*	163^{2}	*152*	*21*	*5.2*	*9.6*	*175*	*47%*	*.303*	*1.50*	*4.47*	*4.59*	*4.93*	*9.1*	*0.9*	*115*	

Breakout: 21% Improve: 37% Collapse: 3% Attrition: 19% MLB: 48% *Comparables: Jon Niese, Arodys Vizcaino, Wade Davis*

The Good: Giolito's curveball, on raw stuff alone, is one of the most promising pitches in prospectdom, a potential 80 grade pitch. His fastball has touched triple-digits and will sometimes comfortably sit in the mid-90s with tremendous downward plane. The change flashes as more than a show-me pitch. He has a good idea of what he wants to do on the mound. There's a lot of past history and previous looks supporting the idea that he's a potential ace.

The Bad: Oh command, where art thou? Command was never the strength of his profile, but it disappeared for him in 2016, leading to huge struggles in the majors. He couldn't spot his fastball very well, leaving both too many balls and too many hittable strikes. He could only throw the curve as a chase pitch, which meant that better hitters just laid off it. Early in the 2016 season, media reports indicated these struggles were the result of overworked mechanics, but it didn't get a whole lot better after Giolito was reported to have gotten past that issue. Just to top it off a bit, his fastball velocity was noticeably down pretty much all season compared to earlier pro looks.

The Irrelevant: Giolito is still eligible for this list, but should be out of prospectdom by the time his uncle's reboot of Twin Peaks hits the air in the second quarter of 2017. Hopefully the central mystery of Season 3 won't be his nephew's missing fastball command.

The Risks: The command might never come around, or it could take years and years and a bunch of teams and pitching coaches. The fastball/curve combination should give him a pretty good relief fallback, at least. As a Tommy John survivor, there's always that little extra bit of risk, too. Also, he's a pitcher. —*Jarrett Seidler*

Major league ETA: Debuted in 2016

Ben Carsley's Fantasy Take: Giolito is still the second-best dynasty pitching prospect in my book (I've been talked into Alex Reyes). The aforementioned command issues are worrisome, but there simply isn't another arm in the minors who comes close to matching Giolito's upside and proximity to the Majors. He might kill your WHIP at first, and the whispers of a future move to the bullpen are scary, but there's also a meaningful chance that he's a true SP1 with 225-plus strikeouts. His median fantasy outcome is Chris Archer, which makes his ceiling pretty special.

3. Reynaldo Lopez, RHP

DOB: 1/4/1994

Height/Weight: 6'0" 185 lbs

Bats/Throws: R/R

Drafted/Acquired: Signed June 2012 by Washington out of the Dominican Republic for $17,000. Acquired from Washington in the Adam Eaton deal.

Previous Ranking(s): #75 (Top 101), #4 (Org) 2016

2016 Stats: 4.91 ERA, 4.58 DRA, 44 IP, 47 H, 22 BB, 42 K at the major league level, 3.27 ERA, 7.09 DRA, 33 IP, 21 H, 10 BB, 26 K at Triple-A Syracuse, 3.18 ERA, 1.50 DRA, 76.1 IP, 69 H, 25 BB, 100 K

The Role: OFP 60—No. 3 starter
Likely 50—Power reliever

YEAR	TEAM	LVL	AGE	W	L	SV	G	GS	IP	H	HR	BB/9	K/9	K	GB%	BABIP	WHIP	ERA	FIP	DRA	VORP	WARP	cFIP	MPH
2014	AUB	A-	20	3	2	0	7	7	36	15	0	3.8	7.8	31	62%	.167	0.83	0.75	3.14	2.79	10.20	1.1	92	
2014	HAG	A	20	4	1	0	9	9	47¹	27	1	2.1	7.4	39	65%	.211	0.80	1.33	2.91	2.92	13.30	1.4	83	
2015	POT	A+	21	6	7	0	19	19	99	93	5	2.5	8.5	94	47%	.321	1.22	4.09	2.95	2.82	24.90	2.7	84	
2016	HAR	AA	22	3	5	0	14	14	76¹	69	7	2.9	11.8	100	43%	.320	1.23	3.18	3.03	1.34	31.90	3.4	63	
2016	SYR	AAA	22	2	2	0	5	5	33	21	6	2.7	7.1	26	33%	.174	0.94	3.27	4.96	5.19	0.60	0.1	102	
2016	WAS	MLB	22	5	3	0	11	6	44	47	4	4.5	8.6	42	43%	.326	1.57	4.91	3.96	4.58	3.20	0.3	105	98.7
2017	*CHA*	*MLB*	*23*	*3*	*3*	*0*	*25*	*7*	*56*	*55*	*6*	*3.6*	*8.0*	*50*	*39%*	*.295*	*1.37*	*4.25*	*4.11*	*4.46*	*4.5*	*0.5*	*100*	
2018	*CHA*	*MLB*	*24*	*8*	*6*	*0*	*62*	*16*	*144¹*	*123*	*17*	*4.7*	*10.4*	*167*	*39%*	*.295*	*1.37*	*3.94*	*4.04*	*4.32*	*14.6*	*1.5*	*98*	

Breakout: 24% Improve: 44% Collapse: 12% Attrition: 22% MLB: 75% *Comparables: Daniel Hudson, Andy Oliver, Robbie Erlin*

The Good: Lopez rode a post-April hot streak in Double-A to Triple-A and eventually an August-September major league residency. That residency included a nine strikeout debut performance against the Dodgers and an 11 strikeout game versus the Braves. His plus arm speed generates a plus-plus fastball, an upper-70s to low-80s curveball that flashes plus, and feel for a potentially average cambio.

The Bad: The walk rate spiked and strike throwing consistency diminished after the promotion. The fastball tends to stay straight. The curveball, its shape and use in the zone, is quite volatile. The changeup can get hard and lose effectiveness. The pitch inefficiency and fastball reliance could limit Lopez to a relief role.

The Irrelevant: Lopez threw his fastest pitch of the year, a 99.7 mph heater, against the Mets on September 12th.

The Risks: If the minor league walk rates and efficiency can follow Lopez to the majors, there's still middle of the rotation potential to be realized. The fallback of being a power reliever who can miss bats isn't a terrible fate either. The fate of being a pitcher though, always makes things a bit more cloudy. *—Adam Hayes*

Major league ETA: Debuted in 2016

Ben Carsley's Fantasy Take: Lopez may have a fairly low chance of actualizing as a no. 3 starter thanks to his size and command issues, but his strikeout potential and MLB ETA (of, you know, now) are too good for fantasy owners to pass up. Don't pencil Lopez into your long-term rotation plans, but hope he turns into a 200-strikeout, high-WHIP no. 4 fantasy starter. A potential future at the back of a bullpen sooner rather than later gives him a lovely additional path to fantasy value, too.

4. Michael Kopech, RHP

DOB: 04/30/1996

Height/Weight: 6'3" 205 lbs.

Bats/Throws: R/R

Drafted/Acquired: Drafted 33rd overall in the 2014 MLB Draft, Mount Pleasant HS (Mount Pleasant, TX); signed for $1.5 million

Previous Ranking(s): #5 (Org.), #98 (Overall)

2016 Stats: 0.00 ERA, 5.51 DRA, 4.1 IP, 4 H, 4 BB, 4 K in 1 game at short-season Lowell, 2.25 ERA, 1.22 DRA, 52 IP, 25 H, 29 BB, 82 K in 11 games at High-A Salem. Acquired from Boston in the Chris Sale deal.

The Role: OFP 60—No. 3 starter or fireballing closer
Likely 50—Major-league setup dude

YEAR	TEAM	LVL	AGE	W	L	SV	G	GS	IP	H	HR	BB/9	K/9	K	GB%	BABIP	WHIP	ERA	FIP	DRA	VORP	WARP	cFIP	MPH
2014	RSX	Rk	18	0	1	0	8	8	13^{2}	11	0	5.9	10.5	16	0%	.314	1.46	4.61	3.14	3.75			97	
2015	GRN	A	19	4	5	0	16	15	65	53	2	3.7	9.7	70	47%	.313	1.23	2.63	3.35	2.92	16.40	1.7	93	
2016	LOW	A-	20	0	0	0	1	1	4^{1}	4	0	8.3	8.3	4	25%	.333	1.85	0.00	4.19	5.51	-0.10	0.0	115	
2016	SLM	A+	20	4	1	0	11	11	52	25	1	5.0	14.2	82	45%	.273	1.04	2.25	2.60	1.07	25.50	2.6	75	
2017	*CHA*	*MLB*	*21*	*3*	*4*	*0*	*11*	*11*	*44^{1}*	*43*	*6*	*5.7*	*8.9*	*44*	*36%*	*.306*	*1.61*	*5.01*	*4.99*	*5.50*	*-0.1*	*0.0*	*128*	
2018	*CHA*	*MLB*	*22*	*5*	*7*	*0*	*23*	*23*	*136^{2}*	*114*	*18*	*6.5*	*11.3*	*171*	*36%*	*.301*	*1.56*	*4.64*	*4.74*	*5.09*	*3.8*	*0.4*	*118*	

Breakout: 18% Improve: 22% Collapse: 2% Attrition: 10% MLB: 25% *Comparables: Alex Reyes, Keyvius Sampson, Luis Severino*

The Good: There aren't much better places to start as a pitching prospect than with a fastball that can touch triple digits. Kopech sits there. He'd be the hardest throwing starter in the majors if he makes it to the majors a starter. He's no one-trick pony either, as the slider shows sharp, two-plane break and the change improved in 2016. He has an ideal starter's build

The Bad: But he's unlikely to stay a starter. There is effort in the delivery with a head whack and there is a reason no starter in baseball sits 99-100. The command profile is fringy, and the fastball lacks wiggle, which granted you care less about when there are three digits in the velocity. The change is improving but needs further improvement. We've already bemoaned vague make-up concerns dogging a player, but breaking your pitching hand punching a teammate is suboptimal.

The Irrelevant: It's not exactly Joe DiMaggio and Marilyn Monroe, but Kopech's girlfriend, Bravo Reality TV bit player Brielle Biermann, does have him beat in the fame department. At least for now.

The Risks: A 100-mph fastball with cover a multitude of sins, chemical or criminal. It is worth noting that the only starter who throws roughly as hard as Kopech is Noah Syndergaard, who has had a series of arm scares over the last 24 months. The fastball/slider combo gives him a pretty high major-league floor even in a pen role, but he is after all, a pitcher (who probably throws harder than man was meant to).

Major league ETA: Late 2018, but faster with a pen move

Ben Carsley's Fantasy Take: Kopech is one of the better sell-high prospects I can think of right now. Everyone is drooling over his stuff, he's likely to post some gaudy numbers in High-A and triple-digit fastballs have seduced many a dynasty enthusiast. See if someone will give you a good MLBer now for Kopech, but don't sell him just to sell. Sure, he might be a reliever, but if he is he'll probably be a closer in time, and if he's not he could strikeout 200-plus batters as a starter. That's three (3) whole pitchers in a row I'm not advocating you avoid at all costs!

5. Zack Collins, C

DOB: 02/06/1995

Height/Weight: 6'3" 220 lbs

Bats/Throws: L/R

Drafted/Acquired: Drafted 10th overall by the White Sox in the 2016 MLB draft, University of Miami (Coral Gables, FL); signed for $3,380,600

Previous Ranking(s): N/A

2016 Stats: .256/.418/.467, 6 HR, 0 SB in 36 games at High-A Winston-Salem

The Role: OFP 60—Bat-first, first-division catcher
Likely 50—Average major league first baseman

YEAR	TEAM	LVL	AGE	PA	R	2B	3B	HR	RBI	BB	K	SB	CS	AVG/OBP/SLG	TAv	VORP	BABIP	BRR	FRAA	WARP
2016	WSX	Rk	21	11	1	0	0	0	0	0	7	0	0	.091/.091/.091	.019	-2.3	.250	0.1	C(3): -0.0	-0.2
2016	WNS	A+	21	153	24	7	0	6	18	33	39	0	0	.258/.418/.467	.302	10.8	.333	-0.4	C(18): -0.6	1.0
2017	*CHA*	*MLB*	*22*	*250*	*27*	*9*	*1*	*8*	*29*	*32*	*80*	*1*	*0*	*.210/.316/.369*	*.241*	*6.1*	*.286*	*-0.3*	*C -0*	*0.6*
2018	*CHA*	*MLB*	*23*	*263*	*33*	*10*	*1*	*9*	*31*	*34*	*83*	*1*	*0*	*.213/.318/.380*	*.246*	*4.8*	*.287*	*-0.5*	*C 0*	*0.5*

Breakout: 2% Improve: 16% Collapse: 4% Attrition: 16% MLB: 33% *Comparables: Derek Norris, Jon Singleton, Chris Parmelee*

The Good: Collins is a potential 25-home-run catcher. There was, uh, one of those last year in baseball. He's a big, strong kid, with above-average bat speed and enough loft to send the ball over the fence from foul pole to foul pole. There's some length as he uncoils to get the plus power, but he has enough of an idea at plate and enough barrel control to project an average hit tool as well. He's got enough arm strength to stick behind the plate, and...well framing is a somewhat teachable skill?

The Bad: During our list-making process, it was very difficult to find people that think Collins can stick behind the plate long term. He can be stiff and unathletic behind the plate and his receiving skills are below-average. The bat can survive a move to first base, but he'd be more of a three true outcomes, second-division starter there due to the swing-and-miss issues.

The Irrelevant: Collins knocked 69 base hits his junior season at Miami.

The Risks: It's a very big fall down the defensive spectrum if Collins can't stick behind the dish. It's also possible the length and loft in the swing get exposed against better professional arms and he's more of a .240 hitter that doesn't get all of the raw pop into games.

Major league ETA: Late 2018/Early 2019 depending on where he ends up defensively

Ben Carsley's Fantasy Take: Collins is a much better fantasy prospect than IRL prospect because we don't care if he's good behind the plate, he just needs to be good enough to log 20-or-so games a year there. Even if he wasn't a backstop, Collins would be a top-100 prospect thanks to his bat. He wouldn't be altogether special at first, but he'd be better than, like, C.J. Cron. Put that type of production behind the plate and you get a potential top-3 fantasy catcher for years, though Collins isn't the type of guy who's going to catch into his 30s.

6. Alec Hansen, RHP

DOB: 10/10/1994

Height/Weight: 6'7" 235 lbs

Bats/Throws: R/R

Drafted/Acquired: Drafted 49th overall by the White Sox in the 2016 MLB draft, University of Oklahoma (Norman, OK), signed for $1,284,500

Previous Ranking(s): N/A

2016 Stats: 2.45 ERA, 3.08 DRA, 11 IP, 11 H, 4 BB, 11 K in Low-A Kannapolis, 1.23 ERA, 1.11 DRA, 36.2 IP, 12 H, 12 BB, 59 K at short-season Great Falls, 0.00 ERA, 2.06 DRA, 7 IP, 1 H, 4 BB, 11 K at complex-level AZL

The Role: OFP 55—Mid-rotation power arm
Likely 50—8th-inning guy

YEAR	TEAM	LVL	AGE	W	L	SV	G	GS	IP	H	HR	BB/9	K/9	K	GB%	BABIP	WHIP	ERA	FIP	DRA	VORP	WARP	cFIP	MPH
2016	WSX	Rk	21	0	0	0	3	3	7	1	0	5.1	14.1	11	70%	.100	0.71	0.00	2.70	2.06	2.80	0.3	79	
2016	GRF	Rk	21	2	0	0	7	7	36²	12	3	2.9	14.5	59	52%	.161	0.65	1.23	3.42	1.11	18.80	1.9	64	
2016	KAN	A	21	0	1	0	2	2	11	11	0	3.3	9.0	11	53%	.344	1.36	2.45	2.76	3.08	2.40	0.3	95	
2017	*CHA*	*MLB*	*22*	*2*	*2*	*0*	*7*	*7*	*32²*	*33*	*5*	*5.4*	*8.7*	*32*	*35%*	*.311*	*1.62*	*5.04*	*5.17*	*5.42*	*0.2*	*0.0*	*129*	
2018	*CHA*	*MLB*	*23*	*8*	*9*	*0*	*29*	*29*	*177²*	*165*	*24*	*5.3*	*10.2*	*201*	*35%*	*.309*	*1.51*	*4.48*	*4.58*	*4.82*	*9.7*	*1.0*	*114*	

Breakout: 5% Improve: 6% Collapse: 2% Attrition: 3% MLB: 8% *Comparables: Alex Wood, Tyler Wilson, Andrew Heaney*

The Good: Hansen's stuff well outpaces your average second-round college pick's. His fastball sits comfortably in the plus velocity band, and he can run it up into the high 90s at times. The pitch shows sink and run as well, coming from a high release point (and a very tall hombre). There's two potential plus breaking balls here. The slider was the party piece as an amateur, but he had more feel for the curve as a pro, a big 11-5 breaker that sits in the upper 70s.

The Bad: Hansen was a second-round pick because he completely forgot how to throw strikes during his junior season. The White Sox and he seem to have remedied that issue somewhat, but given his height and the crossfire and effort in his delivery, the command profile is never going to get much past average. The curveball can flatten out and sit high, the mid-80s slider is a glove-side chase pitch at present, and the change has only made sporadic appearances as a pro.

The Irrelevant: If Hansen had gone 1:1 in this year's draft, he'd be the first Sooner to do so. Bobby Witt and Jon Gray currently hold the record for highest drafted Oklahoma alum. Both went third overall.

The Risks: Hansen looked like a candidate to go at the top of the draft in January. By the end of the minor league season, he looked like a guy who did go at the top of the draft. In between was kind of a disaster though, so he's riskier than even your average pitching prospect—which he is, by the way.

Major league ETA: 2019 I guess?

Ben Carsley's Fantasy Take: Hansen should definitely be in your watch list as he's not far removed from showing stuff that might've made him an early pick in the 2016 draft. But until he shows that stuff consistently, he belongs on waivers.

7. Carson Fulmer, RHP

DOB: 12/13/1993

Height/Weight: 6'1" 190 lbs.

Bats/Throws: R/R

Drafted/Acquired: Drafted eighth overall in the 2015 MLB Draft, Vanderbilt University (TN); signed for $3,470,600

Previous Ranking(s): #2 (Org)

2016 Stats: 8.49 ERA, 4.90 DRA, 11.2 IP, 12 H, 7 BB, 10 K at the major league level, 3.94 ERA, 3.73 DRA, 16 IP, 14 H, 5 BB, 14 K at Triple-A Charlotte, 4.76 ERA, 6.31 DRA, 87 IP, 82 K, 51 BB, 90 K at Double-A Birmingham.

The Role: OFP 60—Major-league closer
Likely 50—Major-league setup dude

YEAR	TEAM	LVL	AGE	W	L	SV	G	GS	IP	H	HR	BB/9	K/9	K	GB%	BABIP	WHIP	ERA	FIP	DRA	VORP	WARP	cFIP	MPH
2015	WSX	Rk	21	0	0	0	1	1	1	1	0	0.0	9.0	1	50%	.500	1.00	0.00	1.82	3.49	0.30	0.0	95	
2015	WNS	A+	21	0	0	0	8	8	22	16	2	3.7	10.2	25	43%	.269	1.14	2.05	3.66	3.61	3.60	0.4	95	
2016	BIR	AA	22	4	9	0	17	17	87	82	7	5.3	9.3	90	45%	.310	1.53	4.76	4.16	6.31	-11.80	-1.3	111	
2016	CHA	MLB	22	0	2	0	8	0	11^2	12	2	5.4	7.7	10	44%	.312	1.63	8.49	5.93	4.90	0.10	0.0	110	95.3
2016	CHR	AAA	22	2	1	0	4	4	16	14	1	2.8	7.9	14	61%	.289	1.19	3.94	3.17	3.73	2.90	0.3	97	
2017	*CHA*	*MLB*	*23*	*1*	*2*	*0*	*20*	*2*	*29*	*29*	*3*	*4.9*	*7.4*	*24*	*42%*	*.296*	*1.55*	*5.15*	*4.63*	*5.21*	*-0.4*	*0.0*	*100*	
2018	*CHA*	*MLB*	*24*	*3*	*2*	*0*	*37*	*3*	*54^2*	*48*	*6*	*5.8*	*9.9*	*60*	*42%*	*.293*	*1.52*	*4.41*	*4.50*	*4.86*	*1.8*	*0.2*	*110*	

Breakout: 7% Improve: 13% Collapse: 4% Attrition: 14% MLB: 18% *Comparables: Tyler Clippard, Nick Maronde, Anthony Lerew*

The Good: Among prospect arms that don't throw in the upper 90s—although he can run it up close—you could make a case Fulmer has one of the best fastballs. It's 93-95 with explosive arm-side run that can almost mimic screwball action. His curveball flashes plus with hard, late break. I'd call it explosive as well, but you shouldn't repeat adjectives like that. Google suggests "incendiary" as an adjective. This is—without a doubt—#thegoodstuff.

The Bad: Fulmer has a high-effort, up-tempo delivery with head violence. The number of walks in the stat line above are not an accident. He struggles to throw strikes consistently with the fastball and the curve. His changeup lags behind the other two pitches. He's added a cutter—as you do with the White Sox—which is a promising pitch, but still a work in progress.

The Irrelevant: Are there any fun facts about Vanderbilt left at this point in list season?

The Risks: Fulmer's probably a reliever in the near-term, and he hasn't thrown enough strikes in the recent past. He's also an undersized pitcher.

Major league ETA: Debuted in 2016

Ben Carsley's Fantasy Take: Fulmer is still a top-100 dynasty prospect thanks to his proximity to the majors and his upside, but there's no doubt that his star has faded considerably. Understand that he might be a reliever, but feel free to value him just as you would, oh, Robert Stephenson. A potential future as a high-strikeout SP5 is still within reach, but I wouldn't bet those odds.

8. Luis Alexander Basabe, OF

DOB: 08/26/1996

Height/Weight: 6'0" 160 lbs.

Bats/Throws: S/R

Drafted/Acquired: Signed August 2012 out of Venezuela for $450,000

Previous Ranking(s): #6 (Org.)

2016 Stats: .258/.325/.447, 12 HR, 25 SB in 105 games at Low-A Greenville, .364/.391/.545, 0 HR, 0 SB in 5 games at High-A Salem. Acquired from Boston in the Chris Sale deal

The Role: OFP 60—Above-average everyday outfielder
Likely 45—Enough pop and glove to play all over the outfield and start in a pinch

YEAR	TEAM	LVL	AGE	PA	R	2B	3B	HR	RBI	BB	K	SB	CS	AVG/OBP/SLG	TAv	VORP	BABIP	BRR	FRAA	WARP
2014	DRS	Rk	17	184	38	7	11	0	26	30	36	13	2	.284/.408/.480	.287	7.6	.365	4.1		0.7
2014	DRS	Rk	17	184	38	7	11	0	26	30	36	13	2	.284/.408/.480	.287	7.6	.365	4.1		0.7
2014	RSX	Rk	17	123	15	5	0	1	13	13	23	2	4	.248/.328/.324	.256	3.1	.298	-2.7		0.6
2014	RSX	Rk	17	123	15	5	0	1	13	13	23	2	4	.248/.328/.324	.256	3.1	.298	-2.7		0.6
2015	LOW	A-	18	256	36	8	3	7	23	32	67	15	4	.243/.340/.401	.273	13.5	.315	4.1	CF(28): 4.6, RF(25): 5.5	2.9
2015	LOW	A-	18	256	36	8	3	7	23	32	67	15	4	.243/.340/.401	.273	13.5	.315	4.1	CF(28): 4.6, RF(25): 5.5	2.9
2016	GRN	A	19	451	61	24	8	12	52	40	116	25	5	.258/.325/.447	.290	27.4	.330	2.7	CF(98): 10.1	4.4
2016	GRN	A	19	451	61	24	8	12	52	40	116	25	5	.258/.325/.447	.290	27.4	.330	2.7	CF(98): 10.1	4.4
2016	SLM	A+	19	23	5	2	1	0	1	1	3	0	0	.364/.391/.545	.320	2.8	.421	0.8	CF(2): 0.1, RF(2): 0.3	0.3
2016	SLM	A+	19	23	5	2	1	0	1	1	3	0	0	.364/.391/.545	.320	2.8	.421	0.8	CF(2): 0.1, RF(2): 0.3	0.3
2017	*CHA*	*MLB*	*20*	*250*	*31*	*9*	*2*	*8*	*25*	*17*	*81*	*7*	*2*	*.211/.269/.367*	*.219*	*-0.1*	*.286*	*0.7*	*CF 6, RF 0*	*0.6*
2018	*CHA*	*MLB*	*21*	*391*	*45*	*15*	*3*	*13*	*46*	*31*	*121*	*11*	*3*	*.222/.286/.391*	*.235*	*2.6*	*.293*	*1.6*	*CF 9, RF 0*	*1.3*

Breakout: 3% Improve: 10% Collapse: 0% Attrition: 5% MLB: 12% *Comparables: Nomar Mazara, Caleb Gindl, Chris Parmelee*

The Good: Basabe is a premium athlete with potential above-average grades on four tools. He's an above-average runner with a good second gear. There's above-average raw in the frame, even as a teenager, although it only plays in games from the left side at present. There's enough arm for any spot in the outfield, but the athleticism and improving instincts make him a potentially above-average center fielder. We are quickly veering into Lake Wobegon territory now.

The Bad: Basabe has some interesting tools on both sides of the ball, but he is also still quite raw on both sides as well. The approach is aggressive from both sides and there's swing-and-miss against A-ball spin from both sides too. The right-handed offensive tools are less developed, not uncommon for a young switch hitter. The defensive skills still need refinement.

The Irrelevant: Multiple times while discussing Basabe internally I referred to the wrong Basabe. At least they are on other teams now.

The Risks: Basabe is still a high-risk prospect. 2017 could be a big breakout year, or he could suffer through a summer swoon against more advanced arms in Double-A. There is not one clear carrying tool for the profile yet—admittedly a lot to ask of teen-ager—so the development path may be bumpier in the future than it was in 2016.

Major league ETA: 2019

Ben Carsley's Fantasy Take: This is your last chance to buy lowish on Basabe. He comes with his fair share of risk, but gambling on power/speed guys in the mid-minors is a tried-and-true dynasty strategy. In a down year for dynasty prospects, there's a chance Basabe sneaks onto the back of our top-100 list, and if not he'd almost certainly be top-125.

9. Zack Burdi, RHP

DOB: 3.9/1995

Height/Weight: 6'3" 205 lbs

Bats/Throws: R/R

Drafted/Acquired: Draft 26th overall by the White Sox in the 2016 MLB draft, University of Louisville (Louisville, KY); signed for $2,128,500

Previous Ranking(s): N/A

2016 Stats: 2.25 ERA, 3.42 DRA, 16 IP, 9 H, 11 BB, 22 K at Triple-A Charlotte, 3.94 ERA, 3.73 DRA, 16 IP, 7 H, 9 BB, 24 K at Double-A Birmingham, 5.40 ERA, 3.83 DRA, 5 IP, 6 H, 0 BB, 4 K at High-A Winston-Salem

The Role: OFP 55—Good late-inning arm
Likely 50—Standard fireballing 8th-inning type

YEAR	TEAM	LVL	AGE	W	L	SV	G	GS	IP	H	HR	BB/9	K/9	K	GB%	BABIP	WHIP	ERA	FIP	DRA	VORP	WARP	cFIP	MPH
2016	WSX	Rk	21	0	0	0	1	0	1	1	0	0.0	9.0	1	100%	.333	1.00	0.00	2.13	4.22	0.10	0.0	93	
2016	WNS	A+	21	0	0	0	4	0	5	6	1	0.0	7.2	4	40%	.357	1.20	5.40	4.55	3.83	0.70	0.1	95	
2016	BIR	AA	21	0	0	0	12	0	16	7	2	5.1	13.5	24	63%	.179	1.00	3.94	3.82	3.73	1.80	0.2	89	
2016	CHR	AAA	21	1	0	1	9	0	16	9	0	6.2	12.4	22	47%	.265	1.25	2.25	2.48	3.42	2.70	0.3	89	
2017	*CHA*	*MLB*	*22*	*1*	*1*	*0*	*23*	*0*	*23*	*23*	*3*	*4.5*	*9.0*	*24*	*48%*	*.295*	*1.44*	*4.85*	*4.43*	*4.94*	*0.2*	*0.0*	*100*	
2018	*CHA*	*MLB*	*23*	*2*	*1*	*1*	*44*	*0*	*47*	*37*	*6*	*5.5*	*11.5*	*60*	*48%*	*.287*	*1.39*	*4.03*	*4.11*	*4.45*	*3.1*	*0.3*	*100*	

Breakout: 16% Improve: 16% Collapse: 4% Attrition: 10% MLB: 22% *Comparables: Danny Barnes, Alex Claudio, Akeel Morris*

The Good: I generally bristle at the idea of drafting a reliever in the first round—perhaps a function of being a Mets fan during the Omar Minaya years—but if you are going to draft a no-doubt reliever early in the Rule 4, picking the guy that touches 100 and has a present plus slider is the one to take. Burdi checks both those boxes, The heater isn't arrow-straight either, as he gets some hard arm-side run from his low-three-quarters slot. The slider is a potential plus-plus wipeout offering with additional refinement.

The Bad: Burdi's never going to have the world's finest command and control. The delivery is high-effort with a whirlwind of torque. Lower arm slot gives lefties a long look, and while he has a better changeup than you'd expect from this profile, it isn't going to be a meaningful part of his late-inning arsenal. He might be a bit of a tightrope act as a reliever against major-league hitters.

The Irrelevant: Burdi cites Buca de Beppo, a family-style Italian chain with a location in Louisville, as his favorite restaurant. He does looks like a man who likes his carbs, but we encourage him to check out Ricobene's once he hits the South Side.

The Risks: He's just about major-league-ready. He was always going to be a reliever all the way, so really there isn't anything to men...oh right, he's a pitcher.

Major league ETA: 2017

Ben Carsley's Fantasy Take: Friends don't let friends draft reliever prospects.

Likely 50—Standard fireballing 8th-inning type

10. Dane Dunning, RHP

DOB: 12/20/1994

Height/Weight: 6'4" 200 lbs

Bats/Throws: R/R

Drafted/Acquired: Drafted 29th overall in the 2016 MLB draft, University of Florida (FL), signed for $2 million. Acquired from Washington in the Adam Eaton deal.

Previous Ranking(s): N/A

2016 Stats: 2.14 ERA, 2.93 DRA, 33.2 IP, 26 H, 7 BB, 29 K at Low-A Auburn

The Role: OFP 50—Fourth starter or set-up man
Likely 45—Fifth starter or reliable middle reliever

YEAR	TEAM	LVL	AGE	W	L	SV	G	GS	IP	H	HR	BB/9	K/9	K	GB%	BABIP	WHIP	ERA	FIP	DRA	VORP	WARP	cFIP	MPH
2016	NAT	Rk	21	0	0	0	1	1	2	0	0	0.0	13.5	3	100%	.000	0.00	0.00	0.31	2.82	0.60	0.1	86	
2016	NAT	Rk	21	0	0	0	1	1	2	0	0	0.0	13.5	3	100%	.000	0.00	0.00	0.31	2.82	0.60	0.1	86	
2016	AUB	A-	21	3	2	0	7	7	33^2	26	1	1.9	7.8	29	65%	.263	0.98	2.14	2.56	2.33	10.90	1.2	83	
2016	AUB	A-	21	3	2	0	7	7	33^2	26	1	1.9	7.8	29	65%	.263	0.98	2.14	2.56	2.33	10.90	1.2	83	
2017	*CHA*	*MLB*	*22*	*2*	*3*	*0*	*7*	*7*	32^2	*39*	*5*	*4.2*	*5.9*	*21*	*50%*	*.313*	*1.65*	*5.39*	*5.29*	*5.80*	*-1.2*	*-0.1*	*139*	
2018	*CHA*	*MLB*	*23*	*7*	*8*	*0*	*25*	*25*	148^2	*155*	*21*	*4.0*	*7.7*	*126*	*50%*	*.305*	*1.49*	*4.62*	*4.72*	*4.97*	*6.5*	*0.7*	*119*	

Breakout: 1% Improve: 1% Collapse: 0% Attrition: 1% MLB: 2% *Comparables: Tyler Wilson, Wilking Rodriguez, Andrew Heaney*

The Good: Shows strikeout potential, reliable command of his low to mid-90s fastball with late life. Clean mechanics paired with a deceptive delivery created by a late break in his hands pair well with his effective changeup.

The Bad: Having pitched out of the bullpen due the Florida Gators' overstocked pool of arms, there are legitimate questions as to how Dunning will hold up as a starter. His 11-5 curveball hasn't shown the promise of his other pitches, and failing to get a handle on it could force a permanent relocation to the pen.

The Irrelevant: Dunning will often pitch wearing those strange hybrid glasses/goggles. Word is still out on his bespectacled splits.

The Risks: Without much starting experience, Dunning may have trouble pitching deep into games. Failing to command his curveball would limit him to a fastball/change repertoire that would function fine out of the bullpen but likely prevent him from starting. Also, he's a pitcher.

Major league ETA: 2018 —Will Haines

Ben Carsley's Fantasy Take: Think of all the other things you could do with a roster spot instead of wasting it on a potential back-end starter who's several years away. You could hold on to a sleeper closer candidate. Maybe stash a speedster who can pad your SB totals when your starters are sitting. Heck, you could get really crazy and even use it to stream a back-end starter who could help you right now, rather than one who might help you years down the line. You can pass on Dunning.

OTHERS OF NOTE:

#11

Spencer Adams, RHP

10 prospects is a pretty arbitrary number. In some cases it may understate how good a system is. The White Sox are not one of those systems. It's a pretty clean delineation. But Spencer Adams can feel a little hard done perhaps. He didn't really do anything wrong to drop off the top ten—other than be in a system that traded for six shiny new prospects with more upside. He made it all the way to Double-A as a 20-year-old and showed off his potential above-average fastball/slider combo along the way. He throws strikes by the bucketful, although at some point he's going to have to miss a few more bats. The control is ahead of the command at present as well. On the plus side, I am more confident he's a starter than a lot of the arms on the actual top ten. The delivery is compact, and he's a good athlete who repeats well. I just don't know if he is much of an impact one.

The tools merchant

Micker Adolfo, OF

Although the pressure on the bat is no less heavy than left field, there is just something more aesthetically pleasing about the right field profile. Adolfo certainly fits the mold. He's tall, athletic, and garners plus or better grades on both his raw power and throwing arm. It's easy to look at him in uniform and figure out why he got 1.6 million out of the D.R. as a 16-year-old. Unfortunately the tools haven't translated to the field yet. He's spent parts of three seasons in the Complex League, where injuries have kept him off the field and he's struggled to make contact when on it. The White Sox are not known for their conservative development tracks though, and Adolfo spend half the year in the Sally League where those swing-and-miss issues were amplified even more. He'll be only 20 this year, so it's melodramatic to suggest that time is running out, but eventually he will have to hit. The right field profile does put pressure on the bat after all.

The parade of ex-2016 Top Ten White Sox continues

Trey Michalczewski, 3B

Michalczewski might have found himself on the outside looking in on the Top Ten even before the White Sox added five Top 101 prospects this offseason. He's had above-average hit and power potential thrown on him for years, but after a season in Double-A, the hit tool looks more like a 4, and the power is still yet to show up. He's average-ish at third and still only 21—I'm sensing a theme in this range—but at a certain point this becomes about what you can do rather than what you might do someday. That point is often Double-A, and while Michalczewski will get another crack at the Southern League, the tools need to actualize and soon.

The factor on the farm

Jake Peter, IF/OF

The IF/OF designation shortchanges Peter's defensive versatility. He played all four infield positions and both outfield corners in 2016. He's going to need those swiss army knife abilities, because there probably isn't enough at the plate here to make him a major-league starter. You can probably guess the profile just from the "he played six different positions" line. Peter doesn't have much power, but offers a strong approach at the plate, some line drives, and good footspeed and baserunning instincts. He is taller than you'd guess based on that description though. Peter's already spent half a season in Triple-A, and with the White Sox in—let's call it the lower part of the contention cycle—they could use a player like this to plug in wherever needed on any given day of the 162. It's a long season.

3?

Courtney Hawkins, OF

Mort was right.

TOP 10 TALENTS 25 AND UNDER (BORN 4/1/91 OR LATER)

1. Carlos Rodon	6. Michael Kopech
2. Tim Anderson	7. Zack Collins
3. Yoan Moncada	8. Alec Hansen
4. Lucas Giolito	9. Carson Fulmer
5. Reynaldo Lopez	10. Luis Alexander Basabe

Carlos Rodon was so feted coming into his junior year of college that once he struggled with his velocity and command he was suddenly considered a disappointment and slid to the White Sox at third overall in the 2014 draft. Then he blitzed through High-A and Triple-A, skipping Birmingham altogether, overwhelming batters with raw stuff in the form of his mid-90s velocity from the left side and his infamous slider. He has now pitched over 300 innings in the majors against only 38 in the minors, for his career. Thus, Rodon went from perceived underachiever on draft day straight to a major leaguer learning on the job, skipping time to build up hype in the minors.

On the surface, it didn't look like Rodon improved from 2015 to 2016, as he gave up more home runs, was more hittable, and his ERA rose from 3.75 to 4.04. If you look deeper, however, he also shaved his walk percentage from 11.7 to 7.6 while posting a cFIP of 87 in the majors to go with a 3.44 DRA. That cFIP was ahead of Rick Porcello's and Madison Bumgarner's, while virtually tied with Cole Hamels and Masahiro Tanaka. Rodon was also a victim of the White Sox' ghastly pitch framing, and some attributed his strong second half to switching from Dioner Navarro's butchery to Omar Narvaez's mediocre competence, as well as heavier use of an improving change. Rodon himself credited Narvaez for helping him backdoor his slider for called strikes instead of its utility being limited to swinging strikes out of the zone. Barely 24-years-old, Rodon is developing into the frontline starter he was long expected to be—he's just done it very quietly.

There are arguments to put Moncada ahead of Tim Anderson, and even Rodon, as his power potential and batting eye give him a huge edge in terms of offensive ceiling. Still, despite Anderson's troubling lack of control of the zone, he held his own in 431 major-league plate appearances while continuing to progress defensively at shortstop such that it looks like he will be able to stick there after all.

Not the physical specimen Moncada is, Anderson is still a freak athlete in his own right—with plus speed—who plays a more valuable position defensively. He has also demonstrated an ability to improve his control of the zone after being given time to adjust to new levels in the minors, despite aggressive promotions. This gives hope to the idea that he will be a batting average and speed-fueled asset on offense as well. And for now—unlike Moncada—Anderson has performed in the majors.

—Nick Schaefer

CINCINNATI REDS

The State of the System: *Cincinnati added a very nice name at the top with the second-overall pick, but it was an up-and-down year for the rest of the system. It lacks impact names past the top two, but it is a deep organization with some interesting 2017 breakout candidates.*

THE TOP TEN

1. 3B Nick Senzel	6. C Tyler Stephenson
2. LHP Amir Garrett	7. OF Taylor Trammell
3. RHP Luis Castillo	8. OF Aristides Aquino
4. LF Jesse Winker	9. RHP Antonio Santillan
5. RHP Robert Stephenson	10. 2B Shedric Long

The Big Question: How long should a rebuild take?

As you set out for Ithaca
hope the voyage is a long one,
full of adventure, full of discovery.

In Western mythology, Orpheus is one of only a few mortals granted passage to the underworld. But the quest to bring his wife Eurydice back to life comes to a tragic end. He charms Hades and pulls his beloved to the brink of earth, only to look over his shoulder and see her descend again.

Such was the Cincinnati bullpen's plight last season, watching the trajectory of 103 of the team's 258 home runs—both major league records. Reviewing the Reds' recent history is commensurate with reading multiple Greek tragedies at once. The Sisyphean task facing a young pitching staff and the league's worst by PWARP; sundry Achilles' heels (or elbows, knees and shoulders); and one final playoff push in 2015 that fell as swiftly as young Icarus.

It was a painful but unsurprising step in the process best known as rebuilding. Walt Jocketty preferred the term retooling, as if he had to buy a new belt sander when he forgot where his old one was. Whatever the PR-friendly term to counter the insidious label "tanking"—rebuilding, reloading, restocking—the underlying concept has been well established.

There are a handful of teams actively pursuing an overhaul and another half-dozen either starting or winding down their own. In this space, you'll soon read about the White Sox, who didn't quite bottom out but gave their prospect list a shot in the arm, and the long-term consequences of the Royals' short-term bet.

But every case is different as clubs borrow from other front office philosophies. The Braves sold off their young, controllable core for younger, more controllable prospects. With four top-10 draft picks in as many years, the Cubs developed hitters while buying their eventual championship rotation. The Phillies, bringing their blossoming team to Cincinnati on Opening Day, finally ended up on the right side of their high-stakes game of catch and release. Meanwhile, the Reds are content with building around Joey Votto, leaning on their pitching prospects and waiting for a pair of No. 2 overall draft picks to make their debuts. But with their National League counterparts flourishing, when can the Reds expect to compete?

Jeff Sullivan pegged the number at four years in terms of turning a cellar dweller into a postseason team. The Astros averaged 104 losses from 2011 to 2014 before reaching the Divisional Series. Theo Epstein's Cubs lost 101 games in his first year as president of baseball operations, and that story likely ends in Cooperstown. This will be the Reds' second year of full investment in a rebuild but arguably their third overall. Despite acquiring Anthony DeSclafani and Eugenio Suarez after the 2014 season, the teardown didn't begin until the following All-Star break. By targeting players in the upper minors or those with some major-league seasoning, the Reds hoped to shave a year off the process, but it came at a cost.

Laistrygonians and Cyclops,
wild Poseidon—you won't encounter them
unless you bring them along inside your soul,
unless your soul sets them up in front of you.

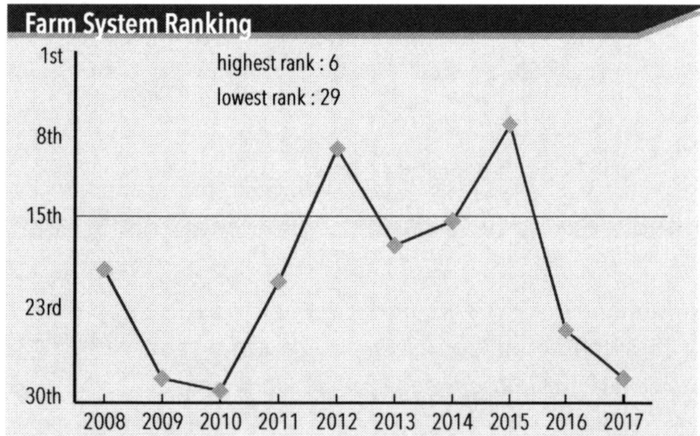

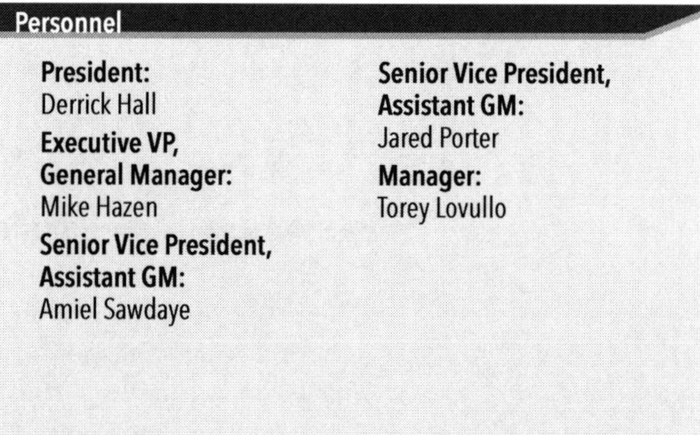
Personnel

President:
Derrick Hall

Executive VP, General Manager:
Mike Hazen

Senior Vice President, Assistant GM:
Amiel Sawdaye

Senior Vice President, Assistant GM:
Jared Porter

Manager:
Torey Lovullo

Constantine P. Cavafy, one of the foremost Greek poets of the twentieth century, continued the theme set in Homer's epic in his 1911 work "Ithaca." The island has a significance larger than life, cherished more for the journey and the demons travelers must conquer along the way than for what awaits. Aroldis Chapman was a generational arm; with all due respect, Rookie Davis is not, but that shouldn't be held against him. The team couldn't pitch long-term contract flexibility to potential suitors, trading Johnny Cueto, Mike Leake and Marlon Byrd just before they hit free agency. Chapman and Todd Frazier soon followed, dealt at their nadir in the winter for critically panned packages.

Though the Reds lack the splashy, high-upside players that populate top-100 lists, they added the kind of depth on which small-market teams rely. But the club made greater strides in gaining focus and fresh perspective, described by Cavafy as "harbors seen for the first time." Dick Williams beefed up the club's minor league operations in his first year as general manager, incorporating mental skills coaching and leadership training into the team's player development strategy. The front office also made a much-needed investment in their analytics department, prioritizing the individualized approach and "culture of flexibility" that Brendan Gawlowski discussed here in 2015.

And if you find her poor, Ithaca won't have fooled you.
Wise as you will have become, so full of experience,
you will have understood by then what these Ithacas mean.

Even if the win-loss record doesn't reflect it, the Reds are better off today than their last postseason team. As Jeff Quinton wrote, though, anyone can copy the Cubs' winning model but few will replicate its success. The next step is staving off the stagnation of Kansas City and Pittsburgh, making the most of a short window and keeping the pace in a top-heavy division. This team will most likely finish under .500, but the Reds are already fighting a winning battle for 2018 and beyond.

—Kourage Kundahl

1. Nick Senzel, 3B

DOB: 6/29/1995

Height/Weight: 6'1" 205 lbs.

Bats/Throws: R/R

Drafted/Acquired: Drafted second overall in the 2016 MLB Draft, University of Tennessee (Knoxville, TN); signed for $6.2 million

Previous Ranking(s): N/A

2016 Stats: .152/.293/.182, 0 HR, 3 SB in 10 games at short-season Billings, .329/.415/.567, 7 HR, 15 SB in 58 games at low-A Dayton

The Role: OFP 60—First-division third baseman
Likely 55—Above-average third baseman

YEAR	TEAM	LVL	AGE	PA	R	2B	3B	HR	RBI	BB	K	SB	CS	AVG/OBP/SLG	TAv	VORP	BABIP	BRR	FRAA	WARP
2016	BIL	Rk	21	41	3	1	0	0	4	6	5	3	0	.152/.293/.182	.196	-0.2	.172	0.3	3B(10): 1.0	0.0
2016	DYT	A	21	251	38	23	3	7	36	32	49	15	7	.329/.415/.567	.364	34.2	.392	1.6	3B(56): 3.1	4.1
2017	*CIN*	*MLB*	*22*	*250*	*31*	*11*	*1*	*9*	*30*	*23*	*66*	*7*	*3*	*.234/.309/.406*	*.243*	*3.3*	*.288*	*-0.1*	*3B 2*	*0.6*
2018	*CIN*	*MLB*	*23*	*268*	*33*	*12*	*1*	*10*	*33*	*24*	*71*	*7*	*4*	*.230/.303/.407*	*.254*	*4.8*	*.282*	*0.3*	*3B 3*	*0.8*

Breakout: 5% Improve: 30% Collapse: 3% Attrition: 29% MLB: 48% *Comparables: Matt Davidson, Alex Liddi, Lonnie Chisenhall*

The Good: Senzel received the biggest bonus in the 2016 draft class, and he backed up the paycheck on the field. He's a potential five-tool third baseman with plus hit and above-average power grades, making him a potential middle-of-the-order bat at the hot corner. His defensive tools aren't quite as exciting—not that you'd care at this point—but he's a competent glove at third with a plus arm.

The Bad: It's a balanced profile, which isn't bad per se, but he lacks an impact carrying tool. Might be more of a good regular than a perennial all-star type. Power might play more as average long-term, and he might fit best as a No. 6 hitter on a first-division team.

The Irrelevant: Senzel isn't the rangiest third baseman you'll find, but he can make plays all over the diamond (and in the dugout).

The Risks: Senzel is about as safe a bet as you can find in A-ball. While he lacks the ceiling of the elite class of prospects, he has an advanced hit tool and should be a solid contributor both at the plate and on the dirt. He could also move very quickly, and a major-league debut in 2017 is not impossible, although the Reds have no incentive to push him through the minors.

Major league ETA: Early 2018

Ben Carsley's Fantasy Take: Sounds good to me! Senzel serves as a badly needed injection of upside and probability for a collection of third base dynasty prospects that's the weakest it's been in years. He's probably the best dynasty prospect from the last draft, and he's a no-doubt top-50 name right now. Sure, you don't have to squint to see the ceiling, but if Senzel emerges as, oh, I don't know, 2016 Anthony Rendon (.270, 20 homers, 12 steals), no one will be complaining.

2. Amir Garrett, LHP

DOB: 05/03/1992

Height/Weight: 6'5" 215 lbs.

Bats/Throws: L/L

Drafted/Acquired: Drafted in the 22nd round of the 2011 MLB Draft, Henderson International School (Henderson, NV); signed for $1 million

Previous Ranking(s): #4 (Org.), #77 (Overall)

2016 Stats: 1.75 ERA, 3.21 DRA, 77 IP, 51 H, 28 BB, 78 K in 13 games at double-A Pensacola, 3.46 ERA, 4.44 DRA, 67.2 IP, 48 H, 31 BB, 54 K in 12 games at triple-A Louisville

The Role: OFP 60—No. 3 starter
Likely 55—Above-average starter or late-inning arm

YEAR	TEAM	LVL	AGE	W	L	SV	G	GS	IP	H	HR	BB/9	K/9	K	GB%	BABIP	WHIP	ERA	FIP	DRA	VORP	WARP	cFIP	MPH
2014	DYT	A	22	7	8	0	27	27	133^{1}	115	11	3.4	8.6	127	50%	.282	1.25	3.64	3.87	3.61	27.20	2.8	97	
2015	DAY	A+	23	9	7	0	26	26	140^{1}	117	4	3.5	8.5	133	45%	.298	1.23	2.44	2.90	3.59	23.20	2.5	93	
2016	PEN	AA	24	5	3	0	13	12	77	51	0	3.3	9.1	78	50%	.252	1.03	1.75	2.50	3.21	15.90	1.7	87	
2016	LOU	AAA	24	2	5	0	12	11	67^{2}	48	6	4.1	7.2	54	49%	.231	1.17	3.46	4.14	4.44	6.50	0.7	98	
MLB	*25*	*2*	*3*	*0*	*27*	*5*	*47*	*48*	*6*	*4.5*	*6.7*	*36*	*42%*	*.289*	*1.48*	*5.12*	*4.93*	*5.03*	*0.2*	*0.0*	*100*			
MLB	*26*	*5*	*4*	*0*	*58*	*10*	*109*	*84*	*13*	*5.8*	*9.4*	*114*	*42%*	*.283*	*1.42*	*4.93*	*5.06*	*5.42*	*-0.8*	*-0.1*	*127*			

Breakout: 11% Improve: 19% Collapse: 14% Attrition: 26% MLB: 36% *Comparables: George Kontos, Gus Schlosser, Josh Smith*

The Good: Do you like athletic pitchers? Of course you do. Garrett was a swingman on the hardwood for the Red Storm, and the athleticism translates to the mound. Your average NCAA 3 doesn't have a 95-mph fastball though. Garrett can touch even higher and the offering has late arm-side life. The slider flashes plus with hard, late tilt. Even though he has already advanced to Triple A, there is more projection left than your average International League arm given how late Garrett came to full-time pitching.

The Bad: His delivery has a bit of crossfire to it, and the arm action can be slingy. Those are two qualities you often associate with relief arms. Also associated with relief arms: a below-average changeup. Garrett's is "developing," but at present it doesn't "do much." Additional command refinement is needed.

The Irrelevant: "Jeffrey, do you happen to have an Amir Garrett dunk montage handy?" "Yes, yes I do."

The Risks: The main risk here is that Garrett's command and changeup issues force him to the bullpen. He's a potential late-inning arm there, but it's not enough of an impact relief profile to make you prefer it to the starting one.

Major league ETA: Late 2017

Ben Carsley's Fantasy Take: Garrett is close enough to the majors and has a high-enough upside that we can feel good investing in him despite the bullpen concerns. He's got a future as a dynasty SP4/5 who doesn't do anything particularly well or particularly poorly when it comes to strikeouts, ERA and WHIP. That's not super exciting, but unless your league has a low innings cap there's plenty of value in an innings eater who eats innings at an above league-average rate. Don't believe me? Josh Tomlin was the 53rd-best fantasy starter last year. Garrett is nothing like Tomlin, I'm just saying the bar's not as high as you think it is.

3. Luis Castillo, RHP

DOB: 12/12/1992

Height/Weight: 6'2" 170 lbs.

Bats/Throws: R/R

Drafted/Acquired: Signed in December 2011 out of Dominican Republic by the San Francisco Giants for $15,000; acquired from the Marlins for Dan Straily

Previous Ranking(s): N/A

2016 Stats: 2.07 ERA, 2.17 DRA, 117.2 IP, 18 BB, 92 K in 23 games at high-A Jupiter, 3.86 ERA, 5.68 DRA, 14 IP, 7 BB, 12 K, in 3 games at double-A Jacksonville

The Role: 60 OFP—Mid-rotation starter, late innings reliever
50 OFP—Back-end starter, middle innings reliever

YEAR	TEAM	LVL	AGE	W	L	SV	G	GS	IP	H	HR	BB/9	K/9	K	GB%	BABIP	WHIP	ERA	FIP	DRA	VORP	WARP	cFIP	MPH
2014	AUG	A	21	2	2	10	48	0	58^{2}	56	6	3.8	10.1	66	46%	.316	1.38	3.07	4.00	2.77	14.90	1.5	88	
2015	GRB	A	22	4	3	4	25	7	63^{1}	59	1	2.7	9.0	63	53%	.326	1.23	2.98	2.74	1.89	22.30	2.4	76	
2015	JUP	A+	22	2	3	0	10	9	43^{2}	44	3	2.9	6.4	31	52%	.308	1.33	3.50	3.67	4.39	3.20	0.4	100	
2016	JUP	A+	23	8	4	0	23	21	117^{2}	95	2	1.4	7.0	91	50%	.271	0.96	2.07	2.46	2.29	41.10	4.2	81	
2016	JAX	AA	23	0	2	0	3	3	14	12	1	4.5	7.7	12	42%	.262	1.36	3.86	4.25	5.76	-1.00	-0.1	106	
2017	*MIA*	*MLB*	*24*	*6*	*5*	*1*	*47*	*14*	*104^{2}*	*112*	*13*	*3.2*	*6.1*	*71*	*41%*	*.319*	*1.43*	*4.55*	*4.59*	*5.40*	*-0.1*	*0.0*	*127*	
2018	*MIA*	*MLB*	*25*	*4*	*4*	*1*	*32*	*10*	*93^{1}*	*89*	*12*	*4.2*	*8.2*	*85*	*41%*	*.316*	*1.42*	*4.31*	*4.78*	*5.11*	*2.7*	*0.3*	*119*	

Breakout: 4% Improve: 7% Collapse: 2% Attrition: 7% MLB: 15% *Comparables: Mayckol Guaipe, Chase Anderson, Randy Wells*

The Good: After pitching primarily as a reliever with the Giants, Castillo has flourished as a starter, showcasing his premium arm strength and ability to hold velocity late in games. In velocity the pitch plays as an 80 sitting 97-99 and touching 101 with above-average control. He has an easy, repeatable delivery with above-average arm speed and a smooth arm action. His slider flashes plus with hard tilt and bite. His changeup is an effective third offering against left-handers.

The Bad: While his fastball has elite velocity, it lacks movement and plane so it can be hittable in the zone. His slider is inconsistent as it gets slurvy and shows more fringe-average than plus. He telegraphs his changeup and he struggles with command, often left up in the zone. More a strike-thrower than a command artist.

The Irrelevant: K-Rod is still in shock because of this.

The Risks: Was older for High A, secondary pitches need to become more consistent for an everyday big-league spot, lack of consistent changeup could force a bullpen move sooner rather than later is a pitcher.

Major league ETA: Early 2018 —Steve Givarz

Ben Carsley's Fantasy Take: Did anyone else read the above and get a distinct Joe Kelly vibe? Luis Castillo has Great Stuff (TM), and he's close enough to the majors that you could easily make the argument for taking him over Garrett in dynasty leagues. Still, the relatively limited upside and the somewhat likely chance he ends up in the bullpen conspire to limit Castillo to a back-of-the-top-100 name, if that.

4. Jesse Winker, OF

DOB: 08/17/1993

Height/Weight: 6'3" 210 lbs.

Bats/Throws: L/L

Drafted/Acquired: Drafted 49th overall in the 2012 MLB Draft, Olympia HS, (Orlando, FL); signed for $1 million

Previous Ranking(s): #3 (Org.), #50 (Overall)

2016 Stats: .462/.533/.923, 2 HR, 0 SB in 4 games at AZL Complex, .303/.397/.384, 3 HR, 0 SB in 106 games at triple-A Louisville

The Role: OFP 55—High BA/OBP everyday left fielder
Likely 50—Average everyday left fielder

YEAR	TEAM	LVL	AGE	PA	R	2B	3B	HR	RBI	BB	K	SB	CS	AVG/OBP/SLG	TAv	VORP	BABIP	BRR	FRAA	WARP
2014	BAK	A+	20	249	42	15	0	13	49	40	46	5	1	.317/.426/.580	.319	19.3	.349	-2.2	LF(46): -2.9, LF(2): -2.9	1.5
2014	PEN	AA	20	92	15	5	0	2	8	14	22	0	0	.208/.326/.351	.256	1.9	.259	0.4	LF(20): 1.5	0.4
2015	PEN	AA	21	526	69	24	2	13	55	74	83	8	4	.282/.390/.433	.308	33.7	.320	-2.0	LF(83): -6.3, RF(40): -3.6	2.8
2016	CIN	Rk	22	15	6	0	0	2	6	2	4	0	0	.462/.533/.923	.490	4.3	.571	0.2	LF(4): -0.5	0.4
2016	LOU	AAA	22	448	39	22	0	3	45	59	59	0	0	.303/.397/.384	.288	20.4	.347	-1.0	RF(52): 0.1, LF(46): -3.0	1.9
2017	*CIN*	*MLB*	*23*	*192*	*22*	*8*	*0*	*6*	*23*	*23*	*38*	*0*	*0*	*.259/.352/.419*	*.270*	*6.9*	*.300*	*-0.4*	*RF -1, LF -0*	*0.5*
2018	*CIN*	*MLB*	*24*	*372*	*50*	*18*	*0*	*12*	*46*	*45*	*77*	*1*	*0*	*.262/.355/.432*	*.282*	*15.1*	*.306*	*-0.9*	*RF -1, LF 0*	*1.5*

Breakout: 4% Improve: 22% Collapse: 11% Attrition: 20% MLB: 42% *Comparables: Adam Eaton, Caleb Gindl, Jaff Decker*

The Good: Winker kept doing Winker things in 2016, hitting .300 as one of the youngest players in the International League. He has an easy plus hit tool that he pairs with a strong approach at the plate. There's more power in the profile—due to a slight uppercut and above-average bat speed—than he showed this year as he battled wrist issues. He is a safe bet to be an above-average offensive player in the majors despite a below-average power projection, even once the wrist heels.

The Bad: He's a left fielder. The arm is accurate enough he could probably be okay in right field, but it's not strong enough to make that the more likely corner outfield landing spot. He's a fine left fielder, but he's not going to win any Gold Gloves, so you are really betting on the hit tool. As patient as he is, without more pop than he showed in 2016, his on-base ability might suffer against major-league arms.

The Irrelevant: Winker looks set to become the second Olympia High School grad to make the majors, following in the footsteps of future-best-SS-in-the-AL-now-1B, Brad Miller.

The Risks: Winker still could have a smidge of physical projection left, but he is otherwise a finished, polished product for good and for ill. The one crimp in the profile here might be his recovery from his wrist issues.

Major league ETA: 2017

Ben Carsley's Fantasy Take: Winker is a better fantasy prospect than an IRL prospect, as I think he's a safe bet to hit well in the majors. It's not a sexy profile, but a future as an AVG-driven OF4 with 15-20 homers is well within his range, sort of like a modern-day Melky Cabrera. Basically, the deeper your league is the more valuable Winker is, because he'll give you a modest boost in four categories. Just don't be afraid to aim higher if you're in one of those weird, stupid leagues where each team only rosters three prospects or something (I've seen it).

5. Robert Stephenson, RHP

DOB: 02/24/1993

Height/Weight: 6'2" 200 lbs.

Bats/Throws: R/R

Drafted/Acquired: Drafted 27th overall in the 2011 MLB Draft, Alhambra HS (Martinez, CA); signed for $2 million

Previous Ranking(s): #1 (Org.), #30 (Overall)

2016 Stats: 6.08 ERA, 6.34 DRA, 37 IP, 41 H, 19 BB, 31 K in eight games at major league level, 4.41 ERA, 8.76 DRA, 136.2 IP, 115 H, 71 BB, 120 K in 24 games at triple-A Louisville

The Role: OFP 55—High-end setup/low-end closer
Likely 50—Eighth-inning guy

YEAR	TEAM	LVL	AGE	W	L	SV	G	GS	IP	H	HR	BB/9	K/9	K	GB%	BABIP	WHIP	ERA	FIP	DRA	VORP	WARP	cFIP	MPH
2014	PEN	AA	21	7	10	0	27	26	136^2	114	18	4.9	9.2	140	38%	.264	1.38	4.74	4.58	6.09	-13.30	-1.4	99	
2015	PEN	AA	22	4	7	0	14	14	78^1	53	8	4.9	10.2	89	39%	.249	1.23	3.68	4.16	3.25	16.10	1.7	88	
2015	LOU	AAA	22	4	4	0	11	11	55^2	51	2	4.4	8.2	51	41%	.306	1.40	4.04	3.35	6.32	-6.30	-0.6	104	
2016	LOU	AAA	23	8	9	0	24	24	136^2	115	17	4.7	7.9	120	42%	.259	1.36	4.41	4.65	8.76	-51.80	-5.3	114	
2016	CIN	MLB	23	2	3	0	8	8	37	41	9	4.6	7.5	31	35%	.299	1.62	6.08	6.54	6.34	-4.00	-0.4	126	95.7
CIN	*MLB*	*24*	*5*	*7*	*0*	*19*	*19*	*95*	*92*	*12*	*4.3*	*7.6*	*80*	*37%*	*.287*	*1.43*	*4.75*	*4.72*	*4.86*	*3.5*	*0.4*	*100*		
CIN	*MLB*	*25*	*9*	*11*	*0*	*31*	*31*	*198*	*143*	*23*	*5.6*	*10.5*	*232*	*37%*	*.277*	*1.34*	*4.50*	*4.61*	*4.98*	*10.1*	*1.0*	*116*		

Breakout: 16% Improve: 29% Collapse: 22% Attrition: 33% MLB: 64% *Comparables: Michael Bowden, Neil Ramirez, Daryl Thompson*

The Good: Stephenson has #thegoodstuff. If you catch him on the right day, he will flash three plus pitches, including a fastball that can touch 96, a downer 11-5 curve, and a hard change that can be a swing-and-miss pitch to both righties and lefties when he is getting it to tumble down in the zone.

The Bad: So he should be way higher on this list, right? Well, he has trouble getting any of those offerings in the zone consistently, and when he is in the zone, he lives in the upper half. That proved to not work as well this year against the high-level hitters. Stephenson also relies too much on his fastball, and struggles to put away hitters at times despite his major-league-quality stuff. At this point the profile will play best in the bullpen, and it sounds like the Reds have come to a similar conclusion.

The Irrelevant: Major-league hitters batted .367 and slugged .663 against Stephenson's fastball in 2016. Mike Trout batted .303 and slugged .560 against fastballs in 2016.

The Risks: Stephenson has already logged a fair amount of innings in the upper minors and even the majors, but there is still a chance that the below-average command and control profile blows up on him even in a short-relief role. The stuff really should carry the profile anyway though. It is #good.

Major league ETA: Debuted in 2016

Ben Carsley's Fantasy Take: If you still own Stephenson in a dynasty league, my advice would be try and sell high-ish on him, as he might still have name value that's disproportionate with what he currently brings to the table. But if we're being honest, you probably already missed your window to sell, which means now you're left holding your breath. Don't look to drop Stephenson if your league rosters 100 prospects, because he's close and there's still a chance Cincinnati might let him start. But don't be afraid to cast him aside for more promising players either, because odds are we're just looking at a high-WHIP reliever. It sounds like his #thegoodstuff isn't as good as Joe Kelly's Great Stuff(TM) anyway.

6. Tyler Stephenson, C

DOB: 08/16/1996

Height/Weight: 6'4" 225 lbs.

Bats/Throws: R/R

Drafted/Acquired: Drafted 11th overall in the 2015 MLB Draft, Kennesaw Mountain HS (Kennesaw, GA); signed for $3.1416 million

Previous Ranking(s): #6 (Org.)

2016 Stats: .250/.348/.450, 1 HR, 0 SB in 5 games at AZL Complex, .216/.278/.324, 3 HR, 0 SB in 39 games at low-A Dayton

The Role: OFP 55—Above-average backstop
Likely 45—Enough pop and glove to be a good backup or second-division starter

YEAR	TEAM	LVL	AGE	PA	R	2B	3B	HR	RBI	BB	K	SB	CS	AVG/OBP/SLG	TAv	VORP	BABIP	BRR	FRAA	WARP
2015	BIL	Rk	18	219	28	15	0	1	16	22	42	0	2	.268/.352/.361	.259	9.3	.338	0.4	C(46): -1.2	0.8
2016	CIN	Rk	19	23	4	1	0	1	2	2	7	0	0	.250/.348/.450	.285	2.1	.333	0.5	C(4): 0.1	0.2
2016	DYT	A	19	153	17	4	1	3	16	12	45	0	0	.216/.278/.324	.225	0.8	.297	0.9	C(27): -1.2	0.0
2017	*CIN*	*MLB*	*20*	*250*	*21*	*9*	*0*	*6*	*26*	*15*	*81*	*0*	*0*	*.198/.252/.323*	*.195*	*-5.6*	*.269*	*-0.5*	*C -1*	*-0.7*
2018	*CIN*	*MLB*	*21*	*302*	*32*	*11*	*0*	*9*	*32*	*20*	*96*	*0*	*0*	*.208/.263/.344*	*.218*	*-3.0*	*.278*	*-0.7*	*C -1*	*-0.4*

Breakout: 1% Improve: 3% Collapse: 0% Attrition: 3% MLB: 5% *Comparables: Francisco Pena, Alex Liddi, Christian Bethancourt*

The Good: Stephenson is a big, strong kid, with potential plus-raw power and enough arm to stick behind the plate assuming further defensive refinement. We'd like to have more to report in this section, but...

The Bad: ...Stephenson missed large chunks of the season with a wrist injury and was compromised by it even when he played. It eventually necessitated surgery. Oh, there was a concussion in there too. So yeah, we will call it a lost season. Not the end of the world when you are 19, but we're not much closer to knowing how well the hit tool or defensive profile will project.

The Irrelevant: Kennesaw, GA is a popular spot for prospects we aren't sure will stick at catcher. We've already written about Kennesaw Mountain State alum Max Pentecost on the Blue Jays list. He's also not the last prospect from Kennesaw on this list.

The Risks: He's a prep catcher, man. A PREP CATCHER. The casino equivalent is those seven-reel video slot machines based on The Walking Dead. I don't understand how those work either. Also he has had a spate of wrist injuries and would be one of the biggest catchers in the majors if he gets to the majors as a catcher.

Major league ETA: 2020

Ben Carsley's Fantasy Take: Waiting on fantasy catching prospects can be frustrating—their progress is often non-linear even as prospects go—but now is a good time to buy low on Stephenson. He's not a top-100 guy yet, but if he hits the way he has the potential to hit, you'll have missed your chance if you wait until next season. Pick him up if your league rosters 150-plus prospects, just feel free to drop him quickly if something tastier comes your way.

7. Taylor Trammell, OF

DOB: 9/13/1997

Height/Weight: 6'2" 195 lbs.

Bats/Throws: L/L

Drafted/Acquired: Drafted 35th overall in the 2016 MLB Draft, Mount Paran Christian School (Kennesaw, GA); signed for $3.2 million

Previous Ranking(s): N/A

2016 Stats: .303/.374/.421, 2 HR, 24 SB in 61 games at short-season Billings

The Role: OFP 55— Good everyday corner outfielder
Likely 45—Good fourth outfielder

YEAR	TEAM	LVL	AGE	PA	R	2B	3B	HR	RBI	BB	K	SB	CS	AVG/OBP/SLG	TAv	VORP	BABIP	BRR	FRAA	WARP
2016	BIL	Rk	18	254	39	9	6	2	34	23	57	24	7	.303/.374/.421	.290	15.4	.396	3.1	LF(39): -0.4, CF(11): 1.8	1.8
2017	*CIN*	*MLB*	*19*	*250*	*24*	*8*	*1*	*5*	*22*	*14*	*86*	*7*	*3*	*.192/.239/.300*	*.184*	*-10.2*	*.274*	*0.4*	*LF 1, CF 0*	*-0.9*
2018	*CIN*	*MLB*	*20*	*326*	*33*	*11*	*2*	*8*	*32*	*20*	*106*	*11*	*4*	*.209/.261/.334*	*.215*	*-5.6*	*.290*	*1.1*	*LF 2, CF 0*	*-0.4*

Breakout: 0% Improve: 6% Collapse: 2% Attrition: 5% MLB: 11% *Comparables: Engel Beltre, Nomar Mazara, Francisco Pena*

The Good: The Reds continued their spending spree later in the 2016 draft, grabbing the toolsy Trammell for top-half-of-the-first-round money with their comp balance pick. The fast-twitch athletic tools jump out of the profile here, but Trammell also showed up in the Pioneer League with more advanced baseball skills than you would expect. He's a plus-plus runner at present, and should stay above-average, if not better, as he fills out. Potentially average or better power given his bat speed and added strength. His profile could take a grade jump if the athleticism begins to show in places other than straight-line speed.

The Bad: As good as they are, those athletic tools might not keep him in center field long term. He's more of a runner at present than an electric baseball athlete, and the bat has a long way to go even considering the successful pro debut in Billings. Despite the big bonus number, he doesn't currently project as an impact player in a corner outfield spot.

The Irrelevant: While not as prodigious as the surnames Johnson, Martinez, or Bonds, Trammells have compiled 58.6 WARP between Alan and Bubba.

The Risks: Toolsy outfielder in rookie ball you say...hmm...yeah, he is gonna be pretty risky.

Major league ETA: 2021

Ben Carsley's Fantasy Take: Yes, if your league roster 200 prospects. Mmmmmmayyyyybe if it rosters 150 prospects. Not if it rosters 100 prospects. He's just too far away.

8. Aristides Aquino, OF

DOB: 4/22/1994

Height/Weight: 6'4" 190 lbs.

Bats/Throws: R/R

Drafted/Acquired: Signed in January 2011 out of the Dominican Republic for $110,000

Previous Ranking(s): N/A

2016 Stats: .273/.327/.519, 23 HR, 11 SB in 125 games at high-A Daytona

The Role: OFP 55—Above-average regular
Likely 45—Fringe/second-division starter

YEAR	TEAM	LVL	AGE	PA	R	2B	3B	HR	RBI	BB	K	SB	CS	AVG/OBP/SLG	TAv	VORP	BABIP	BRR	FRAA	WARP
2014	BIL	Rk	20	307	48	23	5	16	64	15	66	21	5	.292/.342/.577	.325	28.9	.330	2.1		3.2
2015	BIL	Rk	21	54	7	1	3	2	13	2	9	0	1	.308/.333/.558	.284	2.0	.341	-0.4	RF(11): 0.3	0.2
2015	DYT	A	21	249	25	9	3	5	27	11	53	6	1	.234/.281/.364	.236	0.1	.280	2.0	RF(60): -0.1	0.1
2016	DAY	A+	22	526	69	26	12	23	79	34	104	11	7	.273/.327/.519	.282	22.9	.304	1.3	RF(123): 27.1	4.5
2017	*CIN*	*MLB*	*23*	*250*	*28*	*10*	*2*	*11*	*34*	*12*	*68*	*2*	*1*	*.228/.272/.428*	*.232*	*-0.5*	*.272*	*0.0*	*RF 3*	*0.3*
2018	*CIN*	*MLB*	*24*	*293*	*36*	*12*	*3*	*13*	*40*	*14*	*78*	*3*	*2*	*.233/.278/.436*	*.251*	*2.6*	*.278*	*0.1*	*RF 3*	*0.7*

Breakout: 1% Improve: 8% Collapse: 2% Attrition: 5% MLB: 14% *Comparables: Bryce Brentz, Yorman Rodriguez, Scott Schebler*

The Good: Aquino, who has spotlighted as a name to watch in the 2016 and 2015 versions of this list, broke out this past season. His plus-raw power translated in a tough hitting environment and could play at full utility with his plus bat speed and loft. His plus bat speed and quick hands help him catch up to velo and is an aggressive fastball swinger. He is also a plus runner, which is better than what his size suggests. His plus arm is accurate and plays all over the outfield.

The Bad: He is an aggressive hitter, lacking plate discipline, and has trouble making contact. His swing has length and a big leg kick and load can disrupt his overall timing. His defense is below-average at present, and while he has the speed to play CF he struggles with reads and routes, leaving him to a corner-outfield spot. Has a tendency to air it out and throw behind runners, allowing them to move up.

The Irrelevant: Aristides was praised by Socrates as "an exceptional instance of good leadership." I cannot confirm if Socrates Brito agrees.

The Risks: Reds fans might have seen this ballad before with the likes of Yorman Rodriguez, or Jonathan Reynoso. Loud tools, struggles to make contact and lacks plate discipline. His defensive skills could make him a liability and be more of a DH. Missed most of 2015, and a year of development, with a broken ulna and radius.

Major league ETA: Late 2018 —Steve Givarz

Ben Carsley's Fantasy Take: I get the sense that Aquino is pretty anonymous in dynasty circles, and while he shouldn't be a household name he's worth paying attention to. The contact issues are scary, as The Risks portfolio reminds us with tales of prospects past, but betting on players with plus-raw power and plus speed in the mid-to-high minors is a sound strategy. Consider grabbing Aquino if your league rosters 175-200 minor leaguers; he's one of the more intriguing names in that range.

9. Antonio Santillan, RHP

DOB: 04/15/1997

Height/Weight: 6'3" 240 lbs.

Bats/Throws: R/R

Drafted/Acquired: Drafted 49th overall in the 2015 MLB Draft, Seguin HS (Arlington, TX); signed for $1.35 million

Previous Ranking(s): #10 (Org.)

2016 Stats: 3.92 ERA, 2.51 DRA, 39 IP, 32 H, 16 BB, 46 K in 8 games at short-season Billings, 6.82 ERA, 3.99 DRA, 30.1 IP, 27 H, 24 BB, 38 K in 7 games at low-A Dayton

The Role: OFP 55—No. 3 Starter/Closer
Likely 45—Up/Down reliever

YEAR	TEAM	LVL	AGE	W	L	SV	G	GS	IP	H	HR	BB/9	K/9	K	GB%	BABIP	WHIP	ERA	FIP	DRA	VORP	WARP	cFIP	MPH
2015	CIN	Rk	18	0	2	0	8	7	19^2	15	1	5.0	8.7	19	40%	.275	1.32	5.03	4.68	5.39	1.00	0.1	114	
2016	BIL	Rk	19	1	0	0	8	8	39	32	4	3.7	10.6	46	46%	.292	1.23	3.92	4.71	2.51	13.90	1.4	91	
2016	DYT	A	19	2	3	0	7	7	30^1	27	3	7.1	11.3	38	38%	.338	1.68	6.82	4.83	3.99	3.50	0.4	108	
CIN	*MLB*	*20*	*2*	*5*	*0*	*12*	*12*	*50^1*	*55*	*10*	*6.3*	*6.6*	*37*	*25%*	*.314*	*1.79*	*6.47*	*6.50*	*7.09*	*-8.5*	*-0.9*	*168*		
CIN	*MLB*	*21*	*5*	*10*	*0*	*24*	*24*	*144*	*141*	*28*	*6.8*	*9.2*	*147*	*25%*	*.321*	*1.73*	*6.22*	*6.48*	*6.82*	*-14.2*	*-1.5*	*163*		

Breakout: 0% Improve: 0% Collapse: 0% Attrition: 2% MLB: 2% *Comparables: Miguel Castro, Alex Reyes, Parker Bridwell*

The Good: Santillan looks the part of a power arm that could head a rotation, and he has two big pitches to back that up. His fastball has touched 98 in starts and can sit 94-96 with impressive life. His curveball routinely receives plus grades, with its 11/5 shape and plus depth, arriving in the low-80s. He is a tremendous athlete and has impressive strength to hold his velocity deep into games.

The Bad: Santillan struggles to throw strikes. His high-effort, crossfire delivery has been tamped down since he signed, but still has a lot of moving parts. He will lose all semblance of control at times. He lacks feel for a changeup and it is a distant third offering.

The Irrelevant: The Texas Tech 2015 recruiting class had three players taken in the top 50 between Santillan, Josh Naylor, and Trent Clark.

The Risks: He's still a pitcher, and one that struggles to throw strikes consistently. His delivery is high-effort and he can lose it at times with the strike zone. His lack of a third pitch could consign him to the bullpen.

Major league ETA: 2019 —Steve Givarz

Ben Carsley's Fantasy Take: Santillan basically has the default loadout for "power arm" in the low-to-mid minors. His strike-out potential and reasonable upside make him worthy of your watch list, but the probability that he's a reliever and his distance from the majors limit his present dynasty value.

10. Shedric Long, 2B

DOB: 8/22/1995

Height/Weight: 5'8" 180 lbs.

Bats/Throws: L/R

Drafted/Acquired: Drafted 375th overall in the 2013 MLB Draft, Jacksonville HS (Jacksonville, AL); signed for $100,000

Previous Ranking(s): N/A

2016 Stats: .281/.371/.457, 11 HR, 16 SB in 94 games at single-A Dayton, .322/.371/.503, 4 HR, 5 SB in 38 games at high-A Daytona

The Role: OFP 50—Average second baseman
Likely 40—Useful utility infielder

YEAR	TEAM	LVL	AGE	PA	R	2B	3B	HR	RBI	BB	K	SB	CS	AVG/OBP/SLG	TAv	VORP	BABIP	BRR	FRAA	WARP
2014	BIL	Rk	18	93	6	3	0	0	6	5	18	2	1	.172/.217/.207	.198	-0.4	.217	-0.4		-0.1
2015	DYT	A	19	173	22	7	2	6	16	18	31	2	3	.283/.363/.474	.293	6.7	.322	-2.4	2B(23): -0.7, SS(1): 0.1	0.7
2016	DYT	A	20	389	47	24	1	11	45	44	85	16	3	.281/.371/.457	.311	32.3	.346	3.2	2B(82): 2.1, 3B(3): -0.6	3.7
2016	DAY	A+	20	159	22	6	4	4	30	10	35	5	1	.322/.371/.503	.299	12.2	.393	1.3	2B(38): 3.0	1.6
2017	*CIN*	*MLB*	*21*	*250*	*32*	*10*	*1*	*9*	*29*	*20*	*68*	*3*	*1*	*.236/.303/.418*	*.242*	*5.1*	*.290*	*0.0*	*2B -0, 3B -0*	*0.5*
2018	*CIN*	*MLB*	*22*	*375*	*48*	*15*	*2*	*15*	*49*	*30*	*98*	*4*	*1*	*.243/.310/.431*	*.262*	*12.4*	*.293*	*0.0*	*2B 0, 3B 0*	*1.3*

Breakout: 5% Improve: 18% Collapse: 3% Attrition: 13% MLB: 30% *Comparables: Dilson Herrera, Eddie Rosario, Brett Lawrie*

The Good: As much as we'd like to see an 70-speed catcher in the majors, it isn't a surprise Long moved out into the infield. What might be a surprise is the pop he found in 2016 in rather unfriendly hitting environments. He has above-average bat speed and average raw power. That's impressive from a dude his size, and useful up the middle. Oh yeah, and he's got top-of-the-scale speed. Because of the weird development path, there is positive risk in the profile. This could very well be the start of a break-out.

The Bad: The swing is noisy and long, and the hit tool might play to below-average at higher levels, limiting the in-game power. As a converted catcher, Long is...well, built like a catcher. The speed is plus-plus, but the other athletic tools are fringy, so he's not as good a defender as you might think at second, although he should be fine there. He's still figuring out how to turn his speed into a weapon on the bases.

The Irrelevant: The single-season record for steals as a catcher is 36, set by the Royals John Wathan in 1982.

The Risks: I like to say that unusual prospects carry unusual risks, and Long is certainly an unusual prospect, but this risk profile is rather usual. The hit tool will need to allow the burgeoning raw power to play in games, or he will only be a speedy bench option with some pop.

Major league ETA: Late 2018

Ben Carsley's Fantasy Take: At the risk of repeating myself, Long is another one for the watch list. His speed and relative proximity to the majors make him interesting, but the odds are too great for us to get excited yet. But if you want to argue "speed, though," well, I'd listen.

OTHERS OF NOTE:

#11

Ian Kahaloa, RHP

Kahaloa has an advanced feel for pitching for a teenager. His fastball is 92-94 and can touch 96 in games with above-average run. His slider has power break and depth and can be an above-average offering down the line. He has feel for the change—it shows similar action to his fastball and could be an average offering. And he can throw all three pitches for strikes. If we were more confident he was a starter in the long term, he'd be up in the Top 10, but he doesn't have ideal size, and lacks downhill plane and extension on his pitches. His changeup is mostly projection right now, and his command is behind his control with his fastball. Has only played at short-season thus far. He has had various injuries throughout his career, including an issue with his elbow that lowered his signing bonus. He missed most of spring training with an oblique injury, and left his last start of the year with a forearm issue. So, yeah, he's also a pitcher. While he's unlikely to unseat Sid Fernandez as the best Hawaiian-born hurler, Kahaloa could eventually be a useful major league bullpen arm.

The guy who needs to hit some more

Calten Daal, SS/2B

Dall missed significant time with a right shoulder strain in 2016, but when he was on the field it was more of the same from the speedy middle infielder. It's 20 power—Daal has hit two home runs and 20 doubles in almost 1,000 pro plate appearances—but he can hit a bit, run a bit, and play both middle infield positions. It's likely a utility profile, but if there was actually offensive progress made in 2016, he might be able to carve out a career as an eight-hole hitter on a second-division team. That sounds like a damning with faint praise, but it isn't, we swear.

The hard-throwing Italians

Sal Romano, RHP & Nick Travieso, RHP

A pair of 22-year-olds with plus fastballs and shots to fit into the back of a major league rotation, the question for both is if the command profiles will improve enough for them to start. Travieso continued to struggle with that part in 2016, and his overall stuff has taken a step backward since he was the 14th overall pick in 2012. Romano—a 23rd round pick a year earlier—has leapfrogged him this year on the back of a fastball he can run up to 97, a solid curve, and improving command. He is a big human with a big heater. Another year of refinement will make him an easy top-10 selection and give me more confidence he is a long-term major league starter. For now, let's also call him #11.

The park factor of note

Phil Ervin, OF

Much like hoping a movie didn't give everything away in the trailer, you wonder if Phillip Ervin could live up to the expectations he set in his rookie season. The outfielder still struggles to hit for average but posted a .312 TAv and .761 OPS in his second tour of the Southern League, both among the best at the level. Though he'll have to work to push his hit tool to average, the former first-rounder still offers an intriguing mix of power and speed. The latter contributed to a career-high 36 stolen bases but doesn't translate to center field. As for the former, it's worth noting his incredibly lopsided home-road splits. With the left field fences in Pensacola pushed back from 325 to 342 feet, the pull hitter was a victim of his home park—he hit .191/.348/.312 in Pensacola and .282/.376/.477 everywhere else. There might be room for improvement at triple-A Louisville; at the moment, he's a fourth outfielder with a chance for something more. *—Kourage Kundahl*

Steve's Guy

Tyler Mahle, RHP

More of a steady player than a sexy player, Mahle nonetheless could be a solid contributor in the not-too-distant future. He lacks remaining projection at this point, but his fastball should be an above-average offering at peak. His arsenal plays up because of his ability to pound the zone, and place his fastball where he wants it. His slider shows the most promise of his secondaries and could be a bat-misser at the highest level. *—Steve Givarz*

The consistently inconsistent

Keury Mella, RHP

Acquired in the 2015 deadline for Mike Leake, Mella has showcased potential, but struggled to put it all together consistently. His fastball and slider will both show above-average grades on a good day, but he has struggled to miss bats and barrels thus far. His fastball has above-average movement and can be tough to control for him at times. His stuff doesn't translate as well in a bullpen if he isn't throwing strikes, so he needs to gain some more consistency before re-cementing his top 10 status. *—Steve Givarz*

TOP 10 TALENTS 25 AND UNDER (BORN 4/1/91 OR LATER)

1. Nick Senzel	6. Brandon Finnegan
2. Eugenio Suarez	7. Cody Reed
3. Amir Garrett	8. Robert Stephenson
4. Luis Castillo	9. Michael Lorenzen
5. Jesse Winker	10. Jose Peraza

It's not too thrilling, is it? The exciting guys—Senzel, Garrett, maybe Winker—already got coverage by Jeff and co. above. The rest of the bunch feel, well, pretty Cincinnati. The Reds have somehow fallen out of the national baseball conversation over the last few years–just ask Ben and Sam–by producing perfectly good ballplayers and trading them to other teams for average-ish returns as part of a drawn-out pseudo-rebuild. Something is keeping this team from going whole-hog into a Phillies-and-Braves-style rebuild, for better or for worse. Jay Bruce is gone ahead of free agency, but what about Zack Cozart? Could a Billy Hamilton deal finally bring back the sort of impact prospect they haven't had since the Mat Latos trade? While sometimes it makes sense to bet big on a mediocre core that could shine with a few lucky breaks, it feels as if this Reds team requires a few lucky breaks just to break even, never mind having to share a division with Chicago and St. Louis. Let's hope for 85 wins next year! Blah.

The top talents 25-and-under for this team also seem mediocre; this isn't a squad with some transcendent talent or even someone to peg as a future four-win contributor in the bunch. It's a group led by a steady hand in the infield, possessed of a few interesting pitching contributors, and culminating in a couple of guys who could top out as average up-the-middle dudes or bottom out as fringe big-leaguers.

Eugenio Suarez was the return for Alfredo Simon heading to Detroit, a brilliant deal for Cincy that has worked out just swimmingly. (For the Reds, at least. The Tigers ... not so much.) Although Suarez teased All-Star-level performance back in a partial season in 2015, his 2016 performance reflected the work of a ho-hum average big-league infielder. This is definitely not damning with faint praise, this is a legitimate plaudit for a third baseman with pop and circumstance (read: power and a little versatility). He's not a chased-by-chainsaw-wielding-lions nightmare, and he's not the incredible dream of flying over the Grand Canyon while winning a Nobel Prize. He's a good, restful night's sleep ... something we all need and perhaps don't value as much as we should.

Then there's the brace of remaining Reds lefties who came back as part of the Johnny Cueto trade. *(Bon voyage, John Lamb!)* Brandon Finnegan was supposed to be the headliner/highlight of that deal, and I guess he still is, but when you trade away a pitcher like Johnny Cueto for three lefties, you must hope you're getting a least a No. 3 starter back. Finnegan could still get there, but there's work to be done. He was the most present Reds starter a season ago—he made 31 starts among the dross and maybes that was the team's young-and-unproven 2016 crop of starters—but he was hardly the best. His 5.43 DRA made for a below-replacement pitcher, despite his below-4.00 ERA, and there were far, far too many fly balls for anyone to be comfortable. Cody Reed on the other hand, had the opposite problem: His ERA was atrocious (7.36), but his DRA was delicious (3.93). By the metric that best predicts future performance, he was above-average in his 10 starts, but the metric that best predicts another shot in the majors... not so good.

Michael Lorenzen checks in next, and could be better known as the best part of an incredibly shoddy Reds bullpen last year. (Sorry, Rasiel Iglesias!) Recently converted from starting, Lorenzen looked like a dollar-store ripoff of Mark Melancon from a performance perspective: His 64 percent ground-ball rate was great, and he struck out almost a batter per inning to match up with that. Homers were a bit of a problem—when he allowed a fly ball, it left the park almost one-fourth of the time—but he appears to be a solid setup arm so long as his mid-90s cutter and sinker hold up over the long haul.

Then there are the curious cases of Jose Peraza and the just-missed Dilson Herrera, both blocked at their best position—second base—until the day Ohio institution

Brandon Phillips was dealt to Atlanta. Both now stand a chance at becoming a productive regular. Peraza's more likely to shine in a super-utility role given his speed and nascent versatility, but Herrera's got the more advanced offensive skills. Certainly, neither is the type of foundational up-the-middle-player that you'd build a team around, but one could imagine a world where Herrera is an effective role-50 second baseman with offensive upside and where Peraza is the type of super-utility player that managers love and statheads prefer to Kris Negron-esque can't-hit-a-lick alternatives. If you prefer them to the present-reliever value of Lorenzen above, well, that's pretty reasonable, too. They're not sexy profiles—especially as the returns for long-time Reds sluggers like Todd Frazier and Jay Bruce—but hey, this is Cincinnati: a well-documented medium place for medium persons.

—Bryan Grosnick

CLEVELAND INDIANS

The State of the System: *"Flags fly forever, baby! Okay, well, it's not the exact flag they wanted. But they also still have Andrew Miller and a very nice one-two punch at the top of the system."*

THE TOP TEN

1. C Francisco Mejia	6. OF Will Benson
2. RHP Triston McKenzie	7. 1B Bobby Bradley
3. OF Bradley Zimmer	8. LHP Brady Aiken
4. LHP Juan Hillman	9. SS Yu-Cheng Chang
5. OF Greg Allen	10. RHP Adam Plutko

The Big Question: Should an amateur pitcher send in an MRI to teams?

I could have addressed this question in the introduction to just about any team list. The minors are littered with pitching prospects that have lost time to elbow injuries, and plenty of teams have had to "renegotiate" a bonus after a post-draft physical. Cleveland draws this topic because, well (A) there isn't a ton else to talk about in what's now a fringe-average system, and (B) Well it is, but you know what I mean. His entire saga had already become a flashpoint for these kind of conversations long before Cleveland found him atop their 2015 draft board. What came after is a matter for down below. Up here, I want to discuss how the "before" might have changed the balance of power in the draft.

Commissioner Manfred floated the idea of a pre-draft medical combine for all amateurs last year, and a test balloon made its way into the new CBA in the form of a voluntary predraft MRI for pitchers. I am approaching the age when I would be hypothetically old enough to have a draft-eligible child—le sigh—and I'm fairly certain I would strongly recommend he not participate in this. There's an undercurrent of "well, if there's nothing wrong with your elbow, what do you have to hide?" to the whole proceedings. A clean MRI, the argument follows, could help your draft stock. But that only really works if other pitchers send in balky scan results, which seems...unlikely, no? If enough of the top pitching prospects don't, I suppose a sense of vague uncertainty—see that above undercurrent—might have the same effect, but you aren't really being rewarded for your "health," but rather seeing others in your class being punished for suspicions about theirs.

And then there is the old baseball cliché that you can always find something on an MRI. The framework assumes, quite naively, that teams would be unable and/or unwilling to manipulate the results. The problem is, there really isn't a mechanism in place to stop an organization from drafting a kid and say, "yeah we took you at pick 17, but we do have some concerns about the MRI." Maybe you are a high school arm with a Vanderbilt commitment and can tell them to go pound sand, but maybe you are Anthony Kay and out almost a million bucks because you can't negotiate with anyone else. Maybe the "medical concern" even got accidentally leaked.

From the team's perspective, I suppose imperfect knowledge beats no knowledge. But a clean MRI today is no guarantee of future health, and sometimes Jon Lester pitches for years with a grenade in his elbow. I joke about "being a pitcher" being a notable risk for a prospect—one we are probably both tired of at this point—but I think my underlying point here is that we really have no idea which pitchers will get hurt and why it will happen. All we know is that pitchers get hurt an awful lot.

None of this helps Brady Aiken of course, or Mac Marshall, or Jacob Nix. It feels a brutish thing to give the Astros post-TJ plaudits for not signing Aiken, to praise their calculus. They were 'right,' but I don't know if that should be incentivized.

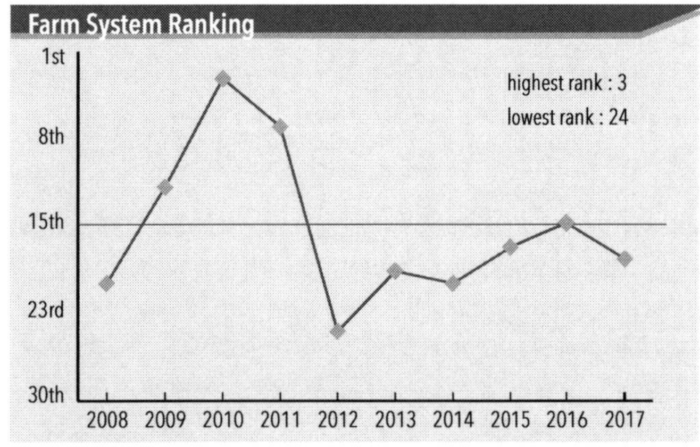

Personnel

President:
Chris Antonetti

General Manager:
Mike Chernoff

Assistant General Manager:
Carter Hawkins

Manager:
Terry Francona

BP Alumni:
Max Marchi
Ethan Purser
Steffan Segui
Keith Woolner

1. Francisco Mejia, C

DOB: 10/27/1995

Height/Weight: 5'10" 175 lbs.

Bats/Throws: S/R

Drafted/Acquired: Signed out of the Dominican Republic in July 2012 for $350,000

Previous Ranking(s): #9 (Org.)

2016 Stats: .347/.384/.531, 7 HR, 1 SB in 60 games at Low-A Lake County, .333/.380/.488, 4 HR, 1 SB in 42 games at High-A Lynchburg

The Role: OFP 60—First-division starting catcher
Likely 55—Above-average major league catcher

YEAR	TEAM	LVL	AGE	PA	R	2B	3B	HR	RBI	BB	K	SB	CS	AVG/OBP/SLG	TAv	VORP	BABIP	BRR	FRAA	WARP
2014	MHV	A-	18	274	32	17	4	2	36	18	47	2	4	.282/.339/.407	.277	15.3	.337	0.0	C(52): 2.2	1.8
2015	LKC	A	19	446	45	13	0	9	53	38	78	4	1	.243/.324/.345	.259	15.1	.281	-1.8	C(94): 4.5	2.1
2016	LKC	A	20	259	41	17	3	7	51	15	39	1	0	.347/.384/.531	.328	29.7	.388	2.3	C(52): 1.4	3.4
2016	LYN	A+	20	184	22	12	1	4	29	13	24	1	2	.333/.380/.488	.308	16.8	.366	-0.1	C(35): 0.5	1.8
2017	*CLE*	*MLB*	*21*	*250*	*25*	*12*	*1*	*8*	*30*	*14*	*57*	*0*	*0*	*.250/.296/.405*	*.232*	*4.3*	*.297*	*-0.4*	*C 0*	*0.5*
2018	*CLE*	*MLB*	*22*	*320*	*38*	*15*	*1*	*10*	*39*	*18*	*72*	*0*	*0*	*.258/.307/.419*	*.242*	*5.0*	*.306*	*-0.7*	*C 0*	*0.6*

Breakout: 3% Improve: 9% Collapse: 0% Attrition: 9% MLB: 17% *Comparables: Travis d'Arnaud, Austin Romine, Christian Vazquez*

The Good: A 50-game hit streak is pretty good, right? There's always going to be a bit of luck and happenstance involved in a long hitting streak, but the underlying tool here is what we want, and oh yeah, it is pretty good too. Mejia's stroke is short and strong from both sides of the plate. There's plus bat speed here and with it the potential for double-digit home run pop. He's improved rapidly behind the plate and he has a plus-plus arm to back up solid receiving skills.

The Bad: If you want to nitpick, Mejia has a very aggressive approach, and it's not impossible upper-minors arms are able to front-foot him at times. He makes a lot of contact, but not all of it is good contact, he'll drop the back shoulder and pop balls up. He runs like a catcher.

The Irrelevant: Maybe it's not quite as impressive as the longer one, but Mejia will start 2017 riding an eight-game hit streak.

The Risks: Catchers are weird, man. Mejia still has to hit in the upper minors. I think he will, but catchers are weird, man.

Major league ETA: Late 2018

Ben Carsley's Fantasy Take: Have I mentioned how much I hate it when Craig Goldstein is right? Our resident Mejia lover has long been the high man on this backstop, and his patience was rewarded in a big way in 2016. Mejia's hit tool is at a premium at the catcher position, and when you factor in his (relative) closeness to the majors and his potential for some power, he starts looking an awful lot like a top-50 guy. Catchers are inherently risky and their development is rarely linear, but Mejia has all the makings of an easy top-10 backstop in due time.

2. Triston McKenzie, RHP

DOB: 08/02/1997

Height/Weight: 6'5" 160 lbs.

Bats/Throws: R/R

Drafted/Acquired/Bonus: Drafted 42nd overall in the 2015 MLB Draft, Royal Palm Beach HS (Palm Beach, FL); signed for $2.3025 million

Previous Ranking(s): #7 (Org.)

2016 Stats: 0.55 ERA, 2.44 DRA, 49.1 IP, 31 H, 16 BB, 55 K in 9 games at short-season Penn League, 3.18 ERA, 1.04 DRA, 34 IP, 27 H, 6 BB, 49 K in 6 games at Low-A Lake County

The Role: OFP 60—No. 3 starter
Likely 50—No. 4 starter

YEAR	TEAM	LVL	AGE	W	L	SV	G	GS	IP	H	HR	BB/9	K/9	K	GB%	BABIP	WHIP	ERA	FIP	DRA	VORP	WARP	cFIP	MPH
2015	CLE	Rk	17	1	1	0	4	3	12	4	0	2.2	12.8	17	48%	.174	0.58	0.75	1.73	2.03	5.00	0.5	76	
2016	MHV	A-	18	4	3	0	9	9	49^{1}	31	2	2.9	10.0	55	37%	.248	0.95	0.55	2.66	2.44	15.40	1.6	81	
2016	LKC	A	18	2	2	0	6	6	34	27	2	1.6	13.0	49	40%	.333	0.97	3.18	1.98	1.04	15.00	1.6	64	
2017	*CLE*	*MLB*	*19*	*3*	*4*	*0*	*10*	*10*	*52*	*59*	*9*	*4.1*	*6.9*	*40*	*47%*	*.309*	*1.59*	*5.23*	*5.33*	*5.60*	*-0.7*	*-0.1*	*131*	
2018	*CLE*	*MLB*	*20*	*4*	*5*	*0*	*15*	*15*	*89^{2}*	*89*	*14*	*4.0*	*8.9*	*89*		*.303*	*1.43*	*4.63*	*4.60*	*4.96*	*4.4*	*0.5*	*115*	

Breakout: 3% Improve: 3% Collapse: 0% Attrition: 2% MLB: 3% *Comparables: Roberto Osuna, Jordan Lyles, Vicente Campos*

The Good: McKenzie checks all the boxes to make me swoon. He's tall, lean, and über projectable. However, he's not the mere conjurings of a rarebit fiend. He's already quite advanced as a pitcher, dominating the Penn and Midwest Leagues while spending most of the season as an 18-year-old. The fastball sits on either side of 90, but features good extension and plane—as you'd expect from a teenaged Stretch Armstrong. His curveball already shows the makings of a swing-and-miss offering at higher levels. It certainly was at the lower ones.

The Bad: Let's dive back into our pocket "teenage changeup" thesaurus—McKenzie has "limited feel for the pitch at present." The curve can have an inconsistent shape at times as well. The velocity can dip into the upper 80s later in outings.

The Irrelevant: The only prior "Triston" in organized baseball was Triston Cortez, who lasted 22 games for Macon of the South Coast Independent League. No word on if he gave a "burn the ships"-type speech.

The Risks: The thing about being a projectable pitcher is you actually have to project at some point. McKenzie has plenty of time to develop, but also a lot of developing to do, so there's a lot of risk in the profile. He'll need a tick or two more on the fastball, and he will have to find some feel for the change. He's also a pitcher.

Major league ETA: 2020

Ben Carsley's Fantasy Take: McKenzie is on the short list of dynasty prospects from the 2015 draft who've improved their stock the most. The reports on him are fairly glowing, and even if the upside isn't legendary, it's high enough to get our attention. Be sure to monitor McKenzie as the year progresses if you roster 100 prospects. If you roster 150 or more, pounce now or forever hold your peace. He has good SP3 upside.

3. Bradley Zimmer, OF

DOB: 11/27/1992

Height/Weight: 6'4" 185 lbs.

Bats/Throws: L/R

Drafted/Acquired: Drafted 21st overall in the 2014 MLB Draft, University of San Francisco (CA); signed for $1.9 million

Previous Ranking(s): #1 (Org.), #23 (Overall)

2016 Stats: .253/.371/.471, 14 HR, 33 SB in 93 games at Double-A Akron, .242/.349/.305, 1 HR, 5 SB in 37 games at Triple-A Columbus

The Role: OFP 60—First-division center fielder who might get "flu-like symptoms" against Madison Bumgarner
Likely 50—Second-division/platoon outfielder

YEAR	TEAM	LVL	AGE	PA	R	2B	3B	HR	RBI	BB	K	SB	CS	AVG/OBP/SLG	TAv	VORP	BABIP	BRR	FRAA	WARP
2014	MHV	A-	21	197	32	11	2	4	30	19	30	11	4	.304/.401/.464	.327	21.9	.348	2.4	CF(42): 1.1	2.4
2014	LKC	A	21	13	4	1	0	2	2	2	3	1	0	.273/.385/.909	.395	2.2	.167	0.1	CF(1): -0.0, RF(1): -0.1	0.2
2015	LYN	A+	22	335	60	17	3	10	39	37	77	32	5	.308/.403/.493	.322	31.3	.388	3.1	CF(41): 6.8, RF(22): -0.1	4.2
2015	AKR	AA	22	214	24	9	1	6	24	18	54	12	2	.219/.313/.374	.257	4.8	.273	-0.2	CF(42): -0.0	0.6
2016	AKR	AA	23	407	58	20	6	14	53	56	115	33	13	.253/.371/.471	.304	30.6	.341	1.8	CF(76): -2.1, RF(9): 1.8	3.5
2016	COH	AAA	23	150	18	5	0	1	9	21	56	5	1	.242/.349/.305	.245	1.4	.423	-0.7	CF(36): 0.8	0.1
2017	*CLE*	*MLB*	*24*	*66*	*9*	*3*	*0*	*2*	*7*	*7*	*21*	*3*	*1*	*.230/.324/.406*	*.255*	*2.3*	*.317*	*0.3*	*CF 1*	*0.3*
2018	*CLE*	*MLB*	*25*	*304*	*39*	*13*	*1*	*11*	*37*	*32*	*99*	*15*	*5*	*.230/.324/.409*	*.248*	*6.7*	*.319*	*1.8*	*CF 4*	*1.2*

Breakout: 5% Improve: 13% Collapse: 8% Attrition: 15% MLB: 28% *Comparables: Joe Benson, Brett Jackson, Jabari Blash*

The Good: Zimmer combines strong physicality—he certainly looks more stout than his listed 185 pounds, in a good way—with a group of advanced baseball skills. He's an easy plus runner with plus raw power. He has a very advanced plate approach and will take more than his fair share of walks. He's awful big to play center long-term, but he tracks the ball well enough out there for now.

The Bad: To be unusually blunt, it's unclear at this point if Zimmer can hit. His swing is long—a combination of a long body with long arms and a long bat path. He's had terrible swing-and-miss problems in the upper minors resulting from this, and it's concerning that he's missing so much and running huge strikeout totals despite being a polished college bat who rarely gets himself out. He's looked particularly hopeless at times against lefties, which is a problem if you want to be a regular, and the struggles open up the possibility of a platoon role in his future. He could end up profiling better in right than center down the road.

The Irrelevant: Zimmer was a teammate for one season with his brother Kyle for the University of San Francisco Dons. Despite having a pair of future first-rounders, the 2012 Dons went 29-30.

The Risks: It's easy to look at a player like Joc Pederson, who has roughly the same strengths and weaknesses and has become a borderline MLB star, but Zimmer is only seven months younger than Pederson and has yet to conquer Triple A. If the hit tool doesn't play, the power and speed will have less opportunity to contribute. At 24, Zimmer is also getting on the older side for a position player prospect who has yet to make the key adjustments.

Major league ETA: Mid-season 2017 —Jarrett Seidler

Ben Carsley's Fantasy Take: Zimmer was viewed as a safe prospect a year ago, but as you can tell from the write-up above, that's no longer the case. There's a pretty wide gap between who Zimmer could be if it all works out and who he'll be if it doesn't in fantasy. The good version could see Zimmer hit .250-260 with 20-plus homers and steals apiece, and would be especially valuable in OBP leagues. The bad Zimmer might not play that often for a first-division team, and could end up posting decent HR/SB stats on a rate basis, but with an average closer to the .220 line. His proximity and upside still make him a solid prospect, but for a guy who was on the cusp of elite dynasty prospect status a year ago, it's a bit disappointing.

4. Juan Hillman LHP

DOB: 05/15/1997

Height/Weight: 6'2" 180 lbs.

Bats/Throws: L/L

Drafted/Acquired/Bonus: Drafted 59th in the 2015 MLB Draft, Olympia HS (Orlando, FL); signed for $825,000

Previous Ranking(s): #8 (Org.)

2016 Stats: 4.43 ERA, 5.09 DRA, 63 IP, 66 H, 24 BB, 47 K in 15 games a short-season Mahoning Valley

The Role: OFP 55—No. 3/4 starter
Likely 45—Back-end starter

YEAR	TEAM	LVL	AGE	W	L	SV	G	GS	IP	H	HR	BB/9	K/9	K	GB%	BABIP	WHIP	ERA	FIP	DRA	VORP	WARP	cFIP	MPH
2015	CLE	Rk	18	0	2	0	8	6	24	26	0	1.9	7.5	20	43%	.347	1.29	4.12	3.15	4.05	4.60	0.4	107	
2016	MHV	A-	19	3	4	0	15	15	63	66	5	3.4	6.7	47	38%	.308	1.43	4.43	4.24	5.09	1.10	0.1	114	
2017	*CLE*	*MLB*	*20*	*2*	*5*	*0*	*11*	*11*	*43^{1}*	*62*	*13*	*5.1*	*3.9*	*19*	*24%*	*.315*	*2.00*	*7.81*	*7.94*	*8.15*	*-12.9*	*-1.3*	*194*	
2018	*CLE*	*MLB*	*21*	*3*	*9*	*0*	*21*	*21*	*120^{2}*	*156*	*33*	*5.3*	*6.3*	*85*	*24%*	*.315*	*1.88*	*7.32*	*7.26*	*7.64*	*-19.9*	*-2.1*	*183*	

Breakout: 0% Improve: 0% Collapse: 0% Attrition: 0% MLB: 0% *Comparables: Jose Torres, Matt Magill, Jose Ramirez*

The Good: Hillman features a deceptive, low-90s fastball that he can spot to either side of the plate. The pitch will show some sink and run down in the zone. He'll occasionally find 95 with the pitch as well. He's a good athlete with a repeatable, up-tempo delivery. The change is potentially above-average. The overall repertoire and command profile is advanced for his age.

The Bad: Hillman's stuff—and especially his velocity—varies from outing to outing. When the fastball isn't down in the zone—or dips into the upper 80s—it's hittable even in short-season. He can lose his feel for the breaking ball and even when it's there the pitch shows early and gets a little loopy. The stuff can dip in games as well, leading me—and others—to wonder if he can hold up as a starter long term.

The Irrelevant: There's a forecasted high of 69 degrees in Orlando today. It is not nearly that nice where I am sitting.

The Risks: Short-season resume, questions about if he can hold up across a starter's workload in-game and across a season. Oh yes, and he's a pitcher.

Major league ETA: 2019

Ben Carsley's Fantasy Take: I believe I've made my feelings on back-end starting prospects abundantly clear. When Hillman is closer to the majors, you can start dabbling if you're in a deeper league. But for right now, his lead time and modest ceiling should keep him out of sight and out of mind for your average dynasty enthusiast. He's in a good system to get the most out of his abilities, though.

5. Greg Allen, OF

DOB: 3/15/1993

Height/Weight: 6'0" 175 lbs.

Bats/Throws: S/R

Drafted/Acquired: Drafted in the sixth round of the 2015 MLB Draft, San Diego State University (San Diego, CA); signed for $200,000

Previous Ranking(s): N/A

2016 Stats: .290/.399/.441, 3 HR, 7 SB in 37 games at Double-A Akron, .298/.424/.402, 4 HR, 38 SB in 92 games at High-A Lynchburg

The Role: OFP 55—Defense-first, solid-average center fielder
Likely 45—High-end fourth outfielder with occasional bouts of second-division starting

YEAR	TEAM	LVL	AGE	PA	R	2B	3B	HR	RBI	BB	K	SB	CS	AVG/OBP/SLG	TAv	VORP	BABIP	BRR	FRAA	WARP
2014	MHV	A-	21	270	46	8	2	0	19	27	26	30	5	.244/.361/.298	.245	0.5	.274	-0.5	RF(14): 3.1, CF(13): -0.6	0.4
2015	LKC	A	22	564	83	27	2	7	45	53	57	43	16	.273/.368/.382	.287	36.4	.297	4.2	CF(116): -1.1, RF(6): -0.2	4.0
2015	LYN	A+	22	16	2	1	0	0	0	2	3	3	0	.154/.313/.231	.214	0.5	.200	1.0	RF(3): -0.2	0.0
2016	LYN	A+	23	432	93	16	4	4	31	58	51	38	7	.298/.424/.402	.309	49.4	.338	13.1	CF(92): 14.7	6.4
2016	AKR	AA	23	174	26	7	3	3	13	19	27	7	6	.290/.399/.441	.310	16.1	.336	2.3	CF(36): 3.5	1.8
2017	*CLE*	*MLB*	*24*	*250*	*35*	*11*	*1*	*6*	*23*	*23*	*45*	*11*	*4*	*.251/.341/.393*	*.246*	*6.2*	*.284*	*0.4*	*CF 1*	*0.9*
2018	*CLE*	*MLB*	*25*	*308*	*37*	*12*	*1*	*7*	*32*	*26*	*60*	*12*	*5*	*.240/.328/.375*	*.237*	*2.4*	*.275*	*1.1*	*CF 2, LF 0*	*0.5*

Breakout: 5% Improve: 12% Collapse: 4% Attrition: 22% MLB: 34% *Comparables: Erik Komatsu, Che-Hsuan Lin, Trevor Crowe*

The Good: Allen is a switch-hitter with a similar swing from both sides of the plate, and it is one built on barrel control and efficiency into the zone at the expense of separation and plane. It's a handsy, whip of a swing, and he's a smart player; he stays back well and fights off difficult pitches, extending at-bats and spoiling quality execution with line drives to all fields. The pesky barrel command pairs with excellent strike zone discipline that helps an already-solid-average hit tool play up with outsized on-base skill. He's an aggressive, plus runner who gets quality releases on his stolen base attempts and can impact the game once on base. The speed plays well in center, where his quick releases and quality angles help the glove threaten plus potential. His arm strength is above-average as well, opening the door to versatility all over the grass.

The Bad: There is very little power to speak of in Allen's game, as both his slight frame and swing mechanics conspire to leave him precious little ability to drive the baseball with any authority. His approach held up through an initial introduction to high-minors pitching last year, but the lack of power may eat into the hit tool after further exposure. He can struggle at times with initial reads in center, and while he'll generally show enough track-and-close to make up for it, there are still some raw edges there.

The Irrelevant: Allen was selected in the sixth round in 2014, one of six San Diego State Aztecs to hear their names called in the draft class. Last June's draft marked just the second time since 1971 that the school failed to produce a single pick.

The Risks: Allen boasts a deep box of tools, along with the baseball I.Q. to bring them to bear on the field. The lack of pop limits his ceiling, but the speed and glove combine with encouraging foundational skills in the box to make him a high-probability contributor at the highest level. He could force a call-up as soon as next summer if the on-base percentage continues to hold.

Major league ETA: Late 2017 —Wilson Karaman

Ben Carsley's Fantasy Take: You know how earlier I said McKenzie was on the short list of prospects who'd helped their fantasy stocks the most since the 2015 draft? Allen might lead that group. He's emerged from relative anonymity to hit well in the mid-to-high minors, and his speed and average give him two potential carrying fantasy tools. Ender Inciarte hit .291 with 16 steals, 85 runs and pretty much no power last season, and that was enough for him to finish as a top-50 OF option. Allen could produce similar numbers in his prime, and he's a valuable pop-up prospect for those of you who play in deep keepers where every (relatively) known prospect quantity was gobbled up long ago.

6. Will Benson, OF

DOB: 6/16/1998

Height/Weight: 6'5" 225 lbs.

Bats/Throws: L/L

Drafted/Acquired: Drafted 14th overall in the 2016 MLB Draft, Westminster HS (Atlanta, GA); signed for $2.5 million

Previous Ranking(s): N/A

2016 Stats: .209/.321/.424, 6 HR, 10 SB in 44 games at complex-level AZL

The Role: OFP 55—Three-true-outcome slugger who doesn't hurt you in the outfield
Likely 40—Strong-side platoon bat

YEAR	TEAM	LVL	AGE	PA	R	2B	3B	HR	RBI	BB	K	SB	CS	AVG/OBP/SLG	TAv	VORP	BABIP	BRR	FRAA	WARP
2016	CLE	Rk	18	184	31	10	3	6	27	22	60	10	2	.209/.321/.424	.285	10.3	.293	2.5	RF(39): -3.0	0.6
2017	*CLE*	*MLB*	*19*	*250*	*24*	*9*	*1*	*7*	*26*	*17*	*93*	*4*	*1*	*.189/.248/.323*	*.192*	*-10.7*	*.277*	*0.1*	*RF -0*	*-1.2*
2018	*CLE*	*MLB*	*20*	*336*	*38*	*13*	*1*	*11*	*38*	*25*	*117*	*6*	*2*	*.209/.272/.365*	*.217*	*-8.4*	*.294*	*0.4*	*RF 0*	*-1.0*

Breakout: 0% Improve: 5% Collapse: 1% Attrition: 4% MLB: 9% *Comparables: Nomar Mazara, Domingo Santana, Engel Beltre*

The Good: Benson is an enormous human being with potential for plus-plus raw power. He struggles to consistently tap into that raw power in games, but even when he shows glimpses, he can put the ball into orbit. He's athletic for someone his size and should be able to cover enough ground in a corner to avoid being a liability. His arm is average at present, but there's enough toolsiness with Benson where there could be room for improvement. He earned free passes at a solid clip in his debut, though it was certainly padded by AZL arms pitching around him.

The Bad: The lack of contact will need to be addressed in order for him to reach the highest levels. He lacks balance at the plate, and his long arms can get too far from the rest of his body, creating a long, loopy swing. Despite impressive athleticism, he still hasn't fully grown into his body, lacking commensurate coordination to control his quick-twitch movements.

The Irrelevant: Benson was committed to Duke before being drafted by Cleveland, and he was reportedly interested in trying to walk on to the school's basketball squad in addition to playing baseball there. Because "basketball is fun," he said, and when you're built like this, why not try?

The Risks: The sky is the ceiling for Benson, but if the hit tool never comes around, he's likely no more than a minor leaguer who puts fans in the seats by hitting baseballs over the fence. It's unlikely his defense will add significant value at any point in his career, so his bat will have to carry him.

Major league ETA: 2021 —Matt Pullman

Ben Carsley's Fantasy Take: Don't let the first-round pedigree fool you; Benson has a long way to go before he even flirts with being a fantasy factor. The tools are attractive and the upside is real, but unless my league rosters around 200 prospects, I'm waiting until the hit tool shows up in games before I take the plunge with Benson. Bret Sayre had him at 35 on his top-50 dynasty signees for 2016, but honestly, that says more about the paucity of impact talent this year than it does Benson.

7. Bobby Bradley, 1B

DOB: 05/29/1996

Height/Weight: 6'1" 225 lbs.

Bats/Throws: L/L

Drafted/Acquired/Bonus: Drafted in the third round of the 2014 MLB Draft, Harrison Central HS (Gulfport, MS); signed for $912,500

Previous Ranking(s): #5 (Org.)

2016 Stats: .235/.344/.466, 29 HR, 3 SB in 131 games at High-A Lynchburg

The Role: OFP 50—Average first baseman of the TTO variety
Likely 45—Second-division starter or lefty bench bat maybe if you aren't carrying 13 pitchers

YEAR	TEAM	LVL	AGE	PA	R	2B	3B	HR	RBI	BB	K	SB	CS	AVG/OBP/SLG	TAv	VORP	BABIP	BRR	FRAA	WARP
2014	CLE	Rk	18	176	39	13	4	8	50	16	36	3	0	.361/.426/.652	.369	19.7	.425	0.3		2.0
2015	LKC	A	19	465	62	15	4	27	92	56	148	3	0	.269/.361/.529	.314	28.1	.352	-2.1	1B(101): 4.8	3.5
2015	LYN	A+	19	9	0	0	0	0	0	1	2	0	0	.000/.111/.000	.089	-1.5	.000	0.0	1B(1): -0.0	-0.2
2016	LYN	A+	20	572	82	23	1	29	102	75	170	3	0	.235/.344/.466	.288	23.4	.293	0.2	1B(116): -5.6	1.8
2017	*CLE*	*MLB*	*21*	*250*	*31*	*9*	*1*	*13*	*37*	*25*	*90*	*0*	*0*	*.217/.299/.441*	*.245*	*0.7*	*.289*	*-0.3*	*1B -1*	*0.0*
2018	*CLE*	*MLB*	*22*	*430*	*61*	*17*	*1*	*23*	*65*	*44*	*152*	*0*	*0*	*.226/.311/.459*	*.253*	*1.5*	*.301*	*-0.9*	*1B -1*	*0.0*

Breakout: 4% Improve: 19% Collapse: 8% Attrition: 12% MLB: 34% *Comparables: Miguel Sano, Matt Olson, Travis Snider*

The Good: Power: You want it, Bobby Bradley has it. He is a big man with strong wrists and some serious loft. You could call it plus-plus raw and I couldn't argue. It's comfortably plus for sure. Ball go far, prospect status go far. Uh, how many more ways can we talk about the pop to stretch out this section? If he keeps hitting bombs, he will keep getting on base enough to buoy what's likely to be a below-average hit tool.

The Bad: You can't argue with the effectiveness of Bradley's swing (at least so far), but it's a weird little thing with a long, low load by his back hip. I suspect he will be vulnerable to better velocity above his hands, something he will see more of in Double-A, and he already expands the zone against A-ball spin. The profile could collapse if he is a .200 hitter at higher levels. He's limited to first base and not going to offer much defensively there.

The Irrelevant: Bradley's 29 home runs is the most by a Lynchburg Hillcat in the 2000s. Yes, I got tired of scrolling back year-by-year on baseball-reference.

The Risks: He may strike out 220 times a year...in Triple-A.

Major league ETA: Late 2018

Ben Carsley's Fantasy Take: I totally understand why Bradley ranks here, but there's an argument to be made that he's the third-best dynasty prospect in this system. The 30 percent strikeout rate is more than a little worrisome, as is the .235 average, but Bradley was just 20 for most of last season, and he did manage to walk a bunch and mash 53 XBH. The floor here is very low because it's entirely possible Bradley never makes it as an everyday starter in the majors. But the ceiling is pretty high, because 30-homer first basemen don't grow on trees. He's a top-100 guy, albeit barely.

8. Brady Aiken, LHP

DOB: 08/16/1995

Height/Weight: 6'4" 205 lbs.

Bats/Throws: L/L

Drafted/Acquired: Drafted 17th overall in the 2015 MLB Draft, IMG Academy (FL); signed for $2.51328 million

Previous Ranking(s): #2 (Org.)

2016 Stats: 7.12 ERA, 3.15 DRA, 24 IP, 32 H, 13 BB, 35 K in 9 games at complex-level AZL, 4.43 ERA, 3.23 DRA, 22.1 IP, 20 H, 8 BB, 22 K in 5 games at short-season Mahoning Valley

The Role: If we gave three grades—but who does that—we'd have to mention the possibility that Aiken regains some of his pre-draft velocity and is suddenly a premium pitching prospect. That is tough to project though, so instead we offer a very unconfident OFP 55—No. 3/4 starter
Likely 40—Middle reliever

YEAR	TEAM	LVL	AGE	W	L	SV	G	GS	IP	H	HR	BB/9	K/9	K	GB%	BABIP	WHIP	ERA	FIP	DRA	VORP	WARP	cFIP	MPH
2016	MHV	A-	19	2	1	0	5	5	22^1	20	3	3.2	8.9	22	43%	.266	1.25	4.43	4.26	3.23	5.00	0.5	94	
2017	*CLE*	*MLB*	*20*	*2*	*3*	*0*	*8*	*8*	31^1	*40*	*8*	*5.6*	*6.1*	*21*	*32%*	*.318*	*1.91*	*6.82*	*7.11*	*7.15*	*-5.9*	*-0.6*	*170*	
2018	*CLE*	*MLB*	*21*	*4*	*9*	*0*	*24*	*24*	142^2	*176*	*32*	*5.5*	*6.7*	*106*	*32%*	*.317*	*1.85*	*6.67*	*6.61*	*6.99*	*-16.2*	*-1.7*	*167*	

Breakout: 0% Improve: 0% Collapse: 0% Attrition: 0% MLB: 0% *Comparables: Jordan Walden, Bryan Morris, Wilking Rodriguez*

The Good: Well, Aiken is throwing again. That's a good thing. His curveball remained intact from his amateur days, and his command of the pitch didn't seem to wane despite the time off and rehab. His fastball regained some of its riding life as the year wore on and worked himself back into form, showing an improving ability to command the heater to all quadrants. The changeup fades on hitters and induces weak contact. Aiken's ability to sequence and command meant he was too advanced for short-season competition. He's filled out significantly compared to his pre-draft days...

The Bad: ...but that hasn't added any velocity. In fact, he's down a few ticks at present, and pitched mostly in the 88–92 range this summer. It's easy to abuse low-level hitters with sequencing and command, and it's worth noting even those batters tagged Aiken in his first season back. His change can arrive a bit firm in the mid-80s, though a tick up in fastball velocity could render that moot.

The Irrelevant: Aiken joined Danny Goodwin and Tim Belcher as 1-1 picks that did not sign.

The Risks: He's a pitcher with Tommy John on his C.V., who hasn't found the velocity he lost in the process. That he's added strength but still has not recovered all of his oomph removes one peg of optimism on which to hang our hats. The broad spectrum of skills and advanced pitchability lend some credence to his case (and some positive risk), but given that he's yet to pitch in full-season ball, caution wins the day.

Major league ETA: 2020 —Craig Goldstein

Ben Carsley's Fantasy Take: Soooooooooo remember those things we said about 2015 draftees? Perhaps none have fallen so far as Aiken, who's not a top-100 name at this point. The upside still remains if the velo comes back, but boy, that's a big if. He can be on your watch list, but I think he'll always be overrated in dynasty thanks to his draft pedigree/relative frame.

9. Yu-Cheng Chang, SS

DOB: 8/18/1995

Height/Weight: 6'1" 175 lbs.

Bats/Throws: R/R

Drafted/Acquired: Signed in June 2013 out of Taiwan for $500,000

Previous Ranking(s): N/A

2016 Stats: .259/.332/.463, 13 HR, 11 SB in 109 games at High-A Lynchburg

The Role: OFP 50—Average infielder...somewhere, probably not shortstop though
Likely 40—Fifth infielder

YEAR	TEAM	LVL	AGE	PA	R	2B	3B	HR	RBI	BB	K	SB	CS	AVG/OBP/SLG	TAv	VORP	BABIP	BRR	FRAA	WARP
2014	CLE	Rk	18	181	39	9	4	6	25	18	28	6	1	.346/.420/.566	.358	11.4	.389	0.8		1.1
2015	LKC	A	19	440	52	16	4	9	52	27	103	5	6	.232/.293/.361	.260	20.1	.288	2.8	SS(99): 11.2	3.3
2016	LYN	A+	20	477	78	30	8	13	70	45	110	11	3	.259/.332/.463	.285	35.1	.316	2.9	SS(104): 0.2	3.6
2017	*CLE*	*MLB*	*21*	*250*	*25*	*11*	*2*	*8*	*30*	*15*	*73*	*2*	*1*	*.224/.276/.392*	*.222*	*1.4*	*.284*	*-0.2*	*SS 3, 2B 0*	*0.4*
2018	*CLE*	*MLB*	*22*	*408*	*48*	*19*	*3*	*14*	*51*	*28*	*116*	*3*	*1*	*.232/.291/.415*	*.236*	*3.8*	*.291*	*-0.4*	*SS 4*	*0.9*

Breakout: 3% Improve: 7% Collapse: 1% Attrition: 8% MLB: 13% *Comparables: Nick Franklin, Trevor Story, Eugenio Suarez*

The Good: Chang's scouting report isn't going to be mistaken for an Iron Maiden hit single, but he has a broad base of offensive and defensive skills that should serve him well in the majors. He has a quick stroke and good enough pitch recognition skills to adjust to offspeed and drive it. There's some extra-base hit power here, although it may play as doubles over homers. He's a fluid defender with an above-average arm.

The Bad: Although reports on Chang's defense were better late in the season, his ultimate defensive home is ideally second or third. He has enough arm for the hot corner and enough athleticism for second, just not enough of either for short. There's some loft in his swing, but it won't be a traditional third base power profile...or a nouveau second base power profile. He might profile best as a 350 plate-appearance utility type.

The Irrelevant: There's a lot of Hillcats on this list, so it's not a huge shock that they won 84 games. Going to be tough to match the sustained success of the 1983-85 Lynchburg squad though. They averaged 93 wins as a Mets affiliate those years, peaking at 96 wins in 1983 on the back of a 100 BB/100 SB season by Lenny Dykstra and 300 strikeouts from Doc Gooden.

The Risks: Potential tweener skillset, no upper minors performance as of yet.

Major league ETA: 2018

Ben Carsley's Fantasy Take: Wait until Chang is more of a lock to remain at short or starts hitting better at higher levels (or both) before you show him a ton of interest. There's not really a carrying fantasy tool here.

10. Adam Plutko, RHP

DOB: 10/3/1991

Height/Weight: 6'3" 200 lbs.

Bats/Throws: R/R

Drafted/Acquired: Drafted in the 11th round in the 2013 MLB Draft, University of California, Los Angeles (Los Angeles, CA); signed for $300,000

Previous Ranking(s): N/A

2016 Stats: 7.36 ERA, 5.55 DRA, 3.2 IP, 5 H, 2 BB, 3 K in 2 games at major league level, 3.27 ERA, 2.12 DRA, 71.2 IP, 64 H, 12 BB, 63 K in 13 games at Double-A Akron, 4.10 ERA, 4.42 DRA, 90 IP, 87 H, 34 BB, 67 K in 15 games at Triple-A Columbus

The Role: OFP 50—No. 4 starter
Likely 40—No. 5 starter/swingman

YEAR	TEAM	LVL	AGE	W	L	SV	G	GS	IP	H	HR	BB/9	K/9	K	GB%	BABIP	WHIP	ERA	FIP	DRA	VORP	WARP	cFIP	MPH
2014	LKC	A	22	3	1	0	10	10	52^2	49	1	2.1	11.3	66	44%	.350	1.16	3.93	1.97	1.86	21.00	2.2	76	
2014	CAR	A+	22	4	9	0	18	18	97	99	11	1.7	7.2	78	33%	.306	1.21	4.08	4.00	4.67	10.00	1.0	97	
2015	LYN	A+	23	4	2	0	8	8	49^2	30	3	0.9	8.5	47	36%	.214	0.70	1.27	2.51	2.06	16.70	1.8	77	
2015	AKR	AA	23	9	5	0	19	19	116^1	96	9	1.8	7.0	90	31%	.256	1.02	2.86	3.37	1.95	40.70	4.4	87	
2016	AKR	AA	24	3	3	0	13	13	71^2	64	5	1.5	7.9	63	35%	.289	1.06	3.27	3.01	2.12	23.70	2.6	83	
2016	COH	AAA	24	6	5	0	15	15	90	87	8	3.4	6.7	67	34%	.293	1.34	4.10	3.97	4.42	9.20	1.0	106	
2016	CLE	MLB	24	0	0	0	2	0	3^2	5	1	4.9	7.4	3	23%	.333	1.91	7.36	6.65	5.55	-0.20	0.0	114	92.9
2017	*CLE*	*MLB*	*25*	*8*	*8*	*0*	*23*	*23*	*133*	*143*	*21*	*3.3*	*6.2*	*92*	*29%*	*.293*	*1.45*	*4.88*	*5.00*	*5.23*	*3.6*	*0.4*	*123*	
2018	*CLE*	*MLB*	*26*	*5*	*7*	*0*	*18*	*18*	*103^1*	*100*	*17*	*4.9*	*9.0*	*104*	*29%*	*.296*	*1.52*	*5.12*	*5.08*	*5.49*	*-0.2*	*0.0*	*128*	

Breakout: 19% Improve: 32% Collapse: 21% Attrition: 41% MLB: 58% *Comparables: Tyler Wilson, Tobi Stoner, Josh Banks*

The Good: Plutko has a collection of four average-ish pitches with pretty good fastball command. He carved up the Eastern League mixing a two-seam and four-seam fastball both of which sit in the low-90s, and a mid-70s curve that can miss bats when it is diving 11-5. He spots the fastball down in the zone well and has good feel for the breaker. The change is already an average offering with some depth to it, and Plutko is comfortable throwing it to both righties and lefties. He gets the most out of his repertoire by mixing sequencing and he has an ideal frame and delivery to start.

The Bad: There's no great shame in having a back-end starter rank tenth in your system. We can't all be the Braves after all. Plutko just isn't all that exciting. It's a collection of four average-ish pitches with pretty good fastball command. He didn't do quite as well against Triple-A bats. The curve might miss enough barrells to let him weave through a major league lineup multiple times, but those mid-70s big breakers don't always fool major-league hitters. The change is just average, and the slider exists primarily to show a different look or just sneak a strike.

The Irrelevant: Apparently it's pronounced "plett-KOH," which...yeah, okay fine. I can't really cast aspersions on how someone chooses to pronounce their last name anyway.

The Risks: Plutko has already debuted in the majors, so the risk here is that he has to nibble a bit more with average stuff, leading to more walks and home runs when he has to come over the plate. Also, he's a pitcher. They get hurt in the majors too.

Major league ETA: Debuted in 2016

Ben Carsley's Fantasy Take: It shouldn't be pronounced "plett-KOH." He shouldn't be on your dynasty roster.

OTHERS OF NOTE:

#11

Nolan Jones, 3B

A quality athlete who has already outgrown shortstop and showed signs of adapting quickly at the hot corner, Jones has a well-balanced profile despite lacking for a true carrying tool. A cold-weather kid, he didn't show innate bat-to-ball skills last summer, but he did show an advanced concept of the strike zone. The power didn't materialize during his debut, but there's clear room for him to put on muscle and address the lack of pop in short order. The hit tool is the big question mark here, but with a bit of development, Jones has a chance to turn into an everyday big league third baseman. *—Matt Pullman*

The factor on the farm

Yandy Diaz, 3B/OF

Ever-shortening major league benches have sent some classic MLB archetypes careening towards extinction. The pure pinch hitter is almost gone, as is the backup first baseman, the pinch runner/defensive caddy, and the third catcher that can play somewhere else. However if you can play all four corners and hit lefties, you will never want for work. I noted in our Eastern League preview that is was a little strange Diaz was sent back to Akron after raking there in 2015. So all he did was rake there again, and then rake in Columbus. The power is not really enough to start in a corner, and the Indians roster doesn't have an obvious fit for him outside of "break glass in case of Jose Ramirez injury," but there is always a role for an effective short-side platoon bat that can play four positions—okay he hasn't played any first base yet, but come on.

Whoa, Nellie

Nellie Rodriguez, 1B

This is a man who comes to the plate with bad intentions. There have been some first base prospects recently—Cody Bellinger and Josh Bell both come to mind—that are athletic players who could play further up the spectrum and have broad-based skills. Nellie Rodriguez is more of what we think of as a first base prospect, a hulking presence with big power and bat speed who goes up there to hit one a country mile with every swing. The rest of the game is a bit rough, but the power could play, and it'll be fun to see him try. Currently behind Bobby Bradley on the organizational depth chart, Nellie might beat him to the majors. *—Jarrett Seidler*

At least he's still left-handed
Rob Kaminsky, LHP

Hey, it turns out the Cardinals don't hit on every draft pick. St. Louis made what looked like a strange trade at the 2015 deadline, shipping their 2013 first-rounder off for a season-and-a-half of platoon corner bat Brandon Moss. The Cleveland prospect version of Kaminsky only bears slight relation to the preternaturally advanced prep lefty of draft time, unfortunately. His once impressive curve has flattened out. He'll throw a kitchen sink's worth of fastballs that go in all kinds of directions, but the velocity is mostly in the mid-high-80s and the command just isn't there. With a lower arm-slot and a curveball that's still enough to give same-side hitters problems, a LOOGY's career may now be what awaits. *—Jarrett Seidler*

The post-hype slee...uh, left field prospect?
Dorssys Paulino, OF

He's baaaaaack! Unfortunately for him, it's as an outfielder. 2012's wunderkind has been through it in the intervening four years, but he's still just 22 (how is he only 22???), and still shows the bat-to-ball that intrigued back when "Gangnam Style" was a thing. The problem is the power never truly developed and doubles pop is a tough profile for a starter in left field, even with Paulino's approach. If he can somehow start putting more balls over the fence, his OBP could push him to a low-end starter's role.
—Craig Goldstein

TOP 10 TALENTS 25 AND UNDER (BORN 4/1/91 OR LATER)

1. Francisco Lindor	6. Bradley Zimmer
2. Francisco Mejia	7. Juan Hillman
3. Triston McKenzie	8. Greg Allen
4. Jose Ramirez	9. Will Benson
5. Tyler Naquin	10. Bobby Bradley

This is the fifth straight year that Francisco Lindor has held the top spot on this list; barring anything disastrous, he should occupy it for two more years to come. And man, is it deserved. The current depth of shortstop talent across the league makes it difficult to anoint one player as clearly the best at the position, but Lindor's argument is just about as strong as any after his second year in the majors. While he's not quite as talented offensively as Carlos Correa or Corey Seager, he's still solidly above average at the plate and makes up for any potential shortcomings with his spectacular defense—courtesy of ridiculous instincts that make just about any play look natural and silky smooth. (He also bests Correa and Seager in all of the various defensive metrics, however much you want to consider those.) Regardless of whether or not he's the best, he's certainly among them, and one of the more exciting players to top an edition of these lists.

The other two big-leaguers on this list both enjoyed breakout seasons in 2016, but it's hard to imagine either continuing to be who they were at their best last year. Jose Ramirez was forced to convert to left field for much of the first half of the season, where he was adequate defensively and on fire offensively—he slashed .331/.393/.497 in the 48 games he spent there. His production wasn't quite as strong with his permanent move back to third base, but he can be a well-rounded switch-hitter who could be Cleveland's long-term answer at the hot corner. Even if the bat regresses, he's a nice utility piece. Tyler Naquin, meanwhile, went from boring fourth outfield prospect to candidate for Rookie of the Year. Though he'd never been known for his bat, he got himself noticed after being called up by hitting .343/.425/.731 through June and July. That didn't last, of course, and his future will more likely be as a platoon guy.

—Emma Baccellieri

COLORADO ROCKIES

The State of the System: *The Rockies system has thinned out at the top a little bit, but it's still chock full o' major-league-ready talent.*

THE TOP TEN

1. SS Brendan Rodgers	6. LHP Kyle Freeland
2. OF Raimel Tapia	7. RHP Antonio Senzatela
3. RHP Jeff Hoffman	8. RHP Ryan Castellani
4. RHP Riley Pint	9. RHP Peter Lambert
5. C Tom Murphy	10. 3B/1B Ryan McMahon

The Big Question: How Do Losers Win?

When you lose consistently as an annual rite of summer, you better have something to show for it. From 2011 to 2015, the Rockies averaged 69 wins a year [ed. note: nice] while finishing more than 24 games out of first in a given season of NL West baseball. The big club has won one playoff game in the last decade, since the 2007 iteration's magical run to World Series, and it has more recently stood idly by as California's perennial powerhouses have duked it out without much interference for divisional supremacy.

Internal inconsistencies in pitching development strategy, coupled with typical injury issues, left the team unable to properly feed a big-league rotation starved by deficiencies in the pool of amenable free market arms. Once the offensive foundations of the Series-running team dissipated, the club struggled to find enough scoring to overcome the lack of preventing that ensued.

The team has drawn well throughout their wander through the wilderness, routinely logging moderately above-average attendance figures in the 2010s. Despite years of predictable mediocrity, Coors Field is a fun park, the baseball's a little weird, and everybody digs the long ball. And for their troubles, Rockie fans were finally rewarded last season with glimpses of a homegrown return to greatness.

It turns out that Colorado has done a couple things well and consistently throughout those years of inconsistent product on the big-league field. The first is identifying solid high draft picks. They've had a keen run of success dating back to the aughts of identifying future major-league talent at the top of their drafts, and that is, really, a fine and underappreciated front office skill. Nolan Arenado (second-rounder in '09), Chad Bettis (second in '10), Tyler Anderson and Trevor Story (first-rounders each in '11), David Dahl and Tom Murphy (10th and 105th overall, respectively, in '12), and Jon Gray (third overall in '13) represent an overwhelming majority of a young core that at least looks the part. All were homegrown draft-and-develop arrivals to Denver.

The most recent drafts have moved into system cornerstone positions now with striking efficiency. Colorado's last three top picks—all top-eight overall picks in their own draft classes—now occupy the first, fourth, and sixth slots on our list. The club's three most recent second-rounders all made the cut, too. We know that somewhere around three in four first-rounders will make it to the majors, and it's a coin flip for second-rounders. Beating those odds consistently, and on a reasonably clustered debut timeline, is a strong recipe for success; and the Rockies appear to be cooking.

The second thing the Rockies have done well is spend money in Latin America. Rolando Fernandez has been with the organization since its Big Bang, and his international classes have produced great consistency on the Dominican academy mounds. Where once the department toiled in modest quarters, plucking needles out of discount bin haystacks, the budgets have been kinder over the past several years. Colorado has cracked the top eleven for international outlays in each of the past three completed signing periods, and they landed a strong Venezuelan class at initially unreported rates in the current one.

In the absence of happy endings at the highest level, the stellar domestic yin and international yang of the scouting department has been the story of this franchise in the current decade, and it makes for an exciting moment on the win curve.

—Wilson Karaman

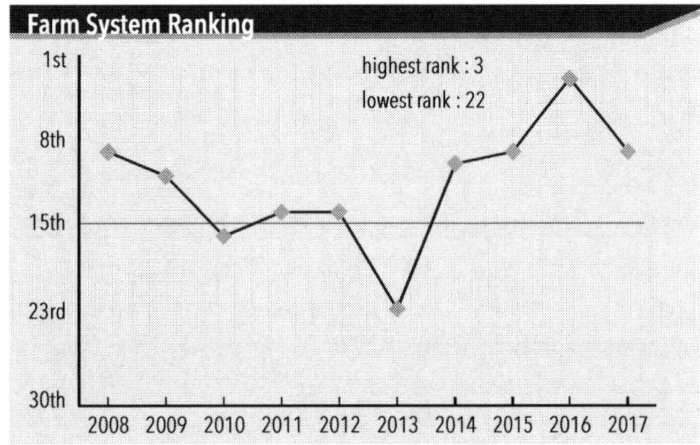

Personnel

General Manager:
Jeff Bridich

Senior Director, Player Development:
Zach Wilson

Assistant General Manager:
Zach Rosenthal

Manager:
Bud Black

BP Alumni:
Marat Biyashev

1. Brendan Rodgers, SS

DOB: 8/9/1996

Height/Weight: 6'0" 180 lbs

Bats/Throws: R/R

Drafted/Acquired: Drafted third overall in the 2015 MLB Draft, Lake Mary HS (Lake Mary, FL); signed for $5.5 million

Previous Ranking(s): #1 (Org), #20 (Top 101)

2016 Stats: .281/.342/.480, 19 HR, 6 SB in 110 games at Low-A Asheville

The Role: OFP 70—All-star shortstop
Likely 60—First division starter on the left side of the diamond

YEAR	TEAM	LVL	AGE	PA	R	2B	3B	HR	RBI	BB	K	SB	CS	AVG/OBP/SLG	TAv	VORP	BABIP	BRR	FRAA	WARP
2015	GJR	Rk	18	159	22	8	2	3	20	15	37	4	3	.273/.340/.420	.267	7.6	.346	0.5	SS(29): 9.8	1.7
2016	ASH	A	19	491	73	31	0	19	73	35	98	6	3	.281/.342/.480	.287	22.4	.319	-2.5	SS(56): -0.2, 2B(24): 0.9	2.5
2017	*COL*	*MLB*	*20*	*250*	*30*	*12*	*1*	*9*	*29*	*14*	*67*	*0*	*0*	*.242/.290/.419*	*.225*	*1.1*	*.296*	*-0.4*	*SS 1, 2B -0*	*0.2*
2018	*COL*	*MLB*	*21*	*356*	*45*	*18*	*1*	*14*	*48*	*21*	*96*	*0*	*0*	*.251/.303/.443*	*.250*	*7.4*	*.309*	*-0.8*	*SS 2, 2B 0*	*1.0*

Breakout: 3% Improve: 11% Collapse: 0% Attrition: 6% MLB: 14% *Comparables: Trevor Story, Alen Hanson, Addison Russell*

The Good: Asheville is a cozy place to hit—and a good BBQ and craft beer town—but Rodgers spent most of the season at 19 and continued to show the above-average hit and power tools that made him a top pick in the 2015 draft. The swing is simple, and Rodgers controls the barrel well. There's enough loft that as he gets stronger the ball should keep carrying over the fence even outside of the Appalachians. If he sticks at shortstop, the total offensive package here could make him a perennial all-star.

The Bad: So about that last part...Rodgers fits into the mushy middle category of "might stick at shortstop." There's enough arm so he could comfortably slide to third if need be, and he'll flash good enough infield actions that you don't have to squint too hard to see him as a passable major league shortstop. The glove is a work in progress though, and if he loses some range in his twenties, a corner may call.

The Irrelevant: Seven shortstops have gone third overall in the draft. Hall of Famer Robin Yount is the leader in the clubhouse, but Manny Machado may have something to say about that over the next decade.

The Risks: There's still a multi-year development horizon here and a reasonable chance he has to slide over to third, which would dampen the overall profile a bit.

Major league ETA: 2019

Ben Carsley's Fantasy Take: Rodgers would be a great fantasy prospect in any organization, but put him in Colorado and whoooo boy, we've got a dynasty gem. Sure, he isn't a total lock to stick at short long term, and he's not a total lock to hit for big-time power in a regular ballpark, but when you're talking about a floor as an infielder with a good bat in Coors, you gotta be excited. I think some are getting a little carried away with Rodgers in dynasty rankings—I won't put him over impact talent that's ready now—but he's a no-shit top-10 guy all the same.

2. Raimel Tapia, OF

DOB: 2/4/1994

Height/Weight: 6'2" 160 lbs

Bats/Throws: L/L

Drafted/Acquired: Signed by Colorado in November 2010 out of the Dominican Republic for $175,000

Previous Ranking(s): #6 (Org), #42 (Top 101)

2016 Stats: .263/.293/.263, 0 HR, 3 SB in 22 games at the major league level, .346/.355/.490, 0 HR, 6 SB in 24 games at Triple-A Albuquerque, .323/.363/.450, 8 HR, 17 SB in 104 games at Double-A Hartford

The Role: OFP 60—Above-average outfielder that challenges for batting titles
Likely 50—Second division starter in a corner that hits but doesn't give you much else

YEAR	TEAM	LVL	AGE	PA	R	2B	3B	HR	RBI	BB	K	SB	CS	AVG/OBP/SLG	TAv	VORP	BABIP	BRR	FRAA	WARP
2014	ASH	A	20	539	93	32	1	9	72	35	90	33	16	.326/.382/.453	.288	31.8	.383	3.1	LF(43): -5.4, CF(42): -3.1	2.1
2015	MOD	A+	21	593	74	34	9	12	71	24	105	26	10	.305/.333/.467	.317	47.6	.350	-0.7	CF(74): 2.1, LF(46): -0.4	5.6
2016	NBR	AA	22	457	79	20	5	8	34	25	49	17	14	.323/.363/.450	.287	25.2	.349	1.4	CF(60): 1.1, RF(22): 5.7	3.6
2016	ABQ	AAA	22	110	14	5	5	0	14	2	12	6	3	.346/.355/.490	.261	2.9	.379	0.0	CF(12): 2.1, LF(8): 1.2	0.6
2016	COL	MLB	22	41	4	0	0	0	3	2	11	3	0	.263/.293/.263	.191	-0.4	.357	1.2	CF(9): 0.1, LF(2): -0.2	0.0
2017	*COL*	*MLB*	*23*	*92*	*10*	*4*	*1*	*2*	*10*	*4*	*18*	*3*	*2*	*.284/.313/.428*	*.240*	*1.3*	*.330*	*0.0*	*LF -0*	*0.1*
2018	*COL*	*MLB*	*24*	*357*	*42*	*17*	*3*	*9*	*43*	*15*	*68*	*11*	*6*	*.287/.320/.443*	*.254*	*7.6*	*.329*	*0.7*	*LF -1*	*0.7*

Breakout: 3% Improve: 13% Collapse: 1% Attrition: 10% MLB: 24% *Comparables: Logan Schafer, Matt Szczur, Gary Brown*

The Good: Tapia's swing inspires the kind of prose usually reserved for describing a certain kind of temperamental Russian piano virtuoso. It induces a mix of awe, confusion, and defensiveness in the observer— what Alex Ross describes as "a furor." His two-strike approach, with a deep crouch that shrinks his strike zone and nearly folds his thin frame in half is a particularly daring interpretation of Rachmaninoff's third piano concerto. This is a blustery description for a potential 70 hit tool, but Tapia has always inspired such flights of fancy from BP prospect writers, and this will likely be our last chance to write about him in these spaces. There also isn't all that much to recommend past the hit tool. It's a really fun hit tool. Otherwise, he's an above-average runner and won't kill you in center field, and the approach at the plate has improved some over the years. He'll now lay off the occasional slider down-and-away, even if he is surely thinking to himself that he could hit it.

The Bad: Tapia's defensive profile fits best in a corner, and he's not going to provide the kind of power you want in that spot. He has plus bat speed, but there isn't much lift in the swing, so you are looking more at a 10-15 home run guy (before the Coors factor). His approach has improved, but he's still very aggressive once he steps in the box. He's been able to consistently make contact at every level so far because of his superior hand-eye coordination, but it's not all good contact, and there's a chance it ends up "less contact" against major-league arms. He may be the least instinctual runner I have ever seen, which makes his speed play down on the basepaths.

The Irrelevant: Tapia's lowest batting average at any minor league stop was .262 as a 17-year-old in the Dominican Summer League.

Major league ETA: Debuted in 2016

The Risks: Tapia already got a cup of coffee, and if he gets crowded out of the Colorado outfield this spring, he may hit .400 in Albuquerque, but if he even if he only hits .280 in the majors, he's just another second-division starter. The hit tool has to play to projection.

Ben Carsley's Fantasy Take: If you know anything about me, you know Tapia is exactly the type of prospect who's long seduced me. Oddly enough, crushing in Triple-A did little to change that. I understand that Tapia shouldn't play center, but that doesn't really matter for our purposes. Even if he "only" hits 15 homers a year, if he's hitting .300 I promise you won't really care. Tapia will be in my top-20 prospects. Honestly, I want to put him even higher. I love him. I miss Mau.

3. Jeff Hoffman, RHP

DOB: 1/8/1993

Height/Weight: 6'3" 185 lbs

Bats/Throws: R/R

Drafted/Acquired: Drafted ninth overall in the 2014 MLB Draft by the Toronto Blue Jays, East Carolina University (NC); signed for $3.0808 million, traded to the Rockies for Troy Tulowitzki.

Previous Ranking(s): #2 (Org), #24 (Top 101)

2016 Stats: 4.88 ERA, 6.27 DRA, 31.1 IP, 37 H, 17 BB, 22 K at the major league level, 4.02 ERA, 2.77 DRA, 118.2 IP, 117 H, 44 BB, 124 K at Triple-A Albuquerque

The Role: OFP 60—Power arm in the middle of your rotation that flashes more at times
Likely 50—No. 4 starter who shouldn't be as hittable as he is

YEAR	TEAM	LVL	AGE	W	L	SV	G	GS	IP	H	HR	BB/9	K/9	K	GB%	BABIP	WHIP	ERA	FIP	DRA	VORP	WARP	cFIP	MPH
2015	DUN	A+	22	3	3	0	11	11	56	59	4	2.4	6.1	38	53%	.329	1.32	3.21	3.70	5.48	-2.50	-0.3	100	
2015	NHP	AA	22	0	0	0	2	2	11^{2}	9	0	1.5	6.2	8	43%	.257	0.94	1.54	2.41	3.09	2.60	0.3	86	
2015	NBR	AA	22	2	2	0	7	7	36^{1}	27	3	2.5	7.2	29	58%	.242	1.02	3.22	3.74	3.18	7.70	0.8	85	
2016	ABQ	AAA	23	6	9	0	22	22	118^{2}	117	11	3.3	9.4	124	44%	.325	1.36	4.02	4.13	2.77	34.00	3.5	80	
2016	COL	MLB	23	0	4	0	8	6	31^{1}	37	7	4.9	6.3	22	51%	.297	1.72	4.88	6.31	6.27	-3.30	-0.3	114	96.8
2017	*COL*	*MLB*	*24*	*7*	*7*	*0*	*21*	*21*	111^{1}	*116*	*13*	*3.4*	*7.3*	*90*	*45%*	*.304*	*1.45*	*4.32*	*4.35*	*4.43*	*9.4*	*1.0*	*100*	
2018	*COL*	*MLB*	*25*	*10*	*10*	*0*	*30*	*30*	188^{1}	*158*	*19*	*4.4*	*10.1*	*210*	*45%*	*.318*	*1.32*	*4.02*	*4.06*	*4.39*	*20.5*	*2.1*	*99*	

Breakout: 26% Improve: 48% Collapse: 12% Attrition: 22% MLB: 74% *Comparables: Mike Foltynewicz, Marco Gonzales, Jon Gray*

The Good: Hoffman's arsenal can go toe-to-toe with any of the best pitching prospects in the minors. His fastball sits in the mid 90s, and he can sink and run the pitch. It can show explosive late life at times, and the velocity comes easily. The slider has passed the curve as his best secondary, but both are potential plus offerings. The slider has sharp two-plane break and he can spot or bury. The mid-80s velocity makes it potentially a true wipeout offering with a bit more refinement. The curve showed more inconsistent than it has in past seasons, but the best ones are 12-6 hammers with big, late downer action. The delivery and body both check the "starting pitcher" boxes.

The Bad: The change is just okay, firm at times, but projects as average with decent tumble. The bigger issue is the command is only average and that might not fly in Coors (though the baseballs will). We generally don't consider offensive environment for prospects—these evaluations happen in a vacuum—but Hoffman's fastball can be too much like the chateaubriand of heaters—center-cut—for any park.

The Irrelevant:

The Risks: Coors Field is a Catherine Wheel designed specifically to torture and break your pitching prospects, but Jon Gray had similarly big stuff and a similarly rough cameo and came out the other side as an above-average major-league arm. I'd expect Hoffman to do the same. The command does need to get better though or he may eventually be consigned to the back of the rotation or the bullpen.

Major league ETA: Debuted in 2016

Ben Carsley's Fantasy Take: Ah yes, the reverse Rodgers. If Hoffman was in (Chris Traeger voice) literally any other organization, he'd probably be a top-50 name. In Colorado he's still good enough to be a top-100 guy, but that maybe undersells the loss of impact potential here. In 14-to-16-team leagues, Hoffman can be started in good matchups on the road next season and maybe against, like, the Padres at home. But you need deeper leagues for Hoffman to have real value, and even then you'll need to be judicious about when you use him. He'll miss bats, though.

4. Riley Pint, RHP

DOB: 11/6/1997

Height/Weight: 6'4" 195 lbs

Bats/Throws: R/R

Drafted/Acquired: Drafted fourth overall in the 2016 MLB draft, St. Thomas Aquinas HS (Overland Park, KS); signed for $4,800,000.

Previous Ranking(s): N/A

2016 Stats: 5.35 ERA, 4.44 DRA, 37 IP, 43 H, 23 BB, 36 SO in short-season Grand Junction

The Role: OFP 60—Power arm in the middle of your rotation
Likely 50—"Effectively wild" no. 4 starter or late-inning arm

YEAR	TEAM	LVL	AGE	W	L	SV	G	GS	IP	H	HR	BB/9	K/9	K	GB%	BABIP	WHIP	ERA	FIP	DRA	VORP	WARP	cFIP	MPH
2016	GJR	Rk	18	1	5	0	11	11	37	43	2	5.6	8.8	36	60%	.383	1.78	5.35	5.46	4.44	5.3	0.5	104	
2017	*COL*	*MLB*	*19*	*2*	*3*	*0*	*9*	*9*	*34*^{1}	*41*	*6*	*3.9*	*7.5*	*28*	*47%*	*.357*	*1.64*	*5.08*	*5.25*	*5.54*	*0.1*	*0.0*	*129*	
2018	*COL*	*MLB*	*20*	*2*	*3*	*0*	*8*	*8*	*48*^{1}	*52*	*7*	*4.2*	*8.7*	*47*		*.345*	*1.54*	*5.04*	*5.09*	*5.50*	*0.2*	*0.0*	*127*	

Breakout: 0% Improve: 0% Collapse: 0% Attrition: 0% MLB: 0% *Comparables: John Lamb, Lance McCullers, Eduardo Rodriguez*

The Good: We're still waiting for the first prep righthander to go 1:1 in the MLB draft. Pint was the most recent Great Right Hope, mostly because he was touching 102. Yeah, that's the good stuff. He may end up with #thegoodstuff as he develops in the pros too. The triple-digit velocity readings may be only an occasional outlier, but his heater sits in the mid 90s, regularly touches higher, and moves enough to make it all shake out as plus-plus. He features both a slider and curve at present, and they can bleed together a bit. I prefer the slider, but these type of things can change rapidly with pro instruction. Anyway, there's enough feel here to project a plus breaker of some taxonomy someday.

The Bad: The changeup [flips through handy pocket book of prep pick changeup descriptors] "shows some promise." He didn't need it much as a high school pitcher in Kansas touching triple digits, so there's some work here to do, but he shows the right arm speed for it, and even now the pitch will flash with some fade. The bigger issue is the delivery is a bit of a project. It's drop-and-drive mechanics with various amounts of drop and drive pitch to pitch, and a fair amount of effort on every pitch. Again, pro instruction can change this, but it's easier to tighten up a curveball than it is to overhaul mechanics. Right now though, the command and control projections are below average.

The Irrelevant: Overland Park was the setting for the award-winning Diablo Cody/Toni Collette Showtime project, The United States of Tara.

The Risks: Pint is a high school pitcher with no pro track record yet, a rough delivery, and one and a half pitches. There's a lot of work to be done, so a lot of risk in the profile.

Major league ETA: 2020

Ben Carsley's Fantasy Take: So basically Jeff Hoffman, but far away? That won't cut it for us quite yet, although Pint should be rostered if your league holds on to 150-plus prospects. Hey, who knows, maybe he'll get traded!

5. Tom Murphy, C

DOB: 4/3/1991

Height/Weight: 6'1" 220 lbs

Bats/Throws: R/R

Drafted/Acquired: Drafted in the third round in the 2012 MLB draft, SUNY Buffalo (Buffalo, NY); signed for $454,000

Previous Ranking(s): N/A

2016 Stats: .273/.347/.659, 5 HR, 1 SB in 21 games at the major league level, .327/.361/.647, 19 HR, 1 SB in 80 games at Triple-A Albuquerque

The Role: OFP 55—Good everyday bat-first catcher
Likely 45—Good backup bat-first catcher

YEAR	TEAM	LVL	AGE	PA	R	2B	3B	HR	RBI	BB	K	SB	CS	AVG/OBP/SLG	TAv	VORP	BABIP	BRR	FRAA	WARP
2014	TUL	AA	23	109	16	4	0	5	15	14	27	0	0	.213/.321/.415	.261	3.8	.242	-0.6	C(23): 1.3	0.5
2015	NBR	AA	24	294	36	17	1	13	44	23	80	5	2	.249/.320/.468	.272	14.8	.306	0.1	C(58): -1.7	1.4
2015	ABQ	AAA	24	136	19	9	2	7	19	5	43	0	1	.271/.301/.535	.266	6.9	.350	0.8	C(27): -1.3	0.6
2015	COL	MLB	24	39	5	1	0	3	9	4	10	0	0	.257/.333/.543	.281	3.0	.273	0.5	C(11): -2.5	0.1
2016	ABQ	AAA	25	322	53	26	7	19	59	16	78	1	1	.327/.361/.647	.321	31.6	.386	-2.2	C(69): 2.1	3.5
2016	COL	MLB	25	49	8	2	0	5	13	4	19	1	0	.273/.347/.659	.290	2.8	.350	-0.7	C(12): 0.4	0.3
2017	*COL*	*MLB*	*26*	*393*	*52*	*20*	*3*	*21*	*60*	*25*	*119*	*1*	*1*	*.256/.309/.504*	*.262*	*18.7*	*.318*	*-0.5*	*C -7*	*0.6*
2018	*COL*	*MLB*	*27*	*438*	*61*	*23*	*3*	*24*	*70*	*29*	*133*	*1*	*1*	*.256/.311/.505*	*.269*	*19.1*	*.321*	*-0.6*	*C -9*	*1.1*

Breakout: 5% Improve: 21% Collapse: 12% Attrition: 30% MLB: 60% *Comparables: Tyler Moore, Zach Walters, Kyle Jensen*

The Good: There is serious pop at the dish here. Granted, the Rockies system doesn't lack for friendly offensive environments, but Murphy could hit a ball over the Sandia Mountains with some friendly tailwinds. Even at sea level, there is 20-home run power in the bat and even more in batting practice. Behind the dish, Murphy won't stand out in any one area, but he is an improved receiver with an above-average arm who should be a capable major-league catcher.

The Bad: There are serious hit tool questions at the dish here. Murphy likes to swing, and the power comes from length and strength. It's an offensive profile where things could go bad as he sees fewer mistakes from major league arms and the book gets out on him. Even if that doesn't happen, the hit tool still tops out at 40 for me, which will limit how much the prodigious pop gets into games while also limiting the ceiling.

The Irrelevant: While at SUNY Buffalo, I hope Murphy managed to take some classes with avant-garde film legend and drone music pioneer, Tony Conrad. The Velvet Underground stories have to be worth the tuition on their own.

The Risks: He's major-league ready and a safe bet to stick at catcher even if he isn't going to top our defensive leaderboards. There's a lot of swing-and-miss here though. If he hits .240, he's a nice starter. If he hits .200, well...

Major league ETA: Debuted in 2015

Ben Carsley's Fantasy Take: Murphy has gone from slightly underrated to slightly overrated in very little time. He's got the pop and home park to make him a potential big-time dynasty asset, but his glove won't keep him in the lineup, and his hit tool might push him straight out of it. He'll be a top-100 guy because fantasy catchers are straight garbage for the most part, but he's not necessarily a great long-term buy.

6. Kyle Freeland, LHP

DOB: 5/14/1993

Height/Weight: 6'3" 170 lbs

Bats/Throws: L/L

Drafted/Acquired: Drafted eighth overall in the 2014 MLB Draft, University of Evansville (IL); signed for $2.3 million

Previous Ranking(s): #9 (Org)

2016 Stats: 3.91 ERA, 3.62 DRA, 74.2 IP, 81 H, 19 BB, 57 K at Triple-A Albuquerque, 3.87 ERA, 3.78 DRA, 88.1 IP, 84 H, 25 BB, 51 K at Double-A Hartford

The Role: OFP 55—Mid-rotation starter
Likely 45—Backend starter for 150 innings a season

YEAR	TEAM	LVL	AGE	W	L	SV	G	GS	IP	H	HR	BB/9	K/9	K	GB%	BABIP	WHIP	ERA	FIP	DRA	VORP	WARP	cFIP	MPH
2014	GJR	Rk	21	1	0	0	5	5	17^1	16	0	1.0	7.8	15	0%	.333	1.04	1.56	2.82	2.71			79	
2014	ASH	A	21	2	0	0	5	5	21^2	14	1	1.7	7.5	18	52%	.220	0.83	0.83	3.08	3.53	4.60	0.5	91	
2015	GJR	Rk	22	0	0	0	2	2	7	2	0	2.6	11.6	9	64%	.143	0.57	0.00	3.29	2.83	2.40	0.2	87	
2015	MOD	A+	22	3	2	0	7	7	39^2	48	5	1.8	4.3	19	49%	.314	1.41	4.76	5.06	5.92	-3.70	-0.4	106	
2016	NBR	AA	23	5	7	0	14	14	88^1	84	9	2.5	5.2	51	53%	.268	1.23	3.87	4.41	3.78	12.90	1.4	102	
2016	ABQ	AAA	23	6	3	0	12	12	73^2	81	7	2.3	7.0	57	55%	.330	1.36	3.91	4.22	3.62	14.10	1.5	82	
2017	*COL*	*MLB*	*24*	*1*	*1*	*0*	*3*	*3*	*15*	*16*	*2*	*3.0*	*5.3*	*9*	*48%*	*.297*	*1.49*	*4.63*	*4.91*	*4.72*	*0.8*	*0.1*	*100*	
2018	*COL*	*MLB*	*25*	*8*	*11*	*0*	*30*	*30*	*188*	*181*	*22*	*4.2*	*8.1*	*168*	*48%*	*.320*	*1.43*	*4.66*	*4.70*	*5.05*	*8.5*	*0.9*	*118*	

Breakout: 17% Improve: 29% Collapse: 12% Attrition: 38% MLB: 51% *Comparables: John Gast, Simon Castro, Edwin Escobar*

The Good: Freeland's repertoire has the potential for an above-average four-pitch mix. Freeland's fastball sits in the low 90s. He sinks it from a low three-quarters slot with good/decent/solid command. The slider is the best of the secondaries, sitting in the upper 80s with late, cutterish movement. The velocity and late action make it a bat-misser. The change and curve both have a chance to be average or better. Freeland's an advanced arm who throws strikes and can throw good ones more often than not.

The Bad: There's some effort in the delivery and Freeland still has the same thinnish frame from draft day. He missed most of

2015 with bone chips and some shoulder "fatigue," so there are going to be durability questions even after a 160-inning 2016 season. The curve and change are potentially average or better, but fringy at present, with the curve more of a backdoor strike or chase pitch. The change doesn't have ideal velo separation, but he can sink it to either side of the plate.

The Irrelevant: The Purple Aces have produced five major leaguers. The best player was Andy Benes, but the best mustache was clearly Sal Fasano's.

The Risks: There's a checkered injury history. The frame and delivery may limit in-season durability as a starter. He needs a little more out of the secondary stuff to slot in the middle of a rotation. And even if that all works out, he's a pitcher.

Major league ETA: 2017

Ben Carsley's Fantasy Take: There are just too many negatives here. I want to believe, but injured + pitcher + Coors is a veritable Swiss slalom course of red flags.

7. Antonio Senzatela, RHP

DOB: 1/21/1995

Height/Weight: 6'1" 180 lbs

Bats/Throws: R/R

Drafted/Acquired: Signed by Colorado in July 2011 out of Venezuela for $250,000

Previous Ranking(s): #8 (Org)

2016 Stats: 1.82 ERA, 2.68 DRA, 34.2 IP, 27 H, 9 BB, 27 K at Double-A Hartford

The Role: OFP 55—Mid-rotation arm or low-end closer
Likely 45—Back-end rotation arm or good middle reliever

YEAR	TEAM	LVL	AGE	W	L	SV	G	GS	IP	H	HR	BB/9	K/9	K	GB%	BABIP	WHIP	ERA	FIP	DRA	VORP	WARP	cFIP	MPH
2014	ASH	A	19	15	2	0	26	26	144^{2}	134	11	2.2	5.5	89	47%	.267	1.18	3.11	4.19	4.73	11.50	1.2	108	
2015	MOD	A+	20	9	9	0	26	26	154	131	10	1.9	8.4	143	47%	.282	1.06	2.51	3.56	2.80	39.00	4.2	88	
2016	NBR	AA	21	4	1	0	7	7	34^{2}	27	1	2.3	7.0	27	44%	.265	1.04	1.82	3.13	3.68	5.50	0.6	94	
2017	*COL*	*MLB*	*22*	*1*	*1*	*0*	*3*	*3*	*15*	*17*	*2*	*3.4*	*5.2*	*9*	*38%*	*.296*	*1.55*	*5.29*	*5.11*	*5.35*	*-0.3*	*0.0*	*100*	
2018	*COL*	*MLB*	*23*	*8*	*11*	*0*	*29*	*29*	*180≤*	*174*	*28*	*4.7*	*8.3*	*167*	*38%*	*.313*	*1.49*	*5.30*	*5.36*	*5.71*	*-2.4*	*-0.2*	*136*	

Breakout: 9% Improve: 23% Collapse: 12% Attrition: 24% MLB: 48% *Comparables: Will Smith, Carlos Carrasco, Jake Buchanan*

The Good: Senzatela has a plus-plus fastball that he can dial up to 97 and will show good east-west life down in the zone. It could be a swing-and-miss pitch for him if the command tightens up due to the deception in his delivery. His slider flashes plus with late two-plane break in the mid-80s. He is a strike thrower who will go after hitters. He's able to find a little extra velocity and stuff when he runs into trouble.

The Bad: Senzatela had a bout of shoulder soreness early in the season and then didn't pitch at all in the second half. That's a pretty big red flag. His fastball velocity—and the stuff more generally—didn't hold up well past 50 pitches and lacks plane. Batters seems more comfortable against the heater than you'd expect. His change is firm and acts like a slower fastball. Will sneak a curve for a strike now and again, but he casts it in order to spot. The offering can bleed into the slider at times and both can get a little soft and slurvy. His arm action can be a bit mechanical and stiff, and Senzatela's uphill delivery has some effort, leading him to overthrow at times. So yeah, it's a fringy command profile.

The Irrelevant:

The Risks: He's an undersized pitcher with a firm change and now some durability questions as well. Even if he's healthy, might be bound for the bullpen.

Major league ETA: Early 2018

Ben Carsley's Fantasy Take: Maybe in a different org. Not in this one, though.

8. Ryan Castellani, RHP

DOB: 4/1/1996

Height/Weight: 6'3" 193 lbs

Bats/Throws: R/R

Drafted/Acquired: Drafted 48th overall in the 2014 MLB draft, Brophy Jesuit, (Phoenix, AZ); signed for $1,100,000

Previous Ranking(s): N/A

2016 Stats: 3.81 ERA, 3.39 DRA, 167.2 IP, 156 H, 50 BB, 142 K for High-A Modesto

The Role: OFP 55—Low no. 3 starter
Likely 45—Back-end starter

YEAR	TEAM	LVL	AGE	W	L	SV	G	GS	IP	H	HR	BB/9	K/9	K	GB%	BABIP	WHIP	ERA	FIP	DRA	VORP	WARP	cFIP	MPH
2014	TRI	A-	18	1	2	0	10	10	37	35	2	2.2	6.1	25	56%	.282	1.19	3.65	4.22	3.73	6.70	0.7	93	
2015	ASH	A	19	2	7	0	27	27	113^{1}	134	5	2.3	7.5	94	49%	.348	1.44	4.45	3.27	3.43	22.60	2.4	95	
2016	MOD	A+	20	7	8	0	26	26	167^{2}	156	8	2.7	7.6	142	55%	.302	1.23	3.81	3.61	3.39	38.80	4.0	89	
2017	*COL*	*MLB*	*21*	*8*	*9*	*0*	*25*	*25*	*128*	*168*	*19*	*3.9*	*4.9*	*70*	*44%*	*.351*	*1.74*	*5.43*	*5.34*	*5.78*	*-3.1*	*-0.3*	*139*	
2018	*COL*	*MLB*	*22*	*5*	*8*	*0*	*21*	*21*	120^{2}	*133*	*18*	*5.1*	*7.9*	*106*	*44%*	*.345*	*1.67*	*5.45*	*5.51*	*5.80*	*-2.7*	*-0.3*	*137*	

Breakout: 9% Improve: 11% Collapse: 6% Attrition: 18% MLB: 21% *Comparables: Will Smith, Tyler Danish, Wilfredo Boscan*

The Good: Castellani's fastball is the big-league kind, with plus two-seam movement and above-average velocity from his three-quarter slot. He generates quality life down in the zone and will cut the pitch for an additional weapon against left-handers. Both secondaries flash above-average, with the changeup running effectively off his fastball plane and the slider showing moderate two-plane bite. There's good baseline athleticism in his delivery, and a tighter arm action works fluidly in spite of some jerk. He has started filling out his 6-foot-3 frame to where he now looks the part of a durable innings-eater.

The Bad: The delivery features some drop and a drifting drive at present. He lacks pitch-to-pitch execution, as the slot wanders and he doesn't always get over his front side. The primary culprit is inconsistent timing; a closed-off landing leaves the glove-side command particularly dodgy, and his mechanics are such that this may be a persistent issue. Castellani's feel to snap off the slider comes and goes, and it's an unrefined pitch that he'll get around and roll. The raw pitch grades play down right now due to command questions.

The Irrelevant: The Castellani were an Iberian tribe that lived on the southern slopes of the Pyrenees around the second century B.C.

The Risks: Castellani has all of the ingredients to develop into a mid-rotation starter, and both the sinking action on his fastball and his secondary arsenal profile well for his potential future home. Last season was the first in which the organization's gloves came off, and he responded with nearly 170 innings of generally sound production. A chief concern about how well he ultimately harnesses and syncs his delivery makes for a wider range of potential outcomes, and that, coupled with the fact that at last glance he was a pitcher, makes him a higher-risk prospect.

Major league ETA: Late 2018 —Wilson Karaman

Ben Carsley's Fantasy Take: Maybe in a different org. Not in this one, though.

9. Peter Lambert, RHP

DOB: 4/18/1997

Height/Weight: 6'2" 185 lbs

Bats/Throws: R/R

Drafted/Acquired: Drafted 44th overall in the 2015 MLB draft, San Dimas HS (San Dimas, CA); signed for $1,495,000.

Previous Ranking(s): N/A

2016 Stats: 3.93 ERA, 2.79 DRA, 126 IP, 125 H, 33 BB, 108 K in Low-A Asheville

The Role: OFP 50—No. 4 starter
Likely 40—No. 5 starter/swingman

YEAR	TEAM	LVL	AGE	W	L	SV	G	GS	IP	H	HR	BB/9	K/9	K	GB%	BABIP	WHIP	ERA	FIP	DRA	VORP	WARP	cFIP	MPH
2015	GJR	Rk	18	0	4	0	8	8	31^{1}	29	3	3.2	7.5	26	54%	.263	1.28	3.45	5.17	3.59	8.00	0.8	98	
2016	ASH	A	19	5	8	0	26	26	126	125	7	2.4	7.7	108	47%	.324	1.25	3.93	3.31	2.79	31.20	3.4	90	
2017	*COL*	*MLB*	*20*	*5*	*6*	*0*	*17*	*17*	*80*	*105*	*15*	*4.0*	*4.9*	*44*	*36%*	*.344*	*1.76*	*5.92*	*5.96*	*6.36*	*-7.1*	*-0.7*	*153*	
2018	*COL*	*MLB*	*21*	*5*	*9*	*0*	*23*	*23*	*136^{1}*	*152*	*23*	*4.6*	*7.5*	*114*	*36%*	*.338*	*1.62*	*5.64*	*5.72*	*6.06*	*-6.0*	*-0.6*	*144*	

Breakout: 3% Improve: 5% Collapse: 2% Attrition: 5% MLB: 8% *Comparables: Casey Kelly, Michael Pineda, Michael Fulmer*

The Good: Lambert is a remarkably advanced arm for a 19-year-old. If I am mentioning command and changeup up here for a teenager, it will usually be something along the lines of "potentially above-average command" or [flips through handy pocket book of prep pick change-up descriptors] "shows some feel" for the change. But Lambert already shows above-average fastball command, and the changeup is his best pitch. He's confident enough with it to work backwards off the cambio, and it's been an out pitch for him in the low minors. The fastball sits in the low 90s, but it plays up at present due to his ability to spot it down in the zone to both sides of the plate. His delivery is repeatable and balanced throughout, and there are no red flags regarding his ability to start.

The Bad: The overall arsenal is only average. He may lack a swing-and-miss pitch at higher levels. The body is still immature, but significant stuff gains are unlikely despite some physical projection remaining. He may be what he is. Present-day fastball/change combo will be too much for A-ball hitters, but command will need to make the stuff play up at higher levels. The slider can miss barrels, but won't miss bats without more two-plane action. The curve is a loopy, show-me, steal a strike pitch that he casts.

The Irrelevant: San Dimas is named after Saint Dismas, who is not officially canonized by the Catholic Church, but is the "penitent thief" mentioned in the Gospels of Mark and Matthew.

The Risks: Lambert has the pitchability—and honestly the stuff as well—to not be too troubled by low minors hitters. There isn't much projection in the stuff though, despite his still being a teenager, so the command will really have to be plus for this to work at higher levels. And there is the matter of being a pitcher and whatnot.

Major league ETA: 2019

Ben Carsley's Fantasy Take: Probably not even in a different org.

10. Ryan McMahon, 3B/1B

DOB: 12/14/1994

Height/Weight: 6'2" 185 lbs

Bats/Throws: L/R

Drafted/Acquired: Drafted 42nd overall in the 2013 MLB Draft, Mater Dei HS (Santa Ana, CA); signed for $1.3276 million

Previous Ranking(s): #3 (Org), #34 (Top 101)

2016 Stats: .242/.325/.399, 12 HR, 11 SB in 133 games at Double-A Hartford

The Role: OFP 50—Average third baseman (for someone other than the Rockies?)
Likely 40—Corner infield bench bat

YEAR	TEAM	LVL	AGE	PA	R	2B	3B	HR	RBI	BB	K	SB	CS	AVG/OBP/SLG	TAv	VORP	BABIP	BRR	FRAA	WARP
2014	ASH	A	19	552	93	46	3	18	102	54	143	8	5	.282/.358/.502	.284	30.7	.360	-0.3	3B(118): 7.9	4.0
2015	MOD	A+	20	556	85	43	6	18	75	49	153	6	13	.300/.372/.520	.358	72.9	.401	1.5	3B(129): 25.2	10.6
2016	NBR	AA	21	535	49	27	5	12	75	55	161	11	6	.242/.325/.399	.265	14.7	.338	1.3	1B(67): -3.2, 3B(67): 5.9	1.9
2017	*COL*	*MLB*	*22*	*250*	*28*	*14*	*1*	*8*	*31*	*21*	*81*	*2*	*2*	*.244/.312/.426*	*.238*	*0.1*	*.338*	*-0.4*	*1B -1, 3B 3*	*0.3*
2018	*COL*	*MLB*	*23*	*397*	*49*	*21*	*2*	*14*	*50*	*32*	*128*	*3*	*3*	*.242/.309/.428*	*.249*	*1.8*	*.332*	*-0.6*	*1B -2, 3B 5*	*0.6*

Breakout: 2% Improve: 21% Collapse: 3% Attrition: 18% MLB: 36% *Comparables: Matt Davidson, Chris Carter, Alex Liddi*

The Good: Despite a down year statistically, McMahon still has the same potential plus game power we've raved about in years past. The swing can get a little long at times, but there is enough bat speed and leverage here to drive balls to all fields. He can handle premium velocity, and the ball jumps off his bat wherever—and this year whenever—he makes good contact. He's still a potentially above-average major-league third baseman, with soft hands, solid actions, and a plus arm.

The Bad: McMahon had a rough transition to Double A. The length and uppercut in his swing got exposed against better stuff and sequencing in the Eastern League, and too often his adjustment was just to drop his shoulder and swing harder. The approach has always been aggressive and there was always a risk the hit tool was going to be fringy, but McMahon looked particularly vulnerable against stuff diving down and away. The transition to half-time first baseman is a work in progress and he looked a little awkward around the bag. It looked better in Fall Ball—and he is athletic enough that he should be plus there in time—but the bat might be truly stretched at first base.

The Irrelevant: Like every other 2016 Yard Goat, McMahon played all 141 games on the road this year. Hopefully the club are Wyndham Rewards members, rated the best hotel rewards program by US News and World Report.

The Risks: The risk profile is a lot higher than it was at this point last year. Double-A can be tough. If he ends up a first baseman due to team need—though he is technically blocked there now too I guess—the bat-to-ball skills will have to get a lot better.

Major league ETA: Early 2018

Ben Carsley's Fantasy Take: Now is a good time to buy low on McMahon in dynasty, but there's a bit of a catch-22 here; if McMahon stays with the Rockies he won't be a third baseman, and if he leaves the Rockies, well, he won't be a Rockie. Still, given the paucity of decent 3B prospects in the minors and his proximity to the majors, McMahon is still a decent gamble.

OTHERS OF NOTE:

#11

German Marquez, RHP

Marquez had a quick rise through Colorado's prospect and organizational ranks in 2016. He made it all the way to Coors, but the stuff is a little short compared to, say, Senzatela's. There's similar profile problems too. His velocity comes a little easier but he sits 93-95 as a starter and doesn't hold it well in starts. The offering is pretty true out of the hand and lacks Senzatela's deception. It could sit higher in short bursts with more effort in the delivery. His breaker also flashes plus; it's an 11-5 downer curve in the low 80s. He gets tight break when he is on top of it, but it can show a bit of a hump out of the hand. His change is firm and he'll slow down his arm to try and turn it over. It's a major-league profile, but Marquez fits better in the pen, and it's not an impact arm there.

The "Lists Are Weird" Guy

Dom Nunez, C

So walk with me for a minute back in time, to a simpler time in December of 2014, when Nunez cracked the Rockies' top ten list with notes of cautious optimism about how the recent catching convert had progressed thus far and was likely to progress further. All he's done since is continue to address pretty much exactly what we suggested he needed to address: quality makeup has driven slow and steady improvement behind the dish, and after sluggish starts at each of his past two years his bat has grown successfully into his level, leading to strong second-half power displays in spite of in-season wilt. That he hasn't managed to reclaim a top-ten anointment is a fault of nothing beyond systemic depth. He lacks for impact tools, but he shows a broad skillset for a backstop, with proper physicality behind the dish and a solid-average arm. And in the box there are ingredients for an average hit tool and playable power not far behind. The 22-year-old still has a good bit of minor-league journey ahead, but he remains on track for a potentially lengthy big-league career. *—Wilson Karaman*

This Doesn't Look How We Thought It Would Look

Forrest Wall, 2B

Billed as one of the more advanced prep bats in the '14 class, Wall's skills in the box have yet to really begin coalescing, despite flashes throughout his at-bats. It's a viscerally appealing swing; he shows an ability to handle the barrel and get into the zone quickly and accurately, and the mechanics from trigger to launch are fluid and generally consistent. His timing remained an issue all season, however, and he struggled to sync the swing consistently to make quality contact against inner-third hard stuff or stay back against anything slower than fastball speed. There's little in the way of swing plane to lift and drive pitches, which puts further pressure on the contact skills actualizing. He looks to be a borderline plus straight-line runner, but the speed plays down on the bases. He posts 50/55 run times, and his breaks on stolen base attempts are still inefficient. The glove is the biggest question mark of all, as he struggled with game speed and fielding fundamentals at times last season. Despite the makings of above-average range and sound body control he doesn't always finish plays, and the arm strength is still on the fringier side for even second base after shoulder surgery several years ago. The club worked him out in center during instructs, and a transition may prove increasingly alluring if the inconsistency on the dirt continues. *—Wilson Karaman*

The Projection...All of the Projection

Pedro Gonzalez, CF

Gonzalez looked like one of the disproportionately elongated stick figures my four-year-old is fond of drawing when he signed a seven-figure deal at 16 a couple summers ago, but he has started to fill in his 6-foot-5 frame with some early man strength, and it remains to be seen just how much of it he'll eventually pack on. He's still long, and he's always going to be, but the body oozes athleticism and future strength that suggests plus power potential at full maturity. His swing is geared to take advantage of it, too, with quality bat speed and plane to drive pitches. It may take him a while to learn to corral it all, however, and the inherent length in his swing will be a battle he'll have to fight throughout his career. His future defensive home is up in the air, with a lot depending on his eventual size. After moving off shortstop and into center field last year, he may very well end up sliding over to right down the line, though early returns suggest he should wind up with plenty of arm for the position. The ceiling here is among the highest of anyone in the system if everything comes more or less together, but it's going to be a long, long time until we find out whether that happens. *—Wilson Karaman*

Steve's Guy

Colton Welker, 3B

The Rockies fourth rounder in this past draft, Welker hit for both average and power while showing off some of his defensive skills in Grand Junction. Welker has good bat to barrel skills, and showed a good eye in his initial foray. The power could be plus when it's all said and done, which pairs well with his plus profile at third base. A below-average runner now, Welker has good instincts and a quality first step and should be an average defender at his peak. A quality performance in Asheville next year could see Welker much higher on this list. *—Steve Givarz*

Wilson's Guy

Parker French, RHP

Let's start with the negatives, because they do exist: French's delivery isn't particularly fluid, with some effort on the way up, some stiffness coming down, and a sometimes-bumpy landing. The raw stuff is limiting in terms of the ceiling, with the lack of a true bat-misser front and center in holding down the OFP. But! Kid pitched very, very well this year in a very, very tough environment, and he was pitching better by season's end than he was pitching at season's beginning. He streamlined the delivery to generate greater repeatability and consistency, and in the process he gained a couple ticks of sitting velocity, up to 92-94 in his final start of the season with loads of sink and quality command down in the zone. The slider took a big step forward as well, as he added a harder cut variant that got up to 88 and showed potential as much-needed auxiliary help against left-handers. He controls the full arsenal, with projection up to plus and command not far behind. Double-A will make for an especially telling test, but he's an underrated arm on account of his boring profile, and one that can force eventual big-league utility with consistent progression. *—Wilson Karaman*

TOP 10 TALENTS 25 AND UNDER (BORN 4/1/91 OR LATER)

1. Nolan Arenado
2. David Dahl
3. Brendan Rodgers
4. Trevor Story
5. Jon Gray
6. Raimel Tapia
7. Jeff Hoffman
8. Riley Pint
9. Tom Murphy
10. Kyle Freeland

Nolan Arenado is eligible for this list by a couple weeks and makes for an easy decision at the top. He's one of the 20 best players in baseball, an elite defender at third with two 40-bomb seasons under his belt—and it's 30-home-run power anywhere on the planet—and should be the cornerstone of the next good Rockies team. He's also getting 30 million bucks for his Arb 2 and 3 seasons as a Super 2 and will eventually be in line for a nine-figure pay day.

There's no zealot like the convert, they say. I was the low man on the prospect team on Dahl heading into the season. He won me over when he flashed way more power for the Yard Goats this season than I'd seen in the past, though I still had questions about how the approach would work in the majors. It, uh, worked pretty well. He's still an aggressive hitter and there's going to be swing-and-miss in the profile, but he's going to do damage when he makes contact. Couple the power surge with strong defense at any of the three outfield spots, plus speed, and a plus arm and he's a no-doubt above-average regular for the 2017 Rockies. They just need make sure an outfield spot stays open for him.

The three through five rankings were tricky. You are balancing a top-tier shortstop prospect with two surefire 2017 major league contributors. Story could easily rank over Rodgers—and I suppose even Dahl—if you think his 2016 breakout is truly a new level of production for him, but his numbers away from Coors Field are very much in line with what I expected from him as a prospect. So considering the environment, you could argue Gray over the two shortstops based on "degree of difficulty" (and I wouldn't be surprised at all if he takes another small step forward this year and looks like the power number three starter we all expected). It's a tough balancing act, and I'd accept an argument for those three in any order.

—Jeffrey Paternostro

DETROIT TIGERS

The State of the System: *"It's another mediocre Tigers system, but they'll probably trade these guys for...oh wait, Dombo's gone. The righty power pitchers are still here though."*

THE TOP TEN

1. RHP Matt Manning	6. OF Jose Azocar
2. OF Christin Stewart	7. OF/3B JaCoby Jones
3. RHP Beau Burrows	8. RHP Spencer Turnbull
4. RHP Joe Jimenez	9. OF Derek Hill
5. LHP Tyler Alexander	10. RHP Adam Ravenelle

The Big Question: What did I miss on Michael Fulmer?

Michael Fulmer is not on this prospect list.

That was a reasonably predictable outcome at the beginning of the 2016 season. He was going to be assigned to Triple-A, but based on his 2015 performance in the Eastern League, it wasn't going to be a long stint. All he needed was a rotation slot to open up. The Tigers entered the season with both Shane Greene and Mike Pelfrey penciled in the rotation. And well…

It also wouldn't be a longshot to predict Fulmer having a successful rookie campaign. He was a Top 100 prospect coming into the year and had finally stayed healthy for a full pro season for the first time since 2012. The slider was in the process of beginning to jump—shocking for a Mets prospect I know—and the velocity was plus and he could reach back for more. It was major-league stuff, and he fit comfortably into that "mid-rotation starter or bullpen arm" bracket depending on the future command and change development.

It would have been tougher to predict his being one of the best pitchers in the American League. Well, at least I didn't. This happens, mind you. I wrote a lot of words about it this year already. This is the type of profile that when it does make good, well there are already a couple plus pitches in there, so the growth can be exponential. I know all of this of course. I just didn't think it would happen to Fulmer.

I can equivocate here. The advanced metrics think he was closer to a number three in 2016. But even if I grant myself that, essentially skipping Triple-A and being a major league three is better than what I expected from Fulmer in 2016, and there is growth potential beyond that. Why? Because I also missed on the stuff.

Specifically I missed on the change. I've written the equivalent of "needs to refine the change" roughly 50 times in this space over the last three months, and sometimes it is just a reps or comfort thing. It seemed to be the case for Fulmer, although he also mentions a slight grip tweak. "You can't teach spin" was a scouting aphorism long before the cargo cult around Statcast popped up. But you can always give a guy a slider or a cutter—which is more or less happened with Fulmer who came out of high school with one of the better curves among prep pitches. But there is more of a continuum with breaking balls. There are good sliders and curves, average ones, fringy ones. Ones that get slurvy, hooks from hell, humpy downers, back-foot behemoths, lollipops and slutters.

The changeup—especially among prospects—seems more like a binary proposition. You either have it or you don't. The latter group may occasionally show some feel for the pitch—another phrase I've regurgitated a few times this winter. But when you see a jump with the pitch, it's often because they were fooling around with a new grip or Johan Santana shows up on rehab and says "hey kid, try this." Perhaps Fulmer was a better candidate to figure it out because of his success with the Warthen slider, more of a grip/pressure pitch.

I also dinged Fulmer a bit too much for his issues staying on the mound in 2013 and 2014. There was a bone spur issue in there, but most of the time was lost to a torn meniscus he later tore a second time. He's a large human, so knee and back issues are worth keeping an eye on, but it there was nothing in there to suggest he was actually injury prone. He has the frame to log innings and despite the Tigers managing his workload down the stretch, there's no reason he can't be a 200-inning workhorse going forward.

Farm System Ranking

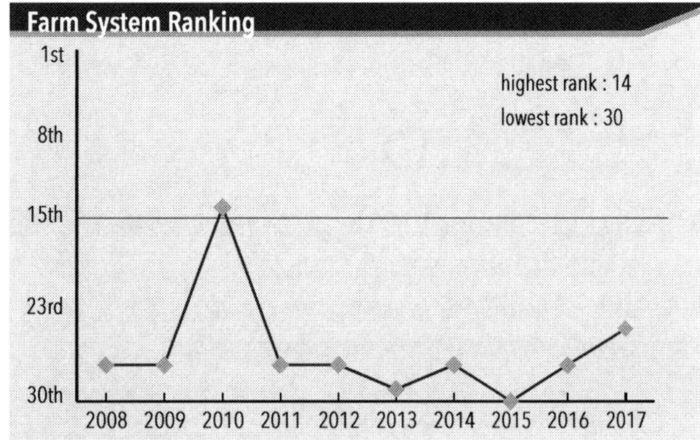

Personnel

EVP, General Manager:
Al Avila

VP, Assistant General Manager:
David Chadd

VP, Assistant General Manager:
John Westhoff

Manager:
Brad Ausmus

BP Alumni:
Andrew Koo
Nick Wheatley-Schaller

Well, he is still a pitcher I guess.

In the end it was a little too easy to pigeonhole Fulmer—and I missed seeing him by a day in the summer of 2015—and I allowed old looks and old prejudices against his health to moderate the very good reports I received. I'll equivocate one more time and suggest that number-three starters have number-two, or even ace seasons all the time. Sometimes it's a real jump and sometimes you are Rick Porcello or R.A. Dickey. But it sure seems like I missed something on Michael Fulmer.

1. Matt Manning, RHP

DOB: 1/28/1998

Height/Weight: 6'6" 190 lbs.

Bats/Throws: R/R

Drafted/Acquired: Drafted ninth overall in the 2016 MLB Draft, Sheldon HS (Sacramento, CA); signed for $3,505,808 million

Previous Ranking(s): N/A

2016 Stats: 3.99 ERA, 1.06 DRA, 29.1 IP, 27 H, 7 BB, 46 K's in 10 games at GCL Tigers

The Role: OFP 60—No. 3 starter
Likely 50—No. 4 starter

YEAR	TEAM	LVL	AGE	W	L	SV	G	GS	IP	H	HR	BB/9	K/9	K	GB%	BABIP	WHIP	ERA	FIP	DRA	VORP	WARP	cFIP	MPH
2016	TGW	Rk	18	0	2	0	10	10	29^{1}	27	2	2.1	14.1	46	38%	.379	1.16	3.99	1.88	1.06	15.20	1.5	66	
2017	*DET*	*MLB*	*19*	*2*	*3*	*0*	*9*	*9*	*32^{2}*	*38*	*6*	*4.1*	*7.4*	*27*	*46%*	*.318*	*1.62*	*5.49*	*5.41*	*5.80*	*-1.2*	*-0.1*	*136*	
2018	*DET*	*MLB*	*20*	*2*	*3*	*0*	*11*	*11*	*67^{2}*	*69*	*12*	*4.3*	*8.8*	*66*	*46%*	*.302*	*1.49*	*5.15*	*5.04*	*5.44*	*0.1*	*0.0*	*128*	

Breakout: 1% Improve: 1% Collapse: 0% Attrition: 1% MLB: 1% *Comparables: Jose Berrios, Roberto Osuna, Adalberto Mejia*

The Good: Manning has the look of a future top-of-the-rotation starter. He has the #goodstuff, including a potential double-plus fastball with above-average life. His steep downhill plane helps the pitch play up. His best secondary offering is the curve, showing 11/5 shape, plus depth, and sharp action. What impresses most is that he can locate the deuce for strikes at the bottom of the zone or bury it to finish off batters. His changeup shows potential due to his arm speed on the offering. All of this comes from a clean and easy arm action, with plus arm speed and a projectable body.

The Bad: While the delivery is clean, there is some effort to it and he can lose his release point from time to time. While it shows potential, the change is a clear third offering that doesn't project to more than average at present. While not skinny, he does need to add weight to his frame to hold up to a season-long workload.

The Irrelevant: We're obligated to show you this video of some of his high school basketball highlights.

The Risks: He's a pitcher...from high school...only one summer of professional baseball under his belt. Needs to add weight to his frame to handle a rotation workload.

Major league ETA: 2020 —Steve Givarz

Ben Carsley's Fantasy Take: If I've said it once, I've said it in at least 26 previous installments; if you're going to gamble on pitching, at least gamble on upside. Manning has plenty of it, and while the long lead time is a bit of a bummer, the potential for fantasy SP2/3 upside makes him worth the wait. He'll be a top-100 dynasty prospect, albeit one near the end of the list.

2. Christin Stewart, OF

DOB: 12/10/1993

Height/Weight: 6'0" 205 lbs.

Bats/Throws: L/R

Drafted/Acquired: Drafted 34th overall in the 2015 MLB Draft, University of Tennessee (Knoxville, TN); signed for $2.0645 million

Previous Ranking(s): #5 (Org.)

2016 Stats: .264/.403/.534, 24 HR, 3 SB in 104 games at High-A Lakeland, .218/.310/.448, 6 HR, 0 SB in 24 games at Double-A Erie

The Role: OFP 55—Bat-First Left-Fielder
Likely 45—DH/Platoon Hitter

YEAR	TEAM	LVL	AGE	PA	R	2B	3B	HR	RBI	BB	K	SB	CS	AVG/OBP/SLG	TAv	VORP	BABIP	BRR	FRAA	WARP
2015	TGR	Rk	21	26	5	2	1	1	2	3	5	2	1	.364/.462/.682	.401	5.1	.438	0.4	LF(6): 0.4	0.5
2015	ONE	A-	21	59	7	2	2	2	11	5	18	0	0	.245/.322/.490	.315	4.0	.313	-0.6	LF(13): -0.3	0.4
2015	WMI	A	21	216	29	9	4	7	31	18	45	3	2	.286/.375/.492	.316	15.9	.338	-0.5	LF(39): -6.5	1.1
2016	LAK	A+	22	442	60	22	1	24	68	74	105	3	1	.264/.403/.534	.323	32.4	.306	-6.6	LF(94): -15.8	1.7
2016	ERI	AA	22	100	17	2	0	6	19	12	26	0	0	.218/.310/.448	.275	4.1	.232	0.7	LF(22): 0.4	0.5
2017	*DET*	*MLB*	*23*	*250*	*31*	*9*	*1*	*12*	*37*	*27*	*74*	*0*	*0*	*.228/.326/.452*	*.263*	*9.1*	*.281*	*-0.2*	*LF -5*	*0.4*
2018	*DET*	*MLB*	*24*	*346*	*48*	*13*	*2*	*16*	*48*	*37*	*102*	*0*	*0*	*.228/.323/.442*	*.260*	*8.0*	*.285*	*-0.5*	*LF -7, RF 0*	*0.1*

Breakout: 3% Improve: 21% Collapse: 6% Attrition: 14% MLB: 48% *Comparables: Jerry Sands, Chris Carter, Joc Pederson*

The Good: Stewart has some of the biggest left-handed raw in the minors (okay maybe Bobby Bradley has more), grading out as an easy plus, if not more. It isn't just a batting practice show either; it can play to plus or better in-game. He has above-average bat speed with quick hands and is able to get extension to pair with his natural strength. While aggressive, Stewart does have a plan of attack and will work counts with the best of them.

The Bad: Despite the bat speed, Stewart's swing has length and he was exposed under the hands. A below-average runner, Stewart is more or less an adventure in the field as he struggles with reads and routes. His arm is below-average as well and, paired with his lack of range, could push him towards DH status sooner rather than later.

The Irrelevant: Stewart's HS alma mater, Providence Christian Academy, has Collin McHugh as the most notable baseball alumnus.

The Risks: His first go-around in Double-A wasn't the smoothest, and all his value is tied to his bat given his defensive status. His aggressive approach could be his undoing as he struggles to get on base.

Major league ETA: 2018 —Steve Givarz

Ben Carsley's Fantasy Take: Well, Stewart is close to the majors, at least. Personally I'm not a big believer in his bat, but the power potential is very real, and if he does end up as a platoon bat, at least he'll be strong-side. If you roster 200 prospects, Stewart should be owned. Mayyyyyybe even if you roster 150 prospects, but I wouldn't feel great about it.

3. Beau Burrows, RHP

DOB: 09/18/1996

Height/Weight: 6'2" 200 lbs.

Bats/Throws: R/R

Drafted/Acquired: Drafted 22nd overall in the 2015 draft, Weatherford HS (Weatherford, TX); signed for $2.154 million

Previous Ranking(s): #3 (Org.)

2016 Stats: 3.15 ERA, 6.06 DRA, 97 IP, 87 H, 30 BB, 67 K in 21 games at Low-A West Michigan

The Role: OFP 55—Mid-rotation starter
Likely 45—Backend starter or useful bullpen piece

YEAR	TEAM	LVL	AGE	W	L	SV	G	GS	IP	H	HR	BB/9	K/9	K	GB%	BABIP	WHIP	ERA	FIP	DRA	VORP	WARP	cFIP	MPH
2015	TGR	Rk	18	1	0	0	10	9	28	18	0	3.5	10.6	33	42%	.277	1.04	1.61	2.33	3.00	8.90	0.9	93	
2016	WMI	A	19	6	4	0	21	20	97	87	2	2.8	6.2	67	42%	.283	1.21	3.15	3.48	6.06	-11.50	-1.3	114	
2017	*DET*	*MLB*	*20*	*3*	*6*	*0*	*15*	*15*	*62¹*	*85*	*15*	*5.0*	*3.0*	*21*	*29%*	*.303*	*1.92*	*7.37*	*7.45*	*7.66*	*-15.2*	*-1.6*	*183*	
2018	*DET*	*MLB*	*21*	*4*	*9*	*0*	*21*	*21*	*126*	*151*	*28*	*6.4*	*5.8*	*81*	*29%*	*.301*	*1.91*	*7.22*	*7.09*	*7.50*	*-20.1*	*-2.1*	*179*	

Breakout: 0% Improve: 0% Collapse: 0% Attrition: 0% MLB: 0% *Comparables: T.J. House, Raul Alcantara, Jeurys Familia*

The Good: Burrows is the second, though far from the last, hard-throwing right-hander in the Tigers' Top Ten. Old habits die hard. He was as high as 97 this year in the Midwest League but more comfortably sits 92-94, where it is a heavy pitch with some arm-side run. Burrows has confidence to throw his curveball at any time, and it sits in the upper-70s and shows some hard 11-5 action. Despite perhaps not having ideal size for a starter, the delivery is clean and repeatable, and there's no mechanical bar to his sticking in a rotation.

The Bad: You'd think a pitcher with his stuff would miss more bats in the Midwest League, but the curve can be more pretty to look at than an effective bat-misser. It can also get slurvy at times and currently is a below-average offering despite an above-average projection. The fastball command is fringy and his velocity bobbed up and down throughout the year. The change has the right arm action and velocity separation, but lacks the movement to miss barrels at present.

The Irrelevant: Burrows will attempt to join Beau Allred and Beau Bell as major leaguers with his given name.

The Risks: He's a teenaged pitcher in A-ball who lacks a bat-missing option at present. Change and command need grade jumps to stay a starter.

Major league ETA: 2020

Ben Carsley's Fantasy Take: As mid-to-back-end starters who are many years from the majors go, I actually like Burrows a good bit. Unfortunately, he's still a mid-rotation starter who's many years from the majors. Put him on your watch list and see how he performs in the low-to-mid minors.

4. Joe Jimenez, RHP

DOB: 01/17/1995

Height/Weight: 6'3" 220 lbs.

Bats/Throws: R/R

Drafted/Acquired: Signed June 24, 2013 out of Puerto Rico as undrafted free agent for $100,000

Previous Ranking(s): #7 (Org.)

2016 Stats: 0.00 ERA, 1.06 ERA, 17.1 IP, 5 H, 5 BB, 28 K in 17 games at High-A Lakeland, 2.18 ERA, 2.30 DRA, 20.2 IP, 12 H, 8 BB, 34 K in 21 games at Double-A Erie, 2.30 ERA, 4.25 DRA, 15.3 IP, 9 H, 4 BB, 16 K in 17 games at Triple-A Toledo

The Role: OFP 55—Potential closer
Likely 50—Eighth-inning reliever

YEAR	TEAM	LVL	AGE	W	L	SV	G	GS	IP	H	HR	BB/9	K/9	K	GB%	BABIP	WHIP	ERA	FIP	DRA	VORP	WARP	cFIP	MPH
2014	ONE	A-	19	3	2	4	23	0	26^{2}	22	1	2.0	13.8	41	44%	.350	1.05	2.70	1.75	1.14	11.30	1.2	64	
2015	WMI	A	20	5	1	17	40	0	43	23	2	2.3	12.8	61	34%	.239	0.79	1.47	1.93	1.08	18.00	1.9	68	
2016	LAK	A+	21	0	0	10	17	0	17^{1}	5	0	2.6	14.5	28	36%	.179	0.58	0.00	1.23	1.06	7.70	0.8	64	
2016	ERI	AA	21	3	2	12	21	0	20^{2}	12	0	3.5	14.8	34	24%	.316	0.97	2.18	1.23	2.30	5.60	0.6	73	
2016	TOL	AAA	21	0	1	8	17	0	15^{2}	9	1	2.3	9.2	16	38%	.205	0.83	2.30	2.72	4.25	1.20	0.1	90	
2017	*DET*	*MLB*	*22*	*2*	*1*	*2*	*37*	*0*	*38^{2}*	*37*	*6*	*3.9*	*8.8*	*38*	*27%*	*.297*	*1.40*	*4.57*	*4.65*	*4.72*	*1.5*	*0.2*	*111*	
2018	*DET*	*MLB*	*23*	*2*	*1*	*2*	*40*	*0*	*45^{1}*	*37*	*6*	*5.1*	*11.3*	*57*	*27%*	*.289*	*1.39*	*4.48*	*4.38*	*4.63*	*2.1*	*0.2*	*108*	

Breakout: 26% Improve: 30% Collapse: 3% Attrition: 9% MLB: 35% *Comparables: Eduardo Sanchez, Alex Claudio, Joe Ortiz*

The Good: A large, physical pitcher, Jimenez's fastball is an easy 80, sitting 96-97 and touching 100 with ease. The pitch has plus boring action, eliciting ugly swings and weak pop-ups on a regular basis. He throws strikes and can spot it to both sides of the plate. His slider is also a plus-to-better offering featuring large break and depth. It has plus action with bite, and given its velo difference (85-86) off the fastball, it can be tough for hitters to time up. His low-three-quarters slot makes it tougher for right-handers to pick up the ball out of his hand.

The Bad: Jimenez does throw a lot of strikes, which is good, but he struggles to command his arsenal at times. He doesn't offer a changeup so he could be somewhat suspect against lefties down the road.

The Irrelevant: Jimenez didn't allow an earned run until his 27th appearance of the season.

The Risks: Tigers fans have seen this dance before with the likes of Bruce Rondon. He is a pitcher with a non-routine arm slot and could have problems at the big-league level unless his command takes a step forward.

Major league ETA: 2017 —Steve Givarz

Ben Carsley's Fantasy Take: Jimenez is either the best or second-best reliever prospect in baseball, depending on how you feel about Frankie Montas. He's not a top-150 dynasty prospect, though. Because he's a reliever.

5. Tyler Alexander, LHP

DOB: 7/14/1994

Height/Weight: 6'2"

Bats/Throws: R/L

Drafted/Acquired: Drafted 65th overall in 2015 MLB Draft, Texas Christian University (Fort Worth, TX); signed for $949,900

Previous Ranking(s): N/A

2016 Stats: 2.21 ERA, 1.69 DRA, 102 IP, 87 H, 16 BB, 82 K in 19 games at High-A Lakeland, 3.15 ERA, 2.88 DRA, 34.1 IP, 36 H, 4 BB, 23 K in 6 games at Double-A Erie

The Role: OFP 50—No. 4 starter
Likely 45—Back-end starter

YEAR	TEAM	LVL	AGE	W	L	SV	G	GS	IP	H	HR	BB/9	K/9	K	GB%	BABIP	WHIP	ERA	FIP	DRA	VORP	WARP	cFIP	MPH
2015	ONE	A-	20	0	2	0	12	12	37	17	3	1.2	8.0	33	67%	.151	0.59	0.97	3.27	2.25	12.40	1.3	76	
2016	LAK	A+	21	6	7	0	19	18	102	87	7	1.4	7.2	82	57%	.268	1.01	2.21	3.10	1.69	42.70	4.4	78	
2016	ERI	AA	21	2	1	0	6	6	34¹	36	4	1.0	6.0	23	49%	.302	1.17	3.15	3.97	2.88	8.40	0.9	94	
2017	*DET*	*MLB*	*22*	*6*	*6*	*0*	*20*	*20*	*93*	*105*	*13*	*2.7*	*5.1*	*53*	*48%*	*.298*	*1.44*	*4.82*	*4.83*	*5.00*	*4.9*	*0.5*	*118*	
2018	*DET*	*MLB*	*23*	*7*	*9*	*0*	*27*	*27*	*163¹*	*156*	*23*	*4.2*	*7.7*	*140*	*48%*	*.284*	*1.42*	*4.92*	*4.80*	*5.10*	*5.3*	*0.5*	*122*	

Breakout: 19% Improve: 33% Collapse: 3% Attrition: 25% MLB: 40% *Comparables: Edwin Escobar, Danny Duffy, Nick Tropeano*

The Good: Alexander might not overpower you with stuff, but he is a dang good pitcher. All of his pitches play up because of his ability to locate and command his arsenal. While his fastball has only average velocity, with average sink he can stymie hitters inside and under their hands. His changeup is an above-average offering because of quality arm speed and late, fading action. He isn't afraid to double up on it, or throw it to left-handed hitters. His slider should be average in the future given his feel and how comfortable he is throwing it.

The Bad: Alexander is maxed out, so he is what he is physically. This is a command-based profile and while he doesn't walk guys, he doesn't project to miss many bats in the future.

The Irrelevant: The Tigers drafted Alexander twice, previously taking him in the 23rd round in 2013 out of high school.

The Risks: He's a pitcher...we've seen lots of command over stuff guys struggle in the big leagues to miss bats and hit spots on a consistent basis. Still a fairly low-risk profile given his overall track record.

Major league ETA: Late 2017 —Steve Givarz

Ben Carsley's Fantasy Take: I ... I don't have anything here. I'm out of ways to say ignore back-end starters. Just do it. Just ignore them.

6. Jose Azocar, OF

DOB: 5/11/1996

Height/Weight: 5'11" 165 lbs.

Bats/Throws: R/R

Drafted/Acquired: Signed October 2012 out of Venezuela for $110,000

Previous Ranking(s): N/A

2016 Stats: .281/.315/.335, 0 HR, 14 SB in 129 games at Low-A West Michigan

The Role: OFP 50—Average center fielder
Likely 40—Extra outfielder

YEAR	TEAM	LVL	AGE	PA	R	2B	3B	HR	RBI	BB	K	SB	CS	AVG/OBP/SLG	TAv	VORP	BABIP	BRR	FRAA	WARP
2014	VTI	Rk	18	269	39	7	6	1	36	11	48	13	5	.340/.373/.428	.164	4.2	.412	1.8		0.9
2015	ONE	A-	19	24	1	1	0	0	0	1	7	0	0	.087/.125/.130	.105	-3.0	.125	0.1	CF(7): 1.3	-0.2
2015	TGR	Rk	19	211	29	10	5	0	29	7	31	6	4	.325/.350/.428	.285	11.7	.380	-1.3	CF(51): 6.4	1.9
2016	WMI	A	20	532	56	11	8	0	51	25	119	14	5	.281/.315/.335	.245	6.0	.366	1.4	RF(68): 3.5, CF(61): -5.4	0.4
2017	*DET*	*MLB*	*21*	*250*	*20*	*8*	*2*	*5*	*25*	*8*	*73*	*1*	*1*	*.225/.250/.338*	*.198*	*-7.6*	*.297*	*0.1*	*RF 0, CF -0*	*-0.8*
2018	*DET*	*MLB*	*22*	*305*	*30*	*10*	*3*	*6*	*30*	*10*	*87*	*1*	*1*	*.232/.260/.352*	*.211*	*-8.2*	*.303*	*0.1*	*RF 0, CF 0*	*-0.9*

Breakout: 3% Improve: 3% Collapse: 1% Attrition: 5% MLB: 5% *Comparables: Destin Hood, Socrates Brito, Avisail Garcia*

The Good: Azocar is a top-of-the-scale runner who can impact the game on the bases and on the grass with his speed. He has enough arm to handle right field if he ends up more of a fourth outfielder in the majors. The profile at the plate is rougher, but there's some projection here. Azocar generates above-average bat speed from a simple swing and could eventually grow into some gap power. Has the speed to take the extra base if that happens.

The Bad: With this kind of profile, you'd expect Azocar to be a high-contact, slap-and-dash type of hitter. That might be the end result, but at present he struggles with spin. If the hit tool doesn't continue to develop, it could be the death knell for the profile because there is well-below-average over-the-fence power here at best.

The Irrelevant: "Azocar" translates as "to pack tightly." Appropriate for the pint-sized outfielder.

The Risks: He was in the Midwest League and didn't hit much. He may not hit enough for more than a bench role, although most teams could use an 80 runner who can play all three outfield positions well.

Major league ETA: 2019

Ben Carsley's Fantasy Take: Azocar should be on every watch list because his speed will make him useful if the bat plays to the point where he can nab playing time. He's too far away to worry about right now, but pay attention to what he does once he gets to High-A.

7. JaCoby Jones, OF/3B

DOB: 05/10/1992

Height/Weight: 6'2" 205 lbs.

Bats/Throws: R/R

Drafted/Acquired: Drafted 87th overall in the 2013 MLB Draft, Louisiana State University (Baton Rouge, LA); signed for $612,000; traded to Detroit from Pittsburgh

Previous Ranking(s): #6 (Org.)

2016 Stats: .214/.214/.321, 0 HR, 0 SB in 13 games at major league level, .312/.393/.597, 4 HR, 2 SB in 20 games at Double-A Erie, .243/.309/.356, 3 HR, 11 SB in 79 games at Triple-A Toledo

The Role: OFP 50—A less athletic Keon Broxton
Likely 40—Useful bench piece that can fake some infield too

YEAR	TEAM	LVL	AGE	PA	R	2B	3B	HR	RBI	BB	K	SB	CS	AVG/OBP/SLG	TAv	VORP	BABIP	BRR	FRAA	WARP
2014	WVA	A	22	501	72	21	3	23	70	33	132	17	9	.288/.347/.503	.291	40.7	.352	5.7	SS(99): 4.1	4.6
2015	ERI	AA	23	160	26	7	2	6	20	17	52	10	3	.250/.331/.463	.282	11.4	.337	1.5	SS(37): 3.6	1.6
2015	BRD	A+	23	423	48	18	3	10	58	31	113	14	4	.253/.313/.396	.261	14.3	.330	-1.8	SS(84): 10.8	2.7
2015	ALT	AA	23	11	2	0	0	0	2	1	0	1	0	.500/.545/.500	.386	2.1	.500	0.3	SS(3): 0.2	0.3
2016	ERI	AA	24	89	11	6	2	4	20	10	23	2	1	.312/.393/.597	.338	9.2	.392	-0.3	3B(9): -0.5, CF(9): 0.8	1.1
2016	TOL	AAA	24	324	33	14	5	3	23	25	97	11	4	.243/.309/.356	.246	6.9	.349	1.8	CF(57): -6.3, 3B(22): -1.2	0.0
2016	DET	MLB	24	28	3	3	0	0	2	0	12	0	0	.214/.214/.321	.171	-1.2	.375	0.5	3B(6): -0.0, CF(5): -0.3	-0.1
2017	*DET*	*MLB*	*25*	*286*	*36*	*11*	*2*	*9*	*29*	*19*	*95*	*7*	*2*	*.224/.281/.389*	*.232*	*2.8*	*.308*	*0.6*	*CF 1*	*0.0*
2018	*DET*	*MLB*	*26*	*411*	*49*	*16*	*3*	*14*	*50*	*29*	*134*	*10*	*4*	*.234/.295/.408*	*.239*	*3.9*	*.319*	*1.0*	*CF 1*	*0.5*

Breakout: 8% Improve: 13% Collapse: 9% Attrition: 32% MLB: 37% *Comparables: Matt Den Dekker, Melky Mesa, Brett Eibner*

The Good: Jones has already spent some time in the majors and offers an intriguing power/speed combination on offense and the ability to play all three outfield positions plus the infield corners. He's an impressive athlete, a plus runner, and he'll show above-average raw power.

The Bad: Jones's swing is long and has exactly one gear, so strikeouts are likely to continue being a problem. He can be overly aggressive at the plate and you can beat him if you change eye levels. The hit tool issues may keep the power from playing in games. His speed plays better on the bases than in the outfield, where he's more "versatile" than "plus." He's playing less third base for a reason too.

The Irrelevant: Jones was also drafted out of high school by the Astros in the 19th round of the 2010 draft. Only one other draftee from that round made the majors, but it's a good one in Adam Eaton.

The Risks: I have no issue with a guy wanting to kick back, relax, and listen to a little Kyuss, but you may feel differently. More concerningly, Jones may never make enough contact against major league pitching. Enjoy Arby's.

Major league ETA: Debuted in 2016

Ben Carsley's Fantasy Take: If Jones gets routine playing time, his power/speed combo makes him a little interesting. Don't hold your breath for him to get said playing time, though; the strikeout issues are real. Hope that Jones blossoms into a low-average, double-digit homer/steal asset, but know that he's more likely to be left to those of you in AL-only formats.

8. Spencer Turnbull, RHP

DOB: 09/18/1992

Height/Weight: 6'3" 215 lbs.

Bats/Throws: R/R

Drafted/Acquired: Drafted 63rd overall in the 2014 MLB Draft, University of Alabama (Tuscaloosa, AL); signed for $900,000

Previous Ranking(s): #4 (Org.)

2016 Stats: 3.38 ERA, 3.78 DRA, 10.2 IP, 3 H, 5 BB, 7 K in 4 games at GCL Tigers West short-season Gulf Coast League, 7.36 ERA, 3.79 DRA, 3.2 IP, 4 H, 1 BB, 5 K in 2 games at GCL Tigers East, 3.00 ERA, 2.78 DRA, 30 IP, 24 H, 10 BB, 27 K in 6 games at High-A Lakeland

The Role: OFP 50—Eighth-inning guy
Likely 40—Sinker/slider middle reliever

YEAR	TEAM	LVL	AGE	W	L	SV	G	GS	IP	H	HR	BB/9	K/9	K	GB%	BABIP	WHIP	ERA	FIP	DRA	VORP	WARP	cFIP	MPH
2014	TGR	Rk	21	0	0	0	1	1	3	2	1	3.0	12.0	4	0%	.200	1.00	3.00	6.17	3.42			90	
2014	ONE	A-	21	0	2	0	11	11	28^1	31	1	4.4	6.0	19	68%	.347	1.59	4.45	4.15	4.30	3.30	0.3	101	
2015	WMI	A	22	11	3	0	22	22	116^2	106	0	4.0	8.2	106	53%	.314	1.35	3.01	3.10	4.41	10.60	1.1	103	
2016	TGR	Rk	23	0	0	0	2	2	3^2	4	2	2.5	12.3	5	50%	.250	1.36	7.36	8.49	3.79	0.80	0.1	98	
2016	TGW	Rk	23	0	1	0	4	4	10^2	3	0	4.2	5.9	7	69%	.115	0.75	3.38	3.41	3.78	2.30	0.2	97	
2016	LAK	A+	23	1	1	0	6	6	30	24	1	3.0	8.1	27	56%	.274	1.13	3.00	2.99	2.78	9.00	0.9	89	
2017	*DET*	*MLB*	*24*	*2*	*3*	*0*	*8*	*8*	*37*	*45*	*6*	*5.5*	*5.0*	*21*	*43%*	*.310*	*1.84*	*6.19*	*6.12*	*6.40*	*-3.8*	*-0.4*	*152*	
2018	*DET*	*MLB*	*25*	*6*	*10*	*0*	*26*	*26*	*154*	*167*	*25*	*6.4*	*7.6*	*130*	*43%*	*.308*	*1.80*	*6.01*	*5.90*	*6.21*	*-9.6*	*-1.0*	*148*	

Breakout: 1% Improve: 4% Collapse: 2% Attrition: 6% MLB: 6% *Comparables: Brock Stewart, Charlie Furbush, Jake Petricka*

The Good: Hey look, the Tigers have another hard-throwing righty in their top ten. Turnbull was touching the upper 90s late in starts in 2015, and despite an injury-plagued 2016, the velocity was back into the mid-90s in the AFL. It's a power sinker that he pairs with a potential above-average slider.

The Bad: He was limited to 50 innings in 2016 with a shoulder issue and then an oblique injury. The first one is going to concern us more down in this section. The curve and change lag behind the other two pitches, making him look more like a standard-issue right-handed bullpen piece given the durability questions. He's already 24 and hasn't pitched in Double-A yet.

The Irrelevant: I was going to make a reference here to the Robert Urich vehicle based on the Robert B. Parker novels, but apparently it was entitled Spenser: For Hire. This is some goddamn Berenstain Bears nonsense.

The Risks: He's a pitcher with a shoulder issue. You can fill in the rest of the section by this point.

Major league ETA: 2018

Ben Carsley's Fantasy Take: He's a pitcher with a shoulder issue. You can fill in the rest of the section by this point.

9. Derek Hill, OF

DOB: 12/30/1995

Height/Weight: 6'2" 195 lbs.

Bats/Throws: R/R

Drafted/Acquired: Drafted 23rd overall in the 2014 MLB Draft, Elk Grove HS (Elk Grove, CA); signed for $2 million

Previous Ranking(s): #2 (Org.)

2016 Stats: .266/.312/.349, 1 HR, 35 SB in 93 games at Low-A West Michigan

The Role: OFP 50—Average center fielder
Likely 40—Speedy bench outfielder

YEAR	TEAM	LVL	AGE	PA	R	2B	3B	HR	RBI	BB	K	SB	CS	AVG/OBP/SLG	TAv	VORP	BABIP	BRR	FRAA	WARP
2014	ONE	A-	18	78	8	1	1	0	3	2	26	2	1	.203/.244/.243	.178	0.0	.313	0.0		0.0
2014	TGR	Rk	18	119	12	2	2	2	11	16	19	9	1	.212/.331/.333	.242	0.0	.241	0.0		0.0
2015	WMI	A	19	235	33	6	5	0	16	20	44	25	7	.238/.305/.314	.258	7.6	.298	1.2	CF(51): 1.7	1.1
2016	WMI	A	20	415	66	17	6	1	31	24	105	35	6	.266/.312/.349	.263	17.8	.361	6.6	CF(54): -7.3, RF(33): 4.1	1.8
2017	*DET*	*MLB*	*21*	*250*	*30*	*9*	*2*	*5*	*19*	*13*	*75*	*12*	*3*	*.216/.258/.332*	*.203*	*-4.5*	*.290*	*1.5*	*CF -2, RF 2*	*-0.5*
2018	*DET*	*MLB*	*22*	*324*	*33*	*11*	*3*	*7*	*33*	*19*	*96*	*16*	*4*	*.222/.271/.353*	*.218*	*-3.3*	*.296*	*2.7*	*CF -2, RF 2*	*-0.4*

Breakout: 3% Improve: 3% Collapse: 0% Attrition: 3% MLB: 5% *Comparables: Xavier Avery, Abraham Almonte, Joe Benson*

The Good: In addition to the usual plethora of right-handed pitching, the Tigers org does not lack for speedy center fielders either. Hill isn't that dissimilar from Azocar. He's a plus-plus runner with a potential plus glove in center field. That's pretty good as future major-league floors go. There's above-average bat speed here. Coupled with a strong approach, he has a good chance to develop into a .260-.270 hitter with some on-base ability at the plate.

The Bad: Which is good, because developing at the plate is a bit of a must-have. He's never going to have much more than gap power. The hit tool only projects to average, which will be fine if it gets there, but there is more swing-and-miss than you'd like from this profile. Part of the issue might just be reps, as Hill's last two seasons have been marred by injuries.

The Irrelevant: Of the Tigers last twelve first round picks, Hill is one of only three non-right-handed pitchers, the other two being Christin Stewart and Nick Castellanos.

The Risks: Like Azocar, the defensive profile gives Hill a very good shot to make it to the majors even if he doesn't hit much. He'll have to hit some though. It's far too early to label him injury-prone, but lack of pro experience does factor in here too.

Major league ETA: 2019

Ben Carsley's Fantasy Take: Hill isn't an exciting fantasy prospect, but he's still probably the fourth- or fifth- fantasy prospect on this list. Like with Azocar, put Hill on your watch list and wait to see how he performs when healthy and when in the mid-minors. Don't let his first-round pedigree fool you into overpaying for him, though.

10. Adam Ravenelle, RHP

DOB: 10/5/1992

Height/Weight: 6'3" 185 lbs.

Bats/Throws: R/R

Drafted/Acquired: Drafted 130th overall in 2014 MLB Draft, Vanderbilt University (Nashville, TN); signed for $412,400

Previous Ranking(s): N/A

2016 Stats: 2.86 ERA, 3.23 DRA, 28.1 IP, 17 H, 17 BB, 34 K in 23 games at High-A Lakeland, 4.85 ERA, 7.36 DRA, 29.2 IP, 30 H, 16 BB, 23 K in 27 games at Double-A Erie

The Role: OFP 50—Eighth-Inning reliever
Likely 40—Middle reliever

YEAR	TEAM	LVL	AGE	W	L	SV	G	GS	IP	H	HR	BB/9	K/9	K	GB%	BABIP	WHIP	ERA	FIP	DRA	VORP	WARP	cFIP	MPH
2014	TGR	Rk	21	0	0	0	1	0	1	0	0	0.0	9.0	1	0%	.000	0.00	0.00	1.50	3.52			93	
2014	WMI	A	21	0	0	1	2	0	3	0	0	0.0	15.0	5	25%	.000	0.00	0.00	0.15	2.85	0.70	0.1	86	
2015	TGR	Rk	22	0	0	0	2	0	4	0	0	6.8	2.2	1	46%	.000	0.75	0.00	5.05	5.44	0.00	0.0	120	
2015	WMI	A	22	2	0	0	19	0	34^1	31	2	5.0	10.5	40	57%	.326	1.46	3.93	3.57	3.37	5.60	0.6	97	
2016	LAK	A+	23	2	1	3	23	0	28^1	17	3	5.4	10.8	34	57%	.219	1.20	2.86	4.24	3.23	5.80	0.6	93	
2016	ERI	AA	23	1	1	1	27	0	29^2	30	4	4.9	7.0	23	60%	.292	1.55	4.85	5.18	7.36	-8.70	-0.9	117	
2017	*DET*	*MLB*	*24*	*2*	*1*	*1*	*41*	*0*	43^2	*50*	*7*	*5.3*	*5.9*	*29*	*50%*	*.303*	*1.73*	*5.78*	*5.80*	*6.02*	*-5.7*	*-0.6*	*142*	
2018	*DET*	*MLB*	*25*	*1*	*0*	*1*	*19*	*0*	26^1	*27*	*4*	*7.0*	*8.4*	*25*	*50%*	*.306*	*1.81*	*5.85*	*5.73*	*6.09*	*-2.9*	*-0.3*	*143*	

Breakout: 2% Improve: 3% Collapse: 0% Attrition: 4% MLB: 4% *Comparables: Scott Oberg, Diego Moreno, Steve Edlefsen*

The Good: While Jimenez also has the #goodstuff, Ravenelle's isn't far behind. His fastball sits 95-98 and routinely touches triple digits. Paired with late movement it can be a tough pitch for batters to square up as he induces weak contact. His slider is a plus offering as well, coming in from 87-91 with sharp break and impressive cut/tilt action.

The Bad: The reason Ravenelle is down here instead of higher with Jimenez is that he doesn't throw strikes on a consistent basis. He routinely misses up with his fastball, and sometimes batters just wait for him to force himself into hitter's counts. The slider can be left in the hitting zone instead of burying it. He has a change but it's a distant third pitch, so it won't be part of his everyday repertoire. He has dealt with various injuries in his career.

The Irrelevant: It seems like we have ranked 30 former Vanderbilt players thus far; I exaggerate slightly but they are really good at producing talented players.

The Risks: He's a pitcher…with an injury history…who doesn't throw strikes on a consistent enough basis.

Major league ETA: 2018 —Steve Givarz

Ben Carsley's Fantasy Take: Ravenelle is a reliever, just like Jimenez. Do you see how under Jimenez I said that even the best (or second) best reliever is not a good fantasy prospect? Well, Ravenelle is a worse reliever prospect than Jimenez. That means, and stay with me here, that Ravenelle is also a worse fantasy prospect than Jimenez, which means that you should not roster Ravenelle, who is a reliever.

OTHERS OF NOTE:

#11
Kyle Funkhouser, RHP

I don't really want to talk about Funkhouser as a "cautionary tale" about pitchers in the draft or anything. So let's just focus on the prospect. He can get up into the mid-90s, but the fastball sat more 91-94 as a pro with some effort to get it to the top end of the velo. The curveball's ahead of the slider for now, although both can get slurvy at times. The change will flash. The story of Funkhouser's 2016 was inconsistency both in college and the pros. 2017 might bring some clarity after a full pro spring and an A-ball assignment. For now, he looks the part of a potential back-end starter, but a guy more likely to end up pitching in the middle innings of baseball games.

We'll always take a shortstop
A.J. Simcox, SS

Signed for $600,000 in the 14th round in 2015, Simcox was pushed aggressively to High-A in his first full season. A smooth defender at short, his plus arm pairs well WITH his smooth actions and quality footwork. Only an average runner, he has surprising lateral range to both sides and the body control to make the tough plays. At the plate, he has average bat speed to pair with his line-drive swing and is able to use the whole field. While he won't be much of an over-the-fence threat, he should be able to hit a fair amount of doubles. While not exciting, players who can play above-average shortstop defense will always be in high demand. *—Steve Givarz*

Dixon Machado, SS

Okay, it says something about the state of this system that I am writing about a guy the Tigers were so wary of playing that they traded for 2016 Erick Aybar—and previous to that were using Mike Aviles. Like Simcox, he's a good defender up-the-middle, and if he could hit even .260—despite well-below-average power—he would never lack for work. And he's done at least that each of the last three years in the minors. The vast majority of those at-bats came in the upper levels in leagues where he was age-appropriate for. I have been thinking a lot lately about how tricky it can be to throw a 5 hit on someone. With Machado though, there were always questions about how he would handle major-league velocity. Hit tool isn't just avoiding Ks, and Machado has never made enough quality contact even in the minors to make him more palatable than the Avileses and Aybars of the world.

The senior sign made good
Michael Gerber, OF

A 15th-round senior who signed for $1,000 in 2014, Gerber has shown that he can be a potential fourth outfielder on a big-league team. While his raw power is above-average, his other tools are around average but play up because of his instincts. He can play all three outfield spots and has the arm strength to cover them all as well. He does have a fair amount of swing-and-miss due to the length in his swing, which could limit his overall utility and point more towards a platoon future. *—Steve Givarz*

The guy who throws 100
Gerson Moreno, RHP

In a shallow system, you might as well just start listing plus shortstops and dudes with 80 fastballs once you get to this point. Moreno is a short right-hander and a reliever all the way, but he stopped throwing strikes once he got to Lakeland, which was always going to be a concern for a guy whose mechanics look like he's a position player called on to finish off a blowout, and whose release point is too often subject to Heisenberg's Uncertainty Principle. There's a slider in there as you'd expect. He snaps it off a bit, and it is really only a glove-side chase pitch at present. There's a late-inning reliever in here somewhere, and seems appropriate to end a Detroit Tigers list with one more righty power arm.

TOP 10 TALENTS 25 AND UNDER (BORN 4/1/91 OR LATER)

1. Nick Castellanos	6. Beau Burrows
2. Michael Fulmer	7. Joe Jimenez
3. Daniel Norris	8. Steven Moya
4. Matt Manning	9. Tyler Alexander
5. Christin Stewart	10. JaCoby Jones

It's become old hat to note the Tigers' moribund farm system, though there are signs of life with the addition of Manning, and the emergence of prospects like Stewart, Burrows, Jimenez, and several hard-throwing and/or tooled-up young Latin American players who are light years away. The Tigers have had a poorly-rated system since the days before they acquired Miguel Cabrera by shipping Cameron Maybin and Andrew Miller out of town.

During this extensive stretch of maintaining a barren farm system, the Tigers have been able to remain competitive thanks to a veteran roster built through trades and free agency, with the occasional player joining the roster in their prime; players like Justin Upton, J.D. Martinez, and lesser talents like Jose Iglesias and James McCann.

While the roster continues to age, the Tigers have expressed an interest in getting younger where they are able to manipulate the roster, and they have done that in part with a couple of prospects from their farm and through recent trades. While Castellanos has seemingly not met expectations to date, he showed tremendous strides in 2016 before hitting the shelf with an injury, and I remain among a cadre of scouts who believe the best is yet to come for the young third baseman. Castellanos' appeal centers almost entirely on his bat, but that bat offers a potential .300 hitter with 20-plus home runs annually, making him a middle-of-the-order threat yet to enter the prime of his career.

The reigning Rookie of the Year, Michael Fulmer was a revelation for Tigers fans last year, flashing electric stuff and the poise and intelligence to adjust throughout his rookie campaign. Even as the high man on Fulmer the last couple of years, I find myself tempering expectations heading into 2017, expecting more of a quality number-three starter than a burgeoning front-of-the-rotation workhorse. Fulmer is going to be a very good major-league pitcher for the foreseeable future, but he does not offer the upside of the potential All-Star third baseman.

Norris offers another high-ceiling arm at a young age, but his history of inconsistency leaves him short of the high-end potential his raw stuff suggests. As a left-hander with firm stuff, Norris could top Fulmer's contributions and value to the Tigers, but that will require an advance in his ability to harness his arsenal from start to start; a development I'm not willing to count on at this point.

For all of the warts on Steven Moya's profile, he still offers potential as a left-handed power bat on the big-league roster, and in a system this thin, that warrants discussion ahead of fifth starter candidates, utility infielders, and a host of raw, non-premium teenage talents. Moya shouldn't elicit much excitement at this stage, barring an unimaginable leap forward in his approach, but remains impossible to write off his ungodly power and the chance that plays enough to contribute in some fashion.

All told, the Tigers are teetering on the brink of "no man's land" where they aren't truly competitive in terms of World Series aspirations, but they have too many bloated contracts and aging talents to strip it down and completely rebuild the roster from the ground up. The gap in the minor league system—a gaping hole from High-A to Triple-A—lacks talent to help augment an expensive roster over the next year or two, leaving the club hoping they stay healthy enough to chase the Indians in the AL Central, but constantly seeking opportunities to move star players and remake their roster on the fly. It's an extremely difficult tightrope to manage, and with a limited track record at the helm, there's no way to know whether General Manager Al Avila is capable of keeping his balance.

—Mark Anderson

HOUSTON ASTROS

The State of the System: *"The Astros might lack for close-to-majors prospects, but they do not lack for prospects."*

THE TOP TEN

1. RHP Francis Martes	6. SS Miguelangel Sierra
2. OF Kyle Tucker	7. OF Ramon Laureano
3. RHP David Paulino	8. OF Derek Fisher
4. RHP Franklin Perez	9. OF Teoscar Hernandez
5. RHP Forrest Whitley	10. OF Daz Cameron

The Big Question: How do you convert minor-league talent into MLB production?

It's amazing how relatively quick the process of rebuilding can be if you commit to it—I mean, really commit to it—and the Astros did nothing if not jump in with both feet. Ownership slashed total payroll expenditures by 15 percent in 2011, then lopped another $17 million off the big-league bill in 2012 on the heels of finishing 40 games out. And then, The Great Bottoming Out in 2013: The franchise cut its big-league player budget by more than half and spent the equivalent of Jason Heyward's 2016 salary on its entire roster, losing 111 games for its trouble and securing its third consecutive top overall pick in the draft.

Broadly speaking, those three drafts (and a fourth in 2014 that included two picks in the top five) injected an absurd amount of talent into Houston's minor-league ranks. By 2013 the franchise cracked the top ten in our Organizational Rankings, and by the following season it was a top-five outfit even after graduating its top prospect from the winter prior. Organizational rankings of 12th in 2015 and eighth in 2016 ensued despite matriculating an absurd and steady stream of talent onto the major-league roster.

Houston added about $26 million in salary commitments last year, which marked a year-to-year jump of about 36 percent from the club's 2015 payroll. That was the second-largest increase of any franchise, behind only the eventual world champions. And the organization certainly hasn't been shy in furthering its financial commitments this offseason, with the additions of Josh Reddick, Carlos Beltran, and Charlie Morton in free agency and the assumption of the next two years of Brian McCann. The $53 million due to Houston's newest residents (plus $20-some-odd million in arbitration raises for a half-dozen existing players) more than offsets the approximately $34 million in free agent losses, and indicates where the front office views themselves on the win curve.

All of this is, of course, setup to the big question facing a team so positioned as these modern-day Astros: what exactly to do when the time comes to compete, and all you've got is this lousy T-shirt, a couple areas of your roster you'd like to strategically improve, and all these prospects stashed below your young core?

Well, we learned one answer with the Ken Giles trade last year. Fresh off the club's first playoff appearance in a decade, General Manager Jeff Luhnow shipped the organization's defending No. 2 (Mark Appel) and No. 3 (Vincent Velasquez) prospects, along with its reigning second-rounder, to Philadelphia in order to obtain just the kind of lockdown relief ace that would've really tied together an already stellar bullpen. It was an aggressive move to strengthen a strength, and while Giles' topline numbers didn't tell an awesome story, his peripherals sure did, and to the extent that the club's performance modeling was accurate, they have so far gotten what they paid for in that deal.

We got a couple more answers earlier this offseason, the first coming when the team exchanged pitcher Albert Abreu for McCann to plug its hole at catcher. This deal was a lower-fi affair—at least in terms of prospect portfolio carnage—on account of the fact that Abreu, while an enticing prospect, is an A-ball arm without an elite, "top prospect" ceiling. He's a solid-average headliner in a salary-acquisition deal such as this, and an encouraging marker of both systemic depth and baseline management aggressiveness.

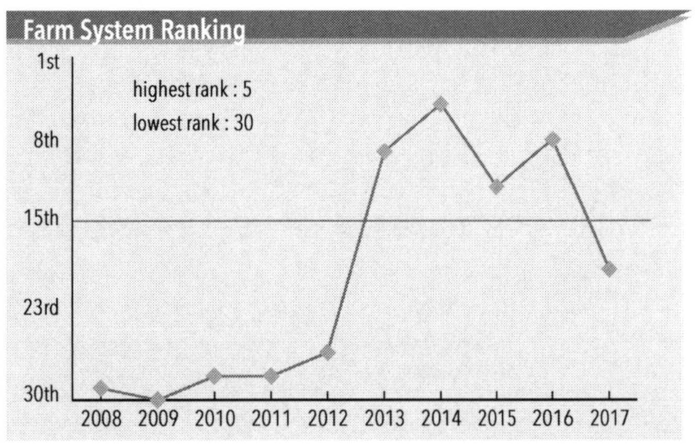

Personnel

General Manager:
Jeff Luhnow

AGM, Scouting and Player Development:
Mike Elias

Special Assistant, Process Improvement:
Sig Mejdal

Director, International:
Oz Ocampo

Manager: A.J. Hinch

BP Alumni:
Tucker Blair
Mike Fast
Kevin Goldstein
Ronit Shah
Colin Wyers

The second answer came when that same management reportedly refused to pony up a package of Joe Musgrove, Francis Martes, and Kyle Tucker (numbers five, six, and eight on the "25 and Under" list below) in a proposed deal with the White Sox for Jose Quintana. Mos Def once warned us that "when you push too hard, even numbers got limits," and this is perhaps an inevitable truth when prognostication is required for evaluation. But in long valuation terms the team may very well have been right to decline such a proposal. Or Quintana could go on to post three surplus WARP to the combined efforts of Musgrove and others occupying the rotation spot he otherwise would have filled. Or perhaps Musgrove himself will outperform a down year from Quintana. Or another, better deal for a starter will emerge later this offseason. Being the general manager of a baseball team, perhaps most especially one on the upside of the win curve right now, is hard. And it is harder still when you leave that question unanswered for another day: What exactly to do with all these prospects stashed below your young core?

—Wilson Karaman

1. Francis Martes, RHP

DOB: 11/24/1995

Height/Weight: 6'1" 225 lbs

Bats/Throws: R/R

Drafted/Acquired: Signed November 2012 by Miami out of the Dominican Republic for $78,000 traded from Miami to Houston in seven-player deal

Previous Ranking(s): #3 (Org.), #63 (Overall)

2016 Stats: 3.30 ERA, 3.72 DRA, 125.1 IP, 104 H, 47 BB, 131 K in 25 games at Double-A Corpus Christi

The Role: 70 OFP—No. 2 starter
60 Likely—No. 3 starter/first-division closer

YEAR	TEAM	LVL	AGE	W	L	SV	G	GS	IP	H	HR	BB/9	K/9	K	GB%	BABIP	WHIP	ERA	FIP	DRA	VORP	WARP	cFIP	MPH
2014	MRL	Rk	18	2	2	0	8	6	33	29	0	5.5	9.0	33	0%	.312	1.48	5.18	3.41	3.84			96	
2014	AST	Rk	18	1	1	0	4	3	11	5	0	2.5	9.8	12	0%	.185	0.73	0.82	2.41	3.62			97	
2015	QUD	A	19	3	2	2	10	8	52	33	1	2.2	7.8	45	48%	.229	0.88	1.04	2.78	3.39	10.20	1.1	92	
2015	LNC	A+	19	4	1	0	6	5	35	31	1	2.1	9.5	37	55%	.309	1.11	2.31	2.81	1.84	12.50	1.4	80	
2015	CCH	AA	19	1	0	0	3	3	14^{2}	19	2	4.3	9.8	16	30%	.386	1.77	4.91	4.32	4.42	1.10	0.1	102	
2016	CCH	AA	20	9	6	0	25	22	125^{1}	104	4	3.4	9.4	131	45%	.296	1.20	3.30	2.73	4.42	9.00	1.0	96	
2017	*HOU*	*MLB*	*21*	*5*	*6*	*0*	*27*	*16*	96^{2}	*103*	*13*	*4.3*	*7.3*	*78*	*40%*	*.304*	*1.54*	*4.81*	*4.83*	*5.55*	*-2.1*	*-0.2*	*128*	
2018	*HOU*	*MLB*	*22*	*7*	*8*	*0*	*27*	*22*	144^{1}	*133*	*21*	*5.6*	*10.0*	*160*	*40%*	*.301*	*1.54*	*4.54*	*4.80*	*5.24*	*2.7*	*0.3*	*120*	

Breakout: 9% Improve: 14% Collapse: 1% Attrition: 13% MLB: 18% *Comparables: John Lamb, Jameson Taillon, Carlos Martinez*

The Good: Martes boasts one of the better top-two pitch combinations in the upper minors, with potential plus-plus grades hanging on both his fastball and curve. Premium arm speed drives an explosive heater into the mid-90s, and he'll knock on triple-digit doors when he reaches back. The pitch has mild natural tailing action and excellent late life, and can miss bats in and above the zone. His hard curveball comes in at slider speed with tight rotation and late 11-5 break, and he has shown to be capable of working it in the zone to steal strikes or taking it below as a potent chase pitch. His firm change made strides with consistency, and flashes as a solid-average complement that works well off the fastball to generate grounders and moderate swing-and-miss.

The Bad: Martes was initially greeted rudely by Double-A hitters when he tried to throw everything by them and though he made strides in refining his approach, he's still transitioning from thrower to pitcher. He can get firm with his landing and jostle himself out of fine command, and his frame is higher maintenance with a thick middle. He's a couple inches shorter than ideal for a power righty, and the fastball can lose plane when elevated.

The Irrelevant: Martes burst onto the prospect scene after posting a 1.04 ERA in 52 innings at Quad Cities in his full-season debut. You know what else burst onto the national scene via the Quad Cities region? The damned railroad, that's what: in 1856 the Rock Island Railroad Company completed construction of the first trans-Mississippi River railroad bridge, connecting Davenport and Rock Island and opening up the west to modernized transit.

The Risks: After the initial adjustment period, Martes acquitted himself impressively as one of the youngest arms in the Texas League. Continued strides with the changeup and command quelled any notion of fast-tracking him as a potentially electric relief ace, though the potential remains as a fallback. Despite all of this, he's a pitcher, so...you know.

Major league ETA: Late 2017/Early 2018 —Wilson Karaman

Ben Carsley's Fantasy Take: Martes is one of my favorite fantasy pitching prospects, as he has the stuff to miss a ton of bats and is not terribly far away from reaching the Majors. I wish he had a better chance of remaining a starter, sure, but the upside he can reach if he's able to do so is very tempting. If it all clicks for Martes, I think we could be looking at a Carlos Carrasco-type weapon and a top-30 fantasy starter. If he falls to the bullpen, he'd be an elite option if he closes. He's the type of dynasty pitcher worth investing in.

2. Kyle Tucker, OF

DOB: 01/17/1997

Height/Weight: 6'4" 195 lbs.

Bats/Throws: L/L

Drafted/Acquired: Drafted fifth overall in the 2015 MLB Draft, Plant HS (Tampa, FL); signed for $4 million

Previous Ranking(s): No. 5 (Org.), no. 93 (Overall)

2016 Stats: .339/.435/.661, 6 HR, 31 SB in 16 games at High-A Lancaster, .276/.348/.402, 3 HR, 1 SB in 101 games at Low-A Quad Cities

The Role: OFP 60—First-division right fielder
Likely 55—Above-average regular

YEAR	TEAM	LVL	AGE	PA	R	2B	3B	HR	RBI	BB	K	SB	CS	AVG/OBP/SLG	TAv	VORP	BABIP	BRR	FRAA	WARP
2015	AST	Rk	18	133	19	3	2	2	13	9	14	4	2	.208/.267/.317	.251	4.4	.219	3.4	RF(17): -2.2, CF(4): 0.7	0.3
2015	GRV	Rk	18	121	11	9	0	1	20	7	15	14	2	.286/.322/.393	.259	2.7	.316	0.6	RF(26): 3.6, CF(1): -0.1	0.6
2016	QUD	A	19	428	43	19	5	6	56	40	75	31	9	.276/.348/.402	.281	20.6	.322	1.3	CF(61): -6.1, LF(17): -0.5	1.8
2016	LNC	A+	19	69	13	6	2	3	13	10	6	1	3	.339/.435/.661	.347	8.0	.340	0.2	RF(6): -0.3, LF(4): 0.1	0.8
2017	*HOU*	*MLB*	*20*	*250*	*28*	*10*	*2*	*6*	*26*	*17*	*62*	*8*	*4*	*.226/.284/.369*	*.229*	*1.4*	*.277*	*0.3*	*CF -2, LF 0*	*0.0*
2018	*HOU*	*MLB*	*21*	*389*	*44*	*17*	*3*	*11*	*43*	*29*	*90*	*13*	*6*	*.235/.296/.388*	*.242*	*4.2*	*.283*	*1.2*	*CF -3, LF 0*	*0.2*

Breakout: 2% Improve: 12% Collapse: 0% Attrition: 4% MLB: 14% *Comparables: Cedric Hunter, Jose Tabata, Anthony Gose*

The Good: Tucker is an advanced hitter, with an old-school setup that relies on a lower hand position at launch and strong wrists to snap the barrel onto plane early and hold it for a long time through the hitting zone. He covers both sides of the plate well despite long limbs, and the hips work well to help him generate bat speed and the plane to drive pitches. He's an instinctual base runner who gets quality reads and gets up to speed quickly, and he's a high-effort player in the field who gets quality reads on contact from anywhere in the outfield. The arm is adequate for right, which is his most likely ultimate landing spot.

The Bad: There is still a significant amount of projection to what his offensive game will ultimately look like, largely on account of his body and questions about how it will fill out. He tends to default to a handsier, one-piece swing at present, and while there is loads of room to add strength, his sloped shoulders and narrower frame leave open the question as to just how much bulk and raw power he'll ultimately develop. The game power should have no trouble reaching at least average at maturity, but how far above that it creeps will have the final say on what the role ceiling ultimately looks like. He's more of an average runner at present, and while his instincts should help him retain most of his defensive and baserunning value, neither is likely to remain a true asset if he does max out physically.

The Irrelevant: Both Kyle and his older brother (and fellow Astro) Preston share an alma mater with Hall of Famer Wade Boggs, one of the great beer drinkers of this or any other era.

The Risks: Tucker succeeded in his full-season debut, culminating with an outstanding 20-game run at High-A to close the year. There are multiple avenues for him to travel en route to creating big-league value, and the tools are wide and deep enough that whatever the ultimate formula looks like has a good chance of adding up to an above-average regular. The gap remaining between his present and projected versions is enough to keep him in a higher-risk bucket, but he has the talent to close that gap in a hurry next season.

Major league ETA: 2018 —Wilson Karaman

Ben Carsley's Fantasy Take: I like gambling on players with Tucker's skillset, but he's a bit rawer than I prefer (says the Nick Williams fan with a straight face) and I'm worried the power/speed combo is more solid than special. That being said, Tucker has moved into the mid-minors and no one really doubts his hit tool, so that's good enough for me. Hope he develops into Hunter Pence and be happy if he develops into Stephen Piscotty.

3. David Paulino, RHP

DOB: 02/06/1994

Height/Weight: 6'7" 215 lbs.

Bats/Throws: R/R

Drafted/Acquired: Signed September 2010 by Detroit out of the Dominican Republic for $75,000; traded from Detroit to Houston for Jose Veras

Previous Ranking(s): No. 9 (Org.)

2016 Stats: 5.14 ERA, 6.31 DRA, 7 IP, 6 H, 3 BB, 2 K in 3 games at major league level, 0.75 ERA, 2.42 K in 14 games at Double-A Corpus Christi, 3.86 ERA, 2.33 DRA, 14 IP, 16 H, 6 BB, 20 K in 3 games at Triple-A Fresno

The Role: OFP 60—No. 3 starter
Likely 50—High-strikeout no. 4 starter

YEAR	TEAM	LVL	AGE	W	L	SV	G	GS	IP	H	HR	BB/9	K/9	K	GB%	BABIP	WHIP	ERA	FIP	DRA	VORP	WARP	cFIP	MPH
2015	TCV	A-	21	1	0	0	2	2	9^{1}	4	0	1.9	9.6	10	59%	.182	0.64	0.00	2.01	2.80	2.60	0.3	86	
2015	QUD	A	21	3	2	0	5	5	28^{2}	21	0	2.2	10.0	32	47%	.292	0.98	1.57	2.00	2.04	10.10	1.1	80	
2015	LNC	A+	21	1	1	1	6	5	29^{1}	24	1	3.1	9.2	30	40%	.295	1.16	4.91	3.40	4.67	1.20	0.1	99	
2016	AST	Rk	22	0	0	0	3	3	12	9	0	1.5	10.5	14	75%	.281	0.92	0.75	1.48	2.14	4.80	0.5	81	
2016	CCH	AA	22	5	2	1	14	9	64	47	3	1.5	10.1	72	40%	.280	0.91	1.83	2.20	2.07	20.80	2.2	75	
2016	FRE	AAA	22	0	2	0	3	3	14	16	1	3.9	12.9	20	45%	.385	1.57	3.86	3.08	3.04	3.60	0.4	88	
2016	*HOU*	*MLB*	*22*	*0*	*1*	*0*	*3*	*1*	*7*	*6*	*0*	*3.9*	*2.6*	*2*	*44%*	*.261*	*1.29*	*5.14*	*4.25*	*6.31*	*-0.90*	*-0.1*	*119*	*94.8*
2018	*HOU*	*MLB*	*24*	*6*	*7*	*0*	*27*	*21*	*141^{2}*	*123*	*19*	*4.4*	*10.7*	*168*	*38%*	*.299*	*1.37*	*3.95*	*4.19*	*4.51*	*11.8*	*1.2*	*103*	

Breakout: 30% Improve: 40% Collapse: 9% Attrition: 27% MLB: 56% *Comparables: Frankie Montas, Macay McBride, Matt Harvey*

The Good: Rare is the 6-foot-7 pitching prospect with the frame of Kevin Garnett who flashes an ability to corral his body coherent, controlled movements and repeat his delivery. But here we are with Paulino, who leverages his height into with quality extension from a high three quarter's slot. His mid-90s fastball will touch 97 with excellent plane and burrowing action down into the zone. The curveball is his best secondary pitch, flashing plus with hard 12-6 action and loads of bite. He shows comfort with and feel for a mid-80s change as well, and while it plays relatively straight he keeps it out of trouble spots and sells it effectively with his arm speed. His angle of attack makes squaring and driving his pitches extremely difficult—he's allowed just six home runs in over 200 professional innings to date.

The Bad: He struggles to finish his delivery, and command lacks, and the curve in particular can lose its shape and hang up as a result. Despite a fast-track advance through the minors, he has yet to prove particularly durable, with Tommy John surgery and a subsequent bout of elbow tendinitis on his resume.

The Irrelevant: Both Paulino and Francis Martes were acquired in trades based on reports by the same pro scout, Alex Jacobs, assigned to cover the Florida back fields as a key component of the organization's overhauled pro-scouting strategy under Kevin Goldstein (#RIP).

The Risks: Paulino's recent history includes questionable durability and a minor discipline issue that cost him a team-sanctioned suspension this past summer. Combined with the fact that he is, at last check, a pitcher, Paulino remains a higher-risk prospect despite being on the cusp of regular big-league reps.

Major league ETA: Debuted in 2016 —Wilson Karaman

Ben Carsley's Fantasy Take: I've warned you to stay away from mid-rotation guys ad nauseam, but this writeup suggests that Paulino is going to miss a hell of a lot of bats, even if his ERA and WHIP conspire to prevent him from reaching true fantasy glory. His short lead time and swing-and-miss stuff make him a solid buy for dynasty leaguers, and he should flirt with a top-100 ranking. Ian Kennedy was a top-40 starter by striking out 180 batters and logging a 3.70 ERA, and that feels right for Paulino. I'm more concerned that he won't log 200 innings consistently than I am that the stuff won't play.

4. Franklin Perez, RHP

DOB: 12/6/1997

Height/Weight: 6'3" 197 lbs.

Bats/Throws: R/R

Drafted/Acquired: Signed in July 2014 out of Venezuela for $1 million

Previous Ranking(s): N/A

2016 Stats: 2.83 ERA, 2.17 DRA, 66.2 IP, 63 H, 19 BB, 75 K in 15 games at Low-A Quad Cities

The Role: OFP 60–Mid-rotation starter
Likely 50–No. 4 starter

YEAR	TEAM	LVL	AGE	W	L	SV	G	GS	IP	H	HR	BB/9	K/9	K	GB%	BABIP	WHIP	ERA	FIP	DRA	VORP	WARP	cFIP	MPH
2015	DAR	Rk	17	1	2	0	11	9	35	34	1	2.8	11.3	44	47%	.359	1.29	4.37	2.35	2.24	13.60	1.3	80	
2015	AST	Rk	17	0	2	0	5	1	15	19	0	1.8	10.2	17	49%	.388	1.47	4.80	1.63	2.43	5.50	0.5	85	
2016	QUD	A	18	3	3	1	15	10	66^{2}	63	1	2.6	10.1	75	39%	.344	1.23	2.84	2.37	2.18	20.20	2.2	81	
2017	*HOU*	*MLB*	*19*	*3*	*3*	*1*	*24*	*8*	50^{2}	*58*	*7*	*4.0*	*7.2*	*41*	*47%*	*.320*	*1.59*	*4.88*	*4.78*	*5.56*	*-2.6*	*-0.3*	*130*	
2018	*HOU*	*MLB*	*20*	*3*	*3*	*0*	*19*	*11*	*93*	*90*	*12*	*3.8*	*9.2*	*95*		*.305*	*1.38*	*3.98*	*4.21*	*4.54*	*5.9*	*0.6*	*104*	

Breakout: 0% Improve: 0% Collapse: 0% Attrition: 0% MLB: 0% *Comparables: Roberto Osuna, Jordan Lyles, Vicente Campos*

The Good: Perez is only 18 and still projectable. He also carved up the Midwest League in 15 starts there this year. That's a rare balance of potential and present in a teenaged arm. His fastball is his most advanced pitch and it is a potential plus pitch. Perez can dial it up to 95 and manipulate the movement in a variety of ways. His change flashes plus with quality deception and fade.

The Bad: Perez is still pretty raw. His mechanics are inconsistent and make the current command profile play down. He won't get punished for it yet, because the stuff is more than good enough to baffle A-ball bats. The curve will flash average but is also inconsistent at present. Although he is still lean right now, the body may require some monitoring.

The Irrelevant: The Quad Cities are composed of Davenport and Bettendorf in Iowa and Rock Island and Moline in Illinois.

The Risks: Perez was one of the youngest players in the Midwest League this year. While that makes his performance all the more impressive, he has a long way to go to the majors and a lot of development time ahead of him. The Astros also kept a tight cap on his usage in games. We could also quibble about the ultimate projection for the curve and command as well, but let's just stick with "He's an 18-year-old pitcher."

Major league ETA: 2020

Ben Carsley's Fantasy Take: You don't get extra points for the "impressive for a pitcher his age" caveat in fantasy. Perez is one to keep an eye on, but at present his lack of super-high ceiling and his lead time make him a fringy dynasty league prospect. He's watch-list worthy, though.

5. Forrest Whitley, RHP

DOB: 9/15/1997

Height/Weight: 6'7" 240 lbs.

Bats/Throws: R/R

Drafted/Acquired: Drafted 17th overall in the 2016 MLB Draft Alamo Heights HS (San Antonio, TX); signed for $3.148 million

Previous Ranking(s): N/A

2016 Stats: 7.36 ERA, 2.25 DRA, 7.1 IP, 8 H, 3 BB, 13 K in 4 games at complex level GCL, 3.18 ERA, 2.87 DRA, 11.1 IP, 11 H, 3 BB, 13 K in 4 games at short-season Greenville

The Role: OFP 55—Mid-rotation arm or late-inning reliever
Likely 45—Backend starter or setup man

YEAR	TEAM	LVL	AGE	W	L	SV	G	GS	IP	H	HR	BB/9	K/9	K	GB%	BABIP	WHIP	ERA	FIP	DRA	VORP	WARP	cFIP	MPH
2015	DAR	Rk	17	1	2	0	11	9	35	34	1	2.8	11.3	44	47%	.359	1.29	4.37	2.35	2.24	13.60	1.3	80	
2015	AST	Rk	17	0	2	0	5	1	15	19	0	1.8	10.2	17	49%	.388	1.47	4.80	1.63	2.43	5.50	0.5	85	
2016	QUD	A	18	3	3	1	15	10	66^{2}	63	1	2.6	10.1	75	39%	.344	1.23	2.84	2.37	2.18	20.20	2.2	81	
2017	*HOU*	*MLB*	*19*	*2*	*2*	*0*	*14*	*7*	*33*	*37*	*5*	*4.0*	*7.7*	*28*	*47%*	*.320*	*1.58*	*4.94*	*4.94*	*5.63*	*-1.0*	*-0.1*	*132*	
2018	*HOU*	*MLB*	*20*	*4*	*5*	*1*	*34*	*18*	141^{2}	*143*	*21*	*3.5*	*8.8*	*139*		*.307*	*1.40*	*4.14*	*4.37*	*4.72*	*6.7*	*0.7*	*108*	

Breakout: 0% Improve: 0% Collapse: 0% Attrition: 0% MLB: 0% *Comparables: Arodys Vizcaino, Will Smith, Jonathan Pettibone*

The Good: The latest in a seemingly never-ending line of long, tall Texan prep arms, Whitley is exactly what you would expect from the paradigm. He runs his fastball up to 97 and gets big plane on the pitch. He pairs it with a power breaker that at its best shows steep 11-5 break.

The Bad: Although he keeps his delivery in line better than your standard 6-foot-7 teenaged arm—if there even is such a thing—Whitley does have long levers and his mechanics can get out of sync. He has "some feel for the changeup," but it is a pitch he has never really needed before. He's well-filled out, especially in his lower half, so there isn't as much projection here as, say, Dustin May.

The Irrelevant: "Long, Tall Texan" is best known as a Beach Boys hit, but it was actually written by Nashville studio musician, Henry Strzlecki.

The Risks: A veritable cornucopia of risks. He is a teenaged arm that needs two secondaries to jump a grade or two. He has no pro track record outside of eight starts in rookie ball. There are potential tall-pitcher issues here, and just general pitcher issues, because he is after all a (tall) pitcher.

Major league ETA: 2021

Ben Carsley's Fantasy Take: To the surprise of no one who's read even one of the previous installments, I think Whitley is too far away and has too modest a ceiling to invest in. Let's wait and see what he looks like in a year or two.

6. Miguelangel Sierra, SS

DOB: 12/02/1997

Height/Weight: 5'11" 175 lbs.

Bats/Throws: R/R

Drafted/Acquired: Signed July 2014 by Houston out of Venezuela for $1 million

Previous Ranking(s): #10 (Org.)

2016 Stats: .289/.386/.620, 11 HR, 6 SB in 31 games at Appy League Greenville, .140/.216/.183, 0 HR, 0 SB in 25 games at short-season Tri-City

The Role: OFP 55—Above-average shortstop
Likely 40—Utility infielder with some pop

YEAR	TEAM	LVL	AGE	PA	R	2B	3B	HR	RBI	BB	K	SB	CS	AVG/OBP/SLG	TAv	VORP	BABIP	BRR	FRAA	WARP
2015	DAR	Rk	17	202	31	17	2	3	19	20	48	8	5	.302/.406/.479	.327	23.3	.400	-0.5	SS(41): 7.5, 3B(1): -0.1	3.0
2015	AST	Rk	17	88	6	2	1	0	1	8	33	4	3	.160/.267/.213	.215	-1.4	.286	-0.7	SS(22): 2.3, 2B(2): -0.3	0.1
2016	GRV	Rk	18	144	23	3	2	11	19	12	40	6	6	.289/.386/.620	.355	21.0	.343	0.3	SS(21): 2.3, 2B(10): -0.9	2.2
2016	TCV	A-	18	102	6	2	1	0	5	7	34	0	3	.140/.216/.183	.172	-6.2	.220	-0.9	SS(24): -3.2	-1.0
2017	*HOU*	*MLB*	*19*	*250*	*26*	*8*	*1*	*6*	*21*	*13*	*98*	*2*	*2*	*.180/.237/.303*	*.193*	*-6.7*	*.274*	*-0.6*	*SS 0, 2B -0*	*-0.7*
2018	*HOU*	*MLB*	*20*	*368*	*39*	*12*	*2*	*11*	*39*	*22*	*139*	*3*	*4*	*.194/.256/.337*	*.212*	*-6.3*	*.286*	*-0.6*	*SS 0, 2B 0*	*-0.7*

Breakout: 0% Improve: 6% Collapse: 2% Attrition: 6% MLB: 13% *Comparables: Raul Mondesi, Elvis Andrus, Domingo Santana*

The Good: Sierra got stronger in the 2015 offseason and the power surge in Greeneville, while aided by the environment, is mostly real. The ball jumps off his bat and he gets some natural loft. He's a good bet to stick at shortstop and has the potential to be a plus glove there with a plus arm.

The Bad: Sierra fell in love with the bombs he was hitting in the thinner air of the Appalachians, and college arms in the NYPL were able to exploit his attempts to hit every pitch across the Hudson River. He's got a little shimmy in his swing, so I wonder how consistent he can keep his upper and lower halves in time, and the ceiling for the hit tool may only be average or solid-average.

The Irrelevant: Although he didn't quite have enough PA to qualify, Sierra would have led the Appy League in slugging by almost 50 points.

The Risks: Sierra just turned 19 and hasn't hit outside of short-season (or even in the Penn League). I have some questions about the ultimate hit tool projection. There's a long and winding road for him to the majors, but at least he is a shortstop and not a pitcher.

Major league ETA: 2021

Ben Carsley's Fantasy Take: There's enough to like about Sierra as a guy to follow as a shortstop who might hit, but he's too far away to invest in right now (depending on league depth). Check back in three months.

7. Ramon Laureano, OF

DOB: 7/15/1994

Height/Weight: 5'11" 185 lbs.

Bats/Throws: R/R

Drafted/Acquired: Drafted 466th Overall in the 2014 MLB Draft Northeast Oklahoma A&M College (Miami, OK); signed for $25,000

Previous Ranking(s): N/A

2016 Stats: .317/.426/.519, 10 HR, 33 SB, in 80 games High-A Lancaster, .323/.432/.548, 5 HR, 10 SB in 36 games at Double-A Corpus Christi

The Role: OFP 55—Above-average outfielder
Likely 45—Second-division starter/quality fourth outfielder

YEAR	TEAM	LVL	AGE	PA	R	2B	3B	HR	RBI	BB	K	SB	CS	AVG/OBP/SLG	TAv	VORP	BABIP	BRR	FRAA	WARP
2014	GRV	Rk	19	61	8	0	0	1	2	7	16	4	0	.189/.283/.245	.216	-0.6	.250	-0.4		-0.1
2015	QUD	A	20	314	43	15	8	4	34	21	83	18	3	.265/.323/.415	.262	8.6	.358	1.8	RF(49): 5.0, CF(15): -1.9	1.5
2016	LNC	A+	21	357	69	19	5	10	60	50	86	33	11	.317/.426/.519	.327	35.1	.411	1.2	CF(30): 3.8, RF(23): 3.2	4.6
2016	CCH	AA	21	148	20	9	2	5	13	20	33	10	3	.323/.432/.548	.356	18.9	.407	1.0	CF(20): 3.1, RF(15): 2.7	2.6
2017	*HOU*	*MLB*	*22*	*250*	*30*	*10*	*2*	*6*	*26*	*24*	*78*	*11*	*4*	*.227/.310/.379*	*.245*	*5.6*	*.316*	*1.0*	*CF 2, RF 1*	*1.0*
2018	*HOU*	*MLB*	*23*	*376*	*44*	*16*	*4*	*10*	*42*	*37*	*120*	*16*	*5*	*.228/.313/.389*	*.250*	*7.4*	*.322*	*2.2*	*CF 3, RF 1*	*1.3*

Breakout: 2% Improve: 25% Collapse: 0% Attrition: 19% MLB: 45% *Comparables: Chris Young, Brett Jackson, Colby Rasmus*

The Good: An unheralded 16th-round pick, Laureano can flat-out play. He led the minors in on-base percentage, and while his Lancaster environs get partial credit, the numbers were largely earned at High-A before notably holding in the wake of his promotion to the Texas League, and he kept right on hitting in the AFL. He gets himself into good counts consistently, and hunts for fastballs when he does. Strong wrists and mild leverage play well with strong plate coverage, enabling damage to all parts of the field. In spite of his modest size he generates fringe-average pop on the back of hard, line-drive contact to the gaps, and plus speed and instincts help him take extra bases on the regular. He shows as a capable defender in all three outfield spots, with particular strength in left and enough arm to handle right.

The Bad: He's not the most natural center fielder, and he can struggle to make quick reads and pick up trajectory there. The speed plays down at times out of the box on account of a high swing finish, and his is a longer stride that can take a few steps to kick into high gear when tracking in the outfield. While there is some pop, it's likely to play more consistently as doubles and triples variety rather than the over-the-fence kind he showed in the California League.

The Irrelevant: Laureano's college program, Northeast Oklahoma A&M, saw three players drafted in the 2014 class, including fellow Astro Dean Deetz (featured below). All three (also including Angels' fifth-rounder Jake Jewell) will attempt to one day leapfrog current Diamondbacks pitching coach Mike Butcher as the school's most famous alumnus.

The Risks: As a pop-up guy with the stigma of Cal League inflation on his resume he'll have to continue to produce against high-minors pitching, though the well-roundedness of his skillset makes him a higher-probability player.

Major league ETA: 2018 —Wilson Karaman

Ben Carsley's Fantasy Take: If you're looking to get in on an offensive prospect your league mates haven't heard of yet, Laureano is not a bad pick. Sure, the upside is modest-ish, but you have to love the approach and with a stint in Double-A already under his belt the lead time here is acceptable, too. The hope is Laureano develops into an OF 3/4 who uses his average, speed, OBP and some homers to serve as a well-rounded asset, albeit one who might not make an impact in any one category. That's still a mighty useful player.

8. Derek Fisher, OF

DOB: 08/21/1993

Height/Weight: 6'1" 210 lbs.

Bats/Throws: L/R

Drafted/Acquired: Drafted 37th overall in the 2014 MLB Draft, University of Virginia (VA); signed for $1.5431 million

Previous Ranking(s): #6 (Org.)

2016 Stats: .245/.373/.431, 16 HR, 23 SB in 102 games at Double-A Corpus Christi, .290/.347/.505, 5 HR, 5 SB in 27 games at Triple-A Fresno

The Role: OFP 55—Above-average left fielder
Likely 45—Second-division left fielder

YEAR	TEAM	LVL	AGE	PA	R	2B	3B	HR	RBI	BB	K	SB	CS	AVG/OBP/SLG	TAv	VORP	BABIP	BRR	FRAA	WARP
2014	AST	Rk	20	4	0	1	0	0	0	1	0	0	0	.667/.750/1.000	.583	1.0	.667	-0.3		0.1
2014	TCV	A-	20	172	31	4	3	2	18	16	35	17	4	.303/.378/.408	.299	10.0	.379	-0.6	LF(38): -1.4, CF(1): -0.1	0.9
2015	QUD	A	21	171	32	11	1	6	24	19	37	8	2	.305/.386/.510	.326	15.7	.370	-0.5	CF(30): -3.4, LF(3): -0.9	1.3
2015	LNC	A+	21	398	74	10	7	16	63	47	95	23	5	.262/.354/.471	.295	27.7	.314	4.3	LF(43): -2.2, CF(35): -2.0	2.7
2016	CCH	AA	22	448	54	13	4	16	59	74	128	23	7	.245/.373/.431	.303	30.0	.329	-0.5	CF(70): -9.0, RF(19): -1.7	2.3
2016	FRE	AAA	22	118	17	8	0	5	17	9	26	5	0	.290/.347/.505	.308	8.2	.338	-0.6	RF(13): -1.8, CF(13): -1.0	0.6
2017	*HOU*	*MLB*	*23*	*250*	*31*	*8*	*2*	*9*	*30*	*29*	*77*	*8*	*2*	*.223/.317/.398*	*.253*	*7.8*	*.299*	*0.8*	*CF -2, RF -1*	*0.6*
2018	*HOU*	*MLB*	*24*	*387*	*47*	*13*	*3*	*12*	*45*	*44*	*122*	*12*	*3*	*.216/.308/.381*	*.247*	*6.4*	*.294*	*1.8*	*CF -3, RF -2*	*0.2*

Breakout: 3% Improve: 22% Collapse: 6% Attrition: 21% MLB: 58% *Comparables: Brett Jackson, Joe Benson, Chris Young*

The Good: Fisher's raw athleticism and underlying tools continue to allow us to dream big dreams. He boasts plus raw power along with speed that rates at least that high, and after a second consecutive 20-20 season—this latest one with the distinction of not being Lancaster-aided—it's fair to say he has shown a consistent ability to apply both tools in games. He sees a lot of pitches and takes a healthy number of walks, which helps drive up his on-base profile. He's an efficient base-stealer, with quality reads and quick breaks, and he has the kind of high-end closing speed that can make up for mistakes on the grass. He's shown some improvement with the glove over the past year, as well.

The Bad: The defense still isn't great, even in a corner, on account of persistent struggles reading trajectory and adjusting his routes. The club continued to give him reps in center in the upper-minors, but he doesn't present as a natural defender with the instincts to hold the position, and the arm is well light for right field (where he also played frequently in 2016). At the plate his swing is geared to generate power, with a noisy load and inconsistent trigger that can compromise his barrel and contribute to swing-and-miss issues that aren't likely to abate. The raw hit tool is unlikely to make it near average, and that compromises the game power.

The Irrelevant: Fisher was named the Pennsylvania State Player of the Year as a high school senior in 2011, leading to a sixth-round selection by the Rangers. That was a weird draft for Texas, whose top four have produced zero value as of this writing. The club also failed to sign its fifth- (Brandon Woodruff), sixth- (Fisher), and seventh- (Max Pentecost) round picks, before inking Kyle Hendricks, Andrew Faulkner, and Jerad Eickhoff (among others) later on.

The Risks: It's an easy crutch to lean on the ol' "he'll go as far as his hit tool takes him" rejoinder, but for a prospect like Fisher it rings especially true. The secondary offensive skills are outstanding, and if he's able to get to enough of his power and get on base often enough to deploy his speed, he has the makings of an above-average regular even in spite of poor batting averages. On the flipside, the defensive profile is suspect enough that if he doesn't max out his offensive value he can just as easily wind up a wildly inconsistent lower-end outfielder with limited utility in left.

Major league ETA: 2017 —Wilson Karaman

Ben Carsley's Fantasy Take: Fisher is a better dynasty prospect than an IRL asset because we don't care where he plays in the outfield so long as he's tolerable enough to play there everyday. Should that happen, Fisher's speed and raw power make him a very enticing gamble, albeit one who might not come with a super-high average. Still, Melvin Upton Jr. just finished as a top-40 outfielder despite hitting .238 because he slugged 20 homers and recorded 27 steals. Fisher's secondary tools might not be that loud, but you get the idea; counting stats make up for a lot.

9. Teoscar Hernandez, OF

DOB: 10/15/1992

Height/Weight: 6'2" 180 lbs.

Bats/Throws: R/R

Drafted/Acquired: Signed February 2011 out of the Dominican Republic for $20,000

Previous Ranking(s): N/A

2016 Stats: .230/.304/.420, 4 HR, 0 SB in 41 games at major league level, .305/.384/.437, 6 HR, 29 SB in 69 games at Double-A Corpus Christi, .313/.365/.500, 4 HR, 5 SB in 38 games at Triple-A Fresno

The Role: OFP 50—Average outfielder
Likely 40—Platoon/bench outfielder

YEAR	TEAM	LVL	AGE	PA	R	2B	3B	HR	RBI	BB	K	SB	CS	AVG/OBP/SLG	TAv	VORP	BABIP	BRR	FRAA	WARP
2014	LNC	A+	21	455	72	33	8	17	75	49	117	31	6	.294/.376/.550	.327	49.3	.374	3.2	CF(82): 3.3, CF(10): 3.3	5.9
2014	CCH	AA	21	98	12	4	1	4	10	2	36	2	3	.284/.299/.474	.291	4.9	.418	-1.0	CF(21): 0.0, RF(2): 0.0	0.6
2015	CCH	AA	22	514	92	12	2	17	48	33	126	33	7	.219/.275/.362	.237	8.6	.261	7.4	CF(80): -2.5, RF(39): 3.2	1.2
2016	CCH	AA	23	322	53	19	0	6	30	32	55	29	11	.305/.384/.437	.304	25.6	.359	4.2	RF(37): -2.0, CF(30): -0.7	2.7
2016	FRE	AAA	23	160	20	9	3	4	23	13	25	5	4	.313/.365/.500	.306	8.7	.350	-2.4	RF(26): 3.7, CF(11): -2.1	0.9
2016	HOU	MLB	23	112	15	7	0	4	11	11	28	0	2	.230/.304/.420	.246	0.6	.275	-0.6	LF(22): -1.7, CF(15): -1.4	-0.2
2017	*HOU*	*MLB*	*24*	*34*	*4*	*2*	*0*	*1*	*4*	*2*	*9*	*1*	*1*	*.234/.287/.392*	*.246*	*0.7*	*.297*	*0.1*	*LF -0*	*0.0*
2018	*HOU*	*MLB*	*25*	*319*	*37*	*15*	*2*	*10*	*38*	*22*	*87*	*13*	*5*	*.242/.297/.412*	*.250*	*6.2*	*.304*	*1.4*	*LF 0*	*0.6*

Breakout: 6% Improve: 27% Collapse: 5% Attrition: 19% MLB: 40% *Comparables: Aaron Cunningham, Moises Sierra, Zoilo Almonte*

The Good: After a disastrous 2015, Hernandez bounced back and hit his way to Houston. He's a plus runner and everything else is within a half-grade or so of average, including an above-average arm that allows him to play all three outfield positions. He'll add enough value at the plate to play in the majors for a good long while. He's ready now for a role in the bigs...

The Bad: ...But it's not an impact profile of any sort. Hernandez might not even be an everyday player. He struggles to consistently make good contact, and the power might play fringe-average at best because of that. He's not ideal as an everyday center fielder despite the speed, which leaves him as a bit of a tweener.

The Irrelevant: Hernandez only got $20,000 as a signing bonus, but he beat outfielder Ariel Ovando—the Astros most expensive signing from that J2 class—to the majors. Ovando is now a pitcher in the Cubs system.

The Risks: He might never hit major league righties enough to hold down an everyday job, but he is otherwise major-league ready.

Major league ETA: Debuted in 2016

Ben Carsley's Fantasy Take: Given how crowded Houston's outfield is and how Hernandez probably profiles best as a bench bat, there's not a ton of hope for him in fantasy unless he gets traded or the Astros outfield suddenly changes. I like his bat and do think he could be of some use in deeper leagues if he gets playing time, but that's a pretty big "if" at this point.

10. Daz Cameron, OF

DOB: 01/15/1997

Height/Weight: 6'2" 185 lbs.

Bats/Throws: R/R

Drafted/Acquired: Drafted 37th overall in the 2015 MLB Draft, Eagle's Landing Christian Academy (McDonough, GA); signed for $4 million

Previous Ranking(s): #4 (Org.), #85 (Overall)

2016 Stats: .278/.352/.418, 2 HR, 8 SB in 19 games at short-season Tri-City, .143/.221/.221, 0 HR, 4 SB in 21 games at Low-A Quad Cities

The Role: OFP 50—Average center fielder
Likely 40—Fourth outfielder

YEAR	TEAM	LVL	AGE	PA	R	2B	3B	HR	RBI	BB	K	SB	CS	AVG/OBP/SLG	TAv	VORP	BABIP	BRR	FRAA	WARP
2015	AST	Rk	18	87	14	2	0	0	6	9	18	13	4	.222/.326/.250	.262	4.7	.286	2.0	CF(17): -1.7	0.3
2015	GRV	Rk	18	124	20	2	3	0	11	16	31	11	6	.272/.372/.350	.296	9.4	.384	0.6	CF(22): 2.2, LF(6): -0.6	1.1
2016	QUD	A	19	87	5	2	2	0	6	8	33	4	3	.143/.221/.221	.170	-5.4	.244	0.1	CF(10): -0.7, LF(6): -0.5	-0.7
2016	TCV	A-	19	89	13	3	1	2	14	6	26	8	2	.278/.352/.418	.285	4.7	.392	0.0	CF(15): -0.1, LF(2): -0.4	0.5
2017	*HOU*	*MLB*	*20*	*250*	*29*	*8*	*1*	*4*	*17*	*16*	*95*	*9*	*6*	*.178/.237/.278*	*.184*	*-10.0*	*.274*	*0.2*	*CF 1, LF 0*	*-1.0*
2018	*HOU*	*MLB*	*21*	*315*	*30*	*10*	*2*	*6*	*27*	*23*	*113*	*13*	*8*	*.189/.255/.297*	*.200*	*-9.6*	*.283*	*1.1*	*CF 1, LF 0*	*-0.9*

Breakout: 1% Improve: 2% Collapse: 0% Attrition: 1% MLB: 3% *Comparables: Joe Benson, Engel Beltre, Alex Liddi*

The Good: He's still only 19 and played better once the Astros sent him to the more age-appropriate Penn League and found more consistency with his swing. The tool set won't wow you, but he's a potentially solid-average center fielder with plus speed, and at the plate he could develop into an average hitter with 10-home-run pop.

The Bad: He's a solid center fielder, but he isn't his pops there, so the glove won't carry the profile. Cameron's not going to develop his father's power either. Man, it's gotta be tough following the career path of your Hall-of-Very-Good paterfamilias, because jamokes like me keep comping you to him. Even after he righted the ship in short season, there's still a fair bit of swing-and-miss in the profile.

The Irrelevant: The four million smackers that Daz got as a bonus is a full 100 times more than his father, Mike Cameron, got from the White Sox as an 18th round pick.

The Risks: Cameron struggled in his first taste of full-season ball, and if he misses even a little on the ultimate offensive tool grade projections, he may end up more of a fourth outfielder type, as he lacks an obvious carrying tool. On the positive risk side, reports suggest he was putting it together at the plate before a broken index finger ended his season early.

Major league ETA: 2020

Ben Carsley's Fantasy Take: Cameron has name value because of his bloodlines and draft position, but 2016 was not an inspiring year. He's not worth dropping or actively looking to move on from, but know that you're dealing with damaged dynasty goods.

OTHERS OF NOTE:

"The Guy We Wish Was, Like, Two Inches Taller and 30 Pounds Bigger"

Garrett Stubbs, C

Stubbs emerged as an impressive backstop at USC, blending intelligence, quality receiving, and an excellent approach into consistent productivity on both sides of the ball en route to winning the Johnny Bench Award in his senior season. The rub? At 5-foot-10, 175 pounds, he is, shall we say, slight for the position. Stubbs has done pretty much the exact same things as a pro that he did in college. He takes excellent, controlled at-bats, rarely expanding the zone. His simple swing produces solid contact, and while he lacks for much in the way of power, he's a smart hitter who uses the whole field. He's sneaky-quick for a catcher as well, with solid-average run times and the instincts to pick off the occasional bag. He shouldered a well below-average catching load last year, but he excelled behind the dish when he played. What he lacks in size he makes up with agility, and his quiet receiving is an asset on the margins of the zone. The legs have quality spring, and paired with his above-average arm helped drive a 51 percent caught-stealing rate for the season. The Astros plan to loosen the reigns and test his durability with an everyday role at Double-A next year, and we'll all learn together if the frame can hold up to the rigors of a full season sweating under the tools of ignorance. There is no talk as of now about adding any other positions to the portfolio, though he played some center, second, and third in college, and the athleticism leaves open the possibility for a later date if full-time catching proves too much for the body to handle. —*Wilson Karaman*

The bonus babies (emphasis on babies)

Jonathan Arauz, SS

A switch-hitting shortstop, Arauz is a ways away from contributing to a big league team, but still has a lot of tools and projection remaining. A smooth defender at short, he isn't the fastest runner but has good instincts and footwork to project as an average-to-better defender. There is good feel for the barrel as well as above-average bat speed which project him to be an average-to-better hitter down the road. The road for Arauz is long, but patience is a virtue, and might be a top-10 guy next year with a strong performance in full-season ball. *—Steve Givarz*

Gilberto Celestino, CF

Like Arauz, Celestino has a nice balance of maturity for his age and enough remaining projection to raise the eyebrows of the more tool-inclined evaluator. Also like Arauz, Celestino is a good bet to stick up-the-middle, as he is a plus runner that already has feel for his routes. The approach also is solid for a dude that can't even buy Marlboros yet, and I was inclined to maybe sneak him onto the back end of the Top 10. In the end he isn't quite there yet, and there is some wisdom in our patience here, but I fully expect Celestino to have forced the issue by the time I start writing the 2018 Astros list.

The boom or bust (emphasis on boom)

J.D. Davis, 3B

Davis gave you more of the same in 2016. The fact that he was able to repeat his particular brand of success in Double-A is heartening, but his particular brand of success is the type that requires a Triple-A test and a...uh...Quadruple-A test as well. There is big power, and commensurate swing and miss. If he already didn't have a summer gig they could have sent him down to San Padre Island to keep beachgoers cool with his mighty hacks. He's still a little rough at third base and will be 24 next year. There's still a reasonable shot at a bat-first—well, really pop-first—everyday third baseman here, but there's still a few more exams to pass.

The "One Day It Might All Click For Him" Guy

Dean Deetz, RHP

To close, or not to close? That is the primary question for Deetz's developmental path, and it is one for which the organization does not yet have an answer. He has some of the best pure stuff in the system, highlighted by a gnarly fastball that sits mid-90s as a starter with movement and late life in the zone. His mid-80s change shows good velocity separation and plus movement, and the pitch can generate silly swings and weak contact when he executes it down in the zone. He rounds out the arsenal with a hard, tight low-80s curve that bites late with quality lateral movement to stay off barrels. All three pitches will flash plus, but rarely will they do so simultaneously or with any regularity. The mechanical consistency and focus to execute wavers from inning to inning (and sometimes batter to batter), but the athleticism and arm action both suggest the potential for rapid improvement, and he'll hint at nascent command throughout starts in spite of wonky control. He tantalized with a pair of dynamic starts to close the year after an end-of-season promotion to Double-A, and those efforts might just be enough to keep him in a starting role...for now. What we do know is that he's a very interesting power arm to keep an eye on, with the potential to impact the big-league bullpen in the second half of '17. *—Wilson Karaman*

TOP 10 TALENTS 25 AND UNDER (BORN 4/1/91 OR LATER)

1. Carlos Correa
2. Alex Bregman
3. Lance McCullers
4. A.J. Reed
5. Francis Martes
6. Kyle Tucker
7. Michael Feliz
8. Joe Musgrove
9. David Paulino
10. Franklin Perez

First, we say farewell to the aged: Jose Altuve, Ken Giles, and Jake Marisnick—two, four, and ten last year—all leave this year's edition of the list in consequence of their advanced years. On the whole, though, there's not much that's changed at the top. Correa, one of the five best position players in baseball, is at the top of the list. Bregman and McCullers have switched places, more because of something Bregman did (put up a .270 TAv in the big-leagues as a 22-year-old) than anything McCullers did wrong. This is a very strong top three.

After three, though, things get complicated. A.J. Reed at four could look very good in a year—after all, this is a guy who's done nasty, nasty things to minor-league pitching, and is still only 23—or it could look a little high. He didn't do much to boost his stock in 141 big-league plate appearances last year, and the strikeout rate (34 percent) is especially concerning. One more year like that, and he'll drop way down this list, and not because of his age. Live up to his potential? He could bump up above McCullers, though probably not above Bregman.

Martes and Tucker you know about, and both are strong talents who'll be making a difference in Houston sooner rather than later. Though he's a reliever, Feliz has the advantage of actually having pitched in the big leagues (a quality he shares with Joe Musgrove), and having struck out 13.2 per 9 last year across 65 innings of work. Musgrove is far -ess impressive, but did just fine last year and should do fine the next, too. Paulino and Perez are two young pitchers, but good ones, and their talent probably eclipses that of the two ranked above them. Perez has a very good chance of staying a starter going forward.

—Rian Watt

KANSAS CITY ROYALS

The State of the System: *It's the five-through-14 of a pretty good system. Unfortunately it is missing the top four.*

THE TOP TEN

1. 3B/OF Hunter Dozier	6. OF Khalil Lee
2. RHP Josh Staumont	7. RHP Scott Blewett
3. LHP Matt Strahm	8. C Meibrys Viloria
4. RHP A.J. Puckett	9. OF Seuly Matias
5. OF Jorge Bonifacio	10. RHP Miguel Almonte

The Big Question: How do you keep a core?

Teams go through cycles. They can't compete for eternity, and father time is undefeated in this game—although I am suspicious of Bartolo Colon. As we examine the Royals now, the core that won them a championship will soon be a shell of themselves. Lorenzo Cain, Alcides Escobar, Eric Hosmer, and Mike Moustakas will be free agents after this season. James Shields, Johnny Cueto, and Edinson Volquez were all too expensive to stay in Kansas City. Wade Davis was traded for Jorge Soler. The two biggest contracts on the payroll belong to players both over 30 years old. The sudden passing of the team's most visibly passionate star, Yordano Ventura, leaves Danny Duffy as the top arm, and one of the few young players who will be sticking around long-term.

The under 25 players isn't awe-inspiring, and neither is this farm system.

So where does all of this leave us? Due to their championship runs, the once hyped Royals farm system is now very weak. The trades of Sean Manaea, Wil Myers, Brandon Finnegan, Cody Reed, Jake Odorizzi, Mike Montgomery, and John Lamb all could have been contributors to the current core, but Flags Fly Forever. The organization has also had to pick much lower than in years past, lowering their draft pool value and the amount of talent available to them. So how does one keep maintain a core? We've witnessed how Kansas City built it, and added to it for the pennant races. But after a disappointing 81-81 season what do you do now? They have already made two trades, and some low-cost free agent signings in Jason Hammel and Brandon Moss. They seem poised to give this core one more opportunity, and given the state of the division, they have a realistic chance. The White Sox have been stripped down, the Twins took a step back, and the Tigers have an older core, and could be looking to strip payroll. Which leaves the Royals against the Indians, the new kids on the block, the defending American League champions. But there are wild cards! The Royals have good luck in those!

The four free-agents-to-be mentioned at the top of this essay are likely to depart. The payroll restrictions on the team means they can't possibly bring them all back at market rate. What does one do? If they find themselves competing and need to look to trades to improve the roster what do they have to sell? Do they have another core ready to take over from this current one? Let's look at this from our perspective.

- Hunter Dozier and Raul Mondesi, both have warts and problems that suggest they might not be capable of everyday status.
- Josh Staumont looks like a reliever, not a starter.
- Whit Merrifield looks poised to come back to earth after his hot start and is more a useful bench player than everyday contributor.
- Kyle Zimmer will miss another year of development after his Thoracic Outlet surgery in June.
- A.J. Puckett, Scott Blewett, Ashe Russell, Eric Skoglund are more back of the rotation starters than mid-to-front rotation starters.
- Ryan O'Hearn and Jorge Bonifacio are platoon/bench options in all likelihood.
- Bubba Starling! Still hasn't hit. More fifth outfielder/reserve than starter.

Cores can be cobbled together, but you only have a certain amount of time with them before things go awry. When presented with the option to maintain and give it another go versus selling off, there is no wrong answer.

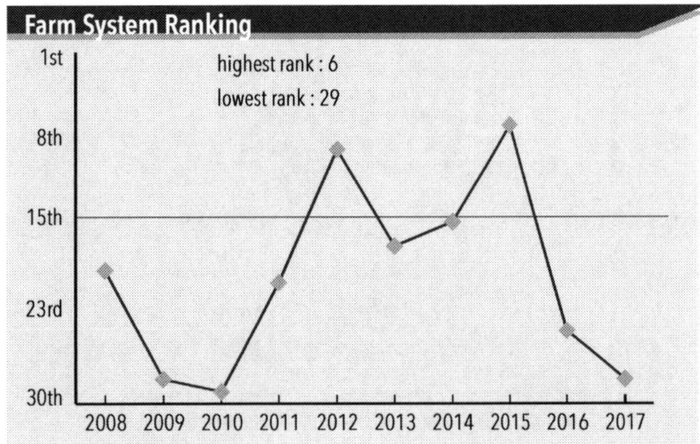

Personnel

General Manager:
Dayton Moore

AGM, Player Personnel:
J.J. Picollo

AGM, MLB and International Ops:
Rene Francisco

Assistant General Manager:
Scott Sharp

Manager:
Ned Yost

BP Alumni:
Mike Groopman
Daniel Mack

Most times, teams will take the option of giving it another go because Flags Fly Forever and winning and competing is better for business.

The Royals made amends to the fans after almost 30 years between World Series Championships. The Royals might have earned forgiveness for spending nearly three decades out of the playoffs with their back-to-back World Series runs, culminating in a championship in 2015. They'll have to hope it suffices for at least the next few years too, because it could get bleak.

—Steve Givarz

1. Hunter Dozier, 3B/OF

DOB: 08/22/1991

Height/Weight: 6'4" 220 lbs.

Bats/Throws: R/R

Drafted/Acquired: Drafted eighth overall in the 2013 MLB Draft, Stephen F. Austin State University (TX); signed for $2,200,000

Previous Ranking(s): #10 (Org)

2016 Stats: .211/.286/.263, 0 HR, 0 SB in 8 games at MLB level, .294/.357/.506, 15 HR, 3 SB in 103 games at Triple-A Omaha, .305/.400/.642, 8 HR, 4 SB in 26 games at double-A Northwest Arkansas

The Role: OFP 55—A cromulent starting third baseman
Likely 50—Second-division starter or good four corners utility player

YEAR	TEAM	LVL	AGE	PA	R	2B	3B	HR	RBI	BB	K	SB	CS	AVG/OBP/SLG	TAv	VORP	BABIP	BRR	FRAA	WARP
2014	WIL	A+	22	267	36	18	0	4	39	35	56	7	3	.295/.397/.429	.324	29.4	.371	2.2	3B(62): -7.8	2.2
2014	NWA	AA	22	267	33	12	0	4	21	31	70	3	2	.209/.303/.312	.222	-1.4	.280	0.9	3B(61): -6.2	-0.8
2015	NWA	AA	23	523	65	27	1	12	53	45	151	6	2	.213/.281/.349	.241	3.8	.283	-0.7	3B(115): -4.2	0.0
2016	NWA	AA	24	110	14	8	0	8	21	14	23	4	0	.305/.400/.642	.365	14.5	.328	0.1	3B(19): -0.3, LF(6): -1.3	1.4
2016	OMA	AAA	24	434	65	36	1	15	54	40	100	3	1	.294/.357/.506	.304	31.6	.358	0.9	3B(63): -6.3, RF(14): 0.9	2.6
2016	KCA	MLB	24	21	4	1	0	0	1	2	8	0	0	.211/.286/.263	.236	-0.2	.364	0.0	RF(7): -0.3	0.0
2017	*KCA*	*MLB*	*25*	*250*	*26*	*13*	*1*	*7*	*30*	*21*	*72*	*1*	*0*	*.233/.301/.393*	*.241*	*2.2*	*.305*	*-0.3*	*3B -3, RF 1*	*0.0*
2018	*KCA*	*MLB*	*26*	*381*	*44*	*20*	*1*	*11*	*43*	*33*	*110*	*2*	*1*	*.229/.299/.388*	*.241*	*0.1*	*.300*	*-0.6*	*3B -4, RF 2*	*-0.3*

Breakout: 10% Improve: 16% Collapse: 13% Attrition: 32% MLB: 37% *Comparables: Matthew Brown, Luke Hughes, Russ Canzler*

The Good: It might feel like we've been all over the place on Hunter Dozier—he's ranked sixth, fifth, tenth, and now first in the system rankings—but his stock is basically right where it was in our 2014 and 2015 rankings, just in a much weaker system. Once again right on the fringes of 101 discussion (more on that in the future), Dozier rediscovered how to hit in 2016, finally conquering Double A and continuing on in the PCL and a cup of coffee in the bigs. The profile is the same as it ever was: potential for an average hit tool, above-average raw power that finally turned into some game power this year, a plus arm, and a fine glove at third despite being a big fellow. All sounds pretty good, right?

The Bad: Dozier completely forgot how to hit in the second half of 2014 and more or less all of 2015, getting stuck playing footsie with the Mendoza Line in the Texas League. The hit tool and approach have always been the question marks here, and he's been known to look bad when he looks bad. We didn't give up on him and he certainly put it back together, but there's definitely some questions about what kind of contact he'll make in the majors. For the defense-conscious Royals, he's currently stuck behind Mike Moustakas and Cheslor Cuthbert at third; Dozier's best path to immediate playing time early in 2017 was probably in right, where he's been blocked by the acquisition of Jorge Soler.

The Irrelevant: Dozier is already the all-time leader in at-bats for players drafted out of Stephen F. Austin, with his 19 overtaking former Cardinal Steven Hill's 13.

The Risks: The risk is more in the profile than the player. At the very least Dozier should be good enough for a long career as a utility player, but shortened benches have made the corner utility/platoon player a fading institution in baseball. As a college pick who has moved slowly, he's old for a hitting prospect yet to establish himself.

Major-league ETA: Debuted in 2016 —Jarrett Seidler

Ben Carsley's Fantasy Take: Dozier has ETA in his favor, but I'd like to see the power and hit tool play up more consistently before going too crazy. If it all clicks, we're looking at a 20-homer third baseman whose average won't kill you. But there are so many versions of Dozier that are worse than that that it's tough to give him a wholehearted endorsement. He's right on the cusp of the dynasty 101, just as he's on the cusp of the IRL 101, but look for him to have a very hot-and-cold fantasy career..

2. Josh Staumont, RHP

DOB: 12/21/1993

Height/Weight: 6'3" 200 lbs

Bats/Throws: R/R

Drafted/Acquired: Drafted 64th overall in the 2015 MLB draft, Azusa Pacific (Azusa, CA); signed for $964,600.

Previous Ranking(s): N/A

2016 Stats: 3.04 ERA, 4.25 DRA, 50.1 IP, 42 H, 37 BB, 73 K at double-A Northwest Arkansas, 5.05 ERA, 6.84 DRA, 73 IP, 62 H, 67 BB, 94 K at high-A Wilmington

The Role: OFP 55—Good eighth-inning guy
Likely 45—Eighth-inning guy that makes you really, really nervous

YEAR	TEAM	LVL	AGE	W	L	SV	G	GS	IP	H	HR	BB/9	K/9	K	GB%	BABIP	WHIP	ERA	FIP	DRA	VORP	WARP	cFIP	MPH
2015	ROY	Rk	21	0	0	0	4	3	8^{2}	3	0	8.3	7.3	7	73%	.136	1.27	0.00	5.32	7.31	-1.70	-0.2	120	
2015	IDA	Rk	21	3	1	1	14	1	31^{1}	18	0	6.9	14.6	51	70%	.316	1.34	3.16	3.38	1.63	13.70	1.3	78	
2016	WIL	A+	22	2	10	0	18	15	73	62	3	8.3	11.6	94	46%	.328	1.77	5.05	4.55	6.84	-11.40	-1.2	113	
2016	NWA	AA	22	2	1	0	11	11	50^{1}	42	2	6.6	13.1	73	42%	.364	1.57	3.04	3.24	4.25	4.70	0.5	103	
2017	*KCA*	*MLB*	*23*	*4*	*6*	*1*	*36*	*16*	90^{1}	*95*	*12*	*7.2*	*8.7*	*88*	*40%*	*.321*	*1.85*	*5.43*	*5.52*	*5.98*	*-7.8*	*-0.8*	*139*	
2018	*KCA*	*MLB*	*24*	*2*	*3*	*0*	*16*	*9*	67^{1}	*66*	*9*	*8.1*	*10.6*	*79*	*40%*	*.328*	*1.88*	*5.26*	*5.44*	*5.79*	*-2.4*	*-0.2*	*134*	

Breakout: 1% Improve: 3% Collapse: 2% Attrition: 2% MLB: 7% *Comparables: Ethan Martin, Jae Kuk Ryu, Michael Ynoa*

The Good: We assemble 30 team lists, and I can count the number of pitchers we've covered with two potential 70-grade offerings without needing any help from Antonio Alfonseca. Staumont's stuff is nastay, and that extra 'a' is not a typo. The fastball sits in the mid-90s and can approach triple digits. He can run it or cut it down in the zone, and the sucker moves. His curveball is a hard downer with big depth and late run. It's a true swing-and-miss offering. His delivery suggests he should be able to throw more strikes than he does...at some point...maybe.

The Bad: We don't have the data, but I imagine Staumont's release point plot on Brooks Baseball would resemble a late period Mondrian. He has an incredibly fast arm, but rarely gets the ball out of his hand in the same spot. He can miss with a fastball in any direction and throw a curve behind a batter or spike it. When he has to get one over, the fastball can be more 93-94 and arrow-straight. The curve is inconsistent and will ride high with less depth. The change is firm though improving. It's really hard to project enough command/control here for him to start in the majors.

The Irrelevant: For an NAIA school, Azusa Pacific is quite the baseball hotbed. Current major league alums include Kirk Nieuwenhuis and Stephen Vogt.

The Risks: No matter what level you play at, you only get four balls to work with. Also, he's a pitcher

Major-league ETA: 2018, maybe faster as a reliever, but maybe not

Ben Carsley's Fantasy Take: The strikeout potential here makes Staumont more interesting to use than is the average reliever prospect, but at the end of the day, he's a reliever prospect, even if he's still masquerading as a starter. It ... it doesn't get much better from here.

3. Matt Strahm, LHP

DOB: 11/12/1991

Height/Weight: 6'3" 185 lbs

Bats/Throws: R/L

Drafted/Acquired: Drafted in the 21st round of the 2012 MLB entry draft, Neosho County Community College (Chanute, KS); signed for $100,000

Previous Ranking(s): N/A

2016 Stats: 1.23 ERA, 2.91 DRA, 22 IP, 13 H, 11 BB, 30 K at the MLB level, 3.43 ERA, 2.35 DRA, 102.1 IP, 102 H, 23 BB, 107 K at double-A Northwest Arkansas

The Role: OFP 55—Good 8th-inning guy
Likely 45—8th-inning guy with merely plus nervousness

YEAR	TEAM	LVL	AGE	W	L	SV	G	GS	IP	H	HR	BB/9	K/9	K	GB%	BABIP	WHIP	ERA	FIP	DRA	VORP	WARP	cFIP	MPH
2014	IDA	Rk	22	1	0	1	10	1	19^{2}	10	1	4.6	12.4	27	0%	.225	1.02	2.29	3.62	2.32			84	
2015	LEX	A	23	2	1	4	14	0	26	12	1	4.2	13.2	38	48%	.234	0.92	2.08	2.68	1.65	9.20	1.0	76	
2015	WIL	A+	23	1	6	1	15	11	68	48	7	2.5	11.0	83	37%	.255	0.99	2.78	3.21	2.13	21.80	2.4	83	
2016	NWA	AA	24	3	8	0	22	18	102^{1}	102	14	2.0	9.4	107	40%	.320	1.22	3.43	3.72	2.35	30.90	3.3	80	
2016	KCA	MLB	24	2	2	0	21	0	22	13	0	4.5	12.3	30	50%	.283	1.09	1.23	2.02	2.91	5.00	0.5	80	96.8
2017	*KCA*	*MLB*	*25*	*3*	*3*	*0*	*54*	*0*	*57*	*54*	*6*	*3.3*	*8.4*	*54*	*36%*	*.296*	*1.31*	*3.83*	*3.90*	*4.23*	*4.9*	*0.5*	*96*	
2018	*KCA*	*MLB*	*26*	*9*	*10*	*0*	*30*	*30*	*187*	*170*	*26*	*4.3*	*10.7*	*222*	*36%*	*.306*	*1.39*	*4.03*	*4.22*	*4.53*	*15.6*	*1.6*	*104*	

Breakout: 36% Improve: 47% Collapse: 19% Attrition: 28% MLB: 78% *Comparables: Scott Elbert, Jae Kuk Ryu, Antonio Bastardo*

The Good: Strahm is a 91-to-95-and-a-slider guy, which maybe isn't great if he is your third-best prospect, but he is better than the standard version of this type. He's left-handed for one, and he can run the pitch arm-side or get it to bore in on righties. He can throw it to all four quadrants of the zone, and it can be a swing-and-miss pitch when he elevates it. In addition to the slider—which he threw more as a starter in the minors than he did in his MLB cup of coffee—he'll show a curve and a change, both of which are within a shout of average.

The Bad: 2016 was Strahm's first pro season as a full-time starter, and while the performance in Double A was quite good, he's likely a reliever in the end. The delivery has some crossfire and some effort to it and the secondaries aren't good enough to turn over a major-league lineup multiple times. The curve can get a little loopy or a little slurvy, although it is a good weapon against lefties out of the pen. The change is good enough for him to crossover as a reliever, due to his arm speed, velocity separation, and the overall deception in his delivery, but it is more of a straight change, only occasionally showing a little late armside fade.

The Irrelevant: Strahm was the fifth Royals 21st-round pick to make the majors, joining Irving Falu, Jason Simontacchi, Lance Carter, and the immortal Larry Sutton.

The Risks: He's unlikely to be quite as good a reliever going forward as he was in 2016, but he should be a pretty good reliever. There was a bout of bicep tendinitis toward the end of the season, and he's already got Tommy John on his resume. And at the end of the day, he is still a pitcher.

Major-league ETA: Debuted in 2016

Ben Carsley's Fantasy Take: Maybe I didn't make myself clear above. Let's try again. The year is 2019. Strahm has established himself as a solid back-of-the-bullpen asset. You're browsing for sleeper closer options, and his name pops up. "Why not," you think to yourself. "He's a lefty and he's got good stuff." So you're glad you picked up Strahm in 2017, and you're glad to stash him on your bench. Saves were overvalued in your draft and you refused to pay up. You need to make gambles like this. So there Strahm sits, missing some bats and allowing some runs, but earning holds instead of saves. Ned Yost thinks The Seventh Inning Belongs to Strahm, you see, and you're starting to get nervous. Should you drop Strahm for another set-up man? For a back-of-the-top-150 prospect? For a swing starter? But you've waited so long ... You don't know. You can't decide. The anxiety is crippling. And so there Strahm sits, collecting Ks and allowing some runs, occupying a roster spot you don't really need but could sort of use. This is the future that awaits you if you draft Strahm. Or Staumont. Or any other reliever prospect. But you're too smart for that. You won't draft reliever prospects. Because reliever prospects aren't here to help. They're here to hurt you, now and in the future, in the past and the present. *(I think we might have lost Ben- j.p.)*

4. A.J. Puckett, RHP

DOB: 5/27/1995

Height/Weight: 6'4" 200 lbs

Bats/Throws: R/R

Drafted/Acquired: Drafted 67th overall in the 2016 MLB draft, Pepperdine University (Malibu, CA); signed for $1,200,000.

Previous Ranking(s): N/A

2016 Stats: 3.66 ERA, 4.28 DRA, 51.2 IP, 42 H, 15 BB, 37 K at Low-A Lexington, 3.86 ERA, 2.93 DRA, 7 IP, 8 H, 0 BB, 8 K at complex-level AZL

The Role: OFP 50—Average MLB starter
Likely 40—Fifth starter/swingman

YEAR	TEAM	LVL	AGE	W	L	SV	G	GS	IP	H	HR	BB/9	K/9	K	GB%	BABIP	WHIP	ERA	FIP	DRA	VORP	WARP	cFIP	MPH
2016	ROY	Rk	21	0	1	0	2	2	7	8	1	0.0	10.3	8	48%	.318	1.14	3.86	4.13	2.93	2.20	0.2	86	
2016	LEX	A	21	2	3	0	11	11	51²	42	4	2.6	6.4	37	52%	.259	1.10	3.66	3.96	4.28	4.20	0.5	103	
2017	*KCA*	*MLB*	*22*	*1*	*3*	*0*	*8*	*8*	*35*	*46*	*6*	*4.8*	*3.7*	*14*	*38%*	*.309*	*1.84*	*6.39*	*6.35*	*7.03*	*-6.1*	*-0.6*	*167*	
2018	*KCA*	*MLB*	*23*	*3*	*5*	*0*	*13*	*13*	*74²*	*89*	*13*	*6.0*	*6.2*	*51*	*38%*	*.315*	*1.86*	*5.93*	*6.13*	*6.52*	*-6.9*	*-0.7*	*153*	

Breakout: 1% Improve: 2% Collapse: 0% Attrition: 2% MLB: 2% *Comparables: Cody Anderson, Chad Bettis, Michael Ynoa*

The Good: Puckett has the frame and delivery of a man purpose-built to munch innings. The fastball is potentially solid-average. He can dial it up to 95 and holds his velocity deep into starts. He can do a few different things with his curve, manipulating its shape within its mid-to-upper-70s velo band. He has a changeup. He'll throw his changeup. It's not bad for a guy coming out of college.

The Bad: I have run through all the even-barely-clever ways to describe average-stuff righties at this point. Puckett is another one, which maybe isn't great if he is the fourth-best prosp...well, you know. The fastball doesn't wiggle much. Both the secondaries are inconsistent and lack much in the way of projection. There's enough curve and change here to start, but neither looks to be a bat-misser.

The Irrelevant: Pepperdine was founded by George Pepperdine, who made his money with the Western Auto Supply Company.

The Risks: Without an out pitch or a ton of fastball, he might get knocked around in the upper minors. Yawn, he's a pitcher.

Major-league ETA: Late 2018

Ben Carsley's Fantasy Take: Puckett might be worth something as a streaming starter once he's actually in the majors, but he's not worth rostering now. Please rely on A.J. Puk to fulfill all of your A.J. Puk/Puckett dynasty needs.

5. Jorge Bonifacio, OF

DOB: 06/04/1993

Height/Weight: 6'1" 195 lbs

Bats/Throws: R/R

Drafted/Acquired: Signed in December 2009 out of the Dominican Republic for $135,000.

Previous Ranking(s): N/A

2016 Stats: .277/.351/.461, 19 HR, 6 SB in 134 games at Triple-A Omaha

The Role: OFP 50—Average corner outfielder
Likely 40—Platoon/bench outfielder

YEAR	TEAM	LVL	AGE	PA	R	2B	3B	HR	RBI	BB	K	SB	CS	AVG/OBP/SLG	TAv	VORP	BABIP	BRR	FRAA	WARP
2014	NWA	AA	21	566	49	20	4	4	51	50	127	8	3	.230/.302/.309	.232	-3.3	.295	3.3	RF(125): -14.5, LF(2): -0.1	-1.7
2015	NWA	AA	22	536	60	30	2	17	64	42	126	3	2	.240/.305/.416	.256	7.1	.287	0.1	RF(97): -7.9, LF(18): -1.7	0.0
2016	OMA	AAA	23	558	82	22	6	19	86	51	130	6	2	.277/.351/.461	.290	29.3	.339	1.2	RF(72): 12.7, LF(50): 6.2	4.3
2017	*KCA*	*MLB*	*24*	*250*	*25*	*11*	*2*	*7*	*28*	*18*	*66*	*1*	*0*	*.233/.294/.382*	*.233*	*0.3*	*.295*	*-0.2*	*RF -2, LF -0*	*-0.2*
2018	*KCA*	*MLB*	*25*	*344*	*40*	*15*	*2*	*10*	*40*	*26*	*90*	*1*	*1*	*.240/.305/.399*	*.245*	*1.4*	*.302*	*-0.4*	*RF -2, LF 0*	*-0.1*

Breakout: 4% Improve: 13% Collapse: 5% Attrition: 19% MLB: 21% *Comparables: Scott Van Slyke, Tyler Austin, Chris Pettit*

The Good: After 1,200 decidedly mediocre Double-A plate appearances, Bonifacio regained a little prospect sheen in 2016. The favorable hitting environments of the Pacific Coast League didn't hurt, but Bonifacio's above-raw power continued to show up more in games, and he looked more like a potential MLB-quality Three True Outcomes right fielder, where his plus arm will also be an asset.

The Bad: None of the above might matter if he doesn't hit and, well, he might not hit. The swing can get long with some wrap, and is grooved at the best of times. He doesn't offer much else in terms of athletic tools. The power will have to play.

The Irrelevant: Bonifacio was actually on a KG-era prospect list, the last person who thought coming up with 300 of these was a productive use of time, so I will just borrow his from 2011: In 2011, Bonifacio went just 7-for-48 (.146) when leading off an inning in the Appy League, but hit .319 in all other at-bats.

The Risks: He might not hit enough to carry a corner outfield profile. There isn't a ton of bench utility since he is right-handed and defensively limited.

Major-league ETA: 2017

Ben Carsley's Fantasy Take: Bonifacio is close enough to the majors that he's of some use to us, and the combination of his power and proximity make him a borderline top-150 prospect. But, as mentioned above, he's probably just a short-side platoon bat, and if he does settle into that role he'll only be of use in AL-only formats. You could do worse when it comes to short-term speculative buys, though.

6. Khalil Lee, OF

DOB: 06/26/1998

Height/Weight: 5'10" 170 lbs

Bats/Throws: L/L

Drafted/Acquired: Drafted in the 3rd round (103rd overall) in the 2016 MLB draft, Flint Hill HS (Oakton, VA); signed for $750,000.

Previous Ranking(s): N/A

2016 Stats: .269/.396/.484, 6 HR, 8 SB in 49 games at complex-level AZL

The Role: OFP 50—Average center fielder with some pop
Likely 40—Bench outfielder

YEAR	TEAM	LVL	AGE	PA	R	2B	3B	HR	RBI	BB	K	SB	CS	AVG/OBP/SLG	TAv	VORP	BABIP	BRR	FRAA	WARP
2016	ROY	Rk	18	222	43	9	6	6	29	33	57	8	4	.269/.396/.484	.318	17.6	.358	-0.5	CF(23): -2.9, RF(15): -2.7	1.3
2017	*KCA*	*MLB*	*19*	*250*	*22*	*8*	*1*	*6*	*25*	*20*	*88*	*1*	*1*	*.191/.262/.314*	*.202*	*-6.6*	*.277*	*-0.2*	*CF -0, RF -0*	*-0.8*
2018	*KCA*	*MLB*	*20*	*341*	*38*	*11*	*2*	*10*	*36*	*29*	*113*	*2*	*1*	*.208/.284/.353*	*.224*	*-4.5*	*.291*	*-0.3*	*CF -1, RF 0*	*-0.6*

Breakout: 0% Improve: 8% Collapse: 2% Attrition: 7% MLB: 15% *Comparables: Nomar Mazara, Domingo Santana, Engel Beltre*

The Good: Lee has the kind of athleticism you expect from a player who was considered a two-way draft prospect. He also has the kind of arm. He has a shot to stick in center field despite not being as burner. There's at least average power in the profile.

The Bad: Lee's already starting to get a little thick in his lower half, and he might have to slide over to right field in his twenties. The profile is very, very raw at the plate, and there are questions about the ultimate hit tool here because of the potential for future swing-and-miss issues. He has present swing-and-miss issues as he will sell out for that pop.

The Irrelevant: Khalil translates to "friend" in Arabic.

The Risks: He's only played in the complex and some teams liked him better as a pitcher. At least he's not a pitcher (anymore).

Major-league ETA: 2021

Ben Carsley's Fantasy Take: Lee sure is far away from the majors. I hate to repeat myself, but check back in 2018 or so.

7. Scott Blewett, LHP

DOB: 04/10/1996

Height/Weight: 6'6" 210 lbs.

Bats/Throws: R/R

Drafted/Acquired: Drafted 56th overall in the 2014 MLB Draft, Baker HS (Baldwinsville, NY); signed for $1.8 million

Previous Ranking(s): #9 (Org)

2016 Stats: 4.31 ERA, 3.52 DRA, 129.1 IP, 138 H, 51 BB, 121 K at Low-A Lexington

The Role: OFP 50—No. 4 starter or setup
Likely 40—Solid middle reliever

YEAR	TEAM	LVL	AGE	W	L	SV	G	GS	IP	H	HR	BB/9	K/9	K	GB%	BABIP	WHIP	ERA	FIP	DRA	VORP	WARP	cFIP	MPH
2014	BNC	Rk	18	1	2	0	8	7	28	27	3	4.8	9.3	29	0%	.316	1.50	4.82	4.82	4.36			106	
2015	LEX	A	19	3	5	0	18	18	81[1]	88	6	2.7	6.6	60	48%	.317	1.38	5.20	3.96	3.80	12.80	1.4	97	
2016	LEX	A	20	8	11	0	25	25	129[1]	138	10	3.5	8.4	121	47%	.338	1.46	4.31	3.90	3.52	21.60	2.4	100	
2017	*KCA*	*MLB*	*21*	*4*	*8*	*0*	*19*	*19*	*91*	*120*	*16*	*5.1*	*4.6*	*46*	*36%*	*.322*	*1.89*	*6.23*	*6.27*	*6.79*	*-13.3*	*-1.4*	*162*	
2018	*KCA*	*MLB*	*22*	*5*	*9*	*0*	*22*	*22*	*131[2]*	*144*	*21*	*6.1*	*7.8*	*114*	*36%*	*.314*	*1.78*	*5.53*	*5.73*	*6.03*	*-6.6*	*-0.7*	*143*	

Breakout: 4% Improve: 4% Collapse: 1% Attrition: 5% MLB: 6% *Comparables: Casey Crosby, Edwin Diaz, German Marquez*

The Good: Blewett has the makings of two plus pitches in his fastball and curve. The fastball bumps 95 and can show good life down in the zone and is a weapon when he elevates it out of his high release point. The curve at its best is a 12-6 downer that has hard, late break. He can play with the shape and velocity to spot it as well.

The Bad: How do you feel about Josh Staumont with better command but worse stuff? Blewett's long frame and near over-the-top release point means he can struggle to stay on top of his offerings and locate below batter's necklines. Better hitters won't chase those as often as A-ball hitters have. He'll miss armside and up and then yank one, the kind of stuff you often see with young pitchers in the low minors. The curveball can vacillate between 12-6 and 11-5 and he can snap it off at times. It will also lose depth and ride high when he is struggling with his release point. The change is a work in progress with a below-average projection.

The Irrelevant: Blewett potentially could be the second MLB pitcher from Baldwinsville, NY, joining Jason Grilli.

The Risks: He's a tall pitcher in A-ball with command and third-pitch issues. There's a long development horizon here and plenty that could go wrong.

Major-league ETA: 2020

Ben Carsley's Fantasy Take: If I revisit Reliever Name Foreshadowing in a few years, I expect Blewett to earn at least 8/10 Riskes.

8. Meibrys Viloria, C

DOB: 02/15/1997

Height/Weight: 5'11" 175 lbs

Bats/Throws: L/R

Drafted/Acquired: Signed in July 2013 out of Colombia for $460,000.

Previous Ranking(s): N/A

2016 Stats: .376/.436/.606, 6 HR, 1 SB in 58 games at rookie-level Idaho Falls

The Role: OFP 50—Average MLB catcher
Likely 40—Backup backstop

YEAR	TEAM	LVL	AGE	PA	R	2B	3B	HR	RBI	BB	K	SB	CS	AVG/OBP/SLG	TAv	VORP	BABIP	BRR	FRAA	WARP
2014	BNC	Rk	17	51	4	2	0	1	5	10	10	0	0	.200/.373/.325	.210	-0.7	.241	0.0		0.0
2014	DRY	Rk	17	129	16	8	1	2	20	14	18	1	1	.306/.383/.450	.258	-0.1	.344	-0.4		0.0
2015	BNC	Rk	18	172	20	0	0	0	16	17	23	0	0	.260/.335/.260	.219	-1.8	.302	0.5	C(27): 0.2	-0.2
2016	IDA	Rk	19	259	54	28	3	6	55	20	36	1	1	.376/.436/.606	.353	40.0	.418	2.3	C(50): -0.8	3.9
2017	*KCA*	*MLB*	*20*	*250*	*20*	*10*	*1*	*4*	*24*	*14*	*73*	*0*	*0*	*.208/.258/.314*	*.198*	*-4.2*	*.278*	*-0.4*	*C -0*	*-0.5*
2018	*KCA*	*MLB*	*21*	*294*	*30*	*12*	*1*	*6*	*28*	*17*	*83*	*0*	*0*	*.220/.271/.338*	*.214*	*-3.8*	*.288*	*-0.6*	*C 0*	*-0.4*

Breakout: 1% Improve: 4% Collapse: 0% Attrition: 2% MLB: 5% *Comparables: Carson Kelly, Francisco Pena, Christian Bethancourt*

The Good: Viloria is potentially a plus hitter that can stick behind the plate and bop some doubles. He's miles away from that right now, but you don't have to do much more than that to be an everyday backstop.

The Bad: When Kiley McDaniel was at FanGraphs he wrote a piece purporting that minor league shortstops fall into one of three buckets "definitely a shortstop," "not a shortstop," and "maybe a shortstop," with that last bucket being by far the largest. I think that applies to catchers as well and Viloria sits nicely in the mushy middle here. The arm is fine, the other stuff is still a bit rough at present, and there probably isn't a plus glove in here regardless.

The Irrelevant: I'm not a particular proponent of European football chants moving into the ballpark, but "My Viloria, my Viloria, even I'll adore you my Viloria" would be a winner.

The Risks: A scout quote we got during this whole process was "Low-A catchers are impossible." Viloria is a rookie ball catcher.

Major-league ETA: 2021

Ben Carsley's Fantasy Take: Viloria is one of my favorite dynasty sleepers. He's way too far away to even flirt with top-100 status, but if you're in really deep leagues and you're looking for a flier, you can pop him. Just be itchy with the trigger finger if another better prospect comes along, because Viloria's lead time and position make him a high-risk asset.

9. Seuly Matias, OF

DOB: 09/04/1998

Height/Weight: 6'3" 200 lbs

Bats/Throws: R/R

Drafted/Acquired: Signed in July 2015 out of the Dominican Republic for $2,250,000

Previous Ranking(s): N/A

2016 Stats: .250/.348/.477, 8 HR, 2 SB in 46 games at complex-level AZL, .125/.222/.167, 0 HR, 0 SB in 7 games at rookie ball in the DSL

The Role: OFP 50—Exciting second-division regular right fielder
Likely 40—Power bench bat

YEAR	TEAM	LVL	AGE	PA	R	2B	3B	HR	RBI	BB	K	SB	CS	AVG/OBP/SLG	TAv	VORP	BABIP	BRR	FRAA	WARP
2016	DRY	Rk	17	27	2	1	0	0	2	2	13	0	0	.125/.222/.167	.330	0.2	.273	0.0	CF(7): 0.5	0.0
2016	ROY	Rk	17	198	32	11	2	8	29	22	73	2	4	.250/.348/.477	.288	9.4	.385	-0.3	CF(23): -2.0, RF(19): 0.1	0.9
2017	*KCA*	*MLB*	*18*	*250*	*20*	*8*	*1*	*6*	*25*	*15*	*102*	*0*	*0*	*.178/.235/.297*	*.186*	*-11.0*	*.282*	*-0.4*	*CF -0, RF 0*	*-1.2*
2018	*KCA*	*MLB*	*19*	*229*	*22*	*7*	*1*	*6*	*22*	*14*	*94*	*0*	*0*	*.180/.235/.306*	*.191*	*-11.0*	*.283*	*-0.5*	*CF 0, RF 0*	*-1.2*

Breakout: 0% Improve: 0% Collapse: 0% Attrition: 0% MLB: 0% *Comparables: Raul Mondesi, Wilmer Flores*

The Good: Matias has two standout tools: serious pop and a hose for an arm. He's athletic but not remarkably fast, which allows him to play a sufficient center field for the time being. Odds are he'll be a right fielder before too long, where has the potential to be an above-average defender. He has a vicious swing that generates excellent bat speed and a distinct sound off the barrel. Despite finishing the season with an alarmingly high strikeout rate, he limited his punchouts to under 26 percent over the final month of play, showing major strides in his first year in the States. Matias has shown patience at the plate, taking walks at a rate that lends stability to his otherwise risky profile.

The Bad: The aforementioned strikeout rate—like most toolsy teenage prospects, Matias' career will be defined by the development of his bat-to-ball ability. The whiffs are primarily caused by him swinging with reckless abandon, as opposed to an inability to lay off pitches out of the zone. There's also a very real chance his frame doesn't allow for much more muscle growth, which would limit his otherwise impressive raw power.

The Irrelevant: Matias shares a birthday with Ken "Hawk" Harrelson, Doyle Alexander, Mike Piazza, Sun-woo Kim, Pat Neshek, and Beyoncé.

The Risks: It's easier to list the things about Matias that aren't risky: 1) he can throw baseballs really hard and really far. The risk is tremendous with any 18 year old, but particularly so for a corner outfielder with a 37-percent strikeout rate in complex-level ball.

Major-league ETA: 2020 —Matt Pullman

Ben Carsley's Fantasy Take: Again, check back in 2019. But don't hold your breath.

10. Miguel Almonte, RHP

DOB: 4/4/1993

Height/Weight: 6'2" 180 lbs

Bats/Throws: R/R

Drafted/Acquired: Signed in November 2010 by Kansas City out of the Dominican Republic for $25,000

Previous Ranking(s): #6 (Org)

2016 Stats: 5.55 ERA, 8.72 DRA, 60 IP, 62 H, 42 BB, 57 K at triple-A Omaha, 7.31 ERA, 4.60 DRA, 16 IP, 24 H, 4 BB, 15 K at double-A Northwest Arkansas

The Role: OFP 45—seventh-inning guy
Likely 40—Middle reliever

YEAR	TEAM	LVL	AGE	W	L	SV	G	GS	IP	H	HR	BB/9	K/9	K	GB%	BABIP	WHIP	ERA	FIP	DRA	VORP	WARP	cFIP	MPH
2014	WIL	A+	21	6	8	0	23	22	110^{1}	107	9	2.6	8.2	101	48%	.316	1.26	4.49	3.92	3.65	23.70	2.4	94	
2015	NWA	AA	22	4	4	0	17	17	67	65	4	3.6	7.4	55	43%	.307	1.37	4.03	4.00	4.90	1.40	0.2	103	
2015	OMA	AAA	22	2	2	0	11	6	36^{2}	33	3	3.7	10.1	41	43%	.323	1.31	5.40	3.90	3.77	5.90	0.6	91	
2015	KCA	MLB	22	0	2	0	9	0	8^{2}	7	4	7.3	10.4	10	52%	.158	1.62	6.23	9.57	4.20	0.50	0.1	103	98.9
2016	OMA	AAA	23	3	7	0	21	12	60	63	5	6.3	8.6	57	49%	.335	1.75	5.55	5.15	8.72	-23.10	-2.4	121	
2016	NWA	AA	23	2	1	0	11	0	16	24	4	2.2	8.4	15	41%	.400	1.75	7.31	5.31	4.60	0.20	0.0	97	
2017	*KCA*	*MLB*	*24*	*3*	*4*	*0*	*36*	*6*	*65*	*70*	*7*	*4.4*	*6.5*	*47*	*42%*	*.302*	*1.57*	*4.99*	*4.78*	*5.24*	*-0.7*	*-0.1*	*100*	
2018	*KCA*	*MLB*	*25*	*4*	*4*	*0*	*49*	*8*	*90^{1}*	*87*	*11*	*5.8*	*9.2*	*93*	*42%*	*.308*	*1.60*	*4.62*	*4.82*	*5.17*	*0.9*	*0.1*	*118*	

Breakout: 13% Improve: 24% Collapse: 20% Attrition: 33% MLB: 53% *Comparables: Esmil Rogers, Daniel Wright, Charles Brewer*

The Good: A move to the pen late in the season kept the embers of Almonte's prospect status faintly glowing—a poor Royals system doesn't hurt either. The velocity was back into the mid-to-upper 90s late in the season and in winter ball. His change rebounded some, showing hard, late sink again.

The Bad: Hey it's another Royals pitching prospect that might not throw enough strikes. The curve is below average, but that's less of an issue now that he's a pen arm I guess, as is the high-effort delivery. The fastball command is still well-below-average.

The Irrelevant: Your author keeps referring to him Yohan Almonte—who was briefly a marginal Mets prospect in the early-2010s off a good Brooklyn season—in his head. Only one more list to go!

The Risks: The risk is he's still an Omaha shuttle arm this time next year. Or he gets hurt because he's a pitcher.

Major-league ETA: Debuted in 2015

Ben Carsley's Fantasy Take: I believe I've made my feelings on reliever prospects known.

OTHERS OF NOTE:

Kyle Zimmer, RHP

Zimmer is easily the best talent on this list, but he's had three straight lost seasons due to recurring shoulder problems. Like Matt Harvey and Phil Hughes, his shoulder issues got a new underlying diagnosis in 2016: thoracic outlet syndrome. Rustin Dodd of the Kansas City Star reported that Zimmer should be "good to go" for spring training, but it's completely impossible to know what's left. At his best, he looked like a developing number two; a four-pitch starter with command, an explosive fastball sitting in the mid-90s and touching higher, and a wipeout curve. He could look like anything from that to a double-A reliever now (and all the points in between), and it wouldn't be surprising. *—Jarrett Seidler*

Eric Skoglund, LHP

Skoglund is both healthy and throws strikes, making him a bit of a sui generis pitching prospect in the Royals system. Unfortunately the stuff isn't much to write home about. He's a long, lean lefty with some deception from his herky-jerky delivery. There's three average pitches he slings from a lowish armslot. The control is ahead of the command, and the stuff can be far too hittable when he catches the fat part of the plate. Still, he is 6-foot-6 and left-handed, and you can't teach that (Venditte is only 6-foot-1). Skoglund likely will settle in somewhere along the fifth starter/swingman/LOOGy continuum.

Donnie Dewees, CF

The Cubs second-rounder in 2015, Dewees has thus far showed that he can hit in pro ball. He features plus bat speed and has a line-drive swing that is conducive to spraying the ball all over the field. He controls the strike zone well and can work counts as well. A plus runner, Dewees projects as an average defender in center and an above-average one in left. There isn't much home-run power to speak of given his swing path and lack of loft, but he should have plenty of extra-base hits. The profile is more fourth outfielder than first-division starter, but a solid performance in Double A could jump him into the Top 10 next season. *—Steve Givarz*

Jeison Guzman, SS

A glove-first shortstop with instincts and range, Guzman's bat will have to evolve for him to develop into a big-league regular. His hands are quick, both in the field and at the plate, and he has a clean arm action delivering the ball from shortstop. While "glove-first" might apply, that doesn't mean he's a lock to stick at the six. His body could easily push him off the position down the line, as good as his glove and hands might be. All things considered, he profiles as a utility infielder, though his glove could carry him long enough to see the bat come around. While he does a good job employing his lower-half in his swing, the contact ability could prove insufficient to ever reach the show. *—Matt Pullman*

Chase Vallot, C

Prep catchers can go in a lot of different directions, but Vallot has gone in a fairly predictable one. A 2015 full-season ball assignment for the 18-year-old went poorly, although he flashed plus power and a strong arm. A repeat assignment to Lexington to round out his teenage years resulted in *more* of the same. The swing here is a little stiff and very long, so the K's aren't likely to be more manageable at higher levels. But he's got a decent shot to catch, just turned 20, and has hit a bunch of bombs off older college arms. The situation warrants continued monitoring.

TOP 10 TALENTS 25 AND UNDER (BORN 4/1/91 OR LATER)

1. Jorge Soler	6. Cheslor Cuthbert
2. Raul Mondesi	7. A.J. Puckett
3. Hunter Dozier	8. Jorge Bonifacio
4. Josh Staumont	9. Khalil Lee
5. Matt Strahm	10. Scott Blewett

Rings rest upon the fingers of players who littered the Royals Top 25-and-under list in the past in exchange for players like Sean Manaea, Brandon Finnegan and Cody Reed, all of whom undoubtedly would have topped this list. In addition, the accidental death of Yordano Ventura took the Royals top talent in the system off the list, leaving one of the weakest farm systems we've seen in the Dayton Moore era to fill out the backend of a less-inspiring list.

The true talent in this list and in the organization lies in players like Jorge Soler, Raul Mondesi, Josh Staumont and a player not on the list, Kyle Zimmer. Those four players represent large ceilings that, if the Royals are lucky enough to catch with three or more, all of them could help propel them to more playoff runs.

The Jorge Soler deal for one season of Wade Davis wasn't the return that some Royals fans had hoped for but, in Soler, Kansas City is acquiring four years of team control and a large ceiling for a closer that was somewhat risky to return anything if arm problems had reappeared. The Cuban has flashed signs of his immense talent in the second half last season with Chicago and in a small sample in 2014 2014, along with a tremendous September and playoff run for the Cubs in 2015. It will be Royals outfield coach Rusty Kuntz's job to iron out the defensive kinks in the outfielder's game, no easy task while playing in one of the largest outfields in the league, but one the front office is betting improves with regular playing time and focus once penciled into a starting spot everyday. If you're buying Soler's improved plate discipline last season combined with his power, then he undoubtedly will be one of the keys to the middle of the Royals lineup this season and going forward.

Last year's top prospect, Raul Mondesi, struggled mightily in his major-league debut thanks to his Royals-esque plate discipline that saw him offer at 43 percent of balls outside of the zone in his 149 plate appearances. This was after an abbreviated minor league season due to a 50-game PED suspension. The tools are still there for Mondesi with elite speed, athleticism, his father's arm and surprising power from the left side. The lack of pitch recognition and discipline were exposed, and Mondesi's defensive gifts aren't allowed to shine on the right side of the diamond while Alcides Escobar mans shortstop. Will the front office continue to push Mondesi this season into a starting spot at the MLB level or will they decide to finally slow things down with a triple-A slot and let him work on the weaknesses in his game?

While Mondesi's struggles came at the major-league level, Dozier's came in 2014 and 2015 in the minors, but an adjustment in his hip movement and a cut-down swing allowed Hunter to unlock his natural strength to connect on 68 extra-base hits in 129 minor-league games. With Mike Moustakas possibly on his way toward free agency, Dozier likely will compete with Cuthbert for the third-base job, or move over to first base where his plus power could still play in the possible absence of Eric Hosmer.

While four of the players mentioned above feature large ceilings the Royals have a couple of higher floor players in Strahm and Cuthbert. At worst with Strahm it appears the Royals have a power lefty from the pen who was spectacular in his MLB debut flashing his plus fastball and solid curveball. It appears that Strahm felt more and more comfortable with his changeup as his debut wore on, using it more in September than his curve to excellent results. If that pitch comes forward, the Royals have a possibility of a No. 3 starter developed from within to combine with Danny Duffy. While Cuthbert and Dozier have taken slow-burn paths to the majors, they appear to be second tier-regulars while young and affordable.

While currently in the lower third of farm systems in the league, the Royals could see a bounceback coming thanks to the drafting of Puckett and Lee, along with additional prospects coming from their 2015 international signing class that landed stateside this past year, plus an additional prospect or two landing next year. With those additions, combined with a larger draft pool (14th in '17), and trade additions should the Royals flip other core stars at the deadline, readers could see a major overhaul in this list come 2018.

—Clint Scoles

LOS ANGELES ANGELS

The State of the System: *"And as it tells its sorry tale / In harrowing detail / Its hollowness will haunt you"*
— The Decemberists: "Los Angeles, I'm Yours"

THE TOP TEN

1. OF Jahmai Jones	6. OF Brandon Marsh
2. 1B Matt Thaiss	7. RHP Grayson Long
3. C Taylor Ward	8. SS Nonie Williams
4. LHP Nate Smith	9. RHP Keynan Middleton
5. SS David Fletcher	10. RHP Jose Campos

The Big Question: How low can you go in other systems and find an Angels Top Ten prospect?

The Angels may not have the worst system in baseball anymore. It's still really bad though. I've already expounded at length on how you get to having one of the worst systems in baseball, and the Angels check every box there. So I won't repeat myself. Instead, I will turn it over to the staff to find prospects deep in other systems that would make the 2017 Angels Top Ten list…

Steve's Guy

Malquin Canelo, SS (Philadelphia Phillies)

With a plus arm, lateral range to both sides, and natural instincts, Canelo can play a really good shortstop. He is also a plus runner, which helps him beat out some balls in the infield, he just needs to hit a little. He lacks bat speed, and his slight frame isn't going to contribute much to over the fence power. His swing path is short and he makes a fair amount of contact, so you're hoping for enough to carve out a viable bench role. That's not nothing, but in a deep Phillies system, he might not even make the top 20. *—Steve Givarz*

Matt's Guy

Nabil Crismatt, RHP (New York Mets) (N.B. I didn't even have to assign him this *—j.p.*)

A soft-bodied 6-foot-1 righty who can be described as crafty. The 21-year-old Colombian native opened the season as a swingman in the Penn League, featuring a fastball operating at 88-91, touching 93 later in the season. He has advanced feel for his changeup, but his third offering is a pedestrian, low-70s, lollipop curve. Despite a lack of overpowering stuff, his pitchability and command allowed him to register 74 strikeouts in 65 ⅔ innings across three levels, while walking just seven batters. He made four appearances in the Sally League, going at least 6 ⅔ innings in each, while posting a sparkling 0.00 DRA. He capped off his modest breakout campaign with a six-inning, one-run spot start for Double-A Binghamton. He's the type of arm that can get lost in the shuffle of even an average system like the Mets', landing at no. 27 on their BP local list, but given the state of the Angels' farm, Crismatt would garner consideration for the last few spots of the top-10. *—Matt Pullman*

Craig's Guy

Imani Abdullah, RHP (Los Angeles Dodgers)

Abdullah was a high-school golfer who transitioned to pitching late, but netted just under $650,000 from the Dodgers as an 11th-round pick in 2015. He's got the height you look for in a pitcher at 6-foot-4, and uses his extension to make his 90-94 mph fastball all the more potent. He gets good life on the pitch as well, and while he'll show the ability to generate steep plane, he's prone to leaving pitches up in the zone as well. His secondaries include a looping curveball that doesn't have the requisite snap to miss bats at present and a firm change, both of which need significant work. Still, a 20-year-old, with this frame and projectability, who can fill the zone with a potent fastball wouldn't look out of place on this list. He's about as raw as they come, which is why he's more in the late teens as a Dodgers prospect, but the Angels system lacks pitchers with his potential. *—Craig Goldstein*

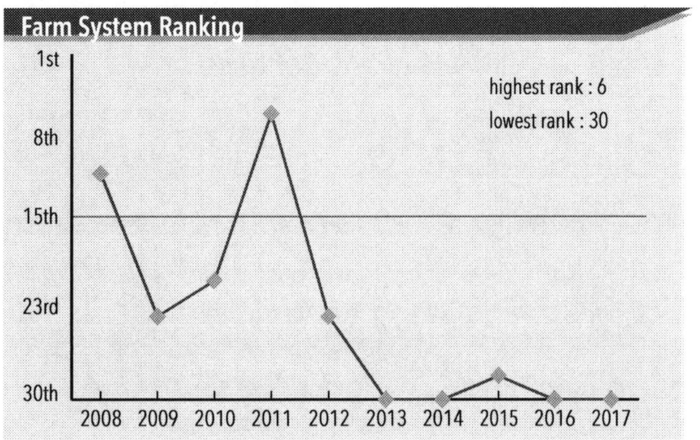

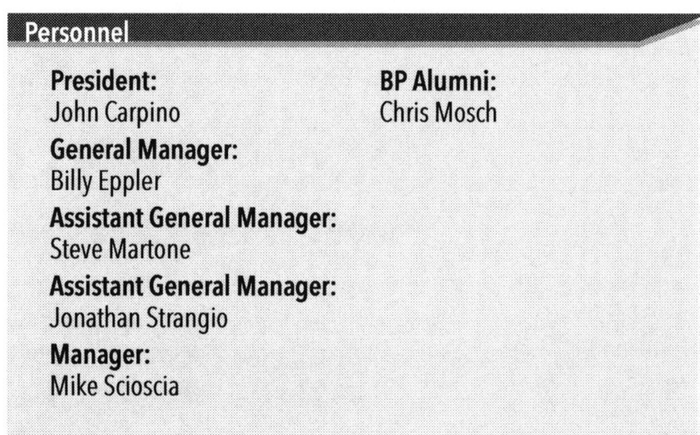
Personnel

President:
John Carpino

General Manager:
Billy Eppler

Assistant General Manager:
Steve Martone

Assistant General Manager:
Jonathan Strangio

Manager:
Mike Scioscia

BP Alumni:
Chris Mosch

Jarrett's Guy

Kyle Higashioka, C (New York Yankees)

Higashioka first reached Double-A Trenton in June 2012, and didn't actually graduate the level until this year. He's been exposed to multiple Rule 5 drafts. Last offseason, he declared minor-league free agency after hitting .254/.305/.375 for High-A Tampa, which made him freely available to any organization for a non-roster invite and a living wage. He re-signed with the Yankees. Despite all that, he'd make this Angels list with room to spare. Then again, Jose Campos is actually on this list, and he was ingloriously dumped off the Yankees 40-man at midseason for Tyler Clippard on his way to being an Angels waiver claim.

After years of injuries and stagnation, Higashioka showed up in 2016 as a quality catch-and-throw guy with good pop. He's also a very good receiver and framer, which meshes with his excellent FRAA numbers. The Yankees added him to the 40-man early to protect him from not just Rule 5 but another run at free agency, where he'd have surely done better than a random NRI, and he'll be battling Austin Romine for the role as Gary Sanchez's backup. There's at least a role 4 backup catcher here, and pending continued health, maybe a little more. How different is that from Taylor Ward, really? *—Jarrett Seidler*

Jeffrey's Guy

Ronald Herrera, RHP (New York Yankees)

Before I saw Herrera for Trenton this year, I got this message from a colleague "He's every short Double-A starter you've ever seen." It's not a bad description, but Herrera's got a bit more pitchability and a bit less stuff than that familiar trope. The fastball sits in the low-90s, although he has to ramp up the effort to keep it there later in starts, and he can lose his command of it armside. He has a full four-pitch mix, including a humpy curve and a slurvy slider. The change has a chance to be above-average with nice split action. It's inconsistent, but he can miss bats with it. The delivery is slow-slow-fast with effort at the end, and the frame/stamina suggests that he's a reliever in the end, although he has a better chance to start than guys in this cohort. He doesn't make the Yankees Top 20—it's an obscenely deep system—but he'd be in the back end of a top 20 on your average team's prospect list. The Angels are not your average team. He makes their Top 10.

1. Jahmai Jones, OF

DOB: 08/04/1997

Height/Weight: 5'11" 200 lbs.

Bats/Throws: R/R

Drafted/Acquired: Drafted 70th overall in the 2015 MLB Draft, Wesleyan HS (Norcross, GA); signed for $1.1 million

Previous Ranking(s): #2 (Org) 2016

2016 Stats: .321/.404/.459, 3 HR, 19 SB in 48 games at rookie ball in Orem, .242/.294/.306, 1 HR, 1 SB in 16 games at Low-A Burlington

The Role: OFP 60—Above-average center fielder
Likely 50—Average outfielder

YEAR	TEAM	LVL	AGE	PA	R	2B	3B	HR	RBI	BB	K	SB	CS	AVG/OBP/SLG	TAv	VORP	BABIP	BRR	FRAA	WARP
2015	ANG	Rk	17	183	28	6	2	2	20	17	33	16	7	.244/.330/.344	.271	10.8	.294	2.7	CF(38): -3.0, RF(2): -0.4	0.8
2016	ORM	Rk	18	226	49	12	3	3	20	21	29	19	6	.321/.404/.459	.322	23.7	.364	1.3	CF(41): -5.0, RF(4): -0.6	2.0
2016	BUR	A	18	70	8	1	0	1	10	5	13	1	0	.242/.294/.306	.219	-0.8	.286	0.2	CF(8): -0.9, RF(4): 1.6	-0.2
2017	*ANA*	*MLB*	*19*	*250*	*27*	*8*	*1*	*6*	*21*	*14*	*73*	*4*	*2*	*.204/.256/.318*	*.203*	*-5.5*	*.266*	*0.0*	*CF -1, RF -0*	*-0.7*
2018	*ANA*	*MLB*	*20*	*369*	*40*	*12*	*1*	*10*	*39*	*24*	*101*	*6*	*3*	*.221/.277/.352*	*.224*	*-3.1*	*.279*	*0.3*	*CF -2, RF 0*	*-0.6*

Breakout: 0% Improve: 7% Collapse: 2% Attrition: 6% MLB: 13% *Comparables: Engel Beltre, Nomar Mazara, Elvis Andrus*

The Good: Look, this hasn't been a good system since Howie Kendrick and Erick Aybar were eligible, but Jones is a good outfield prospect. He's a plus runner who could be an asset in center field once he gets more reps (he's only been a full time outfielder as a professional). The swing is simple and direct, and he's strong enough to do damage even without a traditional power hitter's stroke. I think there's more power in here too, as you'll see it when he gets a bit longer in batting practice. Advanced baseball IQ for his experience level.

The Bad: Jones is athletic, but it's "athletic strong safety," and there may not be quite enough speed for center once he gets into his twenties. The power is mostly theoretical at present. He's still raw and the profile could go a number of ways in the next two years.

The Irrelevant: While I think he looks like a strong safety, Jones was actually an all-state wide receiver in high school. He's not the last Georgia high school wide receiver on this list either.

The Risks: We don't know if this works in full-season ball yet. More collection of tools than baseball player at present. Possible future corner profile.

Major league ETA: 2020

Ben Carsley's Fantasy Take: Jones has a carrying fantasy tool in his speed and enough else to be of substantial interest to us. He's years away and is very high risk, but as far as low minors gambles go, Jones is an attractive one. It's too early to try and project stats or through any comparable lines out there, but Jones is a definite top-150 fantasy prospect and could flirt with the back of the top-100.

2. Matt Thaiss, 1B

DOB: 05/06/1995

Height/Weight: 6'0" 195 lbs

Bats/Throws: L/R

Drafted/Acquired: Drafted 16th overall in the 2016 MLB Draft, University of Virginia; signed for $2,150,000

Previous Ranking(s): N/A

2016 Stats: .276/.351/.427, 4 HR, 1 SB in 52 games at Low-A Burlington, 338/.394/.569, 2 HR, 2 SB in 15 games at rookie-level Orem

The Role: OFP 50—Average first baseman
Likely 40—Fringe starter/lefty bench bat

YEAR	TEAM	LVL	AGE	PA	R	2B	3B	HR	RBI	BB	K	SB	CS	AVG/OBP/SLG	TAv	VORP	BABIP	BRR	FRAA	WARP
2016	ORM	Rk	21	71	16	7	1	2	12	4	4	2	4	.338/.394/.569	.282	2.2	.339	0.2	1B(15): 0.7	0.3
2016	BUR	A	21	226	24	12	3	4	31	22	28	1	0	.276/.351/.427	.293	5.8	.302	-3.6	1B(43): 5.3	1.2
2017	*ANA*	*MLB*	*22*	*250*	*24*	*10*	*1*	*7*	*29*	*17*	*58*	*1*	*0*	*.226/.285/.372*	*.230*	*-3.1*	*.269*	*-0.3*	*1B 5*	*0.2*
2018	*ANA*	*MLB*	*23*	*287*	*33*	*12*	*1*	*9*	*33*	*21*	*67*	*1*	*0*	*.231/.293/.389*	*.242*	*-2.2*	*.274*	*-0.5*	*1B 6*	*0.4*

Breakout: 5% Improve: 18% Collapse: 2% Attrition: 20% MLB: 24% *Comparables: Nick Evans, James Loney, Chris Marrero*

The Good: Thaiss was the best-hitting catcher available in this year's draft class. That's not just damning with faint praise. The hit tool is potentially plus, due to a combination of above-average hand-eye, barrel control and bat speed. His approach is advanced. He's already shown some pull power in professional games and will show it to all fields in batting practice. You can dream on 15-20 home run power at maturity. Thaiss has an above-average arm, because he was once a catcher. Oh yeah, about that.

The Bad: Thaiss was a catcher. He is now a first baseman. Those two positions have very different offensive bars to get over. He's not even a good first baseman yet, although he has the physical tools to be average there with more reps. His power may only end up as a 40 or 45. That's plenty if you are a catcher, but I direct you to those first two sentences again.

The Irrelevant: University of Virginia hitters have a reputation for good plate discipline. The highest OBP for a Cavalier alum belongs to Brandon Guyer (.349), who edges out Ryan Zimmerman.

The Risks: As a first baseman, there will be pressure on the bat to reach a 60/50 projection. He will also have to—you know—learn how to play first base. I've been told it's incredibly hard.

Major league ETA: 2019

Ben Carsley's Fantasy Take: Look, I've been pretty hard on fantasy first baseman prospects to this point, but this list is gonna have a whole lotta negative, so let's stay positive here. Thaiss' power needs to take a step forward and it's a bummer that he can't catch, but I've espoused the virtues of betting on hit tools before, and Thaiss has a good one. Consider him a top-125ish fantasy prospect and hope he grows into some more pop as he gets closer to the majors. He could be a top-20 fantasy first baseman or at least a usable CI in time.

3. Taylor Ward, C

DOB: 12/14/1993

Height/Weight: 6'1" 180 lbs.

Bats/Throws: R/R

Drafted/Acquired: Drafted 26th overall in the 2015 MLB Draft, Fresno State University; signed for $1.67 million

Previous Ranking(s): #4 (Org) 2016

2016 Stats: 249/.323/.337, 10 HR, 0 SB in 123 games at High-A Inland Empire

The Role: OFP 50—Average Starting Catcher
Likely 40—Average Backup Catcher

YEAR	TEAM	LVL	AGE	PA	R	2B	3B	HR	RBI	BB	K	SB	CS	AVG/OBP/SLG	TAv	VORP	BABIP	BRR	FRAA	WARP
2015	ORM	Rk	21	141	20	4	1	2	19	29	8	5	2	.349/.489/.459	.333	14.8	.360	-3.1	C(29): -0.2	1.4
2015	BUR	A	21	103	10	3	0	1	12	10	15	1	1	.348/.412/.413	.296	7.8	.408	0.1	C(20): -0.6	0.8
2016	INL	A+	22	529	61	11	0	10	56	48	81	0	0	.249/.323/.337	.240	9.4	.279	1.4	C(90): 4.1	1.4
2017	*ANA*	*MLB*	*23*	*250*	*24*	*8*	*0*	*6*	*27*	*20*	*55*	*0*	*0*	*.225/.292/.345*	*.225*	*2.2*	*.266*	*-0.5*	*C 0*	*0.3*
2018	*ANA*	*MLB*	*24*	*268*	*31*	*8*	*0*	*7*	*28*	*22*	*56*	*0*	*0*	*.232/.300/.356*	*.234*	*1.8*	*.271*	*-0.7*	*C 0*	*0.2*

Breakout: 3% Improve: 11% Collapse: 1% Attrition: 33% MLB: 39% *Comparables: Tucker Barnhart, Steve Clevenger, Carlos Perez*

The Good: Ward made steady progress across the board at High-A, showcasing maturity and the aptitude to incorporate adjustments on the fly. An aggressive opposite-field approach gave way to greater selectivity and pull-side attention as the season wore on, and Ward started tapping into fringe-average power more consistently. The on-base percentage can play up if demonstrated gains in zone command hold. Behind the plate, Ward's pop is smooth and his arm plus, helping drive a 38-percent caught-stealing percentage. He improved as a pitch-framer and receiver, and he's athletic enough to develop his agility and blocking technique as well.

The Bad: The receiving and bat are both still rawer than you'd expect from a collegiate first-rounder. He can struggle to implement a game plan behind the plate, and showed vulnerability to routine sequencing at it. His tendency to punch the ball to right is born out in swings that will frequently lose the hips and drag the barrel through the zone. It's a fringe-average offensive profile, and the glove still carries a moderate amount of projection to get to average.

The Irrelevant: Ward hails from Dayton, Ohio, home of the Reds' Class-A affiliate Dayton Dragons, who in 2011 broke the all-time record among North American professional sports franchises by selling out their 815th consecutive game at Fifth Third Field.

The Risks: The arm is a standout tool, but the rest of the package lacks for impact and he remains relatively raw even after a full season at High-A. There's a path to starting at the big-league level, but it's narrower than you'd like out of a first-round investment.

Major league ETA: 2019 —Wilson Karaman

Ben Carsley's Fantasy Take: Can't you just pick up Drew Butera or something.

4. Nate Smith, LHP

DOB: 08/28/1991

Height/Weight: 6'3" 205 lbs.

Bats/Throws: L/L

Drafted/Acquired: Drafted in the eighth round of the 2013 MLB Draft, Furman University; signed for $12,000

Previous Ranking(s): #9 (Org) 2016

2016 Stats: 4.61 ERA, 4.77 DRA, 150.1 IP, 166 H, 44 BB, 122 SO at Triple-A Salt Lake

The Role: OFP 50—No. 4 Starter
Likely 40—No. 5 Starter/Swingman

YEAR	TEAM	LVL	AGE	W	L	SV	G	GS	IP	H	HR	BB/9	K/9	K	GB%	BABIP	WHIP	ERA	FIP	DRA	VORP	WARP	cFIP	MPH
2014	INL	A+	22	6	3	0	10	10	55²	41	3	2.3	8.2	51	0%	.250	0.99	3.07	3.36					
2014	ARK	AA	22	5	3	0	11	11	62¹	48	3	4.3	9.7	67	34%	.290	1.25	2.89	3.04	3.82	9.80	1.0	96	
2015	ARK	AA	23	8	4	0	17	17	101²	82	10	2.5	7.2	81	44%	.247	1.08	2.48	3.90	3.64	16.40	1.8	92	
2015	SLC	AAA	23	2	4	0	7	7	36	48	7	3.8	5.8	23	42%	.320	1.75	7.75	6.10	5.16	0.60	0.1	109	
2016	SLC	AAA	24	8	9	0	26	26	150¹	166	18	2.6	7.3	122	40%	.324	1.40	4.61	4.61	3.83	25.30	2.6	99	
2017	*ANA*	*MLB*	*25*	*2*	*2*	*0*	*10*	*5*	*30*	*32*	*4*	*3.2*	*6.2*	*21*	*37%*	*.291*	*1.38*	*4.67*	*4.71*	*4.97*	*0.9*	*0.1*	*100*	
2018	*ANA*	*MLB*	*26*	*6*	*5*	*1*	*50*	*13*	*118*	*104*	*16*	*5.0*	*9.4*	*124*	*37%*	*.283*	*1.43*	*4.63*	*4.65*	*5.01*	*3.6*	*0.4*	*116*	

Breakout: 18% Improve: 34% Collapse: 8% Attrition: 37% MLB: 56% *Comparables: Logan Verrett, Matt Andriese, Rudy Owens*

The Good: Smith has some natural deception that helps his modest fastball play up a bit. He repeats well in spite of his long arm action, flashing solid-average command of a fairly deep four-pitch arsenal. The change is an above-average pitch that can play to plus at maturity, thanks to advanced feel, consistent salesmanship with his arm speed, and above-average tumble. He's made strides in developing a slider, which can flash average with moderate bat-missing potential.

The Bad: The fastball will sometimes fail to scrape 90 in a given start, and tops out around 91. The deficit of raw stuff can lead to nibbling, and he'll struggle to take hitters out of the zone and put them away. His feel for spin comes and goes, with the curve in particular tending to show with some loop, and his reliance on in-zone command leaves him a thinner margin for error. A fly ball pitcher, he's shown some vulnerability to the long ball.

The Irrelevant: In 2017 he'll attempt to become the second Nate Smith to grace a big-league roster, joining Baltimore's Nathaniel Beverly Smith, who logged 11 plate appearances in 1962 and retired with 0.2 WARP to his name.

Major league ETA: 2017 —Wilson Karaman

Ben Carsley's Fantasy Take: Jones is just a tiny bit relevant because of his proximity to the Majors, but that's the only thing he's got going for him for our purposes. It doesn't get better from here, friends.

5. David Fletcher, SS

DOB: 05/31/1994

Height/Weight: 5'10" 175 lbs

Bats/Throws: R/R

Drafted/Acquired: Drafted in the 6th round (195th overall) in the 2015 MLB Draft, Loyola Marymount University (Los Angeles, CA); signed for $406,900

Previous Ranking(s): N/A

2016 Stats: .300/.325/.375, 0 HR, 1 SB in 20 games at Double-A Arkansas, .275/.321/.346, 3 HR, 15 SB in 78 games at High-A Inland Empire

The Role: OFP 45—Second-division second-sacker
Likely 40—Utility Infielder

YEAR	TEAM	LVL	AGE	PA	R	2B	3B	HR	RBI	BB	K	SB	CS	AVG/OBP/SLG	TAv	VORP	BABIP	BRR	FRAA	WARP
2015	BUR	A	21	135	18	4	1	1	10	12	13	6	1	.283/.358/.358	.263	8.2	.311	2.6	SS(29): 2.0, 2B(3): 0.4	1.1
2015	ORM	Rk	21	180	28	12	4	0	30	16	9	11	4	.331/.391/.456	.293	15.9	.346	1.3	SS(37): -1.2	1.4
2016	INL	A+	22	355	42	12	1	3	31	22	43	15	3	.275/.321/.346	.254	11.7	.307	1.6	SS(47): -6.0, 2B(28): -0.2	0.6
2016	ARK	AA	22	83	10	6	0	0	6	3	13	1	0	.300/.325/.375	.277	5.0	.358	0.6	SS(18): 2.2	0.8
2017	*ANA*	*MLB*	*23*	*250*	*27*	*10*	*1*	*5*	*22*	*13*	*48*	*4*	*1*	*.239/.282/.350*	*.221*	*1.2*	*.277*	*0.1*	*SS -1, 2B 0*	*0.0*
2018	*ANA*	*MLB*	*24*	*286*	*30*	*11*	*1*	*6*	*29*	*16*	*55*	*4*	*1*	*.242/.288/.358*	*.230*	*1.0*	*.279*	*0.3*	*SS -1, 2B 0*	*0.0*

Breakout: 5% Improve: 21% Collapse: 11% Attrition: 24% MLB: 37% *Comparables: Juniel Querecuto, Ramiro Pena, Justin Sellers*

The Good: Insert all of the synonyms for small dudes who are better players than their raw tools. Fletcher is a grinder, and he's scrappy, and fine, he's basically David Eckstein with a couple extra inches. Fletcher draws high praise for his baseball aptitude. His quick feet and reactions help him break well on balls in both directions, and he's a fundamentally sound fielder with a swift transfer and consistent accuracy from different angles at short. He plays above his raw speed on the bases, getting good reads and consistently solid jumps. In the box his quiet setup and tight launch angle keep him short to the ball, driving a solid contact profile with all of the skills to log an epic 16-pitch at-bat someday.

The Bad: He lacks for strength or projection, and there are physical limits that leave him borderline on the left side. His throws are max effort affairs, and his average speed holds his range at short in check. It's a profile that looks a lot better at second, and the club has already begun to give him reps at the keystone. He doesn't engage his lower half in the box, and combined with a flat path there's very little power to speak of, which puts an awful lot of pressure on a hit tool that's just okay.

The Irrelevant: Fletcher has the chance to become the fourth graduate of Cypress High School to make it to the majors. Troy O'Leary is the school's all-time leader in WARP produced (6.3), Ken Griffey Jr. swing comps, and home runs in playoff elimination games (3).

The Risks: Still fairly high despite a solid Double-A debut on account of profile limitation. Fletcher is a max-effort guy who's more likely than not to extract every drop of talent out of himself, but a tool set with a couple fives and not much else affords him less rope as he advances.

Major league ETA: 2018 —Wilson Karaman

Ben Carsley's Fantasy Take: So, like, Jace Peterson with less power? We're all set.

6. Brandon Marsh, OF

DOB: 12/18/1997

Height/Weight: 6'2" 190 lbs

Bats/Throws: L/R

Drafted/Acquired: Drafted in the 2nd round (60th overall) in the 2016 MLB draft, Buford High School (Buford, GA); signed for $1,073,300

Previous Ranking(s): N/A

2016 Stats: N/A

The Role: OFP 50—Average major league outfielder
Likely 40—Fourth outfielder that can play all three spots

YEAR	TEAM	LVL	AGE	PA	R	2B	3B	HR	RBI	BB	K	SB	CS	AVG/OBP/SLG	TAv	VORP	BABIP	BRR	FRAA	WARP
2017	*ANA*	*MLB*	*19*	*250*	*28*	*8*	*1*	*6*	*25*	*29*	*42*	*4*	*1*	*.227/.322/.353*	*.243*	*5.3*	*.251*	*-0.1*		*0.6*

Breakout: 0% Improve: 22% Collapse: 9% Attrition: 16% MLB: 38% *Comparables: Wayne Causey, Ed Kranepool, Jurickson Profar*

The Good: Are you still with us? Okay, good, because there are some intriguing tools here. Marsh has a lean, athletic frame with projection left. He's a plus runner with a plus arm. There's already some power in the swing, and it could grow into above-average pop as he enters his twenties. He has the physical tools to potentially stick up the middle.

The Bad: This is gonna take a while. Like Mike Trout will be on his next nine figure contract before Marsh is able to help the major league squad. There's more "tools" than "baseball skills" here at present. He may not hit. He may not be a center fielder (he was a right fielder in high school).

The Irrelevant: Marsh was part of two state championship football teams as a wide receiver for Buford High.

The Risks: Let's see. He hasn't played a professional game yet. At present, he's more athlete than baseball player. He's on a very long developmental track. And he may eventually be forced to a corner spot.

Major league ETA: 2021

Ben Carsley's Fantasy Take: You're waiting for a train.

7. Grayson Long, RHP

DOB: 5/27/1994

Height/Weight: 6'5" 230 lbs

Bats/Throws: R/R

Drafted/Acquired: Drafted in the 3rd round (104th overall) in the 2015 MLB Draft, Texas A&M University (College Station, TX); signed for $548,600.

Previous Ranking(s): N/A

2016 Stats: 5.14 ERA, 2.83 DRA, 14 IP, 14 H, 4 BB, 15 K at High-A Inland Empire, 1.57 ERA, 2.41 DRA, 40 IP, 27 H, 16 BB, 45 K at Low-A Burlington, 6.55 ERA, 4.30 DRA, 11 IP, 13 H, 5 BB, 10 K at rookie ball in the AZL

The Role: OFP 50—No.4 starter
Likely 40—No. 5 starter

YEAR	TEAM	LVL	AGE	W	L	SV	G	GS	IP	H	HR	BB/9	K/9	K	GB%	BABIP	WHIP	ERA	FIP	DRA	VORP	WARP	cFIP	MPH
2015	ORM	Rk	21	0	0	0	13	12	19^{2}	19	1	4.6	10.1	22	57%	.346	1.47	5.03	4.10	3.61	4.90	0.5	92	
2016	BUR	A	22	3	3	0	8	8	40	27	2	3.6	10.1	45	40%	.258	1.08	1.58	3.08	2.47	11.30	1.2	87	
2016	ANG	Rk	22	0	1	0	4	4	11	13	0	4.1	8.2	10	32%	.382	1.64	6.55	3.67	4.62	1.30	0.1	105	
2016	INL	A+	22	2	1	0	3	3	14	14	5	2.6	9.6	15	32%	.281	1.29	5.14	7.07	4.57	1.40	0.1	106	
2017	*ANA*	*MLB*	*23*	*2*	*4*	*0*	*12*	*12*	42^{2}	*50*	*8*	*5.1*	*6.2*	*30*	*27%*	*.303*	*1.72*	*6.10*	*5.98*	*6.67*	*-5.7*	*-0.6*	*155*	
2018	*ANA*	*MLB*	*24*	*5*	*9*	*0*	*28*	*28*	166^{1}	*165*	*29*	*5.5*	*8.5*	*158*	*27%*	*.295*	*1.61*	*5.44*	*5.47*	*5.95*	*-5.1*	*-0.5*	*138*	

Breakout: 1% Improve: 3% Collapse: 0% Attrition: 0% MLB: 3% *Comparables: Mike McClendon, Steven Matz, Rob Zastryzny*

The Good: Long is a polished college starter. He's not going to fill up the report with 6s, but the stuff is average to solid-average across the board. The fastball sits in the low-90s, but the velocity is sneaky fast and it has some life when he elevates it. His mid-80s change has some fade and he maintains his arm speed well. His slider flashes average with some late 12-6 action at its best. His frame was built to log innings in a rotation.

The Bad: It's just..ya know...it's fine, whatever. It's a backend starter profile. There isn't going to be much more fastball here. The curve and slider are going to be just average, maybe a tick above for the change. The slider can be a bit of a roller and still needs more consistency. The delivery isn't all that athletic, and he can struggle to get the ball down in the zone and with his command generally.

The Irrelevant: Long has excellent taste in neckwear

The Risks: The stuff is solid enough, but we haven't seen it work in Double-A yet. His command issues could give him trouble there (and higher up the ladder). He missed two months with an undisclosed injury, which is always what you want to hear about a pitcher.

Major league ETA: 2018

Ben Carsley's Fantasy Take: A train that will take you far away.

8. Nonie Williams, SS

DOB: 05/22/1998

Height/Weight: 6'2" 200 lbs

Bats/Throws: S/R

Drafted/Acquired: Drafted 96th overall in the 2016 MLB draft, Home-schooled (Kansas City, KS); signed for $620,100

Previous Ranking(s): N/A

2016 Stats: .244/.280/.282, 0 HR, 8 SB in 38 games at rookie-ball in the AZL

The Role: OFP 50—Average regular at SS/CF
Likely 40—Utility player

YEAR	TEAM	LVL	AGE	PA	R	2B	3B	HR	RBI	BB	K	SB	CS	AVG/OBP/SLG	TAv	VORP	BABIP	BRR	FRAA	WARP
2016	ANG	Rk	18	164	23	4	1	0	11	8	40	8	3	.244/.280/.282	.218	2.8	.328	4.5	SS(28): -8.8	-0.6
2017	*ANA*	*MLB*	*19*	*250*	*24*	*8*	*1*	*5*	*20*	*10*	*87*	*3*	*1*	*.187/.223/.290*	*.180*	*-9.6*	*.267*	*-0.1*	*SS -2*	*-1.3*
2018	*ANA*	*MLB*	*20*	*311*	*30*	*10*	*1*	*7*	*30*	*15*	*104*	*4*	*2*	*.201/.243/.321*	*.201*	*-8.1*	*.280*	*0.1*	*SS -3*	*-1.2*

Breakout: 0% Improve: 4% Collapse: 1% Attrition: 4% MLB: 7% *Comparables: Raul Mondesi, Alcides Escobar, Elvis Andrus*

The Good: Nonie certainly looks the part given his body and size. While new to switch-hitting, his swing from both sides is able to produce hard line drives, with more feel from the right side. He flashes above-average raw power from both sides, with a chance for above-average in-game power from the right side. He is a plus runner and flies around when he is under way. His average arm plays up due to a quick release and plays at the six-spot.

The Bad: He is a natural righty and has struggled with his swing from the left-side, as it can get long and he will occasionally cut himself off. His bat-to-ball ability is questionable and might leave his hit tool as a below-average offering. His hands are crude for the infield, as are his actions and instincts, with some scouts projecting him as a future outfielder.

The Irrelevant: Nonie got his nickname after his little sister had difficulty pronouncing "Nolan."

The Risks: Williams is a premium athlete but he is extremely raw, and has struggled with making contact thus far. While he boasts an impressive set of tools, they could struggle to translate in-game, which would leave him more of an athlete than a ballplayer. He's just a dot on the horizon at this point, and is likely to take the long route to the majors.

Major league ETA: 2021 —Steve Givarz

Ben Carsley's Fantasy Take: You know where you hope the train will take you, but you can't be sure.

9. Keynan Middleton, RHP

DOB: 09/12/1993

Height/Weight: 6'2" 185 lbs

Bats/Throws: R/R

Drafted/Acquired: Drafted 95th overall in the 2013 MLB draft, Lane Community College (Eugene, OR); signed for $450,000

Previous Ranking(s): N/A

2016 Stats: 4.91 ERA, 3.90 DRA, 14.2 IP, 14 H, 4 BB, 14 K at Triple-A Salt Lake, 1.20 ERA, 2.99 DRA, 15 IP, 11 H, 4 BB, 18 K at Double-A Arkansas, 3.72 ERA, 1.62 DRA, 36.3 IP, 22 H, 20 BB, 56 K at High-A Inland Empire

The Role: OFP 50—Hard-throwing set-up dude
Likely 40—Effectively wild middle reliever

YEAR	TEAM	LVL	AGE	W	L	SV	G	GS	IP	H	HR	BB/9	K/9	K	GB%	BABIP	WHIP	ERA	FIP	DRA	VORP	WARP	cFIP	MPH
2014	ORM	Rk	20	5	4	0	14	14	67	69	9	4.0	7.1	53	0%	.294	1.48	6.45	5.81	6.41			113	
2015	BUR	A	21	6	11	0	26	26	125^{2}	148	15	3.4	6.3	88	40%	.336	1.55	5.30	4.74	7.94	-37.90	-4.0	124	
2016	INL	A+	22	1	1	0	25	0	36^{1}	22	7	5.0	13.9	56	34%	.227	1.16	3.72	4.79	2.09	12.10	1.2	86	
2016	ARK	AA	22	0	0	6	13	0	15	11	1	2.4	10.8	18	42%	.270	1.00	1.20	2.45	3.06	2.80	0.3	83	
2016	SLC	AAA	22	0	1	2	8	0	14^{2}	14	1	2.5	8.6	14	48%	.302	1.23	4.91	3.52	4.25	1.20	0.1	97	
2017	*ANA*	*MLB*	*23*	*3*	*4*	*0*	*23*	*10*	59^{1}	*72*	*13*	*4.8*	*5.6*	*37*	*32%*	*.304*	*1.75*	*6.50*	*6.44*	*6.99*	*-11.5*	*-1.2*	*166*	
2018	*ANA*	*MLB*	*24*	*4*	*6*	*1*	*35*	*15*	115^{2}	*116*	*25*	*6.0*	*8.8*	*113*	*32%*	*.291*	*1.67*	*6.08*	*6.11*	*6.54*	*-12.6*	*-1.3*	*156*	

Breakout: 5% Improve: 7% Collapse: 0% Attrition: 1% MLB: 7% *Comparables: William Cuevas, Hansel Robles, Mike Dunn*

The Good: A move to the bullpen in 2016 did wonders for Middleton. He reportedly touched triple digits with the fastball, and sits comfortably—though I hesitate to use that adverb given his delivery—in the upper 90s. He gets some added deception from his delivery, which involves him turning his back completely to the hitter. His high 80s slider flashes plus.

The Bad: That delivery isn't going to grant him Greg Maddux's command and control. His delivery is more traditional, but just as violent out of the stretch as well. The slider can get lazy at times and lack sharpness.

The Irrelevant: Mau will be happy to learn that Middleton was also a basketball player in high school.

The Risks: Eh. He's almost major league-ready and he throws 100. That delivery does scare me a bit, as does the fact that he's a pitcher.

Major league ETA: 2017

Ben Carsley's Fantasy Take: Yet it doesn't matter. Now tell me why?

10. Jose Campos, RHP

DOB: 07/27/1992

Height/Weight: 6'3" 230 lbs

Bats/Throws: R/R

Drafted/Acquired: Signed by Seattle out of Venezuela in January 2009, acquired by Anaheim off waivers from the Arizona in November 2016.

Previous Ranking(s): N/A

2016 Stats: 3.02 ERA, 3.73 DRA, 56.2 IP, 45 H, 14 BB, 48 K at Double-A Trenton, 3.60 ERA, 3.98 DRA, 20 IP, 22 H, 5 BB, 15 K at Double-A Mobile, 3.49 ERA, 3.93 DRA, 59.1 IP, 50 H, 23 BB, 56 K at High-A Tampa

The Role: OFP 45—Swingman/longman
Likely 40—Up-and-down reliever

YEAR	TEAM	LVL	AGE	W	L	SV	G	GS	IP	H	HR	BB/9	K/9	K	GB%	BABIP	WHIP	ERA	FIP	DRA	VORP	WARP	cFIP	MPH
2015	YAN	Rk	22	0	1	0	1	1	4^2	8	1	0.0	9.6	5	53%	.438	1.71	5.79	3.94	1.40	2.30	0.2	72	
2015	YAT	Rk	22	0	0	0	1	1	5	2	0	0.0	16.2	9	75%	.250	0.40	0.00	-0.30	1.74	2.30	0.2	69	
2015	TAM	A+	22	3	7	0	11	11	44^2	54	5	2.0	6.2	31	36%	.322	1.43	7.05	3.97	6.15	-5.30	-0.6	111	
2016	TAM	A+	23	4	2	0	10	10	59^1	50	3	3.5	8.5	56	40%	.292	1.23	3.49	3.39	5.02	3.00	0.3	102	
2016	TRN	AA	23	5	1	0	9	9	56^2	45	1	2.2	7.6	48	42%	.277	1.04	3.02	2.74	3.97	7.10	0.8	95	
2016	SWB	AAA	23	0	0	0	1	1	5	8	0	1.8	1.8	1	58%	.421	1.80	1.80	3.37	5.75	-0.20	0.0	110	
2016	MOB	AA	23	1	2	0	4	4	20	22	0	2.2	6.8	15	56%	.355	1.35	3.60	2.87	3.99	2.40	0.3	100	
2016	ARI	MLB	23	0	0	0	1	0	5^2	4	2	3.2	6.4	4	33%	.125	1.06	3.18	7.42	5.61	-0.40	0.0	117	91.3
2016	RNO	AAA	23	0	0	0	1	1	1^2	0	0	0.0	0.0	0	0%	.000	0.00	0.00	3.72	3.82	0.30	0.0	104	
2017	*ANA*	*MLB*	*24*	*6*	*8*	*0*	*22*	*22*	*102*	*116*	*16*	*3.8*	*5.9*	*67*	*36%*	*.302*	*1.55*	*5.28*	*5.23*	*5.64*	*-1.9*	*-0.2*	*135*	
2018	*ANA*	*MLB*	*25*	*4*	*6*	*0*	*16*	*16*	*91^2*	*92*	*14*	*5.2*	*8.6*	*87*	*36%*	*.303*	*1.59*	*5.16*	*5.19*	*5.51*	*-0.3*	*0.0*	*131*	

Breakout: 7% Improve: 9% Collapse: 8% Attrition: 18% MLB: 22% *Comparables: Chris Seddon, Erik Davis, J.A. Happ*

The Good: After stalling for the past three seasons due to injury and inconsistency, Campos conquered two levels before making a brief MLB debut with the Arizona Diamondbacks in August. He has above-average control of his fastball and curveball. His curve grades out as average with 11/5 shape and good downward action. His changeup, ineffective earlier in his career, has become probably his most effective offering as he has quality arm speed and average tumbling action.

The Bad: His command is well behind his control, as he is quite hittable in the zone with all his offerings. He was older for High-A and Double-A, and lacks any remaining physical projection. His body is quite stiff and he isn't the most athletic when fielding his position. Campos has a lengthy injury history including a stress fracture in his right elbow in 2012, Tommy John in 2014, and a fractured right arm in September. This was the first time Campos has cleared the 100-inning mark in professional baseball.

The Irrelevant: Campos 0.0 WARP is higher than the star of the trade, Jesus Montero, who currently has -2.2 WARP.

The Risks: While he has value, being claimed off waivers and being an organization's Top 10 prospect says a lot about your system. The command never gets to better than fringe-average and struggles to maintain major league status. The long injury history leaves causes for concern about his durability. Also concerning is that he's a pitcher.

Major league ETA: Debuted in 2016 —Steve Givarz

Ben Carsley's Fantasy Take: Because we'll be together, looking at a different top-10 soon.

OTHERS OF NOTE:

The rain falls down on last year's man

Joe Gatto, RHP

Everything went wrong for Gatto in 2016. He got shelled in the Midwest League, posting a 7+ ERA in 15 outings before a DL stint. After that, the Angels worked with him in side sessions before instructs to try and fix his issues. It's possible he comes back in 2017 as a brand new pitcher, and a revitalized pitching prospect. But based on what he showed in 2016, a low-90s fastball that can touch 95 but features little movement and a below-average command profile, a slurvy breaking ball that flashes, and a work-in-progress change, we'll need to see better stuff or better results before he makes it back onto the Angels list. He is still young—though 21 is hardly "prospect young" for A-ball—and he's a cold weather arm that you'd suspect would require a more leisurely development path. He still has a good, athletic frame as well. So all hope is not lost. But—politely—it looked bad in 2016, and there were questions about his ability to start even before it all went south.

Yes, he is still eligible for this list

Alex Meyer, RHP

You could make a case that whatever faint glimmer of Alex Meyer's Top 101 prospect flame still remains, that's enough warmth to justify him in the Top 10 in the heat death of the universe that is the Angels farm system. He's still very tall. He still throws hard (though not quite as hard as he did before the arm issues). The curve still flashes plus and can be a wipeout offering at its best. He still doesn't throw enough strikes. He missed most of the year with vague shoulder issues. In 2017, he's likely to be a 27-year-old reliever with a checkered injury history and no track record of commanding the stuff. The 96 mph fastball is nice, but not special in relief nowadays. Seeing him behind Keynan Middleton and Jose Campos is a bit of a shock, but I'm more confident that they have a role on a major league team in 2017 than Meyer.

Steve's Guy

Nathaniel Bertness, LHP

His peripherals might not stand out immediately, but this is a very raw arm whose ceiling is only going to climb as he gets more repetitions. After playing basketball for most of his prep career, Bertness switched to baseball and showed off a promising body and potential skillset. He is wiry with room to grow into his 6-foot-6, 205-pound frame. His average fastball should improve, pairing well with his potential plus changeup and average breaking ball. While it's a long way off, he could jump by leaps and bounds next year. *—Steve Givarz*

"Not an exciting profile" but it's the Angels so

Tyler Carpenter, RHP

While an older arm, Carpenter has showed an interesting arsenal that could play well in a relief role. His average fastball has rise and tail, which isn't something you see from a guy with an over-the-top slot. His slider flashes average with above-average depth and life, but struggled with its consistency in a starting role, it could play higher in a relief role. While not an exciting profile, teams need arms like this and a lot of them out-perform their initial roles and become long-standing relief arms. *—Steve Givarz*

Craig's Guy

Michael Hermosillo, CF

A two-sport conversion, Hermosillo displays impressive athleticism, but is as raw as you'd expect a former running back to be. He can go get it in center field, but his approach at the plate needs significant work, though an optimist could appreciate it given the lack of repetitions. He shows encouraging bat-to-ball ability, as well. This is, as ever, a slow-burn type of guy, but given the system at large, he's a viable lottery ticket, and that ain't nothin'.

The Rule 5 Draft Pick

This is the time of year where teams can gleefully throw a wrench into your prospect lists. Our Red Sox list was up for a cool four days before Dave Dombrowski did his level best to make extra work for me before we can publish the Futures Guide. This is still better than a blockbuster deal involving a team you haven't published on yet. The Angels list is being published the morning of the Rule 5 draft. Normally that's a non-issue. But, well, see everything above. The Angels have 39 players on their 40-man roster and could certainly use a Rule 5 flyer. It's possible they grab a relief arm in the Keynon Middleton range, or an extra infielder a heck of a lot closer to the majors than Nonie Williams. We can't prepare for every eventuality this time of year, but we can tell you that there is a pretty good chance the Angels' system has added a 'noteworthy' prospect by the time you are reading this.

TOP 10 TALENTS 25 AND UNDER (BORN 4/1/91 OR LATER)

1. Mike Trout	6. Taylor Ward
2. Tyler Skaggs	7. Cam Bedrosian
3. Jahmai Jones	8. Nate Smith
4. Matt Thaiss	9. David Fletcher
5. Andrew Heaney	10. Brandon Marsh

Hoo boy. Well, let's start with the positive here, right? And no, use of the singular form was not an accident.

For a seventh consecutive winter, Mike Trout is at the top of the list in this, his final year of eligibility. Surprise, surprise. Trout's 8.7 WARP in 2016 marked his "worst" total for a season since his rookie year in 2012, due overwhelmingly to FRAA shaking its robot fists at Trout's efforts in centerfield. Our fielding metric was among the most pessimistic in rating his defense, and his cost of 6.1 runs marked a 16-run turn for the worse from 2015. It's possible that just maybe the first in-earnest conversations should be taking place about a potential move to left in favor of the newly acquired Cameron Maybin? It's doubtful that conversation actually takes shape, however. At best the statistical universe returns a "reply hazy, try again later" verdict on Trout's glove, and when you combine that with Maybin's own not-exactly-spectacular defensive numbers and not-exactly-durable body, a usurpation by Maybin is unlikely. Beyond that option, it's not like the Angels have anyone else within a Scottish oil tanker's shouting distance who is capable of wresting the position away from Trout anytime soon, either.

Beyond that bar room speculation, let's just allow that WARP number sink in for a second. 8.7. The second-best mark in baseball. He's now finished either first or second in all of Major League Baseball in each of his five full seasons. If you take the eight position players not named Mike Trout who logged the most plate appearances at their respective positions in 2016 for the Angels, and you added up all of their WARP, you'd get 5.5. And by VORP he's been even better, producing the best offensive output in the game in four of the five. He's...uh, he's good?

And it's a really good thing that he is, because the rest of this list is, once again, among the worst in baseball. The Angels arguably battle only the lot put forth by the devastatingly-sans-Jose-Fernandez Marlins for a second straight basement finish, and the club is very certainly among the bottom three in the game for a third consecutive year.

Previous list appearers Nick Tropeano (5), Carlos Perez (8), and Kyle Kubitza (10) all graduated and generated a combined 0.4 WARP last season in Anaheim. That includes a negative effort by Perez and a donut from Kubitza, who hit a combined .212 between the Triple-A affiliates of three organizations and no longer aspires to call the Big A home. Last year's fourth-ranked player, Joe Gatto, had an atrocious season as outlined above, resulting in a tumble far, far away from even this motley collection. Victor Alcantara, last year's number seven, stumbled through a mediocre year at Double-A that saw his stuff decay, his whiff and walk rates follow suit, and ultimately his rotation aspirations fade away. He was subsequently shipped to Detroit for Cameron Maybin on the first day of the off-season.

Of the remnants, Tyler Skaggs appears to have emerged none for the worse from Tommy John surgery and rehabilitation. His fastball showed familiar hop, and his hook produced quality late action to coax grounders at a solid rate once again. He struggled to find consistent control and command, as many Tommy Johnners are wont whilst rust-shaking, but his slow and steady ten-game return to the big-league mound counts as a cautiously optimistic win for a franchise with precious few upon which to hang its hat.

In accordance with the kind of requisite karmic balance befitting an organization so far into the doldrums, however, what went (marginally) up simply had to get offset with a hard thud somewhere, and one of the franchise's only other young pitchers of promise, Andrew Heaney, careened off into the unknown of his own elbow replacement surgery. As of this writing his 2017 figures to stand as a lost season, outside of the possibility for a couple dozen A-ball rehab innings at best next summer. He remains in the middle of this list because, well, we work with what we've got.

The only other ostensible success story from the club's young ranks in 2016 was the emergence of Cam Bedrosian as a potent relief ace in the making. And enthusiasm for even that modest development has to be tempered after the righty lost the final two months of his season to a blood clot in his pitching arm. He showed a vastly improved slider in his time on the bump prior to the injury, though, driving a massive whiff rate that resulted in top-25 DRA and cFIP efforts among pitchers who logged at least his 40 innings.

—Wilson Karaman

LOS ANGELES DODGERS

The State of the System: *The Dodgers graduated two of the top prospects in baseball, traded three pretty good ones, and still have a very good system. Meanwhile, somewhere in the South of France, Frank McCourt is spending too much for a 30-year-old midfielder. Living well is the best revenge.*

THE TOP TEN

1. RHP Yadier Alvarez	6. OF Andrew Toles
2. 1B/OF Cody Bellinger	7. 2B Willie Calhoun
3. OF Alex Verdugo	8. SS Gavin Lux
4. OF Yusniel Diaz	9. RHP Jordan Sheffield
5. RHP Walker Buehler	10. RHP Dustin May

The Big Question: So what do the Dodgers do for an encore?

If you'll pardon the intrusion, I'd like to begin by talking about football for a second, if I may. And not the kind that Paternostro speaks in tongues about on Twitter all the time. I mean the American kind. The New England Patriots clinched their sixth consecutive AFC championship appearance the other day, and it got me to thinking about sustained excellence and strategic execution. Bill Belichick is a defensive coach, first and foremost, and one of his fundamental strategic priorities over the years has been to design week-to-week defensive schemes built around limiting the contributions of his opponent's best offensive skill player. His aim is to remove the opposition's primary advantage, and in so doing force answers from his opposite number to an unpleasant question: how am I going to go about beating you without access to my biggest advantage?

Well, the Dodgers currently find themselves staring down the sleeveless barrel of that conundrum, at least insofar as it relates to talent pipelines and international spending. The new CBA drastically limits the overall pool of money designated to signing international talent, and places hard caps on per-team expenditures. This is, of course, bad news for teams with money to throw at international talent. And that makes it catastrophic news for the Dodgers.

I detailed the club's recent pattern of international largesse last winter, and I noted the front office ramifications of their strategy in another piece around that time. The punchline to both is that the franchise was among the deadliest deadbeats in open revolt against the previous international spending system, advance-staffing in bulk and utilizing its financial girth to cyclically binge on massive amounts of raw talent—talent which played a significant role in building the club's top-ranked system heading into this past season.

Fast forward to the present, and the carbon footprint from the team's most recent pipeline adjustment is starting to set in the skies above, albeit with significant shape-shifting still to be done. Big-dollar investment has placed two players in the current top five, and the complex levels are overflowing with six-or-better-figure talent that already flashes top-of-the-system potential to sustain the run. After signing for more than $5.5 million combined on the first day of the 2015-2016 signing period, Starling Heredia, Ronny Brito, and Oneil Cruz, all turned heads at the team's Dominican complex last summer, while switch-hitting outfielder Carlos Rincon flashed massive power in Arizona after migrating north mid-season. Meanwhile, $6 million Cuban man Omar Estevez flashed across-the-board skills in his own stateside debut. Hell, even Yaisel Sierra, whose $30 million price tag looks like a significant overpay, found velocity and effectiveness after a transition to the bullpen and now looks the part of at least a potentially useful big-league bullpen arm. The last hurrah may be a rager for the record books.

Then again…these Dodgers of today, they're a smart bunch. And a rich bunch. And that combination can make for some difficulties in pinpointing primary advantage. The suggestion of international might as primary separator may not actually end up holding much in the way of water when we jump back up to 30,000 feet.

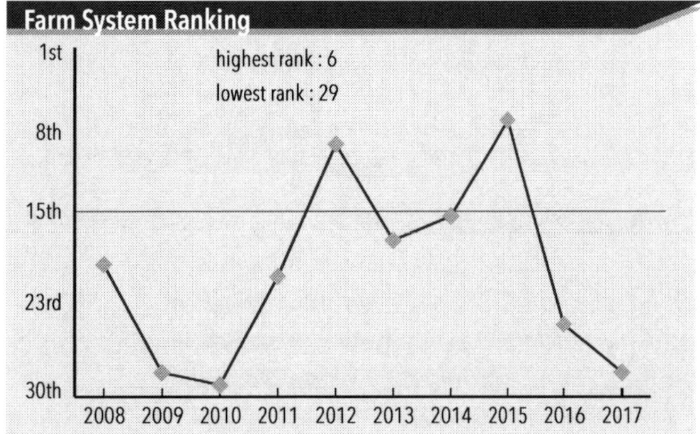

Personnel

President, Baseball Operations:
Andrew Friedman

General Manager:
Farhan Zaidi

SVP, Baseball Operations:
Josh Byrnes

Manager:
Dave Roberts

BP Alumni:
Josh Herzenberg

The early returns on the club's 2016 Rule IV Draft, for example, look just delightful. Five of our 15 player write-ups below involve picks from last summer's class. Even while acknowledging graduation and turnover, it is still somewhat of a remarkable testament to the depth of the Dodgers' board that such digit ink should be spilled on newcomers to the reigning top system in baseball. The preceding draft, for its part, has produced two top-tenners of its own, along with the organization's newly-minted minor league player of the year.

We are too far in the thick of it all to render proper judgment on any of these players, but the early returns on the club's most recent drafting efforts are the good kind. And it's enough to glean hope that the franchise's player development process will remain well-positioned to succeed even with one of its greatest advantages neutralized over the run of the next CBA.

—Wilson Karaman

1. Yadier Alvarez, RHP

DOB: 03/07/1996

Height/Weight: 6'3" 175 lbs.

Bats/Throws: R/R

Drafted/Acquired: Signed July 2015 out of Cuba for $16 million

Previous Ranking(s): #6 (Org.)

2016 Stats: 1.80 ERA, 2.50 DRA, 20 IP, 9 H, 10 BB, 26 K in 5 games at Complex AZL, 2.29 ERA, 1.32 DRA, 39.1 IP, 31 H, 11 BB, 55 K in 9 games at low-A Great Lakes

The Role: OFP 60—No. 3 starter or closer
Likely 55—Mid-rotation starter or late-inning arm

YEAR	TEAM	LVL	AGE	W	L	SV	G	GS	IP	H	HR	BB/9	K/9	K	GB%	BABIP	WHIP	ERA	FIP	DRA	VORP	WARP	cFIP	MPH
2016	DOD	Rk	20	1	1	0	5	5	20	9	0	4.5	11.7	26	64%	.200	0.95	1.80	3.03	2.50	7.10	0.7	88	
2016	GRL	A	20	3	2	0	9	9	39^1	31	1	2.5	12.6	55	50%	.326	1.07	2.29	1.85	1.32	16.20	1.8	67	
2017	*LAN*	*MLB*	*21*	*3*	*3*	*0*	*9*	*9*	40^1	*40*	*5*	*4.3*	*7.6*	*34*	*40%*	*.314*	*1.46*	*4.72*	*4.62*	*5.46*	*0.5*	*0.0*	*128*	
2018	*LAN*	*MLB*	*22*	*7*	*9*	*0*	*29*	*29*	180^2	*155*	*21*	*4.6*	*9.4*	*189*	*40%*	*.308*	*1.37*	*4.19*	*4.54*	*4.85*	*10.2*	*1.1*	*113*	

Breakout: 7% Improve: 7% Collapse: 1% Attrition: 4% MLB: 10% *Comparables: Carl Edwards Jr, Luis Severino, Matt Moore*

The Good: Big arm, good athlete. Fastball has been up to 100, although the velocity can vary depending on when you catch him. Projects as an easy plus-plus pitch regardless and gets some plane and arm-side run when he gets on top of it from his high three-quarters slot. His mid-80s slider projects as plus—flashes there now—with good late bite. His feel for the pitch improved throughout the season. There's still some projection left in his lean, athletic frame. Unlikely he adds much more velocity but some added weight/strength might help tone down some of the effort in his delivery and make everything more repeatable generally.

The Bad: He can fly open at times and struggle with his command. The slider is still inconsistent at present, and the velocity and shape will vary a bit in his outings. He struggles to maintain his arm speed on the change or get it to turn over, although the best will show some good tumble. Below-average projection on the pitch at present could limit his ability to go through a lineup multiple times. He played around with a curve for a different look but there isn't much there yet.

The Irrelevant: Midland, MI is home to the Great Lakes Loons and one of the 90 remaining Big Boy restaurants in America. And 16 million bucks will buy a whole lot of Famous Slim Jims.

The Risks: Alvarez's fastball/slider combo gives him a potential high-leverage reliever fallback role, but there's still some risk here. The changeup needs a grade jump to even have a chance to stick in the rotation, and it's still a little unclear where the fastball will sit over a 180-inning workload. Also, he's a pitcher (who throws really, really hard).

Major league ETA: 2019

Ben Carsley's Fantasy Take: Alvarez is one of the more attractive young arms in the low minors. His floor is fairly low, as you can probably tell from the writeup above, but his fantasy ceiling is a little loftier than the SP3 we see in his prospect writeup thanks to his strikeout potential. He's most certainly a top-75 prospect, and he's got a chance to flirt with the top-50. Big fastballs are a wonderful thing.

2. Cody Bellinger, 1B/OF

DOB: 07/13/1995

Height/Weight: 6'4" 180 lbs.

Bats/Throws: L/L

Drafted/Acquired: Drafted in the fourth round by Los Angeles in the 2013 MLB Draft, Hamilton HS (Chandler, AZ); signed for $700,000

Previous Ranking(s): #9 (Org.)

2016 Stats: .263/.359/.484, 23 HR, 8 SB in 114 games at double-A Tulsa, .545/.583/1.364, 3 HR, 0 SB in 3 games at Triple-A Oklahoma City

The Role: OFP 60—First-division first baseman
Likely 55—Above-average first baseman

YEAR	TEAM	LVL	AGE	PA	R	2B	3B	HR	RBI	BB	K	SB	CS	AVG/OBP/SLG	TAv	VORP	BABIP	BRR	FRAA	WARP
2014	DOD	Rk	18	21	2	1	0	0	0	1	5	0	0	.150/.190/.200	.213	-2.4	.200	-0.6		-0.2
2014	OGD	Rk	18	212	49	13	6	3	34	14	35	8	0	.328/.368/.503	.289	15.7	.381	4.2		1.7
2015	RCU	A+	19	544	97	33	4	30	103	52	150	10	2	.264/.336/.538	.315	39.9	.314	2.5	1B(91): 8.9, CF(26): -0.5	5.3
2016	TUL	AA	20	465	61	17	1	23	65	59	94	8	2	.263/.359/.484	.313	32.0	.287	1.0	1B(81): 0.7, CF(13): -0.6	3.6
2016	OKL	AAA	20	12	5	0	0	3	6	1	0	0	0	.545/.583/1.364	.695	6.0	.375	0.5	1B(3): 0.5	0.7
2017	*LAN*	*MLB*	*21*	*250*	*32*	*10*	*1*	*13*	*38*	*24*	*71*	*2*	*0*	*.236/.314/.465*	*.267*	*7.5*	*.279*	*-0.2*	*1B 2, CF 0*	*1.1*
2018	*LAN*	*MLB*	*22*	*450*	*65*	*19*	*1*	*24*	*69*	*48*	*124*	*3*	*1*	*.241/.325/.477*	*.291*	*20.8*	*.284*	*-0.5*	*1B 4, CF 0*	*2.8*

Breakout: 5% Improve: 23% Collapse: 7% Attrition: 12% MLB: 41% *Comparables: Matt Olson, Jon Singleton, Travis Snider*

The Good: Big kid, big raw, big leverage, big bat speed, big noise. 2016 proved he wasn't just a Cal League mirage. Bellinger's not a traditional corner masher either. He's lean and athletic and has even been spotting Tulsa and OKC in center field from time to time. The power potential is plus-plus, and he could win some gold gloves at first base if that's his ultimate home.

The Bad: Bellinger can sell out to get to that big raw power, and there are potentially big strikeout numbers to go with the big dongs. Minor league arms will pitch around his big bat, but his actual approach lags behind the raw walk totals. He will expand the zone with two strikes. He's not a center fielder, although he should be able to play some corner outfield as well.

The Irrelevant: Five players have played at least 20 games at both first base and center field in the same season this decade: Austin Romine, Wil Myers, Scott Van Slyke, and John Mayberry.

The Risks: Normally this is the spot where I gravely intone about the profile issues with a first base prospect. How the power really has to play in order to achieve that OFP. And all that applies here as well. But man, it sure looks right.

Major League ETA: Late 2017

Ben Carsley's Fantasy Take: I personally prefer Josh Bell because of his floor, but if you want to argue that Bellinger is the best first base prospect, I'll listen. Bellinger has big-time power and big-time production, and while the strikeout issues are real so is the upside. He might only hit .240 or .250, but Bellinger could smash 30 bombs a year. That might come in the OF instead of at 1B, but if that's the case you won't be complaining

3. Alex Verdugo, OF

DOB: 05/15/1996

Height/Weight: 6'0" 205 lbs.

Bats/Throws: L/L

Drafted/Acquired: Drafted 62nd overall in the 2014 MLB Draft, Sahauro HS (Tucson, AZ); signed for $914,600

Previous Ranking(s): #7 (Org.)

2016 Stats: .273/.336/.407, 13 HR, 2 SB in 126 games at double-A Tulsa

The Role: OFP 60—Hit-first center fielder
Likely 50—Second-division right fielder

YEAR	TEAM	LVL	AGE	PA	R	2B	3B	HR	RBI	BB	K	SB	CS	AVG/OBP/SLG	TAv	VORP	BABIP	BRR	FRAA	WARP
2014	DOD	Rk	18	196	28	14	3	3	33	20	14	8	0	.347/.423/.518	.412	17.1	.361	1.3		1.7
2014	OGD	Rk	18	20	3	1	0	0	8	0	4	3	0	.400/.400/.450	.288	1.2	.500	-0.3		0.1
2015	GRL	A	19	444	50	23	2	5	42	17	53	13	5	.295/.325/.394	.258	10.9	.326	-0.7	CF(89): 14.9, RF(11): 1.1	3.1
2015	RCU	A+	19	96	20	9	2	4	19	4	12	1	0	.385/.406/.659	.372	14.1	.408	0.4	CF(23): 1.8	1.8
2016	TUL	AA	20	529	58	23	1	13	63	44	67	2	6	.273/.336/.407	.275	20.8	.292	-1.2	CF(91): -2.5, RF(30): -0.8	1.8
2017	*LAN*	*MLB*	*21*	*250*	*25*	*12*	*1*	*7*	*30*	*14*	*47*	*1*	*1*	*.253/.296/.405*	*.241*	*3.5*	*.286*	*-0.5*	*CF -0, RF -1*	*0.3*
2018	*LAN*	*MLB*	*22*	*394*	*48*	*19*	*2*	*13*	*49*	*25*	*73*	*1*	*1*	*.260/.309/.429*	*.267*	*12.3*	*.290*	*-0.8*	*CF 0, RF -1*	*1.2*

Breakout: 4% Improve: 25% Collapse: 2% Attrition: 19% MLB: 32% *Comparables: Manuel Margot, Joc Pederson, Melky Cabrera*

The Good: Verdugo has thrived despite being young at each level. He has an advanced hit tool that has a good chance to eventually grade out as plus, rarely striking out throughout his minor league career. He combines those bat-to-ball skills with a selective approach, resulting in limited strikeout totals. His gap power should play at major-league average for a corner outfielder, though given his youth, there's time for him to develop more over-the-fence potential. Defensively, he has an absolute cannon for an arm—as well he should given his two-way status at draft time.

The Bad: He's an average runner at present, and isn't expected to contribute much on the base paths. His ultimate home is in right field, where the athleticism will play fine. There's a chance the power doesn't develop, making him more of a gap-to-gap doubles hitter with fringe power. His bat speed can leave evaluators wanting more at times, and he can rely too heavily on his bat-to-ball, leaving him as a slap hitter when he isn't feeling it at the plate.

The Irrelevant: Per Google translate, Verdugo means "executioner" or "hangman."

The Risks: There are a lot of moving parts to his setup in the box, and while it hasn't caused issues so far, it can't yet be ruled out moving forward. His athleticism leaves him on the fringe of being able to stick in center, and the ceiling takes a hit if he shifts to right. If the power doesn't develop and the hit tool takes a step back, he could profile more as a fourth outfielder. There's some positive risk in the hit tool as well, as the arrival of some power paired with his contact rate could make him a dangerous hitter.

Major league ETA: 2018 —Matt Pullman

Ben Carsley's Fantasy Take: I won't lie to you; I have underrated Verdugo's hit tool to this point. There's a chance he gets stuck in a tweener profile, and that would stink, but Verdugo has a solid enough bat and a good enough chance for nice power that we need to pay attention. If it all comes together, we're looking at a high-quality OF3. If the pop never comes or the hit tool doesn't play at the MLB level, you'll be underwhelmed, but that's pretty much true of every prospect. This isn't the most illuminating fantasy writeup of all time, but honestly, there are so many potential versions of Verdugo that I don't quite know what to make of him yet.

4. Yusniel Diaz, OF

DOB: 10/07/1996

Height/Weight: 6'1" 195 lbs.

Bats/Throws: R/R

Drafted/Acquired: Signed November 2015 out of Cuba for $15.5 million

Previous Ranking(s): #8 (Org.)

2016 Stats: .143/.143/.357, 1 HR, 0 SB in 3 games at complex-level AZL, .272/.333/.418, 8 HR, 7 SB in 82 games at high-A Rancho Cucamonga

The Role: OFP 55—Above-average CF
Likely 50—Average regular with some versatility

YEAR	TEAM	LVL	AGE	PA	R	2B	3B	HR	RBI	BB	K	SB	CS	AVG/OBP/SLG	TAv	VORP	BABIP	BRR	FRAA	WARP
2016	DOD	Rk	19	14	2	0	0	1	3	0	3	0	0	.143/.143/.357	.210	-0.2	.100	0.2	CF(2): -0.3	0.0
2016	RCU	A+	19	348	47	8	7	8	54	29	71	7	8	.272/.333/.418	.269	8.7	.326	-2.1	CF(34): -6.3, RF(15): -1.0	0.4
2017	*LAN*	*MLB*	*20*	*250*	*25*	*9*	*2*	*7*	*28*	*16*	*67*	*3*	*2*	*.226/.279/.372*	*.228*	*-0.1*	*.285*	*-0.3*	*CF -2, RF -0*	*-0.2*
2018	*LAN*	*MLB*	*21*	*337*	*39*	*12*	*3*	*10*	*39*	*24*	*85*	*4*	*3*	*.235/.293/.391*	*.252*	*5.7*	*.291*	*-0.2*	*CF -2, RF 0*	*0.4*

Breakout: 3% Improve: 13% Collapse: 0% Attrition: 5% MLB: 15% *Comparables: Anthony Gose, Cedric Hunter, Caleb Gindl*

The Good: Diaz shows across-the-board tools, highlighted by the ingredients for an above-average hit tool. He has outstanding wrist and hand strength, allowing him to thrash the barrel into the zone with above-average bat speed. Coupled with strong pitch recognition skills, the swing-and-miss is limited and he demonstrates advanced survival skills with two strikes. He showed an increased willingness and ability to add situational leverage to his stroke, syncing his lower half better and driving the ball pull-side as the season wore on. He's currently an above-average runner, though he may ultimately settle in at average, and he possesses the physical tools to handle center field capably down the line. He gets high marks for his makeup and quick adjustment during his stateside debut.

The Bad: There aren't a ton of holes to point to in Diaz's game, though the present skillset is of the raw variety. His swing plane tends to stay on the flatter side, and while he showed improvement, he can still be vulnerable on the inner-third thanks to some bat wrap and length into the zone. His feel for timing and exploiting pitchers on the base paths isn't there yet, and he struggles to get clean releases on stolen base attempts. He can lose his game clock and rush plays in the field, and his reads on trajectory in center are inconsistent.

The Irrelevant: There have been 25 men with the surname of Diaz to step between the lines in a big-league game, including three (Aledmys, Edwin, and Dayan) who made their debuts last season.

The Risks: He retains some elements of risk on account of the remaining gap between present and future skill, but his broad base of tools and demonstrated growth and development as one of the youngest regulars in the Cal League lends significant cause for optimism regarding his probability as a future big-league asset.

Major league ETA: 2019 —Wilson Karaman

Ben Carsley's Fantasy Take: At the risk of being too aggressive on lots of Dodgers prospects, I like Diaz. The tools are well-rounded, he's got just enough impact potential to catch my eye and he performed well in his first professional season stateside. If we're talking best-case scenario, Diaz is a five-tool contributor who hits for a good average and contributes meaningfully everywhere else. Worst case, Diaz is ... well ... a really boring modest five-category contributor, like, Dexter Fowler? You could do worse.

5. Walker Buehler, RHP

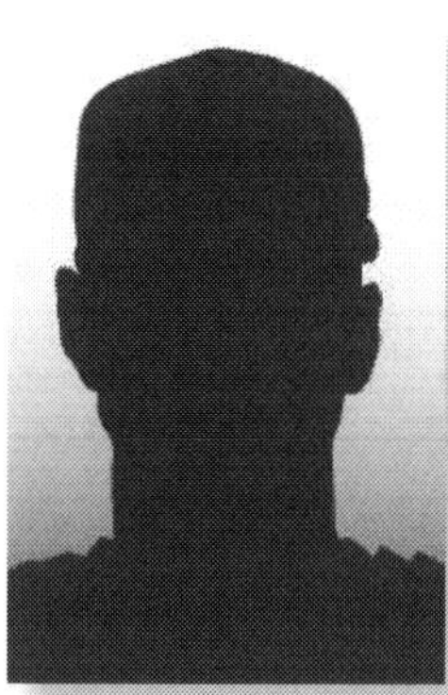

DOB: 7/28/1994

Height/Weight: 6'2" 175 lbs.

Bats/Throws: R/R

Drafted/Acquired: Drafted 24th overall in 2015 MLB Draft, Vanderbilt University (Nashville, TN); signed for $1.78 million

Previous Ranking(s): N/A

2016 Stats: 0.00 ERA, 2.79 DRA, 2 IP, 0 H, 0 BB, 3 K in 1 game at Complex AZL, 0.00 ERA, 4.76 DRA, 3 IP, 0 H, 3 BB, 3 K in low-A Great Lakes

The Role: OFP 60—No. 3 starter
Likely 45—Backend starter with durability issues or good bullpen arm

YEAR	TEAM	LVL	AGE	W	L	SV	G	GS	IP	H	HR	BB/9	K/9	K	GB%	BABIP	WHIP	ERA	FIP	DRA	VORP	WARP	cFIP	MPH
2016	DOD	Rk	21	1	0	0	1	0	2	0	0	0.0	13.5	3	67%	.000	0.00	0.00	1.13	2.79	0.60	0.1	84	
2016	GRL	A	21	0	0	0	2	1	3	0	0	9.0	9.0	3	80%	.000	1.00	0.00	5.48	4.76	0.00	0.0	105	
2017	*LAN*	*MLB*	*22*	*1*	*0*	*1*	*32*	*0*	*33^{2}*	*35*	*6*	*5.4*	*5.7*	*22*	*57%*	*.283*	*1.63*	*6.30*	*6.09*	*7.73*	*-11.9*	*-1.2*	*172*	
2018	*LAN*	*MLB*	*23*	*0*	*0*	*0*	*6*	*0*	*16*	*14*	*3*	*6.0*	*8.0*	*14*	*57%*	*.278*	*1.56*	*5.62*	*6.13*	*6.89*	*-1.6*	*-0.2*	*155*	

Breakout: 3% Improve: 5% Collapse: 0% Attrition: 1% MLB: 5% *Comparables: Ken Giles, Tanner Roark, Emiliano Fruto*

The Good: Buehler had a potential front-of-the-rotation arsenal as an amateur, and his first few pro appearances coming off Tommy John surgery showed it was still in there. He was up to 97 in short bursts and sat in the mid-90 with arm-side run. His curveball and changeup both project as above-average pitches, and his 11-5 breaker has a chance to get better then even that.

The Bad: We can quibble about his command of the stuff in 2016, but he's a year off Tommy John surgery, so whatever. The bigger issue is he has a small, lean frame that may not hold up to the rigors of a major-league starter's workload, and there's already effort in the delivery now. As mentioned, he's already got a major arm surgery under his belt at 22.

The Irrelevant: Walker is the fourth Buehler...Buehler...Buehler....Buehler...in pro baseball. None have made the majors so far.

The Risks: Buehler is only a year removed from surgery, we really don't know if the stuff will come all the way back yet, although (very) early returns are quite good. The professional track record is limited. And he's a recently-injured pitcher.

Major league ETA: 2019

Ben Carsley's Fantasy Take: There's some upside here, but Buehler's recent injury history and potential future as a reliever conspire to limit his fantasy upside. I do love ceilings, so Buehler might be a top-100 guy, but it'll be close, and I'd bet the under.

6. Andrew Toles, OF

DOB: 5/14/1992

Height/Weight: 5'10" 185 lbs.

Bats/Throws: L/R

Drafted/Acquired: Drafted in the third round in 2012 MLB Draft, Chipola Junior College (Chipola, FL); signed for $394,200

Previous Ranking(s): N/A

2016 Stats: .314/.365/.505, 3 HR, 1 SB in 48 games at major league level, .370/.414/.500, 0 HR, 9 SB in 22 games for high-A Rancho Cucamonga, .314/.363/.514, 5 HR, 13 SB in 43 games at double-A Tulsa, .321/.339/.518, 2 HR, 1 SB in 17 games at triple-A Oklahoma City

The Role: OFP 55—Above-average regular on the strength of his speed and defense
Likely 45—Second-division regular/strong-side platoon fourth outfielder

YEAR	TEAM	LVL	AGE	PA	R	2B	3B	HR	RBI	BB	K	SB	CS	AVG/OBP/SLG	TAv	VORP	BABIP	BRR	FRAA	WARP
2014	PCH	A+	22	218	28	10	1	1	13	12	31	18	10	.261/.302/.337	.233	2.4	.300	1.7	CF(46): -2.1	0.1
2014	RAY	Rk	22	25	4	0	1	0	2	0	6	6	0	.292/.320/.375	.252	1.9	.389	1.4		0.2
2016	RCU	A+	24	100	22	8	2	0	9	6	13	9	3	.370/.414/.500	.331	12.5	.430	2.6	LF(9): -1.0, CF(7): 0.6	1.3
2016	TUL	AA	24	190	27	14	3	5	22	12	30	13	3	.314/.363/.514	.323	18.2	.355	1.6	CF(24): -0.7, RF(19): 2.2	2.3
2016	OKL	AAA	24	59	6	5	0	2	7	2	8	1	5	.321/.339/.518	.301	3.2	.340	-0.8	CF(7): 0.9, LF(5): -0.3	0.4
2016	LAN	MLB	24	115	19	9	1	3	16	8	25	1	1	.314/.365/.505	.303	9.5	.385	1.8	LF(18): 2.1, CF(9): -0.3	1.2
2017	*LAN*	*MLB*	*25*	*315*	*38*	*17*	*2*	*8*	*32*	*17*	*67*	*11*	*6*	*.259/.300/.409*	*.251*	*8.0*	*.306*	*0.3*	*LF 3*	*0.8*
2018	*LAN*	*MLB*	*26*	*463*	*54*	*25*	*3*	*13*	*55*	*28*	*101*	*16*	*8*	*.260/.308/.423*	*.265*	*14.9*	*.308*	*1.1*	*LF 4*	*2.0*

Breakout: 12% Improve: 46% Collapse: 12% Attrition: 41% MLB: 78% *Comparables: Jeff Fiorentino, Shane Victorino, Kevin Pillar*

The Good: Toles generates excellent early momentum into his swing, getting the barrel on-plane early, and driving into the zone quickly. His short stroke and quality barrel control produces hard contact against velocity, and he demonstrates an intelligent situational approach at the plate. While he lacks for a ton of loft in the stroke, he has sneaky strength to drive pitches with some carry. His foot speed pushes plus-plus, and he's an instinctual base runner who draws full utility out of the tool when he's on base. The arm is another asset, playing at least to plus (and with more consistent accuracy possibly above it) from left or center fields.

The Bad: Off-field issues have caused a ton of lost developmental time along the way, and his route-running and execution in the outfield wore some of those lost reps last year. He struggles mightily against left-handed pitching, becoming more of a slap-and-dash hitter and struggling to defend as well with two strikes. He likes to extend on the ball, and while he covers the outside corner well as a result there is some ensuing inner-third vulnerability.

The Irrelevant: Chipola College, where Toles wound up after getting kicked off his team at Tennessee, has produced an impressive amount of big-league talent over the years, with alumni tallying north of 18,000 big-league at-bats and hurling more than 1,400 innings. Toles has a long way to go to catch up with current all-time WARP leader Russell Martin, who is sitting on 55.4 as of this writing.

The Risks: Toles' baseball skills were remarkably intact after his return from a year-and-a-half layoff from competition, and he kept right on producing at every stop up to and including Chavez Ravine. The long history of disciplinary issues remain branded to his Permanent Record, though last year's successful reintegration to the game marked a very encouraging development. There are a couple holes in the offensive approach and enough questions about his defensive development that it is wise to continue keeping expectations in check, but he has already proven his worth as a "now" asset who should be able to fill a demonstrable role on the Dodgers' 25-man roster all year, and if he can learn to hit lefties, there is some growth potential there as well.

Major league ETA: Debuted in 2016 —Wilson Karaman

Ben Carsley's Fantasy Take: Toles is probably just a platoon outfielder, and it's hard to make that terribly sexy in fantasy. You might want to own him over the next few years if he's playing and your league is deep, but he's not a franchise maker or breaker.

7. Willie Calhoun, 2B

DOB: 11/4/1994

Height/Weight: 5'8" 187 lbs.

Bats/Throws: L/R

Drafted/Acquired: Drafted in the fourth round in 2015 MLB Draft, Yavapai College (Prescott, AZ); signed for $347,500

Previous Ranking(s): N/A

2016 Stats: .254/.318/.469, 27 HR, 0 SB in 132 games at double-A Tulsa

The Role: OFP 55—High-end bat whose overall value is limited by defensive issues
Likely 45—A 5-foot-8 DH

YEAR	TEAM	LVL	AGE	PA	R	2B	3B	HR	RBI	BB	K	SB	CS	AVG/OBP/SLG	TAv	VORP	BABIP	BRR	FRAA	WARP
2015	OGD	Rk	20	175	28	13	1	7	26	23	18	2	1	.278/.371/.517	.301	9.8	.276	-2.8	2B(33): -7.9	0.2
2015	GRL	A	20	66	9	3	0	1	8	5	7	0	0	.393/.439/.492	.346	7.3	.434	0.0	2B(12): -1.6	0.6
2015	RCU	A+	20	82	11	7	0	3	14	7	13	0	0	.329/.390/.548	.321	8.1	.362	0.9	2B(20): -1.3	0.7
2016	TUL	AA	21	560	75	25	1	27	88	45	65	0	0	.254/.318/.469	.282	26.1	.242	0.3	2B(119): -9.4	1.8
2017	*LAN*	*MLB*	*22*	*250*	*30*	*12*	*0*	*12*	*37*	*18*	*45*	*0*	*0*	*.252/.310/.460*	*.262*	*9.9*	*.264*	*-0.5*	*2B -4*	*0.7*
2018	*LAN*	*MLB*	*23*	*345*	*47*	*16*	*1*	*17*	*51*	*25*	*64*	*0*	*0*	*.255/.312/.469*	*.281*	*17.4*	*.268*	*-0.8*	*2B -5*	*1.3*

Breakout: 5% Improve: 36% Collapse: 8% Attrition: 25% MLB: 62% *Comparables: Lonnie Chisenhall, Jonathan Schoop, Dilson Herrera*

The Good: Calhoun has outstanding pop for a guy his size. He utilizes a low center of gravity and a compact frame to generate double-plus bat speed, giving the ball a distinct sound off his barrel. He's a selective hitter and uses his small strike zone and quick hands to his advantage, keeping his strikeout totals low.

The Bad: The combination of poor athleticism and an unpolished glove makes it a near certainty that Calhoun will provide limited defensive value. He doesn't have a particularly strong arm, and can look awkward when forced to use it outside of routine plays. The lack of speed and poor physique will likely prevent him from contributing much on the basepaths, and his aging curve could be expedited as a result.

The Irrelevant: Kole Calhoun also went to Yavapai College, but they are not related.

The Risks: If Calhoun doesn't hit, he's not a major leaguer. There are additional concerns as to how well his body will age, so while the likely might feel conservative, it is taking into account significant downside-risk.

Major league ETA: Late 2017 —Matt Pullman

BenCarsley's Fantasy Take: I really don't know what to make of Calhoun. I hope he hits because he's a ton of fun, but I'm worried that the defensive profile will prevent him from accumulating bats. Keep following him because he's a fun story, and feel free to pull the trigger if you roster 150-plus prospects, but I can't get more aggressive on him yet.

8. Gavin Lux, SS

DOB: 11/23/1997

Height/Weight: 6'2" 190 lbs.

Bats/Throws: L/R

Drafted/Acquired: Drafted 20th overall in the 2016 MLB Draft from Indian Trail HS (Kenosha, WI); signed for $2,314,500

Previous Ranking(s): N/A

2016 Stats: .281/.365/.385, 0 HR, 1 SB in 48 games at Complex AZL, .387/.441/.484, 0 HR, 1 SB in 8 games at short-season Ogden

The Role: OFP 55—Above-average regular
Likely 45—Defense-first SS who can still contribute with the bat

YEAR	TEAM	LVL	AGE	PA	R	2B	3B	HR	RBI	BB	K	SB	CS	AVG/OBP/SLG	TAv	VORP	BABIP	BRR	FRAA	WARP
2016	DOD	Rk	18	219	34	10	5	0	18	25	43	1	0	.281/.365/.385	.284	14.0	.360	0.4	SS(43): -7.7	0.6
2016	OGD	Rk	18	34	7	3	0	0	3	3	8	1	0	.387/.441/.484	.330	4.1	.522	0.0	SS(8): -1.3	0.3
2017	*LAN*	*MLB*	*19*	*250*	*24*	*9*	*1*	*5*	*21*	*16*	*82*	*0*	*0*	*.195/.247/.303*	*.195*	*-5.7*	*.275*	*-0.3*	*SS -3*	*-0.9*
2018	*LAN*	*MLB*	*20*	*337*	*35*	*12*	*2*	*8*	*33*	*23*	*105*	*0*	*0*	*.209/.267/.335*	*.222*	*-1.7*	*.285*	*-0.4*	*SS -4*	*-0.6*

Breakout: 0% Improve: 4% Collapse: 1% Attrition: 5% MLB: 9% *Comparables: Raul Mondesi, Elvis Andrus, Carlos Triunfel*

The Good: Lux grew into his body from his junior year, adding speed and power to his frame, ultimately becoming the fourth-highest player drafted from Wisconsin. Lux excels defensively with a plus arm, plus actions, and soft quick hands. He could be a plus defender at the six, or any of the infield positions. He features plus bat speed and the loft to potentially slug double-digit home runs at the big-league level.

The Bad: He does have a hitch in his load, which was still present through his first year in pro ball. He is more an average runner, which means he isn't likely to produce much in the way of stolen bases. The power, which showed up in spades this spring, is mostly projection to play to average in-game.

The Irrelevant: His uncle is Augie Schmidt, who was the second-overall pick in the 1982 draft and the Golden Spikes Award Winner at University of New Orleans.

The Risks: Younger player, the power, which showed up in the spring wasn't present in his first full-season. A cold-weather kid, he could have a longer developmental path than others. His body is somewhat filled out, leaving little room for overall projection.

Major league ETA: 2020 —Steve Givarz

Ben Carsley's Fantasy Take: Lux is too far away to start pining over now, but he's got the offensive tools we crave in an infielder. If you separate your watch list into tiers, put him in the first one.

9. Jordan Sheffield, RHP

DOB: 6/1/1995

Height/Weight: 6'0" 185 lbs.

Bats/Throws: R/R

Drafted/Acquired: Drafted 36th overall in 2016 MLB Draft, Vanderbilt University (Nashville, TN); signed for $1.85 million

Previous Ranking(s): N/A

2016 Stats: 0.00 ERA, 4.12 DRA, 1 IP, 0 H, 0 BB, 0 K in 1 game at Complex AZL, 4.09 ERA, 4.42 DRA, 11 IP, 11 H, 6 BB, 13 K in 7 games at Low-A Great Lakes

The Role: OFP 55—Mid-rotation starter or late inning reliever
Likely 45—Set-up guy with durability issues

YEAR	TEAM	LVL	AGE	W	L	SV	G	GS	IP	H	HR	BB/9	K/9	K	GB%	BABIP	WHIP	ERA	FIP	DRA	VORP	WARP	cFIP	MPH
2016	DOD	Rk	21	0	0	0	1	1	1	0	0	0.0	0.0	0	100%	.000	0.00	0.00	4.13	4.12	0.20	0.0	94	
2016	GRL	A	21	0	1	0	7	7	11	11	2	4.9	10.6	13	43%	.346	1.55	4.09	5.39	4.42	0.70	0.1	104	
2017	*LAN*	*MLB*	*22*	*2*	*3*	*0*	*9*	*9*	*33²*	*38*	*7*	*5.2*	*5.8*	*22*	*38%*	*.313*	*1.72*	*6.46*	*6.48*	*7.42*	*-6.9*	*-0.7*	*176*	
2018	*LAN*	*MLB*	*23*	*3*	*7*	*0*	*26*	*26*	*156*	*161*	*30*	*5.4*	*7.4*	*129*	*38%*	*.311*	*1.63*	*5.77*	*6.30*	*6.63*	*-11.5*	*-1.2*	*160*	

Breakout: 3% Improve: 3% Collapse: 0% Attrition: 2% MLB: 4% *Comparables: Wilking Rodriguez, Marco Gonzales, Braden Shipley*

The Good: Sheffield has a power pitcher's arsenal. The fastball regularly bumped 96-97 in short bursts as a pro even after a long NCAA season at Vandy. It sat in the mid-90s as a starter in college and it's a plus offering due to the velocity and some deception in his delivery. He pairs it with a low-80s curve. At its best the breaker will show late, two-plane break although it can show as a flatter, power slurve at times. Both versions are effective at inducing swing-and-miss, and it also projects as a plus offering.

The Bad: Sheffield has a TJ in his medical file already and ticks just about every other box for the "future reliever" tag. It's a high-effort delivery that leaves him prone to command issues. His changeup has some projection due to its dive and velocity (high-80s), but it's his clear third pitch at the moment. Sheffield's fastball doesn't have much in the way of plane or wiggle, and he may not be able to overpower pro hitters with it as easily as he did SEC ones.

The Irrelevant: Sheffield's younger brother, Justus, is in the Yankees system. You may have heard of him.

The Risks: He's an undersized righty (I double-checked this time) with a checkered injury history and a high-effort delivery. Can't quibble with the fastball/curve combo though, and he could move quickly through the minors if he stays healthy. Which he may not, because he's a pitcher.

Major league ETA: Early 2018 as a reliever, late 2018 as a starter

Ben Carsley's Fantasy Take: The Dodgers don't have a great track record with these guys and the upside is very modest. Move along.

10. Dustin May, RHP

DOB: 9/6/1997

Height/Weight: 6'6" 180 lbs

Bats/Throws: R/R Drafted/Acquired: Drafted 101st overall in the 2016 MLB draft, Northwest High School (Justin, TX), signed for $997,500

Previous Ranking(s): N/A

2016 Stats: 3.86 ERA, 2.04 DRA, 30.1 IP, 37 H, 4 BB, 34 K at Complex AZL

The Role: OFP 55—Above-average major league starter
Likely 45—Backend starter with plus-plus hair

YEAR	TEAM	LVL	AGE	W	L	SV	G	GS	IP	H	HR	BB/9	K/9	K	GB%	BABIP	WHIP	ERA	FIP	DRA	VORP	WARP	cFIP	MPH
2016	DOD	Rk	18	0	1	1	10	6	20	37	0	1.2	10.1	34	57%	.394	1.35	3.86	2.56	2.04	11.8	1.2	80	
2017	*LAN*	*MLB*	*19*	*2*	*2*	*1*	*19*	*5*	*36*	*36*	*6*	*3.5*	*8.0*	*32*	*47%*	*.320*	*1.40*	*4.70*	*4.81*	*5.48*	*-0.9*	*-0.1*	*128*	
2018	*LAN*	*MLB*	*20*	*2*	*2*	*0*	*14*	*6*	*58*	*55*	*9*	*3.4*	*8.9*	*57*		*.316*	*1.33*	*4.33*	*4.68*	*5.05*	*1.3*	*0.1*	*118*	

Breakout: 0% Improve: 0% Collapse: 0% Attrition: 0% MLB: 0% *Comparables: Andrew Faulkner, Arodys Vizcaino, Danny Duffy*

The Good: May is a tall Texan who oozes projection. His fastball is already sitting in the low-90s and it's easy to see him ticking up into the mid-90s as he fills out and gets a better feel for his delivery. His breaking ball evolved from a slurvy curveball to a tight, mid-80s slider over the course of 2016, and it's a potential plus offering with a few years of reps. His command of the fastball and the slider is more refined at present than you'd expect from a tall, gangly prep pitcher.

The Bad: The changeup is a clear third pitch, and he'll need a much better one to start. The gap between what he can be and what he is right now is best measured using trigonometric parallax.

The Irrelevant: Given the Yankees needlessly restrictive grooming policies, May should unseat Clint Frazier as having the best ginger locks in baseball.

The Risks: The risks here are substantial. May is very projectable, but he also needs to actually project. He is a long way from the majors, and a lot go wrong in the interim, because he's a pitcher.

Major league ETA: 2020
Ben Carsley's Fantasy Take: May is a good one for your watch list and should arguably be owned if you roster 200 prospects. He could take off fast.

OTHERS OF NOTE:

All of The 5:00 Power

Johan Mieses, OF

If nothing else, Mieses is certainly a living embodiment of the ol' "swing hard in case you hit it" adage. The Dodgers spent a bunch of time last summer tweaking Mieses' setup and launch in order to quiet down copious amounts of early-progression noise and get him quicker into the zone. But in spite of some gains in power utility, the swing-and-miss issues largely persisted as he continued to demonstrate oftentimes wild aggressiveness against anything that was soft or spinning. Mieses is adept at hunting fastballs and punishing mistakes, particularly from lefthanders, but the approach issues remain a significant detriment to his hit tool and, with it, his ultimate projection. He's an all-out ball hawk in the outfield with plenty of arm for right and at least some occasional utility in center still possible. But the reads and feel of a true center fielder aren't there, and the offensive profile points more in the direction of lefty-mashing fourth outfielder than future regular. *—Wilson Karaman*

The Austin Barnes All Star

Will Smith, C

The Dodgers' first pick in the supplemental round last summer, Smith was an advanced college catcher who ended the year with a 25-game run catching and handling multiple infield positions at high-A. As the positional assignments indicate, Smith offers a rare brand of athleticism behind the dish, and it fuels one of the fastest transfers in the minor leagues. His pop technique and arm strength are both assets behind the plate, helping drive a 42 percent caught-stealing rate across three levels after signing. His blocking is still a work in progress, but he shows strong hands and framing potential around the margins of the zone, and the whole package of an above-average defensive catcher is there. The bat's future is somewhat less clear; he grinds out at-bats and gets the barrel into the zone quickly enough to limit swing-and-miss, but he showed some vulnerability to velocity after signing and lacks for much of an "attack mode" at present. His on-base skills should help the hit tool play up, and if they max out the defensive profile is there to usher him into a majority-start role at the highest level. *—Wilson Karaman*

The Helium Potential

Mitchell White, RHP

White snuck up on draft board creators after undergoing Tommy John surgery and a stint in the bullpen at Santa Clara, but the Dodgers saw enough promise in his arsenal and athleticism to pop him in the second round last June. The early returns certainly appeared to validate that decision, albeit across the smallest of samples. His fastball sat 92-94 at season's end with late life and a shared tunnel with a filthy high-80s cutter. The cut features outsized horizontal movement for the velocity and projects as a true plus weapon that can tie up quality left-handed bats. There's above-average depth to his complementary curveball, though the pitch can show with some hump out of his hand. A nascent changeup lags as an under-utilized and undeveloped final piece of the puzzle. White's up-tempo delivery will run into some pace and timing issues at present, but his fluidity and body control is apparent, and it is not at all difficult to envision greater consistency and repeatability coming with more post-surgery reps. Between college and his professional debut he managed to log triple-digit innings, and if the breaking ball and change can continue progressing while the stamina builds, he's a guy with the potential to rise up the ranks quickly over the next 12 months. *—Wilson Karaman*

Wilson's Guy

Brock Stewart, RHP

A former sixth-rounder, Stewart has all the size and stuff you look for to round out a rotation. His four-seamer has ticked up into 93-94 sitting range over the past couple years, and he commands it very well to both sides of the plate with life and above-average movement. He pairs it with a change that can play up into plus range thanks to quality arm speed replication, good drop, and outstanding velocity separation. He struggled to consistently spin the ball in previous minor-league seasons, but his hard slider took a nice step forward this year and showed newfound and intriguing depth across several big-league outings. He's the son of a former coach and current Rays' scout, and his baseball intelligence shows in both repeatable mechanics and his ability to make in-game adjustments. He'll enter 2017 offering quality rotation insurance and/or solid trade value as a ready-now arm. *—Wilson Karaman*

TOP 10 TALENTS 25 AND UNDER (BORN 4/1/91 OR LATER)

1. Corey Seager	6. Jose De Leon
2. Julio Urias	7. Alex Verdugo
3. Joc Pederson	8. Yusniel Diaz
4. Yadier Alvarez	9. Walker Buehler
5. Cody Bellinger	10. Andrew Toles

There are only three Dodgers who qualify for the 25-and-under list who aren't discussed in detail above, but they are a doozy of a trio. Seager followed up a dynamic September cameo with a full-season .320 TAv that led to 6.7 WARP in his first full season (despite a negative FRAA). The top-overall prospect entering the season, Seager claimed an All-Star appearance, a Silver Slugger Award, a Rookie of the Year Award, and finished third in MVP voting. He is, thanks to the free agent/service time relationship, one of the five most valuable assets in baseball at present. The only nagging question is that of how long he'll last at his current position given his size (6-foot-5, 215 pounds), but better defensive positioning should help shore up any loss of range over the next few years, and the bat should be more than enough to carry the profile should he need to slide to third base.

Urias has progressed as linearly as we often tell you that prospects don't, but still continues to confound. He set a career-high in innings pitched, he made his major-league and playoffs debuts, tied for the league lead in pickoffs (in only 77 innings), and generally was a grand success especially when taking age into account. That last part is relevant though. He's now in the major leagues, and while his age relative to level matters when projecting him forward (to a degree), the results he gets in the here and now matter more than ever before, so his DRA of 3.97 should well be noted. It's still an open question as to whether Urias can or will pitch a full slate of innings next year, and how his stuff will hold up to the effects of turning a lineup over a third time (something he largely avoided), how the league will react, and what the effect of a full(er) season will be on the quality of his offerings. He's shown the ability to adapt and handle adversity though, and it's fair to maintain high expectations for him. Even without the ace-level stuff of a Noah Syndergaard, Urias' three-pitch mix and control should allow him to navigate the rigors of the majors well, as he continues to sharpen his fine command and sequencing.

By TAv, Pederson had the second-best offensive performance on the team. People will recall his post-derby swoon in his Jekyll-Hyde rookie campaign, but it's worth noting the adjustments made over the course of the 2016 season. He slashed .260/.380/.520 in the second half of the season, and his FRAA jumped from -21 to -1, culminating in a 3.5-WARP season. Dave Roberts hid him against southpaws (only 77 plate appearances against LHP), which might have contributed to jump in his rate output but also provides a window into where his next area to improve lies. His .469 OPS against same-side pitching leaves a lot of room for growth, and even a jump to merely "bad" against lefties could make him an everyday bat.

—Craig Goldstein

MIAMI MARLINS

The State of the System: *"True is it, that upon the verge I found me*
Of the abysmal valley dolorous,
That gathers thunder of infinite ululations.
Obscure, profound it was, and nebulous,
So that by fixing on its depths my sight
Nothing whatever I discerned therein."
— The Divine Comedy: Inferno: Dante Alighieri
(trans. H.W. Longfellow)

THE TOP TEN

1. LHP Braxton Garrett	6. OF Stone Garrett
2. RHP Luis Castillo	7. OF Thomas Jones
3. RHP Tyler Kolek	8. OF Austin Dean
4. OF Isael Soto	9. IF/OF Yefri Perez
5. 3B Brian Anderson	10. LHP Dillon Peters

The Big Question: And you may ask yourself, "Well, how did I get here?"

I'm not positive yet that the Marlins have the worst farm system in baseball, but they are definitely on the short list to land in the ninth circle of our 2017 org rankings. As prospect writers we spend a lot of time praising and analyzing the good systems. The teams that do it right. The Mets ability to develop pitchers, the Cardinals Way, the teardowns and rebuilds in Chicago and Houston, Atlanta and Philly. The bad systems are just less interesting to write about. But write about them we must. The Marlins get their top 10 prospects and others of note too. Before we get into that though, let's take a look at how you you end up at the bottom of our org rankings.

Trading the prospects you do have

It's possible that up until the last couple of seasons the baseball orthodoxy pendulum swung too far in the direction of overvaluing prospects. Elite prospects, back-end of the top 100 prospects, sleeper prospects, any prospects. Then in July, both World Series teams dealt high-end prospect packages for relievers, something you would have assumed verboten in a sabermetrically-inclined MLB front office. Still, there can be no doubt that when the Indians and Cubs parted with some of their best prospects for Andrew Miller and Aroldis Chapman, that they were getting impact talent in high-leverage innings for a stretch run and the playoffs (and beyond, in Miller's case). The Marlins traded their best prospects for Andrew Cashner and Colin Rea.

Again, there's nothing wrong with trading prospects for major leaguers. That's one very valid way to use your farm system to "produce" major league talent. And at the time Miami needed starting pitching desperately while hanging around the periphery of the NL wild card race. This is not an uncommon move for the Marlins when they are in the "go for it" portion of their contention cycle, known colloquially as #MarlinsTakeover. They've dealt Andrew Heaney for Dee Gordon, a comp balance pick (future prospect I guess) for Bryan Morris, another comp balance picked tossed in with Colin Moran, Francis Martes, and Jake Marisnick for Jarred Cosart (later a throw-in to the Cashner/Rea deal), and international bonus slots to anyone who asked at "your-local-furniture-outlet's-all-things-must-go-President's-Day-sale" prices (more on that in a moment).

Funnily enough, once the Marlins are back in the "ah, fuck it" portion of their contention cycle, they have been very good at rebuilding their org quickly by trading off high-value young regulars, so their 2018 or 2019 org ranking could look a lot rosier after the next fire sale.

Lack of recent success in the draft

The Marlins have been mediocre to bad in recent seasons, so have had the benefit of high draft picks. Conventional

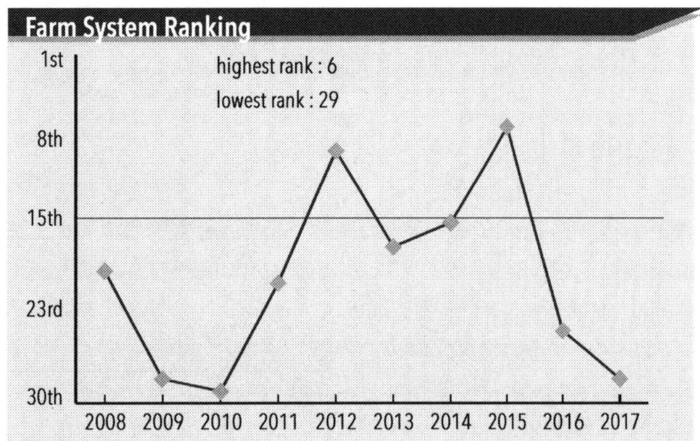

Personnel

President:
Michael Hill

Assistant General Manager:
Mike Berger

VP, Player Development:
Marc DelPiano

Manager:
Don Mattingly

BP Alumni:
Bryan Holcomb
Jason Paré

wisdom suggests you take five years to analyze a draft class, but in the intervening half-decade, you'd hope to see your top picks among your top prospects. That is how it's supposed to work after all. Since the Marlins hit big in 2010 and 2011 on Christian Yelich and Jose Fernandez, they have had seven first-round draft picks. Besides the aforementioned Moran and Heaney (who given their profiles, would have likely graduated in Miami anyway), the Marlins selected Matt Krook, Blake Anderson, Tyler Kolek, Josh Naylor, and Braxton Garrett. If you want to expand to Top 50 picks, we can throw in Colby Suggs, Trevor Williams, Justin Twine, and Brett Lilek.

Garrett and Kolek sit toward the top of the list. So that's good. Even in better systems it isn't outrageous that the seventh-overall pick would be your No. 1 prospect. Kolek had yet to really show the potential you'd expect from the number two-overall pick before his Tommy John surgery this year, but he's a pitcher. This stuff happens. And it's still a 100 mph fastball.

Naylor was the main piece in the Cashner/Rea deal mentioned above, but he was considered a reach at 1.12 in last year's draft. He's a short, physically mature, high school first baseman, and while I liked the offensive profile some when I saw him for Greensboro this Spring, he's not an impact talent or even really a potential Top 101 prospect. Plus, you know, he stabbed a teammate, it was alleged.

Blake Anderson was a prep catcher—danger, Will Robinson!—that the Marlins popped as a compensation pick for not signing Matt Krook the year before. Anderson has been hurt two out of three pro summers and has yet to get out of short-season ball. Krook was an All-American at Oregon as a freshman before losing a year to Tommy John and struggling in his return to the mound this spring. He was a fourth-round selection of the Giants this year. Again, this stuff happens.

It happened to Brett Lilek too, who made only seven starts for Greensboro before being felled by a shoulder strain. Twine was a high school shortstop, now a second baseman, who hasn't hit. Williams made the Pirates pen this year, shipped out for a Colombian teenage arm that is now 21 and missed all of 2016. Colby Suggs was a short, right-handed reliever who is now a short, right-handed reliever coming off Tommy John surgery.

So a lot of their pitchers broke. I don't know how much you can blame talent identification and development for that, but org rankings are outcome-based and the outcomes have been bad. Also I am not entirely convinced that the Miami draft room doesn't look something like this:

A ponderous and somewhat cheap IFA approach

Hoo boy. So the Marlins haven't spent over $600k on a July 2nd signing in the last five years. That $600,000 went to outfielder Anderson Castro in 2014. He has already been released from the organization after spending two summers under the Mendoza Line in their Dominican complex. Their biggest 2015 signing was right fielder Mario Prenza for $550,000. He had his own struggles in Summer ball this year.

It's not fair to lay the issues here at the feet of teenagers though. Non-premier IFA signings can take a little bit of time to develop. So let's hop back to the 2012 class. Those signees would be in their Age 20 season; while far from fully formed baseball players, you'd at least have a better idea of what they are. The biggest signing that year was...uh...$85,000 for Alberto Sanchez, a third baseman who spent one Summer in the Dominican, hit .168, and is currently listed as inactive.

You don't have to break the bank like the Yankees, Cubs, and Padres to get a return on your IFA dollars of course. You don't even have to splurge on a seven-figure hyper-toolsy shortstops every July. Our first four 2017 lists show that you can get a great return on six-figure signings if you scout and develop well. The Marlins could have easily fit Victor Robles, Ronald Acuna, Ozzie Albies, Adonis Medina, and Luis Carpio into even their meager IFA budget. They've also been very active in trading their international bonus slots under the new CBA. Put it all together and you end up with exactly one Marlins-signed IFA in their top 10. And surprise, surprise, he's another right fielder.

They also might want to consider not targeting 16-year-old corner players.

Graduations

This is a natural and good part of the player development cycle. The idea is to turn your prospects into major leaguers with meaningful roles, so you can point to graduations as the system being down for "the right reasons."

The Marlins graduated zero prospects off their 2016 Top 10.

Well that's not it at least.

More "right reasons" in 2017, perhaps?

1. Braxton Garrett, LHP

DOB: 8/5/1997

Height/Weight: 6'3" 190 lbs.

Bats/Throws: L/L

Drafted/Acquired: Drafted seventh overall in the 2016 MLB Draft, Florence HS (Florence, AL); signed for $4.15 million

Previous Ranking(s): Unranked

2016 Stats: N/A

The Role: OFP 60—No. 3 starter
Likely 50—No. 4 starter

The Good: Garrett was the second-best lefty prep arm in the 2016 draft class, and the Marlins went overslot to buy him out of his Vanderbilt commitment. The fastball gets into the low 90s, and it should sit there as he adds strength in his twenties. It's a potential plus pitch, as is the curveball which was as good as any draftee's not named Jason Groome, with a good 1-7 shape and advanced command of the offering. His mechanics are fine, if not without some effort. The frame is ideal for a starter.

The Bad: Despite his lean frame, he's more of an "advanced prep arm" than a projection monster. The fastball may only end up playing at 50 or 55. He's got exactly as a good a changeup at present as you would expect from a high school arm with a monster curve. That is to say, exactly as much as he needs, which is not much.

The Irrelevant: Braxton (Anglo-Saxon in origin, meaning "Brock's town") has risen in popularity as a boy's name from No. 333 the year Garrett was born, to No. 136 in 2016. Damn millennials.

The Risks: He's yet to throw a professional pitch. The developmental horizon is long. He'll eventually need a better changeup. He's a pitcher. So all the standard (high) risks here.

Major league ETA: 2020

Ben Carsley's Fantasy Take: Garrett will get attention in dynasty leagues because of his draft pedigree, but he's more of a decent fantasy asset than anything special. In time Garrett could develop into an SP4/5 in the healthy Jaime Garcia mold. That makes him worth rostering if your league rosters 150 prospects, but if you only roster 100 Garrett is a tougher call.

2. Luis Castillo, RHP

DOB: 12/12/1992

Height/Weight: 6'2" 170 lbs.

Bats/Throws: R/R

Drafted/Acquired: Signed in December 2011 out of Dominican Republic by the San Francisco Giants for $15,000; acquired from the Giants for Casey McGehee

Previous Ranking(s): N/A

2016 Stats: 2.07 ERA, 2.17 DRA, 117.2 IP, 18 BB, 92 K in 23 games at High-A Jupiter, 3.86 ERA, 5.68 DRA, 14 IP, 7 BB, 12 K, in 3 games at Double-A Jacksonville

The Role: 60 OFP—Mid-rotation starter, late innings reliever
50 OFP—Back-end starter, middle innings reliever

YEAR	TEAM	LVL	AGE	W	L	SV	G	GS	IP	H	HR	BB/9	K/9	K	GB%	BABIP	WHIP	ERA	FIP	DRA	VORP	WARP	cFIP	MPH
2014	AUG	A	21	2	2	10	48	0	58^2	56	6	3.8	10.1	66	46%	.316	1.38	3.07	4.00	2.77	14.90	1.5	88	
2015	GRB	A	22	4	3	4	25	7	63^1	59	1	2.7	9.0	63	53%	.326	1.23	2.98	2.74	1.89	22.30	2.4	76	
2015	JUP	A+	22	2	3	0	10	9	43^2	44	3	2.9	6.4	31	52%	.308	1.33	3.50	3.67	4.39	3.20	0.4	100	
2016	JUP	A+	23	8	4	0	23	21	117^2	95	2	1.4	7.0	91	50%	.271	0.96	2.07	2.46	2.29	41.10	4.2	81	
2016	JAX	AA	23	0	2	0	3	3	14	12	1	4.5	7.7	12	42%	.262	1.36	3.86	4.25	5.76	-1.00	-0.1	106	
2017	*MIA*	*MLB*	*24*	*6*	*5*	*1*	*47*	*14*	*104^2*	*112*	*13*	*3.2*	*6.1*	*71*	*41%*	*.319*	*1.43*	*4.55*	*4.59*	*5.40*	*-0.1*	*0.0*	*127*	
2018	*MIA*	*MLB*	*25*	*4*	*4*	*1*	*32*	*10*	*93^1*	*89*	*12*	*4.2*	*8.2*	*85*	*41%*	*.316*	*1.42*	*4.31*	*4.78*	*5.11*	*2.7*	*0.3*	*119*	

Breakout: 4% Improve: 7% Collapse: 2% Attrition: 7% MLB: 15% *Comparables: Mayckol Guaipe, Chase Anderson, Randy Wells*

The Good: After pitching primarily as a reliever with the Giants, Castillo has flourished as a starter, showcasing his premium arm strength and ability to hold velocity late in games. In velocity the pitch plays as an 80 sitting 97-99 and touching 101 with above-average control. He has an easy, repeatable delivery with above-average arm speed and a smooth arm action. His slider flashes plus with hard tilt and bite. His changeup is an effective third offering against left-handers.

The Bad: While his fastball has elite velocity, it lacks movement and plane so it can be hittable in the zone. His slider is inconsistent as it gets slurvy and shows more fringe-average than plus. He telegraphs his changeup and he struggles with command, often left up in the zone. More a strike-thrower than a command artist.

The Irrelevant: K-Rod is still in shock because of this.

The Risks: Was older for High-A, secondary pitches need to become more consistent for an everyday big-league spot, lack of consistent changeup could force a bullpen move sooner rather than later is a pitcher.

Major league ETA: Early 2018 —Steve Givarz

Ben Carsley's Fantasy Take: Did anyone else read the above and get a distinct Joe Kelly vibe? Luis Castillo has Great Stuff (TM), and he's close enough to the Majors that you could easily make the argument for taking him over Garrett in dynasty leagues. Still, the relatively limited upside and the somewhat likely chance he ends up in the bullpen conspire to limit Castillo to a back-of-the-top-100 name, if that.

3. Tyler Kolek, RHP

DOB: 12/15/1995

Height/Weight: 6'5" 260 lbs.

Bats/Throws: R/R

Drafted/Acquired: Drafted second overall in the 2014 MLB Draft, Shepherd HS (Shepherd, TX); signed for $6 million

Previous Ranking(s): #1 (Org.)

2016 Stats: N/A

The Role: OFP 55—Bret comped him to Nate Eovaldi last year and I kind of like that
Likely 45—Frustrating No. 4 starter or hard-throwing seventh inning guy

YEAR	TEAM	LVL	AGE	W	L	SV	G	GS	IP	H	HR	BB/9	K/9	K	GB%	BABIP	WHIP	ERA	FIP	DRA	VORP	WARP	cFIP	MPH
2014	MRL	Rk	18	0	3	0	9	8	22	22	0	5.3	7.4	18	0%	.333	1.59	4.50	3.91	4.76			104	
2015	GRB	A	19	4	10	0	25	25	108^2	108	7	5.1	6.7	81	51%	.298	1.56	4.56	4.87	6.83	-19.40	-2.1	115	
2017	*MIA*	*MLB*	*21*	*2*	*3*	*0*	*8*	*8*	*32^2*	*38*	*5*	*6.1*	*4.7*	*17*	*40%*	*.320*	*1.85*	*6.34*	*6.27*	*7.45*	*-6.8*	*-0.7*	*175*	
2018	*MIA*	*MLB*	*22*	*5*	*10*	*0*	*26*	*26*	*153*	*153*	*24*	*7.2*	*7.9*	*135*	*40%*	*.318*	*1.80*	*5.85*	*6.54*	*6.88*	*-15.1*	*-1.6*	*162*	

Breakout: 2% Improve: 2% Collapse: 0% Attrition: 2% MLB: 3% *Comparables: Dellin Betances, Elvis Araujo, Kyle Lobstein*

The Good: Kolek still has triple-digit heat in his right arm, a frame built to log innings, and a chance for an above-average slider. Unfortunately it is hard to have more here...

The Bad: ...because Kolek missed all of 2016 after undergoing Tommy John surgery. As I wrote in the essay above, this does happen, but it's not ideal for a pitching prospect that was already having some developmental issues. Even assuming he steps back on the field next summer and the stuff returns apace, there will still be lingering questions about Kolek's future role on the mound.

The Irrelevant: Kolek's 100 mph heater is in good company nowadays.

The Risks: Tommy John surgery is common, but it is not routine. It could take some time for the stuff to get all the way back if it ever does, and this is an arm that still needs a lot of pro reps and refinement. The best predictor of future pitcher injuries is past pitcher injuries, yadda yadda yadda. Kolek was risky even before the surgery, as the secondaries needed a lot of work and the control was shaky. And yes, he's still a pitcher.

Major league ETA: 2020

Ben Carsley's Fantasy Take: It doesn't matter how powerful your car's engine is if your car doesn't have tires, a steering wheel, brakes or a transmission. Kolek's fastball and pedigree will keep him on dynasty radars for a while, but if he's on waivers you can wait for him to get healthy and prove TJ didn't rob him of any of his natural talents before putting in a claim.

4. Isael Soto, OF

DOB: 11/02/1996

Height/Weight: 6'0" 180 lbs.

Bats/Throws: L/L

Drafted/Acquired: Signed July 2013 out of the Dominican Republic by the Miami Marlins for $310,000

Previous Ranking(s): #6 (Org.)

2016 Stats: .247/.320/.399, 9 HR, 3 SB in 113 games at Low-A Greensboro

The Role: OFP 50—TTO-type in right field, but enough power to play everyday
Likely 40—Platoon/bench bat

YEAR	TEAM	LVL	AGE	PA	R	2B	3B	HR	RBI	BB	K	SB	CS	AVG/OBP/SLG	TAv	VORP	BABIP	BRR	FRAA	WARP
2014	MRL	Rk	17	199	26	9	1	7	23	10	47	1	2	.251/.302/.426	.311	5.4	.298	-0.3		0.9
2015	GRB	A	18	67	2	1	0	0	1	3	27	0	0	.125/.164/.141	.110	-9.8	.216	-0.8	RF(12): 0.5, CF(3): -0.6	-1.0
2015	MRL	Rk	18	32	3	2	1	1	5	5	6	0	1	.346/.438/.615	.367	2.9	.400	-1.4	RF(2): -0.5	0.2
2015	BAT	A-	18	22	1	0	0	0	0	1	10	0	0	.095/.136/.095	.088	-4.3	.182	-0.7	RF(4): -0.2	-0.5
2016	GRB	A	19	448	51	24	5	9	38	43	115	3	0	.247/.320/.399	.278	13.8	.323	-0.8	RF(101): -1.1	0.7
2017	*MIA*	*MLB*	*20*	*250*	*21*	*9*	*1*	*5*	*24*	*18*	*86*	*0*	*0*	*.193/.254/.312*	*.202*	*-8.6*	*.280*	*-0.3*	*RF -1*	*-1.1*
2018	*MIA*	*MLB*	*21*	*334*	*35*	*13*	*1*	*8*	*33*	*28*	*111*	*0*	*0*	*.203/.272/.334*	*.225*	*-6.3*	*.287*	*-0.5*	*RF -2*	*-0.9*

Breakout: 1% Improve: 3% Collapse: 0% Attrition: 2% MLB: 5% *Comparables: Chris Parmelee, Caleb Gindl, Nomar Mazara*

The Good: In a system that lacks much in the way of bats, Soto's tools stand out. There's plus raw power in the swing, and I'd expect to see it more in games as he adds upper-body strength in his twenties. He's an average runner with a plus arm in right field. He should be a positive defender there with more reps/refinement. There's a semblance of an approach at the plate, if not enough hit tool at present to really put it into action all the time.

The Bad: Soto is raw. Really raw. Overmatched at times in the Sally despite plus bat speed, the swing can be a bit one-gear and he gets pull happy. He's still rough in the outfield. The arm strength is fine for right, but when he doesn't have to air it out, the mechanics can get out of whack and he tends to almost soft toss it. He's runs well at present, but I suspect he will lose some speed as he ages and settle in as a 40 runner. It's a right-field profile either way.

The Irrelevant: Certain minor-league announcers took to calling Soto "Izzy" in 2016, but we won't call it an official nickname until it shows up on his Baseball-Reference page, like the totally legitimate "Millville Meteor."

The Risks: High. He's young, struggled in his first taste of full-season ball, and will have to hit enough to carry a corner outfield profile. I'm not all that confident he will ever hit enough to carry an everyday role.

Major league ETA: 2020

Ben Carsley's Fantasy Take: I knew the Marlins system would be ... uninspiring ... for our purposes, but lolololololol at Isael Soto being the fourth-best prospect in a ranking of anything other than prospects named Isael. Hard pass unless the hit tool starts showing up. The dynasty portion of this list is not gonna get better from here, folks.

5. Brian Anderson, 3B

DOB: 05/19/1993

Height/Weight: 6'3" 185 lbs.

Bats/Throws: R/R

Drafted/Acquired: Drafted 76th overall in the 2014 MLB Draft, University of Arkansas, signed for $600,000

Previous Ranking(s): #9 (Org.)

2016 Stats: .302/.377/.400, 3 HR, 3 SB in 49 games at High-A Jupiter, 243/.330/.359, 8 HR, 0 SB in 86 games at Double-A Jacksonville

The Role: 50 OFP—Solid, if unspectacular starter who won't wow with defensive skills.
40 Likely—Bat-first player who plays other positions.

YEAR	TEAM	LVL	AGE	PA	R	2B	3B	HR	RBI	BB	K	SB	CS	AVG/OBP/SLG	TAv	VORP	BABIP	BRR	FRAA	WARP
2014	BAT	A-	21	85	11	3	1	3	12	6	11	1	1	.273/.333/.455	.271	2.9	.286	-0.1	2B(17): -1.8	0.1
2014	GRB	A	21	172	27	7	0	8	37	13	28	0	0	.314/.378/.516	.324	15.0	.336	-1.6	3B(26): 2.0, 2B(9): 0.4	1.8
2015	JUP	A+	22	530	50	22	2	8	62	40	109	2	2	.235/.304/.340	.269	19.3	.287	-0.9	3B(121): 4.1	2.5
2016	JUP	A+	23	207	27	12	2	3	25	22	38	3	0	.302/.377/.440	.300	13.9	.364	-1.5	3B(47): 8.1	2.3
2016	JAX	AA	23	345	38	9	1	8	40	36	59	0	0	.243/.330/.359	.268	13.7	.274	0.2	3B(85): 12.5	2.8
2017	*MIA*	*MLB*	*24*	*250*	*25*	*10*	*1*	*7*	*29*	*20*	*63*	*0*	*0*	*.230/.297/.379*	*.240*	*2.1*	*.283*	*-0.4*	*3B 5, 1B 0*	*0.8*
2018	*MIA*	*MLB*	*25*	*389*	*46*	*16*	*1*	*12*	*44*	*31*	*101*	*0*	*0*	*.230/.297/.384*	*.254*	*5.4*	*.284*	*-0.8*	*3B 8, 1B 0*	*1.5*

Breakout: 2% Improve: 9% Collapse: 7% Attrition: 13% MLB: 19% *Comparables: Andrew Burns, Adam Duvall, Eric Campbell*

The Good: Anderson fared much better in his second go at High-A, showing improved defense at the hot corner. His plus arm and accuracy plays well at the position and he could be a steady, if not spectacular defender there. His average raw power is starting to show more in games and could play to full utility down the road. He has above-average bat speed through the zone and can work all fields.

The Bad: He did repeat the level after a poor season the year prior, and outside of his arm, his tools all require projection to even get to average. His fielding, while improved, is still clunky. He doesn't have great range and tends to body balls up. Anderson did struggle with advanced arms in his first run at Double-A, and his upside remains more average than impact.

The Irrelevant: In theory, he should surpass the former Chicago White Sox OF Brian Anderson, who has a career -1.0 WARP. Although he has a tougher time passing the former Diamondback LHP Brian Anderson, with a career 14.2 WARP.

The Risks: Anderson isn't getting younger and struggled with his first taste of Double-A. His defense at third might not be palatable enough to ignore if the bat doesn't play higher.

Major league ETA: 2018 —Steve Givarz

Ben Carsley's Fantasy Take: Anderson might be interesting if he's closer to the Majors and has a clear shot at playing time. Still, you don't want to waste a roster spot on someone with the upside of, like, 2016 David Freese.

6. Stone Garrett, OF

DOB: 11/22/1995

Height/Weight: 6'2" 195 lbs.

Bats/Throws: R/R

Drafted/Acquired: Drafted in the eighth round of the 2014 MLB Draft, George Ranch HS (Richmond, TX); signed for $162,400

Previous Ranking(s): #8 (Org.)

2016 Stats: .143/.333/.143, 0 HR, 1 SB in 3 games at Gulf Coast League, .213/.265/.371, 6 HR, 1 SB in 52 games at Low-A Greensboro

The Role: OFP 50— Low-BA/medium-pop outfielder
Likely 30— One of those mid-2000s Phillies prep picks

YEAR	TEAM	LVL	AGE	PA	R	2B	3B	HR	RBI	BB	K	SB	CS	AVG/OBP/SLG	TAv	VORP	BABIP	BRR	FRAA	WARP
2014	MRL	Rk	18	156	17	3	1	0	11	7	31	4	1	.236/.269/.270	.233	-0.3	.297	0.8		-0.1
2015	BAT	A-	19	247	36	18	6	11	46	19	60	8	5	.297/.352/.581	.339	26.7	.355	-1.0	CF(58): -2.9	2.6
2016	MRL	Rk	20	9	1	0	0	0	0	2	3	1	0	.143/.333/.143	.251	0.0	.250	-0.1	RF(2): -0.3	0.0
2016	GRB	A	20	212	21	9	2	6	16	11	71	1	2	.213/.265/.371	.226	-2.2	.300	0.6	LF(33): -2.6, CF(7): 1.5	-0.3
2017	*MIA*	*MLB*	*21*	*250*	*22*	*9*	*1*	*8*	*28*	*13*	*91*	*1*	*1*	*.195/.241/.341*	*.203*	*-7.1*	*.277*	*-0.4*	*LF 0, RF -0*	*-0.7*
2018	*MIA*	*MLB*	*22*	*290*	*30*	*11*	*1*	*9*	*32*	*15*	*105*	*1*	*1*	*.198/.246/.353*	*.217*	*-6.6*	*.277*	*-0.5*	*LF 0, RF 0*	*-0.7*

Breakout: 1% Improve: 1% Collapse: 0% Attrition: 3% MLB: 3% *Comparables: Marcell Ozuna, Trayce Thompson, Andrew Lambo*

The Good: Garrett is a strong kid and that does translate into above-average raw power. You can dream on his wiry frame filling out in his twenties and 20 HR power to come.

The Bad: A "knife prank" gone awry cost Garrett two months of the 2016 season, and he struggled mightily late in the year in his return to Greensboro. He is already playing mostly left field. It's a length-and-strength power profile so there are holes to exploit. He lacks any standout tools other than his raw power.

The Irrelevant: He was born about 40 years too late, but "Stone Garrett" would have been a hell of a ring name in World Class Championship Wrestling. Could easily picture him in the semi-main at the Sportatorium against Geno Hernandez.

The Risks: Like Kolek, Garrett is tricky to evaluate after what essentially amounts to a lost season. All that really means is the high-risk profile from last year (low-minors bat, potential future-corner profile, hit-tool questions) all still apply, and Garrett is just a year older now.

Major league ETA: 2019

Ben Carsley's Fantasy Take: If your dynasty team is thin enough that you need to pick up Stone Garrett maybe you deserve a Josh Naylor "knife prank" too.

7. Thomas Jones, OF

DOB: 8/15/1997

Height/Weight: 6'4" 195 lbs.

Bats/Throws: R/R

Drafted/Acquired: Drafted 84th overall in the 2016 MLB Draft, Laurens HS (Laurens, SC); Signed for $1 million

Previous Ranking(s): N/A

2016 Stats: .234/.380/.313, 0 HR, 6 SB in 19 games at Gulf Coast League

The Role: OFP 50— Low-BA/medium-pop center fielder
Likely 30— One of those mid-2000s Phillies prep picks

YEAR	TEAM	LVL	AGE	PA	R	2B	3B	HR	RBI	BB	K	SB	CS	AVG/OBP/SLG	TAv	VORP	BABIP	BRR	FRAA	WARP
2017	*MIA*	*MLB*	*19*	*250*	*21*	*9*	*1*	*4*	*22*	*17*	*88*	*3*	*1*	*.184/.244/.285*	*.190*	*-8.4*	*.269*	*-0.1*		*-0.9*

Breakout: 0% Improve: 6% Collapse: 2% Attrition: 5% MLB: 12% *Comparables: Nomar Mazara, Engel Beltre, Raul Mondesi*

The Good: The second Vandy commit that the Marlins popped in the 2016 draft, Jones does not have close to Garrett's present polish between the lines, but hoo boy does he have some tools to dream on. How about a 70 run/60 pop CF? Well, we are a long, long way away from that, but it's in there. Jones was a two-sport athlete in high school, and recruited as a college safety. He looks the part, although even on the baseball field he will need to add some muscle to his lean frame to really tap into the power.

The Bad: It's a hell of a projection, but it's all projection. This type of profile has a far-greater range of roles than I can express below. There isn't enough arm here for right field if the center field defense doesn't improve with more reps. I have no idea if he will hit?

The Irrelevant: Thomas Jones is the only currently active "Thomas Jones" in baseball.

The Risks: I'm not separating out future tools this year. I pushed for this after taking over and Jones is a good example of why. I could easily have written "Future Tools: 7 Run, 6 Power, 5 Glove, 5 Arm," but that's misleading because what is the actual likelihood of his achieving that? Where is he likely to fall short if he doesn't reach his OFP? Can he actually hit at all? We only put major-league-average tools or better there, which always felt misleading to me. He could be a 20 hit, and then the power doesn't play to 6, and the rest doesn't really matter.

Tl;dr: He's really risky.

Major league ETA: 2021

Ben Carsley's Fantasy Take: The power/speed combo makes Jones someone to keep an eye on, but if he can't hit, it won't matter. Wait to see if Jones starts hitting or if reports begin to indicate he's figuring it out.

8. Austin Dean, OF

DOB: 10/14/93

Height/Weight: 6'1" 190 lbs

Bats/Throws: R/R

Drafted/Acquired: Drafted in the fourth round in the 2012 MLB Draft, Klein Collins HS (Spring, TX); signed for $367,200

Previous Ranking(s): #7 (Org)

2016 Stats: .238/.307/.375, 11 HR, 1 SB, at Double-A Jacksonville

The Role: OFP 45—Extra/short-side platoon outfielder
Likely 40—Up-and-down righty outfield bat

YEAR	TEAM	LVL	AGE	PA	R	2B	3B	HR	RBI	BB	K	SB	CS	AVG/OBP/SLG	TAv	VORP	BABIP	BRR	FRAA	WARP
2014	GRB	A	20	449	67	20	4	9	58	38	72	4	4	.308/.371/.444	.293	28.5	.354	3.8	LF(81): -12.1, CF(1): -0.3	1.8
2015	JUP	A+	21	578	67	32	2	5	52	39	76	18	10	.268/.318/.366	.285	27.7	.299	2.9	LF(67): -1.4, RF(66): -3.7	2.7
2016	JAX	AA	22	536	60	23	5	11	67	48	110	1	2	.238/.307/.375	.257	8.6	.283	-0.5	LF(115): 1.5, RF(1): -0.1	1.0
2017	*MIA*	*MLB*	*23*	*250*	*24*	*11*	*1*	*6*	*27*	*17*	*60*	*1*	*1*	*.234/.288/.372*	*.235*	*2.0*	*.287*	*-0.4*	*LF -1, RF -0*	*0.1*
2018	*MIA*	*MLB*	*24*	*346*	*37*	*16*	*1*	*8*	*35*	*23*	*82*	*2*	*1*	*.236/.289/.364*	*.245*	*3.0*	*.290*	*-0.6*	*LF -2, RF 0*	*0.1*

Breakout: 0% Improve: 2% Collapse: 1% Attrition: 1% MLB: 6% *Comparables: Tyler Goeddel, Whit Merrifield, Shin-Soo Choo*

The Good: Dean started to hit for more power in Double-A, reaching double-digit home runs for the first time in his pro career. And there is average raw power in there. There's average most things, as everyone of his tools falls within a half grade of 50 either way.

The Bad: But that's not all that exciting when there's an average left field glove in there. Dean's fringy arm and merely average foot speed limits him to that corner, and it's unlikely the power will play in games enough to make him an everyday player there.

The Irrelevant: You wouldn't imagine Austin Dean was all that uncommon a name, but you also wouldn't imagine one of the first google hits for him being a seven-year-old dirt track racer.

The Risks: Medium risk, low reward. Dean probably hits major league lefties well enough to have a bench role on a second-division team, but he already traded off some extra swing-and-miss for double-digit power.

Major league ETA: Early 2018

Ben Carsley's Fantasy Take: If you really need to roster a backup outfielder, at least pick one up who's in the Majors now.

9. Yefri Perez, IF/OF

DOB: 02/24/1991

Height/Weight: 5'11" 170 lbs

Bats/Throws: S/R

Drafted/Acquired: Signed in December 2008 out of the Dominican Republic

Previous Ranking(s): N/A

2016 Stats: .667 .667 1.000, 0 HR, 4 SB in 12 games at the major league level, .259/.334/.308, 1 HR, 39 SB in 84 games at Double-A Jacksonville.

The Role: OFP 40—Fourth outfielder/superutility/useful bench dude
Likely 30—Miami-to-New Orleans shuttle

YEAR	TEAM	LVL	AGE	PA	R	2B	3B	HR	RBI	BB	K	SB	CS	AVG/OBP/SLG	TAv	VORP	BABIP	BRR	FRAA	WARP
2014	GRB	A	23	462	65	17	0	1	29	26	54	30	9	.287/.335/.335	.258	12.2	.326	-0.8	CF(103): -9.9, 2B(12): -0.4	0.2
2015	JUP	A+	24	563	74	10	1	1	22	31	95	71	21	.240/.286/.269	.230	9.6	.290	10.3	CF(133): 13.1	2.5
2016	JAX	AA	25	377	49	7	3	1	28	39	66	39	11	.259/.334/.308	.264	17.7	.315	5.1	CF(62): 0.6, 2B(13): -0.2	1.9
2016	MIA	MLB	25	3	5	1	0	0	0	0	1	4	2	.667/.667/1.000	.612	1.5	1.000	0.3	SS(2): -0.0, 2B(1): -0.0	0.1
2017	*MIA*	*MLB*	*26*	*450*	*53*	*14*	*1*	*5*	*31*	*27*	*103*	*31*	*9*	*.226/.271/.303*	*.215*	*-1.2*	*.282*	*3.4*	*CF 1, 2B 0*	*0.0*
2018	*MIA*	*MLB*	*27*	*273*	*27*	*8*	*1*	*4*	*23*	*17*	*63*	*18*	*6*	*.225/.275/.310*	*.218*	*-1.5*	*.278*	*2.5*	*CF 1, 2B 0*	*-0.1*

The Good: Perez is a 70 runner with plenty of positional flexibility. He's played at every spot on the diamond other than first base and catcher in his minor-league career. He's primarily an outfielder nowadays and he won't kill you in center. He'll hit enough line drives and get on base enough to be serviceable in a once-a-week starting role, or if you need to patch an injury for a couple of weeks.

The Bad: The power sits at the bottom of the scale, and the hit tool isn't good enough for him to nail down an every day role at any of those six positions. This will be his age-26 season, and although he's got a September cup of coffee with Miami, he's only played 84 games above A-ball.

The Irrelevant: Perez is the first Yefri to make the majors. There have been five Geoffreys and five Jefferys, two Jefreys, and one Jefry. There is also a Yeffry de Aza in the Mets system.

The Risks: There might not be enough bat here to be much more than emergency depth, but the athletic tools and positional flexibility likely means plenty of cups of coffee in Perez's near future.

Major league ETA: Debuted in 2016

Ben Carsley's Fantasy Take: There's no point in making a top-300 dynasty prospects list, but were I to make one, Perez still wouldn't be on it.

10. Dillon Peters, LHP

DOB: 8/31/1992

Height/Weight: 5'9" 195 lbs.

Bats/Throws: L/L

Drafted/Acquired: Drafted in the 10th round (287th overall) in the 2014 MLB Draft from the University of Texas (Austin, TX); signed for $175,000

Previous Ranking(s): N/A

The Role: OFP 40—no. 5 starter/first lefty out of pen
Likely 30—Swingman/Longman/LOOGY

YEAR	TEAM	LVL	AGE	W	L	SV	G	GS	IP	H	HR	BB/9	K/9	K	GB%	BABIP	WHIP	ERA	FIP	DRA	VORP	WARP	cFIP	MPH
2015	MRL	Rk	22	1	1	0	4	4	5	10	0	2.0	8.8	13	42%	.303	0.98	0.68	2.25	3.39	3.7	0.4	92	
2015	BAT	A-	22	0	3	0	7	7	46	40	2	2.8	7.7	27	58%	.345	1.58	4.83	3.58	2.77	8.8	0.9	93	
2016	JUP	A+	23	11	6	0	20	20	72	102	2	1.4	7.6	89	60%	.316	1.11	2.46	2.52	2.10	39.8	4.1	83	
2016	JAX	AA	23	3	0	0	4	4	29	17	2	1.6	6.4	16	54%	.231	0.93	1.99	3.58	3.00	5.3	0.6	86	
2017	*MIA*	*MLB*	*24*	*6*	*6*	*0*	*19*	*19*	*95*	*103*	*10*	*2.9*	*6.0*	*64*	*49%*	*.322*	*1.41*	*4.34*	*4.25*	*5.12*	*4.2*	*0.4*	*122*	
2018	*MIA*	*MLB*	*25*	*8*	*10*	*0*	*28*	*28*	*174π*	*164*	*21*	*3.9*	*8.0*	*156*	*49%*	*.311*	*1.38*	*4.15*	*4.65*	*4.89*	*9.8*	*1.0*	*116*	

Breakout: 7% Improve: 11% Collapse: 4% Attrition: 12% MLB: 17% *Comparables: Yohan Flande, Joel Carreno, Chad Green*

2016 Stats: 2.46 ERA, 2.10 DRA, 106 IP, 16 BB, 89 K in 20 games at High-A Jupiter, 1.99 ERA, 3.00 DRA, 22.6 IP 17 H 4 BB 16 K in 4 games at Double-A Jacksonville

The Good: If Luis Castillo was the Marlins breakout pitcher of the year, then Peters wasn't that far behind as he likewise conquered High-A and turned in an impressive debut in Double-A. While lacking in ideal size, his average fastball plays up because of his advanced command of the offering. His curve is a future average-or-better offering, showing tight action with impressive depth given his stature. His changeup is an effective offering as well, mirroring his fastball movement and can locate it against right-handers.

The Bad: Like Castillo, Peters was also old for the level, as he was 23/24 for most of the season. While the curve is effective for strikes, he has had trouble using it as a finishing offering, leaving questions as to whether it is a true swing/miss offering. He lacks ideal size for a rotation spot and already has one Tommy John surgery under him.

The Irrelevant: Peters is the first Texas Longhorn we have ranked on our Top Prospect Series

The Risks: Lacks ideal size for a rotation spot, injury history, relative pop-up arm, hasn't proven it against stiffer competition. He's also a pitcher.

Major league ETA: 2017— Steve Givarz

Ben Carsley's Fantasy Take: There's no point in making a top-500 dynasty prospects list, but were I to make one, Peters still wouldn't be on it.

OTHERS OF NOTE:

I draw the line at coming up with epithets here although I can think of a few

Jeff Brigham, RHP

Acquired in 2015 from the Dodgers for Mat Latos, Brigham has a 70 fastball with a potential above-average slider. Unfortunately his control is below average for a starter and his changeup is a distant third offering. He will be 25 by spring training and like Peters is best suited as a bullpen arm. *—Steve Givarz*

Jarlin Garcia, LHP

Garcia was third in a bad system last year, he's out of the top 10 in a worse system this year. What happened? Well, there was a triceps injury that cost him most of the season, and he wasn't particularly impressive in Double-A when he was healthy. Mostly though, we are just less convinced he is a starter, and the relief profile as a low-90s lefty that can touch higher with a serviceable, but not plus curveball, is more middle relief than late inning.

Andy Beltre, RHP

Another middle reliever? Probably. Beltre has a big arm though, touching 97 for me (other reports even higher) with some run down in the zone. There's a short-but-tight slider here at times, but the fastball is the main weapon. Beltre missed all of 2015 with Tommy John surgery, but after dominating two A-ball levels in 2016, he could be a factor in the Marlins pen as soon as the end of next season. The command profile is problematic, but I could see something like a poor man's Kyle Barraclough eventually. That qualifies as noteworthy here.

TOP 10 TALENTS 25 AND UNDER (BORN 4/1/91 OR LATER)

1. Christian Yelich	6. Brian Anderson
2. Braxton Garrett	7. Stone Garrett
3. Justin Nicolino	8. Tomas Telis
4. Tyler Kolek	9. Thomas Jones
5. Isael Soto	10. Austin Dean

There's a name missing at the top of this list. The sad reality of Jose Fernandez's passing reaches far beyond the implications his death has on the Marlins decision making concerning their roster. Baseball lost a star at a young, young age in tragic and awful fashion. That part can never be understated. But at some point we do have to consider just how much the Marlins will miss him on the baseball field as well. Fernandez was going to be the anchor upon which the Marlins could pin their future. He alone would have improved their future outlook; just look at this list for a visual on how much he changes. Baseball will not forget Fernandez, and the Marlins will miss him in ways we cannot even begin to understand both from a personal level and in a tangible baseball sense.

Christian Yelich married his prodigious contact skills with some power and continued to show excellent plate discipline. He was originally projected to be a 20/20 threat but as Yelich's homers surged, his stolen bases took a step back. Look for more of the same in 2016 in terms of production with the bat. His preternatural bat-to-ball skills allow for a ton of quality contact and the power development is real.

Justin Nicolino illustrates where the Marlins are as an organization pretty well. He's left handed, throws in the high-80s/low-90s and his change is his best secondary pitch. He has command but he doesn't miss bats, which will be an issue as he tries to turn over lineups consistently at the major-league level. There's some value here as a potential swing man but his arsenal is limited and his secondary skills aren't as well developed as a low-velocity starter's have to be to survive in the long term.

Tomas Telis is a backup catcher, but he's here now.

—Mauricio Rubio

MILWAUKEE BREWERS

The State of the System: *This system has everything you want. Top-end impact talent, depth, a mix of pitchers and hitters, youth with upside, guys close to the majors. And Hader even gives you a dude with great hair. Like we said, everything.*

THE TOP TEN

1. CF Lewis Brinson	6. OF Brett Phillips
2. LHP Josh Hader	7. OF Trent Clark
3. OF Corey Ray	8. 3B Lucas Erceg
4. SS Isan Diaz	9. SS Mauricio Dubon
5. RHP Luis Ortiz	10. RHP Cody Ponce

The Big Question: And (again) you may ask yourself, "Well, how did I get here?"

We've already covered how to have one of the worst farm systems in the majors, but we should give equal time to the best systems, of which the Brewers certainly are one. Now, you might think that simply a Costanza-esque plan of just doing the opposite of everything Jeffrey Loria and company do in Miami would be the solution here, and yes, that would work just fine. However, that takes a bit of time, good scouting, better development and of course a dash of luck. And given the steep slope of expected returns in the MLB draft, it might also mean being pretty bad on the major league field for a while.

On this year's Top 101 prospects—available in the 2017 Baseball Prospectus Annual, natch—a full 30 of them currently play for one of four organizations: the Yankees, Braves, White Sox or Brewers. The Braves and the Brewers might not be trying to actively win baseball games at the moment, but they haven't had the bounty of high first-round picks that would boost your system into the top five on their own. The White Sox have been vaguely competitive recently, and the Yankees are the Yankees.

If you are reading these lists, you no doubt have a pretty good idea how all four of those teams got to dominate our Top 101. They did it through high-profile deadline and offseason trades. The Brewers are a particularly noteworthy example of this. Six of their top ten prospects were acquired through trade. They gave up real major-league talent to remake their organization into one of the strongest and deepest in baseball. Jonathan Lucroy was a recent MVP candidate on a very team-friendly contract. Carlos Gomez—when healthy—was a five-tool center fielder on a team-friendly contract. Jean Segura—while not that level of star when dealt—was an everyday up-the-middle player, again, on a team-friendly contract. These weren't the "fleecing the Diamondbacks for Dansby Swanson" variety of trades either. The Gomez trade comes closest to that in hindsight, but it seemed a perfectly reasonable deal for both sides at the time. And the Rangers and Diamondbacks won't regret the production they got out of Lucroy and Segura.

The strange thing about this trend is that while teams have been more willing to part with prospect talent in trades in recent years, there is always the lingering doubt about why an organization is willing to part with one prospect but not another. Why Josh Hader and not David Paulino? Why Lewis Brinson and not Nomar Mazara? Why Isan Diaz and not...well okay there aren't any other Diamondbacks prospects.

This is an offshoot of why "we don't see prospect-for-prospect deals." You have to go back to Matt Garza for Delmon Young, which also is Exhibit A for why you don't see prospect-for-prospect deals. When you are trading for a major-league player, there is much less information asymmetry. Houston will always have a better feel for Brett Phillips than you will, no matter how many crosscheckers and scouting directors saw him in Corpus Christi. Their dossier is longer and deeper. Their staff has lived with him day in and day out.

This is also why you rarely see teams deal for the single best prospect they can get. Maybe Texas would have parted with just Nomar Mazara for Jonathan Lucroy. But if Mazara is just a league-average hitter, then what? The Brewers were on the other side of this, dealing a basket of prospects

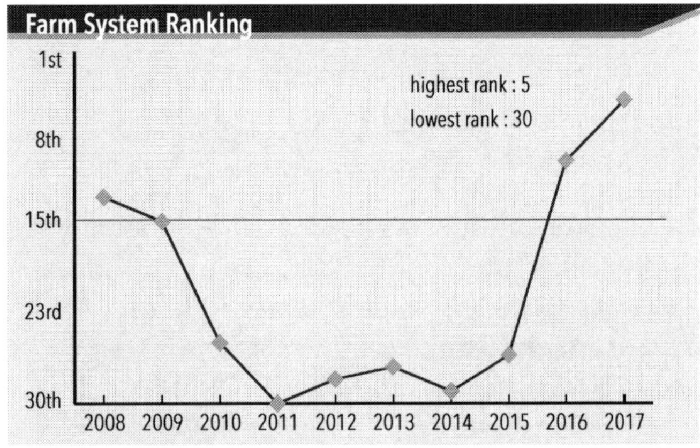

Personnel

General Manager:
David Stearns

VP, Assistant General Manager:
Matt Arnold

Senior Advisor:
Doug Melvin

Manager:
Craig Counsell

BP Alumni:
James Fisher
Adam Hayes
Matt Kleine
Dan Turkenkopf

for Zack Greinke and having the lightly-regarded Lorenzo Cain end up the best of the bunch. This is more art than science, so you want to give yourself as many chances to hit as possible. If Lewis Brinson strikes out 200 times in the majors, maybe Luis Ortiz overshoots his projection and you get a no. 2 starter.

We think the Brewers have a pretty good system. And none of the players in their Top Ten were in the organization on Opening Day 2015. That is an incredibly quick turnaround, but it also may say something about the volatility of the system going forward.

1. Lewis Brinson, CF

DOB: 05/08/1994

Height/Weight: 6'3" 170 lbs.

Bats/Throws: R/R

Drafted/Acquired: Drafted 29th overall by Texas in the 2012 MLB Draft, Coral Springs HS (Coral Springs, FL); signed for $1.625 million. Acquired from Texas in the Jonathan Lucroy deal.

Previous Ranking(s): #15 (Top 101), #3 (Org - Tex)

2016 Stats: 382/.387/.618, 4 HR, 4 SB in 23 games at Triple-A Colorado Springs, .237/.280/.431, 11 HR, 11 SB in 77 games at Double-A Frisco

The Role: OFP 70—Multiple time All-Star center fielder
Likely 55—2016 Leonys Martin

YEAR	TEAM	LVL	AGE	PA	R	2B	3B	HR	RBI	BB	K	SB	CS	AVG/OBP/SLG	TAv	VORP	BABIP	BRR	FRAA	WARP
2014	HIC	A	20	186	36	8	1	10	28	18	46	7	4	.335/.405/.579	.329	22.4	.413	3.0	CF(43): 5.2	2.9
2014	MYR	A+	20	199	17	8	1	3	22	15	50	5	5	.246/.307/.350	.251	2.6	.323	-0.9	CF(33): 2.3 • LF(3): 0.1	0.5
2015	HDS	A+	21	298	51	22	7	13	42	31	64	13	6	.337/.416/.628	.363	39.9	.402	0.9	CF(51): -2.2 • LF(7): 1.0	4.3
2015	FRI	AA	21	121	14	8	1	6	23	6	28	2	1	.291/.328/.545	.301	7.9	.333	-0.3	CF(22): 3.4 • LF(3): 0.3	1.3
2015	ROU	AAA	21	37	9	1	0	1	4	7	6	3	0	.433/.541/.567	.428	7.6	.522	0.3	LF(7): 0.1 • CF(1): -0.2	0.8
2016	CSP	AAA	22	93	14	9	0	4	20	2	21	4	2	.382/.387/.618	.323	8.9	.455	-0.1	CF(23): 6.1	1.6
2016	RNG	Rk	22	15	3	1	0	0	1	2	2	2	0	.231/.333/.308	.275	1.5	.273	0.9	CF(3): -0.2	0.1
2016	FRI	AA	22	326	46	14	6	11	40	17	64	11	4	.237/.280/.431	.244	3.5	.264	-0.4	CF(65): -1.3 • RF(5): -1.3	0.1
2017	*MIL*	*MLB*	*23*	*156*	*20*	*7*	*1*	*6*	*19*	*9*	*42*	*4*	*2*	*.247/.295/.437*	*.255*	*5.0*	*.302*	*0.2*	*CF 3*	*0.7*
2018	*MIL*	*MLB*	*24*	*379*	*47*	*17*	*3*	*15*	*50*	*24*	*103*	*9*	*4*	*.246/.299/.439*	*.263*	*13.0*	*.302*	*0.8*	*CF 8*	*2.2*

Breakout: 4% Improve: 25% Collapse: 4% Attrition: 18% MLB: 48% *Comparables: Michael Choice, Franklin Gutierrez, Kirk Nieuwenhuis*

The Good: If legs are your thing, you're going to like Brinson. He's long, lean and covers large swaths of ground in center, where he's at least a plus defender and borders on plus-plus. Figuring out his bat is a trickier endeavor; he's gone through multiple changes to his swing, both in setup and mechanics in my viewing alone, and who knows what I haven't seen. The constant tinkering appears to have paid off, as he dropped his strikeout rate from 38 percent in Low-A (higher than Gallo that year) to a more manageable percentage in the low-20s. That contact allowed him to tap into his power in the thinner air of Colorado Springs, and he does have plus raw in the tank. Brinson is a potential five-tool guy if the hit tool plays to its fullest.

The Bad: Prior to his inflated BABIP in Colorado Springs, Brinson had struggled in a return engagement to Frisco (Double-A), and there's plenty of reasons why. He hasn't shown the patience in the upper minors that he did early on, and while he has showcased the ability to adjust, his swing can get long and there are exploitable holes. His pitch recognition is still a work in progress.

The Irrelevant: Brinson's .618 slugging in Colorado Springs was good for fourth on the team. 32-year-old swingman Tim Dillard posted a 1.000 slugging, going 2-5 with a bomb.

The Risks: There's a pretty large delta between Brinson's top- and bottom-end outcomes, with much of that output riding on the success of the hit tool. The glove does elevate the floor, but given the abundance of tools, even a second-division starter would feel like a disappointment.

Major league ETA: 2017 —Craig Goldstein

Ben Carsley's Fantasy Take: Do you feel lucky, punk? If it all clicks for Brinson, we're talking a fantasy monster capable of challenging for 20 homers and 30 steals with a tolerable average, putting him squarely in OF1/2 territory. But there's a real risk that Brinson's hit tool will limit the utility of his fantasy speed and power as well as drag down your team's average. Brinson is close to the majors, which helps, but he also strikes me as a player who'll need a few seasons to reach his fantasy prime. I do think that prime will be special, but I think we'll need to slog through quite a few OF4/5 years first.

2. Josh Hader, LHP

Height/Weight: 6'3" 185 lbs

Bats/Throws: L/L

Drafted/Acquired: Drafted in the 19th round of the 2012 MLB draft by Baltimore, Old Mill High School (Millersville, MD), signed for $40,000; Acquired by Milwaukee in the Carlos Gomez deal.

Previous Ranking(s): N/A

2016 Stats: 5.22 ERA, 2.86 DRA, 69 IP, 63 H, 36 BB, 88 K at Triple-A Colorado Springs, 0.95 ERA, 1.57 DRA, 57 IP, 38 H, 19 BB, 73 K at Double-A Biloxi

The Role: OFP 60—No. 3 starter
Likely 55—No. 4 starter/high-leverage relief

YEAR	TEAM	LVL	AGE	W	L	SV	G	GS	IP	H	HR	BB/9	K/9	K	GB%	BABIP	WHIP	ERA	FIP	DRA	VORP	WARP	cFIP	MPH
2014	LNC	A+	20	9	2	2	22	15	103^{1}	76	9	3.3	9.8	112	41%	.254	1.10	2.70	4.10	3.30	25.20	2.5	94	
2014	CCH	AA	20	1	1	0	5	4	20	16	2	7.2	10.8	24	35%	.286	1.60	6.30	4.87	5.62	-1.00	-0.1	110	
2015	CCH	AA	21	3	3	1	17	10	65^{1}	60	5	3.3	9.5	69	42%	.301	1.29	3.17	3.47	3.29	12.70	1.4	89	
2015	BLX	AA	21	1	4	0	7	7	38^{2}	27	3	2.6	11.6	50	47%	.282	0.98	2.79	2.81	1.79	13.90	1.5	63	
2016	BLX	AA	22	2	1	0	11	11	57	38	1	3.0	11.5	73	41%	.291	1.00	0.95	2.14	1.47	23.00	2.5	67	
2016	CSP	AAA	22	1	7	0	14	14	69	63	5	4.7	11.5	88	43%	.345	1.43	5.22	3.81	2.78	19.70	2.0	81	
2017	*MIL*	*MLB*	*23*	*1*	*1*	*0*	*25*	*0*	26^{1}	*23*	*2*	*4.0*	*9.2*	*27*	*38%*	*.288*	*1.27*	*3.63*	*3.59*	*3.95*	*2.9*	*0.3*	*88*	
2018	*MIL*	*MLB*	*24*	*2*	*1*	*0*	*39*	*0*	41^{1}	*28*	*4*	*5.2*	*11.8*	*54*	*38%*	*.295*	*1.26*	*3.62*	*3.74*	*4.03*	*5.0*	*0.5*	*86*	

Breakout: 13% Improve: 23% Collapse: 22% Attrition: 37% MLB: 64% *Comparables: Rafael Montero, Jess Todd, Gio Gonzalez*

The Good: Hader's low arm slot and crossfire delivery create a wildly uncomfortable hitting experience for left-handers, and the combination creates difficult pick-up issues for righties as well. He's added about 25 pounds of good weight over the last couple seasons to help fill out a frame that can be charitably described as "slender," and his well-above-average arm speed helps drive his fastball into sitting position in the mid-90s. He pairs it with an out-pitch slider that gained consistency this season. He'll manipulate shape and take it out of the zone as a true swing-and-miss offering that shows plus projection. Despite some fly-away and volume concerns, Hader's mane rates as a plus weapon, with ample #flow and advanced marketing potential.

The Bad: His changeup made some strides with its consistency this season, but still lags notably as a third pitch, and right-handers crushed him in the hitter-friendly PCL after a second-half promotion. The length in his crossfire delivery leaves him vulnerable to bouts of control issues, and the fine command is never likely to graduate beyond fringe territory. The stuff is awfully tough to hit when it's around the zone, but it remains an open question if he'll be able to repeat well enough to turn over a big-league lineup multiple times. The frame and motion will demand a durability red flag until he proves capable of managing a full-season workload, something he has yet to do with a career high of 126 innings to date.

The Irrelevant: Hader's 15.5 strikeouts-per-nine in 2012 was the highest rate total by any pitcher with at least 20 innings in the Gulf Coast League since back in 1998, when former Marlins org reliever Davis Campos punched out 41 in 23 1/3 innings—good for a 15.8-per-nine rate.

The Risks: Hader's topline numbers took a beating at Colorado Springs, though the stuff remained intact at season's end and he continued to pile up obscene strikeout totals in his first go against Triple-A hitters. The durability and third-pitch questions remain significant enough that he's a higher-risk prospect as a starter, and that makes him a pretty damn high-risk prospect overall, since he is, of course, a pitcher.

Major league ETA: 2017 —Wilson Karaman

Ben Carsley's Fantasy Take: Do you believe that chance is on your side? Hader has the high strikeout potential and short lead time we covet, but there's a chance he's going to be worse for WHIPs than the Sand Snakes. Unfortunately we need pitchers in fantasy so Hader's upside makes him a worthy dynasty target, but you might need to invest in Tums if you own him early in his career. They've taken very different paths to their current levels of prospectdom, but Hader and Sean Newcomb have a lot of similarities for our purposes, if you're just looking for a quick point of reference.

3. Corey Ray, OF

DOB: 9/22/1994

Height/Weight: 5'11" 185 lbs

Bats/Throws: L/L

Drafted/Acquired: Drafted 5th overall in the 2016 MLB Draft, University of Louisville (Louisville, KY), signed for $4,125,000

Previous Ranking(s): N/A

2016 Stats: .247/.307/.385, 5 HR, 9 SB in 57 games at High-A Brevard County

The Role: OFP 60—Above-average outfielder
Likely 50—Average outfielder

YEAR	TEAM	LVL	AGE	PA	R	2B	3B	HR	RBI	BB	K	SB	CS	AVG/OBP/SLG	TAv	VORP	BABIP	BRR	FRAA	WARP
2016	BRV	A+	21	254	24	13	2	5	17	20	54	9	5	.247/.307/.385	.268	3.9	.299	-1.9	CF(40): -4.0	0.0
2016	WIS	A	21	16	2	0	0	0	0	3	4	1	1	.083/.313/.083	.192	-0.3	.125	0.3	CF(3): -0.6	-0.1
2017	*MIL*	*MLB*	*22*	*250*	*31*	*10*	*1*	*8*	*25*	*17*	*69*	*6*	*3*	*.221/.279/.377*	*.223*	*-0.3*	*.277*	*-0.1*	*CF -0*	*-0.1*
2018	*MIL*	*MLB*	*23*	*216*	*25*	*9*	*1*	*7*	*25*	*15*	*60*	*5*	*3*	*.220/.281/.381*	*.238*	*1.4*	*.277*	*0.2*	*CF 0*	*0.1*

Breakout: 2% Improve: 9% Collapse: 0% Attrition: 9% MLB: 18% *Comparables: Daniel Fields, Kirk Nieuwenhuis, Ryan Kalish*

The Good: Ray offers a bit louder athletic tools and a little more upside than you'd normally see in a college corner outfielder. He's got the kind of physique that gets referred to as a "specimen." And with that jeans-selling body comes plus speed and average power potential, especially to his pull side. His swing has some length and noise, but he is athletic enough to make it work and strong enough to generate consistent hard contact. He shows an advanced approach at the plate with solid pitch recognition skills already. His speed is a weapon on the bases.

The Bad: The Brewers moved Ray to center field as a professional after he played mostly right for Louisville. He's fast enough to theoretically handle the position, but not every plus runner can play center (or stays a plus runner into their mid-20s). There will be contact concerns due to his long, leveraged swing. He might be more of a boom-or-bust type hitter who—depending on the boom-to-bust ratio—may or may not play in an outfield corner (likely left since the arm is only average).

The Irrelevant: Ray's favorite restaurant in college was Red Lobster. If he'd asked us, we could have recommended Ed Lee's 610 Magnolia in Old Louisville.

The Risks: Ray has been on team radars forever, so it is interesting that there are still a wide variety of opinions on him within the game. Some see him with star-level outfielder potential, while others don't see more than a good fourth outfielder here. A lot of this will come down to how well the swing works against better arms than those found in the ACC and whether he remains athletic enough to stick in center field. He also had offseason surgery to repair a torn meniscus in his left knee.

Major league ETA: 2018

Ben Carsley's Fantasy Take: Ray is either the best or second-best fantasy prospect from last year's draft, depending on how you think Nick Senzel fits on the Reds. Thanks to his plus speed and the potential for a plus hit tool and plus power, Ray has the raw tools fantasy owners dream about. Sure he comes with some risk, but what prospect doesn't? You should feel good snagging Ray as your league begins to draft and roster newer prospects, and while you'll need to wait a little while your reward should be a speed-heavy OF 2/3.

4. Isan Diaz, SS

DOB: 5/27/1996

Height/Weight: 5'10" 185 lbs

Bats/Throws: L/R

Drafted/Acquired: Drafted 70th overall by the Arizona Diamondbacks in the 2014 MLB Draft, Springfield High School (Springfield, MA), signed for $808,600; Acquired from Arizona in Jean Segura deal.

Previous Ranking(s): N/A

2016 Stats: 264/.358/.469, 20 HR, 11 SB in 135 games for Low-A Wisconsin

The Role: OFP 60—Above-average second baseman
Likely 50—Bat-first regular at the keystone

YEAR	TEAM	LVL	AGE	PA	R	2B	3B	HR	RBI	BB	K	SB	CS	AVG/OBP/SLG	TAv	VORP	BABIP	BRR	FRAA	WARP
2014	DIA	Rk	18	212	22	7	5	3	21	25	56	6	5	.187/.289/.330	.251	1.1	.248	-0.9		0.1
2015	MSO	Rk	19	312	58	25	6	13	51	34	65	12	7	.360/.436/.640	.365	49.1	.434	-1.3	SS(64): -1.5 • 2B(5): 0.2	4.7
2016	WIS	A	20	587	71	34	5	20	75	72	148	11	8	.264/.358/.469	.286	37.6	.332	2.5	SS(90): -0.3 • 2B(41): 1.1	4.2
2017	*MIL*	*MLB*	*21*	*250*	*28*	*10*	*1*	*10*	*32*	*23*	*79*	*1*	*1*	*.216/.293/.398*	*.235*	*3.9*	*.283*	*-0.4*	*SS -1 • 2B 0*	*0.4*
2018	*MIL*	*MLB*	*22*	*438*	*57*	*19*	*1*	*18*	*58*	*44*	*131*	*2*	*2*	*.229/.310/.424*	*.262*	*14.8*	*.294*	*-0.8*	*SS -1 • 2B 0*	*1.5*

Breakout: 5% Improve: 12% Collapse: 4% Attrition: 10% MLB: 25% *Comparables: Corey Seager, Addison Russell, Trevor Story*

The Good: Diaz hit 20 bombs in the chilly confines of the Midwest League while playing most of his games at shortstop. That's pretty, pretty good. The power is real too, despite not having a traditional power-hitting frame. Diaz shows plus raw to the pull side and has extra-base power the other way. Although there is some leverage in the swing path, he makes it work due to advanced barrel feel and pitch recognition. He's a smooth, dependable infield glove despite fringy athletic tools.

The Bad: While he is mostly a shortstop now, his lack of range and only-average arm will force a shift over to second base. He's a below-average runner. You can beat him up in the zone, although he has a knack for contact everywhere else. The power and hit tools may play closer to average against better arms.

The Irrelevant: Isan is traditionally a Hindi name that translates to "bestower of riches." Hard to argue thus far.

The Risks: Diaz has a lot of swing-and-miss to go with that 20-home-run power at present. The swing could get exploited further against advanced arms and cut into the offensive production. The power is for real though, and should carry him to a major-league job in some capacity although our role grades may understate the current risk in the profile.

Major league ETA: Late 2018

Ben Carsley's Fantasy Take: Oh weird, a Brewers fantasy prospect with a high upside and low floor. Diaz has some warts, sure, but you can't ignore a middle infielder with his power, even if he's more likely to spend time at second than at short. Diaz is a comfortable top-100 dynasty prospect, just understand that, as a rawer prospect, his MLB ETA and his fantasy impact ETA might be slightly different.

5. Luis Ortiz, RHP

DOB: 9/22/1995

Height/Weight: 6'3" 230 lbs

Bats/Throws: R/R

Drafted/Acquired: Drafted in the 30th overall by the Texas Rangers in the 2014 MLB draft, Sanger High School (Sanger, California), signed for $1,750,000; Acquired from Texas in the Jonathan Lucroy deal.

Previous Ranking(s): #68 (Top 101), #5 (Org - Tex)

2016 Stats: 1.93 ERA, 6.44 DRA, 23.1 IP, 26 H, 10 BB, 16 K at Double-A Biloxi; 4.08 ERA, 2.78 DRA, 39.2 IP, 47 H, 7 BB, 34 K at Double-A Frisco; 2.60 ERA, 2.80 DRA, 27.2 IP, 23 H, 6 BB, 28 K at High-A High Desert

The Role: OFP 60—No. 3 starter
Likely 50—No. 4 starter

YEAR	TEAM	LVL	AGE	W	L	SV	G	GS	IP	H	HR	BB/9	K/9	K	GB%	BABIP	WHIP	ERA	FIP	DRA	VORP	WARP	cFIP	MPH
2014	RNG	Rk	18	1	1	0	6	5	13^1	12	0	2.0	10.1	15	0%	.343	1.12	2.03	2.68	3.54			95	
2015	HIC	A	19	4	1	0	13	13	50	45	1	1.6	8.3	46	45%	.306	1.08	1.80	2.50	3.35	10.40	1.1	91	
2016	HDS	A+	20	3	2	0	7	6	27^2	23	4	2.0	9.1	28	51%	.264	1.05	2.60	4.22	2.67	8.60	0.9	84	
2016	FRI	AA	20	1	4	1	9	8	39^2	47	3	1.6	7.7	34	47%	.352	1.36	4.08	3.36	2.61	10.80	1.2	94	
2016	BLX	AA	20	2	2	0	6	6	23^1	26	2	3.9	6.2	16	33%	.316	1.54	1.93	4.35	6.51	-3.70	-0.4	123	
2017	*MIL*	*MLB*	*21*	*4*	*6*	*0*	*18*	*18*	71^1	*80*	*12*	*3.3*	*6.0*	*48*	*38%*	*.319*	*1.49*	*5.23*	*5.18*	*5.83*	*-2.1*	*-0.2*	*138*	
2018	*MIL*	*MLB*	*22*	*6*	*10*	*0*	*29*	*29*	*177*	*170*	*28*	*4.3*	*8.7*	*170*	*38%*	*.316*	*1.44*	*4.96*	*5.17*	*5.53*	*0.4*	*0.0*	*131*	

Breakout: 9% Improve: 10% Collapse: 2% Attrition: 11% MLB: 14% *Comparables: Patrick Corbin, Randall Delgado, Vicente Campos*

The Good: A major portion of the Jonathan Lucroy trade, Ortiz isn't the most exciting pitching prospect ever, but advanced command of four solid pitches makes him a valuable piece going forward. His best pitch is a plus fastball, which he throws anywhere from 92 to 97 MPH, and one he can deliberately manipulate to show batters vastly different looks. His slider is his second-best offering, a diving pitch that usually sits in the 83-86 MPH range. He also throws an improving changeup and curveball, both of which he commands well. Ortiz is a very strikeout-heavy pitcher which occasionally gets him into pitch-count trouble, but he reliably gets outs without the ball being put into play.

The Bad: Ortiz has had some arm issues over his short minor league career, and this injury history, paired with his unathletic build, could be a cause for concern going forward. The arm issues are honestly more worrying than his (let's all be blunt here instead of dancing around the words) weight, especially with, as mentioned above, his tendency to pitch to strikeouts instead of contact.

The Irrelevant: On the internet, there exists somewhere video of Ortiz doing a standing jump into the back of a pickup.

The Risks: His history of arm injuries could limit the amount of starts he's capable of throwing, or even push him to relief. Also, he's a pitcher.

Major league ETA: Late 2017 —Kate Morrison

Ben Carsley's Fantasy Take: If you're going to gamble on back-end starters, you could do worse than to invest in ones who are close to the majors and who profile as strikeout-heavy assets. Ortiz's ERA and WHIP might not be elite -- especially in Miller Park -- but if he's striking out a batter per inning, you'll tolerate it. Matt Moore just finished as a top-50 starter by striking out 180 batters, notching a 4.00 ERA and earning 12 wins. Ortiz can do that plenty of times.

6. Brett Phillips, OF

DOB: 5/30/1994

Height/Weight: 6'0" 185 lbs

Bats/Throws: L/R

Drafted/Acquired: Drafted in the sixth round by the Houston Astros in the 2012 MLB draft, Seminole High School (Seminole, FL), signed for $300,000; Acquired from Houston in Carlos Gomez deal.

Previous Ranking(s): #61 (Overall), #2 (Org)

2016 Stats: .229/.332/.397, 16 HR, 12 SB in 124 games at Double-A Biloxi

The Role: OFP 55—Above-average regular
Realistic 45—Second-division outfielder

YEAR	TEAM	LVL	AGE	PA	R	2B	3B	HR	RBI	BB	K	SB	CS	AVG/OBP/SLG	TAv	VORP	BABIP	BRR	FRAA	WARP
2014	QUD	A	20	443	68	21	12	13	58	36	76	18	10	.302/.362/.521	.320	41.2	.341	2.3	RF(60): 6.9 • CF(44): -3.9	4.7
2014	LNC	A+	20	128	19	8	2	4	10	14	20	5	4	.339/.421/.560	.320	11.4	.384	0.3	CF(20): -2.9 • CF(4): -2.9	0.6
2015	LNC	A+	21	322	68	19	7	15	53	22	64	8	6	.320/.379/.588	.328	33.6	.368	3.0	CF(53): 0.6 • RF(9): 0.2	3.8
2015	CCH	AA	21	145	22	8	4	1	18	8	26	7	2	.321/.372/.463	.294	11.6	.393	2.6	CF(28): 5.8 • RF(3): 0.6	2.0
2015	BLX	AA	21	98	14	7	3	0	6	14	30	2	1	.250/.361/.413	.286	6.3	.385	0.8	CF(22): 3.6	1.1
2016	BLX	AA	22	517	60	14	6	16	62	67	154	12	7	.229/.332/.397	.278	24.9	.311	1.5	CF(102): -1.0 • RF(19): -0.2	2.4
2017	*MIL*	*MLB*	*23*	*250*	*32*	*10*	*3*	*8*	*28*	*20*	*72*	*4*	*2*	*.235/.302/.418*	*.242*	*4.3*	*.299*	*0.2*	*CF 0 • RF 1*	*0.7*
2018	*MIL*	*MLB*	*24*	*378*	*45*	*14*	*4*	*12*	*46*	*31*	*108*	*6*	*3*	*.234/.301/.411*	*.252*	*7.2*	*.298*	*0.5*	*CF 1 • RF 2*	*1.1*

Breakout: 1% Improve: 17% Collapse: 3% Attrition: 12% MLB: 34% *Comparables: Kirk Nieuwenhuis, Michael Choice, Franklin Gutierrez*

The Good: Phillips is a dynamic athlete with football pedigree and physicality. He's a plus runner underway, and his max-effort style helps him finish routes well and turn the ball around quickly in the outfield. He charges and ranges well in center, and his marquee tool—a plus-plus firehose of an arm—features velocity and carry aplenty from anywhere on the grass. He's a strong kid with average raw power and the chance to get to it in games, and he'll flash an ability to let the ball travel and drive it to the opposite field. A patient approach helps his on-base profile play above the raw hit tool projection.

The Bad: The on-base profile is important, because Phillips' hit tool may be hard-pressed to scrape fringe-average. His contact rate fell off a cliff at Double-A for a second consecutive season as more advanced pitchers exploited his aggressiveness and mechanical inconsistencies in the box. He gets frequently out of sync, with his lower half losing fluidity and compromising his balance. He'll pull off an outside pitch in one at-bat, then cut himself off inside in the next, and there's ample in-zone swing-and-miss to boot. He lacks a ton of feel for timing pitchers, so the speed utility plays down on the bases on account of poor jumps. He can struggle at times to read trajectories in center as well, particularly on balls hit over his head.

The Irrelevant: A secondary definition of Phillips' nickname, "Maverick," refers to an "unbranded calf or yearling," with both meanings deriving from the same 19th century Texas rancher and engineer, Samuel A. Maverick. His grandson, Maury Maverick, coined the term "gobbledygook" in 1944.

The Risks: There remains a greater variance in potential outcomes here than you'd typically see in a prospect of his pedigree with 750 plate appearances at Double-A under his belt. The significant contact issues and some lingering concern about the glove being ever-so-light for center leave him vulnerable to a tweener tag.

Major league ETA: 2017 —Wilson Karaman

Ben Carsley's Fantasy Take: Phillips is a solid buy-low candidate for fantasy owners because we won't have to wait forever to learn who he truly is, and because his upside is still that of an OF 3/4. There's no sugarcoating how disastrous 2016 was for Phillips' value, though, and while he'll probably still be a top-100 dynasty league prospect, it'll be close. Fortunately, his floor is a bit higher in OBP leagues.

7. Trent Clark, OF

DOB: 11/1/1996

Height/Weight: 6'0" 205 LBS

Bats/Throws: L/L

Drafted/Acquired: Drafted 15th overall in the 2015 MLB draft, Richland High School (North Richland Hills, TX), signed for $2,700,000.

Previous Ranking(s): #99 (Overall), #4 (Org)

2016 Stats: .231/.346/.344, 2 HR, 5 SB in 59 games at Low-A Wisconsin

The Role: OFP 55—Good enough center fielder and two-hitter for a first division team.
Likely 45—Tweener/4th outfielder/second-division starter

YEAR	TEAM	LVL	AGE	PA	R	2B	3B	HR	RBI	BB	K	SB	CS	AVG/OBP/SLG	TAv	VORP	BABIP	BRR	FRAA	WARP
2015	BRR	Rk	18	200	34	7	6	1	16	30	36	20	5	.309/.422/.442	.315	19.2	.388	0.4	CF(40): -1.2 • LF(1): 1.7	2.0
2015	HEL	Rk	18	52	5	0	0	1	5	9	8	5	3	.310/.431/.381	.291	2.7	.364	-0.8	CF(12): -2.0	0.1
2016	WIS	A	19	262	27	15	2	2	24	37	68	5	10	.231/.346/.344	.250	0.8	.325	-4.0	CF(49): 0.8 • LF(10): -1.6	-0.1
2017	*MIL*	*MLB*	*20*	*250*	*29*	*9*	*1*	*5*	*20*	*27*	*77*	*3*	*4*	*.199/.289/.318*	*.213*	*-3.7*	*.276*	*-1.1*	*CF -2 • LF -1*	*-0.6*
2018	*MIL*	*MLB*	*21*	*316*	*36*	*12*	*1*	*7*	*30*	*37*	*93*	*4*	*6*	*.206/.303/.332*	*.235*	*-0.3*	*.278*	*-1.0*	*CF -2 • LF -1*	*-0.3*

Breakout: 1% Improve: 6% Collapse: 0% Attrition: 3% MLB: 8% *Comparables: Joe Benson, Cedric Hunter, Ramon Flores*

The Good: Clark can hit. It's the reason he was a first round pick last year, and it's the reason he remains this high on the Brewers list despite an injury-marred 2016. Clark's swing is unorthodox. Because of his grip and bat path, the swing often gets compared to a golfer's, and it is easy to see why. But the bat stays in the zone for a long time, and Clark is strong enough to drive pitches to all fields. Despite a short stride and load, Clark still generates above-average bat speed and shows advanced pitch recognition for his age. Although there isn't another tool to vigorously praise here, there isn't an obvious weakness in Clark's game either.

The Bad: The bat will have to carry the profile, as Clark lacks a standout tool otherwise. He is only an average runner and may end up in a corner outfield spot—he does have enough arm for right—although his instincts in center help the profile there. He's unlikely to end up with much more than average power, and even that is mostly projecting off his present bat speed and betting on his adding strength in his twenties. Could end up as more of a tweener.

The Irrelevant: Clark is already famous enough to merit recognition on North Richaland Hills Wikipedia sub-heading of "Notable People." He clocks in right under Survivor Season 30 winner, Mike Holloway.

The Risks: Despite being one of the most advanced prep hitters in the 2015 draft class, Clark carries a significant amount of profile risk as a potential corner outfielder without much in the way of power projection. He also lacks minor league performance at present, although we don't ding him too much for struggling at times in the Midwest League as a 19-year-old. He missed time with a hamstring issue this year. Although you wouldn't expect it to linger, it is worth keeping an eye on given the defensive questions.

Major league ETA: 2020

Ben Carsley's Fantasy Take: If you read Clark's writeup and thought "hmm, sounds like a better fantasy prospect than an IRL prospect," you are a smart cookie. Clark's 2016 wasn't inspiring, but his hit tool is and that's the type of profile you want to bet on. Another good buy-low candidate, Clark might be a better fantasy prospect than Phillips at this point, despite the lead time. He could have an Adam Eaton-esque future, albeit with a higher average and lower OBP. Worse comes to worse, he could be 2016 Cameron Maybin; an unexciting but acceptable OF5.

8. Lucas Erceg, 3B

DOB: 05/01/1995

Height/Weight: 6'3" 200 lbs

Bats/Throws: L/R

Drafted/Acquired: Drafted 46th overall in the 2016 MLB draft, Menlo College (Atherton, CA), signed for $1,150,000.

Previous Ranking(s): N/A

2016 Stats: .281/.328/.497, 7 HR, 1 SB in 42 games at Low-A Wisconsin, .400/.452/.552, 2 HR, 8 SB in 26 games at rookie ball in Helena

The Role: OFP 60—First-division third baseman in the mold of Matt Carpenter
Likely 40—Fringe regular/top bench bat

YEAR	TEAM	LVL	AGE	PA	R	2B	3B	HR	RBI	BB	K	SB	CS	AVG/OBP/SLG	TAv	VORP	BABIP	BRR	FRAA	WARP
2016	HEL	Rk	21	115	17	8	1	2	22	8	16	8	1	.400/.452/.552	.333	11.2	.460	1.5	3B(20): 0.3	1.2
2016	WIS	A	21	180	17	9	3	7	29	12	38	1	3	.281/.328/.497	.295	10.4	.325	-0.8	3B(37): -0.5	1.1
2017	*MIL*	*MLB*	*22*	*250*	*25*	*10*	*1*	*9*	*31*	*13*	*71*	*1*	*1*	*.224/.269/.389*	*.222*	*-2.5*	*.279*	*-0.4*	*3B -2*	*-0.5*
2018	*MIL*	*MLB*	*23*	*253*	*30*	*10*	*1*	*10*	*32*	*15*	*72*	*1*	*1*	*.226/.275/.403*	*.241*	*0.3*	*.280*	*-0.5*	*3B -2*	*-0.2*

Breakout: 6% Improve: 14% Collapse: 7% Attrition: 23% MLB: 27% *Comparables: Mat Gamel, Renato Nunez, Brandon Laird*

The Good: Erceg has the natural tools and ability to make this ranking look conservative in a year's time. He boasts a plus-plus arm that unleashed 97-mph fastballs off the mound (and a good curve too), and that plays just fine on the left side of the infield, where he should have an average glove. He's potent at the plate as well, with the potential for a plus hit/plus power combination thanks to above-average bat speed and extreme balance at the plate.

The Bad: The power is mostly pull-side at present, though given his natural hitting ability, he should make use of all fields eventually. He's a below-average runner (possibly well below), and any loss of athleticism would be a negative for a left-side-of-the-infield projection.

The Irrelevant: Erceg may hail from rarely-heard-of Menlo College, but he wasn't the only draftee from the school in 2016, as former teammate Max Dutto was popped by the White Sox in the 10th round.

The Risks: We have written before about not taking vague makeup concerns seriously, but at the risk of being vague, there are serious makeup concerns here. How those concerns play out are going to have a significant impact on Erceg's profile, as someone with his raw tools and abilities doesn't last until the second round without accompanying baggage.

Major league ETA: 2020 —Craig Goldstein

Ben Carsley's Fantasy Take: Thanks to his bat and the position he plays, Erceg is of some importance to us and is probably one of the 15-20 best fantasy prospects from the last draft. That being said, he won't sniff the top-100 and wouldn't be a super safe bet to make the top-150. His risk and his ETA are too much to overcome for us right now.

9. Mauricio Dubon, SS

DOB: 07/19/1994

Height/Weight: 6'0" 160 lbs

Bats/Throws: R/R

Drafted/Acquired: Drafted by the Red Sox in the 25th round of the 2013 MLB draft, Capital Christian High School (Sacramento, CA), signed July 12, 2013; Acquired from Boston in the Tyler Thornburg deal.

Previous Ranking(s): N/A

2016 Stats: .339/.371/.538, 6 HR, 6 SB in 62 games at Double-A Portland, .306/.387/.379, 0 HR, 24 SB in 62 games at High-A Salem.

The Role: OFP 50—Second-division starter at the six
Likely 45—Fifth infielder who won't kill you for a month

YEAR	TEAM	LVL	AGE	PA	R	2B	3B	HR	RBI	BB	K	SB	CS	AVG/OBP/SLG	TAv	VORP	BABIP	BRR	FRAA	WARP
2014	LOW	A-	19	274	40	8	1	3	34	9	26	7	8	.320/.337/.395	.266	14.6	.341	1.6	SS(64): -1.4	1.4
2014	LOW	A-	19	274	40	8	1	3	34	9	26	7	8	.320/.337/.395	.266	14.6	.341	1.6	SS(64): -1.4	1.4
2015	GRN	A	20	262	43	12	3	4	29	18	34	18	4	.301/.354/.428	.294	23.3	.337	6.3	2B(38): 9.0 • SS(18): 1.0	3.5
2015	GRN	A	20	262	43	12	3	4	29	18	34	18	4	.301/.354/.428	.294	23.3	.337	6.3	2B(38): 9.0 • SS(18): 1.0	3.5
2015	SLM	A+	20	269	27	9	0	1	18	23	38	12	3	.274/.343/.325	.240	6.6	.320	2.1	SS(52): -2.1 • 2B(5): 0.1	0.5
2015	SLM	A+	20	269	27	9	0	1	18	23	38	12	3	.274/.343/.325	.240	6.6	.320	2.1	SS(52): -2.1 • 2B(5): 0.1	0.5
2016	SLM	A+	21	279	53	11	3	0	29	33	25	24	4	.306/.387/.379	.289	25.6	.338	5.5	SS(61): -11.3	1.5
2016	SLM	A+	21	279	53	11	3	0	29	33	25	24	4	.306/.387/.379	.289	25.6	.338	5.5	SS(61): -11.3	1.5
2016	PME	AA	21	270	48	20	6	6	40	11	36	6	3	.339/.371/.538	.301	25.7	.374	4.1	SS(62): -6.0	2.1
2016	PME	AA	21	270	48	20	6	6	40	11	36	6	3	.339/.371/.538	.301	25.7	.374	4.1	SS(62): -6.0	2.1
2017	*MIL*	*MLB*	*22*	*250*	*31*	*10*	*2*	*6*	*25*	*14*	*50*	*7*	*2*	*.256/.302/.398*	*.236*	*5.7*	*.295*	*0.5*	*SS -5*	
2018	*MIL*	*MLB*	*23*	*388*	*45*	*15*	*2*	*11*	*45*	*23*	*75*	*10*	*3*	*.261/.309/.409*	*.256*	*13.0*	*.298*	*1.1*	*SS -8 • CF 0*	

Breakout: 6% Improve: 33% Collapse: 9% Attrition: 22% MLB: 51% *Comparables: Tyler Pastornicky, Jorge Polanco, Jean Segura*

The Good: As a 26th-round pick in 2013, Dubon already represents a scouting and player development acquisition win for the Red Sox Brewers by even making this list, but he also could be a major-league contributor in short order. The offensive profile is slash-and-dash, but his quick wrists and bat control allow him to be an asset at the plate without much in the way of power (well at least until he started mashing in Portland). This was Dubon's first season as a full-time shortstop and he has the physical tools to handle the position. He is a plus runner with an above-average arm, and his experience at second and third gives him additional defensive flexibility.

The Bad: The power he flashed in Portland isn't likely to stick around unless he adds more strength to his frame or loft to his plane. Dubon could use some additional strength to generate harder contact generally, as he's not a very physical player at present. You can get him out on soft stuff even if he may not swing through it. There may not be enough bat here to carry a regular profile even at shortstop, because while he is fine there, it isn't a plus glove.

The Irrelevant: When Dubon steps foot on a major-league diamond he will be the second Honduran-born player to do so. The first, Gerald Young, spent parts of eight seasons with the Astros, Rockies, and Cardinals in the late 80s and early 90s.

The Risks: Dubon can handle both middle infield spots, and has enough arm to slide over to third as well. He's hit in Double-A. He may did not have an obvious route to a major-league role in Boston, but he should play in the majors somewhere (Milwaukee) for a while. And because I rarely get to note this, there is some positive risk here if even a bit of the power gains in Double-A are real, although you'll struggle to find people who think they are.

Major league ETA: Late 2017

Ben Carsley's Fantasy Take: The best reason to own Dubon in a dynasty league is if Matt Collins is also in your league and you want to deprive him of one of the three or four things in life that brings him joy. Barring that, Dubon is probably best left on waivers unless you roster in excess of 150 prospects. The hit tool is solid and he can run a bit, too, but when your ceiling is Chris Owings, you need to be assured of playing time to be of much interest.

10. Cody Ponce, RHP

DOB: 4/25/1994

Height/Weight: 6'6" 240 lbs

Bats/Throws: R/R

Drafted/Acquired: Drafted in the 2nd round (55th overall) in the 2015 MLB Draft, Cal Poly Pomona; signed for $1.108 million.

Previous Ranking(s): #9 (Org)

2016 Stats: 5.25 ERA, 2.88 DRA, 72 IP, 84 H, 17 BB, 69 K at High-A Brevard County.

The Role: OFP 50—Average starter or late-inning reliever
Likely 45—No. 4/5 starter or solid pen arm

YEAR	TEAM	LVL	AGE	W	L	SV	G	GS	IP	H	HR	BB/9	K/9	K	GB%	BABIP	WHIP	ERA	FIP	DRA	VORP	WARP	cFIP	MPH
2015	HEL	Rk	21	0	0	0	2	2	5	4	0	0.0	7.2	4	87%	.267	0.80	3.60	2.55	3.03	1.60	0.2	83	
2015	WIS	A	21	2	1	3	12	7	46	43	1	1.8	7.0	36	52%	.300	1.13	2.15	2.77	2.90	11.30	1.2	91	
2016	BRV	A+	22	2	8	0	17	17	72	84	6	2.1	8.6	69	47%	.345	1.40	5.25	3.21	2.93	20.40	2.1	86	
2017	*MIL*	*MLB*	*23*	*3*	*4*	*0*	*20*	*13*	*61^{1}*	*70*	*10*	*3.1*	*5.9*	*40*	*41%*	*.322*	*1.48*	*5.09*	*5.06*	*5.58*	*-0.7*	*-0.1*	*134*	
2018	*MIL*	*MLB*	*24*	*5*	*8*	*0*	*29*	*23*	*151^{2}*	*152*	*24*	*4.0*	*8.0*	*134*	*41%*	*.316*	*1.45*	*5.04*	*5.25*	*5.53*	*-0.1*	*0.0*	*133*	

Breakout: 1% Improve: 2% Collapse: 0% Attrition: 2% MLB: 3% *Comparables: Vidal Nuno, Adam Conley, Tyler Duffey*

The Good: Ponce is a big galoot with a big fastball he can dial into the upper-90s, but more comfortably sits in the solid-average-to-plus velo band. For a large human, he does a good job repeating his delivery and keeping everything on line towards the plate. His curveball has the potential to miss bats, and his change improved in 2016.

The Bad: After missing the first two months of the season with an arm issue, Ponce struggled down the stretch in Advanced-A. His stuff/command was inconsistent throughout the year. Ponce has yet to show that he can handle a starter's workload, and the changeup needs to take a grade jump to keep him in the rotation long term.

The Irrelevant: We can't confirm while at college in Pomona if Ponce ever saw the moon caught high in the branches of the sycamore.

The Risks: Ponce missed time in 2016 with "forearm tightness." That's not great, Bob. But that is the chance you take when you draft a pitcher.

Major league ETA: Late 2018

Ben Carsley's Fantasy Take: The lack of upside and two-year lead time make Ponce a snoozer, especially in this system. You don't need to worry about him unless your league flirts with rostersing 250 prospects. I'd be much more interested in Jacob Nottingham, Devin Williams or Monte Harrison for our purposes.

OTHERS OF NOTE:

We think one of these guys will break out in 2017, just not sure which

Devin Williams, RHP

The Brewers are sitting on two lottery tickets with their 2013 and 2014 second-round prep picks. Williams, the older of the two, has developed slowly, only reaching the Florida State League late this past season. He's your classic projectable righty by type, but he pairs the expected "fastball that touches 95" with an unusually advanced change for his age and experience level. He's heavier now than his listed 165, but still could add good weight and find another tick or two on the fastball. Williams has enough stuff at present to handle A-ball hitters, but the development of a better breaking ball—he throws two at present with the slider being the better and more confident offering—will be the difference between his breaking out and just being another back-end Top 10 candidate this time next year.

Monte Harrison, OF

While Williams 2016 performance for the Timber Rattlers was good, Harrison's was...uh, not. It was always going to be a volatile profile. Harrison was a three-sport athlete in high school, and while his physical tools are bountiful, he has struggled to make consistently good contact at the plate against professional arms. A broken ankle in 2015 and a broken hamate in 2016 have not helped him get the needed professional reps that might sand down some of the rough edges of the profile, either. Still, it's hard to bet against a premium athlete, and if he gets a full healthy season under his belt, he could develop into a legitimate five-tool centerfield prospect. That's maybe a bit too lofty a goal, but we'd settle for his making the top ten next year just so we can drop this into his Irrelevant.

The IFA bonus cautionary tale

Gilbert Lara, SS

Lara got over three million from the Brewers as one of the top prospects in the 2014 July 2nd class. In a system this loaded, it's not a huge deal that he has yet to break into their top ten, but there is some cause for concern here after two mostly anonymous stateside seasons. Slamming an 18-year-old in the Pioneer League is not really our bag, but reports from this summer were not promising either at the plate—where Lara has yet to find a swing that really works for him—or in the field, where he has already outgrown shortstop. This isn't unexpected based on his amateur profile. He was always likely to end up in a corner, but third base would have been more palatable than right field, where he looks more likely to end up at present. He is of course only going to be 19, and it wouldn't have been a big shout to put him up above with the potential breakouts. But as we close the book on a big-spending IFA era, it it is worth noting that more money did not necessarily provide a better hit rate.

There is no such thing as a catching prospect?

Jacob Nottingham, C

2016 was not a kind year to the Sheriff, who struggled mightily and somewhat predictably as one of the youngest regulars in the Southern League. The whiff rate skyrocketed, the aggressive allergy to free passes remained and his calling-card offensive production sagged. That's bad news for a bat-first catching prospect, and Nottingham is nothing if not that. His tight-end frame and hulking physicality leaves him less agile than ideal behind the dish, and he struggled to control the running game despite an above-average arm and technically-sound pop technique. He remains an intriguing name, however, on account of the raw offensive tools, which are highlighted by above-average bat speed and an impressive ability to punish pitches to the opposite field. He'll get another chance to make some requisite adjustments at Double-A next year, and he shouldn't get too far lost in the shuffle of this deep system. —Wilson Karaman

The future reliever who Craig made me take out of the Top Ten

Marcos Diplan, RHP

In defense of Craig—I can't believe I am writing this—this system is also too deep to rank a short, square righty with a fastball that only bumps 94. But I like Diplan, despite him not being my usual type. He gets good extension and better sink on the heater than you'd expect from a pitcher listed at six-foot-even. The slider flashes plus and was a bat-misser for him at both A-ball stops. The change lags behind and he's a six-foot righty so he is probably a future reliever, but we can be too quick to throw that tag on Latin arms, and Diplan has a fair bit of polish and command for a 19-year-old in A-ball.

TOP 10 TALENTS 25 AND UNDER (BORN 4/1/91 OR LATER)

1. Jonathan Villar	6. Domingo Santana
2. Lewis Brinson	7. Corey Ray
3. Orlando Arcia	8. Isan Diaz
4. Zach Davies	9. Corey Knebel
5. Josh Hader	10. Luis Ortiz

For a full-fledged rebuilding club, the Brewers possess ample over-25 talent that's just as interesting, if not more so, than the 25-and-under players listed above. Junior Guerra was a 31-year-old rookie who posted a 2.81 ERA in 2016 and could be one of the hottest arms on the summer market if he proves to be something other than a flash in the pan. Another rookie, Keon Broxton rode a gargantuan second half, highlighted by nine homers and 23 stolen bases, to be a 1.5-win player in just 75 games. Jimmy Nelson is a post-hype sleeper, Wily Peralta continues to make front offices dream with his 96-mph sinker and Eric Thames returns to the majors after socking 124 homers in just three seasons in Korea.

For three years, Jonathan Villar couldn't crack the everyday lineup. He played shortstop, second base, third base, left field and center field for Houston, but never eclipsed the 300-plate appearance threshold. He was excess fat that needed to be trimmed. Prior to the 2016 season, the Astros excised him from the roster, shipping him to Milwaukee for fringe-prospect Cy Sneed. The Brewers handed him the everyday shortstop role and the one-time utilityman suddenly became a star. His 4.8 WARP in 2016 more than doubled his total WARP in his first 658 plate appearances. Skeptics say his .372 BABIP will crash back to earth; however, his plus speed and his historically sky-high BABIP suggest that we're not talking about an inevitable declension narrative.

Lewis Brinson probably has a legitimate claim to be number one on this list. Villar's elite production at the big-league level, though, vaults him above one of the more exciting prospects in the upper minors. The 22-year-old has the tools to be a perennial All-Star. The Brewers have the luxury of patience, which should give him every opportunity to reach that ceiling.

After Villar and Brinson, it's a bit messy. Orlando Arcia lost much of his luster with a disappointing .249 TAv in what should've been a launching pad in Colorado Springs and a .217 TAv in Milwaukee. Still, the raw offensive skillset and the quality defensive package makes him insanely valuable, making him a comfortable number three. Davies gets the nod over Hader due to actual production. The IT-engineer-lookalike had a 3.58 DRA and even had a sub-3.00 ERA over 104.2 innings between May and the beginning of August. Thus, even though Hader is electric, present production should always get the go-ahead.

Domingo Santana mashed 11 homers in just 281 plate appearances and posted an above-average .287 TAv, but his defensive deficiencies detracted from that optimistic story. Corey Ray and Isan Diaz could be special bats if everything clicks. They lack proximity to the majors, though, and both have significant question marks surrounding their respective games. Corey Knebel is a Texan and has the requisite high-octane fastball. He showed an ability to retire both lefties and righties last season and should be the club's closer in April. Luis Ortiz, on the other hand, is a potential mainstay in the middle of the Brewers' rotation.

—J.P. Breen

MINNESOTA TWINS

The State of the System: *Graduations have taken their toll on the system over the last few years, and their highly-drafted arms haven't quite worked out as well—or at least as quickly—as they hoped.*

THE TOP TEN

1. SS Nick Gordon	6. SS Wander Javier
2. LHP Tyler Jay	7. RHP Kohl Stewart
3. RHP Fernando Romero	8. LHP Adalberto Mejia
4. OF Alex Kirilloff	9. C Ben Rortvedt
5. LHP Stephen Gonsalves	10. OF Zach Granite

The Big Question: And you may ask yourself...How do I work this?

At first glance, the 2016 Minnesota Twins certainly did not appear to be a team on the downturn. An 83-79 record the year prior only had them 3 games back of the second wild card position. Their Pythagorean W-L record didn't suggest they were awfully lucky either, as it predicted an 81-81 record. Sure, some players played over their heads (Eddie Rosario, Tyler Duffey, Tommy Milone) and crashed back down. But this was a team on the verge of contention. The talent on the team was homegrown, a farm system we ranked seventh going into the season, Byron Buxton, the number two prospect in baseball was going to play the full season in the bigs. Jose Berrios, Max Kepler, Jorge Polanco, and Byung-Ho Park were going to be contributors to the team that season.

But, unfortunately it all came crashing down with a major-league worst 59-103 record, which was the worst in Minnesota Twins history (based on W-L%). Matthew Trueblood opined on the factors that could go wrong heading into 2016.

"The twins penchant for pitching to contact is one of the most consistent organizational philosophies in baseball. For the last five years, the Twins have had the lowest team strikeout rate in the American League, every year."

As discussed there, the organization was beginning to make strides towards improving that through trades and in the draft. They acquired young, power arms in the draft (Nick Burdi, J.T. Chargois, Jake Reed, and Tyler Jay) and had some successful bullpen arms (Michael Tonkin and Trevor May) but it wasn't enough. Only four qualified Twins relievers had strikeout rates higher than the league average (8.7) in 2016. Exactly zero qualified Twins starters had a strikeout rate higher than the league average (7.8). So this team would have to put the ball in play and hope their defense helps them out in order to have success heading into 2016. But, every pitcher who started a game (not named Ervin Santana) averaged over a hit per inning, well above the 8.8 average in 2016.

In that piece, Matthew boldly predicted...

"When you look up the AL's team strikeout rates at the end of the season, there's a decent chance the Twins will have escaped the cellar."

Matthew was correct...they finished 28th. Matthew, again:

"We had better talk about another thing that has sunk the Twins' efforts to prevent runs over the past handful of seasons—their crummy defense."

The defense was not looking rosy heading into 2016. Yes, Buxton was going to man center field full-time and, in a short 2015 sample, was worth 6.5 FRAA. He and Eddie Rosario would be nice, but the Twins decided to have Miguel Sano play right field, who was worth -2.3 FRAA in 2016. Combine that with an infield defense that produced below average fielding marks across the board, and you get a team that finished third to last in BABIP, third to last in PADE, and last in H/9 (allowed). Add all that to the pitching staff's inability to miss bats and you get a team that allowed the second most runs in baseball (Arizona gave up one more).

You might have noticed that I quoted Talking Heads one-hit wonder "Once in a Lifetime" from the beginning, and to continue quoting them, "And you may ask yourself, where does that highway go?"

The new administration is in a tough position. The most tradeable asset, Brian Dozier, is still a Twin after negotiations

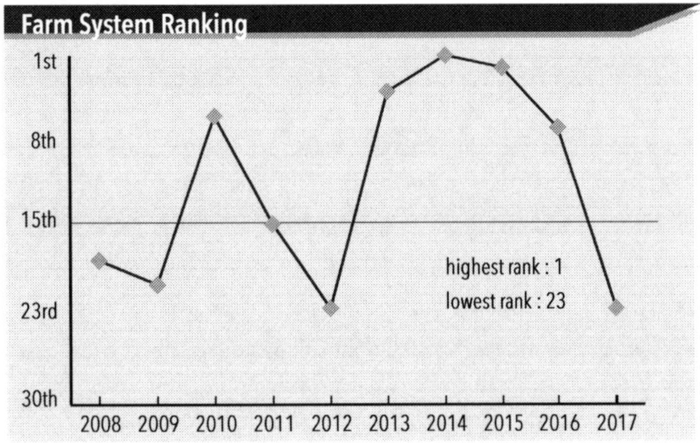

Personnel

EVP, Chief Baseball Officer:
Derek Falvey
SVP, General Manager:
Thad Levine
Assistant General Manager:
Rob Antony
VP, Player Personnel:
Mike Radcliff
Manager:
Paul Molitor

with the Dodgers stalled and they shopped elsewhere. Phil Hughes, Ervin Santana and Glen Perkins are all on the wrong side of 30 and contracts all guaranteed through 2018.

Signing Jason Castro, and his exceptional framing ability are major upgrades over prior catchers Kurt Suzuki, Josmil Pinto, and Juan Centeno. I still believe in Jose Berrios as a potential middle-of-the-rotation-to-better arm. I still believe in all the tools coming together for Byron Buxton. Miguel Sano will play third now, where he could be an average defender. The Twins will have the first pick in the draft, and the largest pool to go with it. Perhaps they can get a bigger return on Dozier mid-season when there are more (or at least more motivated) shoppers than what they could have gotten in the winter. The division outside of Cleveland isn't very competitive. We haven't seen the new regime as active as some others have been, but a new direction is what is needed in Minnesota. —Steve Givarz

—Steve Givarz

1. Nick Gordon, SS

DOB: 10/24/1995

Height/Weight: 6'2" 180 lbs.

Bats/Throws: L/R

Drafted/Acquired: Drafted fifth overall in the 2014 MLB Draft from Olympia HS (Orlando, FL); signed for $3,851,000

Previous Ranking(s): #4 (Org.), #62 (Overall)

2016 Stats: .291/.335/.386, 3 HR 19 SB in 116 games at High-A Fort Myers

The Role: OFP 60—Quality everyday shortstop
Likely 55—Above-average regular

YEAR	TEAM	LVL	AGE	PA	R	2B	3B	HR	RBI	BB	K	SB	CS	AVG/OBP/SLG	TAv	VORP	BABIP	BRR	FRAA	WARP
2014	ELZ	Rk	18	256	46	6	4	1	28	11	45	11	7	.294/.333/.366	.250	9.5	.352	2.4		1.9
2015	CDR	A	19	535	79	23	7	1	58	39	88	25	8	.277/.336/.360	.258	23.0	.333	2.9	SS(118): 8.1	3.3
2016	FTM	A+	20	494	56	23	6	3	52	23	87	19	13	.291/.335/.386	.277	25.2	.353	-2.9	SS(103): 4.3 • 2B(2): -0.1	3.0
2017	*MIN*	*MLB*	*21*	*250*	*28*	*12*	*2*	*5*	*22*	*11*	*61*	*5*	*3*	*.245/.285/.370*	*.224*	*1.8*	*.310*	*-0.1*	*SS 4 • 2B -0*	*0.6*
2018	*MIN*	*MLB*	*22*	*321*	*34*	*15*	*3*	*7*	*33*	*15*	*77*	*6*	*4*	*.250/.292/.384*	*.233*	*2.5*	*.312*	*0.2*	*SS 5 • 2B 0*	*0.8*

Breakout: 4% Improve: 8% Collapse: 0% Attrition: 6% MLB: 12% *Comparables: Yamaico Navarro, Nick Franklin, Orlando Arcia*

The Good: A quality athlete, Gordon has the natural instincts and reactions one likes to see at shortstop. Being a plus runner gives Gordon plus range in the field. Mix in steady hands, a plus arm, and quick transfers, and Gordon projects to be at least an above-average defender at short. At the plate he combines above-average bat speed with a short stroke, quick hands, and and an ability to use the whole field.

The Bad: There isn't much game power to speak of. While he has average raw power with some loft, his swing generates a lot of ground balls and low line drives, playing below-average at present. A plus runner, his base-running skills are quite raw and he gets poor jumps which led to a high amount of caught stealings (13). He has a tendency to chase and while he can make contact with most pitches, it is of the weaker variety.

The Irrelevant: You might have heard of his brother Dee and his father Tom.

The Risks: His speed doesn't help him on the basepaths, mitigating some stolen base value. His power plays further down against major-league arms, leading to some weak overall contact. He starts to expand the zone more and chase for weak contact rather than working overall counts.

Major league ETA: 2019 —Steve Givarz

Ben Carsley's Fantasy Take: You've had ham and cheese sandwiches on white bread that were more exciting than Gordon, but hey, ham and cheese sandwiches get the job done when you're hungry. Gordon is the type of prospect who'll probably never earn a top-10 spot at his position, but who'll probably be a top-20 or top-25 option for a decade. The big drawback here is that a ton of his fantasy value will be derived from his average. In years in which he hits .300, you'll want to own him. If he hits .270? Not so much, at least not unless he ups his baserunning acumen.

2. Tyler Jay, LHP

DOB: 04/19/1994

Height/Weight: 6'1" 180 lbs.

Bats/Throws: L/L

Drafted/Acquired: Drafted sixth overall in the 2015 MLB Draft, University of Illinois; signed for $3.889 million

Previous Ranking(s): #5 (Org.)

2016 Stats: 2.84 ERA, 2.82 DRA, 69.2 IP, 64 H, 21 BB, 68 K in 13 games at High-A Fort Myers, 5.79 ERA, 5.33 DRA, 14 IP, 13 H, 5 BB, 9 K in 5 games at Double-A Chattanooga

The Role: OFP 55—No. 3/4 starter or poor man's Andrew Miller
Likely 50—8th-inning arm

YEAR	TEAM	LVL	AGE	W	L	SV	G	GS	IP	H	HR	BB/9	K/9	K	GB%	BABIP	WHIP	ERA	FIP	DRA	VORP	WARP	cFIP	MPH
2015	FTM	A+	21	0	1	1	19	0	18¹	18	0	3.9	10.8	22	41%	.353	1.42	3.93	2.07	3.83	1.80	0.2	93	
2016	FTM	A+	22	5	5	0	13	13	69²	64	5	2.7	8.8	68	51%	.311	1.22	2.84	3.31	2.82	20.50	2.1	87	
2016	CHT	AA	22	0	0	0	5	2	14	13	2	3.2	5.8	9	50%	.262	1.29	5.79	4.96	5.33	-0.50	-0.1	106	

Breakout: 1% Improve: 1% Collapse: 0% Attrition: 2% MLB: 2% *Comparables: Tyler Duffey, Matthew Bowman, George Kontos*

The Good: Jay has two plus offerings in his fastball and the slider, and both will flash 70-grade at their best. The fastball features natural cut from Jay's three-quarters slot, and can get up into the mid 90s from the left side. The slider shows hard, late run in the upper 80s, although it can lack two-plane break at times. Jay already has advanced command of the offering.

The Bad: Amateur scouts weren't thrilled that Illinois made Jay the closer in 2015, limiting their looks at him. However, Dan Hartleb might have been onto something. Jay is slightly-framed—the uniform literally hangs off of him—and he didn't consistently have the same mid-90s velo as a starter that he showed in short bursts. The changeup is a barrier to starting as well. It shows short, arm-side run, but Jay has trouble getting it over the plate or down in the zone. Crossfire delivery and slingy arm action may limit any further command gains

The Irrelevant: The Chattanooga Lookouts were named for Lookout Mountain, from where you can allegedly see seven different states fromt the same spot.

The Risks: He's a skinny lefty with questions about his ability to start. There's command/change concerns. Oh, and he's a pitcher

Major league ETA: Late 2017 as a reliever, 2018 as a starter

Ben Carsley's Fantasy Take: Nothing ventured, nothing gained. Jay might be a reliever, but if he's a starter he should miss bats. Remember how you viewed (or how you should have viewed, at least) Sean Newcomb at this time last year? That's about how you should view Jay now, just with the ceiling dialed down about 20 percent.

3. Fernando Romero, RHP

DOB: 12/24/1994

Height/Weight: 6'0" 215 lbs.

Bats/Throws: R/R

Drafted/Acquired: Signed November 2011 from the Dominican Republic as an International Free Agent; signed for $260,000

Previous Ranking(s): N/A

2016 Stats: 1.93 ERA 2.76 DRA 28 IP, 18 H, 5 BB, 25K in 5 games at Low-A Cedar Rapids; 1.88 ERA 1.48 DRA, 62.1IP, 48 H, 10 BB, 65 K in 11 games at High-A Fort Myers

The Role: OFP 55—No. 3 starter
Likely 50—No. 4 starter/late-inning reliever

YEAR	TEAM	LVL	AGE	W	L	SV	G	GS	IP	H	HR	BB/9	K/9	K	GB%	BABIP	WHIP	ERA	FIP	DRA	VORP	WARP	cFIP	MPH
2014	CDR	A	19	0	0	0	3	3	12	13	1	3.8	6.8	9	44%	.343	1.50	3.00	4.32	5.29	0.20	0.0	108	
2016	CDR	A	21	4	1	0	5	5	28	18	0	1.6	8.0	25	53%	.250	0.82	1.93	2.33	2.76	7.00	0.8	88	
2016	FTM	A+	21	5	2	0	11	11	62¹	48	1	1.4	9.4	65	58%	.288	0.93	1.88	2.00	1.48	27.70	2.8	67	
2017	*MIN*	*MLB*	*22*	*3*	*3*	*0*	*16*	*9*	*54¹*	*64*	*8*	*3.2*	*6.4*	*38*	*48%*	*.322*	*1.54*	*4.75*	*4.85*	*5.09*	*2.0*	*0.2*	*119*	
2018	*MIN*	*MLB*	*23*	*5*	*5*	*0*	*18*	*15*	*97¹*	*95*	*13*	*3.9*	*8.9*	*96*	*48%*	*.307*	*1.41*	*4.31*	*4.28*	*4.62*	*7.4*	*0.8*	*106*	

Breakout: 15% Improve: 24% Collapse: 1% Attrition: 14% MLB: 27% *Comparables: Liam Hendriks, Andre Rienzo, Alec Asher*

The Good: With a large, broad-shouldered frame, Romero has the build to take the ball every fifth day. His double-plus fastball is explosive life in the zone with arm-side run, making it a difficult pitch to square up. He pairs this with a hard (87-90) power slider with late tilt, and can bury it against right-handers. His changeup isn't far behind, showing quality arm speed and late tumbling action.

The Bad: Romero has missed a lot of time with injuries, including Tommy John in 2014 which wiped out his 2014 and 2015 season. The slider flashes plus, but is inconsistent at present as he is still regaining feel for the offering. His change is mainly projection, flashing average but still sparsely used in games.

The Irrelevant: Fort Myers is named for Confederate Colonel Abraham Myers, who served as quartermaster general during the Civil War.

The Risks: Romero doesn't have many innings under his belt as he's missed time with injuries. He could be a really good bull-pen arm if the change doesn't develop. Body has potential to add bad weight. He's a pitcher with a Tommy John on his resume.

Major league ETA: 2019 —Steve Givarz

Ben Carsley's Fantasy Take: As impressive as his 2016 stats are, Romero scares the crap out of me. I'd wait until he has a big league job to gamble; he's not necessarily the type of player you need to buy now or you'll miss out on. I'm tired of just saying "add him to your watch list," but...

4. Alex Kirilloff, OF

DOB: 11/9/1997

Height/Weight: 6'2" 195 lbs.

Bats/Throws: L/L

Drafted/Acquired: Drafted 15th overall in 2016 MLB Draft, Plum HS (Pittsburgh, PA); signed for $2.8 million

Previous Ranking(s): N/A

2016 Stats: .306/.341/.454, 7 HR, 0 SB in 55 games at short-season Elizabethton

The Role: OFP 60—Above-average corner outfielder
Likely 45—Fourth outfielder/second-division starter with pop

YEAR	TEAM	LVL	AGE	PA	R	2B	3B	HR	RBI	BB	K	SB	CS	AVG/OBP/SLG	TAv	VORP	BABIP	BRR	FRAA	WARP
2016	ELZ	Rk	18	232	33	9	1	7	33	11	32	0	1	.306/.341/.454	.274	9.2	.328	0.8	RF(39): 4.4 • CF(12): -2.8	0.8
2017	*MIN*	*MLB*	*19*	*250*	*21*	*10*	*1*	*7*	*27*	*9*	*74*	*0*	*0*	*.210/.241/.340*	*.193*	*-10.2*	*.273*	*-0.4*	*RF 1 • CF -0*	*-1.1*
2018	*MIN*	*MLB*	*20*	*332*	*36*	*13*	*1*	*10*	*38*	*14*	*92*	*0*	*0*	*.230/.265/.378*	*.218*	*-7.9*	*.289*	*-0.6*	*RF 1 • CF 0*	*-0.8*

Breakout: 0% Improve: 5% Collapse: 2% Attrition: 4% MLB: 9% *Comparables: Nomar Mazara, Engel Beltre, Rougned Odor*

The Good: Kirilloff is a strong kid who already shows power to all fields in games. It's mostly doubles right now, but there is the potential for plus over-the-fence power as he physically matures. There's going to be swing-and-miss here, but he has decent barrel control and should get most of his raw power into games. It's not just a boom-or-bust offensive profile. He's an above-average runner at present, although he will likely slow down in his twenties.

The Bad: Kirilloff is playing all over the grass at present, but will likely settle into right field as he matures, putting additional pressure on the offensive tools. He has some northeast amateur rawness to his game generally, and the power in the swing at present comes from length. There's going to be questions about the ultimate hit tool ceiling until we see him at higher levels.

The Irrelevant: The color plum's hex triplet is #8E4585. The fruit plum was first called such by Pliny the Elder, who you may only know from the beer but was also a Roman naturalist. "Plum" was a nickname for British writer P.G. Wodehouse.

The Risks: He's a cold weather prep bat with a rookie-ball resume and questions about the hit tool. There's a lot of risk here.

Major league ETA: 2020

Ben Carsley's Fantasy Take: Kirilloff is the second-best fantasy prospect in this system and is already flirting with top-101 status. He's got the potential hit tool/power combo we want to see from an outfielder, and while the Northeast stuff means he might take awhile to get going, his ultimate upside is as an OF3.

5. Stephen Gonsalves, LHP

DOB: 7/8/1994

Height/Weight: 6'5" 213 lbs.

Bats/Throws: L/L

Drafted/Acquired: Drafted in the fourth round in the 2013 MLB Draft from Cathedral Catholic HS (San Diego, CA); signed for $700,000

Previous Ranking(s): #8 (Org.)

2016 Stats: 2.33 ERA, 2.26 DRA, 65.2 IP, 43 H, 20 BB, 66K in 11 games at High-A Fort Myers; 1.82 ERA, 3.56 DRA, 74.1 IP, 43 H, 37 BB, 89 K, in 13 games at Double-A Chattanooga

The Role: OFP 55—No. 3 starter
Likely 45—No. 4 starter

YEAR	TEAM	LVL	AGE	W	L	SV	G	GS	IP	H	HR	BB/9	K/9	K	GB%	BABIP	WHIP	ERA	FIP	DRA	VORP	WARP	cFIP	MPH
2014	ELZ	Rk	19	2	0	0	6	6	29	23	1	3.1	8.1	26	0%	.289	1.14	2.79	3.36	4.38			102	
2014	CDR	A	19	2	3	0	8	8	36^{2}	31	1	2.7	10.8	44	36%	.326	1.15	3.19	2.50	2.75	11.00	1.1	90	
2015	CDR	A	20	6	1	0	9	9	55	29	2	2.5	12.6	77	41%	.243	0.80	1.15	2.11	1.09	25.20	2.7	68	
2015	FTM	A+	20	7	2	0	15	15	79^{1}	66	2	4.3	6.2	55	39%	.270	1.31	2.61	3.58	7.82	-24.20	-2.6	124	
2016	FTM	A+	21	5	4	0	11	11	65^{2}	43	2	2.7	9.0	66	48%	.248	0.96	2.33	2.55	2.26	23.50	2.4	84	
2016	CHT	AA	21	8	1	0	13	13	74^{1}	43	1	4.5	10.8	89	38%	.255	1.08	1.82	2.76	3.56	12.70	1.4	92	
2017	*MIN*	*MLB*	*22*	*6*	*7*	*0*	*20*	*20*	104^{1}	*112*	*16*	*4.7*	*7.2*	*84*	*34%*	*.304*	*1.59*	*5.14*	*5.17*	*5.52*	*-0.6*	*-0.1*	*130*	
2018	*MIN*	*MLB*	*23*	*6*	*9*	*0*	*23*	*23*	132^{2}	*119*	*21*	*6.5*	*10.0*	*147*	*34%*	*.291*	*1.62*	*5.32*	*5.30*	*5.71*	*-3.2*	*-0.3*	*133*	

Breakout: 7% Improve: 22% Collapse: 7% Attrition: 19% MLB: 36% *Comparables: Mauricio Robles, Jake Odorizzi, Robbie Ray*

The Good: Built with a frame to eat innings, Gonsalves still has some wiry-ness and physical projection remaining in his body. He employs a low-effort delivery with a three-quarters slot, and a long arm stroke, so the ball jumps on hitters as they struggle to see it out of hand, helping it play up from his average velocity. His changeup is a plus offering with split-like action thrown with arm speed, and its velo difference (76-78) makes it a swing-and-miss offering. His curve shows average potential with fair depth and action.

The Bad: While his delivery is low-effort, it features moving pieces and the long arm stroke could cause some release point issues. His lack of a quality breaking ball could make it tough to reliably get out lefties at the highest level. While he has average-to-better control of his arsenal, his command is behind as he can get loose in the zone with his change.

The Irrelevant: Is it too late to mention that there hasn't been another Gonsalves to make the majors?

The Risks: His lack of a quality breaking ball could be an issue as he turns over lineups as a starter. While he has run somewhat high ground-ball percentages in his career, his BABIP this past year was .251 which could mean he's due for regression.

Major league ETA: 2018 —Steve Givarz

Ben Carsley's Fantasy Take: The MiLB strikeout numbers are pretty, but Gonsalves doesn't profile to miss as many bats in the majors. That places him among the massive glut of back-end fantasy starters who are about a season away, though I admit I like him more than many others in that group. He's probably a top-200 guy.

6. Wander Javier, SS

DOB: 12/29/1998

Height/Weight: 6'1" 165 lbs.

Bats/Throws: R/R

Drafted/Acquired: Signed July 2015 out of the Dominican Republic for $4 million

Previous Ranking(s): N/A

2016 Stats: .308/.400/.654, 2 HR, 0 SB in 9 games in the Dominican Summer League

The Role: OFP 60—First-division shortstop or infielder of some sort, I mean he was seventeen
Likely 45—Something a grade-and-a-half lower than that

The Good: Javier is a potential five-tool shortstop. He has the arm and athleticism to stay on the left side of the infield even if he grows off the 6, and the power potential here would play at either spot on the left side as well.

The Bad: The summer when I was seventeen I worked a crappy job at a now-defunct Northeast retail chain. After a closing shift I would decamp with my high school friends to the local 24-hour-diner where we would discuss our future wildly successful lives outside of our sleepy Connecticut suburb. I would always have a basket of mozzarella sticks, still a comfort food for me to this day, cholesterol be damned. My prospects—heh—laid in writing I was sure. A novelist combining the vaguely autobiographical psychoanalysis of Roth with the quirky postmodernism of Heller. I was writing a novella at the time that was unceremoniously rejected by publishers my Freshman year of college. This is all to say that certainly, without a doubt, Wander Javier is closer to helping a major league baseball team at seventeen than I was. But the distance from the majors becomes best expressed on a logarithmic scale the further away you get. And in that case, he isn't that much closer.

The Irrelevant: When Javier was born, Garth Brooks Double Live was atop the Billboard charts for the fourth straight week, having unseated Alanis Morissette's Supposed Former Infatuation Junkie earlier that month.

The Risks: The tools here are very exciting, but he's a teenager with nine professional games, soooooooooooooo (also he isn't a lock to stick at shortstop which would put more pressure on the bat which is already all projection at this point).

Major league ETA: 2022

Ben Carsley's Fantasy Take: Tools you can dream on with an ETA you should dread. Whether you should bother with Javier at this point in his career depends more on your league setup and where you are in your contention cycle than it does Javier himself, because it's clear he's a lottery ticket. If you have deep MiLB rosters, go for it. If not, I'd suggest gambling on someone closer to the majors. Keep an eye on him, though.

7. Kohl Stewart, RHP

DOB: 10/07/1994

Height/Weight: 6'3" 195 lbs.

Bats/Throws: R/R

Drafted/Acquired: Drafted fourth overall by Minnesota in the 2013 MLB Draft, St. Pius X HS (Houston, TX); signed for $4.544 million

Previous Ranking(s): #7 (Org.)

2016 Stats: 2.61 ERA, 3.52 DRA, 51.2 IP, 39 H, 19 BB, 44 K in 9 games at High-A Fort Myers, 3.03 ERA, 8.77 DRA, 92 IP, 91 H, 44 BB, 47 K in 16 games at Double-A Chattanooga

The Role: OFP 55—No. 3/4 starter
Likely 45—Back-end starter or solid pen arm

YEAR	TEAM	LVL	AGE	W	L	SV	G	GS	IP	H	HR	BB/9	K/9	K	GB%	BABIP	WHIP	ERA	FIP	DRA	VORP	WARP	cFIP	MPH
2014	CDR	A	19	3	5	0	19	19	87	75	4	2.5	6.4	62	57%	.270	1.14	2.59	3.73	4.33	10.80	1.1	101	
2015	FTM	A+	20	7	8	0	22	22	129^1	134	2	3.1	4.9	71	59%	.308	1.38	3.20	3.45	7.69	-37.50	-4.1	115	
2016	FTM	A+	21	3	2	0	9	9	51^2	39	2	3.3	7.7	44	52%	.255	1.12	2.61	3.27	3.52	11.20	1.2	96	
2016	CHT	AA	21	9	6	0	16	16	92	91	4	4.3	4.6	47	54%	.291	1.47	3.03	4.49	8.77	-37.50	-4.1	128	
2017	*MIN*	*MLB*	*22*	*5*	*9*	*0*	*21*	*21*	*109*	*142*	*17*	*4.7*	*3.6*	*44*	*49%*	*.314*	*1.83*	*6.02*	*6.04*	*6.34*	*-10.5*	*-1.1*	*151*	
2018	*MIN*	*MLB*	*23*	*3*	*6*	*0*	*13*	*13*	78^2	*92*	*14*	*6.2*	*6.5*	*57*	*49%*	*.313*	*1.85*	*6.26*	*6.21*	*6.59*	*-8.8*	*-0.9*	*156*	

Breakout: 7% Improve: 9% Collapse: 0% Attrition: 8% MLB: 10% *Comparables: Ryan Webb, Anthony Ortega, Shawn Morimando*

The Good: It just so happened that the Twins list shook out so Stewart ended up seventh again, but his season was more of the same in 2016. The stuff is still quite good. His four-seamer can get up to 95 and has some cut, his low-90s sinker has wicked late movement arm-side and down, there's feel for two breaking balls, a hard slider, and a 12-6 curve. There's also a developing changeup. The delivery is pretty easy and he has the body to start.

The Bad: It just so happened that the Twins list shook out so Stewart ended up seventh again, but his season was more of the same in 2016. He still doesn't miss at many bats as you'd think he would given the arsenal. The two-seamer has so much run at times he has trouble commanding it, or even getting it into the zone. The curve can get a little lazy and loose, the change still needs more development. The profile is in danger of becoming a Twins pitcher. I mean, he's already a Twins pitcher, but he's in danger of becoming a "Twins pitcher."

The Irrelevant: Stewart was also recruited as a football player at Texas A&M, where he may have taken over at QB for Johnny Manziel

The Risks: He's a pitcher without an out pitch at the moment. He's also a pitcher (with a shoulder issue in his recent past).

Major league ETA: 2018

Ben Carsley's Fantasy Take: Stewart still has some fantasy upside thanks to swing-and-miss stuff, but his walk issues and injury history detract some of his value. He could be a high-strikeout, high-WHIP SP5/6, but the odds of him reaching that modest but useful ceiling don't seem great. He'd probably fall somewhere in the 150-175 range among dynasty prospects.

8. Adalberto Mejia, LHP

DOB: 6/20/1993

Height/Weight: 6'3" 195 lbs.

Bats/Throws: L/L

Drafted/Acquired: Signed February 2011 out of the Dominican Republic for $350,000; acquired from San Francisco for Eduardo Nunez

Previous Ranking(s): N/A

2016 Stats: 7.71 ERA, 5.95 DRA, 2.1 IP, 5 H, 1 BB, 0 K in 1 game at major league level, 1.94 ERA, 2.37 DRA, 65 IP, 48 H, 16 BB, 58 K in 11 games at Double-A Richmond, 4.20 ERA, 2.33 DRA, 40.2 IP, 42 H, 11 BB, 43 K in 7 games at Triple-A Sacramento, 3.76 ERA, 2.51 DRA, 26.1 IP, 28 H, 3 BB, 25 K in 4 games at Triple-A Rochester

The Role: OFP 50—4th starter
OFP 45—5th starter/lefty reliever

YEAR	TEAM	LVL	AGE	W	L	SV	G	GS	IP	H	HR	BB/9	K/9	K	GB%	BABIP	WHIP	ERA	FIP	DRA	VORP	WARP	cFIP	MPH
2014	RIC	AA	21	7	9	0	22	21	108	119	9	2.6	6.8	82	36%	.326	1.39	4.67	3.78	5.13	0.90	0.1	102	
2015	RIC	AA	22	5	2	0	12	9	51^1	38	2	3.2	6.7	38	46%	.238	1.09	2.45	3.41	3.73	7.60	0.8	102	
2016	RIC	AA	23	3	2	0	11	11	65	48	4	2.2	8.0	58	48%	.251	0.98	1.94	3.16	2.37	19.70	2.1	76	
2016	SAC	AAA	23	4	1	0	7	7	40^2	42	5	2.4	9.5	43	42%	.327	1.30	4.20	4.02	2.33	13.60	1.4	84	
2016	MIN	MLB	23	0	0	0	1	0	2^1	5	0	3.9	0.0	0	42%	.417	2.57	7.71	4.39	5.97	-0.30	0.0	110	93.2
2016	ROC	AAA	23	2	2	0	4	4	26^1	28	3	1.0	8.5	25	33%	.329	1.18	3.76	3.21	2.51	8.30	0.9	83	
2017	*MIN*	*MLB*	*24*	*2*	*2*	*0*	*15*	*5*	*35*	*37*	*4*	*3.1*	*6.6*	*26*	*37%*	*.297*	*1.41*	*4.28*	*4.28*	*4.64*	*2.2*	*0.2*	*100*	
2018	*MIN*	*MLB*	*25*	*5*	*5*	*0*	*40*	*12*	99^2	*94*	*14*	*4.8*	*9.1*	*100*	*37%*	*.296*	*1.48*	*4.68*	*4.67*	*5.06*	*2.7*	*0.3*	*116*	

Breakout: 23% Improve: 30% Collapse: 16% Attrition: 37% MLB: 55% *Comparables: Jay Jackson, Carlos Rosa, Zach Lee*

The Good: He may have just become a Twin this summer, but Adalberto Mejia has been a Twins Pitcher in spirit for some time now. You know the drill: low-90s with the one, good fastball command, a couple usable offspeed pitches, decent durability and MILB performance. He's close to ready to being able to get MLB hitters out, if not already there. That's a pretty good get for Eduardo Nunez.

The Bad: The downside of the Twins Pitcher profile is lack of obvious upside. The fastball's fine, but there's no real out pitch in the profile, with neither the slider nor the change firmly establishing themselves as a consistently above-average offering. There are a few concerns off the mound as well; Mejia missed the early part of 2015 serving a suspension for a banned stimulant, and it's been quite a few years since he's seen anything remotely close to his listed weight.

The Irrelevant: Mejia is from Bonao in the Dominican Republic, which was originally established as a Spanish colonial fort by Christopher Columbus in 1495.

The Risks: Mejia looks pretty well developed, so there's less positive or negative risk than with most pitchers. Sometimes Twins Pitcher types can lose it at the MLB level and sometimes a secondary pitch develops late, but he probably is what he is. But, he is a pitcher.

Major league ETA: Debuted in 2016 —Jarrett Seidler

Ben Carsley's Fantasy Take: I forgot Adalberto Mejia was a thing. For dynasty purposes, it doesn't really matter that I now remember. Mejia is a fine fantasy spot starter, but that's about the extend of his utility.

Major League ETA: 2017

9. Ben Rortvedt, C

DOB: 9/25/1997

Height/Weight: 5'10" 190 lbs.

Bats/Throws: L/R

Drafted/Acquired: Drafted 56th overall in 2016 MLB Draft, Verona HS (Verona, WI); signed for $900,000

Previous Ranking(s): N/A

2016 Stats: .203/.277/.254, 0 HR, 0 SB in 20 games at GCL Twins, .250/.348/.250, 0 HR, 0 SB in 13 games at short-season Elizabethton

The Role: OFP 50—Average catcher whose pop carries the profile
Likely 40—A less playable version of Evan Gattis maybe? Stuff can happen with prep catchers.

YEAR	TEAM	LVL	AGE	PA	R	2B	3B	HR	RBI	BB	K	SB	CS	AVG/OBP/SLG	TAv	VORP	BABIP	BRR	FRAA	WARP
2016	TWI	Rk	18	66	3	3	0	0	3	5	8	0	0	.203/.277/.254	.235	-0.8	.235	-1.8	C(17): 0.4	0.0
2016	ELZ	Rk	18	47	2	0	0	0	7	5	2	0	0	.250/.348/.250	.268	2.8	.263	0.1	C(13): 0.1	0.3
2017	*MIN*	*MLB*	*19*	*250*	*22*	*10*	*1*	*5*	*23*	*13*	*74*	*1*	*0*	*.206/.251/.321*	*.193*	*-5.2*	*.272*	*-0.3*	*C 0*	*-0.5*
2018	*MIN*	*MLB*	*20*	*261*	*28*	*10*	*1*	*6*	*27*	*16*	*74*	*1*	*0*	*.227/.279/.356*	*.219*	*-1.9*	*.297*	*-0.4*	*C 0*	*-0.2*

Breakout: 0% Improve: 5% Collapse: 2% Attrition: 5% MLB: 10% *Comparables: Francisco Pena, Rougned Odor, Nomar Mazara*

The Good: Rortvedt's a catcher with a potential plus power tool. That'll get you on a top ten list. He has a strong arm. He is young enough there is still plenty of time for him to develop his skills behind the plate.

The Bad: And he'll need to because the "catch" part of "catch-and-throw" is rough at present. His receiving skills are raw, and he can be a bit stiff in general. The length in his swing portends a below-average hit tool.

The Irrelevant: Rortvedt is the highest draft pick the Twins have used on a catcher since Joe Mauer.

The Risks: He's a prep catcher. Catchers are weird, prep catchers often aren't catchers, and Rortvedt isn't exactly starting out with a surefire backstop projection.

Major league ETA: 2021

Ben Carsley's Fantasy Take: If I told you to get in on Tom Murphy four years ago and the only payoff was current-day Tom Murphy, you wouldn't be very happy with me. Wait until Rortvedt is closer.

10. Zach Granite, CF

DOB: 9/17/1992

Height/Weight: 6'1" 175 lbs.

Bats/Throws: L/L

Drafted/Acquired: Drafted 14th round of the 2013 MLB Draft, Seton Hall University (South Orange, NJ); signed for $75,000.

Previous Ranking(s): N/A

2016 Stats: .295/.347/.382, 4 HR, 56 SB in 127 games at Double-A Chattanooga

The Role: OFP 50—Billy Burns/Sam Fuld's good seasons
Likely 40—All their other seasons

YEAR	TEAM	LVL	AGE	PA	R	2B	3B	HR	RBI	BB	K	SB	CS	AVG/OBP/SLG	TAv	VORP	BABIP	BRR	FRAA	WARP
2014	CDR	A	21	85	9	2	2	0	2	4	8	1	4	.291/.321/.367	.255	0.7	.319	-1.2	CF(14): -2.4 • LF(7): -1.3	-0.3
2014	TWI	Rk	21	16	4	0	0	0	0	2	4	3	0	.214/.313/.214	.275	1.0	.300	0.2		0.1
2015	CDR	A	22	83	17	5	1	0	5	12	6	7	1	.358/.463/.463	.358	11.9	.393	1.8	LF(13): 2.1 • CF(4): 0.0	1.5
2015	FTM	A+	22	441	59	10	4	1	26	41	63	21	12	.249/.328/.304	.250	8.5	.294	1.7	CF(64): 5.4 • LF(39): 5.3	2.3
2016	CHT	AA	23	584	86	18	8	4	52	42	43	56	14	.295/.347/.382	.276	33.8	.312	8.2	CF(108): 5.3 • LF(18): 0.6	4.2
2017	*MIN*	*MLB*	*24*	*250*	*34*	*9*	*2*	*5*	*22*	*17*	*40*	*14*	*4*	*.262/.313/.393*	*.236*	*4.9*	*.290*	*1.4*	*CF 1 • LF 1*	*0.7*
2018	*MIN*	*MLB*	*25*	*397*	*45*	*14*	*4*	*9*	*43*	*28*	*63*	*23*	*7*	*.265/.319/.400*	*.244*	*7.8*	*.290*	*3.2*	*CF 2 • LF 1*	*1.1*

Breakout: 6% Improve: 22% Collapse: 5% Attrition: 29% MLB: 44% *Comparables: J.B. Shuck, Matt Szczur, Todd Cunningham*

The Good: A double-plus run paired with a plus glove is a good place to start with any profile, especially in the middle of diamond. Granite can make contact, but it's not as rock-solid (sorry) as you'd like it to be, though he does well to use the whole field in his approach. A top-end outcome could see him as a sparkplug type hitting atop the lineup. He can use his speed plenty well on the bases.

The Bad: There's not much power to be had here, and there's a good chance it limits the overall profile to a fourth outfielder role at best, despite the superlative defense. Even if there's a chance for power in his build, his swing isn't geared to take advantage of it, which imperils his hit tool.

The Irrelevant: Seton Hall's motto is Hazard Zet Forward, translated from Norman as "Despite Hazards, move forward."

The Risks: Given the lack of power, pitchers at the upper levels are going to attack the zone and dare Granite to punish them. Until he proves he can, there's a fair amount of volatility in the profile. If Billy Burns/Sam Fuld types get it done for you, this is the prospect for you.

Major league ETA: 2018 —Craig Goldstein

Ben Carsley's Fantasy Take: Speed and proximity make Granite worthy of some fantasy attention, but the likelihood that he's just a bench player means you can forget him unless you play in very deep AL-only formats. Sort of like if C.J. Cron was a speedy reserve outfielder.

OTHERS OF NOTE:

#11

Felix Jorge, RHP

Jorge is the kind of backend arm with solid-average velo and a full array of average-ish secondary pitches that usually settles in towards the back of these top ten lists. The fastball lacks wiggle, but gets some plane even out of Jorge's six-foot-two frame due to his higher slot and how tall he stays throughout his delivery. The curve will flash 55, the change is fairly advanced, but he may lack an out pitch—Double-A hitters had far less trouble squaring him than A-ball ones. The delivery doesn't use his legs much, which is ironic because his thin frame is about 70 percent legs, but the mechanics and arm action are relatively low effort. He's a back-end guy with some physical projection left. Jorge's an interesting prospect, but not quite a top ten one until he the stuff plays a little better in the upper minors.

Keeping it ?

Nick Burdi, RHP

We could just C+P his brother Zack's entry from the White Sox list and it would be close enough because we've done thirty of these now and our brain is the consistency of Ruhlman's soft scrambled eggs. We could also just C+P his entry from last year since he only threw three innings this year before being sidelined with a bone bruise near his elbow. This is one of the few elbow injuries that doesn't scare us all that much, but Burdi's continued command issues scare us a little more. A healthy Burdi could be up sometime in 2017 as a late-inning reliever with a 80 fastball/60 slider combo. That's not as recherché as it used to be, but still sounds pretty good to us. We don't know why we have lapsed in the first-person plural. It's been a long four months.

The factor on the farm

Daniel Palka, OF

Most organizations have a Daniel Palka. He's a lefty corner guy with platoon issues, good raw pop, and a below-average hit tool that might not make that pop play enough in major league games. It's thin margins for this role. You can make a lot of money in the majors, or you can be riding very long buses from Rochester to Durham for a few years. You'd think Palka would be in the right org to get some big league per diems, as the Twins don't look to be very good for a while, but Minnesota is trying to sort through a glut of corner bats as is. You'd think Palka's immense pull side power would find a major league home eventually. He's more left-handed than the Brad Eldreds and Mike Hessmen that litter the upper minors. But Matt Clark spent the last 18 months thumbing it from the Dominican to Mexico to Japan. And none of those dudes are even C.J. Cron. And I can finally promise you that is the last C.J. Cron mention on these lists.

Worthy of the hullabadoo (it's my last list, you guys)

Akil Badoo, OF

Badoo is your typical post-first-round, high-six-figure prep pick. He's got his flaws. There won't be much in the way of power coming, and he needs to get physically stronger so he can handle better velocity as he moves up the organizational ranks, but he's got the speed and instincts to play center and some feel for hitting. He might just be Zach Granite in five years, but there are far worse fates and far worse prospects.

Or he might be LaMonte Wade

LaMonte Wade, OF

Wade is turning into a bit of a steal for the Twins in the ninth round of last year's draft. His junior year at Maryland was marred by a broken hamate, but more than a year away from the injury he started to show more power than you'd expect this season. That might just be an advanced college bat stinging A-ball pitching, and I'd expect his eye-popping K/BB rates to moderate a bit in Double-A as well, but he's a good athlete who can hit a bit, run a bit, and can play center field once a week. There are far worse fates and far worse prospects, and maybe a bit more upside here than the others ranking would suggest.

TOP 10 TALENTS 25 AND UNDER (BORN 4/1/91 OR LATER)

1. Byron Buxton	6. Nick Gordon
2. Miguel Sano	7. Tyler Jay
3. Jose Berrios	8. Fernando Romero
4. Max Kepler	9. Alex Kirilloff
5. Jorge Polanco	10. Stephen Gonsalves

Much like the awkward in-between state that 20th century American poet Britney Jean Spears spoke of in "I'm Not a Girl, Not Yet a Woman" from her classic Britney collection, the Twins' best long-term building blocks are not prospects, but not yet established stars.

Minnesota's farm system is mediocre at best. However, more than any other team, the Twins show the flaws in evaluating an organization's young talent strictly by prospect-eligible players. Despite losing prospect eligibility Buxton, Berrios, and Polanco are still just 23, making them the same age or younger than one quarter of BP's top 101 prospects. Even Sano and Kepler, at 24, are no older than a dozen top 101 prospects. Minnesota has tumbled down prospect rankings, but the overall collection of young talent remains among the best in baseball and that's evident by the first five names on the 25-and-under list already graduating out of prospect-dom.

Buxton cracked BP's top 10 prospects four times, including ranking first in both 2014 and 2015 before placing second to Corey Seager in 2016. He was rushed to the majors at 21 in a move ex-general manager Terry Ryan has said he regrets, and Buxton's extreme struggles to make contact led to hideous early results followed by endless tinkering by coaches and several trips back to the minors. He never ceased crushing Double-A and Triple-A pitching, and in returning to Minnesota as a September call-up last year it finally clicked. Buxton hit .287/.357/.653 with nine homers, showing upper-deck thump to go with what has always been blazing speed.

Buxton is already a Gold Glove-caliber center fielder, totaling 11.2 Fielding Runs Above Average in 138 games, and his limitless range combined with 20-homer power is enough to make him a very good regular (PECOTA projects him as a top-10 center fielder, with 3.2 WARP). Smoothing out his approach and simply putting bat to ball more often is a key to unlocking greatness. I was a believer before his monster September and I'm certainly a believer now, but Buxton has lots to prove. And he's not alone, as Berrios looked lost in his debut and Sano followed up an excellent rookie year with a disappointing second season that cast some doubt on his being more than a Three True Outcomes designated hitter.

Kepler can be a very strong all-around player and Polanco has solid regular written all over him if the Twins find him a defensive home, but the Buxton/Sano/Berrios trio will tell the story of the rebuild. It's been a long six years in Minnesota and it's time for all of the expensive international signings and high draft picks the Twins have accumulated throughout the prolonged ineptitude to start paying dividends beyond lofty prospect rankings.

—Aaron Gleeman

NEW YORK METS

The State of the System: *The Mets graduated Steven Matz but replaced him with a southpaw with similar upside, Amed Rosario took a step forward into elite prospect-dom, Robert Gsellman had a breakout 2016, and everybody else got a little bit closer to the majors. Better talent past the 10 names on this list means the system is improved overall, but only middle-of-the-pack.*

THE TOP TEN

1. SS Amed Rosario	6. RHP Justin Dunn
2. RHP Robert Gsellman	7. SS Andres Gimenez
3. LHP Thomas Szapucki	8. OF Brandon Nimmo
4. 1B Dominic Smith	9. SS Gavin Cecchini
5. CF Desmond Lindsay	10. RF Wuilmer Becerra

The Big Question: Do we have to change the way we evaluate Mets pitching prospects?

Write what thou see is the whole of the law.

It's a hot, muggy evening in New Britain, Conn. It's only May, and this is unseasonably warm. The Lite-Brite temperature display above the outfield wall reads "98" at game time. The starter for the road team is interesting enough, a live arm with a chance to pitch in the majors. You missed him by a day in A-ball last year, skipping out on a getaway day game. He posted double-digit strikeouts of course.

He struggles in this outing. It happens. He's from Florida. He should be used to this weather, no? But some days you just don't have it. And he is laboring in the heat. The fastball tops out at 94, although you have heard he touches higher. In between the command hiccups, he can change eye levels with it, and the two-seamer has some nice movement. The slider flashes average, but he struggles with consistency, ditto for the change. He's better than your average Double-A starter, but nothing special. Even taking a glass-half-full view on both secondaries, it's hard to see a major-league starter here, although he could be a good fastball-slider righty in the pen if the stuff plays up a bit in short bursts. This all jibes with the general scouting consensus on the pitcher.

Congratulations, you just wrote up Jacob deGrom as a setup man.

So that was a bit of a miss. But if you came to me next March, resume in hand, looking for a gig on the Baseball Prospectus prospect team and were to remark: "you know, I had deGrom as a top of the rotation starter that year, here's my report," I wouldn't hire you. I'd wonder if you actually knew what you were looking at. All prospect writing requires a bit of magical thinking, but I will point you again to the line that opens this essay.

My colleague Jarrett Seidler made this point on our podcast recently, but you could hang your hat on projecting deGrom as a 3, while the rest of us had him as a back-end starter or late-inning reliever. But if you could bottle all the pitch and command jumps needed to get him from that guy on the mound in the Eastern League to the top ten pitcher in baseball he is now, you could turn a whole lot of "Double-A starters with a major-league arm" into "major-league aces."

The deGrom prospect profile is not an uncommon one. I won't go as far to suggest that every team has a Jacob deGrom, but you can usually find an upper-minors arm, hanging out on the periphery of a top-ten list in an average system: A guy with a major-league fastball, college guy with some polish usually, maybe a bit old for the league, secondary stuff that flashes, enough there to get Double-A hitters out, but not to wow you. A future 45 as a starter, maybe the fastball/breaking ball combo plays up in the pen, maybe he's even that third starter if a couple things jump.

But they don't usually all jump. Now somebody has to be the 99th percentile outcome in that cohort, and deGrom happened to be that 1-in-100 longshot. It happens.

And it sure seems to be happening to the Mets a lot lately.

And it happens fast. Jarrett has written about this at length if you want the numbers, but prospect after prospect,

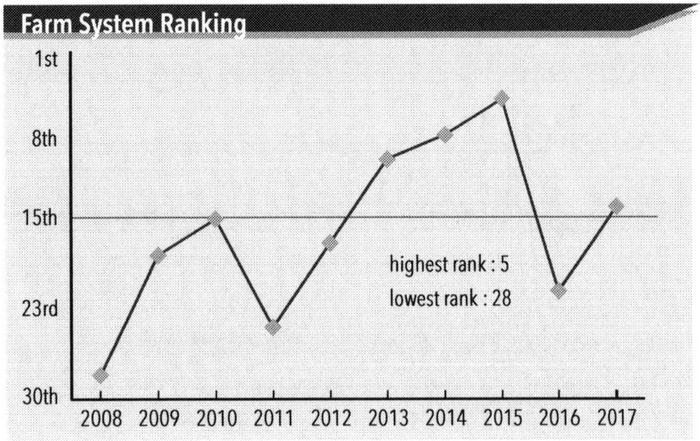

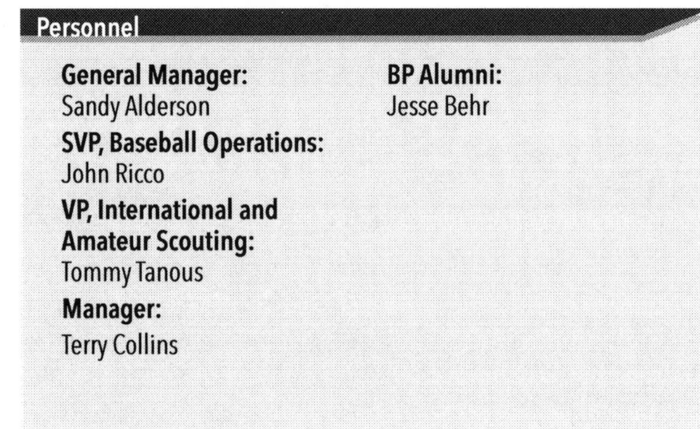

from the elite guys, to the back-end top-100 types, to the Jacob deGroms and Robert Gsellmans, and even the useful org guys, have showed up in the major leagues, if not immediately, then very shortly after debuting, with a velocity spike on their fastball, tightened command, and a plus-or-better slider. It's not a perfect system. Zack Wheeler never quite put it all together before his Tommy John surgery. Rafael Montero went backward, if anything. Jon Niese was always, unfathomably, Jon Niese.

But there's a pattern here. Should we be keeping it in mind, even if it flies in the face of my lead? After all, these pitchers might get traded before they fully actualize these gains (although Michael Fulmer seems to fit in nicely with the proper Mets prospects, and Collin McHugh popped back onto radars due to a velocity/slider jump in Houston). But this is all supposed to take place in a vacuum. You write Mookie Betts up as a second baseman, because that is where he plays, even if he isn't unseating Dustin Pedroia.

I think there is a way to hedge though.

Robert Gsellman is very high on this list. I don't suspect it is spoiling anything to suggest he will be pretty high on our 101. Coming into 2016, he was very much in the range of prospect deGrom. Maybe a bit better chance to stick as a starter, but there wasn't much more upside in a rotation role. But the slider was present in April, even in the cold drizzle in New Hampshire. The velocity ticked up from 2015, now more 91-93 than 89-92. By the time he showed up in the majors, he was sitting 94 and the slider that flashed plus was now plus. He did that for 45 innings, against major-league bats. It happened. We have a better idea of what is possible.

I gave Steven Matz what should have been considered a very aggressive slider grade on the 2016 Mets list. Now the 60 seems perfectly reasonable, but at the time he had thrown exactly eleven sliders in the majors, according to Brooks Baseball. Okay, I watched a lot of Mets baseball then, so I probably saw all eleven. And even by that point, it was a thing you watched for—when was the new Mets pitcher going to start throwing the Warthen slider? But it at least gave you something to hang your hat on. Gsellman didn't even have a slider at that point, so what could you do?

Thomas Szapucki could develop a plus slider in 2020; the arm slot should work. He could be the best of the whole lot. He might just be Jon Niese. Justin Dunn is the kind of raw, hard-throwing arm the Mets player development staff has done well with. He could also be the next Zack Wheeler. It's hard to spot trends. Staffs change quickly, and the sample size of guys in a system that even have a 1 in 100 shot to turn into Jacob deGrom is not significant enough to change the rules.

But if you see it, you can write it.

Here's what we saw:

1. Amed Rosario, SS

DOB: 11/20/1995

Height/Weight: 6'2" 170 lbs.

Bats/Throws: R/R

Drafted/Acquired: Signed July 2nd, 2012 out of the Dominican Republic by the New York Mets for $1.75 million.

Previous Ranking(s): 2016: #2 (Org), #96 (Top 101)

2016 Stats: .341/.392/.481, 2 HR, 6 SB at Double-A Binghamton, .309/.359/.442, 3 HR, 13 SB in 66 games at High-A St. Lucie

The Role: OFP 70—All-Star shortstop
Likely 60—Above-average regular

YEAR	TEAM	LVL	AGE	PA	R	2B	3B	HR	RBI	BB	K	SB	CS	AVG/OBP/SLG	TAv	VORP	BABIP	BRR	FRAA	WARP
2014	SAV	A	18	31	2	0	1	1	4	1	11	0	0	.133/.161/.300	.157	-2.8	.167	-0.1	SS(2): 0.1 • 3B(1): -0.2	-0.3
2014	BRO	A-	18	290	39	11	5	1	23	17	47	7	3	.289/.337/.380	.274	16.4	.345	0.7	SS(64): 2.6	2.0
2015	SLU	A+	19	417	41	20	5	0	25	23	73	12	4	.257/.307/.335	.240	8.8	.316	0.9	SS(102): 13.9	2.5
2015	BIN	AA	19	10	1	0	0	0	1	0	5	1	0	.100/.100/.100	.080	-1.2	.200	0.2	SS(2): 0.4	-0.1
2016	SLU	A+	20	290	27	10	8	3	40	21	36	13	6	.309/.359/.442	.299	24.0	.345	0.5	SS(60): -0.2	2.4
2016	BIN	AA	20	237	38	14	5	2	31	19	51	6	2	.341/.392/.481	.302	20.9	.433	1.7	SS(53): -5.2	1.7
2017	*NYN*	*MLB*	*21*	*250*	*24*	*10*	*2*	*5*	*26*	*14*	*65*	*4*	*1*	*.238/.284/.367*	*.230*	*3.8*	*.305*	*0.2*	*SS 1*	*0.6*
2018	*NYN*	*MLB*	*22*	*358*	*39*	*14*	*4*	*8*	*38*	*22*	*90*	*6*	*2*	*.247/.298/.385*	*.253*	*10.3*	*.312*	*0.5*	*SS 2*	*1.3*

Breakout: 4% Improve: 10% Collapse: 1% Attrition: 9% MLB: 16% *Comparables: Nick Franklin, Alen Hanson, Yamaico Navarro*

The Good: Rosario features a plus arm and a potential plus glove at shortstop. He's turned himself into a 70 runner apparently (I never got anything faster than 4.25 before this season). He smashed two levels this year with the bat despite being one of the youngest players at both stops. He's gone from a glove-first prospect to one with potential plus hit and defensive tools. In the batter's box, quick wrists and plus bat speed allow you to dream on average over-the-fence power someday. Hmm, that's all five tools by my count.

The Bad: If you wanted to pooh-pooh his Florida State League performance, he was repeating the league. That doesn't really work with his Eastern League numbers though, where he posted an .873 OPS. The hand path in his swing is unusual, and major-league arms might be able to find holes. The power projection is almost all projection right now.

The Irrelevant: Rosario was very active on Twitter this season, tagging many of his tweets with the catchphrase "DontBeSurprisedBeReady, or #DBSBR when one needs to save characters.

The Risks: Relatively low considering his age. The defensive tools give him a decent floor, and he hit in Double-A, which makes you more confident in the offensive ones. The ultimate offensive ceiling will decide whether Rosario makes a few all-star games, or just hangs around as a solid regular at the 6.

Major league ETA: Post-Super-2, 2017

Ben Carsley's Fantasy Take: Yes, please. Rosario is an excellent fantasy prospect thanks to his proximity to the majors, his speed, and a hit tool you can truly believe in. He's not necessarily the type of player who will come up and make an immediate fantasy impact, but within a season or two he's capable of producing similarly to 2016 Jose Ramirez, hitting .300 plus with 10-plus homers, 20-plus steals and a whole lotta runs while retaining that sweet, sweet SS eligibility. He's a half-step behind Dansby Swanson and J.P. Crawford because I think they'll produce sooner, but Rosario is right on their heels as a dynasty asset.

2. Robert Gsellman, RHP

DOB: 07/18/1993

Height/Weight: 6'4" 215 lbs.

Bats/Throws: R/R

Drafted/Acquired: Drafted in the 13th round in the 2011 MLB Draft, Westchester HS, (Los Angeles, CA)

Previous Ranking(s): 2016: #9 (org)

2016 Stats: 2.42 ERA, 4.13 DRA, 44.7 IP, 42 H, 42 K, 15 BB at major league level, 2.71 ERA, 5.73 ERA, 4.31 DRA, 48.7 IP, 56 H, 40 K, 16 BB at Triple-A Las Vegas, 3.27 DRA, 66.3 IP, 57 H, 48 K, 15 BB at Double-A Binghamton

The Role: OFP 70—The poor man's Jacob deGrom
Likely 60—Maybe there is such a thing as a mid-rotation starter

YEAR	TEAM	LVL	AGE	W	L	SV	G	GS	IP	H	HR	BB/9	K/9	K	GB%	BABIP	WHIP	ERA	FIP	DRA	VORP	WARP	cFIP	MPH
2014	SAV	A	20	10	6	0	20	20	116^{1}	122	2	2.6	7.1	92	56%	.331	1.34	2.55	3.34	3.48	25.30	2.6	97	
2015	SLU	A+	21	6	0	0	8	8	51	37	1	1.9	6.5	37	61%	.250	0.94	1.76	2.79	2.94	12.10	1.3	90	
2015	BIN	AA	21	7	7	0	16	16	92^{1}	89	4	2.5	4.8	49	54%	.277	1.25	3.51	3.65	4.62	4.90	0.5	105	
2016	BIN	AA	22	3	4	0	11	11	66^{1}	57	2	2.0	6.5	48	57%	.282	1.09	2.71	3.25	3.26	13.50	1.5	91	
2016	LVG	AAA	22	1	5	0	9	9	48^{2}	56	8	3.0	7.4	40	55%	.318	1.48	5.73	5.20	4.17	6.40	0.7	87	
2016	NYN	MLB	22	4	2	0	8	7	44^{2}	42	1	3.0	8.5	42	57%	.325	1.28	2.42	2.67	4.13	6.00	0.6	93	95.9
2017	*NYN*	*MLB*	*23*	*9*	*9*	*0*	*26*	*26*	*148*	*146*	*16*	*3.2*	*6.7*	*111*	*52%*	*.290*	*1.33*	*4.22*	*4.28*	*4.62*	*9.4*	*1.0*	*100*	
2018	*NYN*	*MLB*	*24*	*9*	*9*	*0*	*27*	*27*	*158^{2}*	*125*	*17*	*4.5*	*9.6*	*169*	*52%*	*.292*	*1.29*	*4.00*	*4.29*	*4.62*	*15.6*	*1.6*	*106*	

Breakout: 15% Improve: 28% Collapse: 25% Attrition: 36% MLB: 65% *Comparables: Aaron Poreda, Archie Bradley, Gio Gonzalez*

The Good: Stop us if you have heard this one before: A Mets pitching prospect showed up with a significant uptick in velocity and a heretofore unseen plus slider. Gsellman was flashing these new party pieces in the Spring, but in the majors the sinker velocity averaged higher than he was touching in my April look, and the late bite makes it a borderline plus-plus pitch. His Warthen slider has quickly developed into a swing-and-miss weapon. The addition of the slider has tightened up his curve as well, although it is his clear third offering. He is a big, athletic kid with an easy delivery.

The Bad: Gsellman is still figuring out how to harness the additional fastball velocity, and he occasionally has trouble commanding his sinker's late bite at 95. The slider still needs a bit more consistency. The changeup is below-average, and he prefers to attack lefties with the two breaking balls. It hasn't been an issue so far, but a better change might help the second and third times through the order. He did struggle a bit deeper in starts when he wasn't facing the Phillies.

The Irrelevant: It's pronounced "GUH-zell-man"

The Risks: Gsellman is this high because he has already done it in the majors, admittedly in a sample small enough that he still qualifies for the list at all. He's always looked the part of a major-league arm, but pop-up velocity guys don't always keep their gains, and he'd be a less-exciting pitcher sitting 91-93, if still a good one. Like seemingly every other Mets starter, he's had offseason surgery, although this is for a labrum tear in his non-throwing arm. Also, he's a pitcher.

Major league ETA: Debuted in 2016

Ben Carsley's Fantasy Take: Pop-up pitching prospects are my dynasty kryptonite. I'm terrible at ranking them, though I think everyone is. If Gsellman is truly the pitcher we saw last season, he's a top-20 dynasty prospect well on his way to becoming an SP 2/3. I believe in the Warthen slider, but I'm a bit more skeptical of the fastball gains, and so Gsellman is more likely to be a top-40ish prospect in my book. One thing I'm sure of; you're only getting Gsellman if you go all-in on him, and he's got the type of upside and proximity to the majors that makes him a worthy gamble. Hope you hit on a stud who can flirt with a 3.00 ERA and 200 strikeouts, but still be happy if you get something closer to a Kevin Gausman-type SP 5.

3. Thomas Szapucki, LHP

DOB: 6/12/1996

Height/Weight: 6'2", 205 lbs.

Bats/Throws: L/L

Drafted/Acquired: Drafted in the fifth round of the 2015 draft, William T. Dwyer High School (West Palm Beach, FL), signed for $375,000.

Previous Ranking(s): NR

2016 Stats: 1.27 DRA, 23 IP, 10 H, 39 K, 11 BB at short-season Brooklyn, 0.62 ERA, 1.07 DRA, 29 IP, 16 H, 47 K, 9 BB at rookie ball in Kingsport, 2.35 ERA

The Role: OFP 60—Good Oliver Perez
Likely 50—A healthier Jon Niese

YEAR	TEAM	LVL	AGE	W	L	SV	G	GS	IP	H	HR	BB/9	K/9	K	GB%	BABIP	WHIP	ERA	FIP	DRA	VORP	WARP	cFIP	MPH
2015	MTS	Rk	19	0	0	0	3	0	2^1	5	0	0.0	11.6	3	56%	.556	2.14	15.43	0.73	3.89	0.40	0.0	91	
2016	KNG	Rk	20	2	1	0	5	5	29	16	2	2.8	14.6	47	46%	.255	0.86	0.62	2.35	1.02	15.10	1.5	62	
2016	BRO	A-	20	2	2	0	4	4	23	10	0	4.3	15.3	39	46%	.256	0.91	2.35	1.58	1.15	10.50	1.1	73	
2017	*NYN*	*MLB*	*21*	*2*	*2*	*0*	*6*	*6*	35^2	*32*	*4*	*5.0*	*9.5*	*38*	*27%*	*.322*	*1.46*	*4.42*	*4.31*	*5.03*	*2.1*	*0.2*	*118*	
2018	*NYN*	*MLB*	*22*	*10*	*10*	*0*	*28*	*28*	171^2	*138*	*19*	*4.9*	*10.5*	*200*	*27%*	*.310*	*1.34*	*3.96*	*4.27*	*4.51*	*18.3*	*1.9*	*106*	

Breakout: 4% Improve: 4% Collapse: 0% Attrition: 2% MLB: 5% *Comparables: Carl Edwards Jr, Wilking Rodriguez, Brett Oberholtzer*

The Good: He touches 97 from the left side, and it is a lively pitch he can run and cut. The boring version is particularly tough for righties. The velocity comes easy and the curve flashes plus. He's not just a raw arm-strength guy and has an idea on the mound. His delivery is unorthodox, but the arm action is relatively clean.

The Bad: There is some effort in the upper body, especially out of the stretch. The secondaries only flash and are very raw at present. He's uncomfortable throwing to first and fielding his position. The velocity/stuff wanes deeper into starts.

The Irrelevant: Szapucki finished 20th in the Appalachian League in strikeouts, despite making only five starts there.

The Risks: Szapucki is a potential power-lefty starter, but the risks are substantial. He's only performed in short-season ball and both secondaries need big-grade jumps in order to have major-league utility. His mechanics are unorthodox and he utilizes a low three-quarters arm slot. Back issues limited him to 52 innings in 2016. Also, he's a pitcher.

Major league ETA: 2019

Ben Carsley's Fantasy Take: If you're not already tired of me cautioning you against starters in the low minors, buckle up, because we've got 27 of these suckers left. Szapucki at least has the upside we look for in a dynasty league pitching prospect, and lefties who miss bats like he does will always be en vogue. You could do worse than to take a flier on him in deeper dynasty leagues as there's SP3 upside with a lot of strikeouts here. There's a good chance he turns into a reliever, though.

4. Dominic Smith, 1B

DOB: 6/15/1995

Height/Weight: 6'0", 250 lbs.

Bats/Throws: L/L

Drafted/Acquired: Drafted 11th overall in the 2013 draft, Junipero Serra HS (Gardena, CA), signed for $2,300,000

Previous Ranking(s): 2015: #5 (Org) #86 (Overall)

2016 Stats: .302/.367/.457, 14 HR, 2 SB in 130 games at Double-A Binghamton

The Role: OFP 55—The, oh let's say, 13th-best first baseman in the major leagues
Likely 50—James Loney is such a lazy comp, but...

YEAR	TEAM	LVL	AGE	PA	R	2B	3B	HR	RBI	BB	K	SB	CS	AVG/OBP/SLG	TAv	VORP	BABIP	BRR	FRAA	WARP
2014	SAV	A	19	518	52	26	1	1	44	51	77	5	4	.271/.344/.338	.261	0.9	.321	-4.8	1B(110): -3.1	-0.2
2015	SLU	A+	20	497	58	33	0	6	79	35	75	2	1	.305/.354/.417	.279	7.6	.351	-6.5	1B(104): 9.2	1.8
2016	BIN	AA	21	542	64	29	2	14	91	50	74	2	1	.302/.367/.457	.292	17.6	.329	-5.3	1B(106): 1.1	2.0
2017	*NYN*	*MLB*	*22*	*250*	*25*	*11*	*0*	*7*	*29*	*18*	*56*	*0*	*0*	*.247/.302/.386*	*.242*	*-0.3*	*.295*	*-0.5*	*1B 1*	*0.1*
2018	*NYN*	*MLB*	*23*	*380*	*46*	*18*	*0*	*12*	*45*	*29*	*84*	*0*	*0*	*.253/.312/.407*	*.267*	*6.6*	*.300*	*-1.0*	*1B 2*	*0.9*

Breakout: 6% Improve: 23% Collapse: 5% Attrition: 24% MLB: 36% *Comparables: Nick Evans, Dan Vogelbach, Chris Marrero*

The Good: Smith continued to rake against Double-A pitching. He has good feel for the barrel, and covers both sides of the plate well. The game power flashed at times this year, and he showed more pull-side pop in both games and BP. He has soft hands and a strong, accurate arm on defense.

The Bad: Outside of a three-week stretch in late June/early July, Smith didn't really show the power you'd want out of an everyday first baseman, and his extreme opposite-field approach might limit his overall game power against major-league arms. He will poke or roll over against soft stuff away. The body continues to be high-maintenance.

The Irrelevant: Gardena, CA is quite the hotbed of athletics. Other native sons and daughters include hockey forward Beau Bennett, former Tigers third baseman Enos Cabell, starting pitcher Dock Ellis, running back Gaston Green, Basketball Hall of Famer Lisa Leslie, and pro skateboarder Daewon Song.

The Risks: There's not much risk in the bat; Smith will hit. The risk is in the profile. At the risk of repeating myself from last year, it's tough being a first base prospect. Even his line above, against Double-A pitching in a down Eastern League, would just be average for a major-league first baseman.

Major league ETA: Post-Super-2, 2017

Ben Carsley's Fantasy Take: My internet dad, Bret Sayre, has loved Smith for a long time and I worry this is going to lead to us developing a Tywin/Tyrion Lannister relationship, but alas ... Smith is going to be a major leaguer, and he figures to hit for an okay batting average. That affords him a modicum of fantasy value, but that's pretty much it. Smith doesn't have the power we look for in a fantasy first baseman, nor the speed or super-high average to offset the lack of dingers. Instead, he profiles more as a guy who'll hit .280 with 15-or-so homers and some RBI. That's fine, but it's basically what C.J. Cron did this year and he was only the 26th best fantasy first baseman, per ESPN's Player Rater. Smith is probably a back-of-the-top-150 dynasty prospect just because of his proximity and probability, but he's nothing to get excited over. Beware other owners trying to sell high on him after he puts up comparatively gaudy stats in Las Vegas.

5. Desmond Lindsey, CF

DOB: 01/15/1997

Height/Weight: 6'0" 200 lbs.

Bats/Throws: R/R

Drafted/Acquired: Drafted 53rd overall in the 2015 MLB Draft, Out-of-Door Academy (Sarasota, FL); signed for $1,142,700

Previous Ranking(s): 2015: #7 (Org)

2016 Stats: .297/.418/.450, 4 HR, 3 SB in 32 games at short-season Brooklyn, .364/.562/.455, 0 HR, 0 SB in 5 games at complex-level GCL

The Role: OFP 60—Young Austin Jackson
Likely 45—Older Austin Jackson

YEAR	TEAM	LVL	AGE	PA	R	2B	3B	HR	RBI	BB	K	SB	CS	AVG/OBP/SLG	TAv	VORP	BABIP	BRR	FRAA	WARP
2015	MTS	Rk	18	81	10	4	2	1	6	11	21	3	2	.304/.400/.464	.317	8.1	.426	0.7	CF(16): -0.3	0.8
2015	BRO	A-	18	53	3	3	0	0	7	7	19	0	1	.200/.308/.267	.240	-0.6	.346	-1.0	CF(14): -3.9	-0.5
2016	MTS	Rk	19	16	3	1	0	0	0	5	5	0	0	.364/.563/.455	.409	3.1	.667	0.0	CF(4): -0.7	0.3
2016	BRO	A-	19	134	18	5	0	4	17	20	26	3	1	.297/.418/.450	.345	15.4	.358	-0.1	CF(29): -4.1	1.3
2017	*NYN*	*MLB*	*20*	*250*	*23*	*8*	*1*	*6*	*26*	*22*	*84*	*1*	*0*	*.195/.270/.319*	*.211*	*-3.3*	*.275*	*-0.4*	*CF -4*	*-0.8*
2018	*NYN*	*MLB*	*21*	*295*	*33*	*10*	*1*	*8*	*30*	*29*	*95*	*1*	*0*	*.200/.285/.332*	*.233*	*-0.3*	*.275*	*-0.6*	*CF -4*	*-0.5*

Breakout: 1% Improve: 5% Collapse: 0% Attrition: 3% MLB: 7% *Comparables: Joe Benson, Caleb Gindl, Anthony Gose*

The Good: The Mets thought they got a first-round talent in the second round of the 2015 draft with Lindsay, and he has been as advertised so far. Despite his age, he often looked like a man among boys in the Penn League. He has an advanced approach and hit tool considering his age and experience level and flashed more power this year on Coney Island. When healthy, Lindsay's a plus runner with a shot to stick up the middle.

The Bad: Another spate of lower body injuries kept Lindsay off the field for much of 2016, and he looked compromised at times when he was on it. He has the athletic tools to play center field, but badly needs more reps at the position as his instincts and routes are still raw. There isn't as much projection as you might expect, as Lindsay's frame is already quite mature for his age.

The Irrelevant: Lindsay is the first player ever drafted from Out-of-Door Academy in Sarasota, Florida. The Academy was founded by followers of Belgian educational philosopher, Ovide Decroly.

The Risks: Lindsay is arguably the highest-risk prospect of note in the Mets system, and we are including a guy who hasn't played stateside yet. He's suffered recurring leg injuries since his senior year of high school. He's learning center field as a pro, having been mostly a corner infielder as an amateur. He carries the more banal risks of the profile as well. He doesn't have a track record in full-season ball yet. The tools Lindsay flashes on the field are very exciting, but they've only been flashes so far.

He might end up in left field, where the bat would likely make him more of a tweener.

Major league ETA: 2020

Ben Carsley's Fantasy Take: Lindsay is well-rounded enough that he's worth a shot in deeper dynasty leagues, but his relatively modest ceiling and his distance from the majors limit his value. If it all comes together, Lindsay could be an OF3/4 who hits for a good average with double-digit homer and steal totals. This is a boring caption, but there are only so many ways I can spice up different shades of Austin Jackson.

6. Justin Dunn, RHP

DOB: 9/22/1995

Height/Weight: 6'2" 185lbs.

Bats/Throws: R/R

Drafted/Acquired: Drafted 19th overall in the 2016 draft, Boston College, signed for $2,378,800

Previous Ranking(s): unranked

2016 Stats: 1.50 ERA, 2.89 DRA, 30 IP, 25 H, 35 K, 10 BB in 11 games at short-season Brooklyn

The Role: OFP 55—The Boy Who Comp'd Tom Gordon
Likely 50—The Bullpen Gospels

YEAR	TEAM	LVL	AGE	W	L	SV	G	GS	IP	H	HR	BB/9	K/9	K	GB%	BABIP	WHIP	ERA	FIP	DRA	VORP	WARP	cFIP	MPH
2016	BRO	A-	20	1	1	0	11	8	30	25	1	3.0	10.5	35	46%	.320	1.17	1.50	2.87	3.14	6.70	0.7	91	
2017	*NYN*	*MLB*	*21*	*2*	*3*	*0*	*14*	*7*	*34^{2}*	*38*	*6*	*4.5*	*7.2*	*28*	*31%*	*.322*	*1.59*	*5.58*	*5.40*	*6.37*	*-3.6*	*-0.4*	*153*	
2018	*NYN*	*MLB*	*22*	*5*	*6*	*1*	*38*	*22*	*164^{2}*	*147*	*25*	*3.9*	*8.7*	*158*	*31%*	*.297*	*1.33*	*4.56*	*4.95*	*5.21*	*3.2*	*0.3*	*126*	

Breakout: 0% Improve: 0% Collapse: 0% Attrition: 0% MLB: 0% *Comparables: T.J. McFarland, Vincent Velasquez, Adrian Sampson*

The Good: Dunn thrived when he moved to the rotation this spring for BC. His fastball touches 98, and will show ferocious arm-side life at times. He has a full four-pitch mix with feel for three secondaries. His slider can bump into the mid-80s and will flash plus.

The Bad: Dunn's size (6-foot-2 might be a stretch) and delivery mean bullpen projections will dog him until he proves he can go deep into games and a minor league season. Although he sat in the mid-90s in two or three inning outings for Brooklyn, it is hard to evaluate if he will be able to keep that deeper into starts. His command of the heater can be wild in the zone due to some late torque in his delivery. Secondaries need a lot of refinement, especially the changeup.

The Irrelevant: Dunn went viral on draft night via a video of him hearing his name called while out to dinner with his Boston College teammates.

The Risks: Dunn has a major-league-quality arm, so the risks in the profile have more to do with role. He could move very quickly as a late-inning reliever, but the development time for him to blossom into a mid-rotation arm will be more protracted. He's only been a starter for a few months, and the non-fastball parts of his arsenal are in need of consistency and refinement. We will have a better idea of how this might play out when he gets fully stretched as a starter next year in a full-season level (normally I would have just said "in St. Lucie," but the Mets have never met a prospect they couldn't assign to a lower league than warranted) Also, he's a pitcher.

Major league ETA: 2018

Ben Carsley's Fantasy Take: Dunn is one of the 15-or-so best dynasty prospects from the past draft, a live arm who could take a while to turn into a SP 3/4 or could be a dominant reliever in relatively short order. Let's hope he takes the former route, because his heat and potential for multiple effective secondaires make him a potential high-strikeout starter. It's great for our purposes that Dunn landed with the Mets, an organization that's given us every reason to trust their pitching development in recent seasons. Just be ready to cut ties with him if the Mets decide a fast track to relief is for the best instead. I prefer Dunn to Szapucki, because I think we'll know what he is sooner.

7. Andres Gimenez, SS

DOB: 09/04/1998

Height/Weight: 6'0" 195 lbs.

Bats/Throws: L/R

Drafted/Acquired: Signed in July 2015 out of Venezuela by the New York Mets for $1,200,000

Previous Ranking(s): Unranked

2016 Stats: .350/.469/.523, 3 HR, 13 SB in 62 games at the Dominican Summer League

The Role: OFP 60—Above-average shortstop

YEAR	TEAM	LVL	AGE	PA	R	2B	3B	HR	RBI	BB	K	SB	CS	AVG/OBP/SLG	TAv	VORP	BABIP	BRR	FRAA	WARP
2016	MET	Rk	17	141	24	10	4	1	17	21	13	7	1	.360/.461/.544	.348	6.9	.388	1.0	SS(29): 7.2	1.0
2016	DME	Rk	17	134	28	10	0	2	21	25	9	6	7	.340/.478/.500	.369	20.3	.344	-0.9	SS(19): -2.8 • 2B(12): -1.1	1.6
2017	*NYN*	*MLB*	*18*	*250*	*24*	*9*	*1*	*6*	*26*	*21*	*71*	*2*	*2*	*.211/.284/.339*	*.222*	*0.9*	*.275*	*-0.5*	*SS 0 • 2B 0*	*0.1*
2018	*NYN*	*MLB*	*19*	*268*	*30*	*10*	*1*	*7*	*28*	*22*	*77*	*2*	*2*	*.213/.282/.352*	*.237*	*2.3*	*.274*	*-0.4*	*SS 0 • 2B 0*	*0.3*

Breakout: 0% Improve: 0% Collapse: 0% Attrition: 0% MLB: 0% *Comparables: Raul Mondesi, Wilmer Flores*

The Good: Gimenez has a potential plus hit tool and is an advanced shortstop for his age. He's a good bet to stick at the position and is potentially above-average there. Already gets raves for his high baseball IQ. If all you know about a player is he has a chance to hit .280 and be a good glove at shortstop, well, ignorance of everything else is bliss (and also fine for putting him on a Top 10 list).

The Bad: Gimenez isn't your traditional tooled-up Latin shortstop (you'll find mostly fives and sixes here), so the swing and approach will have to work all the way up the ladder, and the ladder still has a whole lot of rungs on it.

The Irrelevant: While he doesn't have a 2000 birthdate, if you want to feel old, Gimenez was born the same day Google was incorporated.

The Risks: He just turned 18 and has yet to play within the contiguous United States. The risk profile is, uh, extreme.

Major league ETA: 2021

Ben Carsley's Fantasy Take: I'm all about betting on players with good hit tools and it's heartening to hear that Gimenez is likely to stick at short. That being said, the lead time is way too long and the power/speed tools too pedestrian to get worked up about Gimenez right now. Don't forget the name entirely, but move on if your league rosters fewer than 200 minor leaguers.

8. Brandon Nimmo, OF

DOB: 03/27/1993

Height/Weight: 6'3" 205 lbs.

Bats/Throws: L/R

Drafted/Acquired: Drafted 13th overall in the 2011 MLB Draft; Cheyenne East HS (Cheyenne, WY); Signed for $2,100,000

Previous Ranking(s): 2016: #6 (Org)

2016 Stats: .274/.338/.329, 1 HR, 0 SB in 32 games at the major league level, .352/.423/.541, 11 HR, 7 SB in 97 games at Triple-A Las Vegas

The Role: OFP 50—Second-division/platoon outfielder
Likely 45—Fourth outfielder

YEAR	TEAM	LVL	AGE	PA	R	2B	3B	HR	RBI	BB	K	SB	CS	AVG/OBP/SLG	TAv	VORP	BABIP	BRR	FRAA	WARP
2014	SLU	A+	21	279	59	9	5	4	25	50	51	9	3	.322/.448/.458	.318	27.7	.401	1.5	CF(56): -5.1	2.4
2014	BIN	AA	21	279	38	12	4	6	26	36	54	5	1	.238/.339/.396	.258	7.2	.283	0.1	CF(44): -0.8 • LF(21): -3.9	0.4
2015	SLU	A+	22	20	3	1	0	0	2	4	3	0	0	.125/.300/.188	.211	-1.0	.154	-0.4	CF(2): -0.5	-0.2
2015	BIN	AA	22	302	26	12	3	2	16	26	55	0	2	.279/.354/.368	.266	6.1	.343	-3.9	CF(57): -3.6 • RF(10): 0.7	0.4
2015	LVG	AAA	22	112	19	3	1	3	8	18	20	5	4	.264/.393/.418	.284	6.3	.304	0.9	RF(17): 3.9 • CF(13): -0.3	1.0
2016	LVG	AAA	23	444	72	25	8	11	61	46	73	7	8	.352/.423/.541	.304	35.3	.411	2.8	CF(65): 1.5 • LF(23): 1.2	3.9
2016	NYN	MLB	23	80	12	1	0	1	6	6	20	0	0	.274/.338/.329	.267	2.0	.365	-0.4	LF(13): -0.4 • RF(7): -0.1	0.2
2017	*NYN*	*MLB*	*24*	*107*	*11*	*4*	*1*	*2*	*11*	*11*	*26*	*1*	*1*	*.244/.329/.377*	*.259*	*2.9*	*.308*	*-0.2*	*RF 1*	*0.4*
2018	*NYN*	*MLB*	*25*	*336*	*41*	*12*	*2*	*9*	*37*	*35*	*84*	*3*	*3*	*.248/.333/.393*	*.272*	*10.7*	*.313*	*-0.3*	*RF 3*	*1.5*

Breakout: 5% Improve: 24% Collapse: 17% Attrition: 27% MLB: 55% *Comparables: Desmond Jennings, Jaff Decker, Jackie Bradley*

The Good: Nimmo is a less-exciting prospect than he was on draft day 2011, but aren't we all? He still offers you a broad base of baseball skills, including the ability to play all three outfield positions, and a bit of on-base and pop against righties. The less jaded among us may still believe he can convert some of that solid-average raw power he shows in batting practice to game power.

The Bad: At one point there actually was a surfeit of tools and projection here, but five years and multiple lower body injuries later, Nimmo has lost a fair amount of his teenaged athleticism and just never extracted any game power out his swing, despite multiple tweaks to his setup and stride. He struggles picking up the ball against lefties and will need to be hidden against major-league southpaws. Nimmo's stretched in center field nowadays and has settled into the dreaded tweener/fourth outfielder profile.

The Irrelevant: You probably already know that Brandon Nimmo is the first baseball player from Wyoming to be drafted in the first round, but he has a ways to go to be the best player from the Cowboy State. That honor currently belongs to Greg Brock, who played parts of ten seasons with the Dodgers and Brewers, compiling 10 WARP.

The Risks: Nimmo is close to a finished product. He may not offer a sexy OFP anymore, but he can contribute to a major league roster in 2017 and even start for a few weeks in a pinch.

Major league ETA: Debuted in 2016

Ben Carsley's Fantasy Take: If Nimmo grows into some power and plays often as a strong-side platoon bat, he may be worth owning in fantasy someday. Those are two pretty big "ifs," though, and despite his proximity to the majors Nimmo is not a top-150 dynasty prospect. You might be tempted based on his 2016 Triple-A stats, but please remember that offensive performance in Vegas stays in Vegas.

9. Gavin Cecchini, SS

DOB: 12/22/1993

Height/Weight: 6'2" 200 lbs.

Bats/Throws: R/R

Drafted/Acquired: Drafted 12th overall in the 2012 MLB Draft; Alfred M. Barbe HS (Lake Charles, LA); signed for $2,300,000

Previous Ranking(s): 2016: #4 (Org)

2016 Stats: .333/.429/.667, 0 HR, 0 SB in 4 games at the major league level, .325/.390/.448, 8 HR, 4 SB in 117 games at Triple-A Las Vegas

The Role: OFP 50—Average major league second baseman
Likely 40—Utility guy that makes you cringe a bit when he's your Sunday shortstop

YEAR	TEAM	LVL	AGE	PA	R	2B	3B	HR	RBI	BB	K	SB	CS	AVG/OBP/SLG	TAv	VORP	BABIP	BRR	FRAA	WARP
2014	SAV	A	20	259	42	17	4	3	25	25	41	7	1	.259/.333/.408	.276	18.4	.299	3.5	SS(53): 3.4	2.2
2014	SLU	A+	20	271	36	10	1	5	31	32	40	3	3	.236/.325/.352	.246	6.7	.259	0.3	SS(59): -5.1	0.2
2014	BIN	AA	20	4	1	0	0	0	0	0	1	0	0	.250/.250/.250	.184	0.3	.333	0.5	SS(1): 0.1	0.0
2015	BIN	AA	21	485	64	26	4	7	51	42	55	3	4	.317/.377/.442	.300	36.2	.348	-2.3	SS(109): 2.4	4.2
2016	LVG	AAA	22	499	71	27	2	8	55	48	55	4	1	.325/.390/.448	.274	25.2	.357	-2.1	SS(105): -11.5 • 2B(3): 1.2	1.5
2016	NYN	MLB	22	7	2	2	0	0	2	0	2	0	0	.333/.429/.667	.642	2.5	.500	0.0	SS(2): -0.0	0.3
2017	*NYN*	*MLB*	*23*	*62*	*6*	*3*	*0*	*1*	*6*	*5*	*12*	*0*	*0*	*.248/.311/.376*	*.251*	*2.0*	*.289*	*-0.1*	*SS -0*	*0.1*
2018	*NYN*	*MLB*	*24*	*334*	*39*	*14*	*2*	*8*	*37*	*28*	*65*	*1*	*0*	*.252/.318/.393*	*.265*	*12.6*	*.292*	*-0.6*	*SS -1*	*1.3*

Breakout: 6% Improve: 34% Collapse: 4% Attrition: 19% MLB: 46% *Comparables: Brad Miller, Greg Garcia, Chris Taylor*

The Good: Cecchini continued to hit and get on-base in 2016. There has never been a surfeit of tools or projection here, so his performance is going to matter more than for most prospects. He has a contact-oriented swing and enough feel with the bat to be a .270 hitter in the majors. He'd likely be a solid hand at second base, but...

The Bad: Cecchini is not a major-league shortstop. The arm is well-below-average for the position, forcing him to rush his footwork and actions as well. He's sure-handed, but not particularly rangy. Cecchini dropped the leg kick in his swing a couple years ago, and now has only doubles power. It's very possible that he hits an empty .270 when major-league arms decide to attack him more in the zone.

The Irrelevant: Cecchini's full name is Gavin Glenn Christopher Joseph Cecchini. It's a mouthful, though not quite as long as Pablo Diego José Francisco de Paula Juan Nepomuceno María de los Remeidos Cipriano de la Santísima Trinidad Ruiz y Picasso. Neither are close to the record for the longest legal name, which currently stands at 161 words and 898 letters.

The Risks: Like Smith, the risks for Cecchini are more in the profile than future performance. He has hit in the upper minors and is major-league ready, but the bat would be just 'okay' at second base. If he only hits .250, he's just another extra infielder.

Major league ETA: Debuted in 2016

Ben Carsley's Fantasy Take: You're still better off with Garin Cecchini. OK, not really, but unless you've been clamoring for Scooter Gennett with less power, you can take a pass.

10. Wuilmer Becerra, RF

DOB: 10/01/1994

Height/Weight: 6'3" 225 lbs.

Bats/Throws: R/R

Drafted/Acquired: Signed in June 2013 out of Venezuela by the Toronto Blue Jays for $1,300,000

Previous Ranking(s): 2015: #8 (Org)

2016 Stats: .312/.341/.393, 1 HR, 7 SB in 65 games for High-A St. Lucie

The Role: OFP 50—Average right fielder
Likely 40—Lefty masher off the bench

YEAR	TEAM	LVL	AGE	PA	R	2B	3B	HR	RBI	BB	K	SB	CS	AVG/OBP/SLG	TAv	VORP	BABIP	BRR	FRAA	WARP
2014	KNG	Rk	19	228	37	10	2	7	29	14	55	7	3	.300/.351/.469	.295	13.5	.372	-1.4		1.5
2015	SAV	A	20	487	67	27	3	9	63	33	96	16	8	.290/.342/.423	.294	24.8	.351	-0.2	RF(101): -7.2	2.1
2016	SLU	A+	21	263	27	17	0	1	34	9	52	7	1	.312/.341/.393	.268	5.5	.388	0.0	RF(13): -0.3	0.6
2017	*NYN*	*MLB*	*22*	*250*	*24*	*11*	*0*	*6*	*27*	*11*	*71*	*3*	*1*	*.230/.269/.361*	*.222*	*-4.1*	*.299*	*-0.2*	*RF -0*	*-0.5*
2018	*NYN*	*MLB*	*23*	*308*	*33*	*14*	*0*	*8*	*34*	*16*	*89*	*3*	*1*	*.233/.277/.372*	*.241*	*0.3*	*.304*	*-0.3*	*RF 0*	*0.0*

Breakout: 4% Improve: 10% Collapse: 1% Attrition: 13% MLB: 17% *Comparables: Neftali Soto, Nick Evans, Brandon Snyder*

The Good: Man, Becerra is a weird prospect. He looks the part of a big, athletic, dinger-mashing right fielder. And he will show plus raw power in batting practice. He's an above-average runner with a strong throwing arm. And hey, he's cut his strikeouts every year as a professional and hit over .300 this year in the Florida State League. Becerra has cleaned up his swing mechanics over the years and goes up to the plate with a plan. You'd be forgiven for thinking he was close to putting it all together and really breaking out as a prospect...

The Bad: ...but he's stopped hitting for power in games. In 120 games between Kingsport in 2014 and the first half of Savannah in 2015, he hit 15 home runs. He's hit two since. The Mets spread him out at the plate in 2015 and the game power disappeared shortly after. He's been two different prospects in his four years in the Mets system, and if he doesn't figure out a way to meld the two, he won't have much of a major-league future. Some of the power outage could be attributed to a shoulder injury that lingered since spring training and eventually led to him being shut down in the middle of July.

The Irrelevant: Wuilmer Becerra was the Blue Jays "non-elite prospect" in the R.A. Dickey deal. The Mets non-elite prospect? Mike Nickeas.

The Risks: Becerra needs to hit a lot to be a useful bat in a corner outfield spot, and between the power outage and shoulder injury, there will be a lot of unanswered questions about Becerra going into 2017. He will return to St. Lucie as a 22-year-old, so he's no longer as young as you think.

Major league ETA: late 2018

Ben Carsley's Fantasy Take: Becerra is a pure wait-and-see prospect for dynasty leaguers. If he starts hitting for power again, great, pick him up. If not, I promise you'll have forgotten he existed within the next 36 months.

OTHERS OF NOTE:

#11

Luis Carpio, SS/2B

Not all that much has changed from Carpio's profile last year. He still is as polished a teenage player as you will find in the minors. He tracks pitches well, and the ball carries off his bat more than you'd expect. He's a polished defender with great instincts, and already an infield captain as a teenager. In one of those timelines Jerry O'Connell and friends landed in, Carpio had a breakout season in Columbia this year and stacks up well with Isan Diaz among Top 101 middle-infield prospects. In this timeline though, he missed almost all of the season with a torn labrum in his throwing shoulder and was only able to DH in his August cameo in short-season. A missed year tends to lead one to highlight the warts in a profile, and Carpio lacks a standout athletic tool and might have, or could have been destined for second before the shoulder injury. Still, next year will only be his Age-19 season and he could easily find himself back near the top of the 2018 list.

Factor on the "farm"

T.J. Rivera, IF

It's not often you get to write about the No. 5 hitter on a playoff team in this space. In the rare instances where such names are even eligible for these lists, they are up at the tippy top. Sure, you can blame the Mets infield injuries and Terry Collins' obsession with the platoon advantage for Rivera's spot in the wild card game lineup, but the 27-year-old did hit .330 across 100 major league plate appearances. You might now be yelling at me that he should be up there at the tippy top; after all, major-league performance is a big reason that Robert Gsellman is. Ultimately, as much as major-league performance logically leads us more quickly to major-league role projections, we still have to make a call if it is real or not. As I wrote in the Atlanta top 10, more "prospects" make the majors than you think, and a smaller-but-not-insignificant, subset of those hit their first time around the league. Rivera's defensive limitations—he's below-average even at second—and the fact that he was overmatched against better velocity and better breaking stuff, makes me think he isn't much more than a bench option in 2017. That is a major-league role, but it's not what we are pining for during prospect list season.

Okay, he'd probably make the Marlins list.

The pop-up prospect

Tomas Nido, C

Catchers are weird, man. Catching development paths are weirder. So much of their value is tied up in stuff that doesn't appear on a standard scouting report and would be tough to parse from behind home plate anyway. My stopwatch told me that Nido had a pretty good arm. A BP session or two showed you his raw, and prep catchers can take a while to click, even by the standards of catching prospects as a whole. It sure looked like it clicked in 2016 for Nido, as he hit .320 in the Florida State League, and showed a broad base of offensive and defensive skills behind the plate. Double-A will still be a test for the offensive profile, and there likely will be further bumps in the roads in his development, but Nido has forced the Mets into a tricky 40-man roster decision this offseason. He may end up just a good backup with some pop, but there's an intriguing ceiling here now, and you always need more catchers.

Jeffrey's guy

Ali Sanchez, C

Speaking of weird catchers, Sanchez hit .215/.260/.275 in the New York Penn League, and I really struggled with leaving him off the top ten. He was beat up for most of the 2016 season, but that really isn't an excuse, because catchers are always beat up. I still believe in the bat, and he is the catching version of Carpio—incredibly polished behind the plate at all the stuff we can't measure with a stopwatch. Sanchez's arm has always been the big question mark, and he continued to pop well over 2.0 for me this season. It hasn't affected his catch-and-throw numbers yet, but everyone runs in short season, and almost no one really knows what they are doing on the basepaths yet. Then again, all the research we have says controlling the running game is less important than the other things Sanchez seems to do quite well, and the Mets had luck trimming a tenth or two off the pop times of Kevin Plawecki, who had similar throwing issues in the minors. In the end, ranking the dude with a .535 OPS in short-season is something that can make you look really bad in 2019, so let's just call Sanchez a sleeper and move on.

TINSTAAPP, always and forever

Marcos Molina, RHP

Before Thomas Szapucki was even on a Florida follow list, Marcos Molina was shooting up prospect lists based on his own strong Brooklyn campaign. He flashed similar raw stuff to Szapucki, and garnered higher marks for athleticism and polish (and he was a year younger at the same level). He also had famously rough mechanics that put a lot of stress on his arm, and no one was that surprised when he had Tommy John surgery at the end of the 2015 minor-league season. Molina missed all of 2016, and finally reappeared in the AFL with most of his velocity back. But he's only a year removed from the surgery, and there is a ways to go before we get a clearer picture of how much of the front-of-the-rotation is left. The Mets are a bit pressed for time though. Like Nido, the Mets will have to add Molina to the 40-man or else expose him to the Rule 5 draft, and nowadays it is much easier to hide an arm in the bullpen given how short benches have gotten. Two offseasons ago you might have expected Molina to be a slam-dunk add, and maybe even a Top 101 prospect, but you know, he's a pitcher.

TOP 10 TALENTS 25 AND UNDER (BORN 4/1/91 OR LATER)

1. Noah Syndergaard	6. Thomas Szapucki
2. Steven Matz	7. Wilmer Flores
3. Michael Conforto	8. Dominic Smith
4. Amed Rosario	9. Desmond Lindsay
5. Robert Gsellman	10. Justin Dunn

For last year's list, we pointed out that the Mets' strong base of young pitching—Matt Harvey, Jacob deGrom, Jeurys Familia, and Zack Wheeler are all within a few years of being eligible for this list too—set them up for an "extended period of contention." Unfortunately, the downside of reliance on young pitching is that it gets hurt, and boy did the Mets' young pitching get hurt early and often in 2016. Yet all certainly is not lost, as most should be back to full strength or close for 2017, and a new face emerged in Robert Gsellman. Heck, even with all the injuries to the young core, the Mets still nabbed the first wild card slot in the National League.

Noah Syndergaard ranks first on this list for the second consecutive year. Last year, it was more about Harvey and Familia graduating off; this year, Syndergaard is one of the absolute best under-25 players in the game, a true ace in every sense of the word. And the stuff is so good and he's improved so much so fast that it feels like he might yet get better.

Steven Matz was one of the pitchers felled by injury, first pitching through a significant bone spur and later failing to theoretically unrelated shoulder fatigue. Matz has yet to really put together a full, healthy professional season, which raises some obvious durability flags, although all of his varied issues have been unrelated. When healthy, like late in the 2015 season or before the bone spur came in 2016, he's shown the ability to be a No. 2 starter despite occasionally wavering command, with the possibility for even more. Even when compromised and barely throwing his slider after the bone spur, he was still of mid-rotation quality when able to pitch.

Michael Conforto is, perhaps unfairly, viewed as having a lost 2016 season because of his struggles in the major-leagues during the summer months and the apparent loss of confidence in him by manager Terry Collins. But it's easy to forget that he still managed an .804 OPS against righties in the majors amidst a wrist injury and inconsistent playing time, and absolutely demolished Triple-A for 144 plate appearances in a manner that would make anyone short of Barry Bonds blush. He's younger than Bradley Zimmer, for example, a prospect who is rightly still a top prospect but struggled much more mightily in Triple-A than Conforto did in the majors. If you switch around the order of some of these events, but leave the overall package the same, the narrative heavily shifts and Conforto is still viewed as one of baseball's top young emerging stars. We'll see which direction this goes in 2017—if the Mets even open up a spot for him—but the major-league success nudges Conforto just a hair past Amed Rosario.

Yes, Wilmer Flores is still somehow eligible for this list. Flores is what he is: a league-average power bat that crushes lefties and is an excellent defender at first while being fringe to bad/but able to fake everywhere else. Ranking a more-or-less maxed-out average major leaguer against high-upside short-season A dudes is much more art than science, but I ended up dropping Flores behind Thomas Szapucki in light of Wilmer's hamate injury, which has sapped other players' power over the short- and medium-term periods post-injury.

—Jarrett Seidler

NEW YORK YANKEES

The State of the System: *200 million dollar payroll, 200 million prospects.*

THE TOP TEN

1. SS Gleyber Torres	6. RHP James Kaprielian
2. OF Clint Frazier	7. RF Aaron Judge
3. 2B/SS Jorge Mateo	8. RHP Albert Abreu
4. OF Blake Rutherford	9. IF/OF Tyler Wade
5. LHP Justus Sheffield	10. RHP Chance Adams

The Big Question: Are the Yankees responsible for the international draft?

It's CBA time, and the main points of contention between labor and ownership seem to be the qualifying offer and the implementation of an international draft. The MLBPA has never been shy about selling out the interests of non-members to get concessions from ownership—like the elimination of the QO or a 26th roster spot—but an international draft is particularly contentious. Ownership is never above legislating their own cost savings on amateur talent, even as they continue to spend eight and nine figures on the free agent market.

Billionaires trying to legislate cost savings generally need a better media plan than "we want to spend less on the on-field product you consume." The most common way this is couched is with the phrase "competitive balance." This is the same reason the luxury tax exists, and that you occasionally hear talk of instituting a salary cap. The idea being that left to their own devices, the rich teams will just buy all the best players and negatively affect the competitive balance of the league. The Yankees are a useful bogeyman for this, even after some relative belt-tightening under the Steinbrenner filiorum.

Which takes us to the international draft, and specifically the Yanks international free agent class of 2014, where they signed 10 of the top 30 J2 prospects, per Baseball America, and 52 players in total, almost a third of whom they gave six figure or better deals. Insert Simpsons "Think of the Children" dot gif here if you like.

Of course we won't even know if this works for another three or four years. None of the players signed that summer are on this year's top ten list. Many of them haven't even come stateside yet. The best of the class scuffled a bit in Danville as teenagers. The Cubs' recent spending sprees suffer from the same prognostication issues, though the 2013 class is already paying dividends. Of course whether it works or not, there's the optics of it to deal with.

But that means ignoring that the biggest IFA bonuses of the last two classes have been given out by the Rays and the Braves. Or that the Padres have been one of the more aggressive teams internationally under A.J. Preller. Or that the Twins signed Miguel Sano and the A's signed Michael Ynoa. There is plenty of money to go around in the game right now—just ask Jason Castro—and the money going to sixteen-year old Latino kids is the least of it as it is.

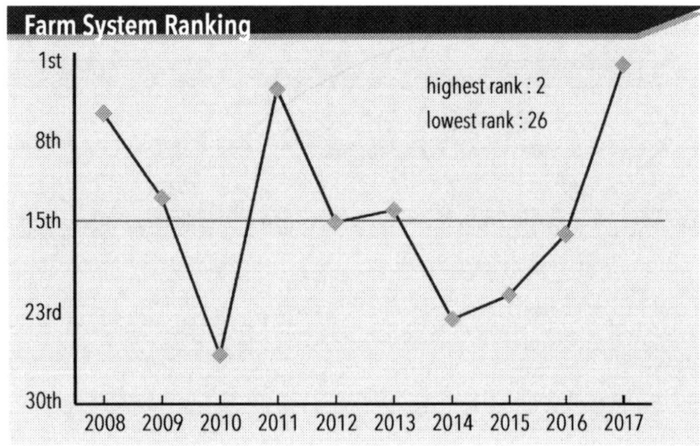

Personnel

General Manager:
Brian Cashman

SVP, Assistant General Manager:
Jean Afterman

Assistant General Manager:
Michael Fishman

Vice President of Baseball Operations:
Tim Naehring

Manager:
Joe Girardi

1. Gleyber Torres, SS

DOB: 12/13/1996

Height/Weight: 6'1" 175 lbs.

Bats/Throws: R/R

Drafted/Acquired: Signed July 2013 by Chicago Cubs out of Venezuela for $1.7 million; acquired from Cubs for Aroldis Chapman

Previous Ranking(s): #1 (Org - Cubs), #41 (overall)

2016 Stats: .275/.359/.433, 9 HR, 19 SB in 94 games at High-A Myrtle Beach, .254/.341/.385, 2 HR, 2 SB in 31 games at High-A Tampa

The Role: OFP 70—All-star infielder...somewhere
Likely 55—Solid regular with some positional flexibility and a nice bat

YEAR	TEAM	LVL	AGE	PA	R	2B	3B	HR	RBI	BB	K	SB	CS	AVG/OBP/SLG	TAv	VORP	BABIP	BRR	FRAA	WARP
2014	CUB	Rk	17	183	33	6	3	1	29	25	33	8	7	.279/.372/.377	.282	7.2	.339	2.3		0.8
2014	BOI	A-	17	32	4	2	3	1	4	4	7	2	0	.393/.469/.786	.373	5.7	.500	0.6	SS(7): 0.4	0.6
2015	SBN	A	18	514	53	24	5	3	62	43	108	22	13	.293/.353/.386	.266	22.1	.373	-2.0	SS(119): -9.3	1.4
2015	MYR	A+	18	24	1	0	0	0	2	1	7	0	1	.174/.208/.174	.151	-2.0	.250	-0.3	SS(7): 0.3	-0.2
2016	MYR	A+	19	409	62	23	3	9	47	42	87	19	10	.275/.359/.433	.282	26.0	.341	0.2	SS(87): 0.9	2.8
2016	TAM	A+	19	138	19	6	2	2	19	16	23	2	3	.254/.341/.385	.279	5.2	.299	-2.9	SS(27): -0.8 • 2B(1): 0.0	0.5
2017	*NYA*	*MLB*	*20*	*250*	*31*	*10*	*1*	*7*	*24*	*18*	*71*	*5*	*3*	*.230/.291/.375*	*.226*	*2.1*	*.300*	*-0.3*	*SS -3 • 2B 0*	*0.0*
2018	*NYA*	*MLB*	*21*	*396*	*47*	*18*	*2*	*12*	*46*	*30*	*113*	*8*	*5*	*.240/.302/.400*	*.239*	*5.1*	*.312*	*0.0*	*SS -4 • 2B 0*	*0.1*

Breakout: 2% Improve: 11% Collapse: 0% Attrition: 5% MLB: 14% *Comparables: Trevor Story, Alen Hanson, Addison Russell*

The Good: Torres was the party piece in the Aroldis Chapman deal, and it is easy to see why. He has an advanced bat for a 19-year-old, plus bat speed with some loft, and he's already strong enough to hit balls out even when not buoyed by the desert air. Potential 6/6 offensive profile. Infield actions are good and the arm is strong enough that it's not impossible he sticks at short, although he'd be below-average there.

The Bad: Torres is unlikely to stick at shortstop even in organizations without Addison Russell or Didi Gregorius. He lacks the first step or overall range—he's a below-average runner—to grade out at average for short, but could be above-average at second or third. There's debate internally over his ultimate power projection. If he's more of a 10-15 home run hitter, that is less enticing if he has to move left or right on the dirt.

The Irrelevant: Gleyber Torres was the 2016 AFL MVP. Other recent winners include Kris Bryant, Greg Bird, and Adam Engel.

The Risks: Torres is only 19 and has yet to Double-A, but he seems less risky than that profile. The hit tool is advanced, and he's an overall polished player as opposed to a "projectable teenager."

Major League ETA: 2018

Ben Carsley's Fantasy Take: I get it. You saw the OFP, you know Torres' name and you're dreaming of his offensive output in Yankee Stadium. I can't blame you. Just keep in mind the very real possibility that Torres won't end up at short, as well as the chance that his power never fully develops. Could you still use a third baseman who hits .280-plus with 15 homers? Of course you could, but you wouldn't say that player is a top-10 dynasty prospect. Torres needs to take a step forward defensively or in terms of pop to enter the upper echelon of truly excellent fantasy prospects. Until then, he'll have to settle for being merely a very good one.

2. Clint Frazier, OF

DOB: 09/06/1994

Height/Weight: 6'1" 190 lbs.

Bats/Throws: R/R

Drafted/Acquired: Drafted fifth overall in the 2013 MLB Draft, Loganville HS (Loganville, GA); signed for $3.5 million; acquired from Indians for Andrew Miller

Previous Ranking(s): #3 (Org - Indians), #53 (overall)

2016 Stats: .238/.238/.333 0 HR, 0 SB in five games at Triple-A Columbus, .228/.278/.396 3 HR, 0 SB in 25 games at Triple-A Scranton Wilkes-Barre, .276/.356/.469, 13 HR, 13 SB in 89 games at Double-A Akron

The Role: OFP 70—A perennial All-Star corner outfielder
Likely 55—Solid regular who always leaves you wondering why he isn't more

YEAR	TEAM	LVL	AGE	PA	R	2B	3B	HR	RBI	BB	K	SB	CS	AVG/OBP/SLG	TAv	VORP	BABIP	BRR	FRAA	WARP
2014	LKC	A	19	542	70	18	6	13	50	56	161	12	6	.266/.349/.411	.277	26.6	.372	0.8	CF(111): -20.7 • RF(1): 0.0	0.8
2015	LYN	A+	20	588	88	36	3	16	72	68	125	15	7	.285/.377/.465	.297	34.5	.348	-2.3	CF(93): -6.5 • RF(35): -0.2	3.2
2016	AKR	AA	21	391	56	25	1	13	48	41	86	13	4	.276/.356/.469	.298	24.3	.331	1.4	RF(31): -1.0 • LF(26): 1.8	2.7
2016	COH	AAA	21	21	2	0	1	0	0	0	6	0	0	.238/.238/.333	.237	-0.2	.333	-0.1	RF(3): 0.1 • LF(2): 0.4	0.0
2016	SWB	AAA	21	108	17	2	3	3	7	7	30	0	0	.228/.278/.396	.248	1.6	.294	0.8	LF(13): -0.8 • RF(6): 1.4	0.2
2017	*NYA*	*MLB*	*22*	*250*	*32*	*10*	*1*	*9*	*28*	*22*	*76*	*3*	*1*	*.233/.307/.407*	*.244*	*3.7*	*.305*	*-0.1*	*RF 0 • LF 1*	*0.5*
2018	*NYA*	*MLB*	*23*	*344*	*42*	*14*	*1*	*11*	*41*	*31*	*105*	*4*	*2*	*.229/.304/.397*	*.242*	*1.6*	*.302*	*0.0*	*RF 0 • LF 2*	*0.3*

Breakout: 1% Improve: 22% Collapse: 1% Attrition: 15% MLB: 40% *Comparables: Joel Guzman, Thomas Neal, Nick Castellanos*

The Good: He has freakish bat speed, and easy plus power with potential for more. He's one of the few right-handed hitters whose swing gets described as pretty or beautiful. Excellent overall athlete, above-average runner, and aggressive, physical player. Looks and feels the part of a superstar. Frazier has as much overall offensive upside as any player still in the minors...

The Bad: ...but for a player that's reached Triple-A without being rushed, he's still fairly far from the upside, especially on the hit tool. There's just too much swing-and-miss still present, and there's no singular, easily fixable cause. He's gotten better at picking up spin, but he's still not great at picking up spin. His swing path is a little shorter to the ball with a quieter pre-swing hitch, but it's still not short and there's still a hitch. And he's toned back the aggressiveness trying to jack everything a mile, but he's still pretty aggressive. Defensively, it looks like he's going to be in a corner full-time by the time he hits The Show.

The Irrelevant: The Yanks leaked a Mike Trout comp for Frazier after trading for him. That seems irrelevant for the purpose of this write-up.

The Risks: The hitting and approach is either going to click at some point, or it won't and he'll always be reaching for an upside that keeps slipping through his fingers. Frazier is talented enough that even if it doesn't all click, we still project him as a likely regular, but low-average corner outfielders that hit for good-but-not-great power aren't exactly special either. There's some downside risk that MLB-quality spin just totally eats his lunch and he's not even that.

Major League ETA: 2017 —Jarrett Seidler

Ben Carsley's Fantasy Take: Bret Sayre and I have been the highest on Frazier among all MiLB enthusiasts for quite some time now. A good performance in Double-A and a trade to an organization that provides favorable offensive contextual factors hasn't changed that, oddly enough. I agree with the sentiment that Frazier is likely to frustrate at times, but if he can do so while hitting 20-plus homers, stealing 10-plus bases and both producing and scoring runs, we'll get over it. Frazier is a legitimate candidate to be an OF2 in his best years, and he's a borderline top-10 overall dynasty asset.

3. Jorge Mateo, SS

DOB: 06/23/1995

Height/Weight: 6'0" 188 lbs.

Bats/Throws: R/R

Drafted/Acquired: Signed January 2012 by the New York Yankees out of the Dominican Republic for $250,000

Previous Ranking(s): #2 (Org.), #65 (Overall)

2016 Stats: .254/.306/.379, 8 HR, 36 SB in 113 games at High-A Tampa

The Role: OFP 60—Quality regular at SS
Likely 50—Regular starter who plays multiple positions including 2B/SS/CF

YEAR	TEAM	LVL	AGE	PA	R	2B	3B	HR	RBI	BB	K	SB	CS	AVG/OBP/SLG	TAv	VORP	BABIP	BRR	FRAA	WARP
2014	YAN	Rk	19	65	14	5	1	0	1	7	17	11	1	.276/.354/.397	.264	4.7	.390	0.8		0.7
2015	CSC	A	20	409	51	18	8	2	33	36	80	71	15	.268/.338/.378	.277	25.5	.338	4.1	SS(79): -0.9	2.6
2015	TAM	A+	20	91	15	5	3	0	7	7	18	11	2	.321/.374/.452	.313	10.6	.409	2.3	SS(20): -0.0	1.1
2016	TAM	A+	21	507	65	16	9	8	47	33	108	36	15	.254/.306/.379	.244	11.8	.313	3.2	SS(62): -4.8 • 2B(40): -0.6	0.6
2017	*NYA*	*MLB*	*22*	*250*	*35*	*9*	*3*	*7*	*22*	*15*	*70*	*15*	*5*	*.225/.273/.371*	*.216*	*1.2*	*.289*	*1.7*	*SS -0 • 2B 0*	*0.1*
2018	*NYA*	*MLB*	*23*	*382*	*43*	*14*	*5*	*11*	*44*	*25*	*103*	*24*	*8*	*.236/.289/.398*	*.233*	*6.0*	*.298*	*3.9*	*SS 0 • 2B 0*	*0.6*

Breakout: 2% Improve: 15% Collapse: 5% Attrition: 10% MLB: 22% *Comparables: Tim Beckham, Chris Nelson, Jonathan Villar*

The Good: With plus bat speed and quick, strong wrists, Mateo isn't your slapper-speed type. He has exceptional bat control, and his approach and discipline improved over the course of the year. There is potential for a plus hit tool but, he still struggles with getting too aggressive, as well as recognizing off-speed. Mateo is a pure 80 runner and his speed is an intimidating force for opponents, forcing defenders to work faster and making them uncomfortable. His plus throwing arm plays well, as does his lateral range in getting to hit balls.

The Bad: While his wrists are strong, Mateo will never develop much over-the-fence power, so he will have to rely on his speed for extra bases. His defense at short is fringe-average currently, as he doesn't have the softest hands and tends to get too quick. He doesn't play the ball on the best hops, causing some awkward moments in the field. Despite top-of-the-scale speed, his baserunning is raw due to poor jumps and reads, as well as better pitcher-catcher pop times. His makeup and discipline have been called into question at times, notably resulting in a two-week suspension this year after he supposedly expressed displeasure that some of his teammates (i.e. Billy Fleming, Abiatal Avelino, Miguel Andujar among others) were promoted to Double-A Trenton before he was.

The Irrelevant: Mateo's 36 stolen bases were a far cry from his 82 last year, which led the minors.

The Risks: Mateo's defensive home is a bit of a question mark following the addition of Gleyber Torres. He needs to make better use of his speed to maximize his potential when he gets on base and wherever it is he ends up defensively. There are some kinks to work out in regards to toning down his approach at the plate.

Major League ETA: Late 2018 —Steve Givarz

Ben Carsley's Fantasy Take: I'm the guy who's gone all-in on Roman Quinn, Jose Peraza, and Billy Hamilton at various points, so you can probably guess how I feel about Mateo. He probably has the best hit tool of the whole bunch, and I'm confident the bat will play enough for Mateo to use his top-end speed. Swiping 40-plus bases covers a lot of sins in fantasy, and Mateo could easily spend many years as a top-10 shortstop or elite MI option. Make like your '90s boy band enthusiast who struggles with homophones and buy, buy, buy.

4. Blake Rutherford, OF

DOB: 5/2/1997

Height/Weight: 6'3" 195 lbs.

Bats/Throws: L/R

Drafted/Acquired: Drafted 18th overall in the 2016 draft, Chaminade College Preparatory School (West Hills, CA); signed for $3.28 million

Previous Ranking(s): N/A

2016 Stats: .382/.440/.618, 2 HR, 0 SB in 25 games at Appalachian League, .240/.333/.400, 1 HR, 0 SB in 8 games at the Gulf Coast League

The Role: OFP 60—First-division outfielder
Likely 50—Second-division outfielder

YEAR	TEAM	LVL	AGE	PA	R	2B	3B	HR	RBI	BB	K	SB	CS	AVG/OBP/SLG	TAv	VORP	BABIP	BRR	FRAA	WARP
2016	PUL	Rk	19	100	13	7	4	2	9	9	24	0	2	.382/.440/.618	.336	7.7	.500	0.5	CF(14): -1.9 • LF(2): -0.2	0.7
2017	*NYA*	*MLB*	*20*	*250*	*25*	*9*	*1*	*7*	*23*	*15*	*85*	*0*	*0*	*.198/.248/.326*	*.195*	*-7.8*	*.276*	*-0.4*	*CF 0 • LF -0*	*-0.8*
2018	*NYA*	*MLB*	*21*	*268*	*29*	*9*	*1*	*7*	*28*	*19*	*87*	*1*	*0*	*.206/.265/.342*	*.211*	*-6.4*	*.281*	*-0.5*	*CF 0 • LF 0*	*-0.7*

Breakout: 1% Improve: 3% Collapse: 0% Attrition: 2% MLB: 4% *Comparables: Joe Benson, Engel Beltre, Chris Parmelee*

The Good: Although he dropped some due to perceived bonus demands, Rutherford was arguably the best prep player in the draft. He has a pure, left-handed hitting stroke, and while there is only average power in his frame at present, he could easily add some strength and pop as he gets older; the hit tool should allow whatever he ends up with to play in games. He's an above-average runner at present, and while I'd expect him to lose a step as he ages and fills out, it's an athletic frame and his speed should settle in at average.

The Bad: Rutherford is only passable in center field at present despite his speed and is likely to move to a corner by the time he steps foot on a major league diamond. He's already 19, and there is some evidence that may limit his ceiling. The profile is more present polish than projection regardless, and while he should be a good regular, he lacks the upside of the names above him.

The Irrelevant: As you'd expect from a Southern California kid, Rutherford is a lifelong Yankees fan.

The Risks: He's only played in rookie ball so far (though you can't poo-poo the results). His season ended a little early with a hamstring issue, which is probably nothing. If he's not a center fielder, there will be—say it with me—increased pressure on the bat.

Major League ETA: 2020

Ben Carsley's Fantasy Take: Rutherford was probably a bit underrated as a dynasty asset headed into the draft. He's several years away, but his hit tool and well-rounded offensive game mean you should buy in on the ground floor. There's no star power here, but a future as an OF3 is very much in play. I continue to be a sucker for dynasty prospects with hit tools as their best assets.

5. Justus Sheffield, LHP

DOB: 05/13/1996

Height/Weight: 5'10" 195 lbs

Bats/Throws: L/L

Drafted/Acquired: Drafted 31st overall in the 2014 MLB Draft, Tullahoma HS (Tullahoma, TN); signed for $1.6 million; acquired from the Indians for Andrew Miller

Previous Ranking(s): #4 (Indians Org.)

2016 Stats: 0.00 ERA, 3.11 DRA, 4 IP, 2 H, 3 BB, 9 K at Double-A Trenton, 3.59 ERA, 3.03 DRA, 95.1 IP, 91 H, 40 BB, 93 K in 19 games at High-A Lynchburg, 1.73 ERA, 3.13 DRA 26 IP, 14 H, 10 BB, 27 K in 5 games at High-A Tampa

The Role: OFP 60—Mid-Rotation Starter
Likely 50—No. 4 Starter/Back-end Reliever

YEAR	TEAM	LVL	AGE	W	L	SV	G	GS	IP	H	HR	BB/9	K/9	K	GB%	BABIP	WHIP	ERA	FIP	DRA	VORP	WARP	cFIP	MPH
2014	CLE	Rk	18	3	1	0	8	4	20^{2}	24	0	3.9	12.6	29	0%	.436	1.60	4.79	2.67	4.50			103	
2015	LKC	A	19	9	4	0	26	26	127^{2}	135	8	2.7	9.7	138	48%	.344	1.36	3.31	2.99	2.47	39.00	4.1	82	
2016	LYN	A+	20	7	5	0	19	19	95^{1}	91	6	3.8	8.8	93	45%	.321	1.37	3.59	3.80	2.80	28.40	2.9	93	
2016	TAM	A+	20	3	1	0	5	5	26	14	0	3.5	9.3	27	45%	.226	0.92	1.73	2.33	3.11	6.80	0.7	94	
2016	TRN	AA	20	0	0	0	1	1	4	2	0	6.8	20.2	9	57%	.286	1.25	0.00	1.11	3.20	0.80	0.1	91	
2017	*NYA*	*MLB*	*21*	*5*	*8*	*0*	*21*	*21*	*99*	*115*	*17*	*4.5*	*6.4*	*70*	*38%*	*.307*	*1.67*	*5.61*	*5.57*	*5.79*	*-3.5*	*-0.4*	*137*	
2018	*NYA*	*MLB*	*22*	*6*	*9*	*0*	*24*	*24*	142^{2}	*144*	*24*	*5.5*	*9.0*	*143*	*38%*	*.302*	*1.62*	*5.49*	*5.33*	*5.67*	*-2.6*	*-0.3*	*134*	

Breakout: 9% Improve: 10% Collapse: 1% Attrition: 5% MLB: 12% *Comparables: Jair Jurrjens, Miguel Almonte, Keyvius Sampson*

The Good: Sheffield reached Double-A in his age-20 season, even with the added hurdle of being traded mid-year, as he was part of the return for Andrew Miller. He works from a three-quarters release with a clean arm action and some effort to the delivery. The fastball sits plus and will touch 95 with bore and sink. The changeup is an average pitch at present, with above-average potential capable of generating swings and misses. He throws a slider that projects as above-average, with a broad velocity range and slurvy break.

The Bad: The control lags behind the command, so there's more feel to his offerings than consistency to throw strikes and limit walks. Both are likely to wind up being fringe-average to average in the best of cases. The offspeed offerings are almost entirely abandoned when the fastball struggles or there is pressure from runners on base.

The Irrelevant: He is not the nephew of Gary Sheffield, which apparently was a thing for a while.

The Risks: There is no clear-cut plus offering beyond the fastball, and the fastball dependency when under duress is a possible signal of the trust (or lack thereof) in the deeper arsenal. There's risk with the control/command growth. The frame is smaller—though athletic—and with some effort to the delivery, the ability to work deep into games is called into question; while only 20, he has yet to complete seven innings in his professional career.

Major League ETA: 2018 —Adam Hayes

Ben Carsley's Fantasy Take: I like Sheffield's fastball and that he's already in Double-A, but right now I don't see a long-term starter here*. I'd be ready to jump on the bandwagon at a moment's notice in case one of the secondaries starts to stand out, but my money is on Sheffield ending up as a reliever. For dynasty purposes, I prefer the next pitcher on this list.

* Publishing this sentence all but assures that Sheffield will develop into a starter. You're welcome, Yankees fans.

6. James Kaprielian, RHP

DOB: 03/02/1994

Height/Weight: 6'4" 200 lbs.

Bats/Throws: R/R

Drafted/Acquired: Drafted 16th overall in the 2015 draft, UCLA; signed for $2.65 million

Previous Ranking(s): N/A

2016 Stats: 1.50 ERA, 1.68 DRA, 18 IP, 8 H, 3 BB, 22 K in 3 games at High-A Tampa

The Role: OFP 60—No. 3 starter in the vein of Chad Billingsley
Likely 50—No.4 starter

YEAR	TEAM	LVL	AGE	W	L	SV	G	GS	IP	H	HR	BB/9	K/9	K	GB%	BABIP	WHIP	ERA	FIP	DRA	VORP	WARP	cFIP	MPH
2015	YAT	Rk	21	0	0	0	2	0	2[1]	2	0	7.7	7.7	2	86%	.286	1.71	11.57	4.16	4.32	0.30	0.0	103	
2015	STA	A-	21	0	1	0	3	3	9	8	0	2.0	12.0	12	56%	.348	1.11	2.00	1.51	2.99	2.30	0.2	85	
2016	TAM	A+	22	2	1	0	3	3	18	8	1	1.5	11.0	22	70%	.179	0.61	1.50	2.03	1.37	8.20	0.8	67	
2017	*NYA*	*MLB*	*23*	*2*	*2*	*0*	*7*	*7*	*34*	*35*	*5*	*3.7*	*7.9*	*30*	*59%*	*.301*	*1.43*	*4.60*	*4.60*	*4.77*	*2.7*	*0.3*	*111*	
2018	*NYA*	*MLB*	*24*	*8*	*9*	*0*	*29*	*29*	*177[2]*	*171*	*26*	*3.5*	*9.1*	*180*	*59%*	*.301*	*1.36*	*4.47*	*4.33*	*4.64*	*12.5*	*1.3*	*108*	

Breakout: 3% Improve: 4% Collapse: 2% Attrition: 3% MLB: 7% *Comparables: Elih Villanueva, Juan Nicasio, Zach McAllister*

The Good: Kaprielian's velocity jumped into the mid-90s in 2016. That's a pretty nice turn of events for a college arm that already got raves for his polish and three potential average-or-better secondary offerings. Kaprielian has an ideal starter's frame although...

The Bad: ...so far he has not had an ideal starter's durability. He made only three starts in Tampa this year before being shut down with elbow inflammation that was later revealed to be a flexor strain. He popped back up in the AFL with the stuff intact, but until he throws a full season in the minors, the risk factor is going to keep him lower than the pitch and command grades would suggest.

The Irrelevant: My comp is not quite as lofty as this one.

The Risks: The good news is Kaprielian didn't need surgery to repair his flexor strain, and the stuff looked as good in the fall as it did in the spring. The bad news is he lost the entire summer, and he is still a pitcher.

Major league ETA: Late 2018

Ben Carsley's Fantasy Take: I mean... Chad Billingsley was good for a while? Kaprielian could move fairly quickly if his AFL stint is any indication, but his injury history is concerning. Still, given the attrition rate of all pitching prospects, you might as well gamble on the ones with upside, and Kaprielian has plenty of it. He should flirt with a top-100 ranking as a potential SP5 who misses bats, albeit one who's still a season away and who comes with some medical red flags.

7. Aaron Judge, RF

DOB: 04/26/1992

Height/Weight: 6'7" 275 lbs.

Bats/Throws: R/R

Drafted/Acquired: Drafted 32nd overall in the 2013 draft, Fresno State University; signed for $1.8 million

Previous Ranking(s): #1 (Org.), #18 (overall)

2016 Stats: .179/.263/.345, 4 HR, 0 SB in 27 games at the major league level, .273/.369/.494, 19 HR, 5 SB in 92 games at Triple-A Scranton

The Role: OFP 55—Solid-Average Corner Outfielder
Likely 50—Second-Division Corner Outfielder

YEAR	TEAM	LVL	AGE	PA	R	2B	3B	HR	RBI	BB	K	SB	CS	AVG/OBP/SLG	TAv	VORP	BABIP	BRR	FRAA	WARP
2014	CSC	A	22	278	36	15	2	9	45	39	59	1	0	.333/.428/.530	.341	25.9	.408	-2.8	RF(55): 1.2	2.9
2014	TAM	A+	22	285	44	9	2	8	33	50	72	0	0	.283/.411/.442	.302	19.9	.377	1.8	RF(61): 7.9	2.9
2015	TRN	AA	23	280	36	16	3	12	44	24	70	1	0	.284/.350/.516	.316	23.0	.345	2.6	RF(52): 9.8	3.7
2015	SWB	AAA	23	260	27	10	0	8	28	29	74	6	2	.224/.308/.373	.247	0.8	.289	-0.2	RF(50): 8.0 • CF(8): -0.5	0.8
2016	SWB	AAA	24	410	62	18	1	19	65	47	98	5	0	.270/.366/.489	.311	31.4	.319	2.8	RF(66): 19.1 • LF(7): -0.7	4.3
2016	NYA	MLB	24	95	10	2	0	4	10	9	42	0	1	.179/.263/.345	.222	-2.5	.282	-0.5	RF(27): -3.4	-0.6
2017	*NYA*	*MLB*	*25*	*465*	*59*	*17*	*1*	*20*	*61*	*50*	*144*	*3*	*1*	*.235/.323/.434*	*.263*	*13.4*	*.306*	*-0.6*	*RF 8*	*1.8*
2018	*NYA*	*MLB*	*26*	*515*	*72*	*20*	*1*	*23*	*72*	*58*	*163*	*3*	*1*	*.237/.331/.443*	*.261*	*9.6*	*.313*	*-0.8*	*RF 8*	*1.9*

Breakout: 5% Improve: 23% Collapse: 7% Attrition: 25% MLB: 57% *Comparables: Jabari Blash, Kyle Jensen, Scott Schebler*

The Good: Judge began the year repeating Triple-A and showed across the board improvement, most notably tapping into his plus-plus raw strength. That power comes from a mature, XXL frame that should make every catcher thankful for the modern collision rules, and pronounced forearm and wrist strength. He received a mid-August promotion and enticed the Yankee fanbase with a home run to dead center in his first game. In the field, Judge profiles as an average corner outfielder with plus arm strength.

The Bad: The bat is more fringy than average. There's a lot of swing and miss to the approach, a natural tradeoff for the power output, that was exposed in his major-league trial. His speed is also fringy and likely to decline as his body ages. Defensively, there's a positional limitation to the corners given the foot speed and some occasionally questionable routes. Additionally, some health question marks surfaced as he lost a month to a knee injury and ended the season on the disabled list with an oblique strain.

The Irrelevant: That first home run was pretty pretty pretty good.

The Risks: Large human beings will have large strike zones; controlling that zone will be a perpetual question mark. The strikeout rate seen in his debut will decrease, but, with a limited hit tool and a swing-and-miss propensity, how much? His size and build are atypical for a position player and, for all the apparent strength, it's difficult to confidently project how the body will hold up to the consistent grind of a season, especially with the injury woes of this past year.

Major league ETA: Debuted in 2016 —Adam Hayes

Ben Carsley's Fantasy Take: Nothing ventured, nothing gained. There's a chance Judge's swing-and-miss precludes him from tapping into his power the way we all want him to. But there's also a chance Judge routinely challenges for 30-plus homers in Yankee Stadium. Per ESPN's Player Rater, Jay Bruce managed to finish as the 33rd-best outfielder last season by hitting .250 with 33 homers and 99 RBI. That type of production could be in play for Judge sooner rather than later, making him an easy top-25 fantasy prospect.

8. Albert Abreu, RHP

DOB: 10/26/1995

Height/Weight: 6'2" 175 lbs.

Bats/Throws: R/R

Drafted/Acquired: Signed in August 2013 by the Houston Astros out of the Dominican Republic for $185,000; acquired from the Astros for Brian McCann

Previous Ranking(s): N/A

2016 Stats: 5.40 ERA, 5.61 DRA, 11.2 IP, 12 H, 9 BB, 11 K in 3 games at High-A Lancaster, 3.50 ERA, 3.68 DRA, 90 IP, 62 H, 49 BB, 104 K in 21 games at Low-A Quad Cities

The Role: OFP 55—Mid-rotation starter who flashes more at times
Likely 45—Backend starter who...flashes more at times

YEAR	TEAM	LVL	AGE	W	L	SV	G	GS	IP	H	HR	BB/9	K/9	K	GB%	BABIP	WHIP	ERA	FIP	DRA	VORP	WARP	cFIP	MPH
2014	DAS	Rk	18	3	2	0	14	14	68	48	1	3.8	7.1	54	0%	.246	1.13	2.78	3.41	4.79			99	
2015	GRV	Rk	19	2	3	1	13	7	46^{2}	35	2	4.1	9.8	51	46%	.282	1.20	2.51	3.56	2.86	14.70	1.4	94	
2016	QUD	A	20	2	8	4	21	14	90	62	5	4.9	10.4	104	49%	.264	1.23	3.50	3.85	3.44	14.80	1.6	96	
2016	LNC	A+	20	1	0	0	3	2	11^{2}	12	2	6.9	8.5	11	41%	.312	1.80	5.40	6.37	5.74	-0.50	0.0	112	
2017	*NYA*	*MLB*	*21*	*3*	*5*	*0*	*27*	*12*	70^{2}	*79*	*12*	*6.5*	*6.4*	*50*	*33%*	*.297*	*1.83*	*6.31*	*6.24*	*6.54*	*-13.5*	*-1.4*	*154*	
2018	*NYA*	*MLB*	*22*	*4*	*7*	*0*	*25*	*17*	129^{1}	*120*	*20*	*7.4*	*10.0*	*144*	*33%*	*.298*	*1.75*	*5.77*	*5.61*	*5.98*	*-6.8*	*-0.7*	*140*	

Breakout: 2% Improve: 2% Collapse: 1% Attrition: 2% MLB: 3% *Comparables: Zach Braddock, Jose Ceda, Ethan Martin*

The Good: Another Yankees prospect with a big fastball, although this one is a very recent addition. Abreu's heater can get up into the mid-90s and it is a wormburning offering with sink and run. All the secondaries improved across 2016, the best of which is a potential plus curveball, but both the slider and change have good shots to be useful major league offerings.

The Bad: The stuff is great. The command of the stuff...well. Abreu struggles to throw strikes with his fastball and his mechanics are generally inconsistent. That is the kind of thing you can iron out, but until he does he will be a bit riskier than you'd expect from a dude with this kind of stuff.

The Irrelevant: The last offseason trade between the Yankees and Astros involved Xavier Hernandez and Andy Stankiewicz.

The Risks: Abreu's stuff is already pretty far along for a guy who has only been able to legally drink for a month. It's a major league arm and a quality one at that, but until he starts to throw more strikes, the ceiling remains lower than you'd think.

Major league ETA: 2019

Ben Carsley's Fantasy Take: On the one hand, Abreu's lack of required further projection is a positive. On the other hand, it means his command is unlikely to take a major step forward, which suggests his strikeout tendencies are likely to come with a high WHIP. There are plenty such pitchers who are still useful for our purposes—Kevin Gausman, Matt Moore, Vincent Velasquez, etc.—but they're more back-end fantasy types in 12-team leagues than rotation stalwarts. And those are top-end projections for Abreu, not his median outcome.

9. Tyler Wade, IF/OF

DOB: 11/23/1994

Height/Weight: 6'1" 185 lbs.

Bats/Throws: L/R

Drafted/Acquired: Drafted in the fourth round of the 2013 draft, Murrieta Valley HS (Murrieta, CA); signed for $371,300

Previous Ranking(s): N/A

2016 Stats: .259/.352/.349, 5 HR, 27 SB in 133 games at Double-A Trenton

The Role: OFP 55—A nifty starting 2B or CF, or even both
Likely 45—A good utility player/second-division starter

YEAR	TEAM	LVL	AGE	PA	R	2B	3B	HR	RBI	BB	K	SB	CS	AVG/OBP/SLG	TAv	VORP	BABIP	BRR	FRAA	WARP
2014	CSC	A	19	576	77	24	6	1	51	57	118	22	13	.272/.350/.349	.260	21.6	.349	1.3	SS(94): 5.7 • 2B(15): -1.1	2.7
2015	TAM	A+	20	418	51	11	5	2	28	39	65	31	15	.280/.349/.353	.274	23.1	.331	2.3	SS(72): 5.8 • 2B(24): -0.9	3.0
2015	TRN	AA	20	117	6	4	0	1	3	2	24	2	1	.204/.224/.265	.198	-2.6	.250	0.3	SS(28): -1.3	-0.4
2016	TRN	AA	21	583	90	16	7	5	27	66	103	27	8	.259/.352/.349	.271	37.6	.317	11.0	SS(91): -6.0 • 2B(38): -0.1	3.4
2017	*NYA*	*MLB*	*22*	*250*	*30*	*8*	*2*	*5*	*22*	*21*	*61*	*7*	*3*	*.233/.302/.353*	*.225*	*2.0*	*.292*	*0.4*	*SS -0 • 2B -0*	*0.1*
2018	*NYA*	*MLB*	*23*	*405*	*46*	*13*	*3*	*9*	*42*	*34*	*98*	*12*	*5*	*.236/.305/.363*	*.231*	*2.6*	*.293*	*1.2*	*SS -1 • 2B -1*	*0.1*

Breakout: 6% Improve: 18% Collapse: 6% Attrition: 15% MLB: 26% *Comparables: Jose Pirela, Ehire Adrianza, Ivan De Jesus*

The Good: He has a very good feel for hitting, and combines it with excellent athleticism. He's a 65 runner down the line and uses it well between the bases. His infield actions are pretty good. The speed and glove could make for a fine defensive center fielder if that's the route the Yankees ultimately go. Wade is a favorite of many scouts and evaluators because of his energy, playing style, and instincts. He'll grow on you the more you see him.

The Bad: The swing isn't geared towards game power at all. That can change, and Wade's built well enough that I don't rule it out, but you have to project 20-30 power as presently constituted. His arm is more erratic than you'd want from a regular shortstop, and the Yankees have a lot of internal competition from superior defensive middle infielders, which is why he's been flirting with the outfield.

The Irrelevant: Murrieta Valley High School also claims tennis star Lindsay Davenport as an alum.

The Risks: Potential lack of an offensive carrying tool combined with a likely defensive role just short of a regular shortstop makes the role projection somewhat tricky. Sometimes, non-elite slash-and-burn types have unexpected difficulties with upper-level pitching. That hasn't happened to Wade quite yet—he's put up unusually consistent slash lines at all of his full-season stops longer than a cup of coffee—and there's probably a major-league utility future there even if it does, but he could be just a utility dude with some bat-to-ball ability and speed. The flip side of that is if something develops into a carrying tool late, watch out.

Major league ETA: Late in 2017 —Jarrett Seidler

Ben Carsley's Fantasy Take: If Wade ends up with a place to play, he could be a sneaky option for fantasy owners thanks to his speed and home ballpark. He should remain on waivers until then, unless your league rosters 200-plus prospects. Utility players can only carry so much fantasy value, even if Wade has clearer paths to value than most of them.

10. Chance Adams, RHP

DOB: 8/10/1994

Height/Weight: 6'0" 215 lbs.

Bats/Throws: R/R

Drafted/Acquired: Drafted 153rd overall in 2015 draft, Dallas Baptist; signed for $330,000

Previous Ranking(s): N/A

2016 Stats: 2.07 ERA, 2.34 DRA, 69.2 IP, 35 H, 24 BB, 71 K in 13 games at Double-A Trenton, 2.65 ERA, 1.36 DRA, 57.2 IP, 41 H, 15 BB, 73 K in 12 games at High-A Tampa

The Role: OFP 55—Mid-rotation starter/late-inning reliever
Likely 45— No. 5 starter

YEAR	TEAM	LVL	AGE	W	L	SV	G	GS	IP	H	HR	BB/9	K/9	K	GB%	BABIP	WHIP	ERA	FIP	DRA	VORP	WARP	cFIP	MPH
2015	STA	A-	20	1	0	0	4	0	9^2	5	0	2.8	12.1	13	43%	.238	0.83	0.93	1.76	3.04	2.00	0.2	86	
2015	CSC	A	20	1	1	0	5	0	11^2	7	0	3.1	12.3	16	64%	.250	0.94	3.09	1.77	2.39	3.20	0.3	84	
2015	TAM	A+	20	1	0	0	5	0	14	12	0	1.3	10.3	16	38%	.324	1.00	1.29	1.74	2.16	4.00	0.4	89	
2016	TAM	A+	21	5	0	0	12	12	57^2	41	4	2.3	11.4	73	42%	.276	0.97	2.65	2.51	1.43	25.90	2.7	70	
2016	TRN	AA	21	8	1	0	13	12	69^2	35	5	3.1	9.2	71	47%	.181	0.85	2.07	3.33	2.74	18.10	2.0	91	
2017	*NYA*	*MLB*	*22*	*1*	*1*	*0*	*14*	*0*	*15*	*14*	*2*	*4.0*	*8.2*	*14*	*39%*	*.285*	*1.30*	*4.29*	*4.61*	*4.38*	*1.1*	*0.1*	*100*	
2018	*NYA*	*MLB*	*23*	*3*	*4*	*0*	*18*	*10*	80^2	*66*	*12*	*5.8*	*10.6*	*95*	*39%*	*.277*	*1.47*	*5.07*	*4.92*	*5.25*	*1.0*	*0.1*	*125*	

Breakout: 18% Improve: 35% Collapse: 9% Attrition: 20% MLB: 49% *Comparables: Johnny Cueto, Hector Rondon, Zach Davies*

The Good: Used exclusively as a reliever in college, Adams first full season saw him transition to the starting rotation where he experienced success, primarily due to advanced control of his fastball and slider. Both pitches grade out as plus, with his slider having plus depth and sharp movement in the zone. His curveball and changeup have improved to the point that they now project as average offerings, giving hitters more to worry about. Adams has a simple, repeatable delivery with a quick, compact arm action.

The Bad: He lacks remaining projection with his body and doesn't have prototypical size for a rotation stalwart. After throwing 94 innings between college and the pros in 2015, Adams jumped to 162 ⅔ in 2016. He still needs to prove he has the durability to repeat as a starting pitcher from year to year. His changeup, while flashing average, has been inconsistent for him and could create problems for him against left-handed hitters.

The Irrelevant: Adams' Chaparral High School (AZ) won back-to-back state titles in 2011 and 2012.

The Risks: He is still a pitcher and has shown some struggles against lefties. He needs to prove he has the durability, especially given the jump in innings pitched. It is more control over command at present, which could lead to a lot of hard contact.

Major league ETA: Late 2017 —Steve Givarz

Ben Carsley's Fantasy Take: Adams is close to the majors, which is in his favor, but his modest ceiling and the probability that he's a back-end arm limit his fantasy usefulness. There's a good ... well ... chance you can still get Adams as a value buy thanks to his pop-up prospect nature, but don't bank on him to be a real difference-maker.

OTHERS OF NOTE:

The lottery ticket

Miguel Andujar, 3B

An entertaining but currently flawed prospect. He's got some real standout abilities—a quick bat, above-average raw power, excellent arm strength—combined with some real rough edges to his game. He'll push what he has to the absolute limit at all times, so on one play he'll make a standout grab followed by a strong throw at the hot corner, only to airmail first base on the next routine grounder. He swings at far too much, but his plate coverage and wrists are good enough that, despite the subpar approach, he wasn't overmatched by Double-A pitching. There's been enough development in Andujar's game since he jumped to full-season ball to hope that the rest smoothes out some more, and he likely has more upside than some of the hitters listed ahead of him. If nothing else, he's a walking highlight reel complete with enthusiasm and hustle, and being a fun player to watch is something too. —Jarrett Seidler

The Yankees have ten of these dudes so we picked one

Jordan Montgomery, LHP

The Yankees plucked Montgomery out of the University of South Carolina in the fourth round of the 2014 draft. Since then, he's dealt. This big left-hander throws from a Josh Collmenter-esque release point, creating a heavy downward angle for all his offerings. The fastball works in the low 90s with very slight side-to-side movement. The changeup and curveball both show average to a tick above, with the former being the better of the two. He also throws a workable fringy slider. All told, this is a strike-thrower working from a hard-to-read angle with major-league value. —Adam Hayes

The tough luck prospect

Dustin Fowler, OF

Fowler was a top-five prospect in an admittedly not quite as good system last year. But he didn't negatively impact his prospect status, hitting .281/.311/.458 in Double-A as a 21-year-old, a bit of an improvement over his A-ball line last year. The added pop was nice, especially if Fowler ends up playing more around the grass as a fourth outfielder. There's still a chance for a major league regular profile here. Fowler can hit a bit and run a bit as well, though his approach will always be on the aggressive side. A .280, 10-homer type with some speed may not be good enough to crack first-division starter status, but he'd still be a top-five prospect in the Orioles and Marlins systems. Just not this one.

The out-of-luck prospect

Billy McKinney, OF

Fowler's drop wasn't as precipitous as McKinney's. A top 101 prospect reduced to role 4 status, and a tough role 4 at that, given he is a left fielder without much in the way of power. McKinney's calling card was always going to be his hit tool, and that deserted him in Double-A this year. It isn't hard to see why. The swing is too long, and he is often out of balance at the plate. The barrel control was good enough to get away with that in the lower minors, but upper level arms were able to exploit his swing. Without a plus hit tool, there just isn't much to see here.

The guys they got for Carlos Beltran

Dillon Tate, RHP & Erik Swanson, RHP

At the deadline, the Yankees rented out Carlos Beltran to the bat-needy Rangers in exchange for a trio of right-handed pitching prospects. The headliner was 2015 fourth-overall pick Dillon Tate, a high-profile name whose prospect value took a swan dive in the first half of the season. (Yankees general manager Brian Cashman called Tate an "asset in distress" upon trading for him.) Tate was way too easy to square up for a top college pick in Low-A, displaying a surprisingly flat fastball that bled velocity as games went on, average-at-best command, and little going on his previously-touted slider or change.

The Yankees made some mechanical tweaks and converted him to relief after acquiring him, and early returns have been good. Reports from late in the season and the Arizona Fall League were that his velocity has returned to the mid-to-high-90s in shorter stints, and the slider and overall deception have played back up as well. Tate could be another in a long line of Yankee power arms out of the pen if things continue to hold together, although given his name and draft slot, it's going to be tempting to take another shot at him in a rotation.

The second prospect was an interesting pop-up arm, 2014 eighth-rounder Erik Swanson. Swanson was pretty far off the radar coming into the 2016 season as a junior college reliever who missed most of 2015 with elbow and forearm injuries. Used as a starter by the Rangers in Low-A, Swanson touched as high as 98 in a June viewing, regularly sitting 91-96. He also flashed a hard slider and a more usable change than one often sees from a power profile at the Low-A level. He's got a big frame and it's pretty easy heat, so Swanson should be more likely to work out in a rotation long-term than Tate at this point, and also has a relief fallback. (The third prospect in the deal, Nick Green, is another low-level arm of some note. The Yankees did quite well in the Beltran deal.)

—Jarrett Seidler

TOP 10 TALENTS 25 AND UNDER (BORN 4/1/91 OR LATER)

1. Gary Sanchez	6. Greg Bird
2. Gleyber Torres	7. Justus Sheffield
3. Clint Frazier	8. James Kaprielian
4. Jorge Mateo	9. Aaron Judge
5. Blake Rutherford	10. Luis Severino

Despite braving 2016 without a single player from last year's list graduating, this edition of the Yankees' 25-and-under list looks remarkably different. And that's a good thing. For the first time in a long while, the Bombers were sellers rather than buyers on the trade market, with General Manager Brian Cashman making the franchise-altering decision to steer the Yankees into a rebuild at last year's deadline.

Cashman kicked things off by first flipping free-agent-to-be Aroldis Chapman to the Cubs for prospects Gleyber Torres, Billy McKinney, and Rashad Crawford (plus reliever Adam Warren). Then he dealt Andrew Miller to Cleveland for Clint Frazier, Justus Sheffield, Ben Heller, and J.P. Feyereisen. And to cap off the fire-sale, he sent Carlos Beltran to the Rangers for Dillon Tate, Erik Swanson, and Nick Green. The Yankees GM took an already impressive farm system, gifted it with multiple new top prospects, and like a phoenix from the ashes allowed a bright future to rise from an incredibly disappointing season. Very soon, the Yankees may be one of the most exciting teams in baseball, and I don't say this just because of a potential "Judge and Justus" pairing.

Heading this year's 25U list is Gary Sanchez, who you may have heard about once or twice this summer. After experiencing a severe case of prospect fatigue and being unfortunately tabbed as The Next Jesus MonteroTM during seven long years in the Yankees' minor leagues, Sanchez hit his way to the big leagues and went on nothing short of an historic run. The Kraken, whom the Yankees finally "released" on opposing pitchers, reached 20 home runs faster than any player since 1930 and capped off a Rookie of the Year-worthy campaign with a .332 TAv and .299/.376/.657 slash line. He also finished with a 2.75 WARP over just 53 games. On defense, Sanchez was average with the glove but threw out 13 runners in 32 attempts with his plus-plus throwing arm. That helped alleviate concerns over his defensive position for the foreseeable future.

Three of the four players on this list following Sanchez are new to the organization—Torres and Frazier via trade, and Rutherford after being taken 18th overall in the draft. It's a testament to just how impactful the trade deadline (and draft) was for the Yankees. The next big-league player is Greg Bird, though he didn't touch the field in 2016 after offseason surgery to repair a torn labrum. Missing the year certainly hurt Bird's standing on this list, but his major-league debut left a lasting impression and gives hope for his 2017.

Hitting .261/.343/.529 in 2015 with a .312 TAv and 11 home runs in 46 games, Bird wasn't quite Gary Sanchez, but it's tough to argue with that kind of production from a then-22-year-old playing through a tear in his labrum. Still, Bird may have less value than most Yankee fans care to admit. His defensive home is limited to first base (injuries as an amateur moved him out from behind the plate) where he's average at best, and he could have issues finding his swing mechanics again after a year off. Regardless, the offensive upside is strong enough to carry him as a first-division regular—he just won't be the star many hoped for after 2015.

Rounding out the bottom of the list are two players who disappointed with the big-league club in 2016: Aaron Judge and Luis Severino. Judge's 44.2 percent strikeout rate will give any evaluator pause, but the 6-foot-7 behemoth has taken time to adjust to new levels in the past and was impressive in Triple-A before his promotion to the show in August. While the risk is higher now than it was before Judge's big-league debut, his upside largely (no pun intended) remains intact and there's little reason to panic just yet.

Panicking about Luis Severino is a bit more understandable, though. The Yankees hoped to have a top of the rotation starter after an electric debut in 2015, but the league figured Severino out last season and the results weren't pretty. The righty's command was fringy at best and his changeup took a step back, allowing opposing batters to sit on the fastball and pummel the secondary pitches hung over the heart of the strike zone. Severino's 5.83 ERA and 4.49 DRA were horrendous, and after a scary arm injury in May, he was banished to Triple-A for two months.

But, there is hope for Severino. The 22-year-old was one of the youngest arms in baseball in his second season (only Julio Urias and Zach Eflin are younger), and his nasty fastball and slider remained intact, as evidenced by a 0.39 ERA and .105 BAA out of the bullpen (after shelving his changeup). If Severino can work the changeup back into his repertoire and refine his command, there's a chance he can look like the pitcher who posted a 2.89 ERA in his rookie season. However, next season could be Severino's last chance at starting, as continued struggles might cause the Yankees to push him to the bullpen full-time where he could be a multi-inning weapon.

—Ben Diamond

OAKLAND ATHLETICS

The State of the System: *The Athletics better hope that there is such a thing as a pitching prospect, because their revitalized system is loaded with them.*

THE TOP TEN

1. SS Franklin Barreto	6. RHP Jharel Cotton
2. RHP Grant Holmes	7. RHP Daulton Jefferies
3. LHP A.J. Puk	8. RHP Daniel Gossett
4. RHP Frankie Montas	9. RHP Dakota Chalmers
5. 3B Matt Chapman	10. RHP Logan Shore

The Big Question: Do the Athletics have a star in their system?

Since Oakland's surprising midseason acquisition spree and subsequent collapse in 2014, the Athletics have been in a holding pattern. That winter, Billy Beane determined that his team's core wasn't strong enough to gear up for another playoff run, and he dealt Josh Donaldson and Jeff Samardzija to contenders. At a glance, the moves seemed to signal Oakland's intention to rebuild. Curiously though, the return packages in both trades were headlined by a big leaguer, not a top prospect. Beane explained his strategy when he discussed his decision to move Donaldson, saying "we wouldn't have done the deal unless it addressed now and the future."

Now and the future. It's a clear statement of purpose, but an odd one in today's game. In an era where most teams clearly define themselves as contenders or rebuilders, Beane chose to straddle the line. The Donaldson and Samardzija trades retrieved Brett Lawrie and Marcus Semien, neither of whom qualified as a rookie, along with a few low-ceiling but big-league ready prospects in Kendall Graveman and Chris Bassitt. These moves kept the Athletics competitive: While Oakland hasn't contended over the past two years, the A's never approached 100 losses nor looked like a team tanking for draft picks.

The troubling side effect is that the A's never received the shot of impact talent their fire sale warranted. From Houston to Atlanta to both sides of Chicago, clubs around the league have exchanged their stars and valuable contributors for bright young players while punting big league wins in an effort to collect top draft picks; the A's, meanwhile, signed Billy Butler and Ryan Madson to solidify their roster.

To be fair, the Donaldson trade did net Franklin Barreto, an enticing prospect who was a bit too young for the national radar back in 2014. And the A's may have made the unsung trade of last year's deadline when they turned two months of Rich Hill and Josh Reddick into Grant Holmes, Frankie Montas and Jharel Cotton. Those four, along with last year's first round pick, A.J. Puk, account for five of Oakland's top six names on our list.

But to rebuild successfully, especially for a shoestring-payroll team like the Athletics, you have to get stars. By trading Donaldson for quarters on the dollar and fielding a mediocre-but-not-terrible big league team, the A's have missed a chance to add a Yoan Moncada or Lucas Giolito-type player to their organization while also limiting their bonus pool money in the draft. While Oakland's farm system is much deeper than it was two years ago, it remains noticeably light on blue chippers. A quick review—skip to the profiles for the nuance—of the top names on the list reveals that most of their top farmhands are high-floor players with limited ceilings.

Holmes has a starter's build, a strong arm, and a deep repertoire, but his command backtracked last season and he looks like more of a mid-rotation starter than a future ace. Montas throws a million miles per hour but he missed almost all of last season, and some evaluators think his stuff will play better in relief. Cotton has reached the big leagues and he'll get outs with a devastating changeup, but he too has a mid-rotation ceiling. Matt Chapman is a glove-first third baseman with some pop; a nice player, but he's Matt Dominguez if the bat falls short. Puk's raw stuff breaks the mold—the southpaw has the highest ceiling among pitchers on this list—but amidst concerns about his athleticism and stiffness in his delivery, some evaluators have cooled on his long-term outlook.

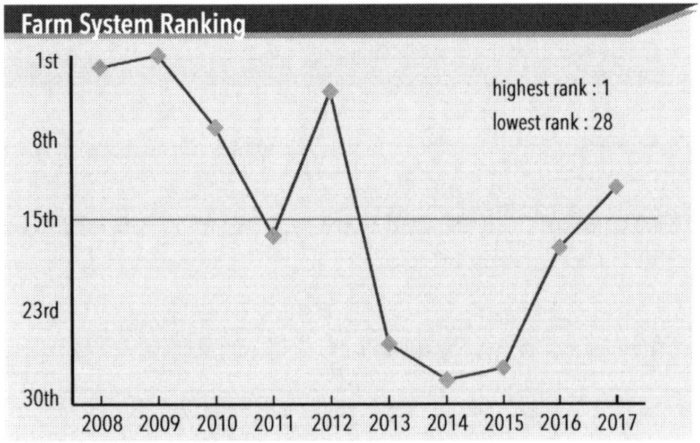

Personnel

EVP, Baseball Operations:
Billy Beane

General Manager:
David Forst

Assistant General Manager:
Dan Kantrovitz

Assistant General Manager:
Billy Owens

Manager:
Bob Melvin

BP Alumni:
Al Skorupa

That leaves Barreto. The jewel of the system, Barreto more than held his own as a 20-year-old in Double A, hitting .281/.340/.414 last season. He's very mature physically for his age and the chances that he's a 60 hit, 50 power player (or a tick better) in the middle of the diamond only increased over the last year. He's going to be a good player for a very long time.

But is he a star to build a team around? It's an open question, and both his youth and feel for hitting against tough competition thus far in his career suggest he could play in his share of All-Star games down the line. The safer bet though is that he's more of a first-division regular than a star; nothing to sneeze at, of course, but that projection makes him more like the best version of the good-not-great types loitering throughout Oakland's system than the next great shortstop in baseball. In short, the A's are stuck right now. Led by Barreto, the A's farm system is good enough to help Oakland continue on its current course, but lacks the upside to change the balance of power in the division. That's a problem for an organization that either can't or won't augment its roster through free agency.

In the next year, Oakland could still get its star: The A's pick sixth in this year's draft and they can still expect a windfall in return for (a healthy) Sonny Gray. If everything goes well, the A's may have one of the best systems in baseball this time next year. But if Gray stays, or if the return package is underwhelming, or if they play it safe in the draft, the farm will likely continue to look as it does for the foreseeable future: strong, but unlikely to bear enough fruit to compete with Houston and Texas for divisional supremacy.

—Brendan Gawlowski

1. Franklin Barreto, SS

DOB: 2/27/1996

Height/Weight: 5'10" 190 lbs.

Bats/Throws: R/R

Drafted/Acquired: Signed July 2012 by Toronto Blue Jays out of Venezuela for $1.45 million; acquired from Blue Jays for Josh Donaldson

Previous Ranking(s): #1 (Org.) #26 (overall)

2016 Stats: .281/.340/.414, 10 HR, 30 SB in 119 games at Double-A Midland, .353/.389/.647 with 1 HR in four games at Triple-A Nashville

The Role: OFP 60—First division shortstop
Likely 55—Above-average regular at shortstop

YEAR	TEAM	LVL	AGE	PA	R	2B	3B	HR	RBI	BB	K	SB	CS	AVG/OBP/SLG	TAv	VORP	BABIP	BRR	FRAA	WARP
2014	VAN	A-	18	328	65	23	4	6	61	26	64	29	5	.311/.384/.481	.314	34.1	.378	2.9	SS(68): -4.5	3.1
2015	STO	A+	19	364	50	22	3	13	47	15	67	8	3	.302/.333/.500	.318	35.7	.337	0.6	SS(86): -14.6	2.3
2016	MID	AA	20	507	63	25	3	10	50	36	90	30	15	.281/.340/.413	.274	27.5	.330	3.1	SS(81): -11.1 • 2B(33): -2.9	1.4
2016	NAS	AAA	20	18	2	0	1	1	3	0	4	0	2	.353/.389/.647	.403	3.4	.417	0.0	SS(4): -0.2	0.3
2017	*OAK*	*MLB*	*21*	*250*	*32*	*11*	*1*	*6*	*24*	*12*	*57*	*9*	*4*	*.249/.292/.392*	*.243*	*6.7*	*.299*	*0.1*	*SS -4 • 2B -1*	*0.2*
2018	*OAK*	*MLB*	*22*	*414*	*47*	*19*	*2*	*11*	*48*	*22*	*91*	*15*	*8*	*.255/.301/.407*	*.254*	*12.3*	*.303*	*1.0*	*SS -7 • 2B -2*	*0.4*

Breakout: 7% Improve: 18% Collapse: 4% Attrition: 16% MLB: 35% *Comparables: Alen Hanson, Addison Russell, Nick Franklin*

The Good: Barreto could have a six hit tool and four other tools that grade average or better at full maturity. He has a quick bat and a good feel for the barrel; his swing is conducive to hitting the ball hard to all fields and he's strong enough to project at least average power down the line. An above-average runner, he's quick enough to be a threat on the bases and has enough lateral range to handle short. Barreto has also worked in at center field and second and should be a defensive asset if he ever has to move off short.

The Bad: Barreto doesn't have any glaring weaknesses in his game, though a few minor flaws could put a small dent in his overall projection. He's not a hacker, but he's aggressive and will need to hit for average to post a good OBP. Physically, he's filling out quickly: He's not as fast as he was two years ago and more growth could push him to second base. His arm plays at short but isn't strong for the position.

The Irrelevant: As he's climbed the minor league ladder, Barreto was the third-youngest everyday player in the Northwest League, California League and Texas League.

The Risks: Barreto's bat is ahead of his glove and while he's improved defensively, he's not a lock to stay at shortstop. Like any player with an average power projection or less, the profile dampens considerably if his hit tool falls short of projections. —Brendan Gawlowski

Major league ETA: Late 2017

Ben Carsley's Fantasy Take: I've been encouraging fantasy owners to buy on Barreto for years. I'm a big believer in his bat, and while I understand he's not a lock at short the reports are slightly more positive than they used to be, and it's not like his value falls off a cliff if he moves to second. The only distressing aspect of the report above is how quickly Barreto is filling out, portending good-but-not-great stolen base totals. Still, I think Barreto can be something like 2016 Jose Ramirez, hitting for a good average with double-digit homers and 20-plus steals. That's makes him a very valuable player as long as he comes with MI eligibility.

2. Grant Holmes, RHP

DOB: 03/22/1996

Height/Weight: 6'1" 215 lbs.

Bats/Throws: L/R

Drafted/Acquired: Drafted 22nd overall by Los Angeles in the 2015 MLB Draft, Conway HS (Conway, SC); signed for $2.5 million; acquired from Dodgers in the Rich Hill deal

Previous Ranking(s): #4 (Org), #40 (Overall)

2016 Stats: 4.02 ERA, 4.32 DRA, 105.1 IP, 103 H, 43 BB, 100 K at High-A Rancho Cucamonga, 6.91 ERA, 4.24 DRA, 28.2 IP, 44 H, 10 BB, 24 K at High-A Stockton

The Role: OFP 60 – No. 3 Starter
Likely 55 – Low No. 3 Starter

YEAR	TEAM	LVL	AGE	W	L	SV	G	GS	IP	H	HR	BB/9	K/9	K	GB%	BABIP	WHIP	ERA	FIP	DRA	VORP	WARP	cFIP	MPH
2014	DOD	Rk	18	1	2	0	7	6	30	20	2	2.1	9.9	33	0%	.243	0.90	3.00	3.60	2.56			83	
2014	OGD	Rk	18	1	1	0	4	4	18^{1}	19	1	2.9	12.3	25	0%	.400	1.36	4.91	3.16	1.48			68	
2015	GRL	A	19	6	4	0	24	24	103^{1}	86	6	4.7	10.2	117	44%	.307	1.35	3.14	3.48	3.26	22.50	2.4	97	
2016	RCU	A+	20	8	4	1	20	18	105^{1}	103	6	3.7	8.5	100	53%	.316	1.39	4.02	3.84	3.00	28.40	2.9	93	
2016	STO	A+	20	3	3	0	6	5	28^{2}	44	4	3.1	7.5	24	60%	.408	1.88	6.91	5.00	3.08	7.50	0.8	93	
2017	*OAK*	*MLB*	*21*	*6*	*8*	*0*	*22*	*22*	105^{2}	*122*	*13*	*4.8*	*5.4*	*64*	*44%*	*.307*	*1.69*	*5.27*	*5.21*	*5.87*	*-4.7*	*-0.5*	*139*	
2018	*OAK*	*MLB*	*22*	*5*	*7*	*0*	*20*	*20*	120^{2}	*119*	*14*	*6.1*	*8.5*	*114*	*44%*	*.306*	*1.66*	*4.70*	*4.96*	*5.24*	*2.5*	*0.3*	*124*	

Breakout: 15% Improve: 16% Collapse: 2% Attrition: 17% MLB: 20% *Comparables: Randall Delgado, Patrick Corbin, Giovanni Soto*

The Good: Holmes' arsenal is built on a couple solid bedrocks in a fastball that can touch 96 and a plus curveball that he deploys with maturity. His four-seamer generates some run and life, and he'll attack the hands with it to generate whiffs and weak contact. He can work in two-seam and cutting variants as well. The curve toggles from 79 to 85, with multiple shapes that feature quality depth and bite. He boasts a frame to wear innings on, and he made strides to address consistency issues in his delivery.

The Bad: There's still a ways to go for Holmes to develop his pitch-to-pitch consistency. He decelerates at the top of his fulcrum, leading to timing issues that can creep up and throw him offline through his drive for stretches. And while his foot strike showed improvement as the season progressed, he'll still land roughly on his heel too often to negatively impact his command. The changeup will flash average, but it is an inconsistent and firm pitch that lags developmentally.

The Irrelevant: The deal that sent Holmes from the Dodgers to Oakland occurred exactly 3,883 days after the Dodgers shipped Milton Bradley to the A's back in 2005 for reigning Texas League Player of the Year Andre Ethier.

The Risks: Holmes spent this past year as one of the youngest pitchers in the California League, and there remains significant development ahead of him. He's a couple inches shorter than the Platonic Ideal of a right-handed pitching prospect, but otherwise he pretty much checks all the boxes to develop into a relatively high-probability, mid-rotation starter. He would merit a high-probability tag, anyway, if he weren't, you know, a pitcher. —Wilson Karaman

Major league ETA: 2018

Ben Carsley's Fantasy Take: Now might be a good time to buy lowish on Holmes. His numbers from the Cal League don't look great, but he was young for the level and, well, it's the Cal League. There's no fantasy ace upside here, but Holmes looks like a good bet to stay in the rotation. I'd like to see him miss more bats, but it's easy to envision him as a no. 5/6 fantasy starter in Oakland, posting a 3.50-3.75 ERA and 180 strikeouts in 200 innings. Part of the appeal with Holmes is that he might be able to surpass 200 innings regularly, though, making him a good compiler unless your league has an IP cap.

3. A.J. Puk, LHP

DOB: 04/25/95

Height/Weight: 6'7" 220 lbs

Bats/Throws: L/L

Drafted/Acquired: Drafted sixth overall in the 2016 MLB draft, University of Florida (Gainesville, FA); signed for $4,069,200

Previous Ranking(s): N/A

2016 Stats: 3.03 ERA, 2.08 DRA, 32.2 IP, 23 H, 12 BB, 40 K at short-season Vermont

The Role: OFP 60—No. 3 starter
Likely 50—No.4 starter

YEAR	TEAM	LVL	AGE	W	L	SV	G	GS	IP	H	HR	BB/9	K/9	K	GB%	BABIP	WHIP	ERA	FIP	DRA	VORP	WARP	cFIP	MPH
2016	VER	A-	21	0	4	0	10	10	32²	23	0	3.3	11.0	40	51%	.271	1.07	3.03	1.92	2.12	11.30	1.2	80	
2017	*OAK*	*MLB*	*22*	*2*	*3*	*0*	*8*	*8*	*33*	*36*	*5*	*4.5*	*7.1*	*26*	*35%*	*.306*	*1.58*	*5.04*	*5.15*	*5.57*	*-0.4*	*0.0*	*133*	
2018	*OAK*	*MLB*	*23*	*6*	*8*	*0*	*29*	*29*	*179¹*	*172*	*23*	*4.2*	*8.3*	*166*	*35%*	*.294*	*1.42*	*4.30*	*4.51*	*4.75*	*9.1*	*0.9*	*113*	

Breakout: 3% Improve: 3% Collapse: 1% Attrition: 2% MLB: 4% *Comparables: Patrick Light, Tyler Wilson, Andrew Heaney*

The Good: Puk is a towering lefty with a fastball that sits in the mid-90s and can touch 98. The pitch has good armside life and Puk can spot it to either side of the plate. It's a swing-and-miss weapon up in the zone. For a tall, lanky southpaw, he already has a pretty good handle on his mechanics. The slider is a potential plus offering as well. He can get it up into the mid-80s and the pitch is difficult to pick up out of his hand even before it shows you its late, two-plane break.

The Bad: The combination of size and stuff—plus a fair amount of polish—makes Puk a potentially elite pitching prospect. Why isn't he quite there yet? Well, as good as the stuff is, it doesn't always show up. He throws strikes, but the command profile still needs refinement. He dealt with a back injury this year that might raise an eyebrow or two among more cautious evaluators until he shows you 120-plus innings in a pro season. The change-up is a potential plus pitch as well, but is mostly arm speed and deception at present.

The Irrelevant: Puk started 12 games at first base for the Gators in 2015.

The Risks: Puk is a big lefty with a big fastball. That mitigates things like the back issue, the inconsistent-at-times stuff, and the lack of a professional track record. A healthy Puk that better harnesses his stuff with a full pro spring could move quite quickly, and that OFP may look low in a year's time. That hasn't happened yet though, and Puk is—after all—still a pitcher.

Major league ETA: Late 2018

Ben Carsley's Fantasy Take: Puk might have a mid-rotation starter tag, but he also comes with considerable strikeout upside if his stuff shows up more often. He's one of the 10 best fantasy prospects from the last draft thanks in part to his landing spot in Oakland, and as mentioned above there's a chance he moves quickly. Essentially, if you want to get in on a guy before he has the "elite fantasy pitching prospect" tag, Puk's a good choice. There's just a chance he never gets there, of course.

4. Frankie Montas, RHP

DOB: 03/21/1993

Height/Weight: 6'2" 225 lbs.

Bats/Throws: R/R

Drafted/Acquired: Signed by Boston out of the Dominican Republic for $75,000 in December 2009; acquired from Dodgers in the Rich Hill Deal

Previous Ranking(s): #5 (Org)

2016 Stats: 2.38 ERA, 2.17 DRA, 11.1 IP, 12 H, 2 BB, 15 K at Triple-A Oklahoma City

The Role: OFP 60—Major league closer
Likely 50—Major league set-up man

YEAR	TEAM	LVL	AGE	W	L	SV	G	GS	IP	H	HR	BB/9	K/9	K	GB%	BABIP	WHIP	ERA	FIP	DRA	VORP	WARP	cFIP	MPH
2014	WNS	A+	21	4	0	0	10	10	62	45	2	2.0	8.1	56	54%	.256	0.95	1.60	2.90	2.09	24.10	2.4	81	
2014	WSX	Rk	21	1	0	0	4	4	14	6	1	4.5	14.8	23	0%	.217	0.93	1.29	3.17	2.23			79	
2014	BIR	AA	21	0	0	0	1	1	5	1	0	1.8	1.8	1	47%	.067	0.40	0.00	3.39	5.68	-0.30	0.0	109	
2015	BIR	AA	22	5	5	0	23	23	112	89	3	3.9	8.7	108	43%	.282	1.22	2.97	3.03	4.30	9.90	1.1	91	
2015	CHA	MLB	22	0	2	0	7	2	15	14	1	5.4	12.0	20	38%	.361	1.53	4.80	3.10	3.71	2.00	0.2	96	99.8
2016	TUL	AA	23	0	0	0	3	1	4^2	2	1	1.9	13.5	7	56%	.125	0.64	1.93	3.61	3.11	0.90	0.1	86	
2016	OKL	AAA	23	0	0	0	4	3	11^1	12	0	1.6	11.9	15	63%	.400	1.24	2.38	1.60	3.17	2.70	0.3	87	
2017	*OAK*	*MLB*	*24*	*2*	*2*	*0*	*30*	*3*	*43*	*40*	*4*	*3.7*	*7.5*	*36*	*42%*	*.291*	*1.34*	*4.07*	*4.02*	*4.49*	*2.9*	*0.3*	*100*	
2018	*OAK*	*MLB*	*25*	*4*	*3*	*0*	*58*	*5*	85^2	*67*	*8*	*4.9*	*10.0*	*95*	*42%*	*.276*	*1.33*	*3.67*	*3.88*	*4.21*	*8.6*	*0.9*	*92*	

Breakout: 20% Improve: 35% Collapse: 15% Attrition: 29% MLB: 55% *Comparables: Sean Nolin, Felix Doubront, Jeurys Familia*

The Good: We've written it before, and we will write it again: There are worse places to start as a pitching prospect than with a triple-digit fastball. Montas has a lightning-fast arm that lights up radar guns, and the delivery isn't as high effort as you'd expect from a dude regularly hitting 100. Montas pairs the blast-furnace heater with a power slider that can get into the 90s. At its best it is a plus pitch with hard, late tilt.

The Bad: Montas threw only 11 innings in-season this year due to a rib injury. The change is a non-factor. Between that and his command issues—the delivery does have some effort—Montas is a reliever all the way. The fastball can flatten out in the triple digits. The slider needs more consistency to be a true major-league bat misser.

The Irrelevant: Montas' first pitch in the majors was a 98 mph fastball. You can't even suggest he was amped up, since he averaged 97 in his 2015 cup of coffee with the White Sox.

The Risks: Montas already has pitched in the majors and has the two-pitch combo to be immediately successful in 2017 in a late-inning role. Without a bit more command, he could end up a frustrating eighth-inning type though. Montas has missed time with the aforementioned rib issue and a knee injury in 2014. No arm issues recently, but he is a pitcher after all.

Major league ETA: Debuted in 2015

Ben Carsley's Fantasy Take: Montas might be the best fantasy reliever prospect, but that's not really a desirable distinction. Montas can rack up the strikeouts, but if he's not closing he's not worth your time. There are enough good arms in Oakland's bullpen ahead of Montas that he's unlikely to be of much use for us this year, though to be fair we all know how quickly bullpens can change.

5. Matt Chapman, 3B

DOB: 04/28/1993

Height/Weight: 6'2" 205 lbs.

Bats/Throws: R/R

Drafted/Acquired: Drafted 25th overall in the 2014 MLB Draft, Cal-State Fullerton, signed for $1.75 million

Previous Ranking(s): #6 (Org)

2016 Stats: .197/.282/.513, 7 HR, 0 SB at Triple-A Nashville, .244/.335/.521, 29 HR, 7 SB in 117 games at Double-A Midland

The Role: OFP 55—Above-Average Third Baseman
Likely 50—Solid Regular

YEAR	TEAM	LVL	AGE	PA	R	2B	3B	HR	RBI	BB	K	SB	CS	AVG/OBP/SLG	TAv	VORP	BABIP	BRR	FRAA	WARP
2014	ATH	Rk	21	15	1	1	1	0	0	1	1	0	0	.429/.467/.643	.490	1.5	.462	0.0		0.1
2014	BLT	A	21	202	22	8	3	5	20	7	46	2	1	.237/.282/.389	.221	-0.8	.288	0.4	3B(21): 2.4	0.2
2014	MID	AA	21	3	0	0	0	0	0	0	0	0	0	.000/.000/.000	.007	-0.7	.000	0.0	3B(1): 0.2	-0.1
2015	STO	A+	22	352	60	21	3	23	57	39	79	4	1	.250/.341/.566	.335	37.5	.257	0.6	3B(77): 11.2	5.3
2016	MID	AA	23	504	78	26	4	29	83	59	147	7	4	.244/.335/.521	.297	35.4	.293	1.8	3B(100): 14.5 • SS(10): 3.6	5.8
2016	NAS	AAA	23	85	14	1	1	7	13	9	26	0	0	.197/.282/.513	.302	6.7	.186	0.2	3B(18): 2.0	0.9
2017	*OAK*	*MLB*	*24*	*250*	*31*	*10*	*1*	*13*	*38*	*23*	*77*	*1*	*1*	*.218/.294/.451*	*.258*	*7.2*	*.262*	*-0.2*	*3B 6 • SS 0*	*1.5*
2018	*OAK*	*MLB*	*25*	*315*	*43*	*12*	*2*	*17*	*47*	*30*	*99*	*2*	*1*	*.213/.292/.446*	*.259*	*6.7*	*.257*	*-0.3*	*3B 8 • SS 0*	*1.6*

Breakout: 4% Improve: 20% Collapse: 18% Attrition: 27% MLB: 48% *Comparables: Mike Olt, Chris Carter, Pedro Alvarez*

The Good: Chapman is one of the better third basemen in the minor leagues, with a defensive package highlighted by a canon of an arm that rates at least a 70. His quick feet and strong instincts drive above-average lateral range, and his receiving is true thanks to soft hands and solid body control. His raw power pushes plus-plus, and he has demonstrated the ability to bring it into games against high-minors pitching. He's a patient hitter who runs deep counts and takes his walks, and his OBP can play above his raw hit tool.

The Bad: The swing generates a ton of extension but retains a good amount of length even after a launch position overhaul during the 2015 season. Couple the mechanics with his patient approach, and he's always likely to run high strikeout totals that threaten to devolve into obscenity. There's also some rigidity in the swing that leaves him frequently underneath pitches, and between the whiffs and weaker fly ball contact the hit tool may have to stretch to a 40. He's a fringe-average runner with effort in the stride, and his body is not one that will get any faster.

The Irrelevant: Chapman was born in Victorville, CA, where Herman Mankiewicz and John Houseman wrote the screenplay for Citizen Kane in 1940. The city also produced a second-rounder in last year's draft, when the Padres selected prep right-hander Reggie Lawson 71st overall.

The Risks: The defensive profile and power potential moderates his risk and portends a big league role, though questions about his contact rates and hit tool leave some variability in the range of outcomes. —Wilson Karaman

Major league ETA: 2017

Ben Carsley's Fantasy Take: Chapman is going to have to mash if he's going to mean anything to fantasy owners, and Oakland is not the easiest place to do so. His ETA, third base eligibility and potential 25-homer power output are marks in his favor, but I'm skeptical the hit tool will play. He's got enough in his favor that he's a top-150 dynasty league prospect, but we're talking about a guy whose ceiling might be 2016 Miguel Sano (.236 average, 25 homers).

6. Jharel Cotton, RHP

DOB: 01/19/1992

Height/Weight: 5'11" 185 lbs.

Bats/Throws: R/R

Drafted/Acquired: Drafted in the 20th round by Los Angeles in the 2011 MLB Draft, East Carolina University (NC); signed for $1,000, acquired from Dodgers in the Rich Hill Deal

Previous Ranking(s): #10 (Org)

2016 Stats: 2.15 ERA, 4.59 DRA, 29.1 IP, 20 H, 4 BB, 23 K at the major league level, 3.41 ERA, 2.63 DRA, 38.1 IP, 28 H, 7 BB, 36 K with Triple-A Nashville, 4.90 ERA, 2.27 DRA, 97.1 IP, 80 H, 32 BB, 119 K with Triple-A Oklahoma City

The Role: OFP 55—No. 3/4 starter
Likely 45—No. 5 starter/middle relief arm

YEAR	TEAM	LVL	AGE	W	L	SV	G	GS	IP	H	HR	BB/9	K/9	K	GB%	BABIP	WHIP	ERA	FIP	DRA	VORP	WARP	cFIP	MPH
2014	RCU	A+	22	6	10	0	25	20	126^{2}	113	18	2.4	9.8	138	45%	.291	1.16	4.05	4.24	1.54	56.80	5.7	70	
2015	GRL	A	23	0	0	0	1	1	3^{1}	4	0	2.7	16.2	6	25%	.500	1.50	5.40	0.70	3.42	0.70	0.1	95	
2015	RCU	A+	23	1	0	0	4	2	22^{1}	14	1	2.8	11.3	28	30%	.265	0.94	1.61	2.79	2.46	6.00	0.6	87	
2015	TUL	AA	23	5	2	0	11	8	62^{2}	49	4	3.0	10.2	71	49%	.296	1.12	2.30	2.87	2.74	15.80	1.7	74	
2015	OKL	AAA	23	0	0	0	5	0	7^{1}	9	0	2.5	11.0	9	43%	.429	1.50	4.91	1.96	3.15	1.40	0.1	93	
2016	OKL	AAA	24	8	5	0	22	16	97^{1}	80	17	3.0	11.0	119	42%	.268	1.15	4.90	4.53	1.92	36.70	3.8	69	
2016	NAS	AAA	24	3	1	0	6	6	38^{1}	28	3	1.6	8.5	36	43%	.248	0.91	2.82	3.41	2.30	12.80	1.3	70	
2016	OAK	MLB	24	2	0	0	5	5	29^{1}	20	4	1.2	7.1	23	36%	.198	0.82	2.15	3.72	4.59	2.50	0.3	103	94.5
2017	*OAK*	*MLB*	*25*	*7*	*8*	*0*	*24*	*24*	*120*	*112*	*12*	*2.9*	*7.5*	*100*	*38%*	*.285*	*1.23*	*3.97*	*3.88*	*4.38*	*11.9*	*1.2*	*100*	
2018	*OAK*	*MLB*	*26*	*8*	*8*	*0*	*25*	*25*	*145^{2}*	*116*	*16*	*4.4*	*10.2*	*165*	*38%*	*.277*	*1.28*	*3.68*	*3.91*	*4.21*	*17.3*	*1.8*	*96*	

Breakout: 11% Improve: 35% Collapse: 22% Attrition: 34% MLB: 72% *Comparables: Rafael Montero, Tim Cooney, Steven Matz*

The Good: When a fastball that can touch the mid-90s is the second-best option in your repertoire, you've got a good place to start. Cotton's changeup boasts more tumble than your dryer and more fade than your favorite jeans. He sells the change with tremendous arm speed and, combined with the deception in his delivery, catches batters on their front foot often. It's a potential plus-plus pitch with a bit more consistency. He's shown the ability to get cut and tail on his fastball at times. His curve has shown significant growth over the last two years and it will show impressive 11-5 shape. He's shown a cutter at the major-league level, and it's a useful addition to his arsenal.

The Bad: He can cut and run his fastball, but generally it lacks movement thanks to a relatively high arm slot, causing the pitch to play down a tick from its above-average velo grade. He needs that angle because he's on the short side for a starting pitcher and sometimes will end up throwing uphill despite the slot. While there's been progress, he can lose feel for his curve and it will get loopy on him. When he doesn't have the third offering, he becomes predictable and homer-prone due to the lack of movement on his fastball.

The Irrelevant: You might think baseball players from the U.S. Virgin Islands are rare (they are), but Cotton wasn't even the first player from the Islands to make his debut in 2016, having been beaten to the punch by Jabari Blash.

The Risks: Cotton is major-league ready, so the risk in his role grades in fairly minimal in that aspect. Still, he gave up four homers in five MLB starts, and that highlights the greatest concern with his current profile. If he can't avoid the long ball as a starter, he could find success out of the pen, with a focus on his two best offerings. Oh and he is a pitcher. —Craig Goldstein

Major league ETA: Debuted in 2016

Ben Carsley's Fantasy Take: You know how I feel about investing in back-end starters, but if you truly feel compelled to do so, at least go for ones who are MLB-ready now. Despite his gaudy strikeout numbers in the minors, Cotton doesn't profile as a strikeout-per-inning guy in the majors. He's also homer-prone, as we read above, but playing in Oakland should help to mitigate that. I could see Cotton settling in as a top-125ish fantasy starter, posting an ERA close to 4.00 and 180 strikeouts in 200 innings. He might be worth streaming at home against weak lineups, but he shouldn't serve as a roster mainstay unless you're in an 18- or 20-team league.

7. Daulton Jefferies, RHP

DOB: 08/2/1995

Height/Weight: 6'0" 180 lbs

Bats/Throws: L/R

Drafted/Acquired: Drafted 37th overall in the 2016 MLB draft, University of California (Berkeley, CA); signed for $1.6 million

Previous Ranking(s): N/A

2016 Stats: 2.38 ERA, 11.1 IP, 11 H, 2 BB, 17 K at rookie ball in the AZL

The Role: OFP 55—No. 3/4 starter
Likely 45—Back-end starter/swingman

YEAR	TEAM	LVL	AGE	W	L	SV	G	GS	IP	H	HR	BB/9	K/9	K	GB%	BABIP	WHIP	ERA	FIP	DRA	VORP	WARP	cFIP	MPH
2017	*OAK*	*MLB*	*21*	*2*	*3*	*0*	*8*	*8*	*33*	*36*	*5*	*4.5*	*7.2*	*27*	*38%*	*.312*	*1.60*	*5.08*	*5.09*	*5.62*	*-0.5*	*-0.1*	*134*	

Breakout: 1% Improve: 1% Collapse: 0% Attrition: 1% MLB: 1% *Comparables: Christian Friedrich, Wilking Rodriguez, Carl Edwards J*

The Good: Jefferies's changeup has shown the ability to miss bats. It sits 85-86 with significant arm-side run, and he throws it with confidence in any count. Despite his stature, Jefferies can still run his low-90s fastball up to 95 with a whippy three-quarters arm action. He's shown the ability to throw strikes consistently and commands both sides of the plate. He's an excellent athlete for the mound and can be expected to field his position well.

The Bad: His longest professional outing was only three innings long. He missed two months of his final collegiate season due to shoulder and calf injuries and didn't make his pro debut until two months after the draft. His mid-80s slider is a work in progress, spinning into a frisbee when left elevated. His short, snappy delivery doesn't look healthy. It's difficult to imagine someone with his frame, arm action, and injury history developing into a perennial 200-inning pitcher.

The Irrelevant: Jefferies played for Team USA along with fellow 2016 Oakland draft picks A.J. Puk and Logan Shore.

The Risks: Like many pitchers, it boils down to health for Jefferies (he is a pitcher). He has a quick arm, a plus changeup, and an advanced feel for pitching, but past shoulder injuries and slight frames don't typically lend themselves to lengthy MLB careers. He profiles more as a back-end starter, but he hasn't shown the durability to create much value from that profile. He lacks the type of stuff that typically plays up out of the bullpen. The odds are seemingly stacked against him, but if his body proves capable of holding up over a full season, he could exceed expectations due to advanced pitchability. —Matt Pullman

Major league ETA: 2019

Ben Carsley's Fantasy Take: There's more to like with Jefferies than with some other really young arms, but there are some serious red flags, too. As tempting as a potential No. 3 starter in Oakland might be, Jefferies' size and injury history place him on the periphery of fantasy relevance at this point. He's a potential fast-riser if he puts some of his workload and durability concerns to bed, though. Well, as much as any pitcher can put those concerns to bed.

8. Daniel Gossett, RHP

DOB: 11/13/1992

Height/Weight: 6'2" 185 lbs

Bats/Throws: R/R

Drafted/Acquired: Drafted in the second round (65th overall) in the 2014 MLB draft, Clemson University (Clemson, SC); signed for $750,000.

Previous Ranking(s): N/A

2016 Stats: 1.98 ERA, 4.16 DRA, 13.2 IP, 10 H, 3 BB, 4 K at Triple-A Nashville, 2.49 ERA, 2.29 DRA, 94 IP, 75 H, 25 BB, 94 K at Double-A Midland, 3.33 ERA, 2.26 DRA, 46 IP, 40 H, 13 BB, 53 K at High-A Stockton

The Role: OFP 50—No.4 starter
Likely 45—No. 4/5 starter

YEAR	TEAM	LVL	AGE	W	L	SV	G	GS	IP	H	HR	BB/9	K/9	K	GB%	BABIP	WHIP	ERA	FIP	DRA	VORP	WARP	cFIP	MPH
2014	VER	A-	21	1	0	0	12	1	24	16	1	0.4	9.4	25	55%	.246	0.71	2.25	2.02	1.64	9.00	0.9	70	
2015	BLT	A	22	5	13	0	27	27	144^{2}	151	16	3.2	7.0	112	49%	.305	1.40	4.73	4.49	5.27	-0.70	-0.1	107	
2016	STO	A+	23	4	1	0	9	9	46	40	4	2.5	10.4	53	54%	.295	1.15	3.33	3.45	2.24	16.60	1.7	76	
2016	MID	AA	23	5	5	0	16	16	94	75	4	2.4	9.0	94	59%	.284	1.06	2.49	2.56	2.90	22.90	2.5	86	
2016	NAS	AAA	23	1	0	0	2	2	13^{2}	10	0	2.0	2.6	4	57%	.227	0.95	1.98	3.79	4.76	0.90	0.1	110	
2017	*OAK*	*MLB*	*24*	*6*	*9*	*0*	*22*	*22*	120^{1}	*132*	*17*	*3.8*	*5.6*	*75*	*47%*	*.294*	*1.52*	*5.09*	*5.08*	*5.66*	*-2.5*	*-0.3*	*136*	
2018	*OAK*	*MLB*	*25*	*6*	*8*	*0*	*21*	*21*	125^{1}	*122*	*19*	*5.0*	*8.4*	*116*	*47%*	*.294*	*1.54*	*4.79*	*5.04*	*5.33*	*1.8*	*0.2*	*127*	

Breakout: 13% Improve: 26% Collapse: 10% Attrition: 24% MLB: 44% *Comparables: Charles Brewer, John Ely, Cesar Valdez*

The Good: Oh, it's another pitcher. Gossett has a better shot to start than the arms directly above him though. He has smoothed out his delivery some since his college days. His fastball sits 92-94 from a high overhead slot, and he can touch higher. He can elevate it up and out of the zone for strikeouts and generally commands it well. The mid-80s change mimics the fastball well out of the hand. He has decent feel for a low-80s curve.

The Bad: Gossett has a slight build and there is some recoil in the delivery to get the velocity. It's not enough to damn him to the bullpen, but it can dampen his command profile. That plus the high slot means he can have issues getting the fastball down in the zone, and it's hittable when he gets it up and not out of the zone. The curve doesn't project as much more than average due to its short 12-6 break. Gossett could lack an out pitch against major league bats.

The Irrelevant: Clemson hasn't had as many major league stars pass through their program as you might think, but the best pitcher to toe their mound is no slouch. It's Jimmy Key, who was worth 55.8 WARP over his 15-year career.

The Risks: While I don't love Gossett's delivery, he threw 150 effective innings this season across three levels and is now knocking on the door of the majors. It's not the sexiest arm on this list, but it may have the best balance of proximity to the majors and probability of remaining a starter. But remember, he is a pitcher.

Major league ETA: Late 2017

Ben Carsley's Fantasy Take: Gossett is close to the majors, which is nice, but he lacks the type of upside we're looking for. I was pretty nice to the first several pitchers on this list so I don't feel bad about this.

9. Dakota Chalmers, RHP

DOB: 10/8/1996

Height/Weight: 6'3" 175 lbs

Bats/Throws: R/R

Drafted/Acquired: Drafted in the third round (97th overall) in the 2015 MLB draft, North Forsyth HS (Cumming, GA), signed for $613,100.

Previous Ranking(s): N/A

2016 Stats: 4.70 ERA, 5.25 DRA, 67 IP, 55 H, 37 BB, 62 K at Low-A Vermont

The Role: OFP 50 – No. 4 Starter
Likely 45 – Setup guy with a big fastball and not a ton else

YEAR	TEAM	LVL	AGE	W	L	SV	G	GS	IP	H	HR	BB/9	K/9	K	GB%	BABIP	WHIP	ERA	FIP	DRA	VORP	WARP	cFIP	MPH
2015	ATH	Rk	18	0	1	0	11	11	20^{1}	15	0	7.5	8.0	18	64%	.273	1.57	2.66	4.70	6.73	-1.90	-0.2	120	
2016	VER	A-	19	5	4	0	15	13	67	55	8	5.0	8.3	62	44%	.253	1.37	4.70	4.90	4.90	2.20	0.2	110	
2017	*OAK*	*MLB*	*20*	*2*	*5*	*0*	*13*	*13*	46^{1}	*56*	*9*	*6.4*	*5.2*	*26*	*34%*	*.302*	*1.92*	*6.86*	*6.79*	*7.53*	*-10.6*	*-1.1*	*178*	
2018	*OAK*	*MLB*	*21*	*3*	*7*	*0*	*18*	*18*	105^{1}	*113*	*20*	*7.0*	*7.3*	*85*	*34%*	*.296*	*1.86*	*6.33*	*6.60*	*6.95*	*-10.6*	*-1.1*	*166*	

Breakout: 0% Improve: 0% Collapse: 0% Attrition: 0% MLB: 0% *Comparables: Neil Ramirez, Matt Magill, Jose Ramirez*

The Good: Chalmers has some of the best pure arm strength in the system, with outstanding acceleration and easy velocity that will creep as high as 97 and run a little bit. There's enough projectability in the frame to suggest a plus-plus pitch if he can command it enough at maturity. He shows some feel for spin, highlighted by a downer low-80s curve, and he made some strides this season in refining a changeup that, while it remains quite raw, shows some projection into average range thanks to the high-end arm speed. He's a smart kid who takes instruction and demonstrates a plan on the bump.

The Bad: The delivery remains very much a work in progress, with balance and pace issues causing poor present repeatability, and violence down the hill that suggests his inconsistency with pitch-to-pitch execution is likely to be a longer-term issue. He can overthink things on the mound sometimes and lose the rhythm and fluidity of his delivery, and he lacks an effective weapon to put away lefties—he walked more of 'em than he struck out at Low-A this year.

The Irrelevant: Chalmers is the highest draft pick out of North Forsythe high school, beating out Mark Doll and Dexter Bobo.

The Risks: The physicality and stuff both suggest plenty of room for positive growth ahead for Chalmers, and there is clear rotation upside. The lack of a full-season debut on his resume, along with present mechanical inconsistencies and a fringy command profile, make Chalmers a higher-risk prospect who will likely require a longer developmental track.

Major league ETA: 2020

Ben Carsley's Fantasy Take: A probable reliever who's several years away from the majors, eh? I'm good.

10. Logan Shore, RHP

DOB: 12/28/1994

Height/Weight: 6'2" 215 lbs.

Bats/Throws: R/R

Drafted/Acquired: Drafted 47th overall in the 2016 MLB Draft from University of Florida (Gainesville, FL); signed for $1.5 Million

Previous Ranking(s): N/A

2016 Stats: 2.57 ERA, 3.46 DRA, 21 IP, 17 H, 7 BB, 21 K in 7 games at Short-Season Vermont

The Role: 50 OFP—No. 4 Starter
Likely 40—No. 5 Starter, Swingman/Longman

YEAR	TEAM	LVL	AGE	W	L	SV	G	GS	IP	H	HR	BB/9	K/9	K	GB%	BABIP	WHIP	ERA	FIP	DRA	VORP	WARP	cFIP	MPH
2016	VER	A-	21	0	2	0	7	7	21	17	1	3.0	9.0	21	50%	.262	1.14	2.57	2.89	3.37	4.40	0.5	94	
2017	*OAK*	*MLB*	*22*	*2*	*3*	*0*	*8*	*8*	*32*	*39*	*6*	*4.8*	*5.3*	*19*	*35%*	*.306*	*1.73*	*5.98*	*6.05*	*6.60*	*-4.0*	*-0.4*	*158*	
2018	*OAK*	*MLB*	*23*	*5*	*8*	*0*	*26*	*26*	*152*[2]	*161*	*24*	*4.6*	*7.0*	*119*	*35%*	*.297*	*1.57*	*5.07*	*5.32*	*5.60*	*-1.5*	*-0.2*	*135*	

Breakout: 2% Improve: 2% Collapse: 0% Attrition: 1% MLB: 2% *Comparables: Wilking Rodriguez, Braden Shipley, Steven Brault*

The Good: While not the first (or second) University of Florida pitcher taken in the draft, Shore was the most successful, serving as the Friday starter and winning the SEC pitcher of the Year award. He can spot his average fastball in all quadrants, helping the pitch play above its velocity. His changeup is a plus offering that features plus sink, and can be thrown to both lefties and righties. His slider showed signs of improvement and could be an average offering.

The Bad: While the slider made improvements, it's still slurvy and inconsistent, leading to questions about whether it can play as average. Shore lacks projection and what you see is pretty much what you get. He's more of a pitchability arm rather than a loud-stuff-arm, which leads to questions about how it will translate as he progresses.

The Irrelevant: Shore was only the second pitcher from Florida to win the SEC pitcher of the Year award, joining Justin Hoyman who won the award in 2004.

The Risks: It could seem like Shore is a relatively safe bet, but there's a chance his combination of pitchability and guts doesn't work out at the upper levels, making him far too hittable. His slider doesn't allow him to turn over lineups as a starter. Also, he's a pitcher. —Steve Givarz

Major league ETA: Late 2018

Ben Carsley's Fantasy Take: Let's just say that if you need to roster Logan Shore at this point in his career, your dynasty team is probably ...

(•_•)

(•_•)>⌐■-■

(⌐■_■)

... washed up. I'm sorry. I'm sorry. I'm trying to delete it.

OTHERS OF NOTE:

The guy we're lower on

Matt Olson, 1B/OF

Once one of Oakland's top prospects and a fringe top-101 candidate, Olson now looks like more of a tweener than an impact hitter. As his power output has declined at the upper levels, the 37 homers he bashed in 2014 now look more like a product of the California League than a blossoming power tool. He doesn't have a quick bat and he's more of a mistake hitter than a real thumper. He'll draw his share of walks — he earned seven free passes in 28 plate appearances during a September cameo last year — but he's more of a passive hitter than a patient one; often he'll take drivable pitches early in counts, and he's always going to strike out a lot. Defensively, he can fake it in a corner, but his best position is at first base, and a cavernous home park won't mask his shortcomings in right field. Olson could conceivably start if the hit tool comes around, but he's more likely to be a nice bench bat than an everyday regular in Oakland. —Brendan Gawlowski

The once and future A

Renato Nuñez, 3B/1B/OF

Nuñez always has felt like a future Athletic. Well to be fair he's a present Athletic, having debuted this past September. And he has a good shot to make the 2017 roster given his pop and defensive...uh...flexibility. He only DH'd during his cup of coffee, but he's a third baseman by trade, having also gotten some minor league reps at first base and left field. Left field might be optimistic as he is a well-below-average runner, and his range at third base is limited. There's also big swing-and-miss in the offensive profile, although it comes with above-average power. While Oakland's system has improved, Nuñez just feels like an A's prospect. He's fringy, but he can plug a hole in your lineup in a few different spots and mash some dingers—especially if they can get him the lion's share of his plate appearances against lefties.

Because we're a sucker for a good glove at the six

Richie Martin, SS

Richie Martin posted a .634 OPS in the Cal League this year. That's not great, Bob. Martin has a pretty good approach at the plate, and a contact-oriented swing, but too often fails to turn that into quality contact. And as he moves up the organizational ladder, his lack of power may lead to better arms challenging the "approach" more. Martin might not need a whole lot more than a .634 OPS to have a major league career though, because he is a heckuva shortstop. His average speed plays up on defense due to a good first step and preternatural infield instincts. The arm is good and the actions are great. The defensive profile immediately pops. He's athletic enough that you can still dream on that leading to some more refinement at the plate, but even if that doesn't come, Martin should collect major league per diem as a backup middle infielder. If he does find a bit more at the dish, he could slot in as a second-division starter at short.

Jeffrey's Guy

Sean Murphy, C

Murphy is the kind of prospect that might sneak onto a top 10 list in a shallower system (or be top five in the Angels system). The Athletics could have gotten a bit of a steal when they popped the big and burly backstop in the third round of the 2016 draft. He's a premium defender behind the plate and there's potentially above-average pop in the profile. A hamate issue marred his 2016 college campaign, and he never really got off the ground in short-season. If the bat never really perks up, Murphy could still have a long career as a major-league backup. But a fully healthy Murphy could shine in 2017 in full-season ball and have a strong case for the top 10 this time next year.

Cistulli's Guy

Max Schrock, 2B

Acquired from Washington in exchange for Marc Rzepczynski this August, Schrock is an undersized second baseman with a short, left-handed stroke. A 2015 13th rounder, the former Gamecock had three standout seasons in the SEC before signing well over slot at $500,000. Standing 5-foot-8, 180 lbs, Schrock has some deceptive strength on his small frame. Featuring a preloaded swing with minimal moving parts, he has an advanced feel for the barrel and present gap-to-gap power. An above-average runner, Schrock is a sum-of-the-parts prospect carried by a plus hit tool. It's easy to see a future big-league reserve here, but potential remains for a second-division regular if the bat continues to develop. —Matt Pullman

TOP 10 TALENTS 25 AND UNDER (BORN 4/1/91 OR LATER)

1. Sean Manaea	**6. Frankie Montas**
2. Franklin Barreto	**7. Matt Chapman**
3. Ryon Healy	**8. Jharel Cotton**
4. Grant Holmes	**9. Daulton Jefferies**
5. A.J. Puk	**10. Daniel Gossett**

Age 25 is somewhat of an arbitrary endpoint. Marcus Semien will be 26 on Opening Day and Sonny Gray 27. Throw those two into the mix and suddenly the A's look like they are a rebuilding team with a strong core of young talent. That is still true, I suppose, but for a perpetually rebuilding team you still want to see a bit more exciting, young, major-league-ready talent at the top of this list.

Sean Manaea put together a healthy, fullish season. That's a good sign given his litany of arm woes going back to his college years. He was pretty good too, showing two above-average secondaries in his change and slider to go with a fastball that can touch 96 from the left side. There are always going to be questions here about his health until he starts rolling off 180-inning campaigns, and the Athletics treated him with kid gloves, especially early in the season. But if the Manaea that showed up in the second half of 2016—when he posted a 2.67 ERA and a 4:1 K:BB ratio—appears in both halves of 2017, the A's might have their No. 2 starter to slot in behind Sonny Gray.

Ryon Healy didn't even get a mench on our 2016 Athletics Top Ten. At the time he was a 23-year-old who had a nice season in Double A but lacked the power you normally associate with a corner infield bat, let alone one that might have to slide over to first. Well, Healy is on our radar now, after mashing his way to the majors in 2016 and hitting 27 home runs across three levels. It turned out he was passable at the hot corner, and when you hit .300 with pop as well, the bat will play anywhere. Healy might not be a .300 hitter long term, but there's enough loud contact in the profile that he'll be an everyday major leaguer long term.

Daniel Mengden made 14 starts for the 2016 A's, a feat the organization might prefer he not repeat in 2017, although he's better than the 6.50 ERA he posted. He might be served by a move to the pen where the stuff might play up. Dillon Overton is your standard issue lefty with a fringy fastball and a good change-up. Less standard is the 4.4 HR/9 he gave up last year. As long as you have a political science major in your fantasy league though, he will live on in the team name The Dillon Overton Window.

—Jeffrey Paternostro

PHILADELPHIA PHILLIES

The State of the System: *Almost all the same names as last year, but another young Latin arm and a first-overall pick have boosted an already strong system in Philadelphia, and the top guns here are all ready to contribute to the major league squad in 2017.*

THE TOP TEN

1. SS J.P. Crawford	6. RHP Adonis Medina
2. C Jorge Alfaro	7. RHP Sixto Sanchez
3. OF Nick Williams	8. OF Roman Quinn
4. OF Mickey Moniak	9. LF Cornelius Randolph
5. RHP Franklyn Kilome	10. Choose Your Own Adventure: The Island of Klentak

The Big Question: How much should we care about 'makeup'?

Makeup is almost certainly the hidden factor as to why some seemingly similarly situated prospects bust while others succeed. Some players have an incredible ability to learn and develop. Some stagnate in situations they should conquer. Yet we have very little ability from the outside to determine which players are high makeup and which ones aren't.

We've often tried. Over the years in these pages, you've seen makeup as a column in our live reports. You've seen it as something we've talked about extensively in prospect lists. Sometimes, it's a euphemism for things we'd rather not talk about, trouble with the law or drug issues or things of that nature. Sometimes it's based on industry scuttlebutt, or information we have off-the-record. Sometimes we hear bad things that we very much believe, but without enough specificity to say exactly what, and the easiest crutch is to talk about the player's bad makeup in somber tones. Sometimes we hear that a player is a sponge and the hardest worker on the planet, and we talk about his great makeup in excited tones. Sometimes, it's just based on a player's posture on the field, or his effort during one play, or other visual cues you pick up around the ballpark.

All of this is probably more useful information to you, the reader, than absolutely nothing, even if we can't always say exactly what we'd like to say. These are absolutely things that we should be using to inform our judgments about prospects—to a degree. Because while we have some information on a player's makeup, it's often very limited. Even major-league organizations can get lost in the fog with makeup, since it's all subjective and we're all human with human biases. And the organizations have the best information possible about their own players.

Which brings us to Nick Williams. As early as 2014, then-BP writer and now Astros scout Tucker Blair obliquely referred to "makeup concerns" in a BP scouting report on Williams, then in the Rangers system, after noting "curious" body language. In one of those moments that makes you realize why certain evaluators get hired by teams, Blair also predicted "it may be portrayed in the wrong light by some in the future."

Williams, after being dealt to the Phillies in the Cole Hamels trade, was assigned to Triple-A Lehigh Valley for the 2016 campaign under the tutelage of veteran minor-league manager Dave Brundage. Brundage publicly benched Williams multiple times over the course of the season, for sins such as not running out routine grounders, showing up opponents, and failing to take an extra base on a flyball. In all honesty, these sorts of benchings are quite common in the minors, but what was uncommon was that the drama played out in the media. Typically, the manager disciplines the player quietly, and the local minor-league press is either kept in the dark or things are kept off the record. Here, both Brundage and Williams gabbed to the media early and often, turning Nick Williams' "bad makeup" into one of the more interesting running plots of the 2016 Phillies, even though it was 70 miles up the Blue Route from Philly in Allentown.

Lost in much of the commentary was another simple

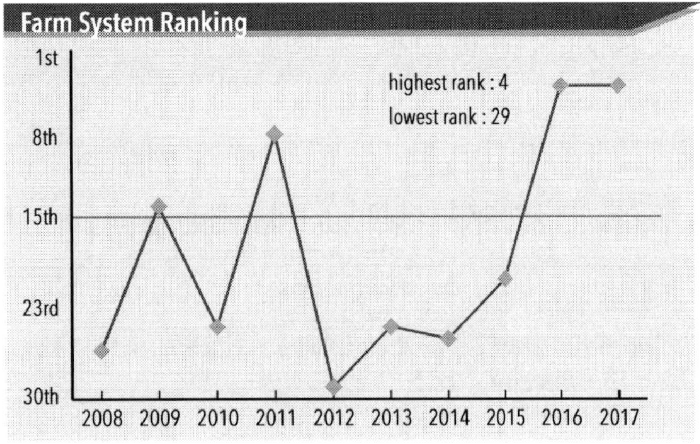

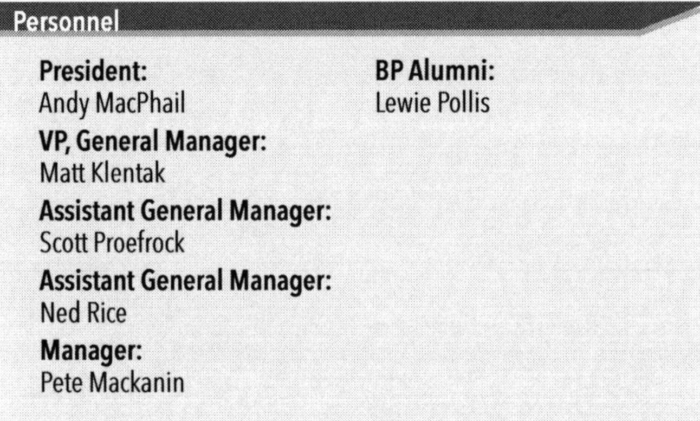
Personnel

President:
Andy MacPhail

VP, General Manager:
Matt Klentak

Assistant General Manager:
Scott Proefrock

Assistant General Manager:
Ned Rice

Manager:
Pete Mackanin

BP Alumni:
Lewie Pollis

truth, that very few players in the majors run out routine plays all the time. Heck, very few players in the minors do either. It's eyewash, fake hustle on plays where 99.9 percent of the time it couldn't matter less whether you run your fastest or put in a representative jog. Moreover, there are times when it's clearly wrong to run everything out, where it puts you at risk of pulling a hamstring or aggravating an existing injury on a play that doesn't matter. Sure, once in awhile you might lose that extra base when the outfielder drops that routine fly, but what never gets mentioned when we talk about all this is that you also might get thrown out trying to advance if said outfielder recovers quickly enough.

What does all of this say about Nick Williams as a prospect? A few more hints emerged after the season ended—Brundage was not retained by the Phillies for 2017, but Williams was also bypassed for a September call-up. It's certainly possible that there are greater underlying issues here that the Phillies organization, or even Brundage, was privy to that us here at Baseball Prospectus are not. But from behind the backstop, I'm much more worried about Williams' late-season regression back to extreme hacker than I am whether he plays with too much flair or too little hustle down the first base line.

—Jarrett Seidler

1. J.P. Crawford, SS

DOB: 01/11/1995

Height/Weight: 6'2" 180 lbs.

Bats/Throws: L/R

Drafted/Acquired: Drafted 16th overall in the 2013 MLB Draft, Lakewood HS (Lakewood, CA); signed for $2,299,300

Previous Ranking(s): 2016: #1 (Org), #3 (overall)

2016 Stats: 244/.328/.318, 4 HR, 7 SB in 87 games at Triple-A Lehigh Valley, .265/.398/.390, 3 HR, 5 SB in 36 games at Double-A Reading

The Role: OFP 70 — All-star shortstop
Likely 60 — Above-average regular

YEAR	TEAM	LVL	AGE	PA	R	2B	3B	HR	RBI	BB	K	SB	CS	AVG/OBP/SLG	TAv	VORP	BABIP	BRR	FRAA	WARP
2014	LWD	A	19	267	37	16	0	3	19	37	37	14	7	.295/.398/.405	.291	21.1	.342	1.2	SS(59): 0.8	2.3
2014	CLR	A+	19	271	32	7	0	8	29	28	37	10	7	.275/.352/.407	.284	15.8	.292	-2.9	SS(62): 0.2	1.6
2015	CLR	A+	20	95	15	1	0	1	8	14	9	5	2	.392/.489/.443	.369	15.1	.435	1.1	SS(20): 0.9	1.7
2015	REA	AA	20	405	53	21	7	5	34	49	45	7	2	.265/.354/.407	.272	21.9	.289	1.0	SS(86): 6.7	3.1
2016	REA	AA	21	166	23	8	0	3	13	30	21	5	3	.265/.398/.390	.283	11.7	.295	1.3	SS(36): 6.0	1.9
2016	LEH	AAA	21	385	40	11	1	4	30	42	59	7	4	.244/.328/.318	.241	10.4	.284	2.1	SS(87): -3.0	0.8
2017	*PHI*	*MLB*	*22*	*186*	*20*	*7*	*1*	*4*	*18*	*20*	*37*	*3*	*1*	*.237/.319/.366*	*.251*	*6.0*	*.278*	*-0.2*	*SS 2*	*0.6*
2018	*PHI*	*MLB*	*23*	*419*	*51*	*16*	*2*	*11*	*46*	*44*	*82*	*6*	*3*	*.244/.325/.383*	*.264*	*16.1*	*.283*	*-0.2*	*SS 4*	*2.2*

Breakout: 9% Improve: 31% Collapse: 10% Attrition: 25% MLB: 47% *Comparables: Ivan De Jesus, Joe Panik, Gavin Cecchini*

The Good: Crawford is a polished, near-complete baseball player on both sides of the ball. He is a plus shortstop, borderline plus-plus, who could compete for Gold Gloves. He won't wow you with the spectacular as much as, say, Francisco Lindor, but he makes everything look easy through outstanding instincts, plus actions, and a plus arm. At the plate he had an advanced approach and works at-bats as well as anyone in the minors, and he is comfortable hitting in any count. He's a potential plus hitter who will get on base more than enough to write him in at the top of a lineup. He is a solid runner, if not a particularly aggressive base-stealer.

The Bad: Crawford's 2016 "feels" disappointing for a top prospect, although I don't know if that is entirely fair. He was a 21-year-old in the International League and did struggle at times against advanced arms with major-league experience and a major-league plan of attack. He'll flash average pull-side power at times, but his swing/approach is geared to line the ball back up the middle, leaving him more of a four-tool than five-tool shortstop.

The Irrelevant: Before Crawford, you have to go back to 2007 and Joe Savery to find a Phillies first-round pick that made that majors. Maybe that actually isn't so irrelevant, at least not to why the Phillies are near the top of our running order for prospect lists.

The Risks: Crawford is the lowest-risk prospect we will cover that hasn't already accrued service time. His defensive profile and strong approach give him a high floor as a major-league contributor, but if his occasional struggles with the bat this year were more than just a blip or an adjustment period against advanced arms, he may "only" be a good regular.

Major league ETA: 2017, post super-2

Ben Carsley's Fantasy Take: Crawford is a better MLB prospect than a fantasy one, but he's still a really good fantasy prospect. Shortstop is a bit deeper than it used to be, but there will always be room for players like Crawford, who could contribute materially across all five fantasy categories and significantly in two of them (AVG, R). If you want to get optimistic, we could be looking at a .300-plus average with 15 homers and steals apiece in his prime, and Crawford's top-of-the-order profile and favorable ballpark factors should aid his runs scored and power stats even more. He's a lock to stay at short, a lock to appear in the majors soon, and a near-lock to hit well. That also makes Crawford a lock for a top-15 spot when our Dynasty 101 list hits later this winter.

2. Jorge Alfaro, C

DOB: 06/11/1993

Height/Weight: 6'2" 225 lbs.

Bats/Throws: R/R

Drafted/Acquired: Signed January 2010 out of Colombia by the Texas Rangers for $1,300,000, traded to Philadelphia in the Cole Hamels deal

Previous Ranking(s): 2016: #8 (Org), #46 (Overall)

2016 Stats: .125/.176/.125, 0 HR, 0 SB in 6 games at the major league level, .285/.325/.458, 15 HR, 3 SB in 97 games at Double-A Reading

The Role: OFP 60 — he could make some All-Star teams
Likely 55 — a solid regular catcher

YEAR	TEAM	LVL	AGE	PA	R	2B	3B	HR	RBI	BB	K	SB	CS	AVG/OBP/SLG	TAv	VORP	BABIP	BRR	FRAA	WARP
2014	MYR	A+	21	437	63	22	5	13	73	23	100	6	5	.261/.318/.440	.268	18.7	.315	-1.7	C(75): -1.0 • 1B(17): 0.0	1.8
2014	FRI	AA	21	99	12	4	0	4	14	6	23	0	0	.261/.343/.443	.271	4.7	.311	0.1	C(15): -1.0 • 1B(1): -0.2	0.4
2015	PHL	Rk	22	6	0	1	0	0	1	0	0	0	0	.500/.667/.750	.498	1.9	.500	0.0	C(2): -0.0	0.2
2015	FRI	AA	22	207	22	15	2	5	21	9	61	2	1	.253/.314/.432	.250	5.5	.347	0.6	C(35): -0.3 • 1B(1): -0.0	0.6
2016	REA	AA	23	435	68	21	2	15	67	22	105	3	2	.285/.325/.458	.268	20.9	.347	-1.5	C(95): 16.5	4.0
2016	PHI	MLB	23	17	0	0	0	0	0	1	8	0	0	.125/.176/.125	.079	-2.5	.250	-0.1	C(4): -0.7	-0.3
2017	*PHI*	*MLB*	*24*	*31*	*3*	*1*	*0*	*1*	*3*	*1*	*10*	*0*	*0*	*.220/.261/.374*	*.228*	*0.4*	*.294*	*-0.1*	*C -0*	*0.0*
2018	*PHI*	*MLB*	*25*	*252*	*28*	*10*	*1*	*9*	*29*	*12*	*82*	*0*	*0*	*.216/.266/.377*	*.236*	*2.3*	*.289*	*-0.5*	*C -2*	*0.0*

Breakout: 4% Improve: 10% Collapse: 5% Attrition: 19% MLB: 20% *Comparables: Lucas May, Max Stassi, Luke Montz*

The Good: His throwing arm is as good as anyone in the game. His raw power is legendary, going back to whispers from Jason Parks (R.I.P.) on Arizona backfields shortly after he signed. His overall hitting ability plays well given the position, and he's specifically improved his ability to hit the ball to all-fields. He's unusually athletic for a catcher, and possesses average-to-above speed. Notice that there's no caveat there, because he runs well in general, not just for a catcher.

The Bad: Alfaro's elite raw power hasn't yet translated well into game power. While that can come late, especially for catchers, his power output in Reading was dwarfed by lesser prospects like Dylan Cozens and Rhys Hoskins. His defensive game has improved greatly since Philadelphia acquired him, but he's not Jonathan Lucroy yet either, and it's still a little up in the air if he ultimately lands at a new position.

The Irrelevant: If Alfaro cracks the BP 101 again this offseason, it'll be his sixth consecutive list.

The Risks: Without that power, the hit tool is just playable and not a carrying tool. He could end up as a medium-pop catch-and-throw guy, or even worse if he ultimately moves off catcher. He's athletic enough to play somewhere like third or right, but would the bat play up enough there? Also, catchers are weird. —Jarrett Seidler

Major league ETA: Debuted in 2016

Ben Carsley's Fantasy Take: If you stuck with Alfaro through his disappointing 2015 season, your patience may soon be rewarded. Catcher remains fantasy's shallowest position. Welington Castillo was the 10th-best fantasy backstop last year per ESPN's Player Rater, and he hit .264 with 14 homers and 68 RBI. Alfaro should eclipse that power output if he gets the playing time, and while he may not aspire to such an average, he could add a few steals to help compensate. There's substantial risk here thanks to the hit tool and less-than-certain defensive future, but given the sad state of fantasy catching and Alfaro's proximity to the majors, he's well worth the gamble.

3. Nick Williams, OF

DOB: 09/09/1993

Height/Weight: 6'3" 195 lbs.

Bats/Throws: L/L

Drafted/Acquired: Drafted 93rd overall in the 2012 MLB Draft by the Texas Rangers, Ball HS (Galveston, TX); signed for $500,000, traded to Philadelphia in the Cole Hamels deal.

Previous Ranking(s): #2 (Org), #23 (Overall)

2016 Stats: .258/.287/.427, 13 HR, 6 SB in 125 games at Triple-A Lehigh Valley

The Role: OFP 60 — First Division Outfielder
Likely 50 — Major League Regular Outfielder

YEAR	TEAM	LVL	AGE	PA	R	2B	3B	HR	RBI	BB	K	SB	CS	AVG/OBP/SLG	TAv	VORP	BABIP	BRR	FRAA	WARP
2014	RNG	Rk	20	14	3	0	1	0	2	1	2	0	0	.308/.357/.462	.278	1.2	.364	0.4		0.2
2014	MYR	A+	20	408	61	28	4	13	68	19	117	5	7	.292/.343/.491	.285	19.2	.391	-1.3	LF(44): -0.9 • CF(25): -3.9	1.5
2014	FRI	AA	20	64	4	2	1	0	4	2	21	1	1	.226/.250/.290	.205	-2.0	.341	0.1	LF(11): -1.6 • CF(4): 0.1	-0.4
2015	REA	AA	21	100	21	5	2	4	10	3	20	3	0	.320/.340/.536	.320	10.4	.370	1.5	CF(21): 0.8	1.2
2015	FRI	AA	21	415	56	21	4	13	45	32	77	10	8	.299/.357/.479	.291	22.6	.346	0.3	LF(45): -0.5 • CF(38): -2.4	2.2
2016	LEH	AAA	22	527	78	33	6	13	64	19	136	6	4	.258/.287/.427	.258	10.7	.325	-0.7	LF(50): 1.2 • CF(38): 1.7	1.4
2017	*PHI*	*MLB*	*23*	*99*	*10*	*5*	*1*	*3*	*12*	*4*	*30*	*1*	*1*	*.240/.272/.411*	*.243*	*1.4*	*.311*	*-0.1*	*LF -0*	*0.1*
2018	*PHI*	*MLB*	*24*	*342*	*40*	*17*	*3*	*12*	*43*	*15*	*99*	*4*	*2*	*.251/.289/.432*	*.262*	*9.3*	*.322*	*-0.1*	*LF 0*	*1.0*

Breakout: 4% Improve: 13% Collapse: 0% Attrition: 8% MLB: 19% *Comparables: Corey Dickerson, Zoilo Almonte, Marc Krauss*

The Good: The entire tool set still flashes average or better in large part due to Williams' pronounced athleticism. While it is a corner outfield profile, the band of variance for questions around his defense and arm narrowed, showing range and advancement in his arm strength. Before wearing down in the last month of the season, Williams put together a very respectable offensive season in his first trip through Triple-A. His bat speed is plus with quick wrists and a short path to the ball. When locked in, he possesses a special ability to barrel balls and make quality contact.

The Bad: After glimpses of improved plate discipline in 2015, the impatient, free-swinging approach at the plate returned. This was especially evident in his susceptibility to expanding the zone on off-speed offerings with two strikes. There was a severe decline in offensive performance in August, though fatigue was more a factor than his skill set being overmatched. Any optimism for a future in center field is likely dwindling given some of the inefficiencies in his routes and reads.

The Irrelevant: Despite having what you'd think would be a fairly common name, Nick Williams has a pretty good chance to be the best Nick Williams to play baseball. It is fortunate that like many Texans he goes by his middle name, rather than his first name. The best Billy Williams is a little bit higher bar to get over in baseball terms.

The Risks: The band of variance is still a band of variance; there's boom and bust to the offensive profile and some questions still exist for the defense. On the plus side, he's still young for Triple-A, and, while he went on the 40-man this winter, there is still time to iron things out. Another trip through the International League should give a better sense of which way the pendulum will swing. - Adam Hayes

Major league ETA: Late 2017

Ben Carsley's Fantasy Take: Williams is the reverse Crawford; he's an even more enticing fantasy prospect than he is a future IRL big leaguer. I've been president of the Nick Williams fan club since I fell in love with his swing in Arizona a few spring trainings ago, and nothing he's done or I've seen since has changed my mind. I will always bet on bat speed and hit tool first in fantasy, and I'm a believer in Williams' potential five-category fantasy future. He'll bring less value to those of you in OBP leagues, but Williams is a potential high-end OF3 in standard formats, capable of mashing 20 homers, stealing double-digit bases and flirting with a .300 average. I'm all in, and you can't stop me, though I reluctantly acknowledge that his floor is pretty low.

4. Mickey Moniak, OF

DOB: 5/13/98

Height/Weight: 6'2" 185 lbs.

Bats/Throws: L/R

Drafted/Acquired: Drafted First Overall in the 2016 MLB Draft by Philadelphia, La Costa Canyon HS (Carlsbad, CA); signed for $6.1 MM

Previous Ranking(s): N/A

2016 Stats: .284/.340/.409, 1 HR, 10 SB in 46 games at complex-level GCL

The Role: OFP 60 — Above-average center fielder
Likely 50 — Average outfielder

YEAR	TEAM	LVL	AGE	PA	R	2B	3B	HR	RBI	BB	K	SB	CS	AVG/OBP/SLG	TAv	VORP	BABIP	BRR	FRAA	WARP
2016	PHL	Rk	18	194	27	11	4	1	28	11	35	10	4	.284/.340/.409	.270	9.4	.345	3.0	CF(30): 4.1 • LF(2): 0.1	1.5
2017	*PHI*	*MLB*	*19*	*250*	*22*	*9*	*1*	*6*	*24*	*10*	*84*	*4*	*2*	*.192/.231/.307*	*.188*	*-9.1*	*.268*	*0.0*	*CF 2 • LF 0*	*-0.8*
2018	*PHI*	*MLB*	*20*	*323*	*33*	*11*	*2*	*8*	*33*	*15*	*103*	*6*	*3*	*.208/.252/.339*	*.216*	*-5.1*	*.282*	*0.3*	*CF 2 • LF 0*	*-0.3*

Breakout: 0% Improve: 5% Collapse: 1% Attrition: 4% MLB: 9% *Comparables: Engel Beltre, Nomar Mazara, Raul Mondesi*

The Good: Moniak might not have been the consensus best talent in the draft, but the Phillies got a relatively safe high school bat at 1-1. Moniak's hit tool was among the best in the draft, featuring a line-drive swing with good barrel control. He is a plus runner with a good shot to stick in center field.

The Bad: He's not a lock to stick in center and doesn't project as a plus defender there. He may not have the arm for right field or the power to be an impact bat in left.

The Irrelevant: Mickey is not short for "Michael," rather "McKenzie," which makes more sense if you actually think about it.

The Risks: Moniak is a prep pick with no professional track record outside of the complex. Hit-tool guys aren't seen as traditionally "risky" profiles, but Moniak doesn't have much to fall back on if he is "only" an average hitter in the end.

Major league ETA: 2020

Ben Carsley's Fantasy Take: Safe doesn't always mean boring! Moniak has the tools to hit .300-plus with 20-plus steals and enough homers to matter in a few years, sort of like Adam Eaton ratched up 10-20 percent. The long lead time and relatively modest upside make him a non-elite fantasy prospect, but still one you should be perfectly content drafting or bidding on as 2016 draftees become eligible in your dynasty league (if they haven't already).

5. Franklyn Kilome, RHP

DOB: 06/25/1995

Height/Weight: 6'6" 175 lbs

Bats/Throws: R/R

Drafted/Acquired: Signed January 2013 by Philadelphia out of the Dominican Republic for $40,000

Previous Ranking(s): #4 (Org), #95 (Overall)

2016 Stats: 3.85 ERA, 4.23 DRA, 114.2 IP, 113 H, 130 K, 50 BB in 23 games at Low-A Lakewood

The Role: OFP 60 — Mid-rotation starter/back-end reliever
Likely 50 — Setup man who feels like he should be more

YEAR	TEAM	LVL	AGE	W	L	SV	G	GS	IP	H	HR	BB/9	K/9	K	GB%	BABIP	WHIP	ERA	FIP	DRA	VORP	WARP	cFIP	MPH
2014	PHL	Rk	19	3	1	0	11	8	40^{1}	36	2	2.5	5.6	25	0%	.264	1.17	3.12	3.80	3.88			98	
2015	WPT	A-	20	3	2	0	11	11	49^{1}	41	1	3.8	6.6	36	57%	.282	1.26	3.28	4.02	5.55	-1.50	-0.2	109	
2016	LWD	A	21	5	8	0	23	23	114^{2}	113	6	3.9	10.2	130	49%	.346	1.42	3.85	3.28	3.98	13.20	1.4	97	
2017	*PHI*	*MLB*	*22*	*4*	*8*	*0*	*18*	*18*	86^{2}	*100*	*15*	*5.1*	*6.1*	*58*	*38%*	*.328*	*1.73*	*5.87*	*5.87*	*6.70*	*-10.9*	*-1.1*	*158*	
2018	*PHI*	*MLB*	*23*	*5*	*9*	*0*	*23*	*23*	137^{2}	*134*	*23*	*6.2*	*8.5*	*129*	*38%*	*.314*	*1.66*	*5.60*	*6.07*	*6.39*	*-10.1*	*-1.0*	*152*	

Breakout: 1% Improve: 1% Collapse: 0% Attrition: 1% MLB: 1% *Comparables: Brian Flynn, Ryan Merritt, Michael Stutes*

The Good: All of the individual pieces are present for a top pitching prospect—when he's on his game. He possesses a fastball that can sit 92-97 and touch a little higher, a curve with easy plus potential, and a change that flashes as more than just an interesting third pitch. He's a tall drink of water with a great power pitcher physique. If you catch him on the right day, you might see a top-of-the-rotation starter kit. There were more right days than wrong days later in the season, which gives hope for in-season progression.

The Bad: When not on his game, Kilome can look like an organizational player. If you show up on the wrong day, you're liable to get a fastball flagging down into the high-80s, off-speeds that won't impress anyone and brutal command problems. As you might suspect, he's often unable to repeat his mechanics. When it goes bad, it goes really bad.

The Irrelevant: Three players have been named Franklyn in baseball history—two were Dominican relievers from the 2000s (Franklyn Gracesqui and Franklyn German), and the third (William Franklyn "Bill" Wolff) pitched one game for the Philadelphia Phillies in September 1902.

The Risks: Absolutely enormous. If anything, OFP undersells the upside, because if it somehow all clicks there really are top-of-the-rotation pieces here. And the likely role oversells the floor, because sometimes these guys can't repeat their mechanics in relief, either. Also, he's a pitcher. —Jarrett Seidler

Major league ETA: 2019

Ben Carsley's Fantasy Take: The "Dominican Clay Buchholz" vibe one gets from reading Kilome's breakdown above might be off-putting, but upside is what we're after when we talk fantasy starters, and Kilome has it. In his Top 101 list from last year, Bret Sayre referred to Kilome's upside as an SP1 and his downside as "The Mariana Trench." That still sounds right to me, though Kilome's strong second half and move into the mid-minors elevates him to borderline top-50 dynasty prospect status.

6. Adonis Medina, RHP

DOB: 12/18/96

Height/Weight: 6'1" 185 lbs.

Bats/Throws: R/R

Drafted/Acquired: Signed May 2015 by Philadelphia out of the Dominican Republic for $70,000

Previous Ranking(s): NR

2016 Stats: 2.92 ERA, 7.66 DRA, 64.2 IP, 47 H, 34 K, 24 BB in 13 games at short-season Williamsport

The Role: OFP 60— Mid-rotation starting pitcher
Likely 50— Back-end starting pitcher or 8th inning guy

YEAR	TEAM	LVL	AGE	W	L	SV	G	GS	IP	H	HR	BB/9	K/9	K	GB%	BABIP	WHIP	ERA	FIP	DRA	VORP	WARP	cFIP	MPH
2014	DPH	Rk	17	2	3	1	11	2	26^{1}	22	0	1.4	7.5	22	0%	.275	0.99	1.37	2.64	3.07			87	
2015	PHL	Rk	18	3	2	0	10	8	45^{1}	42	1	2.4	6.9	35	55%	.304	1.19	2.98	3.23	3.71	10.60	1.0	96	
2016	WPT	A-	19	5	3	0	13	13	64^{2}	47	5	3.3	4.7	34	57%	.214	1.10	2.92	4.66	6.92	-12.10	-1.3	116	
2017	*PHI*	*MLB*	*20*	*2*	*4*	*0*	*16*	*8*	48^{2}	*59*	*10*	*4.7*	*4.2*	*22*	*37%*	*.315*	*1.75*	*6.54*	*6.67*	*7.46*	*-12.0*	*-1.2*	*178*	
2018	*PHI*	*MLB*	*21*	*5*	*9*	*0*	*30*	*20*	140^{2}	*149*	*27*	*5.1*	*6.6*	*103*	*37%*	*.307*	*1.63*	*6.00*	*6.50*	*6.84*	*-16.9*	*-1.7*	*165*	

Breakout: Improve: Collapse: Attrition: MLB: *Comparables:*

The Good: In hindsight, I should have just pulled the trigger on Medina as a top-ten prospect in the system last year. He sports a heavy fastball that regularly touched 95 as a starter in Williamsport and even higher in short bursts. It's a heavy pitch and he shows advanced command of it for a short-season arm. He can pitch just off the fastball when he is going well. His mechanics are repeatable and among as low-impact as you will see for a guy who can dial it up into the mid-90s.

The Bad: While not to the same extent as Kilome, Medina's stuff does vary from outing to outing. His fastball was 89-92 when I saw him, for example, and reports have him as low as 87-90 during the season. His secondaries (curveball and change) are still mostly projection, and until at least one of them turns into a consistent bat-misser, there will be questions about how the profile will fare at higher levels. He doesn't have ideal size for a starting pitcher (although I suspect Medina is now a bit bigger than his signing height and weight listed above).

The Irrelevant: There are currently 11 active Adonises in affiliated baseball. Yeah, more than I thought too.

The Risks: Very High. Medina only has a short-season resume and has to find more consistent velocity and more consistent secondary offerings to reach even his likely outcome. He does have a precocious level of polish and pitchability, more than the young Latin arms on either side of him on this list. But like those two, he's a pitcher.

Major league ETA: 2019

Ben Carsley's Fantasy Take: Wait until Medina is closer to the majors or until he starts profiling as someone with a higher ceiling to bite. You don't want to eat up a roster spot for four or five seasons to end up with an SP6. Dave Stewart does not understand that last sentence.

7. Sixto Sanchez, RHP

DOB: 7/29/98

Height/Weight: 6'0" 185 lbs.

Bats/Throws: R/R

Drafted/Acquired: Signed in February 2015 by Philadelphia out of the Dominican Republic for $35,000

Previous Ranking(s): unranked

2016 Stats: 0.50 ERA, 2.69 DRA, 54 IP, 33 H, 44 K, 8 BB in 11 games at complex-level GCL

The Role: OFP 60— Mid-rotation starting pitcher
Likely 50— 7th/8th inning reliever

YEAR	TEAM	LVL	AGE	W	L	SV	G	GS	IP	H	HR	BB/9	K/9	K	GB%	BABIP	WHIP	ERA	FIP	DRA	VORP	WARP	cFIP	MPH
2015	DPH	Rk	16	1	2	0	11	2	25²	32	0	2.1	6.3	18	48%	.340	1.48	4.56	2.77	3.96	4.60	0.5	92	
2016	PHL	Rk	17	5	0	0	11	11	54	33	0	1.3	7.3	44	57%	.236	0.76	0.50	2.24	3.30	14.50	1.5	84	
2017	*PHI*	*MLB*	*18*	*2*	*2*	*0*	*14*	*6*	*37²*	*38*	*6*	*3.6*	*7.8*	*33*	*47%*	*.320*	*1.42*	*4.74*	*4.79*	*5.50*	*-0.3*	*0.0*	*129*	
2018	*PHI*	*MLB*	*19*	*3*	*3*	*0*	*16*	*8*	*64¹*	*66*	*10*	*3.5*	*9.1*	*65*		*.340*	*1.41*	*4.31*	*4.64*	*5.00*	*2.7*	*0.3*	*116*	

Breakout: 0% Improve: 0% Collapse: 0% Attrition: 0% MLB: 0% *Comparables: Roberto Osuna, Jordan Lyles, Yohander Mendez*

The Good: Sixto has premium arm strength and velocity for someone his age, touching 98 while routinely sitting 93-96. He has a clean, well-balanced delivery with plus arm speed and a smooth arm action. He has good feel for his curveball and, while inconsistent at times, shows above-average potential with 12/6 shape with premium bite and action. He has a good feel for the strike zone and was able to throw his entire arsenal for strikes.

The Bad: Sixto lacks prototypical size for a starting pitcher as he looks closer to 5-foot-10 than 6-feet. His changeup is clearly a third pitch and was only used against lefties sparingly. He has a limited professional track record. While he shows feel for the curveball, he struggled to finish batters with it, leaving it in the zone far too often.

The Irrelevant: After an almost 13-year drought of players named Sixto in affiliated baseball, 2015 saw Sixto Sanchez and Sixto Torres sign professional contracts.

The Risks: Relatively high. While he is still quite young, he has not been challenged against better competition. His lack of size will always be held against him as he moves up the ladder. Also, he's a pitcher. —Steve Givarz

Major league ETA: 2020

Ben Carsley's Fantasy Take: Wait until Sanchez is closer to the majors or until he starts profiling as someone with a higher ceiling to bite. You don't want to eat up a roster spot for four or five seasons to end up with a middle reliever. Terry Ryan does not understand that last sentence.

8. Roman Quinn, OF

DOB: 05/14/1993

Height/Weight: 5'10" 170 lbs.

Bats/Throws: S/R

Drafted/Acquired: Drafted 66th overall in the 2011 draft, Port St. Joe HS (Port St. Joe, FL); signed for $775,000

Previous Ranking(s): #5 (Org)

2016 Stats: .263/.373/.333, 0 HR, 5 SB in 15 games at the major league level, .287/.361/.441, 6 HR, 31 SB in 71 games at Double-A Reading, .500/.522/.591, 0 HR, 5 SB in 6 games at complex-level GCL.

The Role: OFP 55 — Solid-average center fielder
Likely 50 — Average outfielder, when he is actually on the field

YEAR	TEAM	LVL	AGE	PA	R	2B	3B	HR	RBI	BB	K	SB	CS	AVG/OBP/SLG	TAv	VORP	BABIP	BRR	FRAA	WARP
2014	CLR	A+	21	382	51	10	3	7	36	36	80	32	12	.257/.343/.370	.259	15.4	.316	3.1	CF(69): -0.1 • SS(17): -3.1	1.3
2015	REA	AA	22	257	44	6	6	4	15	18	42	29	10	.306/.356/.435	.283	19.6	.360	6.2	CF(58): 2.4	2.5
2016	PHL	Rk	23	24	6	2	0	0	0	1	3	5	1	.500/.522/.591	.402	5.3	.579	1.7	CF(3): -0.1 • LF(2): -0.1	0.5
2016	REA	AA	23	322	58	14	6	6	25	30	68	31	8	.287/.361/.441	.278	24.5	.357	9.6	CF(62): -7.4 • LF(4): -0.9	2.0
2016	PHI	MLB	23	69	10	4	0	0	6	8	19	5	1	.263/.373/.333	.282	3.9	.395	0.8	LF(12): -0.2 • RF(4): 0.0	0.5
2017	*PHI*	*MLB*	*24*	*91*	*12*	*3*	*1*	*2*	*8*	*7*	*24*	*6*	*2*	*.235/.295/.363*	*.238*	*2.0*	*.303*	*0.8*	*CF -0*	*0.1*
2018	*PHI*	*MLB*	*25*	*323*	*37*	*11*	*3*	*8*	*35*	*24*	*89*	*22*	*7*	*.238/.302/.380*	*.249*	*8.6*	*.304*	*3.3*	*CF -1*	*0.8*

Breakout: 12% Improve: 25% Collapse: 2% Attrition: 15% MLB: 41% *Comparables: Reymond Fuentes, Gorkys Hernandez, Kevin Kiermaier*

The Good: Roman Quinn is fast. Like really fast. Like sub-4.0 from both sides of the plate fast. Like fastest real prospect in baseball fast. And he is a real prospect, as he should hit enough, get on base enough and play well enough in center field to make him an ideal table-setter for your lineup. It's a slash-and-dash swing, and he has the speed to beat out almost anything into the 5.5 hole or bunt for a base hit. His speed covers for any sins in the outfield (and we'll get to those), and he has a strong enough throwing arm to handle right field if he ends up in more of a fourth-outfielder role.

The Bad: Despite 80 speed, Quinn is still a little rough in the outfield, especially at tracking balls in the air. He's a slap hitter without much in the way of power, which might be an issue if he ends up in a corner. He has yet to play 100 games in a season, losing time over the years to a ruptured Achilles' tendon and a fractured wrist along with the usual array of sprains and strains. He strikes out a bit more than you'd like out of this profile and more than you'd expect given his simple hitting mechanics. He will expand the zone and chase.

The Irrelevant: Even an unspectacular major-league career should earn Roman more money than 1989 Denzel Washington vehicle The Mighty Quinn, which pulled in just $4.5 million at the box office.

The Risks: Quinn has already debuted in the majors and he's hit wherever (whenever) he has played. But anytime you have as checkered an injury history as Quinn's, you are going to get a reputation as brittle. The injuries haven't sapped his athleticism yet, but it is fair to wonder if his body can handle the rigors of a 162-game major league season.

Major league ETA: Debuted in 2016

Ben Carsley's Fantasy Take: Comping Quinn to Billy Hamilton is super lazy, but what about playing fantasy sports isn't lazy? Hamilton hit .260 with 69 runs (nice) and 58 steals last season, good for a finish as fantasy's 15th-best outfielder. Quinn may not play enough or be quite fast enough to reach such a lofty SB total, but 40-plus steals are well within his reach if he manages to stay on the field. The risk is that Quinn won't be healthy enough to rack up counting stats, but one-trick fantasy ponies can be pretty useful if their one trick is good enough. Jarrod Dyson only got 337 PA this season, but he still swiped 30 bags and finished as a top-60 OF. That seems like a perfectly reasonable median fantasy outcome for Quinn.

9. Cornelius Randolph, LF

DOB: 06/02/1997

Height/Weight: 5'11" 205 lbs.

Bats/Throws: L/R

Drafted/Acquired: Drafted 10th overall in the 2015 MLB Draft, Griffin HS (Griffin, GA); signed for $3,231,300

Previous Ranking(s): #6 (Overall)

2016 Stats: .274/.355/.357, 2 HR, 5 SB in 63 games at Low-A Lakewood, .077/.200/0.77 0 HR, 0 SB in 5 games at complex-level GCL

The Role: OFP 55 — Hit tool carries the day into a good, high-average offensive threat
Likely 50 — Just a regular old bat-first corner outfielder

YEAR	TEAM	LVL	AGE	PA	R	2B	3B	HR	RBI	BB	K	SB	CS	AVG/OBP/SLG	TAv	VORP	BABIP	BRR	FRAA	WARP
2015	PHL	Rk	18	212	34	15	3	1	24	32	32	6	5	.302/.425/.442	.312	18.1	.362	1.3	LF(41): -0.0	1.8
2016	PHL	Rk	19	15	1	0	0	0	0	2	3	0	0	.077/.200/.077	.111	-2.1	.100	0.0	LF(5): -0.4	-0.2
2016	LWD	A	19	276	33	12	1	2	27	26	57	5	4	.274/.355/.357	.297	16.8	.346	1.5	LF(53): -0.7	1.9
2017	*PHI*	*MLB*	*20*	*250*	*23*	*10*	*1*	*5*	*25*	*19*	*72*	*1*	*0*	*.213/.281/.333*	*.220*	*-2.2*	*.284*	*-0.5*	*LF 2*	*0.0*
2018	*PHI*	*MLB*	*21*	*372*	*41*	*15*	*1*	*9*	*38*	*30*	*101*	*1*	*1*	*.224/.295/.352*	*.244*	*2.4*	*.290*	*-0.8*	*LF 3*	*0.6*

Breakout: 1% Improve: 7% Collapse: 0% Attrition: 4% MLB: 9% *Comparables: Ramon Flores, Jeimer Candelario, Caleb Gindl*

The Good: Randolph shows quick hands at the plate and a really good feel for hitting. He's also got a very good sense of the strike zone and an overall idea of what he wants to do at the plate. He kept his head above water at Low-A in his first full season despite battling a bad shoulder injury. Because of the hit tool and overall knack for offense, Randolph has an unusually high floor for a Low-A prospect of his caliber.

The Bad: There isn't much present power, even raw and even in batting practice. Lack of physical projectability might open some questions how much is coming. He's already a LF-only player at age 19. The profile might limit overall upside.

The Irrelevant: If Randolph makes the majors, he'll become just the second MLB draftee out of Griffin High School in Georgia to reach The Show—and both will have been top-ten overall picks (2008 first-overall pick Tim Beckham).

The Risks: Low-to-medium power corner projections are tough unless you hit, and Randolph might only hit. Shoulder injuries can linger and hamper hitting development. —Jarrett Seidler

Major league ETA: 2020

Ben Carsley's Fantasy Take: Randolph's hit tool makes him worthy of our attention, but his lack of power or speed and his distance from the majors make him a fringy bet to appear on our top-100 dynasty list. A future as an OF3 who grows into some pop and uses AVG as a carrying tool is in play, but so are less inspiring fantasy outcomes, such as, oh, I don't know, Lonnie Chisenhall?

10.

You awake from a fitful sleep. You were dreaming, you think. It wasn't a nightmare, but the forms that seemed crystal clear in your mind a moment ago, are now abstract shapes, the connections between them growing more tenuous by the second. You groggily assess your surroundings and realize you are no longer in the bedroom where you laid down to sleep some hours(?) ago. Your bed is the same, but it's four brass posters are now sitting in an empty cave, the rock formations that surround you an unnatural shade of purple.

You should be confused, scared even, but you feel like you have been here before. Are you still dreaming? You get up out of bed, and your legs feel like jelly, but you are strangely compelled to walk toward an eerie green light at the far end of the cavern peaking out from around a dilapidated wooden door.

The door is unlocked and find yourself in a well-appointed library. The floor is old oak, the many bookshelves the same. In the center of the room, behind an almost comically-oversized desk sits a man, his face buried in stacks of paper. He's a young man, about your age, well-dressed in the style of a Ivy League finance major, or maybe economics. His reams of notes are spread across the surface of the desk in a not-quite-haphazard manner, although you imagine it would take you weeks to figure out his filing system. You are trying to decide how best to announce your presence when he dramatically looks up from his work. He doesn't seem surprised that there is a visitor before him. The young man pushes his glasses up further on his nose and begins to assess you.

"Ah, you have arrived. Good, we are nearing our deadline. I am Klentak. You are now on my island of prospects. I am compiling a list. The first nine names were a simple enough task, but I need your help for the last spot. I have many prospects now, and frankly once you get to this point, it all depends on what you want to value. But be warned, the last person to come to this place selected Ben Lively. He now lies at the bottom of a very deep pit."

If you want to take the safe major league future, proceed to "Scott Kingery."

If you don't want to know the terrible truth about this player's hit tool, and just want to sock some dingers, proceed to "Dylan Cozens."

If you are intrigued by Dylan Cozens, but prefer he was older and more Australian, proceed to "Rhys Hoskins."

If you prefer to roll the dice with an 18-year-old pitcher, proceed to "Kevin Gowdy."

10. Scott Kingery, 2B

This 2015 second-round pick spent 2016 mimicking the trajectory of his middle-infield counterpart at the University of Arizona, Kevin Newman. Kingery features a short-to-the-ball bat path and a reactive, all fields approach at the plate. There was more swing and miss at Double-A than the approach should allow for, but Kingery possesses the athleticism to adjust. That same athleticism is on display through his plus-plus speed and plus defense. This small-statured second baseman will see major-league time on the strength of that speed and defense, and could prove to be a solid starter if the bat comes along. - Adam Hayes

10. Dylan Cozens, RF

There's always been at least 70 raw power here, and it jumped forward into games this year. Cozens hit a minor-league leading 40 homers at Double-A Reading, turning the projectable into actual. He hits the ball really hard and far when he squares it up. He has a decent idea of what he wants to do at the plate, especially against righties. He's way more athletic and quick than you'd think given his size, having stolen at least 20 bases each year he's been in full-season ball, and he has a strong throwing arm. While Double-A pitching was no match for him, there's a chance he won't be able to handle major-league velocity and premium breaking stuff.

And 29 of his 40 homers came in the Reading bandbox, so the power actualization, while still real, is less dramatic than it outwardly appears. He doesn't seem to be able to recognize spin against lefties and they currently eat him alive. He's limited to the corner outfield spots already, and his size might ultimately push him to first base. Cozens could be one of those dudes who hits .220 and strikes out 200 times while still helping you, but managers often don't like to play them. - Jarrett Seidler

(They especially don't like to play them when they coldcock teammates in the locker room- JP)

10. Rhys Hoskins, 1B

In 2016, Hoskins tied the previous Reading franchise record for home runs (38) in a single season, yet he does not sit atop that franchise leaderboard as he was outpaced by his teammate Cozens. Hoskins' power spike—he hit 17 across two levels in 2015—was the product of feasting on Eastern League fastballs and playing half of his season in Reading's launchpad, so expectations for a repeat power performance should be tempered. His raw power is above average, but tapping into that power in the future will be heavily dependent on adjusting to off-speed offerings. His hit tool shares the same question of off-speed adjustments, though he has shown patience at the plate and the ability to get on base. It is a first-base-only profile given his slow foot speed and below-average arm, and a fringy profile at that. - Adam Hayes

10. Kevin Gowdy, RHP

YEAR	TEAM	LVL	AGE	W	L	SV	G	GS	IP	H	HR	BB/9	K/9	K	GB%	BABIP	WHIP	ERA	FIP	DRA	VORP	WARP	cFIP	MPH
2016	PHL	Rk	18	0	1	0	4	4	9	9	0	2.0	9.0	9	57%	.300	1.22	4.00	2.31	3.36	2.40	0.2	95	
2017	*PHI*	*MLB*	*19*	*2*	*3*	*0*	*9*	*9*	*35^{2}*	*37*	*6*	*3.7*	*8.1*	*32*	*47%*	*.324*	*1.44*	*4.85*	*4.94*	*5.64*	*-0.3*	*0.0*	*132*	
2018	*PHI*	*MLB*	*20*	*4*	*7*	*0*	*28*	*28*	*168^{1}*	*150*	*24*	*3.5*	*9.6*	*180*		*.313*	*1.28*	*4.10*	*4.42*	*4.77*	*10.1*	*1.0*	*110*	

Breakout: 0% Improve: 0% Collapse: 0% Attrition: 0% MLB: 0% *Comparables: Jeurys Familia, Lucas Giolito, Tyler Glasnow*

Gowdy went two picks after Joey Wentz in the 2016 draft and has a similarly attractive mix of polish and projection in a prep arm. He sits 93-95 now, but you don't have to squint hard to see him ticking up even further as he fills out his lean, 6-foot-4 frame. His slider is a potential plus secondary offering that he can already spot or bury. He carries the usual caveats you'd expect in this profile. He's a long way from the majors, and as an elite prep arm, he hasn't needed to worry all that much about his changeup or command. But despite the lack of a professional track record, there is upside here not all that far off the arms in the top 10 proper.

Ben Carsley's Fantasy Take(s): Gowdy is boring as hell for our purposes. Kingery has enough speed that he's worth monitoring, but the rest of his prospect package is underwhelming enough to limit him to a flyer-type you can land for cheap. Hoskins' proximity and power make him interesting, but he's badly overhyped as a fantasy prospect at present thanks to his prodigious (and unsustainable) Double-A output. That leaves Cozens, who's got power and some speed, but who probably just swung and missed at something as I typed this. I'd bet that Triple-A and MLB arms arrest his development, making this another Cozens you Maeby want to stay away from. Wow that reference is old now.

OTHERS OF NOTE:

Jeffrey's Guy

Arquimedes Gamboa, SS

Signed for $900,000 as part of the Phillies' 2014 J2 class, Gamboa comes straight out of central casting for teenage Venezuelan shortstop. He's an advanced defender with above-average physical tools for the 6 and has the ability to make the difficult play look routine, although he is prone to the occasional head-scratcher on the routine ones. He was overmatched at the plate as an 18-year-old in the Penn League, but there is bat speed from both sides and enough foot speed to grab an extra base on a ball in the gap. Gamboa is a long ways from contributing to a major-league team, and playing at a low level, so all I am looking for is a glimpse or two of something that doesn't look out of place at higher levels or even in the majors. Gamboa gave me more than one or two, and I'll be keeping an eye on him in Lakewood next year.

Steve's Guy

Jhailyn Ortiz, RF

Signed for $4 million as part of their 2015 IFA spending class, Ortiz skipped the DSL and went straight to the GCL to start his professional career. Ortiz is a massive human being, listed at 6-foot-2, 260 pounds, and he could become bigger, in both a positive and negative light as he played the season as a 17-year-old. The calling card here is the power: he has massive amounts of it that is already starting to play in games, albeit at an unchallenging level. He has impressive bat speed to go along with it and shows a good idea for the strike zone, as well as consistency with his swing. Pitchers who have shown the ability to sequence have gotten him to chase and it remains to be seen how he adjusts going forward. Ortiz's arm is above average, but his lack of foot speed and currently poor defensive skills leaves one to wonder about where he ends up on the defensive spectrum. The profile isn't as desirable if he moves to first base, but right field is still in the realm of possibilities if it all goes swimmingly. - Steve Givarz

The guy you were going to ask about in the comments

Jose Pujols, RF

After droning on in my intro to these lists about "upside" you'd think I'd at least include Pujols in our ode to R.A. Montgomery. If you were designing a top prospect from scratch, you could do worse than making him look like Jose Pujols, but in field testing he is more of a Minimum Viable Product. The frame still oozes projection. He's tall, lean and athletic, and when his swing mechanics are working in time, he can put on a show in batting practice. In games the swing is rarely as pretty, with his upper and lower halves often out of sync. And anytime he saw stuff better than your run-of-the-mill Sally League arm he appeared overmatched. He is awkward in the outfield and his athleticism doesn't play up in between the lines as much as you'd expect. You can forgive a bit of rawness in A-ball, more than a bit even, but I just don't see meaningful major-league upside in the package at present.

TOP 10 TALENTS 25 AND UNDER (BORN 4/1/91 OR LATER)

1. Odubel Herrera	6. Nick Williams
2. J.P. Crawford	7. Maikel Franco
3. Vincent Velasquez	8. Mickey Moniak
4. Aaron Nola	9. Jake Thompson
5. Jorge Alfaro	10. Franklyn Kilome

You'll forgive me, as a Phillies fan, for being surprised and baffled at the embarrassment of 25-and-under riches I have to work with while writing this list. I only got five deep into Jeff's prospect list before I had to start making room for the major leaguers, and that's without promising first baseman (and now, after the release of Ryan Howard, presumptive starter) Tommy Joseph as well as two just-over-the-hill breakout candidates in Jerad Eickhoff and Aaron Altherr. So to say this was painful is one part melodramatic and two parts accurate—you have to kill a lot of your babies to get to the 10 best.

So to get there, I tried to be a real Matt Klentak about this. The Phillies' second-year GM has made quite a few moves based on upside—drafting Moniak first overall, trading for Mark Appel (who also missed the top 10 here in his last year of eligibility)—and perhaps an equal number of moves based on floor—drafting Nola, trading for arms like Thompson and Eickhoff. The result is a fairly balanced farm system that, unlike the Phillies' farms that came from the drafts of 2007-2012, does not rely on lottery tickets reaching their 10th-percentile result, but on a balance of risk and reward. As a result, the Phillies of the future shouldn't be abysmally bad even in their worst years, and while that might not bring Cubsian excitement, it's not a bad strategy for contention either.

So with that in mind, balance: at the top of our list I took safety over upside. Understand, though, that Crawford and Odubel Herrera are basically 1A and 1B on this list. One is, as Jeff has noted, a potential All-Star shortstop, the commodity every team dreams of procuring, and the other is a speedy, high-OBP and low-power center fielder. Herrera—the latter, not the former—is yet another successful Phillies Rule 5 pick up the middle, joining Shane Victorino (who memorably stuck with the team) and Ender Inciarte (who memorably did not). He has decent patience, doubles power, speed and strong defense (just ask Cole Hamels about how he maintained his 2015 no-hitter). He's been roughly a four-win player for two years now, and a late-season spell likely brought on by fatigue notwithstanding, he is likely to be a cog in the Phillies' lineup for years to come. He won't be a star, probably, but a four-win outfielder that you can bank? You want one of those.

Below Crawford, but ahead of the quixotic and risky Alfaro, I slotted two starting pitchers who—hyperbole here—will largely determine if the Phillies succeed in their rebuild or not. Velasquez is the riskier of the two, though also the pitcher with the higher ceiling: a double digit K/9 paired with an acceptable walk rate of around 3.0 per nine, Velasquez is exactly the kind of pitcher that, once it clicks for him, could be dominating the NL and in contention for a Cy Young. His stuff is that good. He could also get a shoulder injury or Tommy John and be relegated to a bullpen or fall out of the league entirely. I'd bet more on the former than the latter, but not a lot.

Nola follows Velasquez as his strange mirror image. Slightly lower K/9, slightly lower BB/9, significantly lower HR/9, Nola is the Maddux-arm you can dream on when you're not being realistic about his ceiling but who is more likely to turn into Kyle Hendricks over the long haul. The thing is, Hendricks—a middling strikeout, elite command/control pitcher—is not just useful, but can be extraordinarily valuable. Nola seems destined to be part of the completely obnoxious "Is he a 1 or a 2?" conversation for his career, but let's just say right now: being a 1 or a 2 as a 24-year-old is a pretty darn good outcome.

Then, after Alfaro and Williams, who are, ultimately, all upside until they show that they can do it in the majors for alternate reasons that Jeff has covered above, we have Maikel Franco. Franco, if you remember, was supposed to hit .280/.350/.560 this year. That uh, didn't happen. Franco's low walk rate deflated his OBP, as did his lack of speed on the basepaths. And while he acquitted himself decently at third base, it's unclear if he really has the ability to stick there, particularly with the influx of middle and corner infield prospects the Phillies love to stockpile.

And suddenly, you're looking at a .255/.306/.427 first baseman and softly whispering "Ryan….?" But Franco isn't Howard, and if he can build on his 2015, he could make this low ranking look pretty foolish. How he builds on it, I'm not sure, as it involves outpacing his troubling BABIP and turning outs into hits. So his upside is murky, but it's still upside in the majors, as opposed to Moniak, who has all-world potential but a ton of obstacles to clear before he gets there.

And then, after Moniak we have Jake Thompson. Thompson is hard to figure out, but he has tantalizing ability, largely in the mold of the aforementioned Kyle Hendricks. He did not fare too well in his first taste of the big leagues, but had a pretty nice year in the minors, and 53.2 innings does not a career make. He could totally bottom out and become a mop-up guy or a swing starter, or he could make good on his potential and become a solid No. 3 starter. That ceiling, combined with major-league readiness make him worth putting above higher variance guys like Kilome, Medina and Sanchez, however much pause it gives me.

Klentak has really overhauled this system, though many of the early moves that started him along this path were Ruben Amaro Jr. specials. Still, Amaro's due aside, Klentak's fingerprints are all over this team, and the balance between safety and risk in this exciting 10-under-25 is remarkable when you see it all in one place. Here's hoping there's more upside and less downside for the Phillies and Klentak moving forward.

—Trevor Strunk

PITTSBURGH PIRATES

The State of the System: *This is an incredible top five prospects. Impact talent, arms, bats...oh no don't look down, why did you look down?*

THE TOP TEN

1. OF Austin Meadows	6. 3B Will Craig
2. RHP Tyler Glasnow	7. SS Cole Tucker
3. 1B/OF Josh Bell	8. 3B Ke'Bryan Hayes
4. RHP Mitch Keller	9. LHP Steven Brault
5. SS Kevin Newman	10. LHP Braeden Ogle

The Big Question: Is there such a thing as a mid-rotation starter? (part two of ???)

I have no. 3 starters on the brain again. This seems to happen around this time every year now. I've dispensed with another 101 writeups for the Annual over the faint din of junk food TV— this year it was The Voice and The Voice UK for some inexorable reason, perhaps Ricky Wilson's sartorial sense and piercing blue eyes were a factor. Most of those write-ups, soundtracked by a 40-grade interpretation of a Hozier ballad, were about mid-rotation starters. Because once you get about 20 prospects in—especially in a year where the overall prospect class is shallower than usual—you are dealing with assembly-line-made widgets, a plus fastball affixed here, a potentially plus breaking ball there, command and change expensive optional extras, and absolutely no manufacturer's warranty to speak of.

I've tried Mad Libs, medieval poetic forms, and odes to Dashiell Hammett to break up the monotony of 60 FB, 60 SL, 40 CH, 45 command writeups. Occasionally you will at least get a guy with good hair in the mix. But the drier write-up is the topic this time.

There's really only one prospect on the list below that broadly fits that definition, Mitch Keller. Glasnow is a cut above, although he has similar issues to our oft-repeated no. 3 profile, the fastball is a little sexier, the curveball a little more advanced. The gap between 60 and 70 is significant, even if for both Keller and Glasnow, we are still squinting and projecting a little bit to get it there.

There's another question I am dancing around a bit, as I've generally tried to avoid process stories in this space. But it's more broadly applicable as a question of certitude when making these lists.

How certain are we (am I) that Tyler Glasnow is a better prospect than Mitch Keller?

There is the issue of proximity of course. Keller spent almost the entire season in the South Atlantic League. Glasnow has already earned some major league per diems. Even if we think Keller's stuff can eventually match Glasnow's—and there were some late-season reports that point in that direction—we still have a bird in the hand here. Keller is much riskier, and based on our role grades, not offering more reward.

Okay, well...how confident are we (am I) about a dude's command jumping?

That's the thing with the mid-rotation starter. We usually first point to the lack of a third pitch as the blotch on the resume, but major-league hitters feast on plus fastballs located poorly. And with Glasnow, command isn't even the first hurdle here, we need to backtrack to control. Plus fastballs sure tend to get located poorly when you've walked a couple guys already in the inning.

Mitch Keller's control is quite good. His command isn't bad either, although the aforementioned 60 fastball and curve will paper over command issues in the Sally League. But he can spot his fastball to either side, and it sinks and runs despite his height and stride gap relative to Glasnow. His delivery is simpler and more repeatable—in part due to the stride and height gap, but it's also simpler, full stop. With Glasnow when it comes together though, gosh, can you imagine it?

Well, how confident are we (am I) that it will come together?

At the outset of this year's lists, I wrote about why we always chase upside. Because yes, if it comes together, you can imagine it. And boy, it's pretty good. So Glasnow ranks

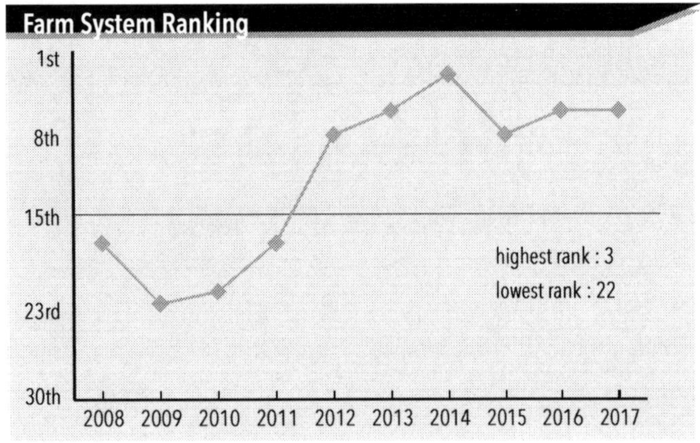

Personnel

President:
Frank Coonelly

EVP, General Manager:
Neal Huntington

Assistant General Manager:
Kevan Graves

Assistant General Manager:
Greg Smith

Assistant General Manager:
Kyle Stark

Manager:
Clint Hurdle

BP Alumni:
Dan Fox
Grant Jones
Stuart Wallace

ahead of Keller. This is hardly apostasy. It is about as cold a take as you will get on these lists. But...it's within, well Jarrett and I have taken to calling it the "fudge factor." It can make a hash of our most carefully-considered prospect rankings, especially when dealing with pitchers. "There is no such thing as a mid-rotation starter" implies we don't know what a mid-rotation starter looks like, which means how the heck are we ranking the twenty of them we are calling "mid-rotation starters" on a national list.

Well, we are, because that's our job. I and others will implore you not to take ordinal rankings too literally. The 19th best prospect turning out worse than the 26th prospect is hardly a scandal. But that fudge factor? It's bigger than you think.

So how certain are we (am I) that Tyler Glasnow is a better prospect than Mitch Keller?

He's higher on the list, man. He's higher on the list.

1. Austin Meadows, OF

DOB: 05/03/1995

Height/Weight: 6'3" 200 lbs

Bats/Throws: L/L

Drafted/Acquired: Drafted ninth overall in the 2013 MLB Draft, Grayson HS (Loganville, GA); signed for $3.0296 million

Previous Ranking(s): #2 (Org.), #22 (Overall)

2016 Stats: .200/.294/.333, 0 HR, 0 SB in 5 games at Low-A West Virginia, .311/.365/.611, 6 HR, 9 SB in 45 games at Double-A Altoona, .214/.297/.460 6 HR, 8 SB in 37 games at Triple-A Indianapolis

The Role: OFP 70— All-star-level outfielder in the Christian Yelich mold
Likely 60—Above-average everyday left fielder

YEAR	TEAM	LVL	AGE	PA	R	2B	3B	HR	RBI	BB	K	SB	CS	AVG/OBP/SLG	TAv	VORP	BABIP	BRR	FRAA	WARP
2014	PIR	Rk	19	6	1	2	1	0	1	2	0	0	0	1.000/1.000/2.000	.827	4.0	1.000	0.0		0.4
2014	BRI	Rk	19	18	2	0	0	0	0	3	3	0	0	.071/.235/.071	.138	-0.8	.091	0.1		-0.1
2014	WVA	A	19	167	18	13	1	3	15	14	30	2	3	.322/.388/.486	.293	10.7	.383	-0.3	CF(38): 0.4	1.2
2015	BRD	A+	20	556	72	22	4	7	54	41	79	20	7	.307/.357/.407	.289	32.0	.351	-0.1	CF(114): -16.4	1.9
2015	ALT	AA	20	28	5	2	3	0	1	2	5	1	0	.360/.429/.680	.375	3.9	.450	-0.2	CF(6): -0.4	0.4
2016	ALT	AA	21	190	33	16	8	6	23	16	32	9	3	.311/.365/.611	.332	19.7	.343	0.8	CF(39): 1.5 • LF(2): -0.6	2.3
2016	WEV	A-	21	17	0	2	0	0	0	2	1	0	0	.200/.294/.333	.217	-0.6	.214	-0.4	CF(5): 0.7 • LF(1): -0.1	0.0
2016	IND	AAA	21	145	16	7	3	6	24	15	34	8	2	.214/.297/.460	.291	9.6	.236	0.9	CF(23): -3.6 • LF(11): -0.3	0.6
2017	*PIT*	*MLB*	*22*	*64*	*8*	*3*	*1*	*2*	*7*	*4*	*14*	*2*	*1*	*.257/.310/.432*	*.256*	*1.8*	*.304*	*0.2*	*CF -0*	*0.1*
2018	*PIT*	*MLB*	*23*	*333*	*41*	*16*	*4*	*11*	*42*	*27*	*76*	*10*	*3*	*.258/.321/.445*	*.270*	*12.6*	*.308*	*1.3*	*CF -2 • RF 0*	*1.2*

Breakout: 4% Improve: 26% Collapse: 1% Attrition: 21% MLB: 56% *Comparables: Joc Pederson, Colby Rasmus, Brett Jackson*

The Good: Meadows has one of the best hit tools in the minors. He's direct to the ball with plus bat speed. He has extra-base hit power to all fields—even more up-the-middle and pull side— and his above-average raw started playing more in games in 2016. Potential .300 hitter in the majors. He's a plus runner who has the athleticism to play a competent center field. Could be a real defensive asset in a corner.

The Bad: The power has only really shown up for one season and may play more as 40 doubles than 20 home runs in the majors due to a swing geared more for line drives. A fringy arm limits him to left field if he isn't a center fielder, and his instincts on the grass haven't advanced to the point where his plus speed makes him a lock to stick up the middle. There's going to be durability questions until he plays a full season.

The Irrelevant: You probably know that both Meadows and Clint Frazier grew up in Loganville, Georgia, but did you also know that actor Kyle Chandler, best known for his role as Gary Hobson on Early Edition, is also a Loganville native?

The Risks: Meadows is just waiting for the Pirates to open up an outfield spot for him at this point. His advanced hit tool should make the transition to facing major-league pitching less bumpy than it is for most. He's been slightly injury prone throughout his minor league career. Needs to show he can hold up for a full 162-game season.

Major league ETA: Late 2017

Ben Carsley's Fantasy Take: Meadows is on the short list of best fantasy prospects in the game. He's a potential five-category fantasy contributor, he's knocking on the doorstep and he shouldn't be a player who needs a few years to figure stuff out before he's usable. The big red flag here is health, but while some of Meadows' boo-boos point to a potential injury-plagued career (the hamstring injuries), some are just dumb bad luck (getting struck in the face by a baseball). Still, I'm reasonably optimistic Meadows can hit .300 with 15 homers and 20 steals on a regular basis, and there's a chance I'm underselling the power. That's OF1/2 territory.

2. Tyler Glasnow, RHP

DOB: 08/23/1993

Height/Weight: 6'8" 225 lbs.

Bats/Throws: R/R

Drafted/Acquired: Drafted in the fifth round of the 2011 MLB Draft, Hart HS (Santa Clarita, CA); signed for $600,000

Previous Ranking(s): #1 (Org.), #11 (Overall)

2016 Stats: 4.24 ERA, 5.07 DRA, 23.1 IP, 22 H, 13 BB, 24 K in 7 games at major league level, 3.00 ERA, 3.99 DRA, 6 IP, 4 H, 6 BB, 11 K in 2 games at Double-A Altoona, 1.87 ERA, 2.80 DRA, 110.2 IP, 65 H, 62 BB, 133 K in 20 games at Triple-A Indianapolis

The Role: OFP 70—No. 2 starter
Likely 60—No. 3 starter that flashes better at times

YEAR	TEAM	LVL	AGE	W	L	SV	G	GS	IP	H	HR	BB/9	K/9	K	GB%	BABIP	WHIP	ERA	FIP	DRA	VORP	WARP	cFIP	MPH
2014	BRD	A+	20	12	5	0	23	23	124^{1}	74	3	4.1	11.4	157	40%	.260	1.05	1.74	2.63	1.66	54.40	5.5	73	
2015	WEV	A-	21	0	1	0	2	2	5^{1}	3	0	3.4	10.1	6	57%	.214	0.94	3.38	2.95	3.77	0.90	0.1	98	
2015	ALT	AA	21	5	3	0	12	12	63	41	2	2.7	11.7	82	42%	.269	0.95	2.43	1.98	1.33	26.30	2.8	58	
2015	IND	AAA	21	2	1	0	8	8	41	33	1	4.8	10.5	48	39%	.314	1.34	2.20	2.82	3.95	6.20	0.6	91	
2016	ALT	AA	22	0	0	0	2	2	6	4	1	9.0	16.5	11	30%	.333	1.67	3.00	4.86	3.99	0.70	0.1	97	
2016	IND	AAA	22	8	3	0	20	20	110^{2}	65	4	5.0	10.8	133	43%	.255	1.15	1.87	2.92	2.80	31.30	3.2	82	
2016	PIT	MLB	22	0	2	0	7	4	23^{1}	22	2	5.0	9.3	24	49%	.317	1.50	4.24	4.30	5.07	0.40	0.0	102	96.8
2017	*PIT*	*MLB*	*23*	*6*	*6*	*0*	*30*	*15*	*95*	*82*	*9*	*4.7*	*9.0*	*96*	*39%*	*.288*	*1.37*	*4.08*	*4.08*	*4.35*	*8.4*	*0.9*	*100*	
2018	*PIT*	*MLB*	*24*	*8*	*8*	*0*	*25*	*25*	144^{2}	*99*	*13*	*5.5*	*11.1*	*178*	*39%*	*.285*	*1.30*	*3.92*	*4.07*	*4.39*	*16.8*	*1.7*	*99*	

Breakout: 19% Improve: 35% Collapse: 23% Attrition: 23% MLB: 74% *Comparables: Gio Gonzalez, Henry Owens, Matt Moore*

The Good: Glasnow has two plus pitches in his repertoire already. A mid-90s fastball that can touch higher and is difficult to elevate due to its extreme downhill plane and arm-side run. The curveball sits around 80 and at its best comes out of the hand like the heater before dropping off the table with 12-6 break. Both pitches can flash plus-plus at times, and he's had outings where the fastball has sat higher and the curve has been unhittable. The stuff is difficult to square even for major-league hitters.

The Bad: Glasnow is 6-foot-8 and mostly legs at that. That is a lot of lower half to get over, and his delivery can often get out of sync. He can struggle to throw strikes with the fastball and his velocity can dip into the low-90s when he is fighting his mechanics. The curve can flatten out to more 11-5 or get spiked. The change is firm and still lags a ways behind the other two offerings.

His general inefficiency tends to shorten his outings.

The Irrelevant: The only taller pitchers to appear in a game for the Pirates are John Holdzkom and Johnny Gee, both of whom were listed at 6-foot-9.

The Risks: Minor league hitters have never been able to hit Glasnow, and he flashed top-of-the-rotation stuff against major league bats as well. You do wonder if he will ever throw enough strikes or have enough overall efficiency in-game to reach that OFP though.

Major league ETA: Debuted in 2016

Ben Carsley's Fantasy Take: Glasnow is going to be frustrating at times—especially early in his career—but the potential payoff is worth the cost of your antacid. The WHIPs will be high, but by god the strikeouts will be, too. An easy top-15 dynasty prospect, Glasnow is in the right organization to make the most of his talents. Yes, there are warts, but the upside is worth the risk.

3. Josh Bell, 1B/OF

DOB: 08/14/1992

Height/Weight: 6'2" 235 lbs.

Bats/Throws: S/R

Drafted/Acquired: Drafted 61st overall in the 2011 MLB Draft, Dallas Jesuit HS (Dallas, TX); signed for $5 million

Previous Ranking(s): #5 (Org.), #49 (Overall)

2016 Stats: .273/.368/.406, 3 HR, 0 SB in 45 games at major league level, .295/.382/.468, 14 HR, 3 SB in 114 games at Triple-A Indianapolis

The Role: OFP 60—First-division regular at first base
Likely 55—Above-average first baseman

YEAR	TEAM	LVL	AGE	PA	R	2B	3B	HR	RBI	BB	K	SB	CS	AVG/OBP/SLG	TAv	VORP	BABIP	BRR	FRAA	WARP
2014	BRD	A+	21	363	45	20	4	9	53	25	43	5	4	.335/.384/.502	.309	23.6	.364	-1.8	RF(62): -9.1	1.5
2014	ALT	AA	21	102	13	2	0	0	7	8	12	4	1	.287/.343/.309	.248	0.7	.329	0.3	RF(19): 2.8	0.4
2015	ALT	AA	22	427	47	17	6	5	60	44	50	7	4	.307/.376/.427	.299	18.9	.335	-2.1	1B(84): -7.5	1.2
2015	IND	AAA	22	145	20	7	3	2	18	21	15	2	0	.347/.441/.504	.325	11.2	.377	-0.1	1B(32): -3.2	0.8
2016	IND	AAA	23	484	57	23	4	14	60	57	74	3	7	.295/.382/.468	.306	24.1	.328	-4.0	1B(96): -3.3 • RF(4): 1.2	2.3
2016	PIT	MLB	23	152	18	8	0	3	19	21	19	0	1	.273/.368/.406	.286	6.4	.294	0.2	1B(23): -0.3 • RF(16): -2.5	0.4
2017	*PIT*	*MLB*	*24*	*542*	*69*	*24*	*4*	*15*	*59*	*54*	*88*	*3*	*3*	*.280/.353/.440*	*.277*	*18.0*	*.313*	*-1.0*	*1B -3*	*1.3*
2018	*PIT*	*MLB*	*25*	*567*	*76*	*26*	*4*	*18*	*72*	*57*	*94*	*3*	*3*	*.285/.360/.460*	*.292*	*24.7*	*.316*	*-0.9*	*1B -3*	*2.3*

Breakout: 3% Improve: 29% Collapse: 16% Attrition: 21% MLB: 66% *Comparables: Conor Jackson, Chris Carter, Ji-Man Choi*

The Good: If you are going to rate this highly as a corner outfield or first base prospect—and a far from spectacular defender either spot at that—you better hit a lot. Bell should. The swing is a little unorthodox, and it's mostly upper body, but he's shown impressive hand-eye and barrel control. He marries this with a good knowledge of the zone and the ability to make hard contract in all four quadrants. He's strong enough to lift balls over the fence too, even though he doesn't use his legs as much as you'd expect from a traditional power hitter. It's not impossible there are some 20-home run seasons at maturity, though I expect him to settle in around 15 in a typical year.

The Bad: Bell doesn't offer much with the glove in the outfield or even at first base. He swings from the, uh, hips, I guess, and you can get him to poke at soft stuff away when his two halves aren't in time. As strong as he is, the swing isn't going to provide the traditional corner power you expect, so the hit tool and approach will have to carry the profile. So far, so good on that front at least.

The Irrelevant: Bell was part of the Pirates record 17 million dollar draft class in 2011. We're guessing that record won't be broken for a while.

The Risks: Bell's bat has proved its mettle in the upper minors, and he held his own during his first pass against major league arms. The profile is a tough one of course, but this is a first base prospect even Ben has to feel good about (or at least not comp to CJ Cron).

Major league ETA: Debuted in 2016

Ben Carsley's Fantasy Take: I think Bell is underrated in fantasy circles. We spend a lot of time focused on what he can't do, but I believe in the hit tool, and I think he'll hit for at least acceptable power. Ok, maybe he's only Brandon Belt 2.0, but Brandon Belt is an eminently usable fantasy prospect.

4. Mitch Keller, RHP

DOB: 04/04/1996

Height/Weight: 6'3" 195 lbs.

Bats/Throws: R/R

Drafted/Acquired: Drafted 64th overall in the 2014 MLB Draft, Xavier HS (Cedar Rapids, IA); signed for $1 million

Previous Ranking(s): #10 (Org.)

2016 Stats: 2.46 ERA, 1.55 DRA, 124.1 IP, 96 H, 18 BB, 131 K in 23 games at Low-A West Virginia, 0.00 ERA, 3.14 DRA, 6 IP, 5 H, 1 BB, 7 K in 1 game at High-A Bradenton

The Role: OFP 60—No.3 starter
Likely 55—No. 3/4 starter

YEAR	TEAM	LVL	AGE	W	L	SV	G	GS	IP	H	HR	BB/9	K/9	K	GB%	BABIP	WHIP	ERA	FIP	DRA	VORP	WARP	cFIP	MPH
2014	PIR	Rk	18	0	0	0	9	8	27^{1}	19	0	4.3	9.5	29	0%	.279	1.17	1.98	3.14	3.08			92	
2015	BRI	Rk	19	0	3	0	6	6	19^{2}	25	1	7.3	11.4	25	49%	.429	2.08	5.49	4.53	4.64	2.70	0.3	105	
2016	WVA	A	20	8	5	0	23	23	124^{1}	96	4	1.3	9.5	131	48%	.284	0.92	2.46	2.41	1.55	47.90	5.3	71	
2016	BRD	A+	20	1	0	0	1	1	6	5	0	1.5	10.5	7	47%	.333	1.00	0.00	1.42	3.14	1.60	0.2	86	
2017	*PIT*	*MLB*	*21*	*5*	*6*	*0*	*19*	*19*	85^{2}	*96*	*12*	*3.2*	*5.9*	*56*	*36%*	*.324*	*1.47*	*4.93*	*4.86*	*5.64*	*-0.7*	*-0.1*	*131*	
2018	*PIT*	*MLB*	*22*	*6*	*9*	*0*	*25*	*25*	145^{1}	*141*	*20*	*4.0*	*8.1*	*131*	*36%*	*.316*	*1.41*	*4.70*	*4.93*	*5.38*	*2.3*	*0.2*	*124*	

Breakout: 18% Improve: 22% Collapse: 3% Attrition: 12% MLB: 26% *Comparables: Robert Stephenson, Luis Severino, Alex Reyes*

The Good: Keller was one of the best arms in the South Atlantic League this year, and the stuff backs up the numbers. His fastball can get up into the mid-90s and was touching higher late in the season. The pitch features both sink and tail and he commands it well to both sides of the plate. His curveball improved throughout the season and was flashing plus-plus by the end of the year. His delivery is about as clean as you will find nowadays, and his body is built for logging innings in a rotation—he's got "da butt" as Experience Unlimited would say.

The Bad: The change is firm at present. It lacks velo separation although it will show some tail at times. He's only shown his best stuff in flashes, to reach his projection it will have to show up more consistently.

The Irrelevant: In addition to an array of minor league sports options and Orchestra Iowa, Cedar Rapids is also home to the National Czech and Slovak Museum.

The Risks: Keller has made exactly one start in the Florida State League, but the combination of stuff and command make him lower risk than you'd expect from that professional resume. The changeup will need to get to passable, but I'm pretty confident in his major league rotation future. But he is a pitcher, so you know.

Major league ETA: Late 2018

Ben Carsley's Fantasy Take: Oh weird, a talented Pirates pitching prospect with a big fastball. Keller may lack the upside of a Glasnow, Jameson Taillon, or Gerrit Cole, but he's plenty talented in his own right. Keller is definitely a top-100 prospect, and I think his stock will rise considerably over the next few months. Buy now.

5. Kevin Newman, SS

DOB: 08/04/1993

Height/Weight: 6'1" 185 lbs.

Bats/Throws: R/R

Drafted/Acquired: Drafted 19th overall in the 2015 MLB Draft, University of Arizona (AZ); signed for $2.175 million

Previous Ranking(s): #4 (Org.)

2016 Stats: .366/.428/.494, 3 HR, 4 SB in 41 games at High-A Bradenton, .288/.361/.378, 2 HR, 6 SB in 61 games at Double-A Altoona

The Role: 55 OFP—Above-average regular, Think Freddy Sanchez
Likely 50—League-average starter, Think Ryan Theriot

YEAR	TEAM	LVL	AGE	PA	R	2B	3B	HR	RBI	BB	K	SB	CS	AVG/OBP/SLG	TAv	VORP	BABIP	BRR	FRAA	WARP
2015	WEV	A-	21	173	25	10	1	2	9	10	22	7	1	.226/.281/.340	.260	5.9	.252	-1.0	SS(38): -6.3	0.0
2015	WVA	A	21	110	14	4	1	0	8	9	8	6	1	.306/.376/.367	.289	7.3	.333	-0.4	SS(23): 0.3	0.8
2016	BRD	A+	22	189	24	10	1	3	24	17	12	4	1	.366/.428/.494	.355	28.1	.375	1.4	SS(38): 1.5	3.0
2016	ALT	AA	22	268	41	11	2	2	28	26	24	6	3	.288/.361/.378	.268	14.8	.308	2.3	SS(60): 0.2	1.6
2017	*PIT*	*MLB*	*23*	*250*	*30*	*11*	*1*	*6*	*25*	*18*	*38*	*2*	*1*	*.267/.327/.404*	*.250*	*8.7*	*.294*	*-0.1*	*SS 0*	*1.0*
2018	*PIT*	*MLB*	*24*	*356*	*42*	*16*	*2*	*9*	*40*	*26*	*54*	*4*	*1*	*.269/.329/.414*	*.268*	*15.1*	*.295*	*-0.1*	*SS 1*	*1.7*

Breakout: 6% Improve: 34% Collapse: 5% Attrition: 19% MLB: 49% *Comparables: Greg Garcia, Chris Taylor, Brad Miller*

The Good: One of the best pure hitters in the minors, Newman has all the things you like in a hitter. Plus bat speed, a line-drive swing, barrel control, an approach to all-fields and pitch recognition. Combine all that and you've got a guy who could be a plus or better hitter at the major-league level. Newman makes adjustments and very rarely swings and misses. While only an average straight-line runner, he is a better runner underway and can take opportunities for extra bases on the basepaths. He works counts well resulting in extra on-base opportunities.

The Bad: While a great hitter, the power is well below-average. He has a quality first step and can get rid of the ball quick, but his footwork isn't pristine, as he lacks explosiveness and flash. His arm, while accurate, tends to lack carry and isn't a threat.

The Irrelevant: Other winners of the Cape Cod League Batting title include Stephen Piscotty, Todd Cunningham, Chris Coghlan, and Conor Gillaspie.

The Risks: While a sound hitter, the major leagues are different and any underperformance of his hit tool lowers his overall value. He is more of a second baseman than shortstop, which puts more pressure on his bat to hold everyday value. If the hit tool doesn't play to our expectation the downside risk is significant.

Major league ETA: 2018 —Steve Givarz

Ben Carsley's Fantasy Take: Freddy Sanchez is a good comp, but if we're going for something more current, I think Newman could be something like 2015 Matt Duffy (the good one), but shortstop-eligible. That'd make him a top-20 option at the position, which means he'd be a good MI in 12- to 14-team leagues. The ceiling isn't sexy, but the floor is high.

6. Will Craig, "3B"

DDOB: 11/16/1994

Height/Weight: 6'3" 212 lbs.

Bats/Throws: R/R

Drafted/Acquired: Drafted 22nd Overall in 2016 MLB Draft, Wake Forest University (Winston-Salem, NC); signed for $2.253 million

Previous Ranking(s): N/A

2016 Stats: .280/.412/.362, 2 HR, 2 SB in 63 games at Low-A West Virginia

The Role: OFP 50—League-average first baseman
Likely 45—Second-division corner

YEAR	TEAM	LVL	AGE	PA	R	2B	3B	HR	RBI	BB	K	SB	CS	AVG/OBP/SLG	TAv	VORP	BABIP	BRR	FRAA	WARP
2016	WEV	A-	21	274	28	12	0	2	23	41	37	2	0	.280/.412/.362	.319	18.8	.322	-1.9	3B(46): 0.2	1.9
2017	*PIT*	*MLB*	*22*	*250*	*24*	*9*	*1*	*5*	*26*	*22*	*62*	*0*	*0*	*.218/.299/.339*	*.220*	*-2.9*	*.273*	*-0.3*	*3B -0*	*-0.4*
2018	*PIT*	*MLB*	*23*	*262*	*30*	*10*	*1*	*6*	*27*	*24*	*63*	*0*	*0*	*.225/.308/.359*	*.243*	*0.9*	*.278*	*-0.5*	*3B 0*	*0.1*

Breakout: 3% Improve: 14% Collapse: 1% Attrition: 17% MLB: 19% *Comparables: Rio Ruiz, Zelous Wheeler, Jeimer Candelario*

The Good: One of the best power-hitting prospects in last year's class, Craig is a patient hitter with a leveraged stroke from the right side that is geared to do damage to the baseball. Strong forearms and wrists work well into the zone, and he has enough bat speed and plane to turn around elevated velocity. There's less swing-and-miss than your typical power prospect, and he strikes out less than you'd expect from a guy who works deep counts. There's potential for an above-average hit tool along with plus power if he develops as the organization has placed a significant bet that he will. His arm is plus from the left side, with velocity that carries line to line.

The Bad: He is very, very slow, with a thick middle and heavy legs that just don't move with any kind of urgency regardless of situation. The range at third is well-below average, and he's extremely unlikely to stay at the position long-term. The strike zone discipline can bleed into passivity, and he has struggled to translate his power into wood-bat games. He can lose his lower half, and with it his ability to generate bat speed and drive the ball with consistent authority.

The Irrelevant: In addition to his former teammate and current Tiger Daniel Norris, Craig shares high school alumni status with Hall of Fame college football coach Steve Spurrier and Col. LeRoy Reeves, who designed the Tennessee state flag in 1905.

The Risks: Significant, especially given his pedigree as a first-round college bat. The club sent him to short-season ball after he signed, where the approach played but the power didn't. His defensive shortcomings put a significant amount of pressure on his bat, and his game power in particular.

Major league ETA: 2019 —Wilson Karaman

Ben Carsley's Fantasy Take: The first section of Craig's "The Bad" section also applies to me, which is never a good sign. The power tool shows some promise, but Craig is definitely a first baseman and might not hit enough to matter for us. He's a top-150 name because the minors are shallow right now, but don't let his first-round status fool you into thinking he's a blue chipper.

7. Cole Tucker, SS

DOB: 07/03/1996

Height/Weight: 6'3" 185 lbs

Bats/Throws: R/R

Drafted/Acquired: Drafted 24th overall in the 2014 MLB Draft, Mountain Pointe HS (Phoenix, AZ); signed for $1.8 million

Previous Ranking(s): #8 (Org.)

2016 Stats: .262/.308/.443, 1 HR, 1 SB in 15 games at Low-A West Virginia, .238/.312/.301, 1 HR, 5 SB in 65 games at High-A Bradenton

The Role: OFP 50—Average everyday shortstop
Likely 45—Fifth infielder/second division starter

YEAR	TEAM	LVL	AGE	PA	R	2B	3B	HR	RBI	BB	K	SB	CS	AVG/OBP/SLG	TAv	VORP	BABIP	BRR	FRAA	WARP
2014	PIR	Rk	17	217	39	6	2	2	13	26	38	13	5	.267/.368/.356	.278	10.2	.329	2.7		1.0
2015	WVA	A	18	329	46	13	3	2	25	16	49	25	6	.293/.322/.377	.269	18.7	.336	3.0	SS(69): 2.8	2.3
2016	WVA	A	19	67	9	4	2	1	2	4	9	1	1	.262/.308/.443	.312	6.5	.294	0.5	SS(15): 2.8	1.0
2016	BRD	A+	19	304	36	12	1	1	25	29	62	5	6	.238/.312/.301	.236	3.1	.306	-1.1	SS(61): 12.6	1.6
2017	*PIT*	*MLB*	*20*	*250*	*27*	*10*	*1*	*4*	*21*	*13*	*60*	*5*	*2*	*.233/.276/.347*	*.211*	*-1.4*	*.288*	*-0.1*	*SS 4*	*0.3*
2018	*PIT*	*MLB*	*21*	*374*	*39*	*15*	*3*	*7*	*38*	*21*	*86*	*7*	*4*	*.244/.289/.369*	*.236*	*3.9*	*.297*	*0.3*	*SS 6*	*1.0*

Breakout: 2% Improve: 11% Collapse: 0% Attrition: 2% MLB: 13% *Comparables: Ruben Tejada, Orlando Arcia, Tim Beckham*

The Good: Tucker features a balanced profile with a chance to stick at shortstop. He's an above-average runner whose speed is an asset on the bases and on the dirt. He shows good hands on the infield and is smooth around the bag despite his long and lanky build. At the plate he has feel for the barrel and strong wrists. The power plays as gap right now, but he could grow into more over-the-fence power as he fills out.

The Bad: Tucker is in that nebulous "could stick at short" category, as opposed to the "slam-dunk shortstop" or "can't stick at shortstop" categories. He's always going to get dinged for his height, although he is nimble generally and gets down low pretty well. He has enough arm for the position even after labrum surgery, but it's not an asset there. He's an aggressive hitter and still needs to grow into game power.

The Irrelevant: Mountain Point HS grads have been drafted eleven times. The best major leaguer so far is C.J. Cron (you can never get away from him, folks).

The Risks: Tucker might end up sliding over to third, which would help the defensive profile a bit, but not so much the prospect profile. There is still a lot of projection here to get to an everyday role.

Major league ETA: 2019

Ben Carsley's Fantasy Take: Meh. Tucker could end up as an ok MI thanks to his speed, but the hit and power tools aren't promising enough for us to fall in love at present. Honestly, I can't shake the feeling that he'll just be Jordy Mercer again but like, 15 percent better.

8. Ke'Bryan Hayes

DOB: 01/28/1997

Height/Weight: 6'1" 210 lbs.

Bats/Throws: R/R

Drafted/Acquired: Drafted 32nd overall in the 2015 MLB Draft, Concordia Lutheran HS (Tomball, TX); signed for $1.855 million

Previous Ranking(s): #9 (Org.)

2016 Stats: .400/.500/.600, 0 HR, 0 SB in 2 games at Gulf Coast League, .263/.319/.393, 6 HR, 6 SB in 65 games at Low-A West Virginia

The Role: OFP 50—Everyday third baseman
Likely 45—Second-division starter/corner infield bench bat

YEAR	TEAM	LVL	AGE	PA	R	2B	3B	HR	RBI	BB	K	SB	CS	AVG/OBP/SLG	TAv	VORP	BABIP	BRR	FRAA	WARP
2015	PIR	Rk	18	175	24	4	1	0	13	22	24	7	1	.333/.434/.375	.308	14.9	.393	0.2	3B(36): 5.9	2.0
2015	WEV	A-	18	52	8	1	0	0	7	6	7	1	1	.220/.320/.244	.296	1.9	.250	-1.7	3B(12): 3.2	0.5
2016	WVA	A	19	276	27	12	1	6	37	16	51	6	5	.263/.319/.393	.290	14.0	.304	-1.5	3B(64): 2.0	1.8
2016	PIR	Rk	19	6	0	1	0	0	0	1	1	0	0	.400/.500/.600	.398	1.1	.500	0.0	3B(2): 0.1	0.1
2017	*PIT*	*MLB*	*20*	*250*	*24*	*10*	*1*	*6*	*27*	*14*	*62*	*2*	*1*	*.231/.283/.361*	*.220*	*-3.0*	*.285*	*-0.4*	*3B 2*	*-0.1*
2018	*PIT*	*MLB*	*21*	*381*	*43*	*17*	*1*	*11*	*43*	*21*	*90*	*3*	*2*	*.244/.294/.388*	*.245*	*2.3*	*.293*	*-0.6*	*3B 3*	*0.6*

Breakout: 1% Improve: 6% Collapse: 0% Attrition: 3% MLB: 7% *Comparables: Cheslor Cuthbert, Jeimer Candelario, Maikel Franco*

The Good: Hayes is a solid third baseman. Moves well laterally despite his size, has good hands, actions, footwork and a plus arm. Potentially an above-average hitter. He'll show good plate coverage and marries it with above-average bat speed. Shows above-average power power at 5 o'clock, although it plays more fringy after dusk.

The Bad: The raw power hasn't really come into games much yet, as he prefers to make line-drive, gap-to-gap contact. He's still finding consistency with his swing at the plate. He's athletic enough for his size, but a below-average runner and not going to get faster. May never develop enough power to be an everyday corner player.

The Irrelevant: His father, Charlie Hayes, was a third baseman of some note.

The Risks: Hayes missed time this year with back and rib issues, which is suboptimal, though we are far from calling it a recurring issue. On the field, you'd like to see him start to turn more of his raw power into game power to carry the corner profile. He's only got an A-ball resume so far.

Major league ETA: 2020

Ben Carsley's Fantasy Take: We're sort of in wait-and-see mode with Hayes until he shows more power. If you start hearing reports about his raw improving or if you see him start to hit for power in games, invest. If not, he falls well short of top-100 prospect status, and would probably fall closer to the 150-175 range.

9. Steven Brault, RHP

DOB: 4/29/1992

Height/Weight: 6'0" 200 lbs.

Bats/Throws: L/L

Drafted/Acquired: Drafted 339th Overall in 2013 MLB Draft, Regis University (Denver, CO); acquired for Travis Snider

Previous Ranking(s): N/A

2016 Stats: 4.86 ERA, 6.21 DRA, 33.1 IP, 45 H, 17 BB, 29 K in 8 games at major league level, 0.00 ERA, 2.55 DRA, 4 IP, 1 H, 0 BB, 5 K in 1 game at Low-A West Virginia, 3.91 ERA, 2.57 DRA, 71.1 IP, 66 H, 35 BB, 81 K in 16 games at Triple-A Indianapolis

The Role: OFP 50—Average starter
Likely 40—No. 5 starter/swingman/up and down arm

YEAR	TEAM	LVL	AGE	W	L	SV	G	GS	IP	H	HR	BB/9	K/9	K	GB%	BABIP	WHIP	ERA	FIP	DRA	VORP	WARP	cFIP	MPH
2014	DEL	A	22	9	8	0	22	21	130	107	4	1.9	8.0	115	50%	.286	1.04	3.05	3.09	2.12	47.70	4.9	86	
2014	FRD	A+	22	2	0	0	3	3	16^{1}	7	0	1.1	5.0	9	56%	.152	0.55	0.55	2.78	2.89	4.90	0.5	91	
2015	BRD	A+	23	4	1	0	13	13	65^{2}	62	3	2.9	6.2	45	52%	.292	1.26	3.02	3.44	4.27	5.90	0.6	103	
2015	ALT	AA	23	9	3	0	15	15	90	72	1	1.9	8.0	80	51%	.273	1.01	2.00	2.37	1.99	31.10	3.4	74	
2016	WEV	A-	24	0	0	0	1	1	4	1	0	0.0	11.2	5	75%	.125	0.25	0.00	0.77	2.55	1.20	0.1	83	
2016	IND	AAA	24	2	7	0	16	15	71^{1}	66	6	4.4	10.2	81	39%	.319	1.42	3.91	3.59	2.57	21.80	2.2	86	
2016	PIT	MLB	24	0	3	0	8	7	33^{1}	45	5	4.6	7.8	29	47%	.354	1.86	4.86	5.11	6.21	-3.20	-0.3	117	93.8
2017	*PIT*	*MLB*	*25*	*6*	*6*	*0*	*16*	*16*	*96*	*97*	*11*	*3.6*	*7.0*	*75*	*43%*	*.295*	*1.41*	*4.40*	*4.42*	*4.70*	*5.2*	*0.5*	*100*	
2018	*PIT*	*MLB*	*26*	*9*	*10*	*0*	*27*	*27*	161^{2}	*128*	*19*	*5.0*	*10.0*	*179*	*43%*	*.298*	*1.35*	*4.36*	*4.56*	*4.92*	*11.2*	*1.2*	*114*	

Breakout: 16% Improve: 30% Collapse: 34% Attrition: 42% MLB: 77% *Comparables: Brandon Workman, Mike Kickham, Andre Rienzo*

The Good: How do you feel about sinker/slider backend lefties? Brault is a classic example of that ilk. He features a low-90s fastball he can throw to either side, the two-seam version shows good arm-side run and some sink. It's an effective pitch when he can keep it down in the zone and spot it away to righties. His best sliders are solid-average with hard, late depth, but he can also play with the shape some and will backdoor it. He's confident in the changeup and will throw it even when he's behind in counts. He maybe shouldn't so much? (we'll get there). There's some deception in his delivery as well.

The Bad: When the fastball isn't down, it's very hittable, and his command profile is more average or a tick above. The slider isn't a consistent bat-misser. The changeup features deceptive arm action, but not much velocity separation and inconsistent fade. He can tend to nibble with his merely average stuff which can get him into trouble and also limit his efficiency.

The Irrelevant: Anything I could include here has likely already been covered in his Reddit AMA.

The Risks: Well, how do you feel about sinker/slider backend lefties?

Major league ETA: Debuted in 2016

Ben Carsley's Fantasy Take: How do fantasy owners feel about sinker/slider backend lefties? They shouldn't feel great, even if the contextual factors are good, as they are with Brault. He might be worth something in very deep leagues as long as he's in the rotation, but Brault doesn't have the upside or staying power to matter for us. I'm sorry.

10. Braeden Ogle, LHP

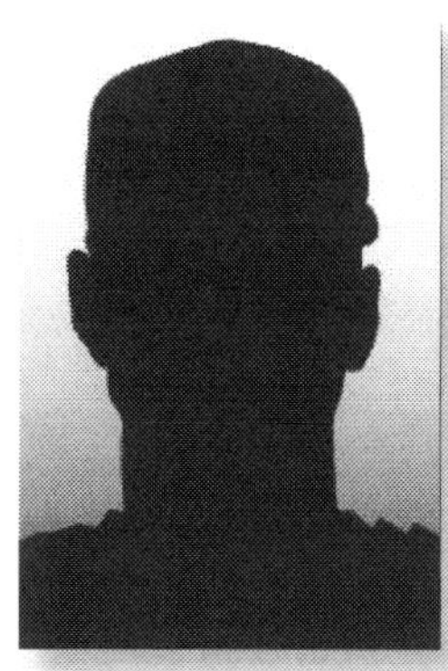

DOB: 7/30/1997

Height/Weight: 6'2" 170 lbs.

Bats/Throws: L/L

Drafted/Acquired: Drafted 135th Overall in 2016 MLB Draft, Jensen Beach HS (Jensen Beach, FL); signed for $800,000

Previous Ranking(s): N/A

2016 Stats: 2.60 ERA, 27.2 IP, 18 H, 11 BB, 20 K in 8 games at Gulf Coast League

The Role: OFP 50—No. 4 starter
Likely 40—No. 5 starter/middle reliever

YEAR	TEAM	LVL	AGE	W	L	SV	G	GS	IP	H	HR	BB/9	K/9	K	GB%	BABIP	WHIP	ERA	FIP	DRA	VORP	WARP	cFIP	MPH
2016	PIR	Rk	18	0	2	0	8	8	27^{2}	18	2	3.6	6.5	20	51%	.211	1.05	2.60	4.11	4.97	2.30	0.2	105	
2017	*PIT*	*MLB*	*19*	*2*	*3*	*0*	*9*	*9*	35^{1}	*38*	*5*	*3.8*	*7.2*	*28*	*47%*	*.329*	*1.50*	*4.92*	*4.82*	*5.55*	*0.1*	*0.0*	*130*	
2018	*PIT*	*MLB*	*20*	*3*	*5*	*0*	*17*	*17*	102^{1}	*101*	*15*	*4.2*	*8.2*	*93*		*.320*	*1.45*	*4.87*	*5.09*	*5.49*	*0.6*	*0.1*	*129*	

Breakout: 0% Improve: 0% Collapse: 0% Attrition: 0% MLB: 0% *Comparables: John Lamb, Akeel Morris, Lance McCullers*

The Good: How do you feel about projectable lefties a loooooong way away from the majors. Ogle fits the bill. He can get his fastball up to 95, but can't really keep it there (and his velocity could be all over the place as an amateur). He shows two different breaking balls and has some feel for spin. The change is...um...projectable.

The Bad: It's a project. The stuff was up and down in the spring, though pro reports were better. Every single pitch mentioned above needs a grade jump or two. This could go in a million different directions in the next 24 months. Some of them are really good though.

The Irrelevant: Ogle is the second Braeden in organized baseball. The first, Braeden Bock played for the upstart Federal League in...just kidding, it's another millennial—Braeden Schlehuber, a catcher in the Braves system.

The Risks: It's a projectable lefty in the Gulf Coast League! And he's a pitcher!

Major league ETA: 2021

Ben Carsley's Fantasy Take: Not yet. And unless the ceiling improves, maybe not ever.

OTHERS OF NOTE:

#11

Taylor Hearn, LHP

The other lefty in the Melancon deal, Hearn could very quickly transfer that designation to Felipe Rivero. He's a tall southpaw that has touched the triple digits and sits in the mid-90s as a starter. He pairs the potential plus-plus heater with a slider that flashes plus at present. The change and the command...well, we can direct you to the essay above. Hearn is still a little raw at present—and is yet to get out of A-ball—so the Pirates still have plenty of time to mold him into a—le sigh—mid-rotation starter, but he could be a weapons-grade southpaw in the bullpen if that fastball hits triple digits more in short bursts. It isn't always that simple, but it's also not a bad fallback position to have.

The factor on the farm

Dovydas Neverauskas, RHP

We often talk about how a fringy starting pitching prospect's stuff might "play up in the pen." We don't always know exactly what that will look like, but are betting on a couple more ticks on the fastball, a sharper slider, and an excising of the other, below-average pitches. What we don't usually expect is what happened to Nerverasukas. Calling the Lithuanian righty a "fringy starting pitching prospect" would be the nicest thing anyone wrote about him in 2015 before his move to the pen. But in the season-and-a-half since his conversion to relief, Neverauskas has gone from "starter that doesn't get out of A-ball" to "2017 major league bullpen option." The fastball jumped from the low 90s to the high 90s, and he pairs it with a hard cutter/slider thing. There likely isn't real late-inning potential here, but major league potential is impressive enough given where we were 18 months ago.

The factor on the farm (for another team)

Jose Osuna, OF/1B

Jose Osuna is in the wrong organization. He's probably not a great fit in a corner outfield spot, but he isn't unseating Austin Meadows or Gregory Polanco on the grass at PNC Park anyway. As it is the Pirates are looking to trade a franchise icon just to make room for Meadows anyway. Osuna also happens to play the same positions as Josh Bell, who is already in the majors and much higher on this list. Now redundancy isn't the worst thing in the world, and you can always use an extra bat like Osuna's. He doesn't have ideal pop for the three positions he can play, but he's strong enough to mash a dinger or 15. And he's not your traditional Triple-A-corner type at the plate, he's got some feel for hitting. You still have to squint hard to get the profile over a 45, but there are teams that could use that. Unfortunately, the Pirates do not appear to be one of them at present.

Catcher development paths are weird, part 785

Elias Diaz, C

Diaz debuted in the Pirates organization in 2009. Zach Duke and Paul Maholm made the most starts for the big club that year. Jack Wilson was their shortstop. I was writing and directing a short musical film about a young father who convinces his son he's a squid (the father, not the son). What I am trying to convey is that catcher development paths are long. Diaz can hit a little bit and is a solid enough backstop, but doesn't really do any one thing well enough to carve out a starter's role. He's had brief brushes with the majors in 2015 and 2016 and now should be fully ready for his long-ordained role in the fraternal order of backup catchers. My film adaptation of Haruki Murakami's short story, "All God's Children Can Dance" however, still remains in pre-production limbo.

Life begins at 20

Yeudy Garcia, RHP

When you sign all the "best" prospects from a country at 16, it's inevitable a few will fall through the cracks. After all, sometimes pitchers add velocity in their late teens. Sometimes a lot of velocity. Garcia signed with the Pirates at 20, so he's always going to be old for his level, but 2016 was more of the same in the Florida State League. It's a big fastball paired with a developing breaker. The background is always going to make one think "late-inning relief arm," and that might well be his eventual major league home, but there's no longer need to make up for lost time, so giving Garcia a shot as a starter in Double-A in 2017 seems like a reasonable plan.

TOP 10 TALENTS 25 AND UNDER (BORN 4/1/91 OR LATER)

1. Gregory Polanco
2. Austin Meadows
3. Jameson Taillon
4. Tyler Glasnow
5. Josh Bell
6. Mitch Keller
7. Kevin Newman
8. Chad Kuhl
9. Will Craig
10. Felipe Rivero

The rich get even richer in the 25-and-under list, and this year's version graduated Gerrit Cole at that. Topping the 2017 edition is former top prospect-turned-2016 breakout star Gregory Polanco. Like his corner outfield mate Starling Marte, Polanco is bordering on outrageously good defensively and probably capable of handling center. Offensively, Polanco is more of a lower-average slugger at present, but don't forget: we rated him as highly as a 60-potential hit as a prospect. The power certainly came around, and he's still growing as a player. If the hit tool comes around, he could yet be a superstar.

Jameson Taillon came back from over two years lost to Tommy John surgery and assorted other injuries to establish himself as a potential top-of-the-rotation starter. A lot of boxes are checked off here to just call him a top-of-the-rotation guy already: dominant fastball/curve combo, development of the change into a viable third pitch, command improvements, long-held expectations that he would get to this level, good performance in both the minors and the majors. Yet we hedge, and accordingly place Taillon third instead of first, in light of the injuries. Though third on this list is a slot still ahead of one of the three best RHP prospects in the game.

Sinkerballer Chad Kuhl popped in the majors fully-formed as a fourth starter in 2016. He doesn't have much upside past that, and it's always a bit of a balancing act on where to rank the present contributors against upside players. We've ranked him just ahead of Will Craig, and just behind Craig slots another player in this boat, Felipe Rivero. Rivero, the primary piece received in the Mark Melancon trade, is a present decent middle-leverage reliever with excellent stuff who has a chance to be a good high-leverage reliever if the command sorts out. One imagines the Pirates will probably get him some saves at some point to be flipped out for the next iteration in the chain.

—Jarrett Seidler

SAN DIEGO PADRES

The State of the System: *They tore it down and built it back up and we are back where we started with a very good and very deep system.*

THE TOP TEN

1. OF Manuel Margot	6. 3B Fernando Tatis Jr.
2. RHP Anderson Espinoza	7. RHP Jacob Nix
3. RHP Cal Quantrill	8. LHP Logan Allen
4. OF Hunter Renfroe	9. OF Jorge Ona
5. LHP Adrian Morejon	10. 2B Luis Urias

The Big Question: Is This 2012 All Over Again?

In 2012, the San Diego Padres had one of the top farm systems in all of baseball. BP's former prospect ace Kevin Goldstein gave the Friars top billing in his annual farm system review, as did ESPN's Keith Law. While the Padres lacked a headlining prospect, San Diego had built an unusually deep system. Goldstein gave nine Padres prospects four-star ratings, and argued that the top seven names in the system were essentially interchangeable.

Fast forward five years, and the situation on the ground is fairly similar. While the Padres don't have the league's top system—spoiler, they're comfortable in the top ten in our organziational rankings—they again boast a deep stable of potentially productive players. The 2012 edition had tons of interesting names, and while this year's may be top-heavy by comparison, in each case San Diego's depth compares well with everyone else's.

Now, let's return to the big question above.

By any reasonable measure, the Padres got very little out of that renowned 2012 crop. The best player on the list, Anthony Rizzo, never played for the Padres again. Jedd Gyorko popped 30 homers last year, but like Rizzo, he did so while plying his trade in the Midwest. Rymer Liriano never developed as a hitter, which is a problem when you're the world's most indifferent corner outfielder. Pitchers Casey Kelly, Joe Wieland, and Robbie Erlin couldn't stay healthy. Joe Ross was traded to the Nationals, and the less said about that deal the better. Cory Spangenberg might be the best player left over, and he's a low-ceiling second basemen coming off of a major quad injury. None of the three-star prospects Goldstein covered developed into big league contributors.

There's no way to sugarcoat the previous paragraph: that's a bad outcome, and it goes a long way towards explaining why the first half of the decade was so forgettable for San Diego. The good players on that list no longer play for the Padres, and the trades that pushed them away were a net negative for the club. The pitchers all got hurt. The toolsy guys didn't hit. The dream of a young, cost-controlled core in San Diego never materialized. Together, the group has produced nearly 30 WARP, but only 2.7 came for the Padres.

As fans of a bad and often rudderless team, Padres partisans might be tempted to lump the present group of youngsters with the disappointments from the past. But in this case, the past has little bearing on the future.

For one thing, there's not much evidence of a scouting or developmental pipeline malfunction. Rizzo, Ross, and Trea Turner may have blossomed elsewhere, but the Padres do not have an institutional blindspot the way that, say, the Mariners had with position players for a decade, or the Orioles do with young pitchers. Moreover, A.J. Preller's ill-advised spending spree in 2015 doesn't prove that the Padres can't obtain young talent; his trades for Manuel Margot and Anderson Espinoza, along with the club's gutsy decision to take Cal Quantrill in the draft last summer, suggests otherwise. Preller was also aggressive in Latin America, spending $25 million on 13 players last summer, including $4 million on blue-chip Dominican shortstop Luis Almanzar.

More specifically, the top of the Padres list features a bunch of fairly safe player-types. Rarely should you assume that a good minor leaguer will become a good major leaguer, but a number of the Padres top prospects are relatively decent bets to contribute. Margot is 22, posted good numbers in Triple-A, and has already debuted. His speed and defensive abilities in center field suit his

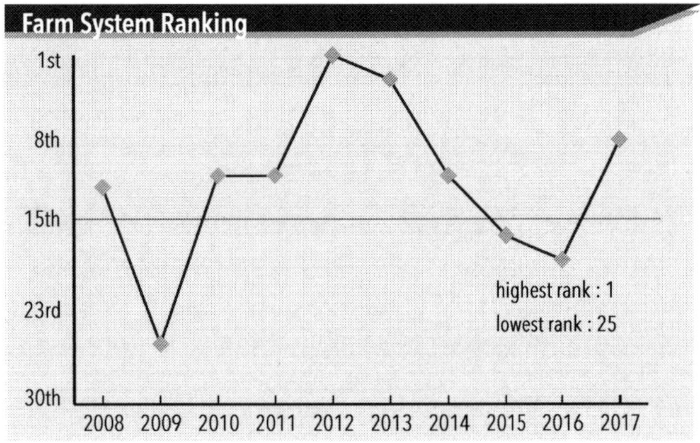

Personnel

EVP, General Manager:
A.J. Preller

VP, Assistant General Manager:
Fred Uhlman Jr.

Assistant General Manager:
Josh Stein

Manager:
Andy Green

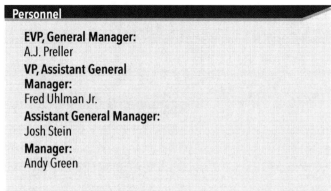

home park perfectly, and he's one of the best center field prospects in baseball. Quantrill's top-of-the-shelf stuff survived Tommy John surgery; while the right-hander may start in Low-A, he should move quickly. Hunter Renfroe has his warts, but like Margot, he's already reached the majors as well. There is no such thing as a safe teenage pitching prospect—but if there was, he would look something like Espinoza, who combines advanced pitchability with three offerings that flash plus or better.

Does any of this resolve the big question above? Of course not; only the ballplayers can sort that out definitively. But with the Padres rebuilding, and another wave of young talent lurking in the system just underneath our purview, the farm system is ascendent and healthy. Over the next five years, the Padres may or may not extract 30 WARP from the talent on our top ten list; much of that will depend on whether there's a hidden superstar in the group. It does seem safe to predict, however, that they'll produce quite a bit more than the 2.7 wins that the last bumper crop delivered to San Diego.

—Brendan Gawlowski

1. Manuel Margot, OF

DOB: 09/28/1994

Height/Weight: 5'11" 170 lbs.

Bats/Throws: R/R

Drafted/Acquired: Signed July 2011 by Boston out of the Dominican Republic for $800,000; acquired by San Diego in Craig Kimbrel trade

Previous Ranking(s): #1 (Org), #14 (Top 101), #16 (Midseason Top 50)

2016 Stats: .243/.243/.405, 0 HR, 2 SB in 10 games at the major league level, .304/.351/.426, 6 HR, 30 SB in 124 games at Triple-A El Paso

The Role: OFP 60—First-division center fielder that hits enough to be a sparkplug at the top of a lineup
Likely 55—Above-average center fielder that hits at the bottom of the lineup.

YEAR	TEAM	LVL	AGE	PA	R	2B	3B	HR	RBI	BB	K	SB	CS	AVG/OBP/SLG	TAv	VORP	BABIP	BRR	FRAA	WARP
2014	GRN	A	19	413	61	20	5	10	45	37	49	39	13	.286/.355/.449	.282	24.8	.309	2.8	CF(96): 8.7	3.6
2014	SLM	A+	19	56	4	5	0	2	14	2	5	3	2	.340/.364/.560	.320	5.4	.333	0.0	CF(16): -0.8	0.5
2015	SLM	A+	20	198	35	6	5	3	17	11	15	20	5	.282/.321/.420	.273	9.6	.289	1.5	CF(42): 5.1	1.7
2015	PME	AA	20	282	38	21	4	3	33	21	36	19	8	.271/.326/.419	.270	13.0	.303	1.9	CF(63): -3.6 • RF(1): 0.1	1.1
2016	ELP	AAA	21	566	98	21	12	6	55	36	64	30	11	.304/.351/.426	.270	30.8	.335	7.9	CF(121): 17.8 • RF(1): 0.2	4.7
2016	SDN	MLB	21	37	4	4	1	0	3	0	7	2	0	.243/.243/.405	.274	2.4	.300	0.8	CF(9): 0.4 • RF(1): 0.1	0.3
2017	*SDN*	*MLB*	*22*	*462*	*58*	*20*	*5*	*9*	*40*	*25*	*84*	*20*	*8*	*.249/.289/.385*	*.241*	*9.4*	*.285*	*2.0*	*CF 11*	*1.7*
2018	*SDN*	*MLB*	*23*	*538*	*59*	*23*	*6*	*12*	*58*	*32*	*96*	*24*	*9*	*.257/.303/.400*	*.257*	*16.9*	*.292*	*3.1*	*CF 13*	*3.2*

Breakout: 3% Improve: 22% Collapse: 10% Attrition: 26% MLB: 44% *Comparables: Ben Revere, Ryan Sweeney, Gerardo Parra*

The Good: Margot is the best bet in the minors to be a plus defensive center fielder. He's a plus-plus runner with good outfield instincts. The speed will play on the bases as well. He's a potential plus hitter and produces above-average bat speed out of a compact, line-drive swing. He covers the plate well and should have no issue with major league velocity.

The Bad: Margot is going to have below-average power in the majors. He can be an aggressive hitter and at times showed some vulnerability to spin in Triple-A. There could be a bit of an adjustment for him against major-league pitching even if his glove is good enough quickly enough to keep him in the lineup. His arm is only average.

The Irrelevant: Margot was the youngest player in the Pacific Coast League on Opening Day. That is actually sort of relevant. Less relevant is he was born the same week as The Scout was released.

The Risks: My colleague Jarrett Seidler is fond of saying that the hardest thing to evaluate is how well a player will hit major-league pitching. He's hit every other level of pitching so far, but as good as the potential glove/speed combo is, if he's not an above-average hitter, the profile just isn't that special.

Major league ETA: Debuted in 2016

Ben Carsley's Fantasy Take: Margot has proximity, MiLB track record and a carrying tool (SB) on his side. He's not the sexiest fantasy prospect in the world because he's unlikely to hit for much power and the average is likely to fluctuate some, but he's as sure a bet as any prospect to be a meaningful contributor, and to meaningfully contribute soon. Expect a tolerable average with 25 steals right away, and know that the average could tick up enough in his prime for Margot to serve as an OF3.

2. Anderson Espinoza, RHP

DOB: 03/09/1998

Height/Weight: 6'0" 160 lbs

Bats/Throws: R/R

Drafted/Acquired: Signed July 2014 out of Venezuela for $1.8 million by the Red Sox; acquired by San Diego in the Drew Pomeranz deal

Previous Ranking(s): #2 (Org), #73 (Top 101), #24 (Midseason Top 50)

2016 Stats: 4.38 ERA, 4.44 DRA, 76 IP, 77 H 27 BB, 72 K at Low-A Greenville, 4.73 ERA, 4.46 DRA, 32.1 IP, 38 H, 8 BB, 28 K at Low-A Fort Wayne

The Role: OFP 60—No. 3 starter
Likely 55—Mid-rotation starter or late-inning reliever

YEAR	TEAM	LVL	AGE	W	L	SV	G	GS	IP	H	HR	BB/9	K/9	K	GB%	BABIP	WHIP	ERA	FIP	DRA	VORP	WARP	cFIP	MPH
2015	DRX	Rk	17	0	0	0	4	4	15	13	0	1.8	12.6	21	64%	.361	1.07	1.20	1.67	1.91	6.60	0.6	81	
2015	RSX	Rk	17	0	1	0	10	10	40	24	0	2.0	9.0	40	71%	.238	0.82	0.68	2.27	2.13	16.70	1.6	79	
2015	GRN	A	17	0	1	0	1	1	3^{1}	4	0	5.4	10.8	4	73%	.364	1.80	8.10	2.88	3.51	0.60	0.1	91	
2016	GRN	A	18	5	8	0	17	17	76	77	2	3.2	8.5	72	49%	.342	1.37	4.38	2.99	4.44	4.70	0.5	97	
2016	FTW	A	18	1	3	0	8	7	32^{1}	38	1	2.2	7.8	28	44%	.363	1.42	4.73	3.17	4.46	2.00	0.2	101	
2017	*SDN*	*MLB*	*19*	*5*	*7*	*0*	*20*	*20*	86^{2}	*91*	*12*	*3.7*	*7.1*	*69*	*47%*	*.323*	*1.46*	*4.71*	*4.71*	*5.47*	*0.9*	*0.1*	*128*	
2018	*SDN*	*MLB*	*20*	*7*	*9*	*0*	*28*	*28*	173^{2}	*162*	*23*	*4.2*	*9.2*	*177*		*.321*	*1.40*	*4.32*	*4.65*	*5.02*	*7.3*	*0.8*	*116*	

Breakout: 0% Improve: 0% Collapse: 0% Attrition: 0% MLB: 0% *Comparables: Manny Banuelos, Tyler Skaggs, Martin Perez*

The Good: Espinoza has a potential plus-plus fastball. He can ramp it up into the upper 90s, and it sits comfortably around 95 with explosive arm-side life. He can work both sides of the plate with it already. The mid-70s curve flashes plus with tight, 11-5 break and improving ability to use it as more than just a chase pitch. The change will also flash plus or even better with extreme velo separation (low-80s) and hard sink and fade. Espinoza has advanced pitchability for his teenaged years and is a complete player on the mound who already has a handle on fielding his position and holding runners.

The Bad: Sometimes his fastball velocity is "only" plus. The command can waver at times due to some inconsistent mechanics. That's the kind of stuff you grow out of, but Espinoza probably won't be growing taller, and he lacks a starter's frame or much in the way of physical projection. Both secondaries flash, but need grade jumps to play to the OFP. The change is particularly inconsistent, but we say that about every 18-year-old on these lists (because it is inevitably true).

The Irrelevant: Not to toot our own horn, but Craig and I successfully predicted the Espinoza-for-Pomeranz trade back in July.

The Risks: Espinoza's numbers as an 18-year-old in A-ball don't concern us much, but I do feel the need to throw a little cold water on the profile. He's a long way from the majors, and there's always going to be reliever whispers dogging a six-foot righty, especially one that has, well, a teenaged frame. He might grow out of that and become an impact starter, but we are a long ways away from that, and a lot can go wrong in the interim.

Major league ETA: 2019

Ben Carsley's Fantasy Take: Don't get caught up in Espinoza's 2016 stats; we're still dealing with a potential front-line starter here. You're familiar with my thoughts on valuing upside over probability when it comes to dynasty starters by now, and Espinoza is teeming with the former. He's still a top-50 fantasy prospect in my book, because if it does work, we're looking at a high-strikeout SP1 who pitches in Petco Park. That, to use an industry term, would be extremely good.

3. Cal Quantrill, RHP

DOB: 2/10/1995

Height/Weight: 6'2" 165 lbs

Bats/Throws: L/R

Drafted/Acquired: Drafted eighth overall in the 2016 MLB draft, Stanford University (Palo Alto, CA); signed for $3,963,045

Previous Ranking(s): N/A

2016 Stats: 17.36 ERA, 9.72 DRA, 4.2 IP, 12 H, 4 BB, 2 K at Low-A Fort Wayne, 1.93 ERA, 1.43 DRA, 18.2 IP, 15 H, 2 BB, 28 K at short-season Tri-City, 5.27 ERA, 2.55 DRA, 13.2 IP, 12 H, 2 BB, 16 K at complex-level AZL

The Role: OFP 60—No. 3 starter
Likely 50—No. 4 starter

YEAR	TEAM	LVL	AGE	W	L	SV	G	GS	IP	H	HR	BB/9	K/9	K	GB%	BABIP	WHIP	ERA	FIP	DRA	VORP	WARP	cFIP	MPH
2016	PDR	Rk	21	0	2	0	5	5	13^{2}	12	0	1.3	10.5	16	49%	.324	1.02	5.27	2.45	2.55	4.80	0.5	81	
2016	TRI	A-	21	0	2	0	5	5	18^{2}	15	0	1.0	13.5	28	56%	.333	0.91	1.93	1.26	1.43	7.90	0.8	70	
2016	FTW	A	21	0	1	0	2	2	4^{2}	12	1	7.7	3.9	2	32%	.524	3.43	17.36	7.98	9.72	-2.40	-0.3	124	
2017	*SDN*	*MLB*	*22*	*2*	*3*	*0*	*9*	*9*	34^{2}	*38*	*6*	*4.1*	*6.9*	*27*	*29%*	*.326*	*1.57*	*5.31*	*5.37*	*6.03*	*-1.8*	*-0.2*	*144*	
2018	*SDN*	*MLB*	*23*	*4*	*7*	*0*	*22*	*22*	131^{2}	*130*	*21*	*4.1*	*8.5*	*124*	*29%*	*.321*	*1.44*	*4.73*	*5.09*	*5.37*	*1.8*	*0.2*	*129*	

Breakout: 1% Improve: 1% Collapse: 0% Attrition: 0% MLB: 1% *Comparables: Wilking Rodriguez, Tyler Wilson, Braden Shipley*

The Good: Quantrill had first-overall-pick type stuff in college, and it looks like it survived his 2015 Tommy John surgery intact. He has three potential above-average pitches in his fastball, curve, and change. His fastball velocity was back to 93-95 by the end of the season, and the pitch has some arm-side run with potentially above-average command. The changeup is his best secondary. It also has plus potential—and already flashes there—and he can throw it for strikes in addition to getting lefties to chase it. The curve is the better of his two breaking balls, an above-average offering he can also spot or bury.

The Bad: Quantrill's 2016 pro debut was essentially a rehab assignment. He didn't throw for Stanford in the Spring as he worked his way back from the surgery. So we're not entirely sure what "Cal Quantrill, pitching prospect," looks like yet. He struggled with his command some this summer. That's not uncommon when you are still less than 24 months out from surgery, but there are also some issues in the delivery that may continue to impede his command. We have no idea if he can handle a starter's workload in the minors—his longest outing of the year was 4 ⅔ innings.

The Irrelevant: Cal's father, Paul, actually started 64 games in the majors, going 16-30 with a 5.03 ERA in those outings.

The Risks: There's a lot of known unknowns here. Quantrill is coming off major arm surgery and has only thrown 50 innings since 2014. We like the profile a lot, and the professional debut was encouraging, but a full 2016 season in the minors will tell us a lot more about where he stands. Until then, he's a pitcher coming off Tommy John surgery.

Major league ETA: 2019

Ben Carsley's Fantasy Take: I believe I just made my thoughts on potential front-end starters in this organization known. Quantrill isn't quite with Espinoza, but you have to love the reports he's getting right now. I don't think Quantrill will end up as a top-50 guy, but he'll certainly be in the top-100, and probably in the top-75. SP1/2s don't grow on trees.

4. Hunter Renfroe, RF

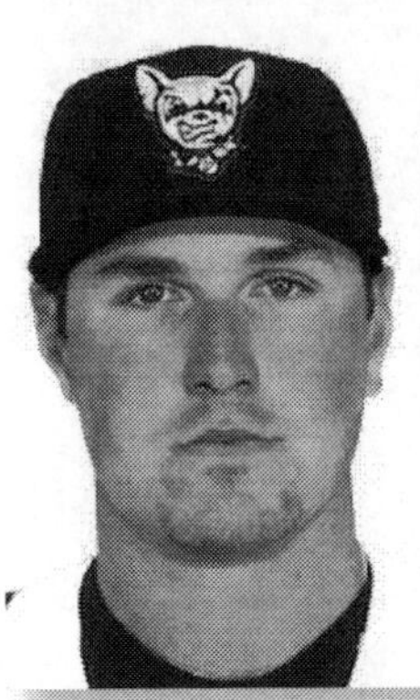

DOB: 1/28/1992

Height/Weight: 6'1" 215 lbs.

Bats/Throws: R/R

Drafted/Acquired: Drafted 13th overall in the 2013 MLB Draft, Mississippi State (Starkville, Mississippi); signed for $2.678 million

Previous Ranking(s): #3 (Org), #90 (Top 101)

2016 Stats: .371/.389/.800, 4 HR, 0 SB in 11 games at the major league level, .306/.336/.557, 30 HR, 5 SB in 133 games at Triple-A El Paso

The Role: OFP 55—Above-average corner masher
Likely 50—Second division starter that swats a few

YEAR	TEAM	LVL	AGE	PA	R	2B	3B	HR	RBI	BB	K	SB	CS	AVG/OBP/SLG	TAv	VORP	BABIP	BRR	FRAA	WARP
2014	LEL	A+	22	316	46	21	3	16	52	28	81	9	3	.295/.370/.565	.340	30.5	.359	-0.3	RF(49): -0.6 • RF(7): -0.6	3.3
2014	SAN	AA	22	251	17	12	0	5	23	25	53	2	1	.232/.307/.353	.244	1.3	.280	-0.5	LF(30): -0.8 • CF(22): -2.4	0.0
2015	SAN	AA	23	463	50	22	3	14	54	33	112	4	1	.259/.313/.425	.259	8.8	.316	1.6	RF(79): 11.9 • CF(8): -1.8	2.2
2015	ELP	AAA	23	95	15	5	2	6	24	4	20	1	0	.333/.358/.633	.314	8.0	.369	0.7	RF(18): 1.3 • CF(3): 0.1	0.9
2016	ELP	AAA	24	563	95	34	5	30	105	22	115	5	2	.306/.336/.557	.277	22.2	.339	1.8	RF(111): 3.7 • CF(12): -1.1	2.4
2016	SDN	MLB	24	36	8	3	0	4	14	1	5	0	0	.371/.389/.800	.404	6.1	.346	0.2	RF(9): 0.6	0.7
2017	*SDN*	*MLB*	*25*	*485*	*54*	*22*	*2*	*21*	*67*	*26*	*132*	*2*	*1*	*.242/.285/.443*	*.253*	*7.9*	*.292*	*-0.6*	*RF 4*	*0.9*
2018	*SDN*	*MLB*	*26*	*490*	*63*	*23*	*2*	*23*	*70*	*31*	*136*	*2*	*1*	*.241/.293/.451*	*.265*	*10.7*	*.291*	*-0.7*	*RF 4*	*1.6*

Breakout: 4% Improve: 25% Collapse: 10% Attrition: 31% MLB: 50% *Comparables: Bryce Brentz, Scott Schebler, Brett Carroll*

The Good: Renfroe is your prototypical right field profile for both good and for...well, we will get to the other part down below. There is potential plus game power in the bat from a long, leveraged swing. He's athletic for his size, and more than enough so to handle the corner outfield spot with a bit of aplomb. The arm is an easy plus.

The Bad: That long, leveraged swing doesn't always hit what it is aiming for. He's got a hitch and a big leg kick, and his swing can get grooved at times, so expect big strikeout numbers. The hit tool might only play to below-average. Usually with this profile you expect three true outcomes, but Renfroe has never really walked much as a professional, despite more than enough power to make minor-league arms nibble a bit. His approach is suspect, and he works himself into bad counts. As for what happens then, well, see above.

The Irrelevant: Renfroe led the Chihuahuas in home runs, but if you combine PCL and MLB bombs, Renfroe's 34 is one behind Ryan Schimpf. This has been a Schimpf Alert.

The Risks: The dingers versus whiffs balance can be a precarious one. Betting on the dingers is always more fun, but the downside risk on Renfroe is substantial as a corner outfielder who isn't going to offer a ton more at the plate than those home runs.

Major league ETA: Debuted in 2016

Ben Carsley's Fantasy Take: The swing-and-miss risk will always be there, but Renfroe improved his approach (or at least his strikeout rate) in Triple-A last season, granting us some hope that Renfroe won't function as a windmill at the next level. If the hit tool does play fantasy owners are in luck, because there's very real power here. If it all clicks, Renfroe could produce like 2016 Yasmany Tomas, flirting with 30 homers and posting a respectable average despite an uninspiring OBP. If he can't make contact like we hope in the majors, well, you know how that story ends.

5. Adrian Morejon, LHP

DOB: 2/27/1999

Height/Weight: 6'0" 165 lbs

Bats/Throws: L/L

Drafted/Acquired: Signed July 2016 out of Cuba for $11 million.

Previous Ranking(s): N/A

2016 Stats: N/A

The Role: OFP 55—Mid-rotation starter with upside
Likely 45—Back-end innings eater/middle reliever

The Good: His delivery is methodical, repeatable, and relatively effortless. He has a strong lower half and an all-around solid build. During instructs his fastball sat 94 across a three-inning start, and he throws a heavy, low-spin changeup with split-like movement, diving down and away to right-handed hitters.

The Bad: He's yet to make an official start as a pro, and he dealt with some arm soreness near the end of instructs. He lacks the height of a prototypical starter, though he makes up for it with the aforementioned sturdy frame.

The Irrelevant: Morejon was MVP of the 15-and-under World Cup in 2014.

The Risks: He's an undersized, teenage pitcher with zero professional innings under his belt.

Major league ETA: 2020 —Matt Pullman

Ben Carsley's Fantasy Take: Morejon ranked in at no. 17 on Bret Sayre's list of the Top 50 dynasty signees for 2016. Floor, polish and probability are the calling cards here, which are slightly more exciting for a pitcher who'll call Petco home than they would be for most other arms. They're still not terribly exciting, though, and while he's mature for a teenager, he's still a teenager. He'll probably end up ranked, like, 82nd on the top-100 in 2019 and I'll be complaining about how boring his profile is.

6. Fernando Tatis, Jr., 3B

DOB: 1/2/1999

Height/Weight: 6'3" 185 lbs

Bats/Throws: R/R

Drafted/Acquired: Signed July 2015 by the White Sox out of the Dominican Republic for $825,000; acquired by San Diego in the James Shields deal.

Previous Ranking(s): N/A

2016 Stats: .273/.306/.455, 0 HR, 1 SB in 12 games at short-season Tri-City, .273/.312/.426, 4 HR, 14 SB in 43 games at rookie ball at complex-level AZL.

The Role: OFP 55—Everyday third baseman with upside
OFP 45—Utility infielder

YEAR	TEAM	LVL	AGE	PA	R	2B	3B	HR	RBI	BB	K	SB	CS	AVG/OBP/SLG	TAv	VORP	BABIP	BRR	FRAA	WARP
2016	PDR	Rk	17	188	35	13	1	4	20	10	44	14	2	.273/.312/.426	.284	12.7	.344	2.0	SS(29): -0.0 • 2B(8): -1.3	1.1
2016	TRI	A-	17	49	4	4	2	0	5	3	13	1	1	.273/.306/.455	.307	4.5	.364	0.4	SS(7): -1.3 • 3B(3): -0.7	0.2
2017	*SDN*	*MLB*	*18*	*250*	*27*	*10*	*1*	*6*	*21*	*10*	*83*	*5*	*2*	*.201/.236/.326*	*.192*	*-6.3*	*.278*	*0.3*	*SS -0 • 2B -0*	*-0.8*
2018	*SDN*	*MLB*	*19*	*257*	*25*	*10*	*1*	*7*	*27*	*10*	*87*	*5*	*2*	*.203/.234/.341*	*.206*	*-5.3*	*.278*	*0.6*	*SS 0 • 2B 0*	*-0.6*

Breakout: 0% Improve: 0% Collapse: 0% Attrition: 0% MLB: 0% *Comparables: Raul Mondesi, Wilmer Flores*

The Good: Tatis has big-league bloodlines and a big-league body. He features a tall, mature frame which could still be growing, along with broad shoulders which allow for plenty of muscle development. That build lends itself to easy power projection, and when combined with an intriguing hit tool for his age, provides plenty of upside potential. He has the upside of a solid-average hit tool given his knack for barreling the ball. He shows smooth actions at shortstop, which make it easy to see him handling a shift to second or third base if he grows out of the position.

The Bad: He has an unrefined approach at the plate, which is understandable given his age. While the upside on his hit tool is above-average, the amount of swing-and-miss built into his swing means he'll likely fall short of that potential. It's highly unlikely he remains a shortstop given his size, but he should be able to stick on the dirt. He's an average runner at present, and given the expected development to his frame, could be a below-average runner before too long.

The Irrelevant: His father, Fernando Tatis, is the only player in MLB history to hit two grand slams in one inning.

The Risks: As with all 18 year olds, there's immense risk. He swings and misses too much and hasn't yet shown a tactical approach at the plate. He could continue to grow, potentially relegating him to the outfield where his profile would be less valuable.

Major league ETA: 2021 —Matt Pullman

Ben Carsley's Fantasy Take: The bloodlines and the bat may not be quite as interesting here as they are with Vladito, but Tatis turned himself into a prospect worth watching in dynasty leagues. He's forever away and has contact issues, but a potential 25-homer hitter at either short or third (probably the latter) is worth monitoring and possibly even worth jumping the gun on early in a league that rosters 200-plus prospects.

7. Jacob Nix, RHP

DOB: 01/09/1996

Height/Weight: 6'4" 220 lbs.

Bats/Throws: R/R

Drafted/Acquired: Drafted in the third round of the 2015 MLB Draft, IMG Academy (Bradenton, FL); signed for $900,000

Previous Ranking(s): #8 (Org)

2016 Stats: 3.93 ERA, 3.50 DRA, 105.1 IP, 115 H, 20 BB, 90 K at Low-A Fort Wayne
The Role: OFP 55—Mid-rotation starter
Likely 45—Backend starter

YEAR	TEAM	LVL	AGE	W	L	SV	G	GS	IP	H	HR	BB/9	K/9	K	GB%	BABIP	WHIP	ERA	FIP	DRA	VORP	WARP	cFIP	MPH
2015	PDR	Rk	19	0	2	0	7	3	19^{2}	23	1	3.2	8.7	19	51%	.355	1.53	5.49	3.92	3.91	4.00	0.4	98	
2016	FTW	A	20	3	7	0	25	25	105^{1}	115	5	1.7	7.7	90	48%	.340	1.28	3.93	3.01	3.50	17.80	2.0	92	
2017	*SDN*	*MLB*	*21*	*4*	*7*	*0*	*17*	*17*	74^{2}	*92*	*13*	*3.7*	*4.7*	*39*	*36%*	*.324*	*1.63*	*5.77*	*5.66*	*6.58*	*-8.4*	*-0.9*	*157*	
2018	*SDN*	*MLB*	*22*	*6*	*9*	*0*	*25*	*25*	148^{1}	*151*	*25*	*4.3*	*7.1*	*118*	*36%*	*.309*	*1.50*	*5.26*	*5.67*	*6.00*	*-5.3*	*-0.5*	*144*	

Breakout: 2% Improve: 2% Collapse: 2% Attrition: 3% MLB: 4% *Comparables: Vance Worley, Felipe Rivero, Roman Mendez*

The Good: Nix still has the big fastball that got him drafted twice. It sits in the mid-90s, touched 97 and he can take a little off of it to add some armside run. He's already comfortable manipulating the pitch in that way. His curveball is potentially above-average, and he is comfortable throwing it to both sides. He'll show feel for a potentially average change as well. His frame is ideal for a starter, and there are no glaring red flags in his delivery.

The Bad: The secondaries still need refinement. The curve can get flatter and sweepy, the change firm at times. Both offerings are inconsistent at present and grade out as below-average. There's some crossfire in the delivery and occasional effort that impacts the command profile, although he has little issue throwing strikes.

The Irrelevant: Nix spent a "gap year" in Bradenton after the Aiken/Astros fallout. Plenty of time to see all the Village of the Arts—the largest arts district on the Gulf Coast—has to offer.

The Risks: Nix is still in A-ball and may lack a true swing-and-miss pitch at the highest level. Also, he's a pitcher.

Major league ETA: 2019

Ben Carsley's Fantasy Take: You know how this goes at this point, and how I feel about mid-rotation upside guys. Does Petco help a little? Sure, and the arsenal is there for him to valuable in a fantasy league, but that "may lack a true swing-and-miss pitch at the highest level" part above bodes poorly for our purposes. Check back next year.

8. Logan Allen, LHP

DOB: 5/23/1997

Height/Weight: 6'3" 200 lbs

Bats/Throws: R/L

Drafted/Acquired: Drafted in the eighth round by the Red Sox in the 2015 MLB Draft, IMG Academy (Bradenton, FL), signed for $725,000; acquired by San Diego in the Craig Kimbrel deal

Previous Ranking(s): N/A

2016 Stats: 3.33 ERA, 4.64 DRA, 54 IP, 48 H, 22 BB, 47 K at Low-A Fort Wayne, 3.00 ERA, 2.52 DRA, 6 IP, 5 H, 1 BB, 8 K at complex-level AZL

The Role: OFP 55—Mid-rotation starter
Likely 45—Back-end starter/middle reliever

YEAR	TEAM	LVL	AGE	W	L	SV	G	GS	IP	H	HR	BB/9	K/9	K	GB%	BABIP	WHIP	ERA	FIP	DRA	VORP	WARP	cFIP	MPH
2015	RSX	Rk	18	0	0	0	7	7	20	12	0	0.4	10.8	24	59%	.261	0.65	0.90	1.05	1.86	9.00	0.9	70	
2015	LOW	A-	18	0	0	0	1	1	4^{1}	6	0	0.0	4.2	2	33%	.333	1.38	2.08	2.59	5.16	0.10	0.0	108	
2016	PDR	Rk	19	0	0	0	3	3	6	5	0	1.5	12.0	8	60%	.333	1.00	3.00	1.96	2.52	2.10	0.2	85	
2016	TRI	A-	19	0	1	0	1	1	2^{1}	4	0	3.9	15.4	4	57%	.571	2.14	7.71	1.63	2.00	0.80	0.1	87	
2016	FTW	A	19	3	4	0	15	11	54	48	2	3.7	7.8	47	38%	.301	1.30	3.33	3.61	4.64	1.80	0.2	109	
2017	*SDN*	*MLB*	*20*	*2*	*4*	*0*	*17*	*11*	44^{2}	*53*	*9*	*5.1*	*5.3*	*27*	*31%*	*.317*	*1.74*	*6.39*	*6.34*	*7.26*	*-9.7*	*-1.0*	*173*	
2018	*SDN*	*MLB*	*21*	*3*	*6*	*0*	*22*	*17*	*115*	*124*	*22*	*5.7*	*7.2*	*92*	*31%*	*.316*	*1.71*	*6.12*	*6.60*	*6.95*	*-11.2*	*-1.2*	*166*	

Breakout: 0% Improve: 0% Collapse: 0% Attrition: 1% MLB: 1% *Comparables: Parker Bridwell, Yohander Mendez, Kyle Drabek*

The Good: He has plus natural stuff, from a fastball with run that touches 95 with regularity, to a low-70s bender which can buckle knees just as often. He has the frame of a big-league workhorse and looks the part of a veteran starter on the mound, working quickly and generally attacking the zone. When he's on, his stuff works downhill and induces ground balls at a very high rate.

The Bad: He's thrown just 86 ⅔ innings since being drafted in 2015, missing a portion of this past season with elbow soreness. His delivery is a bit loud, with some arm stab and significant spine tilt, which can cause him to leave the ball up. His changeup is a generic offering that arrives in the lower 80s with some fade.

The Irrelevant: There is a highly-touted prep lefty from Florida named Logan Allen in this year's draft class, which makes the second such Logan Allen in three years.

The Risks: Health is the foremost risk with all pitchers, but particularly ones who've dealt with elbow issues as recently as this past August. If his command and changeup don't continue to develop, his ceiling is limited to that of a back-end starter.

Major league ETA: 2020 —Matt Pullman

Ben Carsley's Fantasy Take: Allen is a good guy for the watch list. If he performs well in High-A, he could flirt with a top-100 list given his presumed proximity to the Majors and the organization he calls home. It's a bit early to get excited now, though.

9. Jorge Ona, OF

DOB: 12/31/1996

Height/Weight: 6'0" 220 lbs

Bats/Throws: R/R

Drafted/Acquired: Signed July 2016 out of Cuba for $7 million

Previous Ranking(s): N/A

2016 Stats: N/A

The Role: OFP 55—Above-average everyday right fielder
Likely 45—Second division starter/good outfield bench bat

YEAR	TEAM	LVL	AGE	PA	R	2B	3B	HR	RBI	BB	K	SB	CS	AVG/OBP/SLG	TAv	VORP	BABIP	BRR	FRAA	WARP
2017	SDN	MLB	20	250	25	9	1	3	21	25	40	4	1	.233/.313/.329	.227	1.4	.265	0.0		0.2

Breakout: 5% Improve: 21% Collapse: 2% Attrition: 8% MLB: 36% *Comparables: Rusty Staub, Bill Mazeroski, Ed Kirkpatrick*

The Good: The Pads added a second prototypical right fielder to this list in July, albeit a teenaged one much further away from major-league contribution than Renfroe. His swing's shorter than Renfroe's, but generates similar raw power. He has an above-average arm. Like we said, prototypical right fielder.

The Bad: We talked about the "known unknowns" as it applied to Cal Quantrill. There's some unknown unknowns here as well, as Ona won't have played a competitive baseball game for almost two full years when he steps onto the field in 2017, and that's assuming he is assigned to a full-season affiliate. There's likely downsides here beyond just "he may not hit enough for a corner." We just won't know what they are for a little while longer.

The Irrelevant: Ona was part of the Padres 60 million dollar—including penalties—IFA class this year. That's more than enough to buy a season ticket for every single seat at his likely home park, Parkview Field in Fort Wayne. Plenty left over to rent out all the field boxes too.

The Risks: Ona has zero professional track record and projects in a corner spot. He may have similar tools to Renfroe, but this section is the reason he is six spots lower.

Major league ETA: 2020

Ben Carsley's Fantasy Take: He may play second fiddle on this list to Morejon, who also got the bigger bonus, but from a traditional fantasy sense, Ona is the better profile. The reductive way to think about him in dynasty leagues is about 90 percent of Jorge Soler when he came over. As for the non-reductive way, we'll just have to see him play in the States for that, but the power upside is enough to get him strong consideration for the Dynasty 101.

10. Luis Urias, 2B

DOB: 6/3/1997

Height/Weight: 5'9" 160 lbs

Bats/Throws: R/R

Drafted/Acquired: Contract was purchased from the Mexico City Red Devils in December 2013.

Previous Ranking(s): N/A

2016 Stats: .444/.667/.778, 1 HR, 1 SB in 3 games at Triple-A El Paso, .330/.397/.440, 5 HR, 7 SB in 120 games at High-A Lake Elsinore

The Role: 50 OFP—Average second baseman
45 Likely—Second-division starter with utility value

YEAR	TEAM	LVL	AGE	PA	R	2B	3B	HR	RBI	BB	K	SB	CS	AVG/OBP/SLG	TAv	VORP	BABIP	BRR	FRAA	WARP
2014	DPA	Rk	17	11	1	0	0	0	0	1	1	0	0	.100/.182/.100	.115	0.0	.111	0.0		0.0
2014	PDR	Rk	17	179	29	5	1	0	14	18	13	10	6	.310/.393/.355	.304	9.7	.336	1.4		1.3
2015	TRI	A-	18	44	6	1	0	0	1	5	1	3	3	.355/.487/.387	.391	7.3	.367	0.2	2B(6): 0.5 • 3B(1): 0.0	0.8
2015	FTW	A	18	224	28	5	1	0	16	16	18	5	10	.290/.370/.326	.267	6.1	.318	-1.7	2B(38): 0.9 • SS(7): 1.0	1.1
2016	ELP	AAA	19	15	6	0	0	1	3	5	1	1	0	.444/.667/.778	.430	3.2	.429	0.2	2B(3): 0.4	0.4
2016	LEL	A+	19	531	71	26	5	5	52	40	36	7	13	.330/.397/.440	.317	41.6	.348	-5.9	2B(80): 6.0 • SS(22): -3.1	4.6
2017	*SDN*	*MLB*	*20*	*250*	*30*	*11*	*1*	*5*	*24*	*16*	*36*	*2*	*2*	*.268/.331/.397*	*.250*	*6.5*	*.293*	*-0.8*	*2B 3 • SS -1*	*1.0*
2018	*SDN*	*MLB*	*21*	*423*	*52*	*19*	*2*	*10*	*48*	*29*	*58*	*3*	*4*	*.280/.345/.421*	*.278*	*19.6*	*.301*	*-1.2*	*2B 5 • SS -1*	*2.6*

Breakout: 5% Improve: 19% Collapse: 0% Attrition: 6% MLB: 21% *Comparables: Ronald Torreyes, Francisco Lindor, Jurickson Profar*

The Good: Some people exist on this Earth to hit baseballs, and Urias is one of those people. His balance and body control is on display with a long, flowing leg kick that launches a very quick stroke, and he controls the barrel with startling precision. As one of the youngest regulars in the Cal League he showed advanced aptitude recognizing pitches and staying back on balls. The approach is geared to the opposite field and up the middle at present. He made strides defensively at second, getting more decisive in his reads of contact and improving his footwork and transfer, and there's just enough arm strength to warrant the left-side reps the club gave him.

The Bad: There's limited power projection, as he lacks for strength or present interest to drive the ball to the pull side. The pure bat-to-ball may very well be enough to overcome advanced arms challenging him on the inner third as he progresses, but there's some potential vulnerability. His body is pretty well maxed out already, and he's a fringe-average runner with ensuing range limitations that probably keep his profile south of regular left-side utility.

The Irrelevant: Urias was the first teenager to lead the California League in hitting with a minimum of 100 games played since Jose Lopez, who hit .324 in 123 games as an 18-year-old in 2002.

The Risks: A whole lot depends on his hit tool actualizing in full, and as a 19-year-old with all of 15 plate appearances above High-A there are plenty of minor-league hurdles ahead of him. The lack of secondary skills beyond a potentially average glove leaves him a narrower road to run on.

Major league ETA: Late 2018/Early 2019 —Wilson Karaman

Ben Carsley's Fantasy Take: Between the lead time, the organization and the utter lack of secondary tools, it's hard to get terribly excited about Urias. If he hits .280 with low counting stats, that makes him, what, Joe Panik at the very best? I do love bat-first prospects, but there's a limit.

OTHERS OF NOTE:

Wilson's Guy (still)

Javier Guerra, SS

There's really no sugarcoating it: 2016 was a terrible, horrible, no-good, very bad year for Javier Guerra. He'll show the ingredients for some bat-to-ball ability, with quickness into the zone and sound hand-eye coordination, and there's some plane to suggest average potential power down the line. But his mechanics proved wildly inconsistent swing to swing, with an aggressive approach leading to timing and sync issues that he didn't show much progress in addressing. In the field he shows some of the most natural, fluid shortstop actions you'll see, with top-shelf lateral quickness propelling him to decent range in spite of below-average foot speed. He possesses outstanding body control, and his quick transfer can make his already-plus arm play up further still. But he struggled far too often to execute even routine plays to completion, and perhaps most troublingly demonstrated precious little growth or development in gaining better consistency with his fundamentals. The raw material of a very good shortstop is still here, but the tools are very far from actualization. —Wilson Karaman

The second best Marlins prospect

Josh Naylor, 1B

Naylor isn't all that different a prospect than he was in July, but a move from Miami's fallow system to San Diego's bumper crop of prospects isn't going to help his Q rating at all. It also doesn't help that he is a short, stocky, teenaged first baseman. That's a tough profile to overcome, even if I can soften the blow by suggesting he is more athletic than I was expecting. Naylor does have the requisite plus raw power you'd expect--and require–from the profile and showed a semblance of an approach against the older and more advanced full-season arms he faced in his first full pro season. The swing can be a little one-gear, so I wonder if the power ultimately plays in major-league games to the level it does in BP. There's also the matter of the whole "knife prank" incident. It sure seems like the Marlins were selling low on one of their few prospects just to get him out of town. That could tell you something. Of course they have also traded another of their few prospects for two different backend starters. So Miami does make this harder to parse than it should be.

The risks section personified

Michael Gettys, OF

Gettys is perhaps the highest-variance prospect in this system. His physicality immediately jumps off the field, as he boasts premium athleticism in his movements and an ideal frame to fill out with good muscle. The speed should still push plus even at maturity and it plays to full utility in center, where he shows feel for trajectory and tracking ability from gap to gap. His arm is his best asset, with plus-or-better velocity and carry. There's juice in his bat, too: The raw power is above-average at present and may settle in at plus range down the line. But while he made swing changes this year that improved his bat-to-ball, the hit tool projection still remains questionable. He takes an aggressive stride, and coupled with some stiffness in his launch and a thinner angle through the zone, he struggles to make adjustments and swings and misses frequently against soft stuff. When he does make contact there's volume to it, and he's a guy that can bring some power into games even if the hit tool never quite actualizes. Another step or two forward with the bat could raise him onto a first-division trajectory, but Double-A pitching could just as easily abuse him with advanced sequencing and leave him looking more like a speed-and-defense-and-occasional-pop fourth outfielders. —Wilson Karaman

Franchy Cordero, OF

You can copy and paste much of what I just wrote about Michael Gettys into Franchy's section here, and you'd wind up little worse for the wear. Cordero is an outstanding quick-twitch athlete with an explosive stride and some baseline instincts to project average utility in center field. His reads on stolen base attempts aren't great right now, but the crossover is there and he has the physical tools to develop efficiency with experience. There's also sneaky pop here, with above-average bat speed and a leveraged stroke that can lift and drive pitches when he catches them. But his stroke frequently winds up as an arms swing, and he is inconsistent with his barrel control. Neither the approach nor the pitch recognition helps his cause, and the hit tool might never reach even 40 range. There's enough here to project a lo-fi fifth outfielder type of profile even if that's the case, and the athleticism warrants erring on the side of optimism that his slow burn can end at slightly a higher ceiling than that. —Wilson Karaman

Or maybe this guy would have been the second best Marlins prospect

Chris Paddack, RHP

Before the Marlins were trading two of their best prospects for Andrew Cashner and Colin Rea, only to later trade one of them again for Dan Straily after Rea's elbow injury surfaced, they were trading their one breakout prospect of 2016 for Fernando Rodney. Paddack shined in 2016, showing two potential plus pitches in his fastball and change, before a elbow strain put him on the shelf, eventually requiring Tommy John surgery. He likely won't step on a mound again until 2018, but he's young enough that this may just be a bump in the developmental road. He's a potential mid-rotation arm if he can find more consistency and feel for his curveball, but this is why I make the same joke about every pitcher in "The Risks." Well, that and I need something to amuse myself as we crank out ~450 of these player blurbs.

TOP 10 TALENTS 25 AND UNDER (BORN 4/1/91 OR LATER)

1. Manuel Margot	6. Travis Jankowski
2. Anderson Espinoza	7. Luis Perdomo
3. Austin Hedges	8. Adrian Morejon
4. Cal Quantrill	9. Fernando Tatis, Jr.
5. Hunter Renfroe	10. Jacob Nix

Austin Hedges might be the leading candidate for best defensive catcher in the majors by the end of the decade—shoot, he might be the answer by Opening Day. He possesses an exciting, well-rounded set of skills behind the dish, with polished fundamentals, a rocket arm, and plus receiving ability. Even Hedges' bat—long the glaring hole of his profile—rebounded in 2016, as he posted a .301 TAv in the hitter-friendly PCL. The major-league numbers (and most of the minor-league numbers) aren't nearly as encouraging, though, and it'll ultimately be the stick that decides whether he's something more than Brad Ausmus 2.0. He slots in ahead of Quantrill on the strength of his immediacy, the risks of low-level pitchers with surgery on their C.V., and the low bar to clear as a valuable contributor for plus defensive catchers.

Jankowski probably works best as a fleet-footed center fielder, but a shift to left field seems likely whenever the Padres decide to pull the trigger on a permanent Margot call-up. He's less enticing in a corner, sure, but there's a chance the glove makes up for his punch-and-judy offensive approach. Jankowski did show some promising on-base skills in his first extended major-league trial last season, and the base running adds further appeal.

Perdomo, a Rule 5 pick, went from failed mop-up guy to a successful starter in the span of a few months, an unlikely bright spot amid last year's last-place Friars. The numbers still look ugly on the surface, but a closer look reveals plenty of positives. By our numbers, Perdomo was something like a league-average pitcher in 2016, with a 99 cFIP and a 4.02 DRA in 147 innings. He induced ground balls at a 60 percent clip and struck out 2.3 hitters for every one he walked. All this for someone who hadn't pitched past High-A prior to last year, and it's easy to see why there's tepid optimism brewing here.

Catcher/reliever/outfielder Christian Bethancourt just misses the cut, because we're not exactly sure what he is. Reports out of winter ball have him sitting in the mid-90s off the mound. If he can somehow work as a late-inning reliever and a backup to Hedges, he'll be equal parts valuable and fun to watch.

The recently extended Wil Myers graduates from this list off an up-and-down—but, importantly, healthy—campaign where he established himself as a solid gloveman at first and a sneaky good base runner. Cory Spangenberg just narrowly misses the age cutoff for inclusion as well, but he's coming off a year almost entirely lost to a torn left quad, and he's likely to find himself in a positional battle at second base with Roy Hobbs wannabe Ryan Schimpf come spring training.

San Diego has amassed an overwhelming collection of young talent. Even though this group of non-prospect 25-and-unders certainly doesn't rival the league's best, the addition of near-ready minor leaguers like Margot and Renfroe combined with slow-burn teenagers make the Padres an organization on the fast-track back to relevance.

—Dustin Palmateer

SAN FRANCISCO GIANTS

The State of the System: *It's another mediocre Giants system, and they will probably get three more useful regulars out of it then we expect.*

THE TOP TEN

1. RHP Tyler Beede	6. LHP Andrew Suarez
2. SS Christian Arroyo	7. OF Steven Duggar
3. CF Bryan Reynolds	8. OF Sandro Fabian
4. 1B Chris Shaw	9. RHP Joan Gregorio
5. LHP Ty Blach	10. OF Heath Quinn

The Big Question: Why do the Giants always confound our org rankings?

This is the last of the NL West team lists. Next week starts our last division, the AL Central. After that we publish the Top 101 and then finally our organizational rankings. I could have given you the current schedule of prospect team events really at any time or place. But I have been thinking about our org rankings lately, because I need to update the Annual rankings for the website (thanks Reds, Mariners, Marlins, among others).

My philosophy for organizational rankings may be a little different from others. Overall system depth is important of course, but I don't know how much it moves the needle that the Yankees 23rd-best prospect might be a major-league middle reliever or an extra outfielder. You can find those this time of year fairly cheaply on an NRI flyer. That's not to say there isn't value in having a few of those options internally. Because sometimes one of them will outperform that and now you have a fourth outfielder you can start for a month, or an 8th-inning guy. That's a significant major-league role filled and a player development win.

But what I really care about is that the Braves put the vast majority of their Top 10 on our Top 101, and they have 12 guys who might make a top 150. You can say the same thing about the Yankees. That's potential impact talent. Those aren't guys who just get an invite to camp. They're guys who drive their lamborghini that spits fire to camp. And when those guys outperform their projections, they go to all-star games. You build your franchise around them.

I don't think it's a huge spoiler to tell you the Giants don't have any prospects on our Top 101. Or that their recent organizational rankings have been less than...well, let's just go to the handy-dandy chart from this year's Annual.

Now the Giants have won three World Series titles since the last time we ranked them as a Top 10 farm system. They historically haven't been a franchise that splashes the pot a ton in free agency, although that has changed in recent offseasons. If I ask you to name a major recent Giants trade, you might still name the deal that sent Joe Nathan and Francisco Liriano to Minnesota for A.J. Pierzynski. You look at those World Series champions and there are plenty of grey-bearded thirty-somethings having their last great season, so sure, there was some luck involved. But one of the overarching themes of recent success by the bay has been overperforming their org rankings.

And it's not just the Joe Paniks and Brandon Crawfords of the world jumping a grade from second-division starter to first. Every time the Giants have ended up with a touted talent at the top of their otherwise fallow farm, they've hit. Buster Posey wasn't just a very good catcher, he's put together the first half of a Hall of Fame career. The last time the Giants system ranked in our top ten, it was topped by Madison Bumgarner. That worked out pretty well. Brandon Belt went from OFP 60 to MLB 60. Three homegrown stars make up for a world of deficiency elsewhere in your farm system. These are the players that can move the needle for your major league team and that potential should likewise move the needle for our org rankings.

Oh, I guess the follow-up question would be how the Giants are doing it. Well, if I had the answer to that I would not be sitting at my computer trying to fill the last—well, technically first—750 words of a 6000 word prospect list. Those kind of player development secrets are well-guarded and don't show up in your heartwarming spring training human interest profiles on scrappy, overachieving Joe Panik.

I suppose we should at least try to name this phenomenon. We already have "Cardinals Devil Magic," but this feels more like its own thing, rather than an off-brand

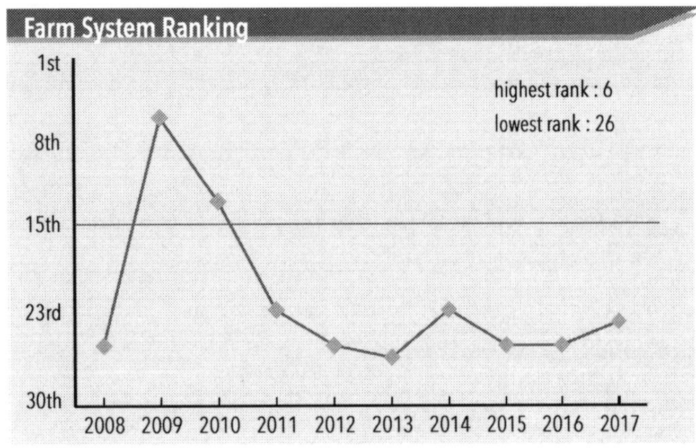

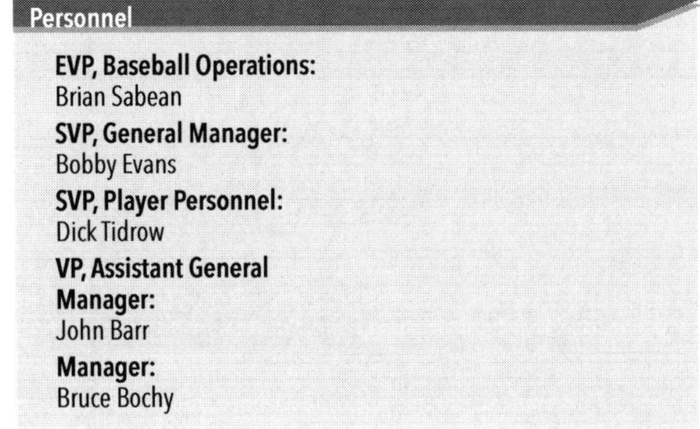
Personnel

EVP, Baseball Operations:
Brian Sabean

SVP, General Manager:
Bobby Evans

SVP, Player Personnel:
Dick Tidrow

VP, Assistant General Manager:
John Barr

Manager:
Bruce Bochy

Missouri demonry like the one that powered the Royals for a few years. The tale of the "San Francisco Voodoo Queen" may have been a myth—and one with ugly roots at that—but do you have a better explanation for Brandon Crawford hitting suddenly hitting twenty home runs in a season?

1. Tyler Beede, RHP

DOB: 05/23/1993

Height/Weight: 6'4" 200 lbs.

Bats/Throws: R/R

Drafted/Acquired: Drafted 14th overall in the 2014 MLB Draft, Vanderbilt University; signed for $2,613,200

Previous Ranking(s): #3 (Org)

2016 Stats: 2.81 ERA, 3.05 DRA, 147.1 IP, 136 H, 53 BB, 135 K at Double-A Richmond

The Role: OFP 55—Mid-rotation starter
Likely 50—Average starter

YEAR	TEAM	LVL	AGE	W	L	SV	G	GS	IP	H	HR	BB/9	K/9	K	GB%	BABIP	WHIP	ERA	FIP	DRA	VORP	WARP	cFIP	MPH
2014	GIA	Rk	21	0	1	0	4	4	8^{2}	8	0	4.2	11.4	11	0%	.348	1.38	3.12	2.87	2.91			95	
2014	SLO	A-	21	0	0	0	2	2	6^{2}	8	0	4.1	9.4	7	65%	.400	1.65	2.70	3.06	3.39	1.50	0.2	92	
2015	SJO	A+	22	2	2	0	9	9	52^{1}	51	2	1.5	6.4	37	64%	.295	1.15	2.24	3.43	2.91	12.60	1.4	85	
2015	RIC	AA	22	3	8	0	13	13	72^{1}	62	4	4.4	6.1	49	60%	.269	1.34	5.23	4.21	7.34	-18.00	-2.0	113	
2016	RIC	AA	23	8	7	0	24	24	147^{1}	136	9	3.2	8.2	135	49%	.309	1.28	2.81	3.48	3.05	33.50	3.6	85	
2017	*SFN*	*MLB*	*24*	*7*	*7*	*0*	*22*	*22*	120^{2}	*119*	*11*	*3.7*	*6.6*	*88*	*49%*	*.313*	*1.40*	*4.19*	*4.20*	*5.00*	*7.5*	*0.8*	*117*	
2018	*SFN*	*MLB*	*25*	*8*	*9*	*0*	*26*	*26*	153^{2}	*139*	*15*	*5.1*	*9.2*	*157*	*49%*	*.326*	*1.47*	*4.06*	*4.52*	*4.84*	*11.4*	*1.2*	*112*	

Breakout: 16% Improve: 30% Collapse: 23% Attrition: 34% MLB: 60% *Comparables: Jake Arrieta, Chad Bettis, Esmil Rogers*

The Good: Beede has had an up-and-down career in both college and the pros since he turned down mucho dinero in the 2011 draft from the Blue Jays. 2016 was his most promising season as a prospect. He still sits in the low 90s—though he can find 95 when he wants—but now offers three different fastball looks: a two-seamer with good arm-side run and a high-80s cutter to complement the four-seam. He can add and subtract with the pitch and his command of all three variants has improved. The curveball is an average-major league offering that flashes plus with good depth despite his three-quarters slot. He has a starter's frame and delivery and gets a lot out of mostly average stuff due to his high mound IQ.

The Bad: The change is pretty flat, although the arm action and velocity separation make it potentially average. It's not going to miss bats though, and it's tough to find another pitch in Beede's repertoire that will get consistent swings-and-misses against major-league hitters. The curve and cutter have the best chance, but the curve can get slurvy and the cutter is still a nascent pitch for him. The overall profile lacks upside.

The Irrelevant: There have been 184 pro baseball players with Vanderbilt ties. The first recorded Vandy alum to play in the majors was Ben Sanders, who spent five seasons as a hurler in the National League, Players League, and American Association from 1888-1892.

The Risks: May lack a putaway pitch at the major-league level. He needs more command refinement or he'll generally be too hittable. He's a starting pitcher of some variety, but we'll put the emphasis on pitcher here, in case you haven't gotten the hint by now.

Major league ETA: Late 2017

Ben Carsley's Fantasy Take: San Francisco is one of the best places for a mid- to back-end starter to end up, but at the end of the day, Beede is still just a mid- to back-end starter. Favorable contextual factors could help Beede play as high as a SP6 in standard leagues some day, but thanks to his lack of big-time strikeout potential, SP6 looks to be his ceiling. He's a top-150 guy, but he won't be in the top-100.

2. Christian Arroyo, SS

DOB: 05/30/1995

Height/Weight: 6'1" 180 lbs.

Bats/Throws: R/R

Drafted/Acquired: Drafted 25th overall in the 2013 MLB Draft, Hernando HS (Brooksville, FL); signed for $1,866,500.

Previous Ranking(s): #1 (Org)

2016 Stats: .274/.316/.373, 3 HR, 1 SB in 119 games at Double-A Richmond

The Role: OFP 55—Bat-first infielder somewhere other than shortstop
Likely 50—Second-division starter

YEAR	TEAM	LVL	AGE	PA	R	2B	3B	HR	RBI	BB	K	SB	CS	AVG/OBP/SLG	TAv	VORP	BABIP	BRR	FRAA	WARP
2014	AUG	A	19	125	10	3	1	1	14	4	22	1	2	.203/.226/.271	.189	-6.6	.237	-0.8	2B(26): 6.7 • SS(5): -0.1	0.0
2014	SLO	A-	19	267	39	14	2	5	48	18	31	6	1	.333/.378/.469	.309	24.7	.360	0.1	SS(58): 3.9	3.0
2015	SJO	A+	20	409	48	28	2	9	42	19	73	5	3	.304/.344/.459	.304	31.8	.355	-2.3	SS(88): -2.5	3.2
2016	RIC	AA	21	517	57	36	1	3	49	29	72	1	1	.274/.316/.373	.254	12.5	.313	-1.3	SS(48): -1.1 • 3B(48): 2.1	1.5
2017	*SFN*	*MLB*	*22*	*250*	*25*	*14*	*1*	*5*	*23*	*11*	*52*	*0*	*0*	*.252/.287/.377*	*.227*	*0.7*	*.301*	*-0.4*	*SS 1 • 3B 1*	*0.4*
2018	*SFN*	*MLB*	*23*	*313*	*34*	*17*	*1*	*7*	*33*	*16*	*67*	*0*	*0*	*.252/.294/.389*	*.247*	*4.1*	*.300*	*-0.7*	*SS 1 • 3B 2*	*0.9*

Breakout: 1% Improve: 12% Collapse: 7% Attrition: 23% MLB: 27% *Comparables: Neil Walker, Josh Vitters, Cheslor Cuthbert*

The Good: The hardest thing to project is if a player will hit major-league pitching. Arroyo has all the tools to do so though. He generates plus bat speed from his strong wrists and forearms and converts it into hard line drives to all fields. We think he's a plus hitter at the highest level. He's a capable infield defender at multiple positions despite not having premium athletic tools.

The Bad: Outside of the hit tool, there isn't all that much to recommend. Power projection is below-average and will come more in doubles than home runs. He played as much third base as shortstop in 2016—and some second base as well—and one of those is his likely long term home, as he lacks the range and athleticism for the 6. He will be solid at the other infield spots, but won't add a ton with his glove. He's an aggressive hitter, and that doesn't always pay off with good contact and limits the on-base ability despite his plus hit tool. He's a below-average runner.

The Irrelevant: There are actually 44 species of flying squirrels, We assume Richmond's mascot is the Southern Flying Squirrel, the only one native to the American South.

The Risks: The bat really needs to play to projection to make the profile viable at third base. His aggressive approach may get exploited by major league arms. There's not much projection left and he lacks athleticism.

Ben Carsley's Fantasy Take: It's lazy to go with player comps—especially with comps to players in the same organization—but is Arroyo materially different than Joe Panik? I don't really think he is, which means he'll be a player you want in TDGX-sized 20-team leagues and a player you can pass on in shallower formats. That being said, he sort of seems destined to become an All-Star with the Cardinals at some point.

3. Bryan Reynolds, CF

DOB: 1/27/1995

Height/Weight: 6'3" 200 lbs

Bats/Throws: S/R

Drafted/Acquired: Drafted 59th overall in the 2016 MLB Draft; Vanderbilt University (Nashville, TN); signed for $1,350,000

Previous Ranking(s): N/A

2016 Stats: .317/.348/.444, 1 HR, 1 SB in 16 games at Low-A Augusta, .312/.368/.500, 5 HR, 2 SB in 40 games at short-season Salem-Keizer

The Role: OFP 50—Average outfielder
Likely 45—Fourth outfielder that won't kill you in center

YEAR	TEAM	LVL	AGE	PA	R	2B	3B	HR	RBI	BB	K	SB	CS	AVG/OBP/SLG	TAv	VORP	BABIP	BRR	FRAA	WARP
2016	SLO	A-	21	171	28	12	1	5	30	11	41	2	0	.312/.368/.500	.301	7.2	.391	0.6	CF(33): -4.5	0.4
2016	AUG	A	21	66	11	5	0	1	8	3	20	1	0	.317/.348/.444	.316	4.3	.452	0.2	CF(11): 1.4	0.6
2017	*SFN*	*MLB*	*22*	*250*	*21*	*10*	*1*	*6*	*26*	*11*	*80*	*0*	*0*	*.214/.253/.339*	*.203*	*-5.3*	*.294*	*-0.3*	*CF -0*	*-0.6*
2018	*SFN*	*MLB*	*23*	*228*	*24*	*10*	*1*	*6*	*24*	*11*	*73*	*0*	*0*	*.221/.265/.364*	*.227*	*-1.5*	*.304*	*-0.4*	*CF 0*	*-0.2*

Breakout: 3% Improve: 4% Collapse: 0% Attrition: 3% MLB: 7% *Comparables: Trayvon Robinson, Michael Taylor, David Dahl*

The Good: Reynolds is your classic not-quite-a-first-rounder college bat. He's a good athlete who already looks the part of a major-league baseball player. He has a broad base of skills, and there really isn't a true weakness in his game. You can throw a 50 or better on all five tools. He should have average power from both sides of the plate, and he's a polished outfielder who already makes good reads and takes good routes to the ball. He could move quite quickly through the minors.

The Bad: Reynolds lacks a clear carrying tool. He's only an average runner at present and if he slows down anymore, he may be forced to a corner despite his advanced instincts on the grass. He swings hard to get to his power, and swung and missed an awful lot against short-season arms. There's concern that it might continue against better arms, as his swing is leveraged and there is some head yank as well. In the end, the overall offensive profile might be light for a corner.

The Irrelevant: In addition to being the alma mater of what feels like half the prospects we have written about so far, Vanderbilt University also has an institute devoted to the study of the card game bridge.

The Risks: The risk here is that Reynolds ends up a tweener—not enough range for center, not enough bat for a corner.

Major league ETA: Late 2018

Ben Carsley's Fantasy Take: Reynolds has OF4/5 upside, but he's so far away from the majors that we don't really need to worry about him yet. If Reynolds' hit tool starts playing better, you can dabble, but honestly he's probably not even in the top-200 range yet. Womp womp.

4. Chris Shaw, 1B

DOB: 10/20/1993

Height/Weight: 6'4" 235 lbs

Bats/Throws: L/R

Drafted/Acquired: Drafted 31st overall in the 2015 MLB Draft, Boston College; signed for $1,400,000

Previous Ranking(s): #7 (Org)

2016 Stats: .246/.309/.414, 5 HR, 0 SB in 60 games at Double-A Richmond, .285/.357/.544, 16 HR, 0 SB in 72 games at High-A San Jose

The Role: OFP 50—Average first baseman
Likely 45—Borderline second-division starter

YEAR	TEAM	LVL	AGE	PA	R	2B	3B	HR	RBI	BB	K	SB	CS	AVG/OBP/SLG	TAv	VORP	BABIP	BRR	FRAA	WARP
2015	SLO	A-	21	200	22	11	0	12	30	19	41	0	0	.287/.360/.551	.305	9.5	.310	-1.8	1B(31): 1.4	1.1
2016	SJO	A+	22	305	47	22	0	16	55	28	70	0	0	.285/.357/.544	.333	24.7	.326	-2.4	1B(52): -0.8	2.5
2016	RIC	AA	22	256	26	16	4	5	30	20	55	0	0	.246/.309/.414	.270	1.6	.299	-3.5	1B(48): -2.3	-0.1
2017	*SFN*	*MLB*	*23*	*250*	*27*	*12*	*2*	*9*	*33*	*18*	*68*	*0*	*0*	*.239/.299/.430*	*.248*	*1.6*	*.296*	*-0.3*	*1B -1 • 3B 0*	*0.1*
2018	*SFN*	*MLB*	*24*	*322*	*41*	*16*	*2*	*13*	*43*	*25*	*85*	*0*	*0*	*.246/.310/.443*	*.271*	*7.2*	*.302*	*-0.6*	*1B -1 • 3B 0*	*0.7*

Breakout: 8% Improve: 22% Collapse: 4% Attrition: 19% MLB: 37% *Comparables: Ike Davis, Jesus Aguilar, Ryan Lavarnway*

The Good: Shaw has power, and lots of it. A big, hulking slugger, he extends on the ball well to crush pitches with plane to the pull side. He has an idea about how to hit, too: he'll hunt fastballs early, but has the good sense to work into the count when he doesn't get one to his liking. He hangs in well against left-handers, indicating potential for more than platoon utility. His defense took at least a half step forward, as he was moving around the bag better by season's end. For whatever it's worth at first, his arm strength is above-average.

The Bad: He's a stiff big, rather than an athletic one. The lower half of his swing is mechanical, with a short stride and some issues with his weight transfer, and he doesn't generate consistent bat speed to catch balls up in the zone or on the inner third. The physical realities limit his hit tool to fringe-average range, and with that bring down the game power potential into something more like above-average territory. He's a bottom-of-the-scale runner, and while the defense did improve last year it still projects to a below-average tool on account of poor mobility and hands that are not the softest.

The Irrelevant: Shaw hails from Stoneham, MA, a few miles down the road from where I grew up, and home to the Stone Zoo. When I was about eight I fed a giraffe there, and it tried to eat my scarf when I lingered too long after handing it a carrot. Not that the experience traumatized me, or anything. I just - AH! Oh...sorry. Thought I saw a giraffe there. Anyway...

The Risks: The profile offers precious little margin for error in his offensive development, and while there's probably enough hit tool here to scrape by as a second-division starter, he's unlikely to get to enough power in games to offset the runs he gives away with the glove to balance out as an average regular.

Major league ETA: Late 2018 —Wilson Karaman

Ben Carsley's Fantasy Take:

5. Ty Blach, LHP

DOB: 10/20/1990

Height/Weight: 6'2" 200 lbs

Bats/Throws: R/L

Drafted/Acquired: Drafted in the fifth round in the 2012 MLB Draft, Creighton University (Omaha, NE); signed for $224,500

Previous Ranking(s): N/A

2016 Stats: 1.06 ERA, 3.97 DRA, 17 IP, 8 H, 5 BB, 10 K at the major league level, 3.43 ERA, 1.48 DRA, 162.2 IP, 147 H, 38 BB, 113 K at Triple-A Sacramento

The Role: OFP 50—Good no. 4 starter
Likely 45—No. 4/5 starter or long reliever/utility pitcher

YEAR	TEAM	LVL	AGE	W	L	SV	G	GS	IP	H	HR	BB/9	K/9	K	GB%	BABIP	WHIP	ERA	FIP	DRA	VORP	WARP	cFIP	MPH
2014	RIC	AA	23	8	8	0	25	25	141	142	8	2.5	5.8	91	47%	.295	1.28	3.13	3.70	2.92	36.10	3.8	97	
2015	SAC	AAA	24	11	12	0	27	27	165^{1}	189	16	1.7	5.1	93	49%	.311	1.33	4.46	4.33	3.40	35.00	3.6	93	
2016	SAC	AAA	25	14	7	0	26	26	162^{2}	147	9	2.1	6.3	113	50%	.280	1.14	3.43	3.79	1.48	69.80	7.2	79	
2016	SFN	MLB	25	1	0	0	4	2	17	8	1	2.6	5.3	10	60%	.152	0.76	1.06	3.66	3.97	2.40	0.2	103	93.1
2017	*SFN*	*MLB*	*26*	*3*	*2*	*0*	*8*	*8*	*40*	*41*	*3*	*2.6*	*5.7*	*25*	*46%*	*.295*	*1.31*	*3.67*	*3.79*	*4.35*	*3.7*	*0.4*	*100*	
2018	*SFN*	*MLB*	*27*	*8*	*9*	*0*	*27*	*27*	163^{2}	*142*	*15*	*3.8*	*8.1*	*148*	*46%*	*.302*	*1.29*	*3.75*	*4.20*	*4.54*	*15.5*	*1.6*	*103*	

Breakout: 8% Improve: 23% Collapse: 22% Attrition: 29% MLB: 52% *Comparables: D.J. Mitchell, Eric Jokisch, Logan Verrett*

The Good: Blach gets easy plus marks—or even better—on both his changeup and his overall command. He throws a heavy fastball that along with the change induces a lot of grounders when it's working well. By the time he made the majors as a September call-up, his velocity had ticked up into the 90-93 range, higher than he's sat for most of his career. He has just enough funk and sling in his motion to create extra deception. He's pitched very well in some sketchy pitching environments over his career, and as you've been reading on the rest of the site this week, this sort of command profile can play up quite a bit in the right circumstances.

The Bad: Having taken three full seasons in the upper-minors as a college pitcher, Blach is already 26, with just two MLB starts plus two more relief appearances under his belt. He'll throw two distinct breaking balls and they're both fringy, although the curve improved some in his second run at Triple-A. But the lack of feel for spin presents questions about whether he'll get enough swings-and-misses in The Show, and doesn't present a slam dunk relief fallback if he doesn't make it starting.

The Irrelevant: Blach may be inexperienced, but he's already outdueled Clayton Kershaw, tossing eight innings of three-hit ball to down the Dodger ace last fall, while adding two hits of his own.

The Risks: He could fail to keep the ball on the ground in the majors, or even just fail to fool anyone at all. He doesn't have a totally clear shot at the 2017 rotation, and again, he's already 26, so time is of the essence. And he's a pitcher.

Major league ETA: Debuted in 2016

Ben Carsley's Fantasy Take: It's easy to envision Blach as a decent spot starter in dynasty, as he might be a sneaky good matchup play against inferior offenses at home. That means you should remember his name, but that he shouldn't occupy one of your minor league roster spots. It could be worse. We could still be talking about the Diamondbacks.

6. Andrew Suarez, LHP

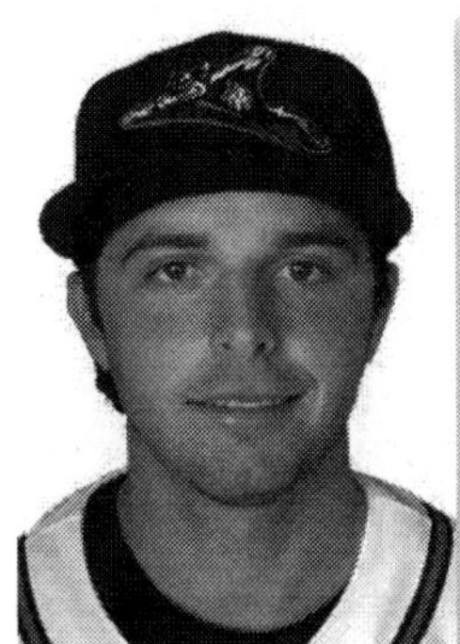

DOB: 9/11/1992

Height/Weight: 6'2" 205 lbs

Bats/Throws: L/L

Drafted/Acquired: Drafted 57th overall in the 2014 MLB draft, University of Miami (Coral Gables, FL); signed for $1,010,100

Previous Ranking(s): N/A

2016 Stats: 3.95 ERA, 2.76 DRA, 114 IP, 129 H, 24 BB, 90 K at Double-A Richmond, 2.43 ERA, 1.33 DRA, 29.2 IP, 25 H, 5 BB, 34 K at High-A San Jose

The Role: OFP 50— No. 4 starter
Likely 40—No. 5 starter/swingman

YEAR	TEAM	LVL	AGE	W	L	SV	G	GS	IP	H	HR	BB/9	K/9	K	GB%	BABIP	WHIP	ERA	FIP	DRA	VORP	WARP	cFIP	MPH
2015	GIA	Rk	22	0	0	0	3	0	5	2	0	1.8	10.8	6	73%	.182	0.60	1.80	2.02	3.49	1.10	0.1	93	
2015	SLO	A-	22	1	0	0	5	5	19^{1}	17	2	0.9	7.0	15	53%	.273	0.98	1.40	3.70	3.63	3.50	0.4	91	
2015	SJO	A+	22	1	0	0	3	3	15	13	2	1.2	9.6	16	46%	.297	1.00	1.80	3.78	2.70	4.00	0.4	87	
2016	SJO	A+	23	2	1	0	5	5	29^{2}	25	2	1.5	10.3	34	61%	.299	1.01	2.43	2.91	1.33	13.70	1.4	74	
2016	RIC	AA	23	7	7	0	19	19	114	129	11	1.9	7.1	90	48%	.332	1.34	3.95	3.72	2.76	29.60	3.2	84	
2017	*SFN*	*MLB*	*24*	*7*	*6*	*0*	*19*	*19*	*106*	*116*	*11*	*2.6*	*6.3*	*74*	*44%*	*.326*	*1.38*	*4.12*	*4.07*	*4.93*	*7.5*	*0.8*	*115*	
2018	*SFN*	*MLB*	*25*	*8*	*9*	*0*	*25*	*25*	*149^{2}*	*146*	*18*	*3.6*	*8.9*	*149*	*44%*	*.332*	*1.38*	*3.81*	*4.28*	*4.56*	*15.6*	*1.6*	*105*	

Breakout: 17% Improve: 27% Collapse: 10% Attrition: 26% MLB: 40% *Comparables: Steven Matz, Hector Noesi, Cory Mazzoni*

The Good: Suarez has a low-90s fastball he can cut or run from his three-quarters slot and he is usually pretty good at keeping down in the zone. He has a full complement of secondary offerings, the best of which is a changeup that he disguises well with his arm action and shows some late fade. He goes to his slider a fair bit, and while it can get a little flat from the arm slot, it is an effective chase pitch with an average projection.

The Bad: The arsenal ranges from fringy to average, depending on the day. The fastball is very hittable when he isn't hitting his spots down. He's only really comfortable commanding the fastball and change armside. The breaking balls can bleed into each other and get slurvy and neither is likely to be a bat-misser in the majors. There's some "funky lefty" in the delivery that tends to make him a little wild in the zone.

The Irrelevant: He's not related to Albert Suarez. This will be more relevant in a moment.

The Risks: Suarez might lack a swing-and-miss offering in the majors. The fastball command might not be good enough to keep hitters from whacking it. This is starting to sound like the Giants have a type. Oh yeah, he's also a pitcher.

Major league ETA: Late 2017

Ben Carsley's Fantasy Take: Here is a snippet of the conversation we had pre-TINO while discussing this Giants list:

George Bissell: Who the hell is Andrew Suarez? Do you mean Albert Suarez?

Craig Goldstein: No ... Albert. Suarez is a common name.

George: I don't understand.

Craig: It ... he ... it doesn't matter. It's not important.

Bret Sayre: Why are we talking about this?

George: So ... so Andrew and Albert are different?

Craig: Seriously, George, it just, it doesn't matter.

7. Steven Duggar, OF

DOB: 11/4/1993

Height/Weight: 6'2" 195 lbs

Bats/Throws: L/R

Drafted/Acquired: Drafted in the sixth round in the 2015 MLB draft, Clemson University (Clemson, SC); signed for $248,800

Previous Ranking(s): N/A

2016 Stats: .321/.391/.432, 1 HR, 9 SB in 60 games at Double-A Richmond, .284/.386/.462, 9 HR, 6 SB in 70 games at High-A San Jose

The Role: OFP 50—Average regular in center
Likely 40—Quality fourth outfielder

YEAR	TEAM	LVL	AGE	PA	R	2B	3B	HR	RBI	BB	K	SB	CS	AVG/OBP/SLG	TAv	VORP	BABIP	BRR	FRAA	WARP
2015	SLO	A-	21	267	40	12	1	1	27	35	52	6	3	.293/.390/.367	.283	12.9	.373	1.4	RF(52): 9.3 • CF(7): -0.9	2.3
2016	SJO	A+	22	311	43	12	4	9	30	44	66	6	7	.284/.386/.462	.323	24.5	.346	-2.2	RF(60): 5.2 • CF(5): -0.2	3.0
2016	RIC	AA	22	276	35	16	4	1	24	28	51	9	7	.321/.391/.432	.327	27.7	.397	1.0	CF(59): 7.1	3.8
2017	*SFN*	*MLB*	*23*	*250*	*30*	*11*	*2*	*5*	*23*	*25*	*62*	*4*	*3*	*.252/.330/.385*	*.250*	*5.3*	*.326*	*-0.4*	*CF 2 • RF 1*	*1.0*
2018	*SFN*	*MLB*	*24*	*387*	*44*	*17*	*3*	*8*	*40*	*38*	*98*	*6*	*4*	*.248/.325/.383*	*.261*	*9.3*	*.322*	*-0.2*	*CF 3 • RF 2*	*1.6*

Breakout: 0% Improve: 20% Collapse: 7% Attrition: 16% MLB: 44% *Comparables: Brian Goodwin, Desmond Jennings, Dexter Fowler*

The Good: Duggar flashes a whole bunch of big league-caliber tools, highlighted by raw speed that rates at least plus and an arm not far behind. He demonstrates an advanced approach at the plate, with quality pitch recognition skills and solid balance that allows for in-swing adjustment. He's quick into the zone with excellent bat-to-ball skills, to where the strikeout rate can remain modest in spite of his proclivity towards working deep into counts. He's stronger than he looks too, and it currently manifests in hard line-drive contact. His range is an asset on the grass, where he has split time between center and right, and should be able to develop into a passable defender in the former.

The Bad: Despite such a big box of tools, they haven't all begun to translate into on-field skills. The swing plane and a limited load relegate his near-average raw power to well-below-average utility in games, and his speed does not translate on the bases, where he remains tentative with his reads and releases on stolen base attempts. The lack of game pop opens up questions about how the on-base skills will translate further up the ladder. He doesn't demonstrate an innate nose for the ball in center, and the profile slides quickly into tweener territory if he has to confine to right field.

The Irrelevant: Duggar's alma mater of Clemson has produced 245 draft picks, with 53 players going on to make it to the majors. 186-game winner Jimmy Key carries the school's flag currently, with over 55 career WARP built across nearly 2,600 big-league innings.

The Risks: Duggar's tools and athleticism make him a high probability prospect to play in the major leagues. How the hit tool holds up at the higher levels will determine a lot here, as will the glove in center. If he winds up on the good side of his developmental bell curve, there are ingredients for a quality regular in center with solid on-base skills and playable speed. But there's little middle ground between that outcome and one in which the hit tool slides back into average range, the speed never quite translates on the bases, and he plays into a bench role at his apex.

Major league ETA: 2018 —Wilson Karaman

Ben Carsley's Fantasy Take: Put Duggar on your watch list, because if the bat starts playing at higher levels, his speed will make him a fantasy-relevant option. He's pretty close to the majors, too, so there could be some decent value to be found on the cheap here over the next season or two.

8. Sandro Fabian, OF

DOB: 3/6/1998

Height/Weight: 6'1" 180 lbs

Bats/Throws: R/R

Drafted/Acquired: Signed July 2014 out of the Dominican Republic for $500,000

Previous Ranking(s): N/A

2016 Stats: .340/.364/.522, 2 HR, 3 SB at rookie ball in the AZL

The Role: OFP 50—Regular corner outfielder with upside
Likely 40—He struggles to play his way out of Double-A

YEAR	TEAM	LVL	AGE	PA	R	2B	3B	HR	RBI	BB	K	SB	CS	AVG/OBP/SLG	TAv	VORP	BABIP	BRR	FRAA	WARP
2015	DGI	Rk	17	286	47	10	2	3	37	15	47	2	0	.269/.348/.364	.264	4.3	.312	-2.8	RF(60): 4.6 • CF(5): 1.4	1.1
2016	GIA	Rk	18	174	30	13	5	2	35	7	28	3	1	.340/.364/.522	.334	16.2	.388	-1.3	RF(40): 2.0 • LF(1): -0.1	1.8
2017	*SFN*	*MLB*	*19*	*250*	*19*	*10*	*1*	*5*	*24*	*7*	*77*	*0*	*0*	*.206/.241/.318*	*.192*	*-11.1*	*.279*	*-0.2*	*RF 1 • LF -0*	*-1.1*
2018	*SFN*	*MLB*	*20*	*355*	*36*	*14*	*3*	*8*	*36*	*13*	*103*	*0*	*0*	*.225/.264/.354*	*.223*	*-7.5*	*.295*	*-0.4*	*RF 1 • LF 0*	*-0.7*

Breakout: 0% Improve: 5% Collapse: 2% Attrition: 4% MLB: 9% *Comparables: Nomar Mazara, Engel Beltre, Raul Mondesi*

The Good: He has an impressive feel for the barrel as a teenager, finishing in the top five in batting average in the AZL this past summer. He has a short, linear stroke without much loft presently. His frame has plenty of room to fill out, and as he matures physically, he could tailor his swing for additional power. He projects as a sure-handed defender in a corner outfield role and his defensive range outplays his speed on the basepaths.

The Bad: He doesn't have an advanced strategy in the box, primarily preying on fastballs in the zone and itching to swing at fastballs out of the zone. He won't be an asset on the basepaths, though it isn't likely he'll be a liability either. While his bat path is short to the ball, his swing mechanics can fall out of sync, resulting in weak contact.

The Irrelevant: Fabian's hometown, Santo Domingo, was discovered by Christopher Columbus's brother, Bartholomew Columbus.

The Risks: He still hasn't celebrated his 19th birthday, so the risks are seemingly endless. He will need to improve his approach as he moves through the minors, and there's a chance his innate bat-to-ball ability will actually hinder the development of his plate discipline. He's already relegated to a corner outfield role, so there's minimal room for error in his offensive development.

Major league ETA: 2021 —Matt Pullman

Ben Carsley's Fantasy Take: Check back in 2019? Check back in 2019.

9. Joan Gregorio, RHP

DOB: 1/12/1992

Height/Weight: 6'7" 180 lbs

Bats/Throws: R/R

Drafted/Acquired: Signed March 2010 out of the Dominican Republic.

Previous Ranking(s): N/A

2016 Stats: 5.28 ERA, 3.15 DRA, 107.1 IP, 112 H, 43 BB, 122 K at Triple-A Sacramento, 2.33 ERA, 1.81 DRA, 27 IP, 15 H, 6 BB, 30 K at Double-A Richmond

The Role: OFP 50—Jon Rauch without the tattoos
Likely 40—Middle reliever with command issues

YEAR	TEAM	LVL	AGE	W	L	SV	G	GS	IP	H	HR	BB/9	K/9	K	GB%	BABIP	WHIP	ERA	FIP	DRA	VORP	WARP	cFIP	MPH
2014	SJO	A+	22	2	2	0	6	5	22²	27	2	5.2	10.7	27	23%	.370	1.76	6.75	4.23	4.10	3.70	0.4	99	
2014	AUG	A	22	2	7	1	13	12	68	50	2	3.6	8.6	65	41%	.259	1.13	3.57	3.47	4.91	3.90	0.4	99	
2015	RIC	AA	23	3	2	1	37	9	78²	64	6	3.7	8.2	72	38%	.272	1.22	3.09	3.69	4.33	5.20	0.6	97	
2016	RIC	AA	24	0	2	0	5	5	27	15	1	2.0	10.0	30	48%	.222	0.78	2.33	2.28	1.81	9.90	1.1	75	
2016	SAC	AAA	24	6	8	0	21	21	107¹	112	13	3.6	10.2	122	37%	.343	1.44	5.28	4.34	3.15	26.20	2.7	89	
2017	*SFN*	*MLB*	*25*	*1*	*1*	*0*	*18*	*0*	*18*	*18*	*2*	*4.1*	*8.3*	*17*	*34%*	*.299*	*1.42*	*3.80*	*4.36*	*4.41*	*1.1*	*0.1*	*100*	
2018	*SFN*	*MLB*	*26*	*2*	*1*	*0*	*30*	*0*	*32*	*26*	*3*	*4.9*	*10.6*	*38*	*34%*	*.311*	*1.34*	*3.56*	*3.97*	*4.27*	*3.0*	*0.3*	*94*	

Breakout: 9% Improve: 23% Collapse: 19% Attrition: 36% MLB: 45% *Comparables: Michael Clevinger, Matt Shoemaker, Tyler Lyons*

The Good: Gregorio's fastball sits in the low-90s and comes in from a tough arm angle. Gregorio gets a deep release point on all his stuff due good extension from his long frame. He can ramp the fastball up into the mid 90s in short bursts as well. His slider flashes plus with hard, late downer action. He's bigger than his listed 180 now, although still fairly thin. He has improved his mechanical consistency since his last go-round as a starter in 2014

The Bad: The changeup is pretty true. The command isn't so great, as the delivery can still get out of sync due to Gregorio's long levers. The slider can be mostly a chase pitch that he starts outside corner and runs away. Although he's been better in his second go-round as a minor league starter, the profile will fit best in a major-league pen.

The Irrelevant: There's never been a Joan in the big leagues. The closest was actually Jack Quinn, who was born in Slovakia, Joannes. He pitched his last game at the age of 50 and won 247 games along the way.

The Risks: Eh, Gregorio is knocking on the door of a major-league role. It's possible that the "tall pitcher" issues will undo his command enough to make him more of an up-and-down relief arm. There's also the threat of "regular pitcher" issues too.

Major league ETA: 2017

Ben Carsley's Fantasy Take: Ty Blach thinks Gregorio is a boring prospect.

10. Heath Quinn, OF

DOB: 6/7/1995

Height/Weight: 6'2" 190 lbs

Bats/Throws: R/R

Drafted/Acquired: Drafted 95th overall in the 2016 MLB Draft, Samford University (Birmingham, AL); signed for $625,900

Previous Ranking(s): N/A

2016 Stats: .353/.421/.412, 0 HR, 0 SB in 4 games at High-A San Jose, .337/.423/.571, 9 HR, 3 SB in 54 games at Short-Season Salem-Keizer

The Role: OFP 50—Second-division regular corner outfielder
Likely 40—Bench bat with some power

YEAR	TEAM	LVL	AGE	PA	R	2B	3B	HR	RBI	BB	K	SB	CS	AVG/OBP/SLG	TAv	VORP	BABIP	BRR	FRAA	WARP
2016	GIA	Rk	21	9	4	1	0	0	0	2	1	0	0	.600/.778/.800	.522	2.7	.750	-0.1	RF(2): -0.2	0.3
2016	SLO	A-	21	239	37	19	1	9	34	26	50	3	0	.337/.423/.571	.352	27.3	.405	1.6	RF(49): 10.5	3.8
2016	SJO	A+	21	19	2	1	0	0	0	2	7	0	0	.353/.421/.412	.310	0.5	.600	-0.8	RF(4): 0.0	0.1
2017	*SFN*	*MLB*	*22*	*250*	*23*	*10*	*1*	*6*	*27*	*17*	*75*	*0*	*0*	*.218/.279/.356*	*.219*	*-4.2*	*.290*	*-0.3*	*RF 1*	*-0.3*
2018	*SFN*	*MLB*	*23*	*188*	*20*	*7*	*1*	*5*	*20*	*13*	*58*	*0*	*0*	*.216/.279/.354*	*.230*	*-2.7*	*.290*	*-0.3*	*RF 1*	*-0.2*

Breakout: 1% Improve: 5% Collapse: 0% Attrition: 5% MLB: 9% *Comparables: Zoilo Almonte, Destin Hood, James Jones*

The Good: There's potential for plus power with a physically-mature frame and moderate loft in his swing. He has impressive overall strength, particularly in his lower half. He's a patient hitter with a refined approach, though his profile is not without some swing and miss. His hit tool could grade out as future average, though even if it falls a grade short, could still allow him to be a future impact bat. His arm is more accurate than it is strong, but it could prove to be average in right field.

The Bad: He won't add value on the basepaths and could have below-average range in the outfield before too long, though he is fundamentally sound defensively. All things considered, if he's going to add value in the field, it's likely in left field, not right field. The aforementioned swing and miss could be an issue down the line.

The Irrelevant: Quinn's alma mater, Samford University, has produced the last two Florida State football coaches, Bobby Bowden and Jimbo Fisher.

The Risks: He's a corner outfielder without supreme defensive ability, so his bat will have to carry him to the big leagues. If his whiff rate continues to grow, he'll have a hard time creating an everyday role for himself.

Major league ETA: 2019 —Matt Pullman

Ben Carsley's Fantasy Take: No one is scrambling to grab Quinn right now. You're fine monitoring his performance and waiting to see if the power and patience translates to the upper minors. Then again, you could go for Quinn now with the hopes of flipping him after he posts what could very well be gaudy Cal League stats. People don't usually take the buy-low, sell-high approach with anonymous dynasty prospects, but if you're into that sort of thing, Quinn's a good candidate for it.

OTHERS OF NOTE:

Pitcher Week, postscript

Ray Black, RHP & Kyle Crick, RHP

An April 2016 BP report by Adam Hayes had Ray Black sitting 97-98 with "lethal" fastball movement, touching 104, and displaying a future above-average slider. Who in baseball can match that stuff, Aroldis Chapman and Noah Syndergaard on their best days? Kyle Crick has worked as high as 94-98 in past looks and was still at 95 this year. He flashes two or even three average or better offspeed pitches depending on the day. What on earth are guys with this kind of stuff doing off in the others section in this thin system?

We sure do talk a lot about command and control. Hell, we've spent this whole week on the site talking about command and control and trying to quantify things and doing all kinds of great research. So it's fitting that at the end of an article at the end of Pitching Week that we meet the opposite of command and control: dudes that have utterly no idea where the ball is going. Minor league hitters can't touch Ray Black at all, but they can opt to leave their bats on their shoulders, because he's walked over a batter per inning for two seasons running. Kyle Crick just double-repeated the Double-A level, and did get under his 2015 walk-an-inning pace, but was generally so bad and uninspiring that it's hard to see how he doesn't end up triple-repeating come 2017; in six minor-league seasons, he's yet to cross below five walks per nine. If anything, these two are even tougher to watch in person than on the stat line, because everything is there for these guys to be great short relievers. Instead, more time on the Richmond Flying Squirrels awaits. —Jarrett Seidler

The guy(s) the Giants will somehow turn into an average regular

C.J. Hinojosa, SS

It feels like Hinojosa would fit better in the Diamondbacks system as a hitter with some feel at the plate, but a slim chance to stick at shortstop. The speed isn't the issue, as he's a plus runner, but his actions aren't fluid and his average arm is a little light for the position. There's a chance the bat could play at second, though. He'll show some pull-side pop at times, and while he strikes out more than you'd expect from this profile, he's comfortable working deep counts and could hit enough to be an average regular at the keystone. The more likely scenario is he settles in as a useful utility infielder, of course.

Jalen Miller, 2B

Miller was always going to be a bit of a project at the plate, but the potential was tantalizing enough for the Giants to pay him a little extra to buy him out of his college commitment in last year's draft. An assignment to full-season ball was always going to be a challenge and Miller struggled all season against the older, more polished arms of the South Atlantic League. It wouldn't be unfair to assume he slid over to second base to make room for Lucius Fox to play shortstop everyday, but he only picked up a handful of starts even after the Bahamian was dealt. Second base was always likely to be his long term home anyway, but that does put more pressure on the bat to develop. He'll get another chance at the South Atlantic League in 2017, but at some point the clock does start ticking on his prospect status, as the tools aren't loud enough to handwave three pro seasons of poor performance.

Austin Slater, OF

Already 24 years old, Slater is going to need to continue to hit to provide value. He can hit a little bit, but there are questions surrounding whether the power he's shown thus far is legitimate. He's produced good exit velocities in the minor leagues, lending some credence to the output, but the minor leagues are not the majors and his short stride, minimal load, and lack of loft could make it more difficult to hit for power against elite arms. He did spend some time at the keystone shortly after being drafted, but he shifted back to the outfield last year, where his arm is playable in a corner and he should be an average defender. If the power isn't legit, he ends up as below-average with both tools at the plate, and more of a reserve outfielder. He might not be more than that even if it is.

TOP 10 TALENTS 25 AND UNDER (BORN 4/1/91 OR LATER)

1. Tyler Beede	6. Steven Okert
2. Christian Arroyo	7. Steven Duggar
3. Bryan Reynolds	8. Sandro Fabian
4. Chris Shaw	9. Joan Gregorio
5. Andrew Suarez	10. Heath Quinn

You're not surprised, are you? The Giants are a team firmly in baseball's middle-age, with just two non-prospects that would qualify for our 25U list: Okert and Trevor Brown. In fact, almost everyone on the projected 25-man roster is between the ages of 26 and 33, with the youngest position player being second baseman Joe Panik. That's fine for today or tomorrow, but things could start to get ugly in 2019. But don't be mistaken, when your stars are Buster Posey, Madison Bumgarner, and the Brandons Belt and Crawford, things are just fine for now. Heck, even Johnny Cueto hasn't made it to his 31st birthday yet, despite the feeling that he's been around forever. Even though there's not much on this particular list, you're not looking at a terrible, aged team on the precipice of a performance cliff. Embrace the now.

So who is Steven Okert, our lone big-league talent on this list? The short answer is that he's a perfectly cromulent second lefty out of the 'pen with the chance to be just a little more. In his short debut with the big club last season he held his own, striking out about a batter per inning over 14 frames. (In case you were wondering, that's just well enough to not pitch during the playoffs.) Going forward there's cause for a little–but not too much–excitement. His stuff has faded a little since the height of his prospectdom, and his velocity isn't quite as crisp as it was during 2014. His best weapon is his slider, but he used it a little more infrequently than you might expect in favor of his fastball and cutter in his limited action this year. And while he can dial it up to the mid-90s, his ceiling is probably a setup guy, and his likely role is a LOOGY. For our purposes, that's plenty good enough to earn a spot in the back half of this list. With Will Smith holding down the southpaw setup role, Okert gets to be the fifth- or sixth-best reliever in a good bullpen, until something else changes.

Let's pad our word count a little by talking about Brown, the only other dude to rate consideration. He doesn't make this list despite getting serious time as the Giants' backup catcher last season, mostly because he's not particularly good. His framing numbers are decidedly below average (-5.4 FRAA), and his bat is nothing to write home about. ("Dearest Abigail, Trevor Brown has below average power."). The Giants obviously wanted to upgrade from him, hence their recent signing of Nick Hundley to be Buster Posey's new reserve. Brown will bounce around for a decade because he's a functional catcher, but you'd rather have everyone else on the list above than a Triple-A backstop.

That's it! That's the entirety of the rest of the Giants' 25-and-under talent! It sure would be nice if someone like Beede or Arroyo pans out, otherwise things could start to get a little dark in a couple of years.

—Bryan Grosnick

SEATTLE MARINERS

The State of the System: *The tenth-best pitching prospect in the Braves system is the fourth-best prospect in this system. Draw your own conclusions.*

THE TOP TEN

1. RF Tyler O'Neill	6. 1B/DH Dan Vogelbach
2. OF Kyle Lewis	7. OF Mitch Haniger
3. RHP Max Povse	8. OF Brayan Hernandez
4. RHP Andrew Moore	9. RHP Dan Altavilla
5. RHP Nick Neidert	10. 3B Joe Rizzo

The Big Question: Do the Mariners have the worst top pitching prospect in baseball?

Ask three evaluators what makes a good pitching prospect, and you may get three different answers. Many will naturally gravitate towards upside, and talk about size, arm strength, velocity, hammer breaking balls, and other terms you could associate with Noah Syndergaard. Some might bring up a pitcher's ability to control his delivery, and to throw quality strikes with all of his pitches. Others will list a combination of stuff and mechanics, with a liberal dash of intangibles alongside.

Ask three evaluators to name the Mariners top pitching prospect, and you may get three responses that break down neatly along the lines described above. We tabbed Luiz Gohara as the top arm in the system [editor's note: before he was subsequently traded], but he didn't exactly run away with the title. He's a teenage fireballer who flashes two decent secondaries, but between concerns about his size, effort level, and lengthy developmental path, there are plenty of red flags in the profile. Reasonable people might prefer Andrew Moore or Max Povse, safer alternatives with a lower ceiling but higher floor.

Ultimately though, none of them are an ideal headliner. At his best, Gohara flashes no. 2-caliber stuff but he's more likely to wind up in the bullpen than on Cy Young ballots. Meanwhile, Moore and Povse will probably start more than a few games in the big leagues at some point, but even forecasting a smooth transition to the majors, it's hard to imagine either becoming more than a no. 4. Are there any other teams with less compelling options at the top of their prospect heap?

Let's break this down visually. Here's a look at the 20 teams who clearly have a better pitching prospect than Seattle:

1	Atlanta	Sean Newcomb
2	Boston	Jason Groome
3	Chicago (AL)	Lucas Giolito
4	Chicago (NL)	Trevor Clifton
5	Cincinnati	Amir Garrett
6	Colorado	Jeff Hoffman
7	Detroit	Matt Manning
8	Houston	Francis Martes
9	Los Angeles (NL)	Yadier Alvarez
10	Milwaukee	Josh Hader
11	New York (AL)	Justus Sheffield
12	New York NL	Robert Gsellman
13	Oakland	Grant Holmes
14	Philadelphia	Franklyn Kilome
15	Pittsburgh	Tyler Glasnow
16	St. Louis	Alex Reyes
17	San Diego	Anderson Espinoza
18	Tampa Bay	Brent Honeywell
19	Texas	Yohander Mendez
20	Washington	Erick Fedde

All of those pitchers are safely on our top 101 list, and while there might be a scout who likes Gohara more than, say, Manning, you probably wouldn't find many of them.

On the next tier down, you again have another group of pitchers who most evaluators would prefer over anyone in Seattle's system. There's a little more room for

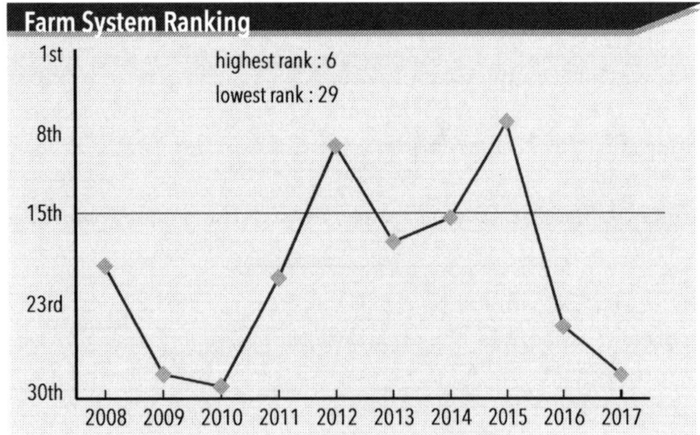

Personnel

EVP, General Manager:
Jerry Dipoto

VP, Assistant General Manager:
Jeff Kingston

VP, Player Personnel:
Tom Allison

Manager:
Scott Servais

BP Alumni:
John Choiniere

disagreement here, but consensus probably sides with the following five names over Gohara or Moore:

21	Cleveland	Triston McKenzie
22	Miami	Braxton Garrett
23	Minnesota	Tyler Jay
24	San Francisco	Tyler Beede
25	Toronto	Sean Reid-Foley

And now we've reached the muck. To end the drama early, Gohara's profile is probably more enticing than anything the Angels have to offer, unless you really value back-end lefties. You could also slot Gohara ahead of Cody Sedlock, Baltimore's top prospect, and a pitcher likely ticketed for a relief role. But he's right there with Arizona's Anthony Banda—a command and control southpaw on the brink of the big leagues—or Kansas City's Josh Staumont, a power arm who walked over 100 hitters in 123 innings last season. To be sure, Gohara is an interesting arm to follow, but a glance at his relative standing among other *top* pitching prospects suggests that the Mariners probably don't have a future all-star on the mound lurking in their system.

But even with one of the worst top pitching prospects in the league, Seattle's pitching situation isn't as dismal as it first appears. For one, the picture is much brighter than it was a year and a half ago, when Gohara ran a 6.20 ERA in the Northwest League, Moore was in short-season ball, Povse was an Atlanta farmhand, and a Google search for Nick Neidert retrieved this as its top image. Incumbents have improved, and new blood from trades and the draft have strengthened a once stagnant system. In Gohara and Neidert, the Mariners have two pitchers who could conceivably pitch in the middle of a rotation someday, and both are coming off strong years in Low-A. There's work ahead, but promise on the horizon.

Seattle also has more young depth in the upper minors this season than they have in years past. In a year where the Mariners were eliminated from playoff contention on the season's penultimate day, fans can only wonder what might have been if the organization hadn't needed Cody Martin, Joe Wieland, and Wade Leblanc to take the ball down the stretch. In Moore, Povse, and, to a lesser extent, Rob Whalen and Ryan Yarbrough, Seattle has several potential back-end arms who can help as soon as 2017. Meanwhile, Dan Altavilla is still prospect eligible and he may see time in the eighth inning this season; fellow youngster Tony Zych could have a meaningful role in relief as well.

Taken together, there's probably more pitching help on the way in Seattle than in Arizona, Kansas City, Baltimore, and Los Angeles, and possibly Miami as well. That doesn't make this a good system for pitching, but the trajectory of the organization's pitching depth is heading in the right direction. If Seattle's development staff has another good year, the theme of this essay could look dated pretty quickly.

—Brendan Gawlowski

1. Tyler O'Neill, RF

DOB: 06/22/1995

Height/Weight: 5'11" 210 lbs.

Bats/Throws: R/R

Drafted/Acquired/Bonus: Drafted in the third round of the 2013 MLB draft, Garibaldi SS (Maple Ridge, BC); signed for $650,000

Previous Ranking(s): #9 (Org.)

2016 Stats: .293/.374/.508, 24 HR, 12 SB in 130 games at Double-A Jackson

The Role: OFP 55—Above-average regular in right field.
Likely 50—Average regular in right field.

YEAR	TEAM	LVL	AGE	PA	R	2B	3B	HR	RBI	BB	K	SB	CS	AVG/OBP/SLG	TAv	VORP	BABIP	BRR	FRAA	WARP
2014	MRN	Rk	19	2	0	0	0	0	0	0	1	0	0	.000/.000/.000	-.001	-0.1	.000	0.0		0.0
2014	EVE	A-	19	11	2	2	0	0	2	1	5	0	0	.400/.455/.600	.400	2.0	.800	0.2	LF(2): -0.6	0.2
2014	CLN	A	19	245	31	9	0	13	38	20	79	5	0	.247/.322/.466	.294	13.7	.320	0.3	LF(36): -3.2, RF(13): 1.2	1.3
2015	BAK	A+	20	449	68	21	2	32	87	29	137	16	5	.260/.316/.558	.322	34.6	.303	-0.7	RF(39): -1.1, LF(35): -0.5	3.5
2016	WTN	AA	21	575	68	26	4	24	102	62	150	12	2	.293/.374/.508	.327	47.3	.364	-0.8	RF(108): -6.6, LF(5): -0.3	4.2
2017	*SEA*	*MLB*	*22*	*250*	*32*	*9*	*1*	*14*	*38*	*18*	*84*	*3*	*1*	*.235/.299/.461*	*.260*	*6.6*	*.303*	*0.0*	*RF -2, LF 0*	*0.5*
2018	*SEA*	*MLB*	*23*	*339*	*47*	*13*	*1*	*18*	*52*	*26*	*111*	*4*	*1*	*.238/.306/.466*	*.265*	*8.0*	*.304*	*-0.1*	*RF -3, LF 0*	*0.6*

The Good: O'Neill's carrying tool is his power. It's 70 raw and if everything clicks, he has the pop to hit 30 homers in the big leagues. His power stems from his frame: he's a big man, a workout warrior with thick wrists and forearms, and plus bat speed to go along with it. He's capable of driving the ball out to all fields and he has a swing that lets him do it. He's not the world's most patient hitter, but it's encouraging that his walk rate climbed in Double-A last season (while reducing his strikeouts, no less). While he's not a burner, he's an average runner, if not a tick better than that. He also has a very strong arm.

The Bad: The list of successful big-league hitters who ran a minor league strikeout rate north of 25 percent is short, and O'Neill flirts with the line between a strikeout-prone slugger and a guy who just swings and misses too often. He struggles with pitch recognition, and as an aggressive hitter, he's particularly susceptible to spin down and out of the strike zone. He swings hard, and once he gets going, he struggles to make mid-pitch adjustments. These flaws won't necessarily sink him, but there's work ahead. Defensively, he's playable in right but he won't win any gold gloves.

The Irrelevant: O'Neill played for the same select baseball team as Brett Lawrie—the Langley Blaze—albeit several years apart.

The Risks: There's a decent chance that he won't make enough contact for the bat to play in an everyday role. He has also (accidentally) injured himself out of frustration; make of that what you will.

Major league ETA: Late 2017 —Brendan Gawlowski

Ben Carsley's Fantasy Take: The risks are real, but so too is the power upside, and you're best served gambling on someone as close to the majors as O'Neill is. Don't count on him for a great average, but O'Neill could hit 20-plus bombs without sinking you in any other categories, sort of like Marcell Ozuna. That'd make him a solid OF 4/5, though if the swing-and-miss gets too bad we could be looking at more of a fantasy bench bat here. He'll flirt with being a top-50 fantasy prospect.

2. Kyle Lewis, OF

DOB: 7/13/1995

Height/Weight: 6'4" 210 lbs.

Bats/Throws: R/R

Drafted/Acquired: Drafted 11th overall in 2016 MLB Draft, Mercer University (Macon, GA); signed for $3.286 million

Previous Ranking(s): N/A

2016 Stats: .299/.385/.530, 3 HR, 3 SB in 30 games at short-season Everett

The Role: OFP 55—Above-average regular in right field
Likely 50—Average regular in right field

YEAR	TEAM	LVL	AGE	PA	R	2B	3B	HR	RBI	BB	K	SB	CS	AVG/OBP/SLG	TAv	VORP	BABIP	BRR	FRAA	WARP
2016	EVE	A-	20	135	26	8	5	3	26	16	22	3	0	.299/.385/.530	.342	12.8	.344	-1.2	CF(27): -1.1	1.4
2017	*SEA*	*MLB*	*21*	*250*	*23*	*9*	*1*	*7*	*27*	*16*	*71*	*1*	*0*	*.209/.266/.345*	*.212*	*-2.7*	*.268*	*-0.2*	*CF 1*	*-0.2*
2018	*SEA*	*MLB*	*22*	*299*	*33*	*11*	*2*	*9*	*33*	*20*	*82*	*1*	*0*	*.218/.276/.369*	*.226*	*-2.1*	*.274*	*-0.3*	*CF 1*	*-0.1*

Breakout: 2% Improve: 5% Collapse: 0% Attrition: 3% MLB: 5% *Comparables: Abraham Almonte, Domonic Brown, Daniel Fields*

The Good: Lewis is a five-tool talent. At the plate, he's quick to the ball and he has enough loft in his swing to project at least above-average power at the highest level, provided that he fills out a bit more. He's a patient and disciplined hitter who likes to work the count; he'll strike out fairly often but also draw his share of walks. He's an average runner with a plus arm, and if he comes back healthy, there's a shot he sticks in center field. Unfortunately…

The Bad: …A brutal knee injury last summer casts legitimate doubt on his ability to hang in center. He was never a lock to stay up the middle and this setback could push him over to right field sooner rather than later. The bat should still play, but it projects as more "good" than "star" in a corner.

The Irrelevant: Lewis was the first player ever selected in the first round out of Mercer University. Pat Creech, the 32nd overall pick in 1973, is the only other MU Bear selected before the third round.

The Risks: It's difficult to project Lewis's future role, given what we know about his knee. If everything went well in surgery and proceeds smoothly in his rehab, there's a chance he'll be the same guy who was drafted last summer. Sadly, we won't know much until he gets back on the field.

Major league ETA: 2019

Ben Carsley's Fantasy Take: Bret Sayre ranked Lewis as the fifth-best fantasy prospect from the 2016 draft, and his well-rounded skillset makes it hard to disagree. It doesn't really matter for our purposes that Lewis might not be a center fielder so long as his glove is good enough to let him play somewhere in the outfield every day. His fantasy future actually doesn't look too different from O'Neill's, but Lewis has a slightly better hit tool and slightly less power. Hopefully he can still run a bit after the knee injury.

3. Max Povse, RHP

DOB: 8/23/1993

Height/Weight: 6'8" 185 lbs.

Bats/Throws: R/R

Drafted/Acquired: Drafted 102nd overall in the 2014 MLB Draft, University of North Carolina at Greensboro (Greensboro, NC); signed for $425,000; acquired from Braves for Alex Jackson and Tyler Pike

Previous Ranking(s): N/A

2016 Stats: 3.71 ERA, 1.46 DRA, 87.1 IP, 89 H, 17 BB, 91 K in 15 games at High-A Carolina, 2.93 ERA, 3.47 DRA, 70.2 IP, 61 H, 12 BB, 48 K in 11 games at Double-A Mississippi

The Role: OFP 50—No. 4 starter
Likely 45—No. 4/5 starter

YEAR	TEAM	LVL	AGE	W	L	SV	G	GS	IP	H	HR	BB/9	K/9	K	GB%	BABIP	WHIP	ERA	FIP	DRA	VORP	WARP	cFIP	MPH
2014	DNV	Rk	20	4	2	0	12	11	47^1	42	1	2.1	7.0	37	0%	.285	1.12	3.42	3.10	4.36			102	
2015	ROM	A	21	4	2	0	12	12	59^2	50	2	2.4	7.5	50	45%	.279	1.11	2.56	3.20	2.71	16.70	1.8	90	
2015	CAR	A+	21	1	3	0	5	5	18^1	24	0	3.4	4.9	10	52%	.364	1.69	9.33	3.80	4.70	0.80	0.1	103	
2016	CAR	A+	22	5	5	0	15	15	87^1	89	5	1.8	9.4	91	56%	.337	1.21	3.71	2.86	1.39	39.70	4.1	65	
2016	MIS	AA	22	4	1	0	11	11	70^2	61	4	1.5	6.1	48	50%	.268	1.03	2.93	3.46	3.30	14.10	1.5	99	
2017	*SEA*	*MLB*	*23*	*7*	*8*	*0*	*22*	*22*	112^2	*127*	*17*	*3.0*	*5.6*	*70*	*45%*	*.298*	*1.46*	*4.92*	*4.95*	*5.30*	*2.1*	*0.2*	*126*	
2018	*SEA*	*MLB*	*24*	*6*	*8*	*0*	*21*	*21*	125^1	*126*	*20*	*4.3*	*8.1*	*113*	*45%*	*.298*	*1.48*	*4.91*	*4.98*	*5.29*	*2.2*	*0.2*	*126*	

Breakout: 9% Improve: 15% Collapse: 7% Attrition: 24% MLB: 31% *Comparables: Scott Diamond, Garrett Richards, Dallas Beeler*

The Good: Povse is an advanced, polished arm, with three potential major-league quality offerings. The fastball sits in the low 90s, but the pitch plays up due to the plane and boring movement he gets from it. There's a decent amount of deception too. The curve and change both have a chance to be average or maybe a tick above.

The Bad: Povse throws strikes, but his length, limbs, and uphill delivery all give plenty of opportunities for the mechanics to go awry. He's more control than command at present. We are at the start of the section of the Mariners list now where the arms may lack an out pitch in the majors.

The Irrelevant: 6-foot-8 is very tall for a pitcher, but he won't be the tallest pitcher in the majors. That honor still belongs to Chris Young, who measures 6-foot-10.

The Risks: Povse is a polished strikethrower, who is just a bit of command refinement away from being a back-of-the-rotation major league arm. It's not super-exciting, but he's close to the majors and relatively low risk. As long as you ignore that he is a pitcher.

Major league ETA: Late 2017

Ben Carsley's Fantasy Take: There are worse back-end starter prospects in the mid-minors to bet on. But there are so, so many better prospects. Unfortunately, this sentiment is about to become a theme...

4. Andrew Moore, RHP

DOB: 6/2/1994

Height/Weight: 6'0" 185 lbs.

Bats/Throws: R/R

Drafted/Acquired: Drafted 72nd overall in the 2015 MLB Draft, Oregon State University (Corvallis, OR); signed for $800,000

Previous Ranking(s): N/A

2016 Stats: 1.65 ERA, 3.09 DRA, 54.2 IP, 36 H, 13 BB, 47 K in 9 games at High-A Bakersfield, 3.16 ERA, 3.41 DRA, 108.1 IP, 112 H, 18 BB, 86 K in 19 games at Double-A Jackson

The Role: OFP 50—No. 4 starter
Likely 45—No. 5 starter/swing man

YEAR	TEAM	LVL	AGE	W	L	SV	G	GS	IP	H	HR	BB/9	K/9	K	GB%	BABIP	WHIP	ERA	FIP	DRA	VORP	WARP	cFIP	MPH
2015	EVE	A-	21	1	1	0	14	8	39	37	2	0.5	9.9	43	46%	.340	1.00	2.08	2.29	1.39	16.10	1.7	65	
2016	BAK	A+	22	3	1	0	9	9	54^2	36	2	2.1	7.7	47	45%	.230	0.90	1.65	3.18	3.01	15.00	1.5	93	
2016	WTN	AA	22	9	3	0	19	19	108^1	112	9	1.5	7.1	86	36%	.320	1.20	3.16	3.34	2.34	33.20	3.6	90	
2017	*SEA*	*MLB*	*23*	*7*	*7*	*0*	*22*	*22*	110^2	*122*	*17*	*2.8*	*5.8*	*71*	*33%*	*.295*	*1.41*	*4.83*	*4.86*	*5.16*	*3.8*	*0.4*	*124*	
2018	*SEA*	*MLB*	*24*	*6*	*7*	*0*	*19*	*19*	*113*	*112*	*18*	*4.1*	*8.4*	*105*	*33%*	*.297*	*1.44*	*4.80*	*4.88*	*5.13*	*3.7*	*0.4*	*124*	

Breakout: 10% Improve: 13% Collapse: 2% Attrition: 18% MLB: 27% *Comparables: Kendry Flores, Sean Nolin, Dan Straily*

The Good: Moore will go as far as his command takes him, and fortunately, he's adept at locating all four of his pitches throughout the strike zone. As with most Driveline guys, he has an up-tempo delivery, but he repeats it extremely effectively and his motion makes him difficult to time. He also maintains his arm speed well on all of his offerings; taken together, the net effect makes Moore more effective than the sum of his parts. His changeup and curve both play within a tick of average depending on the day.

The Bad: I hesitate to say that any of Moore's pitches are "bad," but if you watched a machine programmed to replicate his arsenal, you probably wouldn't walk away overly impressed. He sits in the low-90s with his fastball, touching a bit higher, and he likes to work up in the zone with the pitch. Moore's slider is behind his other off-speed pitches; it's not clear whether he'll have an out pitch against elite bats.

The Irrelevant: Moore spent the offseason as target practice for Dan Straily.

The Risks: Moore might not miss too many bats, and if Safeco plays like the launching pad it was last season, he faces an uphill battle to stick as a pitch-to-contact starter.

Major league ETA: 2018, possibly late 2017 —Brendan Gawlowski

Ben Carsley's Fantasy Take: Fun fact: I work in SEO for my real-life job and I can tell you that Google hates duplicate content. This is the only thing that prevents me from writing the same exact thing about back-end starting prospects on every single one of these lists. Stay away.

5. Nick Neidert, RHP

DOB: 11/20/1996

Height/Weight: 6'1" 180 lbs.

Bats/Throws: R/R

Drafted/Acquired: Drafted 60th overall in the 2015 MLB Draft Peachtree HS (Peachtree, GA); signed for $1.2 million

Previous Ranking(s): #10 (Org.)

2016 Stats: 2.57 ERA, 3.33 DRA, 91 IP, 75 H, 13 BB, 69 K in 19 games at Low-A Clinton

The Role: OFP 50—No. 4 starter
Likely 45—Back-end starter or good middle reliever

YEAR	TEAM	LVL	AGE	W	L	SV	G	GS	IP	H	HR	BB/9	K/9	K	GB%	BABIP	WHIP	ERA	FIP	DRA	VORP	WARP	cFIP	MPH
2015	MRN	Rk	18	0	2	0	11	11	35¹	25	1	2.3	5.9	23	67%	.235	0.96	1.53	3.65	3.27	10.30	1.0	92	
2016	CLN	A	19	7	3	0	19	19	91	75	7	1.3	6.8	69	41%	.262	0.97	2.57	3.59	3.90	11.30	1.2	99	
2017	*SEA*	*MLB*	*20*	*3*	*6*	*0*	*14*	*14*	*59*	*74*	*14*	*3.6*	*4.1*	*27*	*36%*	*.292*	*1.65*	*6.53*	*6.66*	*7.08*	*-10.6*	*-1.1*	*170*	
2018	*SEA*	*MLB*	*21*	*5*	*10*	*0*	*25*	*25*	*147*	*168*	*32*	*4.5*	*7.1*	*116*	*36%*	*.302*	*1.65*	*6.06*	*6.14*	*6.57*	*-13.2*	*-1.4*	*157*	

Breakout: 1% Improve: 1% Collapse: 1% Attrition: 3% MLB: 4% *Comparables: Michael Fulmer, Robbie Ray, Jeurys Familia*

The Good: I could save us all some time by copy/pasting the Moore and Povse reports here, but there are some subtle differences I suppose. Neidert is a bit rawer, but the stuff is better on balance. Neidert can get his fastball up to the mid-90s and it is lively pitch when he can get it down in the zone. The curveball will flash solid-average. The change and the slider both have a chance to be major league offerings.

The Bad: Neidert's delivery plays a little taller than his listed 6-foot-1, but the fastball can lack plane. There's some effort in the delivery, and his control is better than his command, and he can be wild in the zone with the fastball. He doesn't always get the fastball down and it is very hittable up in the zone. The curve can show early and get a little humpy. The change flashes, but is too firm at present.

The Irrelevant: Per TripAdvisor, the top thing to do in Peachtree, GA is "Golf Cart Paths." It has 160 reviews as of publication.

The Risks: The Mariners managed Neidert's innings carefully in 2016, so there will be some questions to how the frame and delivery hold up to a starter's workload until it...holds up to starter's workload. There isn't a clear out pitch at present, although I think the curve could get there. The fastball may get squared more in the upper minors without command improvements. The total package might end up playing better in short bursts. And oh, yeah, he's a pitcher.

Major league ETA: 2019

Ben Carsley's Fantasy Take: Fun fact: I work in SEO for my real-life job and I can tell you that Google hates duplicate content. This is the only thing that prevents me from writing the same exact thing about back-end starting prospects on every single one of these lists. Stay away.

6. Dan Vogelbach, 1B/DH

DOB: 12/17/1992

Height/Weight: 6'0" 250 lbs.

Bats/Throws: L/R

Drafted/Acquired: Drafted 68th Overall in the 2011 MLB Draft, Bishop Verot HS (Fort Myers, FL); signed for $1.6 million; acquired from Cubs for Mike Montgomery and Jordan Pries

Previous Ranking(s): N/A

2016 Stats: .083/.154/.083, 0 HR, 0 SB in 8 games at major league level, .318/.425/.548, 16 HR, 0 SB in 89 games at Triple-A Iowa, .240/.404/.422, 7 HR, 0 SB in 44 games at Triple-A Tacoma

The Role: OFP 50—Average regular at DH
Likely 45—Bench bat

YEAR	TEAM	LVL	AGE	PA	R	2B	3B	HR	RBI	BB	K	SB	CS	AVG/OBP/SLG	TAv	VORP	BABIP	BRR	FRAA	WARP
2014	DAY	A+	21	560	71	28	1	16	76	66	91	4	4	.268/.357/.429	.280	15.3	.296	-3.1	1B(103): -9.9	0.6
2015	CUB	Rk	22	17	4	2	0	0	0	6	1	0	0	.455/.647/.636	.429	3.3	.500	-0.1	1B(3): 0.2	0.3
2015	TEN	AA	22	313	41	16	1	7	39	57	61	1	1	.272/.403/.425	.310	16.0	.330	-3.0	1B(75): 1.4	1.9
2016	IOW	AAA	23	365	53	18	2	16	64	55	67	0	0	.318/.425/.548	.349	35.7	.362	-1.8	1B(76): -3.0	3.4
2016	TAC	AAA	23	198	26	7	0	7	32	42	34	0	0	.240/.404/.422	.308	8.9	.263	-3.1	1B(25): -0.9	0.8
2016	SEA	MLB	23	13	0	0	0	0	0	1	6	0	0	.083/.154/.083	.102	-2.3	.167	-0.4	1B(4): -0.3	-0.3
2017	*SEA*	*MLB*	*24*	*237*	*28*	*9*	*0*	*9*	*31*	*32*	*55*	*0*	*0*	*.242/.347/.424*	*.275*	*7.1*	*.285*	*-0.6*	*1B -2*	*0.4*
2018	*SEA*	*MLB*	*25*	*454*	*64*	*18*	*1*	*19*	*61*	*59*	*107*	*0*	*0*	*.248/.350/.441*	*.276*	*12.5*	*.293*	*-1.2*	*1B -4*	*0.9*

Breakout: 2% Improve: 15% Collapse: 14% Attrition: 24% MLB: 47% *Comparables: Chris Carter, Ji-Man Choi, Travis Shaw*

The Good: Vogelbach can really hit. He's a disciplined hitter with excellent strike zone judgment, and his swing covers both halves of the plate. He's a huge guy with loft in his swing, and above-average bat speed, all of which translates into plus raw power. He started tapping into it in games pretty regularly last season, and he has the potential to launch 25-plus homers as a big leaguer. He won't win many batting titles—too many strikeouts and he's not legging out many infield grounders—but he makes a lot of hard contact and should post a strong on-base percentage. Vogelbach has also earned a lot of praise for his make-up, and he's a very high-effort player on the field.

The Bad: Despite the defensive improvements he's made in recent years, Vogelbach's best position is designated hitter. The Mariners plan to use him at first base, and he's playable there, but he's a 20 runner and his lack of range on grounders and pop-ups will become apparent quickly. At the plate, the walks and power come with plenty of strikeouts, and he hasn't hit quite as many homers as you'd think given his frame and raw power.

The Irrelevant: According to Kiley McDaniel, Vogelbach avidly reads critiques about his game; hello Dan!

The Risks: There's compelling evidence that the strike zone is bigger in the majors than in Triple-A, and that could make life difficult for a guy like Vogelbach. There's also a bias against pure-DH types, as many managers prefer to cycle players through the DH slot to reduce wear and tear. Together, those factors could pinch Vogelbach's value to a big-league team.

Major league ETA: Debuted in 2016 —Brendan Gawlowski

Ben Carsley's Fantasy Take: This ranking is a personal affront to the respective honors of me, Bret and Wilson Karaman. But for real, Vogelbach is the personification of the difference between fantasy value and IRL value. Sure, the ceiling isn't elite here, but Vogelbach has a high floor as a modest source of power and AVG, even if he's only eligible at UT. He's probably the third-best (and maybe the second-best) fantasy prospect on this list, and he's definitely a top-100 dynasty prospect as an MLB-ready bat who could hit .280 with 20 homers. He'll be more valuable in OBP leagues, too.

7. Mitch Haniger, OF

DOB: 12/23/1990

Height/Weight: 6'2" 215 lbs.

Bats/Throws: R/R

Drafted/Acquired: Drafted 38th overall in the 2012 MLB Draft Cal Poly State-San Luis Obispo; signed for $1.2 million. Acquired from Diamondbacks for Ketel Marte and Taijuan Walker

Previous Ranking(s): N/A

2016 Stats: .294/.407/.462, 5 HR, 4 SB in 55 games at Double-A Mobile; .341/.428/.670, 20 HR, 8 SB in 74 games at Triple-A Reno; .229/.309/.404, 5 HR, 0 SB in 34 games for the Arizona Diamondbacks

The Role: OFP 50—Mashing corner outfielder
Likely 45—Mashing bench bat

YEAR	TEAM	LVL	AGE	PA	R	2B	3B	HR	RBI	BB	K	SB	CS	AVG/OBP/SLG	TAv	VORP	BABIP	BRR	FRAA	WARP
2014	DIA	Rk	23	16	4	1	0	1	4	1	6	0	0	.200/.250/.467	.222	-0.3	.250	0.1		0.0
2014	MOB	AA	23	30	5	3	0	0	5	3	4	0	0	.333/.433/.458	.362	4.6	.381	0.9	RF(7): 0.5	0.6
2014	HUN	AA	23	271	41	7	1	10	34	19	41	4	0	.255/.316/.416	.281	11.3	.267	-0.4	RF(47): -3.9, CF(25): -0.4	0.9
2015	MOB	AA	24	174	23	10	1	1	19	16	32	4	4	.281/.351/.379	.281	8.6	.341	0.2	CF(38): -2.6, LF(12): 1.4	0.9
2015	VIS	A+	24	226	40	16	3	12	36	17	39	8	2	.332/.381/.619	.368	30.7	.353	1.4	RF(24): 1.8, CF(21): -1.2	3.4
2016	MOB	AA	25	236	21	14	2	5	30	30	37	4	3	.294/.407/.462	.317	17.9	.340	-0.9	LF(32): 0.9, CF(16): -0.6	1.5
2016	RNO	AAA	25	312	58	20	3	20	64	39	62	8	1	.341/.428/.670	.360	43.5	.373	3.4	RF(34): 2.9, CF(34): -0.8	4.6
2016	ARI	MLB	25	123	9	2	1	5	17	12	27	0	0	.229/.309/.404	.250	2.3	.256	0.2	CF(22): 1.3, LF(9): -0.0	0.4
2017	*SEA*	*MLB*	*26*	*529*	*67*	*22*	*2*	*22*	*69*	*46*	*120*	*6*	*2*	*.253/.326/.448*	*.275*	*21.6*	*.291*	*-0.4*	*RF -3, LF -1*	*1.4*
2018	*SEA*	*MLB*	*27*	*522*	*71*	*22*	*2*	*22*	*71*	*48*	*123*	*5*	*2*	*.255/.333/.452*	*.273*	*16.8*	*.298*	*-0.3*	*RF -3, LF -1*	*1.4*

Breakout: 4% Improve: 35% Collapse: 16% Attrition: 28% MLB: 74% *Comparables: Casper Wells, Ben Francisco, Chip Ambres*

The Good: With the help of Bob Tewksbary, Haniger tweaked his swing in 2016 and the results were striking. He added a leg kick, lowered his hands, and then lowered the boom on the upper minors. Reno and the PCL may exaggerate the effects some, but there is legit above-average power in the profile now. He's not a complete disaster in center field, and has the arm strength to slide over to right field if necessary.

The Bad: He's a step or two too slow for an everyday up-the-middle role, and those swing changes may not be enough to carry a right field profile in the majors. The swing-and-miss has never been excessive in his pro career, but he was always over-age, and I do wonder if major-league arms will be able to exploit some of the new timing mechanisms in his swing. He will need to hit a lot to carry a corner outfield profile.

The Irrelevant: It took me at least a year to stop thinking that Bob Tewksbary the hitting instructor was Bob Tewksbury the pitching savant. Yes, it didn't make sense to me even at the time.

The Risks: We aren't saying Haniger is a Quad-A player, but if he were a Quad-A player, his 2016 would be in line with that profile. He doesn't qualify for the 25U list so banking on further improvement might be foolhardy.

Major league ETA: Debuted in 2016

Ben Carsley's Fantasy Take: If you play in a 16-team AL-only league with 40 man rosters, run, don't walk, to pick up Haniger. Otherwise you're good.

8. Brayan Hernandez, OF

DOB: 9/11/1997

Height/Weight: 6'2" 175 lbs.

Bats/Throws: S/R

Drafted/Acquired: Signed in July 2014 out of Venezuela for $1.85 million

Previous Ranking(s): N/A

2016 Stats: .285/.324/.400, 1 HR, 9 SB in 33 games at complex level AZL

The Role: OFP 50—Average major-league corner outfielder
Likely 40—Tweener bench outfielder

YEAR	TEAM	LVL	AGE	PA	R	2B	3B	HR	RBI	BB	K	SB	CS	AVG/OBP/SLG	TAv	VORP	BABIP	BRR	FRAA	WARP
2015	MCO	Rk	17	196	32	8	2	2	22	18	44	9	6	.224/.295/.328	.243	4.5	.287	2.2	CF(43): -1.8, RF(6): -0.3	0.3
2016	DMR	Rk	18	146	30	6	2	5	15	10	23	12	2	.278/.331/.466	.316	12.6	.302	1.1	CF(30): 0.7	1.4
2016	MRN	Rk	18	140	13	8	2	1	19	7	36	9	3	.285/.324/.400	.274	6.1	.383	0.5	CF(17): -1.0, RF(15): -0.5	0.3
2017	*SEA*	*MLB*	*19*	*250*	*27*	*8*	*1*	*7*	*22*	*10*	*87*	*5*	*2*	*.193/.227/.319*	*.188*	*-9.4*	*.266*	*0.2*	*CF -0, RF -0*	*-1.1*
2018	*SEA*	*MLB*	*20*	*357*	*37*	*12*	*2*	*11*	*39*	*16*	*116*	*8*	*4*	*.209/.248/.350*	*.209*	*-8.7*	*.279*	*0.7*	*CF 0, RF 0*	*-1.0*

Breakout: 0% Improve: 5% Collapse: 1% Attrition: 4% MLB: 9% *Comparables: Engel Beltre, Nomar Mazara, Raul Mondesi*

The Good: Hernandez is a wiry-strong, twitchy athlete. His loose hands and strong wrists help create above-average bat speed which results in loud contact off the bat. He's a plus runner with a solid second gear and the type of bouncy first step that creates the range necessary to track fly balls in the gap.

The Bad: His present feel for the barrel would get picked apart at the higher levels of the minors. He seems to cheat in order to keep up with velocity, resulting in ugly swings out on his front foot against fringe breaking stuff. Defensively, he split time between center field and right field in the AZL, signaling his ultimate positional destination is likely an outfield corner.

The Irrelevant: While age-appropriate for complex ball, Hernandez's youth isn't so extreme to make you contemplate your own mortality, but then again Event Horizon had just come out when he was born.

The Risks: Hernandez is your prototypical flame out candidate. He has the tools to be a big leaguer, but he hasn't shown the bat-to-ball skills to make him a true top prospect. His offensive profile would play much better up the middle, as he may not hit enough to warrant an everyday role in a corner.

Major league ETA: 2021

Ben Carsley's Fantasy Take: Hernandez is a good one for your watch list, but that's about the extent of his fantasy value at the moment.

9. Dan Altavilla, RHP

DOB: 9/8/1992

Height/Weight: 5'11" 200 lbs

Bats/Throws: R/R

Drafted/Acquired: Drafted in the fifth round of the 2014 MLB Draft, Mercyhurst College; signed for $250,000

Previous Ranking(s): N/A

2016 Stats: 1.91 ERA, 3.01 DRA, 56.2 IP, 40 H, 22 BB, 65 K in 43 games at Double-A West Tennessee, 0.73 ERA, 4.64 DRA, 12.1 IP, 10 H, 1 BB, 11 K in 15 games at the major league level

The Role: OFP 45—7th inning guy
Likely 40—Solid enough middle reliever

The Good: When writing about a marginal starting pitching prospect, my cohort will often fall back on the hoary cliché of "maybe his stuff will play up in the bullpen." But hey, sometimes that really works. After two middling years in A-ball, as a short right-handed starter, the Mariners let Altavilla loose in the pen and it, uh, really worked. In relief Altavilla works off an upper-90s fastball with incredible armside life and a high-80s slider he can spot or chase. He has a better change than you'd expect from this type of prospect: it's a bit firm at 90, but shows some arm-side fade and he isn't afraid to throw it.

The Bad: Altavilla is bullpen-only and a short righthander without much in the way of projection. He is what he is in other words. At present the slider is too inconsistent to project a late-inning role. His command is below-average although that gets covered for by the raw velocity and movement of the stuff.

The Irrelevant: Mercyhurst's mascot is Luke the Laker, who appears to be a distant cousin of Steely McBeam.

The Risks: Altavilla is a major-league-ready reliever with a good shot of breaking camp with the Mariners this year. I suppose there is the risk that Jerry DiPoto will trade him because he is, after all, a Mariner. Oh, and he's also a pitcher.

Major league ETA: Debuted in 2016
Ben Carsley's Fantasy Take: Fish for saves elsewhere.

10. Joe Rizzo, 3B

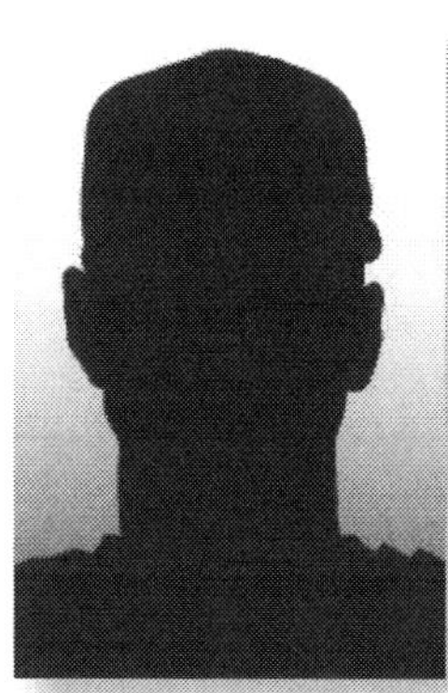

DOB: 3/31/1998

Height/Weight: 194 lbs

Bats/Throws: L/R

Drafted/Acquired: Drafted 50th overall in the 2016 MLB draft, Oakton HS (Vienna, VA), signed for $1,750,000.

Previous Ranking(s): N/A

2016 Stats: .291/.355/.392, 2 HR, 2 SB at rookie ball in the AZL.

The Role: OFP 45—Second-division starter at the hot corner
Likely 40—Matt Dominguez probably should have taken the extension

The Good: Rizzo is a natural third baseman with good hands, smooth actions, and an above-average arm. He has above-average raw and a good shot to get enough of that in games for the bat to play in a corner.

The Bad: Rizzo is less of a natural hitter. He struggles with offspeed above and beyond even what you would expect from a second-round prep bat. The pretty left-handed swing breaks down against spin. The power potential is still just potential and hasn't shown up in games yet.

The Irrelevant: Rizzo was born in Hackensack, NJ, the subject of Fountains of Wayne's best track, "Hackensack."

The Risks: It may take a while for the profile to come together—if it ever does—and Rizzo has only played in the complex so far. There are questions about hit tool and pitch recognition. You don't play third basemen just for their glove.

Major league ETA: 2021

Ben Carsley's Fantasy Take: N/A, but you already knew that.

OTHERS OF NOTE:

The guy we're bored with

D.J. Peterson, 3B/1B

Yeah, it's not fair, but the epithet is a paraphrase of my response in our Slack channel when someone suggested D.J. Peterson was still a Top Ten Mariners prospect. 2016 was a nice bounceback after a disastrous 2015, but the Mariners aren't even really pretending he's a third baseman anymore. And at first base, the 50 hit/50 power combo isn't all that exciting. Seattle has made rumblings that they might try him in a corner outfield spot as well, which...good luck to all parties involved I guess. The veneer of positional flexibility could make him a useful four corners righty bat, and there's still some second-division starter upside here even at first, but I'm just bored with D.J. Peterson. Prospect writers can be fickle that way.

Matt's Guy

Christopher Torres, SS

Torres is a scrappy switch-hitting shortstop with more feel for the barrel from the left side. He's a plus runner with some idea for the strike zone, taking close pitches and spitting on marginal two-strike offerings. He struck out more than one would hope for complex-level ball, and he isn't the type of natural defender that makes him a lock to stick at shortstop. Like most prospects who still haven't celebrated their 19th birthdays, there's quite a bit of risk to Torres's profile. He lacks the upside of some of his AZL teammates, but there's a reasonable path to becoming a big-league utility man. —Matt Pullman

TOP 10 TALENTS 25 AND UNDER (BORN 4/1/91 OR LATER)

1. Edwin Diaz	6. Nick Neidert
2. Tyler O'Neill	7. Dan Vogelbach
3. Kyle Lewis	8. Brayan Hernandez
4. Max Povse	9. Dan Altavilla
5. Andrew Moore	10. Joe Rizzo

As you can see from this list, the Mariners are very light on young talent. That's not altogether surprising: with Robinson Cano, Felix Hernandez, Nelson Cruz, Kyle Seager, and Hisashi Iwakuma, this is a team with a strong core of veterans, built to win now—or perhaps more accurately, built to win two years ago. Seattle isn't entirely devoid of young major-league talent; after all, Diaz is the closer, and Diesel Dan Altavilla could eventually handle the eighth. Boog Powell is hanging around in Triple-A as a fourth outfield type. Tony Zych and James Paxton are still in their mid-20s. Clearly though, this is an old team.

So what does an old team built to win now do with a 22-year-old gas-spitter like Diaz in the back of the bullpen? For now, he'll close games for a team still hoping to sneak into the playoffs while the stars remain, well, stars. Provided that his command issues last September were the product of fatigue and not the onset of a serious control problem, he should thrive in the role. Relievers around the league dominated the sport with high-octane fastballs and tight sliders, and for a few months last summer, nobody epitomized the trend quite like Diaz. The electric right-hander touched 102 mph, sat pretty close to that number, and simply devastated hitters after a midseason promotion from Double-A. He struck out 88 batters in 51 innings last year, including 12 of the 16 men he faced in one memorable two-week stretch of June. He had a few bumps, but for the most part, Diaz was legit.

Long term, the answer to the above question is more complicated. The Mariners, whatever their merits now, will probably not be a good team in 2019. Almost all of their impact players will either be gone or in their 30's, and while there are a few promising players on our top ten, the next great Mariners team will not feature many of the names above in prominent roles. To reset the organization, Seattle will probably have to rebuild in the coming years. We don't know how much value they'll be able to obtain in return for members of their soon-to-be-aging core but given the size of the contracts involved, the safe guess is "not a ton." We're dealing with hypotheticals on top of hypotheticals, but it's not hard to project a situation where Diaz soon becomes one of Seattle's most valuable trade chips, if he is not already.

Coming off of a postseason shaped by dominant relief pitching, the market for relievers is scorching right now. Andrew Miller and Aroldis Chapman both commanded large returns in midseason trades last year, while Mark Melancon and Kenley Jansen just signed $60- and $80-million contracts, respectively. Provided that Diaz stays healthy and effective and solidifies his reputation as an elite reliever Jerry Dipoto could soon find himself in a position where he can extract a king's ransom for Diaz. And given that we're talking about a young, hard-throwing pitcher—one who wore down in the second half of last season, no less—there must be a certain amount of incentive to move him sooner rather than later. Closers are a luxury on a bad team, and if Miller's acquisition serves as any guide, the guess here is that an inexpensive talent like Diaz will return quite a package from a contender looking for a velocity injection.

Mariners fans should enjoy Diaz's exploits while they can. Seattle has enough talent on the roster to give it a go in 2017, and if the rest of the team clicks, Diaz can be a valuable part of a winning ball club this year. In all likelihood though, his long term future lies elsewhere. He's at the top of our 25U list this season; soon, he may be directly responsible for his replacement.

—Brendan Gawlowski

ST LOUIS CARDINALS

The State of the System: *It's a pretty good system. A little better than middle-of-the-pack. It's also difficult to sum up pithily here.*

THE TOP TEN

1. RHP Alex Reyes	6. RHP Dakota Hudson
2. RHP Sandy Alcantara	7. RHP Luke Weaver
3. SS Delvin Perez	8. OF Harrison Bader
4. C Carson Kelly	9. RHP Jordan Hicks
5. CF Magneuris Sierra	10. RHP Jack Flaherty

The Big Question: Who is the next beneficiary of the Cardinals Devil Magic?

Ranking Cardinals prospects is a fool's errand. Aledmys Diaz appears nowhere on last year's list. Matt Carpenter never ranked higher than eighth. Tommy Pham's only appearance on a BP Prospect list was penned by Kevin Goldstein (he checked in at #18). Jedd Gyorko was basically one more bad season away from being legally declared dead so his surviving relatives could finally collect the insurance money. They even gainfully employed a Hampshire College graduate in work that didn't involve collecting lost tennis balls and turning them into art or something.

So am I going to sit here agog when Harrison Bader turns into Matt Holliday or Austin Gomber suddenly sits 94-96? I am not.

But in the interest of covering all our bases, here are some off-the-board candidates that might benefit from the Midwestern dark arts:

Connor Jones adds a few ticks on his fastball

Jones was a durable college starter with above-average fastball velocity and the usual menagerie of secondary offerings. But what if all of a sudden he sat 95-97? That would be weird, right? Adding that kind of velocity in your early-20s? Not for the Cardinals. They've already pulled that bit of legerdemain once with Michael Wacha.

Jesse Jenner has a major league career as a backstop

Even in my younger years, covering only one organization's farm system to the point of superfluity, I couldn't bring myself to get too concerned with a 10k senior-sign catcher. You always need catchers from an organizational standpoint, but those guys tend to bounce around A-ball as backups for a few years and then move into coaching.

However, the organization I covered wasn't the Cardinals.

Jenner is on that path—bouncing around as a backup between three levels while posting an OPS of .600-something—so don't be surprised at all when he pops up in the Top Ten like Carson Kelly in a year. It's a profile the Cardinals do well with.

Nick Plummer comes back in 2017 and looks like an above-average corner outfielder

No, we haven't forgotten about Plummer, the Cardinals' first-round pick in 2015. He missed all of 2016 with hand and wrist issues that required multiple surgeries. Maybe he comes back with a bionic hand. It's the Cardinals. They do well with that profile. That profile being dudes with bionic hands.

Bryce Denton literally makes a pact with a demon

Denton, the Cards second round pick in 2015, has potentially above-average hit and power tools, but big questions about his ultimate defensive home. The bat looks a lot better at third base, so what if he were accompanied by a small demon that could field like Ken Boyer?

"Why, the signiory of Embden shall be mine.
When Mephistophilis shall stand by me,
What ball can get by me, Denton? Thou art out
Cast no more doubts. Come, Mephistophilis,
And bring a plus glove from great Lucifer;
Is't not first pitch? Come, Mephistophilis,
Veni, veni, Mephistophile!"

As for the rest...

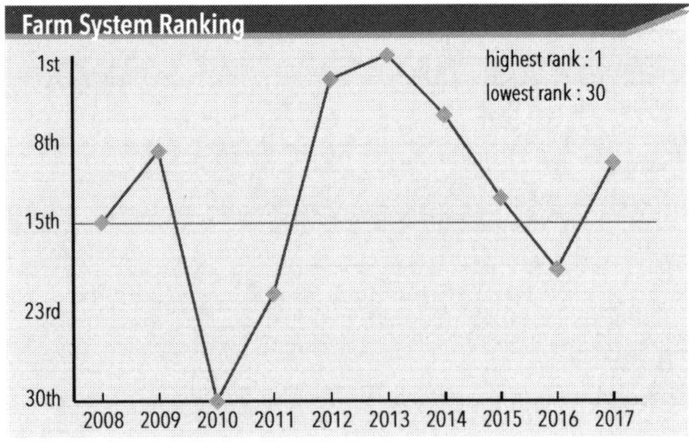

Personnel

SVP, General Manager:
John Mozeliak

Assistant General Manager:
Mike Girsch

Manager:
Mike Matheny

BP Alumni:
Zach Mortimer
Mauricio Rubio

1. Alex Reyes, RHP

DOB: 08/29/1994

Height/Weight: 6'3" 175 lbs.

Bats/Throws: R/R

Drafted/Acquired: Signed December 2012 by St. Louis out of the Dominican Republic for $950,000

Previous Ranking(s): #1 (Org), #10 (Overall), #8 (Midseason Top 50)

2016 Stats: 1.57 ERA, 3.72 DRA, 46 IP, 33 H, 23 BB, 52 K at the major league level, 4.96 ERA, 2.36 DRA, 65.1 IP, 63 H, 32 BB, 93 K in Triple-A Memphis

The Role: OFP 70—Front-of-the-rotation starter
Likely 60—No. 3 starter or high-end closer

YEAR	TEAM	LVL	AGE	W	L	SV	G	GS	IP	H	HR	BB/9	K/9	K	GB%	BABIP	WHIP	ERA	FIP	DRA	VORP	WARP	cFIP	MPH
2014	PEO	A	19	7	7	0	21	21	109^1	82	6	5.0	11.3	137	40%	.295	1.31	3.62	3.45	3.04	29.20	3.0	94	
2015	CRD	Rk	20	0	0	0	1	1	3	0	0	0.0	9.0	3	0%	.000	0.00	0.00	2.30	3.52	0.80	0.1	94	
2015	PMB	A+	20	2	5	0	13	13	63^2	49	0	4.4	13.6	96	46%	.371	1.26	2.26	1.75	1.07	28.40	3.1	70	
2015	SFD	AA	20	3	2	0	8	8	34^2	21	1	4.7	13.5	52	44%	.286	1.12	3.12	2.32	2.01	11.90	1.3	70	
2016	MEM	AAA	21	2	3	0	14	14	65^1	63	6	4.4	12.8	93	42%	.365	1.45	4.96	3.72	2.36	21.70	2.2	71	
2016	SLN	MLB	21	4	1	1	12	5	46	33	1	4.5	10.2	52	44%	.283	1.22	1.57	2.71	3.72	7.70	0.8	94	100.1
2017	*SLN*	*MLB*	*22*	*8*	*7*	*0*	*23*	*23*	*122*	*111*	*13*	*4.2*	*9.6*	*130*	*39%*	*.326*	*1.38*	*4.03*	*3.88*	*4.42*	*15.5*	*1.6*	*100*	
2018	*SLN*	*MLB*	*23*	*10*	*10*	*0*	*32*	*32*	*203*	*155*	*19*	*4.5*	*11.2*	*253*	*39%*	*.311*	*1.27*	*3.62*	*3.70*	*3.97*	*29.4*	*3.0*	*89*	

Breakout: 23% Improve: 41% Collapse: 10% Attrition: 22% MLB: 66% *Comparables: Trevor Bauer, Luis Severino, Shelby Miller*

The Good: Reyes's fastball is an 80-grade offering. It sits in the upper-90s, can touch triple digits, and features life to both sides. When he elevates it, the pitch is criminally unfair. His curve flashes plus-plus and dives off the deck with late 12-6 movement at its best. The change has made strides in 2016 and will flash plus with good sink at times. The overall arsenal is potentially one of the best in baseball—not the minors, baseball.

The Bad: Reyes still struggles to throw as many strikes as you'd like from a frontline starter. The delivery should be repeatable, but he hasn't unlocked that part yet and both his control and command are fringy. The curve can flatten out or be more of a bury pitch when he doesn't have feel for it. The change is too often straight and firm and is more of an average pitch at present.

The Irrelevant: Reyes topped out at 87 mph in high school. That's, uh, pretty irrelevant now.

The Risks: The stuff is there to start, whether the command/efficiency allows him to pitch at the top of the rotation is still unanswered. Whatever role he ends up in, he's going to be good. Unless he gets hurt, because, yeah, he's a pitcher.

Major league ETA: Debuted in 2016

Ben Carsley's Fantasy Take: You see that big ol' 70 and that ETA of "already debuted?" Those factors make Reyes incredibly sexy for our purposes, even if he is a pitcher. The WHIP might be a little ugly early in his career-- hell, maybe for all of his career-- but pitchers who can miss in excess of a bat per inning don't grow on trees. If it all clicks, Reyes could very well be the next Chris Archer, or maybe healthy Carlos Carrasco. He's a likely closer if he moves to the pen, so he's got multiple paths to big-time fantasy value. It's just not fair how the Cardinals find one of these guys every two or three years.

Major league ETA: 2017

2. Sandy Alcantara, RHP

DOB: 8/7/1995

Height/Weight: 6'4" 170 lbs

Bats/Throws: R/R

Drafted/Acquired: Signed in July 2013 by St. Louis out of the Dominican Republic for $125,000

Previous Ranking(s): N/A

2016 Stats: 3.62 ERA, 4.36 DRA, 32.1 25 H, 14 BB, 24 K in High-A Palm Beach, 4.08 ERA, 2.28 DRA, 90.1 IP, 78 H, 45 BB, 119 K in Low-A Peoria

The Role: OFP 60—No. 3 starter/closer
Likely 50—No. 4 starter/set-up

YEAR	TEAM	LVL	AGE	W	L	SV	G	GS	IP	H	HR	BB/9	K/9	K	GB%	BABIP	WHIP	ERA	FIP	DRA	VORP	WARP	cFIP	MPH
2014	DCA	Rk	18	1	9	0	12	11	56^{2}	56	1	3.0	8.7	55	0%	.329	1.32	3.97	2.96	3.47			91	
2015	CRD	Rk	19	4	4	0	12	12	64^{1}	59	3	2.8	7.1	51	59%	.298	1.23	3.22	3.48	3.68	15.70	1.5	93	
2016	PEO	A	20	5	7	0	17	17	90^{1}	78	4	4.5	11.9	119	46%	.333	1.36	4.08	3.21	2.28	27.40	3.0	88	
2016	PMB	A+	20	0	4	0	6	6	32^{1}	25	0	3.9	9.5	34	52%	.294	1.21	3.62	2.54	4.36	4.00	0.4	94	
2017	*SLN*	*MLB*	*21*	*5*	*7*	*0*	*18*	*18*	*95*	*103*	*13*	*5.3*	*6.5*	*69*	*38%*	*.323*	*1.67*	*5.52*	*5.37*	*6.15*	*-6.2*	*-0.6*	*143*	
2018	*SLN*	*MLB*	*22*	*8*	*11*	*0*	*28*	*28*	*172^{2}*	*157*	*24*	*5.7*	*8.9*	*171*	*38%*	*.312*	*1.55*	*5.21*	*5.41*	*5.80*	*-3.9*	*-0.4*	*136*	

Breakout: 5% Improve: 5% Collapse: 1% Attrition: 4% MLB: 6% *Comparables: Reynaldo Lopez, Daniel Norris, Matt Moore*

The Good: Hey, it's another triple-digit fastball. Alcantara has touched 100 this year, and his heater sits in the high 90s. It's a heavy pitch with good life down in the zone and he can elevate it for Ks as needed. His curve will flash above-average with 11-5 shape. He may still get bigger and stronger in his early 20s. He has the body and delivery to start.

The Bad: Everything else is pretty raw. He commands the fastball better than either secondary, and the fastball command is still a little rough. The curve is well-below-average and a work in progress. It can flatten out as often as it gets swings-and-misses. He has a straight change that he'll show feel and fade with, but he tends to slow everything down to utilize it.

The Irrelevant: Alcantara shares a birthday with both Queen Elizabeth I of England and Corbin Bernsen.

The Risks: Alcantara is really raw, still in A-ball and needs big grade jumps on the secondaries to stick in a rotation. And oh yeah, he's a pitcher (who throws 100).

Major league ETA: Late 2018

Ben Carsley's Fantasy Take: What ... what is it with BP and Corbin Bernsen? Anyway, Alcantara is one of the more exciting fantasy pitching prospects in the mid-minors. The control needs refinement (stop me if you've heard that before), but he's got big-time strikeout potential (stop me if you've heard that before). A future as a fantasy SP3 who detracts from your WHIP but gives you plenty of Ks is very much possible. It's just not fair how the Cardinals find one of these guys ever two or three years.

3. Delvin Perez, SS

DOB: 11/24/1998

Height/Weight: 6'3" 175 lbs

Bats/Throws: R/R

Drafted/Acquired: Drafted 23rd overall in the 2016 MLB Draft, International Baseball Academy (Ceiba, PR); Signed for $2,222,500.

Previous Ranking(s): N/A

2016 Stats: .294/.352/.393, 0 HR, 12 SB in 43 games at complex-level GCL

The Role: OFP 60—First-division shortstop
Likely 50—Average shortstop

YEAR	TEAM	LVL	AGE	PA	R	2B	3B	HR	RBI	BB	K	SB	CS	AVG/OBP/SLG	TAv	VORP	BABIP	BRR	FRAA	WARP
2016	CRD	Rk	17	180	19	8	4	0	19	12	28	12	1	.294/.352/.393	.285	13.0	.353	0.8	SS(40): -3.5 • CF(1): -0.1	1.0
2017	*SLN*	*MLB*	*18*	*250*	*25*	*10*	*1*	*5*	*20*	*11*	*76*	*4*	*1*	*.204/.242/.314*	*.190*	*-6.3*	*.275*	*0.2*	*SS -1 • CF -0*	*-0.7*
2018	*SLN*	*MLB*	*19*	*246*	*23*	*10*	*1*	*6*	*24*	*10*	*77*	*3*	*1*	*.206/.240/.334*	*.205*	*-5.1*	*.275*	*0.3*	*SS 0 • CF 0*	*-0.6*

Breakout: 0% Improve: 0% Collapse: 0% Attrition: 0% MLB: 0% *Comparables: Raul Mondesi, Wilmer Flores*

The Good: Perez is a potential five-tool shortstop. He's a good bet to stick at shortstop and even be above-average there despite his size. The athletic tools are ahead of the offensive ones at present, but he has a chance for average-or-better grades in both hit and power as he matures. Would show plus raw power even at 17.

The Bad: Perez tumbled down draft boards after testing positive for a performance-enhancing drug, but he was a divisive prospect even before that. There were makeup concerns centered on his perceived effort on the field. Weight that info how you like. The ultimate power projection is fuzzy and very much depends on who you talk to about him. Offensive tools may only end up "good for shortstop" rather than "good for baseball players."

The Irrelevant: Ceiba has yet to produce a major league baseball player, but two champion boxers, Carlos Santos and McJoe Arroyo, hail from there.

The Risks: He is a teenaged shortstop with a complex league resume, makeup concerns, and a failed drug test. Even if you only care about the first part—which is a valid stance—he's extremely risky.

Major league ETA: 2020

Ben Carsley's Fantasy Take: Perez is risky, but I think the dynasty community may be a little too down on him after his failed test. At the end of the day, there aren't many first-division shortstop prospects in systems as good at developing prospects as the Cardinals. Bret Sayre had Perez down at 23 in his Top-50 signees ranking, but he'd be about 10 spots higher for me. I'm not entirely sure if that makes him a top-100 prospect yet, but if not it makes him close.

4. Carson Kelly, C

DOB: 7/14/1994

Height/Weight: 6'2" 220 lbs

Bats/Throws: R/R

Drafted/Acquired: Drafted 86th overall in the 2012 MLB draft, Westview High School (Portland, OR); signed for $1,600,000

Previous Ranking(s): N/A

2016 Stats: .154/.214/.231, 0 HR, 0 SB in 10 games at the major league level, .292/.352/.381, 0 HR, 0 SB in 32 games at Triple-A Memphis, .287/.338/.403, 6 HR, 0 SB in 64 games with Double-A Springfield

The Role: OFP 55—Above-average major league catcher
Likely 50—Glove-first everyday backstop you pencil in the eight-hole

YEAR	TEAM	LVL	AGE	PA	R	2B	3B	HR	RBI	BB	K	SB	CS	AVG/OBP/SLG	TAv	VORP	BABIP	BRR	FRAA	WARP
2014	PEO	A	19	415	41	17	4	6	49	37	54	1	0	.248/.326/.366	.264	15.9	.274	-2.2	C(79): -0.7	1.6
2015	PMB	A+	20	419	30	18	1	8	51	22	64	0	0	.219/.263/.332	.223	1.2	.239	-1.0	C(104): 1.3	0.3
2016	SFD	AA	21	236	29	7	0	6	18	14	46	0	1	.287/.338/.403	.283	14.4	.339	-0.9	C(60): 8.7	2.5
2016	MEM	AAA	21	126	14	10	0	0	14	11	17	0	0	.292/.352/.381	.261	5.8	.340	-0.1	C(32): 2.5	0.9
2016	SLN	MLB	21	14	1	1	0	0	1	0	2	0	0	.154/.214/.231	.204	-0.4	.182	-0.2	C(10): -0.0	-0.1
2017	*SLN*	*MLB*	*22*	*250*	*23*	*11*	*1*	*6*	*28*	*15*	*49*	*0*	*0*	*.236/.287/.372*	*.226*	*2.8*	*.270*	*-0.5*	*C 1*	*0.4*
2018	*SLN*	*MLB*	*23*	*294*	*34*	*13*	*1*	*9*	*34*	*18*	*59*	*0*	*0*	*.244/.297/.396*	*.249*	*6.5*	*.278*	*-0.7*	*C 1*	*0.8*

Breakout: 6% Improve: 17% Collapse: 10% Attrition: 21% MLB: 33% *Comparables: Bryan Anderson, J.R. Murphy, Hector Sanchez*

The Good: Before the season kicked off, Kit House wrote this about Kelly in our Texas League preview: "He's either a method actor who started hitting like a catcher to accommodate the change in role, or he's trying to establish his character's defensive motivation before a break-out at the plate in act III." Well, the offensive climax for Kelly arrived in 2016. Okay, he still will never be Buster Posey with the bat, but he started hitting more line drives with his simple, inside-out swing, and the hits followed. Even before he started posting a .700+ OPS, Kelly had a good shot at a major-league role on the strength of his glove. He has an above-average arm and he draws raves for his receiving and the way he handles his pitching staff.

The Bad: This was his first season hitting at this level since short-season ball. The power is well-below-average. He's not going to be an offensive force and fits best at the bottom of the lineup. He runs like a catcher.

The Irrelevant: Kelly didn't spend much time in Memphis, but we do hope he got to visit the Stax Museum and its 17,000 sq. ft. of Soul Music exhibits.

The Risks: Kelly's hit in the upper minors and there's no doubt the glove will play at the highest level. There's always some short-term risk in the bat as new major-league catchers have a lot on their plate. There is some positive risk here too if we are underrating the total defensive profile, which we do at times since catchers are weird, man.

Major league ETA: Debuted in 2016

Ben Carsley's Fantasy Take: It sounds like Kelly's glove will keep him in the lineup, which is good, but the total lack of power and the hit tool that's more "good for a catcher" than "good" really limit his upside. Maybe he's an AVG/R-driven top-20 backstop who's relevant in TDGX-sized 20-team dynasty leagues, but that's his ceiling.

5. Magneuris Sierra, CF

DOB: 04/07/1996

Height/Weight: 5'11" 160 lbs.

Bats/Throws: L/L

Drafted/Acquired: Signed July 2012 by St. Louis out of the Dominican Republic for $105,000

Previous Ranking(s): #3 (Org)

2016 Stats: .307/.335/.395, 3 HR, 31 SB in 122 games at Low-A Peoria

The Role: OFP 60—First-division center fielder carried by his speed and glove.
Likely 45—Platoon or fourth outfielder

YEAR	TEAM	LVL	AGE	PA	R	2B	3B	HR	RBI	BB	K	SB	CS	AVG/OBP/SLG	TAv	VORP	BABIP	BRR	FRAA	WARP
2014	CRD	Rk	18	223	42	12	3	2	30	16	30	13	3	.386/.434/.505	.327	30.6	.444	3.1		3.8
2015	PEO	A	19	190	19	1	3	1	7	7	52	4	5	.191/.219/.247	.177	-11.8	.260	-1.2	CF(50): 4.9	-0.6
2015	JCY	Rk	19	239	38	8	0	3	15	19	42	15	2	.315/.371/.394	.285	15.6	.378	1.0	CF(53): 5.2	2.1
2016	PEO	A	20	562	78	29	4	3	60	22	97	31	17	.307/.335/.395	.284	31.4	.367	1.7	CF(121): 1.7	3.7
2017	*SLN*	*MLB*	*21*	*250*	*27*	*10*	*1*	*5*	*20*	*8*	*64*	*6*	*4*	*.230/.255/.338*	*.202*	*-5.7*	*.289*	*-0.3*	*CF 1*	*-0.5*
2018	*SLN*	*MLB*	*22*	*364*	*37*	*14*	*2*	*7*	*36*	*14*	*92*	*9*	*6*	*.242/.273/.358*	*.226*	*-2.4*	*.303*	*0.2*	*CF 2 • LF 0*	*0.0*

Breakout: 4% Improve: 6% Collapse: 0% Attrition: 4% MLB: 6% *Comparables: Reymond Fuentes, Engel Beltre, Gorkys Hernandez*

The Good: Sierra's second pass at the Midwest League went better than his first, and he flashed premium athletic tools along with an improving performance at the dish. He's a plus-plus runner with a plus arm. That's a pretty good starting point for an above-average everyday center fielder. He's simplified his swing at the plate, and while he can yank one down the line every once in awhile, his swing is geared more for slash and dash. When you run as well as he does though, that's just fine. There's still some physical projection left as well.

The Bad: The gap between the possible and the present is large. As fast as Sierra is, he's still quite raw on the bases and in center. Not a big deal for a 20-year-old in the Midwest League, but we are projecting a lot here even on the defensive side. At the plate, he's never going to offer much in the way of pop, and he still struggles with spin specifically and lefties generally. Again, not unusual at this point on the development curve, but there are a lot of ways this profile can go wrong.

The Irrelevant: If you search for just "Magneuris," every single hit on the first page is for Sierra. I only used Google, so no idea what crazy stuff Bing might spit out.

The Risks: You can just read "The Bad" section again. That should about cover it.

Ben Carsley's Fantasy Take: The thing about speed is that it's good and we need it. Also, as an SEO in my real job, I can tell you that whatever Bing would spit out would just be a slightly less relevant version of what Google told you. Only 14 players had 30 or more steals last season. Only 14 more met or surpassed the 20-steal mark. Ender Inciarte hit .291 with just 16 steals and was a top-50 option. That's not meant to be a direct comparison, but rather to hammer home that speed forgives a lot of sins in fantasy. In this case, it's likely to make Sierra a top-150 prospect despite his flaws and his distance from the majors.

6. Dakota Hudson, RHP

DOB: 9/15/1994

Height/Weight: 6'5" 215 lbs

Bats/Throws: R/R

Drafted/Acquired: Drafted 34th overall in the 2016 MLB draft, Mississippi State (Starkville, MS); Signed for $2,000,000

Previous Ranking(s): N/A

2016 Stats: 0.96 ERA, 4.63 DRA, 9.1 IP, 6 H, 7 BB, 10 K at High-A Palm Beach, 0.00 ERA, 1.35 DRA, 4 IP, 4 H, 0 BB, 9 K at complex-level GCL

The Role: OFP 55—Low No. 3 starter
Likely 50—High-leverage reliever

YEAR	TEAM	LVL	AGE	W	L	SV	G	GS	IP	H	HR	BB/9	K/9	K	GB%	BABIP	WHIP	ERA	FIP	DRA	VORP	WARP	cFIP	MPH
2016	CRD	Rk	21	1	0	0	4	1	4	4	0	0.0	20.2	9	62%	.500	1.00	0.00	-0.44	1.71	1.60	0.2	75	
2016	PMB	A+	21	1	1	3	8	0	9^1	6	0	6.8	9.6	10	91%	.261	1.39	0.96	3.36	4.63	0.50	0.0	104	
2017	*SLN*	*MLB*	*22*	*2*	*0*	*1*	*32*	*0*	34^1	*36*	*5*	*5.3*	*6.5*	*25*	*72%*	*.319*	*1.65*	*5.46*	*5.48*	*6.20*	*-4.1*	*-0.4*	*142*	
2018	*SLN*	*MLB*	*23*	*1*	*0*	*1*	*27*	*0*	32^2	*29*	*4*	*5.3*	*8.3*	*30*	*72%*	*.298*	*1.47*	*4.95*	*5.14*	*5.62*	*-1.6*	*-0.2*	*129*	

Breakout: 0% Improve: 0% Collapse: 0% Attrition: 0% MLB: 0% *Comparables: Michael Lorenzen, Evan Scribner, Zach Stewart*

The Good: Hudson boasted one of the deepest arsenals in the draft class, with four pitches that offer potential big-league utility. The fastball sits in the mid-90s with mild run, and he pairs it with a nasty slider/cutter hybrid in the upper-80s. The latter pitch features nasty tilt and is a swing-and-miss pitch against right-handed hitters. He'll use it equal-opportunity to bore in hard on left-handed hitters as well, giving him a pitch to pair with an average-flashing changeup to manage his splits. He'll toggle a curveball between the upper-70s and low-80s as well, and he's adept at dropping the pitch in for early strikes. The frame is a good'n for any pitcher, but especially the startin' kind.

The Bad: There's some jingle and jangle to his delivery. He doesn't always harness a powerful early build of momentum and channel it efficiently downhill, and his mild crossfire adds some length to an already-longer arm action. He's made strides to streamline his mechanics, but fine command is unlikely to ever be an asset, and the control may never gain startering consistency. The fastball has some mild run to it, but can lack for life and in-zone command, while the curve often sets an early trajectory and fails to bite late.

The Irrelevant: Hudson is to date the only baseball player from Sequatchie County High School to ever get drafted.

The Risks: Well, normally this is where we'd note that he's a pitcher, and one with command and control flags at that. But since he was a collegiate arm with big stuff that the Cardinals snagged towards the top of the draft, we instead have to assume that he'll be successfully matriculating into the St. Louis rotation at some point next season. The fastball and filthy cutter/slider thing could play in potentially devastating fashion out of the bullpen, and given the command and control questions they may ultimately have to.

Major league ETA: 2018 —Wilson Karaman

Ben Carsley's Fantasy Take: I have already written the best thing I've ever written about Dakota Hudson and have nothing else to add about yet another mid-rotation starter who's not terribly close to the majors.

7. Luke Weaver, RHP

DOB: 08/21/1993

Height/Weight: 6'2" 170 lbs.

Bats/Throws: R/R

Drafted/Acquired: Drafted 27th overall in the 2014 MLB Draft, Florida State University (FL); signed for $1.843 million

Previous Ranking(s): #7 (Org)

2016 Stats: 5.70 ERA, 4.22 DRA, 36.1 IP, 46 H, 12 BB, 45 K at the major league level, 0.00 ERA, 4.49 DRA, 6 IP, 2 H, 2 BB, 4 K at Triple-A Memphis, 1.40 ERA, 1.14 DRA, 77 IP, 63 H, 10 BB, 88 K at Double-A Springfield

The Role: OFP 55—No. 3/4 starter
Likely 45—Backend starter

YEAR	TEAM	LVL	AGE	W	L	SV	G	GS	IP	H	HR	BB/9	K/9	K	GB%	BABIP	WHIP	ERA	FIP	DRA	VORP	WARP	cFIP	MPH
2014	CRD	Rk	20	0	0	0	4	4	6	4	0	0.0	13.5	9	0%	.333	0.67	0.00	1.00	2.13			75	
2014	PMB	A+	20	0	1	0	2	2	3^1	11	1	10.8	8.1	3	24%	.625	4.50	21.60	9.09	8.05	-0.90	-0.1	118	
2015	PMB	A+	21	8	5	0	19	19	105^1	98	2	1.6	7.5	88	46%	.303	1.11	1.62	2.28	2.75	27.30	3.0	84	
2016	SFD	AA	22	6	3	0	12	12	77	63	4	1.2	10.3	88	40%	.289	0.95	1.40	2.04	1.14	33.90	3.7	61	
2016	MEM	AAA	22	1	0	0	1	1	6	2	0	3.0	6.0	4	38%	.125	0.67	0.00	3.39	4.49	0.60	0.1	104	
2016	SLN	MLB	22	1	4	0	9	8	36^1	46	7	3.0	11.1	45	37%	.386	1.60	5.70	4.37	4.22	4.60	0.5	99	94.9
2017	*SLN*	*MLB*	*23*	*6*	*7*	*0*	*34*	*16*	*103*	*109*	*14*	*2.9*	*7.7*	*89*	*37%*	*.302*	*1.39*	*4.41*	*4.29*	*4.50*	*7.4*	*0.8*	*100*	
2018	*SLN*	*MLB*	*24*	*8*	*7*	*0*	*53*	*20*	*151*	*130*	*18*	*3.3*	*9.6*	*161*	*37%*	*.306*	*1.23*	*3.96*	*4.04*	*4.35*	*16.7*	*1.7*	*99*	

Breakout: 27% Improve: 53% Collapse: 14% Attrition: 27% MLB: 77% *Comparables: Daniel Norris, Danny Duffy, Mike Minor*

The Good: Weaver is an athletic righty with a fastball he can run up into the mid-90s and an easy plus change with good fade, arm action, and velo separation. He is comfortable throwing the cambio to either side of the plate and to both righties and lefties. His delivery is a little unorthodox, but he repeats it well enough to start.

The Bad: Neither of Weaver's breaking balls is even average, and he threw them very sparingly in the majors, leaving him a bit of a two-pitch pitcher. His fastball command isn't good enough yet to make that approach viable against major-league hitters, especially when he is operating more in the 91-93 range. His changeup is very good, but not so good he can throw it as often as he does and not have occasional long ball issues.

The Irrelevant: As of publication, Weaver has the third best K/9 in Cardinals history (min. 30 IP).

The Risks: Weaver only qualifies for this list by 14 innings. You would have preferred he be better in those major-league games, but he's already there. He is still a pitcher though.

Major league ETA: Debuted in 2016

Ben Carsley's Fantasy Take: I'm acknowledging that the Cardinals generally tend to make the most out of these guys, but there's still not much in Weaver's profile that excites me terribly. He could be useful in spot starts, but he's not someone I'm interested in rostering in 16-team leagues.

8. Harrison Bader, OF

DOB: 6/3/1994

Height/Weight: 6'0" 195 lbs

Bats/Throws: R/R

Drafted/Acquired: Drafted in the third round in the 2015 MLB draft, University of Florida (Gainesville, FL); signed for $400,000.

Previous Ranking(s): N/A

2016 Stats: .231/.298/.354, 3 HR, 2 SB in 29 games at Triple-A Memphis, .283/.351/.497, 16 HR, 11 SB in 82 games as Double-A Springfield.

The Role: OFP 55—Above-average regular in center field
Likely 45—Platoon corner bat

YEAR	TEAM	LVL	AGE	PA	R	2B	3B	HR	RBI	BB	K	SB	CS	AVG/OBP/SLG	TAv	VORP	BABIP	BRR	FRAA	WARP
2015	SCO	A-	21	30	6	2	0	2	4	0	5	2	0	.379/.400/.655	.356	4.0	.409	0.5	LF(4): -0.2 • RF(3): -0.5	0.4
2015	PEO	A	21	228	34	11	2	9	28	15	44	15	6	.301/.364/.505	.310	21.3	.344	3.4	CF(42): 8.1 • LF(7): 3.9	3.7
2016	MEM	AAA	22	161	22	7	1	3	17	11	38	2	3	.231/.298/.354	.249	2.5	.292	-0.1	CF(26): 1.2 • LF(16): 0.5	0.5
2016	SFD	AA	22	356	48	12	4	16	41	25	93	11	10	.283/.351/.497	.312	29.5	.349	0.7	CF(77): -0.5 • RF(4): -0.5	3.0
2017	*SLN*	*MLB*	*23*	*250*	*35*	*10*	*1*	*10*	*30*	*16*	*67*	*5*	*4*	*.246/.306/.433*	*.252*	*6.6*	*.302*	*-0.5*	*CF 3 • LF 1*	*1.1*
2018	*SLN*	*MLB*	*24*	*346*	*43*	*13*	*2*	*13*	*44*	*22*	*94*	*7*	*5*	*.240/.300/.420*	*.261*	*9.3*	*.296*	*-0.1*	*CF 5 • LF 1*	*1.6*

Breakout: 4% Improve: 26% Collapse: 4% Attrition: 22% MLB: 54% *Comparables: Michael Choice, Joe Benson, Brett Jackson*

The Good: Harrison responded extremely well to an aggressive assignment, heading to Double-A in his first full season. His approach at the plate is balanced, as he looks to take pitches and use his hands and bat speed to drive balls to all fields. A plus runner, he glides in the field and can be a plus defender in the corners, or an above-average one in CF. Long-ball power showed up in 2016, and could play to average at peak. Absolutely hammered left-handed pitchers.

The Bad: The rest of his tools require projection to get to average. The profile is more solid than flashy, as he won't often wow you in the field. The power could play down in the big leagues and be more of the extra-base variety rather than over the fence. The relative violence in his swing could limit his ability to make contact on a consistent basis. Even with the breakout season, Bader was only marginally effective against right-handed pitchers, which could limit his utility at the major-league level.

The Irrelevant: There has never been a big leaguer with the first name Harrison. But we could have two debut next year with Bader and Rockies LHP Harrison Musgrave.

The Risks: Limited sample in pro ball, the relative violence in his swing, more polished than flashy profile. The power plays down and is more of a tweener for everyday production.

Major league ETA: 2017 —Steve Givarz

Ben Carsley's Fantasy Take: There's a strong argument to be made that Bader is the fourth-best fantasy prospect in this system, because he's not a glove-first catcher, not a pitcher, and you'll know what he is long before you unravel the mystery that is Sierra. Bader might be a bit overrated in our circle because of his Double-A stats, but he's close enough to the majors with a reasonable enough path to playing time (as a lefty-masher) that he has value in deep leagues. Hope for a top-50 OF and be happy to settle for a really solid fantasy bench bat.

9. Jordan Hicks, RHP

DOB: 9/6/1996

Height/Weight: 6'2" 185 lbs

Bats/Throws: R/R

Drafted/Acquired: Drafted in the third round in the 2015 MLB draft, Cypress Creek (Houston, TX); signed for $600,000

Previous Ranking(s): N/A

2016 Stats: 1.76 ERA, 4.91 DRA, 30.2 IP, 25 H, 16 BB, 22 K at short-season State College, 4.20 ERA, 5.75 DRA, 30 IP, 33 H, 13 BB, 20 K at short-season Johnson City

The Role: OFP 55—Low-end no. 3 starter or late-inning arm
Likely 45—Back-end starter or 7th inning guy

YEAR	TEAM	LVL	AGE	W	L	SV	G	GS	IP	H	HR	BB/9	K/9	K	GB%	BABIP	WHIP	ERA	FIP	DRA	VORP	WARP	cFIP	MPH
2016	JCY	Rk	19	2	1	0	6	6	30	33	1	3.9	6.0	20	57%	.344	1.53	4.20	4.56	5.75	-0.10	0.0	111	
2016	SCO	A-	19	4	1	0	6	6	30^{2}	25	0	4.7	6.5	22	66%	.269	1.34	1.76	3.60	4.91	1.10	0.1	104	
2017	*SLN*	*MLB*	*20*	*2*	*3*	*0*	*8*	*8*	*41*	*50*	*7*	*5.7*	*4.1*	*19*	*39%*	*.322*	*1.85*	*6.47*	*6.46*	*7.26*	*-7.7*	*-0.8*	*168*	
2018	*SLN*	*MLB*	*21*	*4*	*8*	*0*	*18*	*18*	*105*	*115*	*17*	*5.8*	*5.9*	*69*	*39%*	*.316*	*1.74*	*6.22*	*6.50*	*6.98*	*-14.2*	*-1.5*	*163*	

Breakout: 0% Improve: 0% Collapse: 0% Attrition: 0% MLB: 0% *Comparables: Jose Urena, Neil Ramirez, Adrian Houser*

The Good: Hicks signed late in 2015 so had to wait until this year to make his pro debut. He quickly made up for the lost time, however, coming out firing with a mid-90s fastball and a low-80s curveball that could be a bat-misser at the highest level due to it's tight spin. The fastball/breaker combo is potentially plus.

The Bad: He was a 19-year-old, former third-round prep pick in short-season ball. How good do you think the changeup is right now? Exactly. It's a mid-80s pitch that projects as average but it has a long way to go. The command profile is going to need some improving as well, and his ultimate home might be the bullpen.

The Irrelevant: The best player to be selected with the 105th overall pick was Cliff Lee, popped by the Expos in 2000.

The Risks: (siren emoji) SHORT-SEASON PITCHER (siren emoji)

Major league ETA: 2020

Ben Carsley's Fantasy Take: Please check back at this time next year.

10. Jack Flaherty, RHP

DOB: 10/15/1995

Height/Weight: 6'4" 200 lbs

Bats/Throws: R/R

Drafted/Acquired: Drafted 34th overall in the 2014 MLB Draft, Harvard-Westlake School (Los Angeles, CA); signed for $2 million

Previous Ranking(s): #2 (Org)

2016 Stats: 3.56 ERA, 2.72 DRA, 134 IP, 129 H, 45 BB, 126 K in High-A Palm Beach

The Role: OFP 50—Average major-league starter
Likely 45—No. 4/5 starter

YEAR	TEAM	LVL	AGE	W	L	SV	G	GS	IP	H	HR	BB/9	K/9	K	GB%	BABIP	WHIP	ERA	FIP	DRA	VORP	WARP	cFIP	MPH
2014	CRD	Rk	18	1	1	0	8	6	22^{2}	18	1	1.6	11.1	28	0%	.293	0.97	1.59	2.53	1.57			73	
2015	PEO	A	19	9	3	0	18	18	95	92	2	2.9	9.2	97	37%	.330	1.29	2.84	2.83	2.94	24.10	2.6	93	
2016	PMB	A+	20	5	9	0	24	23	134	129	8	3.0	8.5	126	49%	.316	1.30	3.56	3.20	2.72	40.70	4.2	88	
2017	*SLN*	*MLB*	*21*	*6*	*7*	*0*	*21*	*21*	107^{2}	*122*	*17*	*3.9*	*6.2*	*75*	*37%*	*.326*	*1.56*	*5.25*	*5.17*	*5.75*	*-2.2*	*-0.2*	*136*	
2018	*SLN*	*MLB*	*22*	*7*	*10*	*0*	*25*	*25*	148^{1}	*148*	*23*	*4.6*	*8.3*	*137*	*37%*	*.322*	*1.52*	*5.20*	*5.37*	*5.70*	*-2.0*	*-0.2*	*136*	

Breakout: 9% Improve: 11% Collapse: 3% Attrition: 12% MLB: 15% *Comparables: Daniel Corcino, Randall Delgado, German Marquez*

The Good: Flaherty has an advanced arsenal for his age with three average-or-a-tick-above pitches that he can throw for strikes. He has the frame and delivery you look for in a starter.

The Bad: Flaherty should warm up to Luniz's "I've Got Five on it," because that also describes the scouting report here. The sum of the parts can make this kind of profile play up a bit, but there is a fine margin for error, and he may get hit harder against higher level bats.

The Irrelevant: Harvard-Westlake has been quite the professional baseball finishing school in recent years, but their most productive major-league alum so far is Brennan Boesch, who has been worth a mere 1.3 WARP in the bigs.

The Risks: Pitchers without obvious out pitches sometimes find the upper minors trickier than A-ball. Pitchers also get hurt. And he's a pitcher.

Major league ETA: Late 2018

Ben Carsley's Fantasy Take: I look forward to the Cardinal's top-10 list next season, when we'll value Flaherty just as we value Weaver now, albeit for different reasons.

OTHERS OF NOTE:

#11

Junior Fernandez, RHP

Fernandez is yet another Cardinals arm who can touch 100, but he's down here and not above because of his lack of command and consistent off-speed offerings. Fernandez is very athletic, with a simple delivery and quick arm speed to go with his projectable body. While he touches higher, the fastball sits primarily 93-96 but tends to lack life and it can be hittable when in the zone. His changeup is his preferred go-to option and he sells it well with consistent arm speed and plus fading action. His slider is slurvy, but while he doesn't have a lot of feel for the spin right now it could grow into an average pitch because of his youth and athleticism. His command of the arsenal needs to improve, but he has a long road ahead of him and the whole package could be as good as Alcantara's in the end. —Steve Givarz

#12

Edmundo Sosa, SS

If you want another Cardinals Devil Magic candidate, Sosa wouldn't be a bad one. On the surface the profile isn't too exciting, especially after a down year with the bat in A-ball. The tools don't jump out at shortstop, although he's serviceable enough there. There may be some strength and commensurate doubles power to come, and although Sosa profiles best as a good fifth infielder that can play either spot up-the-middle, if he suddenly turns into Aledmys Diaz, don't say we didn't warn you.

The greatest trick the devil ever pulled was changing corner dudes into shortstops

Paul deJong, 3B

Selected in the fourth round of the 2015 draft out of Illinois State University, deJong went from the Redbirds to the Cardinals organization. Playing almost exclusively shortstop in the Arizona Fall League, deJong showcased the ability to fill the position in an emergency role, something which could prove necessary for his overall profile to work at the major-league level. There's some over-the-fence power power here, which he demonstrated by hitting the fifth-most home runs (22) in the Texas League this summer. However, he combines average-at-best bat speed with an unrefined feel for the barrel in what can only project as a below-average hit tool at the moment. Of course, it is the Cardinals. —Matt Pullman

Would you prefer one in left-handed?

Austin Gomber, LHP

Gomber is in the same vein as Weaver and Flaherty, but he's a big southpaw! The fastball sits in the low-90s, and he commands it well enough while pairing it with a potentially above-average change. The breaking ball lags behind. Yes, it might literally be left-handed Luke Weaver, though the stuff is a little bit lighter all told, and he's only conquered Double-A. But you know, the Cardinals do well with this type of...okay, you get it by now.

The Cardinals do really well with this type of profile, you guys

Dylan Carlson, OF

A project, as first-rounders go, Carlson could pay off handsomely in time. The switch-hitting first baseman is transitioning to the outfield, including taking 41 of his 50 games post-signing in center. He has the tools to make the transition stick, and it's likely the Cardinals will give him that opportunity. If he can't handle center, his above-average arm should fit in a corner and the reports on his defense at first were positive, in a worst case scenario. He's more consistent from the left side of the plate, but is aggressive in attacking the ball from both sides. While he is more strength than bat speed at present, there's enough projection in his frame to get both to plus if it all comes together, with plus power/above-average hit a possibility. The likelihood is something less than that, of course, but he's a fun gamble in a system that excels at getting the most out of hitters.

—Craig Goldstein

TOP 10 TALENTS 25 AND UNDER (BORN 4/1/91 OR LATER)

1. Carlos Martinez	6. Michael Wacha
2. Alex Reyes	7. Delvin Perez
3. Stephen Piscotty	8. Carson Kelly
4. Sandy Alcantara	9. Magneuris Sierra
5. Randal Grichuk	10. Dakota Hudson

This list was more fun to write last year. At the time, the Cardinals had six big leaguers in the top seven spaces (Kolten Wong and Trevor Rosenthal accompanied the four holdovers listed above). The group took a collective step back in 2016 though, as Wong and Grichuk spent part of 2016 in Triple-A, while Rosenthal lost his job and Wacha spent September buried in the bullpen. While all six remain a part of St. Louis' core, many have a slightly cloudier future with the team than they did 12 months ago.

That comment doesn't apply to Martinez, who spent 2016 solidifying his transformation from backend reliever to staff ace. The right-hander can miss bats with all four of his offerings, and his deep arsenal allows him to dominate when he has his best stuff (he allowed one run or fewer in 13 of 31 starts) and survive when he does not (he only conceded more than four runs twice). Martinez will be 25 for all but a fortnight of the 2017 season and he's poised to emerge as one of the best pitchers in the National League. Phrased differently, if Reyes can match Martinez's production, the Cardinals and their fans should be thrilled.

Piscotty was the rare bird who escaped Stanford with his bat intact. The program has notoriously wrecked many a promising hitter's swing, but the erstwhile and current Cardinal has been one of the most solid hitters in the league since debuting in July of 2015: in 905 career plate appearances, Piscotty is batting .282/.348/.467. That doesn't make him a star, but with good defense in right, he's the latest first-division regular in an organization that produces them by the bushel.

Few men embody contemporary baseball quite like Grichuk, a player whose high strikeout, low walk, and plus power skill set has found a comfortable home in the 21st century. In an unconventional experiment, Grichuk tried to have his cake and eat it too last season, as he actively attempted to reduce his strikeouts and take more walks (h/t Corinne Landrey). Technically he succeeded, but the small improvements in his walk and strikeout rates came packaged with a massive drop in power. Following a brief demotion to Memphis, Grichuk recommenced playing caveman baseball, to more success:

Grichuk before demotion: .206/.279/.392, 8 homers, 54 SO, 18 BB in 225 PA

Grichuk after demotion: .269/.300/.554, 17 homers, 87 SO, 10 BB in 253 PA

Even with all the strikeouts, that second line was good enough to keep him in the lineup down the stretch. This year, he'll have to sustain that production over a full season, and there will be more pressure than ever on his bat. After signing Dexter Fowler, St. Louis no longer needs to shoehorn Grichuk into center field; Grichuk will in turn slide to left, where the organization will have less patience if he falls into a prolonged slump. He'll probably hold the job, at least for this season, but there's an upper bound to how often you can strike out while remaining an offensive threat and Grichuk will always flirt with the threshold.

It's not clear that Wacha belongs on this list right now. A poor finish to the 2015 season, marred by uncharacteristically poor command and control, seeped into 2016. His velocity dropped a tick from the previous season, he posted the highest ERA and walk rate of his career, and perhaps of most concern, he missed time with shoulder inflammation. That's the bad news. The good news is that his stuff remains intact and that neither his DRA nor his FIP strayed far from his career norms. More than a year ago, Jeff Sullivan noticed that Wacha's release point was unusually high at the tail end of 2015, and the right-hander had an even more pronounced case of spinal tilt last season. Whether that's intentional, an unconscious response to a barking shoulder, or entirely unrelated to his command problems, we can't know for sure. Regardless, Wacha is an enigma. We can't rule out a return to the bullpen for him in 2017, nor dismiss the possibility that he recaptures his all-star form from 2015. He's a splash of volatility on a team that's pretty projectable elsewhere.

The Cardinals have a few other young contributors who bear a quick mention here. Matthew Bowman will still be 25 on opening day, and while he's a Role 40 player, he was a nice find in last year's Rule 5 Draft. Sam Tuivailala throws hard, and if he learns to throw strikes, he could log meaningful innings in relief. Mike Mayers had a debut to forget, but he touches the mid-90s out of the rotation, and could step into a swing role this season.

The lesson here is that, like always, the Cardinals are loaded with young talent. Declining numbers from Wong, Rosenthal, and Wacha shouldn't detract from the potential aces sitting at the top of the rotation, or that Piscotty probably has an all-star appearance or two ahead of him. Turns out, St. Louis is still pretty good at this.

—Brendan Gawlowski

TAMPA BAY RAYS

The State of the System: *A strong one-two punch at the top, an interesting mix of upside and major-league-ready behind it, but in total a solid, rather than spectacular system.*

THE TOP TEN

1. SS Willy Adames	6. RHP Jacob Faria
2. RHP Brent Honeywell	7. RHP Chih-Wei Hu
3. RHP Jose De Leon	8. RHP Austin Franklin
4. 3B Joshua Lowe	9. SS Daniel Robertson
5. 1B/OF Jake Bauers	10. 1B Casey Gillaspie

The Big Question: What went wrong in the 2011 draft?

It's 2011 (as you may have gathered).

The Rays are in the middle of a contention cycle that will see them make the playoffs four out of six years, never winning fewer than 84 games over that period. They've built an inexpensive, mostly homegrown core of young players. They are a small market success story. Books will be written about this run.

A good chunk of that homegrown core was built out of high-first-round picks, when the team wasn't so good and wasn't even called the Rays. The Rays haven't had so many of those lately and that last one was Tim Beckham, who's still a ways off from the majors. Oh, and they had a pre-draft deal with Buster Posey that year. That's already looking bad. Last year they had three first-round picks that they spent on two prep outfielders and a prep catcher. There's time to develop those players, but that young core is getting expensive, and that is going to be a problem sooner than the developmental horizon for a high school catcher.

As luck would have it though, the Rays have figured out how to game the Elias rankings and loaded up on compensation picks. Ten picks in the first 60. This is ludicrous. Or maybe it's the new *Moneyball* …

Five years on is a good time to look back at a draft class. Of those ten, none appear on this year's top ten list. Three have made the majors, but only one looks like he will have a meaningful impact on the 2017 Rays team and beyond. The system is starting to come out of a relatively fallow period, but the lifeline of the major-league Rays, young, cost-controlled major league starters hasn't been there in recent years, and it's shown.

To recap:

1.24: Taylor Guerrieri: A Top 10— and Top 101—prospect as recently as last year, Guerrieri dropped to the Rays in part due to makeup concerns. It was the normal prospect pitfalls that felled him though, a Tommy John surgery and declining stuff. He does make the others of note.

1.31: Mikie Mahtook: An advanced college bat that spent parts of four season in the upper minors before making his debut with the Rays as a 25-year-old. Despite a fast start in 2015, he's been a replacement-level outfielder on balance. The jury is still out, but it's 10-2 in favor of an extra bench outfielder and the holdouts are waffling. He got part-time at-bats with the Tigers in April.

1.32: Jake Hager: A prep shortstop that never really hit and eventually moved off shortstop after an ankle injury cost him a full season.

1s.38: Brandon Martin: Another prep shortstop, never got out of A-ball.

1s.41: Tyler Goeddel: A prep third baseman that moved to the outfield and then got plucked in the Rule 5 by the Phillies after his first season in Double A. It didn't go very well.

1s.42: Jeff Ames: JuCo righty. The Rays had a reputation for taking things very slowly with their arms, and Ames is no exception. Eventually got moved to the pen in 2015 where he hasn't thrown enough strikes. Fun fact: I saw Jeff Ames outduel Luis Mateo in the NYPL playoffs in 2012. I thought he was clearly the better pitching prospect. Turns out I was right, and also turns out that it doesn't matter.

Farm System Ranking

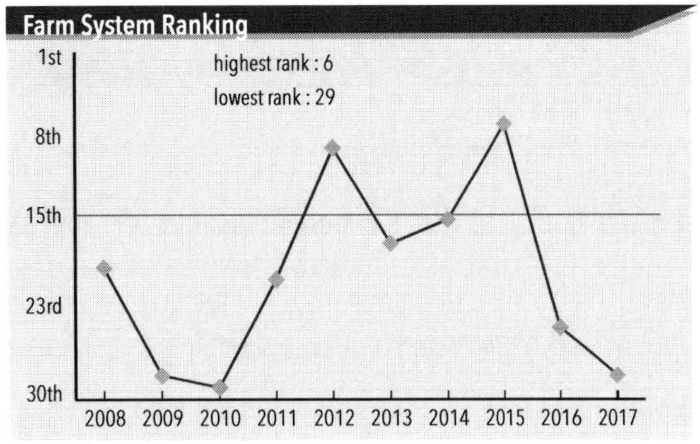

Personnel

President of Baseball Operations:
Matt Silverman

Senior Vice President:
Chaim Bloom

SVP, General Manager:
Erik Neander

Manager:
Kevin Cash

BP Alumni:
Bradley Ankrom
Chaim Bloom
James Click
Jason Cole
Shawn Hoffman
Tim Steggall

1s.52: Blake Snell: Prep lefty. Was the number one prospect in the system last year. Looks like a mid-rotation arm with the potential for more. Ding ding ding.
1s.56: Kes Carter: College outfielder, released after the 2015 season after posting a .590 OPS in Double A as a 25-year-old. Spent 2016 playing Indy ball in Fargo, which seems apropos because he sounds like he should be a bit player on the FX series.
1s.59: Grayson Garvin: College lefty, never really been healthy.
1s.60: James Harris: Prep outfielder, never hit, was released and glommed on with the Athletics. Finally hit a little ... in the Cal League.

This was also the last year of suggested slotting, where the only punishment for spending over slot was a frosty phone call from the Commissioner's Office. The Rays only went over a million dollars for three of these ten picks. Guerrieri was the highest at $1,600,000. They spent a little under nine million for the lot of them. Even at the time, it was widely considered to be an overly conservative approach given their bounty of picks. The Rays could have easily spent twice that with little impact on their bottom line. I imagine they consider Blake Snell well worth the nine million dollar outlay by himself. And they'd be right.

But they have to do better than that.

1. Willy Adames, SS

DOB: 09/02/1995

Height/Weight: 6'1" 180 lbs

Bats/Throws: R/R

Drafted/Acquired: Signed July 2012 out of Dominican Republic for $420,000; traded from Detroit to Tampa Bay in David Price deal

Previous Ranking(s): #30 (Midseason Top 50), #54 (Top 101), #2 (Org) 2016

2016 Stats: .274/.372/.430, 11 HR, 13 SB in 132 games at double-A Montgomery

The Role: OFP 60—Above-average shortstop
Likely 55—A low-res Ben Zobrist facsimile

YEAR	TEAM	LVL	AGE	PA	R	2B	3B	HR	RBI	BB	K	SB	CS	AVG/OBP/SLG	TAv	VORP	BABIP	BRR	FRAA	WARP
2014	WMI	A	18	400	40	14	12	6	50	39	96	3	6	.269/.346/.428	.307	37.4	.353	0.7	SS(97): -0.7	3.8
2014	BGR	A	18	114	15	5	2	2	11	15	30	3	0	.278/.377/.433	.292	10.4	.379	2.1	SS(25): -3.0	0.8
2015	PCH	A+	19	456	51	24	6	4	46	54	123	10	1	.258/.342/.379	.275	23.1	.356	-0.6	SS(97): 4.7	3.0
2016	MNT	AA	20	568	89	31	6	11	57	74	121	13	6	.274/.372/.430	.303	47.0	.342	2.4	SS(112): 2.0	5.3
2017	*TBA*	*MLB*	*21*	*250*	*25*	*10*	*2*	*6*	*27*	*26*	*77*	*2*	*1*	*.225/.307/.371*	*.243*	*6.7*	*.312*	*0.0*	*SS 1*	*0.8*
2018	*TBA*	*MLB*	*22*	*459*	*55*	*20*	*4*	*12*	*51*	*49*	*134*	*4*	*2*	*.237/.322/.395*	*.256*	*14.1*	*.320*	*0.0*	*SS 1*	*1.7*

Breakout: 6% Improve: 14% Collapse: 3% Attrition: 11% MLB: 30% *Comparables: Addison Russell, Corey Seager, Trevor Story*

The Good: They say that art imitates life, but the Willy Adames trade was more an example of the converse being true. It is possible that in this case the Rays knew something more than the rest of us, since Adames' stock has only gone up since the deal that brought him to national attention. 2016 was a breakout of sorts, as Adames started to show more game power to pair with an improving approach and solid hit tool. You can see him as a 15-home-run bat now, and that's still nothing to sneeze at if Adames can stick at shortstop, and that's looking like a real possibility now. It may end up a fringy glove at the 6, as he won't wow you with the spectacular or flash premium athletic tools—although the arm is plus—but he may be able to hack it there.

The Bad: It's also possible Adames has to move to second or third, That would be bad. It's not the death knell, but there isn't a standout tool on the offensive side that would make the bat more than "fine" further down the defensive spectrum. I'm less comfortable with throwing a 45 on the game power than others, although it is in there.

The Irrelevant: Once Adames makes the majors, he will be the sixth major leaguer to have been involved in a David Price trade, well unless Jairo Labourt gets there first.

The Risks: Adames added power as a 21-year-old in Double A and otherwise conquered the level as well. There's still a bit of a wrap in his swing and some commensurate swing and miss that might get exploited by better arms. Still, there's enough loud contact in the profile and enough facility on the left side of the infield to be more confident there is a major league regular here now.

Major league ETA: It's the Rays, so post-Super 2, 2018

Ben Carsley's Fantasy Take: Adames is clearly trending in the right direction when it comes to fantasy. He's getting better at the plate as he gets closer to the Majors, and we know that he'll play somewhere in the infield. Still, Adames isn't an elite dynasty prospect, and he's not particularly close. If he maxes out based on the attributes we read above, he's what, 2016 Alemdys Diaz (.300, 17 homers)? That's a very useful fantasy asset to be sure, but when your ceiling is as a low-end SS or a mid-tier MI, there's only so high you can rank, even when you're knocking on the majors' doorstep.

2. Brent Honeywell, RHP

DOB: 03/31/1995

Height/Weight: 6'2" 180 lbs

Bats/Throws: R/R

Drafted/Acquired: Drafted 72nd overall in the 2014 MLB Draft, Walters State Community College (TN); signed for $797,500

Previous Ranking(s): #52 (Top 101), #3 (Org) 2016

2016 Stats: 2.28 ERA, 3.12 DRA, 59.1 IP, 51 H, 14 BB, 53 K at double-A Montgomery, 2.41 ERA, 1.25 DRA, 56 IP, 43 H, 11 BB, 64 K at high-A Charlotte.

The Role: OFP 60—No. 3 starter, possibly more if the premium velocity holds
Likely 55—No. 4 starter

YEAR	TEAM	LVL	AGE	W	L	SV	G	GS	IP	H	HR	BB/9	K/9	K	GB%	BABIP	WHIP	ERA	FIP	DRA	VORP	WARP	cFIP	MPH
2014	PRI	Rk	19	2	1	0	9	8	33^{2}	19	1	1.6	10.7	40	0%	.225	0.74	1.07	2.20	1.92			72	
2015	BGR	A	20	4	4	0	12	12	65	53	3	1.7	10.5	76	39%	.299	1.00	2.91	2.40	1.52	26.80	2.8	75	
2015	PCH	A+	20	5	2	0	12	12	65^{1}	57	2	2.1	7.3	53	49%	.291	1.10	3.44	2.72	2.87	16.00	1.7	87	
2016	PCH	A+	21	4	1	0	10	10	56	43	5	1.8	10.3	64	33%	.279	0.96	2.41	2.77	1.30	26.00	2.7	75	
2016	MNT	AA	21	3	2	0	10	10	59^{1}	51	4	2.1	8.0	53	29%	.287	1.10	2.28	3.17	2.32	18.30	2.0	86	
2017	*TBA*	*MLB*	*22*	*5*	*6*	*0*	*18*	*18*	*92*	*96*	*14*	*3.3*	*7.6*	*77*	*30%*	*.297*	*1.41*	*4.63*	*4.67*	*5.15*	*3.3*	*0.3*	*122*	
2018	*TBA*	*MLB*	*23*	*9*	*10*	*0*	*30*	*30*	*185*	*163*	*27*	*4.6*	*10.3*	*211*	*30%*	*.290*	*1.39*	*4.23*	*4.41*	*4.71*	*13.2*	*1.4*	*110*	

Breakout: 14% Improve: 29% Collapse: 2% Attrition: 18% MLB: 36% *Comparables: Trevor May, Rafael Montero, Reynaldo Lopez*

The Good: His screwball tends to get top billing, but his most valuable asset might be his confidence on (and off) the mound. Honeywell isn't afraid of anyone, and he has the arsenal to back it up. His fastball touched the upper-90s in the AFL and his ever-famous screwball gives him a plus secondary offering that plays well off that heat. If he keeps that velocity in 2017 our OFP below may end up light. The screwball is a bat-misser with hard fade and tumble. He'll mix in a change and a curve both of which could get to average with added consistency. Honeywell loves to work the bottom of the zone, but knows he can elevate with his harder stuff when he needs a whiff.

The Bad: Honeywell's fastball command could be refined, and while he's athletic and repeats his delivery well, there is a bit of a head whack that can cause some in-zone looseness. It's nothing that can't be addressed. His curve is relatively new, so there's some potential additional growth, but as it stands now it's more of a change-of-pace strike-stealer than it is a swing-and-miss offering.

The Irrelevant: You know by now that he is the nephew of Iron Mike Marshall.

The Risks: The screwball is more than just a novelty, with legitimate movement but if it's something hitters learn to track better—or if he just doesn't have it one day—his other secondaries won't necessarily carry him. If he can't refine the command on his fastball, the velocity is going to need to remain elite, because major-league hitters can punish mid-90s fastballs when they aren't placed well. Also, he's a pitcher.

Major league ETA: Early 2018 —Craig Goldstein

Ben Carsley's Fantasy Take: Congrats to those of you who listened to Craig Goldstein and hopped on the Honeywell bandwagon a few seasons ago. He's not an elite fantasy prospect because he doesn't figure to miss bats like a true fantasy ace would, but Honeywell certainly looks the part of a reasonable SP4/5 who already has a track record of success in Double A. Once Honeywell is established in the majors, expect him to flirt with a mid-3.00s ERA and 180-plus strikeouts with a non-elite but tolerable WHIP. He's firmly entrenched as a top-50 dynasty prospect, albeit probably closer to 50 than 20.

3. Jose De Leon, RHP

DOB: 08/07/1992

Height/Weight: 6'2" 185 lbs.

Bats/Throws: R/R

Drafted/Acquired: Drafted in the 24th round by Los Angeles in the 2013 MLB Draft, Southern University; signed for $35,000; acquired from the Dodgers for Logan Forsythe

Previous Ranking(s): #3 (Org.)

2016 Stats: 6.35 ERA, 5.25 DRA, 17 IP, 19 H, 7 BB, 15 K, in 4 games at major league level, 2.61 ERA, 1.36 DRA, 86.1 IP, 61 H, 20 BB, 111 K in 16 games at triple-A Oklahoma City

The Role: OFP 55—Mid-rotation starter who misses a bunch of bats
Likely 50—Homer-prone no. 4 starter

YEAR	TEAM	LVL	AGE	W	L	SV	G	GS	IP	H	HR	BB/9	K/9	K	GB%	BABIP	WHIP	ERA	FIP	DRA	VORP	WARP	cFIP	MPH
2014	OGD	Rk	21	5	0	0	10	8	54^1	44	2	3.1	12.8	77	0%	.333	1.16	2.65	2.95	0.92			64	
2014	GRL	A	21	2	0	0	4	4	22^2	14	1	0.8	16.7	42	31%	.317	0.71	1.19	0.62	0.51	12.40	1.3	48	
2015	RCU	A+	22	4	1	0	7	7	37^2	26	1	1.9	13.9	58	45%	.325	0.90	1.67	2.00	0.76	18.10	2.0	56	
2015	TUL	AA	22	2	6	0	16	16	76^2	61	11	3.4	12.3	105	36%	.294	1.17	3.64	3.64	1.40	31.40	3.4	67	
2016	OKL	AAA	23	7	1	0	16	16	86^1	61	9	2.1	11.6	111	36%	.259	0.94	2.61	3.23	1.36	38.20	3.9	63	
2016	LAN	MLB	23	2	0	0	4	4	17	19	5	3.7	7.9	15	46%	.280	1.53	6.35	7.01	5.25	0.20	0.0	111	94.5
2017	*TBA*	*MLB*	*24*	*2*	*1*	*0*	*13*	*3*	*25*	*22*	*3*	*3.5*	*9.6*	*27*	*35%*	*.292*	*1.24*	*3.49*	*3.87*	*4.05*	*3.2*	*0.3*	*89*	
2018	*TBA*	*MLB*	*25*	*7*	*5*	*1*	*68*	*14*	*138^1*	*97*	*13*	*4.6*	*12.5*	*191*	*35%*	*.281*	*1.21*	*3.02*	*3.26*	*3.59*	*23.3*	*2.4*	*73*	

Breakout: 25% Improve: 47% Collapse: 15% Attrition: 21% MLB: 74% *Comparables: Scott Elbert, Eric Surkamp, Tyler Thornburg*

The Good: Armed with an above-average fastball, plus change, and adequate slider, De Leon's top virtue is his ability to pound the zone with any offering. His fastball rests in the 90-93 band with occasional tail. He can run it up as 96, though that's rare. Hitters tend to react late to it, though there's not a ton of deception in the delivery, his mechanics are free and easy which might fool them. The cambio is the best offering in his arsenal, featuring plenty of depth and tumble.

The Bad: The fastball tends to lose its wiggle at higher velocities, so when he reaches back for a little extra, it tends to be too true. He likes to pitch up in the zone with the fastball and while this nets him swings and misses, it makes him homer prone as well. De Leon's slider plays more fringy than average, due to its inconsistency, and if he's not missing bats with it, hitters can sit on the change. His propensity to be around the zone without premium stuff contributes to his struggles with the longball as well. He'll show a curveball in the mid-70s here and there, but it's more of an option for sequencing than an integral part of his arsenal.

The Irrelevant: When he was in Little League he had the nickname "Nomar" after Garciaparra. We can thank Vin Scully for that one.

The Risks: De Leon had a relatively extended major-league trial for a prospect, so there are few timeline issues. The risks are whether MLB hitters will pick up on his fastball better than minor leaguers did, and if he's one of those guys who might be around the zone a little too much. The MiLB numbers are daunting, but the stuff belies more of a mid-rotation profile. He is, though, a pitcher.

Major league ETA: Debuted in 2016 —Craig Goldstein

Ben Carsley's Fantasy Take: You know what? I like De Leon. Sure, he might just be a mid-rotation starter, but I think he'll be a damn good one, and I think his floor is just fine, too. At the end of the day you need pitchers in fantasy (unfortunately), and while De Leon's ceiling won't leave you with vertigo, his floor will make you feel cozy and safe. It's ok to like him. He won't hurt you. (He's a pitcher, so ...)

Major League ETA: 2017

4. Joshua Lowe, 3B

DOB: 02/02/1998

Height/Weight: 6'4" 190 lbs

Bats/Throws: L/R

Drafted/Acquired: Drafted 13th overall in 2016 MLB Draft, Pope HS (Marietta, GA); signed for $2,597,500

Previous Ranking(s): N/A

2016 Stats: .237/.360/.400, 3 HR, 1 SB in 26 games at rookie ball in Princeton, .258/.386/.409, 2 HR, 1 SB in 28 games at rookie ball in the GCL.

The Role: OFP 60—Above-average major league third baseman
Likely 50—Boom or bust corner bat, with enough boom to make it play

YEAR	TEAM	LVL	AGE	PA	R	2B	3B	HR	RBI	BB	K	SB	CS	AVG/OBP/SLG	TAv	VORP	BABIP	BRR	FRAA	WARP
2016	RAY	Rk	18	114	14	6	1	2	15	20	27	1	1	.258/.386/.409	.309	10.5	.338	0.9	3B(22): 0.9	1.1
2016	PRI	Rk	18	100	11	0	2	3	11	17	32	1	1	.238/.360/.400	.284	6.2	.333	0.4	3B(23): -3.2	0.3
2017	*TBA*	*MLB*	*19*	*250*	*21*	*7*	*1*	*6*	*24*	*22*	*93*	*0*	*0*	*.177/.253/.291*	*.196*	*-8.9*	*.267*	*-0.4*	*3B -2*	*-1.2*
2018	*TBA*	*MLB*	*20*	*334*	*36*	*10*	*1*	*9*	*33*	*32*	*118*	*0*	*0*	*.194/.273/.325*	*.216*	*-7.9*	*.281*	*-0.6*	*3B -3*	*-1.2*

Breakout: 0% Improve: 7% Collapse: 3% Attrition: 8% MLB: 15% *Comparables: Nomar Mazara, Domingo Santana, Raul Mondesi*

The Good: Lowe is a tall drink of water with a projectable frame. He already has an aesthetically pleasing lefty power stroke with high-end bat speed, and more game power should come as he fills out. It makes *the sound* in batting practice even at present and Lowe had as much raw pop as any player in his draft class. He's relatively new to third base but he has the tools for the hot corner as he is a good athlete with a plus arm.

The Bad: The bat speed is impressive, but there is still length-and-strength to tap into his power at present and that will lead to swing-and-miss. He's relatively new to third base, and it shows. Depending on how the skills and body develop he may have to move back to the outfield, and that would end with him in right field. You know what that means by now.

The Irrelevant: His brother Nathaniel was also drafted by the Rays in June, although he had to wait until the 13th round to hear his name called.

The Risks: Blaise Pascal once opined: "Il n'est pas certain que tout soit incertain" or "It is not certain that everything is uncertain. Pascal never had to write about 18-year-old prep bats with big raw and questionable hit tools though.

Major league ETA: 2021

Ben Carsley's Fantasy Take: Lowe was one of the 20-or-so best fantasy prospects from the 2016 draft, but he's got a long way to go. It's great to hear the praise for his bat and to learn there could be some more pop coming down the line, but Lowe's not a lock to stay at third and has a long lead time. Third base is a really shallow position for dynasty league prospects, but I think Lowe would still find himself outside the top-10 there. The hope is he develops into something like 2016 Jake Lamb (.249, 29 homers, 91 RBI) with a slightly better average, but there are lots of less favorable outcomes still on the table, too.

5. Jake Bauers, 1B/OF

DOB: 10/21/1995

Height/Weight: 6'1" 195 lbs

Bats/Throws: L/L

Drafted/Acquired: Drafted in the seventh round (208th overall) by San Diego, Marina HS (Huntington Beach, CA); signed for $240,000; acquired by Tampa Bay in deal for Wil Myers.

Previous Ranking(s): N/A

2016 Stats: .274/.370/.420, 14 HR, 10 SB at double-A Montgomery

The Role: OFP 55— Solid-average major league first baseman
Likely 45— Platoon three corners bat

YEAR	TEAM	LVL	AGE	PA	R	2B	3B	HR	RBI	BB	K	SB	CS	AVG/OBP/SLG	TAv	VORP	BABIP	BRR	FRAA	WARP
2014	FTW	A	18	467	59	18	3	8	64	51	80	5	6	.296/.376/.414	.284	17.4	.347	0.9	1B(103): 8.6	2.7
2015	PCH	A+	19	249	33	14	2	6	38	29	33	2	3	.267/.357/.433	.298	13.1	.291	1.2	1B(52): -4.9	0.9
2015	MNT	AA	19	285	36	18	0	5	36	21	41	6	3	.276/.329/.405	.267	7.0	.307	2.3	1B(61): -1.8	0.6
2016	MNT	AA	20	581	79	28	1	14	78	73	89	10	6	.274/.370/.420	.301	33.6	.305	2.1	RF(62): 5.7, 1B(57): 0.1	4.1
2017	*TBA*	*MLB*	*21*	*250*	*27*	*11*	*0*	*7*	*29*	*23*	*56*	*2*	*1*	*.240/.314/.390*	*.249*	*2.5*	*.284*	*-0.5*	*RF 3, 1B -0*	*0.5*
2018	*TBA*	*MLB*	*22*	*406*	*51*	*18*	*1*	*13*	*49*	*40*	*89*	*3*	*2*	*.250/.327/.416*	*.263*	*6.9*	*.293*	*-0.7*	*RF 4, 1B 0*	*1.2*

Breakout: 3% Improve: 18% Collapse: 0% Attrition: 8% MLB: 23% *Comparables: Wil Myers, Nomar Mazara, Joc Pederson*

The Good: Bauers can hit. He'll need to (more on that in a minute), but the lefty has the ability to spray line drives to all fields with over-the-fence power to the pull side. He has an advanced approach and enough present-day power to keep pitchers from challenging him too recklessly. He's still only 20 and could add more strength to the natural loft in his swing and end up with average pop. Even if that doesn't come, he profiles as an above-average hitter who gets on base.

The Bad: Even with all that, if he doesn't hit 15-20 home runs, it's a tough profile at first base or corner outfield (and he played mostly first base down the stretch). He's below-average on the grass. He's a good glove at first base, but the problem with being a good glove at first base is it means you're a first baseman. He's a below-average runner, as you might have gathered. The track record for 6', 180-pound first baseman is not particularly long recently, and there is a reason for that.

The Irrelevant: It's getting late, so will you accept a hackneyed 24 reference?

The Risks: The 20-year-old Bauers had a nice season in Double A, giving back little of his production from 2015. That's an important test to pass, and you can be reasonably confident there is a major-league-quality bat in there. Whether that major-league-quality bat is a first-base-quality bat is still an unknown.

Major league ETA: 2018

Ben Carsley's Fantasy Take: Look, we've been over this when we discussed Dom Smith and Trey Mancini, but I'll mention it again; first base isn't as deep a fantasy position as it used to be. Brandon Belt hit .275 with 17 homers and was the 21st-best first baseman, per ESPN's Player Rater. C.J. Cron (him again?) hit .278 with 16 homers in less playing time and finished at 26th. Go a little further down the ladder and Travis Shaw ranked at 31 by hitting .242 with 16 homers. It's just not that tough to be relevant in a 16-teamer anymore, and I think Bauers can firmly enter that Cron-to-Shaw range. Is that exciting? God no. Is Bauers a top-100 dynasty prospect? No. But top-200? Probably, nestled in alongside Smith, Sam Travis and other light-power, decent-bat first basemen.

6. Jacob Faria, RHP

DOB: 07/30/1993

Height/Weight: 6'4" 200 lbs.

Bats/Throws: R/R

Drafted/Acquired: Drafted in the 10th round of the 2011 MLB Draft, Gahr HS (Cerritos, CA); signed for $150,000

Previous Ranking(s): #10 (Org) 2016

2016 Stats: 3.72 ERA, 4.93 DRA, 67.2 IP, 46 H, 32 BB, 64 K at triple-A Durham, 4.21 ERA, 2.17 DRA, 83.1 IP, 64 H, 34 BB, 93 K at double-A Montgomery

The Role: OFP 55— A-little-bit-above-league-average-innings-muncher (it doesn't make a good acronym, sorry)
Likely 45— Run-of-the-mill backend starter

YEAR	TEAM	LVL	AGE	W	L	SV	G	GS	IP	H	HR	BB/9	K/9	K	GB%	BABIP	WHIP	ERA	FIP	DRA	VORP	WARP	cFIP	MPH
2014	BGR	A	20	7	9	0	23	23	119^{2}	113	9	2.4	8.0	107	44%	.300	1.21	3.46	3.55	3.57	25.00	2.6	97	
2015	PCH	A+	21	10	1	0	12	10	74^{1}	51	1	2.7	7.6	63	40%	.253	0.98	1.33	2.53	3.27	14.40	1.6	92	
2015	MNT	AA	21	7	3	0	13	13	75^{1}	52	5	3.6	11.5	96	33%	.278	1.09	2.51	2.85	1.79	27.60	3.0	72	
2016	MNT	AA	22	1	6	0	14	14	83^{1}	64	5	3.9	10.0	93	42%	.282	1.20	4.21	3.20	2.79	21.30	2.3	87	
2016	DUR	AAA	22	4	4	0	13	13	67^{2}	46	7	4.3	8.5	64	40%	.227	1.15	3.72	4.08	4.75	4.50	0.5	103	
2017	*TBA*	*MLB*	*23*	*4*	*4*	*0*	*38*	*8*	*71*	*66*	*9*	*4.2*	*8.1*	*64*	*34%*	*.284*	*1.37*	*4.47*	*4.53*	*4.89*	*2.1*	*0.2*	*100*	
2018	*TBA*	*MLB*	*24*	*6*	*5*	*0*	*64*	*12*	124^{2}	*99*	*15*	*6.1*	*11.3*	*156*	*34%*	*.286*	*1.48*	*4.29*	*4.45*	*4.80*	*5.9*	*0.6*	*109*	

Breakout: 11% Improve: 21% Collapse: 21% Attrition: 32% MLB: 51% *Comparables: Jake Odorizzi, Robert Stephenson, Neil Ramirez*

The Good: Faria has a pair of potential above-average major-league offerings in his fastball and change. He can get the fastball up around 95, although it sits more in the low-90s. When he can get it down in the zone it will show plane and arm-side run from his high-three-quarters slot. The change shows late sink as well and the arm speed provides deception. Faria has a square, athletic build that is made to log innings.

The Bad: The curveball flashes average when he gets on top of it and gets 12-6 break down out of the zone. Too often it is spiked or just sort of floats in dick-high. Faria is very upright throughout his delivery and that can negatively affect his command and specifically his ability to get the fastball down in the zone. I don't know if either secondary will be a true put-away pitch in the majors, and there isn't any one thing that jumps out at you as a carrying tool, though the sum total of the parts works out pretty well.

The Irrelevant: Faria has his Christmas shopping already well underway.

The Risks: Faria is pretty polished, already spent time in Triple A, and has enough fastball and enough feel for the two secondaries to be major-league ready in short order. He is, though, still a pitcher.

Major league ETA: Post-Super-2, 2017

Ben Carsley's Fantasy Take: There are so, so, so, so many Jacob Farias. Granted this one is poised to pitch in a good park, but if you really want someone with this profile go pick up like, I don't know, Mike Leake or something.

7. Chih-Wei Hu, RHP

DOB: 11/04/1993

Height/Weight: 6'1" 230 lbs

Bats/Throws: R/R

Drafted/Acquired: Signed by Minnesota in August 2012 out of Taiwan for $220,000; acquired by Tampa Bay in deal for Kevin Jepsen.

Previous Ranking(s): N/A

2016 Stats: 2.59 ERA, 3.63 DRA, 142.2 IP, 128 H, 36 BB, 107 K for double-A Montgomery.

The Role: OFP 55— Command-and-control no. 4 starter or quirky setup arm
Likely 45— A little-bit-too-hittable no. 5 starter

YEAR	TEAM	LVL	AGE	W	L	SV	G	GS	IP	H	HR	BB/9	K/9	K	GB%	BABIP	WHIP	ERA	FIP	DRA	VORP	WARP	cFIP	MPH
2014	ELZ	Rk	20	1	0	0	3	3	16	7	0	1.1	9.0	16	0%	.179	0.56	1.69	2.13	2.65			82	
2014	CDR	A	20	7	2	0	10	9	55	40	0	2.1	7.9	48	47%	.260	0.96	2.29	2.50	3.52	11.50	1.2	98	
2015	ROC	AAA	21	1	0	0	1	1	6	2	0	6.0	9.0	6	50%	.143	1.00	1.50	3.16	5.27	0.00	0.0	104	
2015	FTM	A+	21	5	3	0	15	15	84^{2}	79	5	2.0	7.8	73	40%	.303	1.16	2.44	2.99	3.78	12.10	1.3	89	
2015	PCH	A+	21	0	3	1	5	4	18^{1}	23	1	3.9	9.8	20	55%	.407	1.69	7.36	3.00	3.85	2.50	0.3	90	
2016	DUR	AAA	22	0	1	0	1	1	4^{2}	7	1	3.9	13.5	7	15%	.500	1.93	7.71	4.24	3.33	1.00	0.1	91	
2016	MNT	AA	22	7	8	0	24	24	142^{2}	128	7	2.3	6.8	107	44%	.283	1.15	2.59	3.28	3.39	27.10	2.9	92	
2017	*TBA*	*MLB*	*23*	*6*	*8*	*0*	*21*	*21*	113^{1}	*123*	*17*	*3.2*	*6.2*	*78*	*37%*	*.296*	*1.45*	*4.84*	*4.88*	*5.37*	*1.3*	*0.1*	*128*	
2018	*TBA*	*MLB*	*24*	*6*	*7*	*0*	*19*	*19*	112^{1}	*106*	*17*	*4.3*	*9.0*	*112*	*37%*	*.294*	*1.43*	*4.51*	*4.69*	*5.00*	*5.4*	*0.6*	*118*	

Breakout: 15% Improve: 19% Collapse: 10% Attrition: 25% MLB: 36% *Comparables: A.J. Cole, Sean Gilmartin, Jameson Taillon*

The Good: Hu offers a five-pitch mix including a palm ball (although he throws it sparingly) and is comfortable mixing his full repertoire and working backwards. It's a command-and-control, pitchability profile, but Hu makes it work. This in large part due to his ability to spot a deceptive low-90s fastball to all four quadrants of the strike zone. The fastball showed more mid-90s in short burst, which may give you more hope for a strong relief fallback then you would otherwise expect from the profile

The Bad: There's nothing in that five-pitch mix that's a slam dunk plus offering. The palm ball is probably the closest, as he can touch 90 with it and it falls right off the shelf. Neither breaking ball projects as a bat-misser, and in general, I wonder how many major-league bats Hu will miss. I am intrigued by the potential FB/PB combo in short bursts (I've never had to abbreviate palm ball before, PB? PA? PLM?).

The Irrelevant: It's always difficult to tell with the baseball cap, but it sure looked like Hu was sporting a mullet for part of the season with Montgomery.

The Risks: Hu is what we would generally describe as an "advanced" arm, and he passed the Double-A test in 2016, but that doesn't mean he is low risk. The lack of a clear out pitch and sporting only an average fastball means higher level bats may knock him around more than the ones in the Southern League. And on top of all that, he's a pitcher.

Major league ETA: Late 2017

Ben Carsley's Fantasy Take: Hu is relatively close to the Majors, I'll give him that, but the profile just doesn't excite. If he ends up starting in Tampa he could be an acceptable streamer thanks to the favorable home ballpark, but he can remain safely off dynasty radars for now.

8. Austin Franklin, RHP

DOB: 10/02/1997

Height/Weight: 6'3" 215 lbs

Bats/Throws: R/R

Drafted/Acquired: Drafted in the 3rd round (90th overall) in 2016 MLB draft, Paxton HS (Paxton, FL), signed for $597,500

Previous Ranking(s): N/A

2016 Stats: 2.70 ERA, 3.34 DRA, 43.1 IP, 30 H, 16 BB, 40 K at rookie ball in the GCL

The Role: OFP 55—Mid-rotation innings eater who flashes the potential for more
Likely 45—Back-end starter/setup man. Check back in two years.

YEAR	TEAM	LVL	AGE	W	L	SV	G	GS	IP	H	HR	BB/9	K/9	K	GB%	BABIP	WHIP	ERA	FIP	DRA	VORP	WARP	cFIP	MPH
2016	RAY	Rk	18	1	2	1	11	9	43¹	30	0	3.3	8.3	40	42%	.254	1.06	2.70	2.71	4.19	7.00	0.7	99	
2017	*TBA*	*MLB*	*19*	*2*	*2*	*0*	*12*	*6*	*33¹*	*36*	*5*	*4.1*	*7.8*	*29*	*47%*	*.308*	*1.53*	*4.97*	*4.86*	*5.56*	*-0.9*	*-0.1*	*130*	
2018	*TBA*	*MLB*	*20*	*4*	*5*	*0*	*22*	*16*	*117²*	*108*	*19*	*4.7*	*9.1*	*120*		*.286*	*1.44*	*4.72*	*4.89*	*5.28*	*1.2*	*0.1*	*124*	

Breakout: 0% Improve: 0% Collapse: 0% Attrition: 0% MLB: 0% *Comparables: Joe Musgrove, Eduardo Rodriguez, Tyler Glasnow*

The Good: Prep arm with a sinking fastball that's already touching 94, and sits in the low-90s. He can locate to both sides of the plate. His best pitch might be his power curveball that flashed above-average prior to the draft, and even better in instructs. The changeup is nascent but he has feel for it. Has starter size, skillset.

The Bad: Franklin will drift at times which can wreak havoc on his command. The fastball can dip into the upper-80s when he tires. The changeup shows promise but the minors (and bullpens) are littered with pitchers who had two viable offerings and a "developing" cambio.

The Irrelevant: Franklin fired off two no-hitters in his senior season.

The Risks: Multitudes. He has yet to throw above complex-league ball. "Flashing plus" does not equal "plus." The changeup might never come. The mechanics might render him too inconsistent to start, though they appear fixable and he's yet to receive a full season of professional coaching. Also, he's a pitcher.

Major league ETA: 2022 —Craig Goldstein

Ben Carsley's Fantasy Take: If you want to add Franklin to your watch list or list of sleepers and monitor his performance in 2017, knock yourself out. If you waste a roster spot on him right now, you have no one but yourself to blame.

9. Daniel Robertson, SS

DOB: 03/22/1994

Height/Weight: 6'1" 205 lbs

Bats/Throws: R/R

Drafted/Acquired: Drafted 34th overall by Oakland in the 2012 MLB Draft, Upland HS (Upland, CA); signed for $1.5 million; acquired by Tampa Bay in deal for Ben Zobrist.

Previous Ranking(s): #7 (Org) 2016

2016 Stats: .259/.358/.356, 5 HR, 2 SB in 118 games at triple-A Durham

The Role: OFP 50— League average infielder buoyed by OBP and positional flexibility
Likely 45— Standard issue "good utility" guy.

YEAR	TEAM	LVL	AGE	PA	R	2B	3B	HR	RBI	BB	K	SB	CS	AVG/OBP/SLG	TAv	VORP	BABIP	BRR	FRAA	WARP
2014	STO	A+	20	642	110	37	3	15	60	72	94	4	4	.310/.402/.471	.308	61.0	.349	3.0	SS(115): 0.8, 2B(7): -0.7	6.2
2015	RAY	Rk	21	12	2	0	0	0	0	3	2	1	0	.125/.417/.125	.250	0.4	.167	0.1	SS(3): -0.3	0.0
2015	MNT	AA	21	347	49	20	5	4	41	33	58	2	3	.274/.363/.415	.306	29.7	.324	0.8	SS(69): 3.7	3.6
2016	DUR	AAA	22	511	50	21	3	5	43	58	100	2	1	.259/.358/.356	.260	18.5	.322	-0.3	SS(75): 1.8, 2B(21): 2.0	2.5
2017	*TBA*	*MLB*	*23*	*63*	*6*	*3*	*0*	*1*	*6*	*6*	*14*	*0*	*0*	*.237/.321/.357*	*.254*	*1.8*	*.294*	*-0.1*	*2B 0*	*0.2*
2018	*TBA*	*MLB*	*24*	*359*	*42*	*15*	*2*	*7*	*37*	*31*	*84*	*0*	*0*	*.240/.322/.371*	*.252*	*7.6*	*.300*	*-0.6*	*2B 1*	*0.9*

Breakout: 4% Improve: 24% Collapse: 4% Attrition: 16% MLB: 36% *Comparables: Greg Garcia, Chris Taylor, Tyler Saladino*

The Good: This isn't an exciting profile. Hmm, this is a bad lede for The Good section. I think Robertson will hit some. The swing is simple, but he gets good extension and has some feel for the barrel. He'll hit line drives and get on base for you, .270 with some doubles perhaps. He can play three different infield positions. This isn't an exciting profile, but Robertson is likely a major-league contributor for the Rays in 2017.

The Bad: Although he still mostly played shortstop in 2016, Robertson also spent time at second and third. He has the arm for third, but the offensive profile may fit better at second. That's not really a compliment. He's a below-average runner and that shows on the dirt although he's a polished defender otherwise. He's never hit for any sort of power outside of the Cal League— and you are unlikely to wring much more out of his swing plane— which was less of an issue when he was playing shortstop more.

The Irrelevant: The most-recently-of-the-Mariners (now with Cleveland) Dan(iel) Robertson has a bit of a head start on this Daniel, but just a bit.

The Risks: It's pretty low, but warrants mentioning that prospects with just "solid' hit tools and not much power stop drawing walks once major league arms realize they have just solid hit tools and not much power, without the 50 or 60 walks a year, Robertson's offensive profile could collapse and he could look more like an up-and-down extra infielder.

Ben Carsley's Fantasy Take: I used to be pretty high on Robertson as a potential top-15 second baseman with decent all-around stats, but the offensive stagnation has all but killed any real fantasy value here. It'd be different if Robertson had the natural tools we look for and just got stuck in the high minors, but, well, you can read the above. Does it sound like he has the natural tools to you? He might still be a top-200 prospect based on proximity, but that's a mighty fall from where he ranked 18 months ago.

Major league ETA: Early 2017

10. Casey Gillaspie, 1B

DOB: 01/25/1993

Height/Weight: 6'4" 240 lbs

Bats/Throws: S/L

Drafted/Acquired: Drafted 20th overall in the 2014 MLB draft, Wichita State University (KS), signed for $2,035,500.

Previous Ranking(s): N/A

2016 Stats: .307/.389/.520, 7 HR in 47 games for triple-A Durham, .270/.387/.454, 11 HR, 5 SB in 85 games for double-A Montgomery

The Role: OFP 50— Average first baseman
Likely 45— Fringy/second division starter

YEAR	TEAM	LVL	AGE	PA	R	2B	3B	HR	RBI	BB	K	SB	CS	AVG/OBP/SLG	TAv	VORP	BABIP	BRR	FRAA	WARP
2014	HUD	A-	21	308	27	16	1	7	42	42	65	2	3	.262/.364/.411	.268	2.8	.321	-2.5	1B(63): 0.2	0.3
2015	BGR	A	22	268	37	11	0	16	44	28	43	4	0	.278/.358/.530	.307	12.5	.275	-3.1	1B(60): 1.5	1.5
2015	RAY	Rk	22	7	0	0	0	0	0	0	2	0	0	.000/.143/.000	.087	-1.3	.000	0.0	1B(1): 0.1	-0.1
2015	PCH	A+	22	45	3	0	1	1	4	4	9	0	0	.146/.222/.268	.181	-3.8	.161	-0.7	1B(12): -0.6	-0.5
2016	MNT	AA	23	357	51	21	0	11	41	58	79	5	1	.270/.387/.454	.314	20.4	.327	-2.6	1B(77): 2.0	2.4
2016	DUR	AAA	23	203	27	13	2	7	23	22	38	0	1	.307/.389/.520	.313	14.5	.358	1.2	1B(45): -0.3	1.5
2017	*TBA*	*MLB*	*24*	*250*	*30*	*10*	*1*	*10*	*34*	*29*	*66*	*0*	*0*	*.234/.326/.426*	*.264*	*5.4*	*.285*	*-0.4*	*1B 1*	*0.7*
2018	*TBA*	*MLB*	*25*	*367*	*49*	*16*	*1*	*15*	*48*	*41*	*100*	*0*	*0*	*.235/.324/.427*	*.265*	*5.8*	*.290*	*-0.8*	*1B 1*	*0.8*

Breakout: 1% Improve: 12% Collapse: 13% Attrition: 20% MLB: 33% *Comparables: Travis Shaw, Jesus Aguilar, Andy Wilkins*

The Good: Gillaspie drew an aggressive assignment to Double A this year. Okay, well, he's 23 so it doesn't sound that aggressive, but he'd only spent 77 games in full-season ball prior to landing in Montgomery this April. He'd make it to Triple A before the end of the year, hit .300 there and raise his previous power ceiling. He's still a first base prospect, but there's a potential 55 hit/55 power profile in here, and that is ... something.

The Bad: It's hard to poo-poo the performance much, so let's talk about the profile. He's still a burly first baseman with some length in the swing. He doesn't offer much more than the bat, and if it falls even a little short, it's tough to find a bench role for that guy. He doesn't have the innate hitting ability of Bauers, so despite more raw the game power might play down, though the four spot gap probably overstates the difference in profiles.

The Irrelevant: Yep, Conor's brother.

The Risks: Like Bauers, he's hit in the upper minors. Unlike Bauers he doesn't even offer the bare minimum of wrong-end-of-the-defensive-spectrum positional flexibility, so if he stops hitting...that's gonna be a problem.

Ben Carsley's Fantasy Take: Read what I wrote for Bauers, then factor in that Gillaspie is another tier behind him. That's a compliment compared to how I felt about his fantasy future when he was drafted, but it's still not really a compliment.

Major league ETA: Post-super-2, 2017

OTHERS OF NOTE:

#11

Kevin Padlo, 3B

Poor Kevin Padlo, not only did he have to change orgs, but he swapped out a 2016 return engagement in Asheville, with its good barbeque, craft beer, and friendly hitting environs for one in Bowling Green, Kentucky. Undeterred, Padlo showed off some real pop as a 19-year-old in a tough offensive environment, and the power is already playing to all fields. He also profiles as a potential above-average third baseman, much in the mold of Joshua Lowe, with solid athletic tools and a strong throwing arm. Like Lowe there is a ways to go to get to that major league OFP. The polite way to describe Padlo's swing would be something along the lines of: "Well, he doesn't get cheated up there." It has some length and he struggles to change gears against offspeed. The overall profile is still very raw and the development time will be long. But the power—and potential major league reward—here is real.

A blurb by Martin Scorsese

Adrian Rondon, SS

"Jeffrey, you should be seduced by Rondon's profile more than you are."

Actually, I think I've been seduced by his profile more than I should be. There's an easy vision here, one of big bonus numbers and future power-hitting shortstops. If the devil were to tempt me...well, The Last Temptation of Christ style, he could do worse than a lifetime of summers spent watching 17-year-old shortstops hitting bombs in the Appy League. There's a couple problems in this instance though. For one, Rondon isn't likely to stick at shortstop and was already playing third base in instructs, and the approach is still very raw at the plate. The latter of those issues could resolve itself in time, but we have already ranked one third baseman with big raw, solid third base athletic tools, and questions about the swing and approach. He did it in the Midwest League. Rondon has more upside than Padlo, but...get back to me in a year.

And speaking of Jesus

Jesus Sanchez, OF

Sanchez was signed out of the same J2 class as Rondon at one-tenth the cost. And if keeping Rondon out of the top ten doesn't make me look bad next year, doing the same Sanchez sure might. Like Rondon, he's a long way away from the majors and likely doesn't stick up the middle. Also like Rondon, there is very real power here and a more advanced hit tool at present. There's a stateside track record here now too, so it's a bit of a copout to get back to me in a year, since there are plenty in my shoes that would tell you it's better be a year early on a guy than a year late, but...get back to me in a year.

Most likely to be played by Morgan Freeman

Lucius Fox, SS

I assume you all know they backstory and the bonus number by now. You're probably even aware he didn't play a game for a Tampa affiliate because of an undisclosed—by the Giants— foot injury he suffered in Augusta. It's unfair to say this of an 18-year-old, but it's unlikely Fox will live up to the high seven-figure bonus. After all, if the odds were better, the Giants wouldn't have been inclined to trade him for the "serviceable no. 4 starter" version of Matt Moore. Fox was overmatched at the plate in the Sally this year, but he has the skillset to be a major-league regular at shortstop. He's an above-average runner, whose speed plays up even more on the basepaths, and he has the actions and athleticism for short, although he struggles with the game speed at present. It's easy to conclude that Fox should have been eased into pro baseball in the complex and then a short-season assignment, and that may well be the case, but it was going to be a long development path regardless, and as I wrote earlier, prospects don't advance along a y = x slope.

The guy we're lower on than others

Garrett Whitley, OF

I must confess to the audience my biases. Being based in the northeast I have had multiple conversations behind the backstop about Garrett Whitley over the last couple years. None of them have gone well for Garrett Whitley's odds of making this Top Ten list. There's the potential for four above-average tools here, and I've droned on about the importance of making upside bets on prospect lists. But you have to have some confidence in the potential, or else you are just frittering your money away on the "match the dealer" bonus. A different metaphor: In my film school days I had a collection of paperback tomes advising you on how to make your first feature film. The democratization of film technology has long since rendered them all obsolete anyway, but one piece of what I'd consider somewhat bizarre advice stuck with me. I'll paraphrase to the best of my memory: Audiences will put up with an odd cut or a slightly out of focus shot (who was the audience for this book exactly?), but if the audio track is fuzzy or noisy or out of sync, you will completely lose them. If you don't think Whitley is a center fielder, or that the raw power will never fully show up in games, you can still make a case for him in the Top Ten, but if you don't think he'll hit...

The ex-101 guy

Taylor Guerrieri, RHP

Guerrieri landed on the Top 101 in 2013 and then again in 2016, after proving he could make it through a season without injury. We wrote of him previously that the question will rest on health, and not stuff and now he's put together a healthy season and he's nowhere to be seen. What gives? Well, velocity, to start. Guerrieri continued to pound the zone in 2016, but the velocity dropped from plus to pedestrian, and hitters noticed, as he struggled to miss bats. The curve is still there, but the fastball seemed to be a developmental focus at times, and his change lags behind even the reduced fastball. Guerrieri's walk and strikeout rates are trending in the wrong direction, and while those are ancillary to the stuff... the stuff is mitigated at present. Without a rebound in velocity, he might be bullpen bound. —Craig Goldstein

The fifth starter

Ryan Yarbrough, LHP

Yarbrough isn't that far off the arms in the middle of the Top Ten, but he lacks even their fourth starter potential. Perhaps we are splitting hairs; a back-end starter is a back-end starter. But Yarbrough is what he is—there just isn't much room for growth here. His fastball sits in the low-90s. He pairs it with a solid change and below-average curveball. He throws strikes with all three. He performed well in Double A. You know this profile. Yarbrough may be a bit better prospect than your dime-a-dozen command lefty with a good change, but not enough to sneak into the Top Ten this year.

TOP 10 TALENTS 25 AND UNDER (BORN 4/1/91 OR LATER)

1. Blake Snell	6. Jake Bauers
2. Willy Adames	7. Jacob Faria
3. Brent Honeywell	8. Chih-Wei Hu
4. Jose De Leon	9. Austin Franklin
5. Josh Lowe	10. Daniel Robertson

You know the Rays. I'm not saying you know every player on the roster—quick, name four relief pitchers from the 2016 team!—but you know their modus operandi. You know how they're designed. Cursed with a payroll just north of your family's monthly budget, this is a team that builds by acquiring young, cost-controlled players via trade, getting the most out of them for a couple of seasons, then trading them for more young, cost-controlled players. Sometimes they'll develop a player of their own, but then that guy gets traded for more young, cost-controlled players. Rarely they'll sign a free agent, but then they'll try to trade that guy for a young, cost-controlled player.

Today's Rays are loaded with, you guessed it, young, cost-controlled players. What's going to make this 25U list easy, and rather short is this: literally only one of them is under the age of 25. Aside from Old Man Evan Longoria (entering his age-31 season) and sophomore left-handed starter Blake Snell (entering his age-24 season), this team is entirely composed of players that are playing the upcoming year at an age between 26 and 30. It's a very strange hegemony of age, with so many members of the team born within that same five-year window and literally all of them within seven years and change–Longoria was born on October 7, 1985 and Snell on December 4, 1992. It makes one wonder if their clubhouse is exceptionally tight-knit given the weird lack of age-based stratification. With few veterans and almost no one who has ever hit free agency, does the common ground in age and/or service time make the dugout more collaborative, or are they all competing for the same spots? Inquiring minds want to know.

Anyway, we should briefly go over our outlier and the head of the team's 25U list in Snell. After his 2015 Year of Helium, Snell clocked in as the No. 21 prospect on BP's 2016 rankings, a left-hander with dynamic stuff and a vicious fastball. Expected to burst onto the scene last season, he instead struggled to harness his gifts, walking more than five batters per nine and failing to go deep into many games. The raw stuff is still there, and it can be magnificent at times to watch his slider make professional hitters look like that weird kid from little league. But efficiency and adequacy do not yet go hand-in-hand, and averaging less than five innings per start still kind of sucks, even in today's two-times-through-the-order world of baseball.

So yes, we're limited to Blake Snell, then the rest of our prospect team's list. It's not all that exciting. You know, that's actually a reasonable tagline for the team's hopes in the coming year. Your 2017 Tampa Bay Rays: It's not all that exciting! Season tickets on sale now!

—Bryan Grosnick

TEXAS RANGERS

The State of the System: *The Rangers system is remarkably consistent in the kind of dudes it has. There's just fewer of them at the moment.*

THE TOP TEN

1. LHP Yohander Mendez	6. SS Yeyson Yrizarri
2. RHP Ariel Jurado	7. 1B Ronald Guzman
3. CF Leody Taveras	8. LHP Cole Ragans
4. SS Anderson Tejeda	9. IF Josh Morgan
5. LHP Brett Martin	10. LHP Andrew Faulkner

The Big Question: Proximity over potential?

As long as we have had prospect lists, we've had arguments on how to create those prospect lists. What tools get greater consideration than others? How does age come into play? What about time at (and success in) varying levels of the minor league experience? Do we give any credence to funny names, or, wait, no, I'm being told "funny names" is an entirely different list.

While the Rangers' system is nowhere near as impressive as it was a few years ago (or even, technically, last year), they still have a quartet of players that encapsulate the fundamental questions at the bottom of these debates: What is better: proximity to major league production, or pure, raw (untested) talent?

When we deal with proximity, we are often handcuffed by a lower ceiling just by the virtue of knowing more about the players flaws. Yohander Mendez and Ariel Jurado bear that banner for experience in this discussion, at the oh-so-advanced ages of 21 and 20, respectively. Mendez has already had his first taste of the major leagues, though it didn't exactly go swimmingly, and has demonstrated success at the highest levels of the minor leagues for the last two seasons. Jurado, an elite sinkerballer, had success in pitcher-unfriendly High Desert, and despite some struggles in Double-A Frisco, has consistently impressed scouts and evaluators alike with his maturity and approach.

If it weren't for the other two youngsters in this system, Leody Taveras and Anderson Tejeda, it would be an absolute no-brainer to crown Mendez and Jurado the top and second best prospect in the Texas system. They're both a season (or less, depending on performance) from consistent major league appearances, they're both pitchers in a pitcher-less system, and they're young. There's still room for growth and improvement, but both pitchers have shown signs of what they'll be in the future, and that future is pretty good. Definitely not aces, but solid pitchers who will put up solid performances.

As for Taveras and Tejeda, what makes them so special? Here, it's all about potential. If Mendez and Jurado are solid, solidity (in the prospect world) can sometimes be boring. We can see, at this point, that Mendez and Jurado lack the projection to break their molds and turn into stars, but that is balanced by a more evidence-based body of work. We can hold in our mind's eye both their shortcomings and their successes against advanced competition. If these two fielders are anything, they're incredibly exciting, bursting with unknown potential and the signs of potential stardom. Taveras and Tejeda have shown glimmers of stardom, and it is easy to imagine them soaring above a path fraught with risks. Their ultimate ceilings are seemingly inversely proportional to the amount of experience they have. When a player has yet to fail (or fail convincingly), it's much easier to assume greatness. After all, everyone loves a future star, especially those of us tasked with creating prospect lists.

Taveras, a Dominican outfield prospect signed in 2015, gets fantastic reviews from those who have been lucky enough to see him either in the AZL or with the Spokane Indians. He, per reports, demonstrates a similar ability to read the game as the Rangers' other ridiculous youngster, Nomar Mazara, and while Mazara was already in Low-A at age 18, it wouldn't be inconceivable to see Taveras take a similar path through the minor leagues. Of course, there have also been guys with great game understanding and sweet swings who have gotten to the crafty pitchers in Double-A and never quite figured it out, but why borrow trouble? The same goes for talented (but out-of-nowhere)

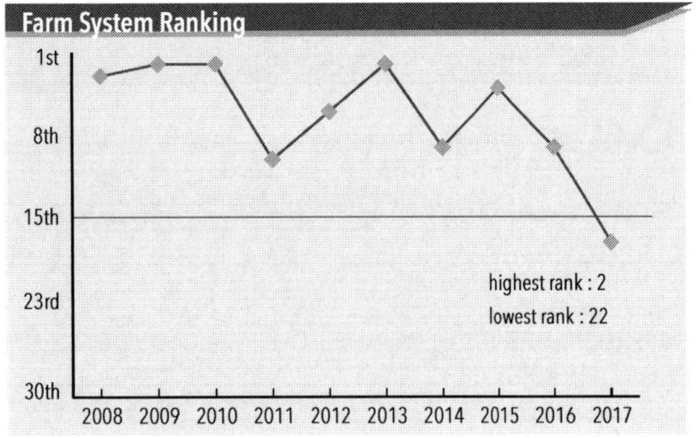

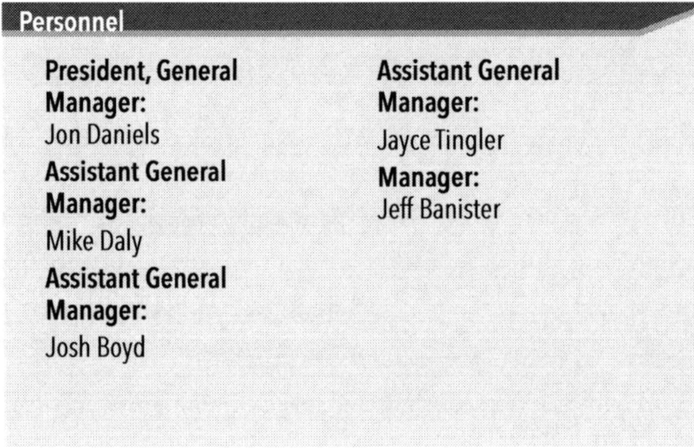

Personnel

President, General Manager:
Jon Daniels

Assistant General Manager:
Mike Daly

Assistant General Manager:
Josh Boyd

Assistant General Manager:
Jayce Tingler

Manager:
Jeff Banister

infielder Tejeda, who might take his NWL power surge up the levels, or might never hit more than seven homers in a season again.

So, we have two experienced pitchers with proven success, but a low chance of stardom, and two inexperienced hitters with boundless energy and the projections of a million "I saw them first!"s to choose from. Either choice is defendable, as would have been the decision to reject the paradigm of rankings and simply list everyone alphabetically. Since that's not allowed, though, we must make a decision. Do we go with near or far, offense or pitching, solidity or excitement?

For me, and for this ranking, what it comes down to is the fact that a farm system exists to create value for the major league team. There is no title, no trophy for "the best farm system." Prospects exist to either become major leaguers, or to show enough major-league potential to be traded for more major-league value. That isn't to say that having a solid farm system isn't an added benefit (I mean, just look at the trouble the Los Angeles Angels are in), and that there isn't intrinsic value in being a talented but unproven prospect. However, there is simply more value, and more proven value, in a set of players who - at only two or three years older! - find themselves knocking on the door to the major leagues, as not just replacement level relievers, but positive contributors.

—Kate Morrison

1. Yohander Mendez, LHP

DOB: 01/17/1995

Height/Weight: 6'4" 180 lbs.

Bats/Throws: L/L

Drafted/Acquired: Signed July 2011 by Texas out of the Dominican Republic for $1.5 million

Previous Ranking(s): #8 (Org.)

2016 Stats: 18.00 ERA, 6.96 DRA, 3 IP, 5 H, 2 BB, 0 K in 2 games at major league level, 2.45 ERA, 1.69 DRA, 33 IP, 21 H, 11 BB, 45 K in 7 games at High-A High Desert, 3.09 ERA, 2.55 DRA, 46.2 IP, 39 H, 14 BB, 46 K in 10 games at Double-A Frisco, 0.57 ERA, 5.64 DRA, 31.1 IP, 12 H, 16 BB, 22 K in 7 games at Triple-A Round Rock

The Role: OFP 55—No. 3 starter
Likely 50—No. 4 starter

YEAR	TEAM	LVL	AGE	W	L	SV	G	GS	IP	H	HR	BB/9	K/9	K	GB%	BABIP	WHIP	ERA	FIP	DRA	VORP	WARP	cFIP	MPH
2014	RNG	Rk	19	0	1	0	3	3	5^{2}	8	0	3.2	11.1	7	0%	.444	1.76	4.76	2.62	3.63			97	
2014	HIC	A	19	3	0	0	7	6	31	26	4	0.6	8.1	28	52%	.268	0.90	2.32	3.65	2.81	9.00	0.9	80	
2015	HIC	A	20	3	3	3	21	8	66^{1}	57	2	2.0	10.0	74	54%	.312	1.09	2.44	2.41	1.49	26.20	2.8	75	
2016	HDS	A+	21	4	1	0	7	7	33	21	2	3.0	12.3	45	51%	.264	0.97	2.45	2.77	1.35	15.10	1.6	71	
2016	FRI	AA	21	4	1	0	10	10	46^{2}	39	2	2.7	8.9	46	47%	.296	1.14	3.09	2.92	2.91	11.30	1.2	90	
2016	ROU	AAA	21	4	1	0	7	4	31^{1}	12	0	4.6	6.3	22	40%	.150	0.89	0.57	3.94	5.92	-2.50	-0.3	112	
2016	TEX	MLB	21	0	0	0	2	0	3	5	0	6.0	0.0	0	33%	.333	2.33	18.00	5.11	6.96	-0.70	-0.1	123	95
2017	*TEX*	*MLB*	*22*	*3*	*3*	*0*	*29*	*5*	*51*	*52*	*6*	*3.8*	*6.4*	*37*	*41%*	*.291*	*1.44*	*4.72*	*4.71*	*4.90*	*1.4*	*0.1*	*100*	
2018	*TEX*	*MLB*	*23*	*3*	*3*	*0*	*37*	*7*	*72^{1}*	*63*	*9*	*5.9*	*9.3*	*75*	*41%*	*.282*	*1.52*	*4.90*	*4.90*	*5.30*	*-0.2*	*0.0*	*123*	

Breakout: 16% Improve: 35% Collapse: 13% Attrition: 26% MLB: 56% *Comparables: Aaron Poreda, Johnny Cueto, Jake Thompson*

The Good: Mendez is as solid a pitching prospect as they come, if not exactly ace material. At only 21, he has both the arsenal and the command to be a valuable part of the Rangers' future. He sits 90-93 with his fastball, which he can get some good sinking action on, and despite the lack of premium velocity, he can still fool batters with the pitch. His best pitch, however, is his changeup, which he throws with the same deceptive delivery as his fastball, making it incredibly difficult for hitters to pick up until it's too late for them to do anything about it. Mendez developed a slider on his trip through the minors, and while it's still his weakest pitch, he's been able to manipulate its depth enough to use it as a workable third pitch. The sum here is greater than the parts, however, especially when you add in Mendez's ability to pitch thoughtfully, working off hitters' weaknesses, as seen in his sub-1.00 Triple-A ERA.

The Bad: In his September cup of coffee, Mendez didn't exactly wow spectators with his performance. In his very first appearance, he allowed five runs on four hits over an inning of work, aided by a likely nerves-induced uncharacteristic lack of command. Additionally, Mendez only pitched six innings in a game twice in 2016, leading to questions about his durability. While Texas may have simply been trying to protect their best chance at developing a starter since Martin Perez, there are definitely valid concerns about Mendez's future ability to go three times through the order.

The Irrelevant: Mendez's 0.57 ERA in the PCL was the lowest (min 30 IP) since Tim Lincecum posted a 0.29 in 2007.

The Risks: With pitchers, there are always risks. Inherent injury specter aside, Mendez could take longer to adjust to the climes of the major leagues than expected, leading to similar up-and-down issues suffered by someone like Chi Chi Gonzalez.

Major league ETA: Debuted in 2016. —Kate Morrison

Ben Carsley's Fantasy Take: As hard as I push the "don't waste roster spots on backend starters" rule, those of you in deeper fantasy leagues will need to roster the no. 3/4 starters of the world to field competitive teams. If your league dictates that you must roster such players, Mendez is as solid a prospect among them as you'll find. It's a bummer for our purposes that he'll pitch in Texas, but Mendez has the tools to contribute modestly but meaningfully in all non-save pitcher categories. I don't expect the ERA or WHIP to be wonderful at first, but eventually Mendez should settle in as a mid-to-high-3s ERA guy with something like 170 strikeouts in 200 innings. It's not exciting, but it's not terribly far off from what Matt Moore did in 2016, and he was a top-50 starter. Plus, Mendez should have a more tolerable WHIP.

2. Ariel Jurado, RHP

DOB: 1/30/1996,

Height/Weight: 6'1" 180 lbs.

Bats/Throws: R/R

Drafted/Acquired: Signed December 2012 by Texas out of Panama for $50,000

Previous Ranking(s): N/A

2016 Stats: 3.86 ERA, 79.1 IP, 83 H, 24 BB, 71 K in 16 games at High-A High Desert, 3.30 ERA, 43.2 IP, 44 H, 10 BB, 35 K in 8 games at Double-A Frisco

The Role: OFP 55—No. 3/4 starter
Likely 50—No. 4 starter

YEAR	TEAM	LVL	AGE	W	L	SV	G	GS	IP	H	HR	BB/9	K/9	K	GB%	BABIP	WHIP	ERA	FIP	DRA	VORP	WARP	cFIP	MPH
2014	RNG	Rk	18	2	1	0	14	3	38^{2}	35	1	1.9	8.1	35	0%	.293	1.11	1.63	3.25	3.53			91	
2015	HIC	A	19	12	1	0	22	15	99	92	5	1.1	8.6	95	61%	.314	1.05	2.45	2.62	1.27	42.60	4.5	63	
2016	HDS	A+	20	7	2	0	16	16	79^{1}	83	4	2.7	8.1	71	64%	.342	1.35	3.86	3.53	1.93	31.20	3.2	79	
2016	FRI	AA	20	1	4	0	8	6	43^{2}	44	3	2.1	7.2	35	53%	.315	1.24	3.30	3.29	3.27	8.40	0.9	90	
2017	*TEX*	*MLB*	*21*	*6*	*5*	*1*	*35*	*15*	94^{2}	*110*	*10*	*3.5*	*5.3*	*55*	*52%*	*.314*	*1.54*	*4.55*	*4.64*	*4.87*	*5.9*	*0.6*	*114*	
2018	*TEX*	*MLB*	*22*	*6*	*6*	*0*	*29*	*18*	139^{1}	*145*	*14*	*4.6*	*7.7*	*120*	*52%*	*.315*	*1.54*	*4.44*	*4.45*	*4.75*	*8.3*	*0.9*	*110*	

Breakout: 9% Improve: 15% Collapse: 4% Attrition: 14% MLB: 22% *Comparables: Justin Nicolino, Jarrod Parker, Zach Davies*

The Good: Jurado pitches like he's 25, not a few days away from 21. Some pitchers like to stalk around the mound, overflowing with emotions. Some use that as a cover for lesser stuff, or use it to help pump themselves up to access their best gear. Jurado doesn't do that, or really need to. He's a quiet mound presence who's just going to go out there and put the ball exactly where he wants to. Command is usually one of the last things to mature in a pitching prospect, but for Jurado, it's something he's demonstrated since the day the Rangers signed him out of Panama. It helps that he has a decent arsenal of pitches to apply it to: a heavy, sinking fastball; an improving changeup, a well-handled curveball that he manipulates, and a slider that he uses sparingly, but effectively. His fastball is the only consistently above-average offering, but his changeup has flashed in that range as well.

The Bad: Jurado doesn't have the velocity expected of a right-handed pitcher. He sits around 90-94, which is fine, but not ideal in this day and age of velocity being everything. It's also not likely that there's more velocity in the body, as he's fairly filled out without much projection left. His 123 total innings in 2016 is far and away the highest number of innings he's thrown as a professional, so his durability is still fairly untested.

The Irrelevant: Mariano Rivera is inarguably the best pitcher born in Panama, but he is not the one with the lowest ERA, that currently belongs to Padres catcher Christian Bethancourt.

The Risks: The command is great, but the stuff has to be there. While Jurado's not had much trouble with keeping his minor league teams in a position to win, his sinker-heavy philosophy means he does have to have a good defense around him to be truly successful. If he does have that good defense, it's double-play central. If he doesn't, get used to "in play, run(s)." Also, he's a pitcher.

Major league ETA: 2018 —Kate Morrison

Ben Carsley's Fantasy Take: A lot of what was said about Mendez is relevant here too, but Jurado is farther away and has a slightly lower ceiling. That means he'll miss out in joining Mendez on the top-100 list, but if we extended our ranking by another 25 he'd be there. I say that now, but the lack of plus stuff and the future home in Texas gives me pause ... I'm sorry I hate your prospects, I don't know why they picked me for this either.

3. Leody Taveras, CF

DOB: 9/8/1998

Height/Weight: 6'1" 170 lbs.

Bats/Throws: S/R

Drafted/Acquired: Signed July 2015 out of the Dominican Republic for $2.1 million

Previous Ranking(s): N/A

2016 Stats: .278/.329/.382, 1 HR, 11 SB in 33 games at Arizona League, .228/.271/.293, 0 HR, 3 SB in 29 games at short-season Spokane

The Role: OFP 60—First-division center fielder
Likely 45—Reserve outfielder

YEAR	TEAM	LVL	AGE	PA	R	2B	3B	HR	RBI	BB	K	SB	CS	AVG/OBP/SLG	TAv	VORP	BABIP	BRR	FRAA	WARP
2016	DRN	Rk	17	45	6	2	2	0	9	6	5	4	3	.385/.467/.538	.326	1.5	.441	-2.1	CF(7): -1.0 • RF(2): -0.5	0.0
2016	RNG	Rk	17	155	22	6	3	1	15	11	24	11	4	.278/.329/.382	.253	3.4	.328	-0.3	CF(31): -3.1 • RF(3): -0.2	-0.2
2016	SPO	A-	17	133	14	6	1	0	9	8	26	3	1	.228/.271/.293	.253	2.4	.283	-0.3	CF(26): 2.0 • RF(1): -0.4	0.3
2017	*TEX*	*MLB*	*18*	*250*	*26*	*9*	*1*	*5*	*21*	*12*	*71*	*4*	*2*	*.211/.250/.323*	*.195*	*-7.2*	*.278*	*-0.1*	*CF -1 • RF -0*	*-0.9*
2018	*TEX*	*MLB*	*19*	*281*	*27*	*11*	*2*	*6*	*28*	*12*	*81*	*4*	*2*	*.213/.249/.336*	*.204*	*-8.1*	*.277*	*0.2*	*CF -2 • RF 0*	*-1.1*

Breakout: 0% Improve: 0% Collapse: 0% Attrition: 0% MLB: 0% *Comparables: Raul Mondesi, Wilmer Flores*

The Good: Taveras is an excellent athlete. A plus runner, Taveras also has explosive wrists, a quick first step, and a lean frame that should allow him to add good weight as he physically matures. At the plate, he has excellent bat speed and a good feel for the barrel. He hits the ball well to all fields, and while neither the stroke nor his size is conducive to huge power now, he could have average power or a tick better a decade from now. Defensively, his speed, route running ability, and plus arm strength will all play well in center field.

The Bad: Taveras is such a young pup that he hasn't really shown many glaring weaknesses in his game. If we're going to nitpick: his swing can get stiff, and his mechanics at the plate are noisy, both of which could become problematic if he can't iron that out between now and adulthood.

The Irrelevant: Leody is the younger cousin of former big league outfielder Willy Taveras.

The Risks: Taveras was a 17-year-old in short-season ball last year; we don't know whether he'll leave the sport to take up a career in teaching, much less whether he'll grow into his power projection.

Major league ETA: 2020 —Brendan Gawlowski

Ben Carsley's Fantasy Take: The lead time hurts Taveras' value, but he's got the kind of upside we're looking for. It's probably too early to say he's in consideration for the top 100--and it's definitely too early to try and project out any stats--but now's the time to buy. I'd put him somewhere on the 12-to-15 range in this list.

4. Anderson Tejeda, SS

DOB: 4/1/1998

Height/Weight: 5'11" 160 lbs.

Bats/Throws: L/R

Drafted/Acquired: Signed September 2014 out of the Dominican Republic for $100,000

Previous Ranking(s): N/A

2016 Stats: .293/.331/.496/ 1 HR, 1 SB in 32 games at Arizona League, .277/.313/.553, 8 HR, 1 SB in 23 games at short-season Spokane

The Role: OFP 60—First-division regular
Likely 45—Utility infielder

YEAR	TEAM	LVL	AGE	PA	R	2B	3B	HR	RBI	BB	K	SB	CS	AVG/OBP/SLG	TAv	VORP	BABIP	BRR	FRAA	WARP
2015	DRG	Rk	17	55	4	2	2	0	8	8	11	2	2	.277/.382/.404	.269	2.9	.361	0.5	2B(10): -0.2 • SS(4): -0.2	0.2
2015	DRN	Rk	17	180	32	17	4	4	32	17	38	7	5	.323/.397/.557	.335	21.7	.402	-0.5	SS(29): -0.3 • 2B(8): -0.5	2.1
2016	DRG	Rk	18	47	9	2	3	1	7	5	4	5	0	.262/.340/.524	.338	5.7	.270	-0.1	SS(8): 1.7 • 3B(1): 0.1	0.8
2016	RNG	Rk	18	142	22	12	6	1	21	8	36	1	0	.293/.331/.496	.305	12.2	.392	-0.4	SS(20): -3.9 • 2B(12): -0.3	0.8
2016	SPO	A-	18	99	15	0	1	8	19	5	33	1	0	.277/.313/.553	.285	6.6	.340	0.5	SS(17): -1.8 • 2B(3): -0.3	0.5
2017	*TEX*	*MLB*	*19*	*250*	*23*	*9*	*2*	*8*	*28*	*12*	*85*	*1*	*1*	*.206/.247/.355*	*.202*	*-4.0*	*.282*	*-0.1*	*SS -0 • 2B 0*	*-0.5*
2018	*TEX*	*MLB*	*20*	*369*	*42*	*13*	*3*	*13*	*44*	*20*	*119*	*2*	*1*	*.221/.267/.391*	*.225*	*-1.1*	*.294*	*-0.1*	*SS 0 • 2B 0*	*-0.1*

Breakout: 0% Improve: 6% Collapse: 2% Attrition: 6% MLB: 13% *Comparables: Raul Mondesi, Nomar Mazara, Carlos Correa*

The Good: For a teenager, Tejeda is very advanced. He's not the biggest guy in the world, but with a quick bat, strong forearms, and a swing geared to put the ball in the air, he's already taking his above-average raw power into games. While there's plenty of swing and miss in his game at present, he's capable of hitting the ball hard to all fields. In the field, he's a bit error-prone but he has good instincts and a plus arm. While he's played all three infield positions thus far, he's being groomed as a shortstop for now.

The Bad: Tejeda is a very aggressive hitter who goes up swinging and likes to end at-bats on his terms; if he doesn't curb that instinct, many of them will end in weak contact. He's also a fastball-first hitter still learning to recognize spin.

The Irrelevant: If we can agree that a single batting practice session is essentially irrelevant in the grand scheme of his career, it is irrelevant that Tejeda launched ball after ball into the right field bleachers prior to a game at Safeco Field last season. Irrelevant, but impressive.

The Risks: Given his advanced skill set and position, Tejeda is a safer bet than most teenagers to have a big-league career. Of course, we are talking about a free-swinging teenager in short-season ball, so there's still plenty that can go wrong.

Major league ETA: 2020 —Brendan Gawlowski

Ben Carsley's Fantasy Take: In a lot of ways it's crazy to suggest favoring a guy like Tejeda over a guy like Jurado in dynasty, but there's a strong argument for it. Yes, he is a lottery ticket, but at least he's one of the super shiny ones you sneak into cards for milestone birthdays.

5. Brett Martin, LHP

DOB: 4/28/1995

Height/Weight: 6'4" 190 lbs.

Bats/Throws: L/L

Drafted/Acquired: Drafted in the fourth round of the 2014 MLB Draft, Walters State Community College (Morristown, TN); signed for $475,000

Previous Ranking(s): N/A

2016 Stats: 4.53 ERA, 3.58 DRA, 43.2 IP, 58 H, 14 BB, 48 K in 9 games at Low-A Hickory, 3.86 ERA, 2.02 DRA, 2.1 IP, 3 H, 0 BB, 6 K in 2 games at complex-level AZL, 4.24 ERA, 4.92 DRA, 23.1 IP, 24 H, 7 BB, 16 K in 6 games at High-A High Desert

The Role: OFP 55—No. 3/4 starter
Likely 45—Backend starter

YEAR	TEAM	LVL	AGE	W	L	SV	G	GS	IP	H	HR	BB/9	K/9	K	GB%	BABIP	WHIP	ERA	FIP	DRA	VORP	WARP	cFIP	MPH
2014	RNG	Rk	19	1	4	1	15	6	35	36	3	3.1	10.0	39	0%	.333	1.37	5.40	4.11	3.34			94	
2015	HIC	A	20	5	6	0	20	18	95^{1}	92	6	2.5	6.8	72	49%	.306	1.24	3.49	3.67	5.17	0.10	0.0	105	
2016	HIC	A	21	2	3	0	9	9	43^{2}	58	3	2.9	9.9	48	53%	.404	1.65	4.53	3.06	3.18	8.90	1.0	91	
2016	RNG	Rk	21	0	0	0	2	2	2^{1}	3	0	0.0	23.1	6	60%	.600	1.29	3.86	-1.01	1.88	1.00	0.1	79	
2016	HDS	A+	21	2	1	0	6	6	23^{1}	24	3	2.7	6.2	16	55%	.292	1.33	4.24	4.91	3.90	4.10	0.4	99	
2017	*TEX*	*MLB*	*22*	*3*	*5*	*0*	*20*	*12*	58^{2}	*78*	*11*	*4.7*	*4.0*	*26*	*41%*	*.319*	*1.85*	*6.25*	*6.36*	*6.60*	*-9.3*	*-1.0*	*157*	
2018	*TEX*	*MLB*	*23*	*4*	*7*	*0*	*23*	*17*	116^{2}	*136*	*21*	*6.0*	*6.7*	*87*	*41%*	*.315*	*1.83*	*6.14*	*6.13*	*6.48*	*-10.0*	*-1.0*	*154*	

Breakout: 1% Improve: 1% Collapse: 0% Attrition: 1% MLB: 1% *Comparables: Jeff Locke, Drake Britton, Adrian Sampson*

The Good: Martin isn't that far off of Mendez and Jurado in terms of stuff, he just has a few more developmental hurdles to clear. He has a plus fastball from the left side that gets good plane and angle from his height and high slot. His breaking ball is a hard slurve that he can spot to either side of the plate, and could be a bat-misser at higher levels with more consistent command and shape. Martin fills out his repertoire with a potentially average change. He's a good athlete although you don't really see that in his mechanics. There might be a bit of projection still left in the frame and delivery.

The Bad: Martin has a slight hesitation in his delivery and remains tall throughout. He throws strikes, but his command is below average at present and he especially struggles to consistently gets his fastball down in the zone. It can be a very hittable pitch. The slurvy breaking ball flattens out and the change needs further development. At present there isn't an obvious out pitch in the majors.

The Irrelevant: Martin is bidding to be the second player from Walters State Community College to make the majors. The first, Ryan Kelly, made 17 appearances out of the Braves pen in 2015.

The Risks: I'll be interested to see how Martin's stuff, especially the fastball, plays in Double-A. He's a lefty with a plus fastball and a useable breaker, so he has a better shot at the majors than your average A-ball arm. But he is a pitcher.

Major league ETA: Late 2018

Ben Carsley's Fantasy Take: Maybe we'll view Martin next year the way we view Mendez now, but until then he can remain on waivers unless your league rosters 200-plus prospects.

6. Yeyson Yrizarri, SS

DOB: 2/2/1997

Height/Weight: 6'0" 175 lbs.

Bats/Throws: R/R

Drafted/Acquired: Signed July 2013 out of Venezuela for $1.35 million

Previous Ranking(s): N/A

2016 Stats: .269/.292/.389, 7 HR, 20 SB in 118 games at Low-A Hickory

The Role: OFP 55—First-division MLB shortstop
Likely 40—Toolsy utility guy that's just a hair from putting it together

YEAR	TEAM	LVL	AGE	PA	R	2B	3B	HR	RBI	BB	K	SB	CS	AVG/OBP/SLG	TAv	VORP	BABIP	BRR	FRAA	WARP
2014	DRG	Rk	17	48	7	3	1	0	6	3	4	1	1	.302/.354/.419	.272	0.0	.325	0.0		0.0
2014	RNG	Rk	17	206	23	13	1	1	19	9	36	5	3	.237/.275/.332	.202	1.2	.282	1.5		0.4
2015	ROU	AAA	18	34	2	1	1	0	4	1	5	0	1	.273/.294/.364	.196	-1.4	.321	-0.5	SS(9): -1.2	-0.3
2015	SPO	A-	18	257	27	10	1	2	29	6	46	8	6	.265/.290/.339	.240	4.8	.318	0.0	SS(57): 0.3 • 2B(5): -0.7	0.5
2016	HIC	A	19	479	53	27	3	7	53	9	91	20	15	.269/.292/.389	.266	20.4	.318	-1.5	SS(116): 13.9	3.8
2017	*TEX*	*MLB*	*20*	*250*	*24*	*11*	*1*	*5*	*25*	*5*	*64*	*5*	*4*	*.229/.253/.351*	*.203*	*-3.7*	*.286*	*-0.5*	*SS 3*	*-0.1*
2018	*TEX*	*MLB*	*21*	*394*	*40*	*17*	*2*	*9*	*42*	*9*	*96*	*8*	*7*	*.243/.268/.376*	*.221*	*-2.1*	*.298*	*-0.2*	*SS 5*	*0.3*

Breakout: 1% Improve: 7% Collapse: 0% Attrition: 2% MLB: 13% *Comparables: Chris Owings, Raul Mondesi, Tim Beckham*

The Good: He's as tooled out as tooled out can be. He's got a beautiful swing from the right side, certainly the type of swing you can imagine hitting for a solid major-league average some day. Tremendous bat speed hints at the potential for some future power. His arm strength is plus-plus and pairs well with solid infield actions, a parlay with good odds to stay at short. While he can make just about any throw, Yrizzari can get a bit scattershot. He's athletic and graceful on the baseball field, and an above-average runner to boot. It's always worth noting when we hit one of these organizational strengths that the Rangers have done unusually well developing this kind of profile recently.

The Bad: There must be something pretty bad for us to be ranking him this low, right? He's got no earthly idea what to swing at yet, leading to a 9/91 BB/K ratio at Low-A this year. In my looks, I didn't see a player horribly fooled by spin and sequencing, more a player far too aggressive. He'll have to learn what he can and can't barrel, or he's going to end up as a good Double-A player and no more.

The Irrelevant: As you probably know, the two hotbeds of international free agency are Venezuela and the Dominican Republic. Both can claim Yrizarri, who is Venezuelan by birth but was raised in the Dominican, setting up an interesting potential fight for his services in the 2021 WBC.

The Risks: Extreme. The OFP/Likely sort of system that we use doesn't work terribly well for the Yeyson Yrizarris of the world unless you use huge gaps that would make this list look silly. Calling him a 55/40, while "true" in the sense of how we use the numbers, vastly understates the delta between reasonable outcomes for extreme tools guys with one glaring issue like Yrizarri. There's a decent chance it all works out and he's Rougned Odor, in which case that 55 role is a tick and change low, and there's an even bigger chance he's a role 20 or 30 that never figures out what to swing at, like Engel Beltre. (It was harder to find a toolsy Rangers international guy that didn't figure it out at all than you'd think.)

Major league ETA: 2020 —Jarrett Seidler

Ben Carsley's Fantasy Take: As noted above, Yrizarri is certainly in the right system for someone with his profile. The odds of fantasy payoff are so low here that it's tough to get super excited right now, but Yrizarri should be on everyone's watch list. If it looks like he's starting to put it together or if more positive reports about his hit tool start trickling in, pounce.

7. Ronald Guzman, 1B

DOB: 10/20/1994

Height/Weight: 6'5" 205 lbs.

Bats/Throws: L/L

Drafted/Acquired: Signed July 2011 out of the Dominican Republic for $3.45 million

Previous Ranking(s): N/A

2016 Stats: .288/.348/.477, 15 HR, 2 SB in 102 games at Double-A Frisco, .216/.266/.330, 1 HR, 0 SB in 25 games at Triple-A Round Rock

The Role: OFP 55—Everyday first baseman
Likely 45—Fringy platoon 1B/DH

YEAR	TEAM	LVL	AGE	PA	R	2B	3B	HR	RBI	BB	K	SB	CS	AVG/OBP/SLG	TAv	VORP	BABIP	BRR	FRAA	WARP
2014	HIC	A	19	492	46	32	0	6	63	37	107	6	3	.218/.283/.330	.226	-14.4	.270	-1.5	1B(115): -10.5 • LF(2): 0.3	-2.5
2015	HIC	A	20	104	10	3	0	3	14	6	15	2	0	.309/.346/.433	.287	3.8	.338	-0.2	1B(24): -0.5	0.3
2015	HDS	A+	20	452	54	25	7	9	73	27	101	3	0	.277/.319/.434	.257	2.0	.343	-1.2	1B(106): 0.2	0.2
2016	FRI	AA	21	416	51	16	5	15	56	33	82	2	1	.288/.348/.477	.296	16.6	.331	-2.5	1B(95): 4.0	2.2
2016	ROU	AAA	21	95	9	5	1	1	11	6	23	0	1	.216/.266/.330	.211	-5.4	.281	-1.6	1B(20): -1.6	-0.7
2017	*TEX*	*MLB*	*22*	*33*	*3*	*1*	*0*	*1*	*3*	*2*	*8*	*0*	*0*	*.225/.272/.355*	*.218*	*-0.9*	*.284*	*0.0*	*1B -0*	*-0.1*
2018	*TEX*	*MLB*	*23*	*316*	*35*	*14*	*2*	*9*	*35*	*21*	*82*	*0*	*0*	*.234/.288/.381*	*.229*	*-6.6*	*.293*	*-0.6*	*1B -2*	*-0.9*

Breakout: 3% Improve: 5% Collapse: 1% Attrition: 8% MLB: 9% *Comparables: Brandon Snyder, Russ Canzler, Nick Evans*

The Good: Sometimes, it just takes a little while for an athlete to grow into their body and be able to make all the muscles work in unison, even with diligent work. Guzman appears to finally be at that point, an exciting development for fans of giant first basemen who can do the splits. Across Double- and Triple-A this season, Guzman showed a highly improved feel for the strike zone, a better understanding of his bat, and the ability to hit for the above-average power that he'd been projected to have since

Jason Parks first wrote about him in 2012. How much power he'll have will hinge on his hit tool which could play to above-average, but is often mitigated by his length.

The Bad: He's still going to strike out a heck of a lot, and he needs another full year of seasoning before he can be an answer to the Rangers' current first-base conundrum. He's also, as I said earlier this year, "tethered to first base like an astronaut to the International Space Station." First base prospects have to hit, and hit for power, and do both consistently, or they'll get replaced with someone who's not a good defender at their original position but who does do all those things.

The Irrelevant: Guzman was the second of the Rangers' big-time bonus kids in 2011, following Nomar Mazara, but after that year, many thought he might be the better prospect.

The Risks: His upside is first base only, and while there shouldn't be any issue with him remaining there, it's a strain on roster flexibility to have a player who can only play first or DH. Additionally, the Rangers already have a big power, big kid with strikeout issues who hasn't yet overcome them at the major-league level, and the jump between the upper minors and major-league pitching is still quite a gulf.

Major league ETA: 2018 —Kate Morrison

Ben Carsley's Fantasy Take: Well C.J. Cron doesn't really have big time strikeout issues anymore so I'm sort of at a loss. If Guzman hits 20-plus homers and can muster a .260-270ish average, well, production like that would've made him a top-20ish first base play in 2016; the position really isn't as deep as it used to be. Let's hope the power ticks up and makes him a more legitimate future fantasy weapon, because as it stands right now Guzman probably isn't going to get on base quite enough to be a great play for us.

8. Cole Ragans, LHP

DOB: 12/12/1997

Height/Weight: 6'4" 190 lbs.

Bats/Throws: L/L

Drafted/Acquired: Drafted 30th Overall in the 2016 MLB Draft, North Florida Christian HS (Jacksonville, FL), signed for $2,003,400

Previous Ranking(s): N/A

2016 Stats: 4.70 ERA 7.2 IP 11 H 6 BB 9 K in 4 games at complex-level AZL

The Role: OFP 55—No. 3/4 starter
Likely 45—Back-end starter/relief arm

The Good: An athletic lefty, Ragans has a quality arsenal with remaining room for projection. He has advanced command of his fastball that was up to 95 during the summer. His ability to locate the pitch lets it play higher than its velo, and it could be a plus to plus-plus pitch in time. His curveball shows quality downer action and spin, and even when he doesn't have a great feel for it, he can still locate for strikes. You could project his changeup to average as he already has feel for it and mixed it in during his amateur career.

The Bad: While athletic, his slot, a high three-quarters to almost over the top isn't natural and creates a lot of spine tilt for extra plane. His feel for the curveball is inconsistent, and he throws a lot of spinners to the plate. His changeup is mostly projection and arm speed as there isn't a lot of movement to it.

The Irrelevant: Ragans became the highest drafted player out of North Florida Christian HS this past summer, beating out 2014 third-rounder Matt Railey.

The Risks: His control backed up on him during his initial exposure, and he needs to add weight to his body to hold up over the season. His inconsistent feel for off-speed with the high-three-quarters slot can pose some challenges down the road. Not only is he a pitcher, he is a high school pitcher.

Major league ETA: 2020 —Steve Givarz

Ben Carsley's Fantasy Take: Let's check back in 2019?

9. Josh Morgan, IF

DOB: 11/16/1995

Height/Weight: 5'11" 185 lbs.

Bats/Throws: R/R

Drafted/Acquired: Drafted 95th Overall in 2014 MLB Draft, Lutheran HS (Orange, CA); signed for $800,000

Previous Ranking(s): #7 (Org.)

2016 Stats: .300/.367/.394, 7 HR, 4 SB in 128 games at High-A High Desert

The Role: OFP 50—Second-division infield starter
Likely 40—Utility infielder

YEAR	TEAM	LVL	AGE	PA	R	2B	3B	HR	RBI	BB	K	SB	CS	AVG/OBP/SLG	TAv	VORP	BABIP	BRR	FRAA	WARP
2014	RNG	Rk	18	141	26	2	1	0	10	19	13	2	2	.336/.468/.372	.235	0.5	.380	0.5		0.1
2014	SPO	A-	18	102	11	1	0	0	9	10	10	1	1	.303/.392/.315	.280	4.9	.342	-0.6	2B(13): 0.0 • SS(10): -1.3	0.4
2015	HIC	A	19	416	59	15	1	3	36	45	53	9	4	.288/.385/.362	.298	32.6	.330	2.0	3B(50): 2.0 • SS(44): -0.6	3.6
2016	HDS	A+	20	533	74	19	2	7	64	44	61	4	2	.300/.367/.394	.264	20.0	.328	-0.3	3B(84): 1.4 • SS(29): 3.8	2.5
2017	*TEX*	*MLB*	*21*	*250*	*24*	*9*	*1*	*4*	*23*	*19*	*48*	*0*	*0*	*.243/.312/.345*	*.226*	*-0.1*	*.288*	*-0.4*	*3B -0 • SS 0*	*0.0*
2018	*TEX*	*MLB*	*22*	*408*	*46*	*15*	*1*	*7*	*40*	*31*	*74*	*0*	*0*	*.254/.322/.361*	*.238*	*0.9*	*.296*	*-0.8*	*3B 0 • SS 0*	*0.1*

Breakout: 3% Improve: 9% Collapse: 3% Attrition: 8% MLB: 16% *Comparables: Cheslor Cuthbert, Rio Ruiz, Michael Brantley*

The Good: Morgan is a natural hitter, with a compact, level stroke that sprays line drives and hard ground balls all over the yard. He goes to the plate with a plan, offering a selective approach that keeps him in the zone and limits his swing-and-miss. He's a smooth defender at second and third alike, with solid lateral agility, fluidity to the ball, and soft hands. His range is stretched at short, but he converts outs on balls he can get to and offers steady versatility on the dirt. He flirted with catching at instructs for a second consecutive season, and may get a crack at some in-game reps behind the dish in 2017.

The Bad: Despite a developed frame with some strength to it, the swing and approach severely curtails any power potential. He puts the ball on the ground a lot, and as a fringe-average runner he isn't poised to take full advantage of the profile. He'll work counts, but he wants to hit. The combination leaves his offensive value tethered entirely to his hit tool actualizing in full, and with a defensive profile that is as valuable for its breadth more than its depth, his path beyond a solid utility role on someone's bench isn't the clearest.

The Irrelevant: The race to become the third prep pick from Orange Lutheran High School to reach the majors will likely come down to Morgan and former teammate Jason Martin, drafted in the eighth round by Houston a year ahead of Morgan. Both spent full, successful seasons in the California League in 2016.

The Risks: Morgan has been pushed aggressively and responded well to date, and his solid-if-unspectacular hitting and defensive skills make him a high-floor player capable of contributing solid value to a big-league club though versatility. The frame and barrel instincts leave open the possibility of a regular role down the line, but there is significant projection to that outcome.

Major league ETA: 2019 —Wilson Karaman

Ben Carsley's Fantasy Take: As much as I rag on the current dynasty prospect landscape, we're not at the point where we need to roster utility infielders.

10. Andrew Faulkner, LHP

DOB: 09/12/1992

Height/Weight: 6'3" 200 lbs.

Bats/Throws: R/L

Drafted/Acquired: Drafted in the 14th round of the 2011 MLB Draft, South Aiken HS (Aiken, SC); signed for $125,000

Previous Ranking(s): #10 (Org.)

2016 Stats: 6.75 ERA, 5.89 DRA, 6.2 IP, 8 H, 4 BB, 1 K in 9 games at major league level, 3.97 ERA, 4.78 DRA, 45.1 IP, 39 H, 20 BB, 39 K in 41 games at Triple-A Round Rock

The Role: OFP 50—Nice late-inning bullpen piece
Likely 40—A guy that bounces between Round Rock and Arlington some more

YEAR	TEAM	LVL	AGE	W	L	SV	G	GS	IP	H	HR	BB/9	K/9	K	GB%	BABIP	WHIP	ERA	FIP	DRA	VORP	WARP	cFIP	MPH
2014	MYR	A+	21	10	1	1	21	18	104^{1}	86	1	2.7	8.6	100	46%	.298	1.12	2.07	2.70	2.31	37.70	3.8	82	
2014	FRI	AA	21	2	4	0	7	6	30^{2}	28	3	4.1	9.7	33	48%	.298	1.37	4.99	3.61	4.21	3.30	0.3	98	
2015	FRI	AA	22	7	4	1	28	15	92^{1}	84	9	4.6	8.8	90	42%	.291	1.42	4.19	4.34	3.70	13.60	1.5	106	
2015	ROU	AAA	22	0	0	0	6	0	8	2	0	1.1	14.6	13	25%	.167	0.38	0.00	0.72	1.92	2.70	0.3	77	
2015	TEX	MLB	22	0	0	0	11	0	9^{2}	8	2	2.8	9.3	10	48%	.240	1.14	2.79	4.66	4.22	0.50	0.1	98	95.6
2016	ROU	AAA	23	5	3	4	41	1	45^{1}	39	3	4.0	7.7	39	46%	.279	1.30	3.97	4.51	5.24	-1.30	-0.1	110	
2016	TEX	MLB	23	0	0	0	9	0	23	8	3	5.4	1.4	1	41%	.208	1.80	6.75	10.45	6.62	-1.2	-0.1	122	94.6
2017	*TEX*	*MLB*	*24*	*1*	*1*	*0*	*19*	*0*	20^{1}	*21*	*2*	*4.0*	*6.6*	*15*	*40%*	*.293*	*1.46*	*4.67*	*4.46*	*4.80*	*0.5*	*0.0*	*100*	
2018	*TEX*	*MLB*	*25*	*2*	*1*	*0*	*31*	*0*	32^{2}	*29*	*3*	*5.7*	*9.4*	*34*	*40%*	*.298*	*1.53*	*4.54*	*4.54*	*4.91*	*0.5*	*0.1*	*110*	

Breakout: 22%   Improve: 30%   Collapse: 16%   Attrition: 34%   MLB: 52%   *Comparables: Zach Phillips, Juan Morillo, Yoervis Medina*

The Good: He's lefthanded! He has some nice pitches! He has a deceptive delivery that lets him make the most of both of the previous two things! Faulkner relies on a sinking fastball, a fringy changeup, and a solid breaking ball to get his outs, and releases all of his pitches similarly, giving a hitter a indistinguishable look out of the hand.

The Bad: While Faulkner's first stop in the major leagues was by all accounts a success, he regressed in 2016, struggling to record outs at the beginning of the season and being demoted to Triple-A. A September outing showed some improvement, but he'll need to prove that he can handle major-league bats consistently to be a contender for 2017 bullpen innings.

The Irrelevant: It's a shade under three hours from Round Rock to Globe Park, assuming normal traffic.

The Risks: He's a lefty (pitcher) without a consistent out pitch, and big-league batters are really good at their jobs.

Major league ETA: Debuted in 2015. —Kate Morrison

Ben Carsley's Fantasy Take: If you really want to ruin Faulkner just go see James Franco's As I Lay Dying.

OTHERS OF NOTE:

The big fastball

Connor Sadzeck, RHP

Connor Sadzeck may yet be due a breakout year, but time is ticking away on the big right-hander's chance to remain a legitimate starting candidate. A big dude with a big fastball, Sadzeck has the raw stuff (in his last game of 2016, he hit 100 in the sixth inning) that would make one think he could blow any hitter away, but the lack of both deception and life on the pitch means that incoming velocity is alarmingly likely to turn into exit velocity. He complements that fastball with his best pitch, a curveball he can manipulate the depth on when he has a good handle on it, and augments that with a changeup that has shown some improvement, but is still far and away his weakest pitch. Sadezck's biggest struggles in his two years at Double-A Frisco are with consistency, finding the upper-middle point between dominating a lineup and letting everything get hit. If he can't show some improvement in that area, expect Texas to move him to the bullpen sooner rather than later, and see what use he can get out of the massive fastball with fewer innings to concentrate on. —Kate Morrison

*The guy we *think* is going to be 22 on Christmas*

Jairo Beras, OF

Beras is a physical specimen who sticks right on out from the crowd, with length and wiry strength for days. His 6-foot-6 frame is by no means done maturing, and he already possesses plus raw power with the leverage and swing plane to take advantage of it. Unfortunately, he still lacks much in the way of an approach to see it actualize consistently in games at present. A noisy launch, poor timing, and raw pitch recognition all conspire to hold down the hit tool and, with it, the game power. He made some progress this year in refining his plan of attack, particularly in hitting counts, where he became more selectively aggressive. He boasts a surprising first gear for a man of his dimensions, and the raw speed sits a tick above average right now. The routes are inefficient at present, and he's still learning how to harness his size into coordinated track-and-close efforts. You can see the raw ingredients of a power-hitting right fielder, but they're still strewn about the kitchen counter. —Wilson Karaman

The Future Manager

Jose Trevino, C

If we handed out grades for field generalship, Trevino would rate at least a 70 with rumblings of a true future 80. He was the heartbeat of the California League champions at High Desert, setting the club's tone with his intensity and leadership behind the dish. All of the intangibles you look for in a catching prospect are present in Trevino, and the tangibles ain't bad either. He offers a nice blend of size and agility, and the defensive package is excellent across the board: He goes and gets balls in the dirt, the framing work is solid, and he controls the running game (48 percent caught-stealing) with sound technique and an above-average arm. He's a highly aggressive hitter in the zone, with quality bat-to-ball skills in spite of some length to his swing, and there's some nascent power to all fields. The bat will determine whether he develops into an average regular or not, but even if the stick winds up a little light Trevino is a high-probability guy to find big-league work for a long time as a quality backup catcher. —Wilson Karaman

The lottery ticket

Kyle Roberts, LHP

A fifth-rounder in this past draft, Roberts has three really good things going for him:

1. He's 6-foot-6.
2. He's left-handed.
3. He has touched 98 and sits 91-94.

While those are all really good, there are a lot of hurdles for him to overcome. His slider can flash plus, but is incredibly inconsistent at this point. His changeup is sparsely used and like other young players he needs to gain feel for the offering. He struggles to maintain the mechanics in his delivery and is quite lean, so he needs to add muscle. The upside here is tremendous; a potential no.3 starter or late-inning arm, but this is a long-term project who needs coaching and time to blossom. —Steve Givarz

TOP 10 TALENTS 25 AND UNDER (BORN 4/1/91 OR LATER)

1. Nomar Mazara	6. Yohander Mendez
2. Rougned Odor	7. Ariel Jurado
3. Joey Gallo	8. Leody Taveras
4. Jurickson Profar	9. Anderson Tejeda
5. Martin Perez	10. Chi Chi Gonzalez

Nomar Mazara had one of the quieter graduations you'll see from a global top-five prospect in 2016, neither failing nor making huge noise. He was just about average in every facet of the game, which sounds like a knock, but the dude got called up at 20. Being major-league average in a season that contains your 21st birthday while having huge offensive tools and getting constant praise for your makeup is a sign that you're a potential superstar.

Rougned Odor often gets criticized for what he can't do, which is walk. I'm reminded here of the old Up and In credo that overlooking hitting ability to focus on walk rate can be misguided. And Rougned Odor is turning into an extra base machine while playing quality defense at second. That's a very good player even if he's only walking 20 or 25 times a year.

For awhile, it looked like Joey Gallo was going to stay just under the at-bat threshold we use to determine prospect eligibility, and regain his spot as Texas's top prospect. But the Rangers clinched the division a little early, so Adrian Beltre took a few extra days off, and thus Gallo finished with four at-bats too many to still be a prospect. This saved us some big internal arguments over his placement in the 101. The combination of Beltre's extension and Mitch Moreland's departure should leave Gallo as the starting first baseman, which is a bit of a waste of his second 80 tool (arm) but at least should give him regular at-bats to let the first 80 tool (power) shine.

Yes, Jurickson Profar and Martin Perez are still eligible for this list. No, I'm not sure how either, but I checked the birthdays and that's what they say. After a month-and-a-half reestablishing his ability to play shortstop regularly in Triple-A, Profar returned to the majors in largely the same super-utility role he'd played in 2013. It was a mixed bag. Like Gallo, Profar could use a regular position and playing time. Unlike Gallo, that remains unlikely with the Rangers running out star players at Profar's three most plausible positions. Perez, eligible here by just a handful of days, has settled in as a solid mid-rotation arm, the current third starter that the Rangers are constantly trying (without success) to demote to a fourth starter.

Chi Chi Gonzalez just makes the back of this list over Delino DeShields and Alex Claudio. Chi Chi struggled in 2016 in both the majors and minors, yet the potential on his sinker/slider combination that made him our 29th-ranked prospect in baseball just two years ago still remains. There's a chance left for success here, but he's running out of time.

—Jarrett Seidler

TORONTO BLUE JAYS

The State of the System: *Almost everyone on the 2015 list either graduated or got dealt. That's what happens when a team is gunning for its first flag in decades.*

THE TOP TEN

1. RHP Sean Reid-Foley	6. SS Richard Urena
2. OF Anthony Alford	7. RHP T.J. Zeuch
3. 3B Vladimir Guerrero, Jr.	8. 1B Rowdy Tellez
4. RHP Conner Greene	9. C Max Pentecost
5. RHP Jonathan Harris	10. SS Bo Bichette

The Big Question: What the heck are we supposed to do with Lourdes Gurriel?

You write and compile enough of these lists and you get a feel for the various prospect "types;" the plus fastball fourth starter with not much else, the 91-95 with a slider relief arm, the plus power and big swing-and-miss first baseman, the toolsy shortstop a ways away, the potential tweener outfielder. You mentally catalog them. You like some in the categories better than others. You like some categories better than others. None of these are the elite guys. Those are the easy ranks.

Even in a system not as flat in talent at the top as the Blue Jays—most systems, really— the difference between your fifth-best prospect (your plus fastball fourth starter) and your tenth-best prospect (the toolsy shortstop a ways away) isn't going to be significant. It's within the fudge factor. Lourdes Gurriel is better than the fifth prospect in this system. I think.

I'm supposed to have a more specific answer to this, right? It's literally my job. I made a joke about it in the intro to our lists. All I have to do is give you ordinal rankings. I can't even use the Yu Darvish or Jose Abreu cards. It's likely Gurriel will need at least some minor league time. More than a perfunctory few weeks like his older brother. He's a prospect by our standards. I think.

The Blue Jays have indicated they plan to start him at shortstop for now. He's played there, along with some second, first, and a bit of outfield. He was one of the best players in the Serie Nacional in 2015, his last season there. The league is usually compared to Advanced-A. A 21-year-old—probably not a shortstop—mashing in the Carolina League gets your attention. That could be Yoan Moncada, but it could be Max Schrock. And Gurriel specifically is tougher to pin down because he doesn't have huge tools. He's not popping a 45-inch vertical and then roasting a pig on YouTube. He plays well in games, but doesn't shine in showcases. And we don't know how quickly or how well he'll be able to play in major league games. He hasn't played in any games in a full year.

What do I think?

I don't think he's a shortstop, although I see no harm in trying him there. I expected him to get more than $22 million. That probably means something. I guess the play here is something like OFP 55/Likely 45, maybe at second base, probably other positions as well at the low end, certainly high risk either way. But it still feels like a dart throw. I'm sure I've ranked prospects like Gurriel already in this process. I'm just not sure which ones.

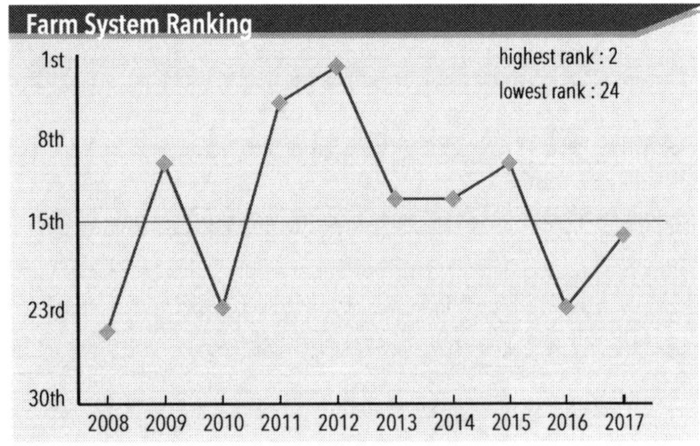

Personnel

President:
Mark Shapiro

General Manager:
Ross Atkins

VP, Baseball Operations:
Ben Cherington

Assistant General Manager:
Tony LaCava

Assistant General Manager:
Andrew Tinnish

Assistant General Manager:
Joe Sheehan

Manager:
John Gibbons

BP Alumni:
Matt Bishoff
Dan Evans

1. Sean Reid-Foley, RHP

DOB: 8/30/1995

Height/Weight: 6'3" 220 lbs

Bats/Throws: R/R

Drafted/Acquired: Drafted 49th overall in the 2014 draft, Sandalwood HS (Jacksonville, FL); signed for $1.1288 million

2016 Stats: 2.95 ERA, 3.44 DRA, 58 IP, 43 H, 22 BB, 59 K in 11 games at Low-A Lansing, 2.67 ERA, 1.33 DRA, 57.1, 35 H, 16 BB, 71 K in 10 games at High-A Dunedin

The Role: OFP 55—Low-end no. 3 starter
Likely 50—No. 4 starter or 8th inning arm

YEAR	TEAM	LVL	AGE	W	L	SV	G	GS	IP	H	HR	BB/9	K/9	K	GB%	BABIP	WHIP	ERA	FIP	DRA	VORP	WARP	cFIP	MPH
2014	BLJ	Rk	18	1	2	0	9	6	22^2	21	0	4.0	9.9	25	0%	.339	1.37	4.76	2.75	2.83			86	
2015	DUN	A+	19	1	5	0	8	8	32^2	25	1	6.6	9.6	35	45%	.279	1.50	5.23	3.81	7.91	-10.30	-1.1	120	
2015	LNS	A	19	3	5	0	17	17	63^1	57	3	6.1	12.8	90	46%	.355	1.58	3.69	3.44	2.37	20.10	2.1	93	
2016	LNS	A	20	4	3	0	11	11	58	43	2	3.4	9.2	59	52%	.277	1.12	2.95	3.08	3.24	11.40	1.3	92	
2016	DUN	A+	20	6	2	0	10	10	57^1	35	2	2.5	11.1	71	49%	.254	0.89	2.67	2.12	1.04	28.30	2.9	63	
2017	*TOR*	*MLB*	*21*	*5*	*6*	*0*	*19*	*19*	*85*	*88*	*12*	*5.4*	*7.1*	*67*	*39%*	*.296*	*1.64*	*5.38*	*5.32*	*5.60*	*-1.2*	*-0.1*	*133*	
2018	*TOR*	*MLB*	*22*	*6*	*8*	*0*	*24*	*24*	*141*	*130*	*21*	*6.6*	*9.7*	*152*	*39%*	*.297*	*1.65*	*5.37*	*5.28*	*5.59*	*-1.4*	*-0.1*	*133*	

Breakout: 11% Improve: 16% Collapse: 1% Attrition: 8% MLB: 17% *Comparables: Jose Berrios, Keyvius Sampson, Danny Duffy*

The Good: Reid-Foley's fastball grades out as plus, sitting 92-94, and up to 97 in shorter spurts, and he controls the pitch well. He features a pair of breaking balls, a potential above-average slider with good tilt and bite, and a potential average curveball with 11/5 shape and fair action. His frame is built to log innings and still has some physical projection remaining. His delivery has been simplified in order to throw more strikes.

The Bad: His durability hasn't been the best; missing time in the past three seasons with various injuries. He cups his hand over the ball, which can lead to some inconsistencies with the breaking balls. His arm action is compact but messy, further putting his rotation potential in question. His changeup is almost a non-factor right now as he struggles with his feel for it. He's more of a control than command guy at present.

The Irrelevant: It's a battle between Reid-Foley, and Trae Santos as to who will become the second major leaguer born from Guam; they would join former Blue Jay John Hattig, who debuted in 2006.

The Risks: Reid-Foley has questions about his rotation potential given his arm action, his command, lack of changeup, and durability. This was the first year for him consistently throwing strikes, and it remains to be seen if those gains will come forward.

Major league ETA: 2018 —Steve Givarz

Ben Carsley's Fantasy Take: Ah yes, the vaunted Blue Jays-Guam pipeline. I've liked Reid-Foley for a while, but in the end his durability issues, lack of premium upside, and potential hitter-friendly home of Toronto put a serious cap on his fantasy value. He's just starting to enter the national consciousness as a good prospect so you can pop him if your league rosters 150 prospects, but don't get carried away just because he tops the Blue Jays list here.

2. Anthony Alford, CF

DOB: 7/20/1994

Height/Weight: 6'1" 205 lbs

Bats/Throws: R/R

Drafted/Acquired: Drafted in the third round of the 2012 draft, Petal HS (Petal, MS); signed for $750,000

Previous Ranking(s): #1 (Org.), #44 (Overall)

2016 Stats: .236/.344/.378, 9 HR, 18 SB in 92 games at High-A Dunedin

The Role: OFP 55—Above-average regular in CF
Likely 50—Average regular in the OF

YEAR	TEAM	LVL	AGE	PA	R	2B	3B	HR	RBI	BB	K	SB	CS	AVG/OBP/SLG	TAv	VORP	BABIP	BRR	FRAA	WARP
2014	BLU	Rk	19	35	5	0	0	1	2	5	13	1	0	.207/.343/.310	.235	0.3	.333	0.2		-0.1
2014	LNS	A	19	25	3	1	0	1	3	0	8	4	0	.320/.320/.480	.287	2.2	.438	0.8	CF(4): -0.5	0.2
2015	LNS	A	20	232	49	14	1	1	16	39	60	12	1	.293/.418/.394	.287	19.7	.419	6.5	CF(47): -4.7	1.7
2015	DUN	A+	20	255	42	11	6	3	19	28	49	15	6	.302/.380/.444	.299	21.3	.374	4.1	CF(55): -0.4	2.4
2016	DUN	A+	21	401	53	17	2	9	44	53	117	18	6	.236/.344/.378	.261	15.0	.327	2.3	CF(84): 1.6 • LF(6): 1.6	1.6
2017	*TOR*	*MLB*	*22*	*250*	*31*	*10*	*1*	*6*	*23*	*28*	*80*	*7*	*2*	*.219/.312/.359*	*.232*	*2.4*	*.311*	*0.3*	*CF 2 • RF 0*	*0.5*
2018	*TOR*	*MLB*	*23*	*336*	*39*	*14*	*2*	*8*	*35*	*38*	*108*	*9*	*3*	*.219/.313/.361*	*.235*	*1.1*	*.313*	*0.8*	*CF 2 • RF 0*	*0.4*

Breakout: 1% Improve: 18% Collapse: 0% Attrition: 12% MLB: 34% *Comparables: Michael Saunders, Brett Jackson, Chris Young*

The Good: Alford has an impressive, athletic body, one that looks like it can still play on a football field. A double-plus runner, his speed is a weapon both on the bases and in the field. A potential above-average defender in center, Alford makes good reads and covers ground extremely well. At the plate his plus bat speed, paired with a smooth, line-drive stroke allows him to cover the zone and square up pitches.

The Bad: Alford did catch the injury bug last year, missing most of the season with a dislocated right kneecap, as well as a concussion. While smooth, that line-drive swing is flat and doesn't produce much power, and might not play higher than below average at full utility. His outfield routes aren't the most consistent as he uses his speed to help make up for his mistakes. His base-running ability is still rather raw as he needs to take better advantage of jumps and reads.

The Irrelevant: Anthony Alford played in the US Army All American bowl as a high school quarterback.

The Risks: Injuries hit Alford hard, missing almost two months of the season when he needed a lot of development time. The hit tool lags behind and becomes more of a defensive replacement/fourth outfielder than everyday player. He hasn't been tested at the higher-levels.

Major league ETA: 2018 —Steve Givarz

Ben Carsley's Fantasy Take: The top fantasy prospect in the system, Alford's stock took a hit in 2016 but he's still a borderline top-100 dynasty prospect. His plus-plus speed will be of immediate interest as soon as he makes the majors, though his hit tool will determine whether Alford will be more of the 20-steal or 30-steal outfielder variety. If it all goes well, Alford could end up looking something like 2015 Delino Deshields, hitting .260 with 20-plus steals and a few bombs to settle in as a solid OF4. If Alford's hit tool doesn't take a step forward, he's more of the 2016 Travis Jankowski type, which is actually still somewhat usable if you're in a 16-team league.

3. Vladimir Guerrero, Jr., 3B

DOB: 3/16/1999

Height/Weight:.6'1" 210 lbs

Bats/Throws: R/R

Drafted/Acquired: Signed by the Blue Jays in July 2015 out of the Dominican Republic for $3.9 million

Previous Ranking(s): #5 (Org.)

2016 Stats: .271/.359/.449, 8 HR, 15 SB in 62 games at short-season Bluefield

The Role: OFP 60—Above-average major league first baseman
Likely 45—Second-division starter at first base

YEAR	TEAM	LVL	AGE	PA	R	2B	3B	HR	RBI	BB	K	SB	CS	AVG/OBP/SLG	TAv	VORP	BABIP	BRR	FRAA	WARP
2016	BLU	Rk	17	276	32	12	3	8	46	33	35	15	5	.271/.359/.449	.294	20.0	.283	1.5	3B(50): -10.4	1.0
2017	*TOR*	*MLB*	*18*	*250*	*24*	*10*	*1*	*6*	*26*	*18*	*73*	*4*	*2*	*.208/.266/.339*	*.205*	*-6.6*	*.273*	*-0.1*	*3B -4*	*-1.1*
2018	*TOR*	*MLB*	*19*	*260*	*28*	*11*	*1*	*7*	*27*	*18*	*77*	*4*	*2*	*.210/.265/.351*	*.213*	*-6.7*	*.273*	*0.0*	*3B -4*	*-1.1*

Breakout: 0% Improve: 0% Collapse: 0% Attrition: 0% MLB: 0% *Comparables: Raul Mondesi, Wilmer Flores*

The Good: He doesn't look like his father, and putting a Hall of Fame comp on him, bloodlines or no, would be irresponsible. However you'd be forgiven, if you caught Vladito on the right day, for seeing a bit of the same controlled violence that marked his father's swing. He already has plus raw as a teenager, and it isn't hard to see him finding another grade of raw as he enters his twenties. He has enough feel for the barrel, even when swinging out of his shoes like his pops, to make the power play in games too.

The Bad: I do wonder if he rates as highly on this list with a different last name, although baseball bloodlines can be important. I guess you can dream big and imagine Vlad, Jr. one day hitting like his father, but that is where the comp will have to end. He's already a large human being, with a very thick midsection and lower half. At 17. He's likely a first baseman in the end and that will put an awful lot of pressure on the offensive profile to have a strong patrilineal influence. The stolen bases are more an artifact of every Tom, Dick, and Vladdy being able to steal in the low minors. He's already a below-average runner.

The Irrelevant: Vlad's baseball family is almost as prolific as Gory's pro wrestling clan at this point. In addition to Vlad Jr., nephews Gregory Guerrero and Gabby Guerrero are both kicking around the minors, Gregory with the Mets, and Gabby with the Diamondbacks.

The Risks: Vladito's precocious performance as a 17-year-old in the Appalachian League is nice and all, but he's still a future first baseman in short-season ball. This could go any which way in the coming years.

Major league ETA: 2021

Ben Carsley's Fantasy Take: It's disappointing to learn that Guerrero is so unlikely to stick at third base. You know how I feel about fantasy first basemen, after all. Guerrero's offensive upside remains decent enough that he might sneak onto a top-150 list, but he's likely to be overvalued due to his name, as mentioned above. That makes him a good sell-high candidate if you own him, because waiting four-plus seasons for a non-elite first baseman just isn't worth it.

4. Conner Greene, RHP

DOB: 4/4/1995

Height/Weight: 6'3" 165 lbs

Bats/Throws: R/R

Drafted/Acquired: Drafted in the seventh round of the 2013 draft, Santa Monica HS (Santa Monica, CA); signed for for $100,000

Previous Ranking(s): #2 (Org.), #100 (Overall)

2016 Stats: 2.90 ERA, 6.94 DRA, 77.2 IP, 74 H, 38 BB, 51 K in 15 games at High-A Dunedin, 4.19 ERA, 5.79 DRA, 68.2 IP, 57 H, 33 BB, 48 K in 12 games at Double-A New Hampshire

The Role: OFP 55—Low-end mid rotation arm/high-end late inning reliever
Likely 50—Cromulent 8th inning guy

YEAR	TEAM	LVL	AGE	W	L	SV	G	GS	IP	H	HR	BB/9	K/9	K	GB%	BABIP	WHIP	ERA	FIP	DRA	VORP	WARP	cFIP	MPH
2014	BLJ	Rk	19	2	2	0	7	4	31^{2}	25	2	1.7	8.5	30	0%	.271	0.98	1.99	3.09	2.70			84	
2014	BLU	Rk	19	1	2	0	6	5	27^{2}	26	1	3.9	6.8	21	0%	.298	1.37	4.23	3.93	6.33			109	
2015	LNS	A	20	7	3	0	14	14	67^{1}	75	4	2.5	8.7	65	38%	.364	1.40	3.88	3.22	3.29	14.50	1.5	96	
2015	DUN	A+	20	2	3	0	7	7	40	36	1	1.8	7.9	35	55%	.297	1.10	2.25	2.34	2.39	12.00	1.3	83	
2015	NHP	AA	20	3	1	0	5	5	25	25	1	4.3	5.4	15	55%	.304	1.48	4.68	4.15	6.64	-4.30	-0.5	115	
2016	DUN	A+	21	4	4	0	15	15	77^{2}	74	5	4.4	5.9	51	53%	.283	1.44	2.90	4.36	5.89	-3.60	-0.4	112	
2016	NHP	AA	21	6	5	0	12	12	68^{2}	57	5	4.3	6.3	48	50%	.256	1.31	4.19	4.48	6.49	-10.60	-1.1	114	
2017	*TOR*	*MLB*	*22*	*6*	*9*	*0*	*23*	*23*	115^{1}	*133*	*19*	*4.9*	*4.9*	*63*	*44%*	*.296*	*1.70*	*5.99*	*5.96*	*6.31*	*-10.8*	*-1.1*	*149*	
2018	*TOR*	*MLB*	*23*	*3*	*6*	*0*	*14*	*14*	79^{2}	*81*	*12*	*6.8*	*8.2*	*73*	*44%*	*.303*	*1.77*	*5.94*	*5.84*	*6.26*	*-6.0*	*-0.6*	*147*	

Breakout: 7% Improve: 12% Collapse: 1% Attrition: 9% MLB: 17% *Comparables: Matt Harrison, Joe Ross, Zach Phillips*

The Good: Greene has big arm speed and a big fastball. He sits in the mid-90s as a starter and can ratchet it up higher. It's a heavy pitch, and he has had success spotting it down in the zone. The changeup is advanced and flashes plus with good velocity separation, fade, and sink. There could still be a bit more projection in the frame.

The Bad: There is just enough effort in the delivery, and just enough commensurate control issues to make you think that Greene is better suited in a late-inning role. The second pitch being the changeup makes the relief profile a little more unusual—and unusual profiles can mean unusual risks—but the fastball is good enough that it doesn't worry me all that much, and the curveball isn't a non-factor and could play up in short bursts. His slot can wander on the secondaries as well.

The Irrelevant: Can confirm that your Senior Prospect Writer demanded we keep the same Greene headshot this year. Why? Just look at it.

The Risks: It's a plus-plus fastball and potential plus change. That gets you to the majors if nothing else, even in this era of high velocity. The command/control issues put a bit of a damper on the party, and may force Greene into relief, but he's still a major-league arm in that role, and the profile might even play up past the OFP with a bump from the pen move. Or he could get hurt, because he's a pitcher.

Major league ETA: Early 2018, could be up late this year as a pen arm

Ben Carsley's Fantasy Take: A low-end mid-rotation arm in Toronto whose future may very well come in relief? Nah. Nah, I say.

5. Jon Harris, RHP

DOB: 10/16/1993

Height/Weight: 6'3" 160 lbs

Bats/Throws: R/R

Drafted/Acquired: Drafted 29th overall in the 2015 draft, Missouri State University (MO); signed for $1.9448 million

Previous Ranking(s): #3 (Org.)

2016 Stats: 2.23 ERA, 4.23 DRA, 84.2 IP, 74 H, 24 BB, 73 K in 16 games at Low-A Lansing, 3.60 ERA, 5.44 DRA, 45 IP, 37 H, 14 BB, 26 K in 8 games at High-A Dunedin

The Role: OFP 55—Low-end mid-rotation arm
Likely 50—League average innings muncher

YEAR	TEAM	LVL	AGE	W	L	SV	G	GS	IP	H	HR	BB/9	K/9	K	GB%	BABIP	WHIP	ERA	FIP	DRA	VORP	WARP	cFIP	MPH
2015	VAN	A-	21	0	5	0	12	11	36	48	1	5.2	8.0	32	43%	.388	1.92	6.75	4.02	6.47	-4.90	-0.5	116	
2016	LNS	A	22	8	2	0	16	16	84^{2}	74	1	2.6	7.8	73	50%	.296	1.16	2.23	2.93	4.21	7.60	0.8	97	
2016	DUN	A+	22	3	2	0	8	8	45	37	2	2.8	5.2	26	51%	.252	1.13	3.60	3.67	4.70	3.90	0.4	106	
2017	*TOR*	*MLB*	*23*	*5*	*7*	*0*	*18*	*18*	85^{1}	*105*	*16*	*4.9*	*4.1*	*39*	*40%*	*.299*	*1.78*	*6.39*	*6.40*	*6.63*	*-11.0*	*-1.1*	*159*	
2018	*TOR*	*MLB*	*24*	*5*	*10*	*0*	*23*	*23*	*136*	*147*	*24*	*6.5*	*7.0*	*105*	*40%*	*.297*	*1.80*	*6.30*	*6.21*	*6.54*	*-13.2*	*-1.4*	*156*	

Breakout: 2% Improve: 2% Collapse: 0% Attrition: 2% MLB: 2% *Comparables: Joseph Colon, Justin Marks, Ryan Cook*

The Good: There's nothing that will jump out at you in Harris's arsenal, but he offers a full four-pitch mix with a potential plus fastball with some armside hop. Harris can run the heater up into the mid-90s and works comfortably 92-94. All three of his secondaries have a chance to be average or better. The slider can get flat and cutter-like at times, but Harris can also get it up over 90. The curve is a 12-6 breaker from his high three-quarters slot, could be an out pitch for him, but the feel is inconsistent and it can roll and show early. He has a starter's frame and mechanics.

The Bad: The change is the fourth pitch here, and although it flashes average with some tumble and run, it's too often firm. The control outpaces the command at present. Needs to throw more good strikes with the fastball. The secondaries all have a chance to be average or better, but there isn't much more in the future profile than that—we weren't kidding about all the 55s—and they still have a ways to go to get there. Despite his lean frame, there isn't much more projection in the body if you were betting on that off the listed height and weight.

The Irrelevant: Harris didn't get out of the first inning of his first start in Lansing this season. He was pretty good after that though.

The Risks: It's a very average risk profile. He hasn't pitched in Double-A yet, but there's enough stuff and pitchability here to have some immediate success at the level. The command needs to tighten up, but we think it probably will. Oh, and he's a pitcher, but that part will never change.

Major league ETA: 2018

Ben Carsley's Fantasy Take: A low-end mid-rotation arm in Toronto who's not even knocking on the doorstep of the majors yet? Nah. Nah, I say.

6. Richard Urena, SS

DOB: 2/26/1996

Height/Weight: 6'1" 170 lbs

Bats/Throws: S/R

Drafted/Acquired: Signed by the Blue Jays in July 2012 out of the Dominican Republic for $725,000

Previous Ranking(s): #7 (Org.)

2016 Stats: .305/.351/.447, 8 HR, 9 SB in in 97 games at High-A Dunedin, .266/.282/.395, 0 HR, 0 SB in 30 games at Double-A New Hampshire

The Role: OFP 55—Above-average regular at SS
Likely 50—Regular at multiple positions

YEAR	TEAM	LVL	AGE	PA	R	2B	3B	HR	RBI	BB	K	SB	CS	AVG/OBP/SLG	TAv	VORP	BABIP	BRR	FRAA	WARP
2014	BLU	Rk	18	237	35	15	2	2	20	16	51	5	4	.318/.363/.433	.288	22.5	.406	1.6		2.5
2014	VAN	A-	18	37	3	2	1	0	5	3	5	1	0	.242/.297/.364	.261	1.2	.276	0.0	2B(5): -0.2 • 3B(3): -0.9	0.0
2015	DUN	A+	19	128	9	3	1	1	8	3	26	3	1	.250/.268/.315	.228	0.9	.309	0.0	SS(30): -2.6	-0.2
2015	LNS	A	19	408	62	13	4	15	58	13	84	5	5	.266/.289/.438	.254	15.7	.299	1.9	SS(90): -9.4	0.7
2016	DUN	A+	20	431	52	18	7	8	41	25	64	9	6	.305/.351/.447	.266	17.0	.346	-1.3	SS(79): 0.1	1.8
2016	NHP	AA	20	132	14	6	5	0	18	4	19	0	2	.266/.282/.395	.256	5.3	.306	0.7	SS(29): -0.8	0.5
2017	*TOR*	*MLB*	*21*	*250*	*28*	*10*	*3*	*8*	*27*	*8*	*61*	*1*	*1*	*.240/.268/.402*	*.221*	*1.1*	*.287*	*-0.1*	*SS -2*	*-0.1*
2018	*TOR*	*MLB*	*22*	*357*	*39*	*15*	*4*	*11*	*42*	*15*	*86*	*2*	*2*	*.242/.276/.408*	*.229*	*0.9*	*.288*	*-0.2*	*SS -3*	*-0.2*

Breakout: 6% Improve: 8% Collapse: 1% Attrition: 8% MLB: 12% *Comparables: Chris Owings, Nick Franklin, Yamaico Navarro*

The Good: A switch-hitter, Urena has above-average bat speed from both sides, with an aggressive approach and quick hands. He has good bat-to-ball ability and can spray towards the whole field. His plus arm plays well at shortstop with good carry and strength. While an average runner down the line, he has a good second gear and flies around the base-paths. Has present strength to put a charge into baseballs with considerable loft. He reads balls well at short with good lateral range to both sides and instincts.

The Bad: Urena lacks body control while at short, as he can rush and not be in the best position to play hops. He also has struggled with his backhand at times. While he has strength, there isn't much physical projection left, which could limit his power to below-average. While he has a plus arm, his accuracy suffers when he rushes his throws. His swing from the right side is longer and can cut himself off. He can get overly aggressive at the plate and sells out for power. He is just an average runner down the line.

The Irrelevant: On August 10, Urena set a New Hampshire record with three triples in one game.

The Risks: Urena is still very young, and didn't do that well in his first foray in Double-A. He has raw defensive skills that might not play at the six down the road. His aggressive approach could leave him vulnerable to better stuff at the higher levels, which means he might not hit enough for an everyday role at short.

Major league ETA: 2018 —Steve Givarz

Ben Carsley's Fantasy Take: If you're going to gamble on a raw player, you might as well gamble on a shortstop. Urena lacks any standout fantasy tool, but if he can stick at short the bar is fairly low, albeit higher than it was a few seasons ago. He might not be as closer to seeing regular MLB playing time as his position in Double-A would have you believe, but Urena could be a solid across-the-board contributor in the middle infield by late 2019 or 2020. Pick him up and hope you landed Asdrubal Cabrera.

7. T.J. Zeuch, RHP

DOB: 8/1/1995

Height/Weight: 6'7" 225 lbs.

Bats/Throws: R/R

Drafted/Acquired: Drafted 21st overall in the 2016 MLB Draft, University of Pittsburgh (PA); signed for $2.175 million

Previous Ranking(s): N/A

2016 Stats: 0.00 ERA, 0.00 DRA, 3 IP, 0 H, 0 BB, 2 K in 1 game at the Gulf Coast League, 3.52 ERA, 2.51 DRA, 23 IP, 21 H, 5 BB, 22 K in 6 games at short-season Vancouver, 9.00 ERA, 1.98 DRA, 8 IP, 10 H, 2 BB, 14 K in 2 games at Low-A Lansing

The Role: OFP 55—Good no.4 starter
Likely 45—Good no. 5 starter

YEAR	TEAM	LVL	AGE	W	L	SV	G	GS	IP	H	HR	BB/9	K/9	K	GB%	BABIP	WHIP	ERA	FIP	DRA	VORP	WARP	cFIP	MPH
2016	VAN	A-	20	0	1	0	6	6	23	21	1	2.0	8.6	22	70%	.317	1.13	3.52	3.08	2.40	7.30	0.8	82	
2016	LNS	A	20	0	1	0	2	2	8	10	1	2.2	15.8	14	65%	.474	1.50	9.00	3.48	1.91	2.80	0.3	77	
2017	*TOR*	*MLB*	*21*	*2*	*2*	*0*	*8*	*8*	*32^{2}*	*37*	*5*	*4.4*	*6.0*	*22*	*57%*	*.308*	*1.63*	*5.23*	*5.41*	*5.41*	*0.2*	*0.0*	*129*	
2018	*TOR*	*MLB*	*22*	*6*	*8*	*0*	*27*	*27*	*161^{2}*	*163*	*20*	*4.8*	*8.2*	*147*	*57%*	*.306*	*1.54*	*4.79*	*4.70*	*4.95*	*6.6*	*0.7*	*118*	

Breakout: 2% Improve: 2% Collapse: 0% Attrition: 1% MLB: 2% *Comparables: Carl Edwards Jr, Nick Tropeano, Wilking Rodriguez*

The Good: Zeuch is a bit of an odd duck, a very tall righty with a pretty easy delivery and generally repeatable mechanics. The fastball is in the low 90s at present, but he gets some plane from his height and slot, and there could be more velocity in there as he touched 97 in college. Zeuch has an advanced curveball with good 11-5 shape. He can throw strikes with his full four-pitch mix.

The Bad: The stuff isn't that sexy, and it is unlikely to get much sexier. The slider and change are below-average at present. He can struggle with "tall pitcher syndrome" at times, not always finishing his delivery, which can lead to command issues.

The Irrelevant: T.J.'s father, Tim played two games with the Victoria Mussels, but missed being teammates with Bill Murray by a couple seasons.

The Risks: Zeuch is a polished college arm that should move up the organizational ladder quickly. There isn't a ton of ceiling, and the usual pitcher risks apply, but I also don't see the profile really being challenged until the highest level of the minors, if even then.

Major league ETA: Late 2018

Ben Carsley's Fantasy Take: A low-end mid-rotation arm in Toronto who's not even knocking on the doorstep of the majors yet? This is the worst remake of Groundhog Day ever.

8. Rowdy Tellez, 1B

DOB: 3/16/1995

Height/Weight: 6'4" 245 lbs

Bats/Throws: L/L

Drafted/Acquired: Drafted in the 30th round, 2013 draft, out of Elk Grove HS (CA); signed for $850,000

Previous Ranking(s): #8 (Org.)

2016 Stats: .297/.387/.530, 23 HR, 4 SB in 124 games at Double-A New Hampshire

The Role: OFP 55—Everyday bopper at first
Likely 45—Second-division starter/lefty power bat off the bench

YEAR	TEAM	LVL	AGE	PA	R	2B	3B	HR	RBI	BB	K	SB	CS	AVG/OBP/SLG	TAv	VORP	BABIP	BRR	FRAA	WARP
2014	BLU	Rk	19	218	26	11	1	4	36	19	27	3	2	.293/.358/.424	.289	12.0	.315	2.3		0.5
2014	LNS	A	19	49	6	0	0	2	7	7	10	0	0	.357/.449/.500	.369	6.5	.433	0.3	1B(8): -0.1	0.7
2015	LNS	A	20	299	36	19	0	7	49	24	56	2	2	.296/.351/.444	.290	7.7	.346	-4.4	1B(51): 2.0	1.0
2015	DUN	A+	20	148	17	5	0	7	28	14	28	3	0	.275/.338/.473	.275	4.2	.293	0.6	1B(24): 0.7	0.5
2016	NHP	AA	21	514	71	29	2	23	81	63	92	4	3	.297/.387/.530	.310	29.8	.324	-0.9	1B(101): -5.0	2.7
2017	*TOR*	*MLB*	*22*	*34*	*4*	*2*	*0*	*1*	*5*	*3*	*8*	*0*	*0*	*.250/.325/.450*	*.266*	*0.7*	*.293*	*-0.1*	*1B -0*	*0.0*
2018	*TOR*	*MLB*	*23*	*290*	*40*	*15*	*1*	*13*	*42*	*30*	*71*	*0*	*0*	*.251/.333/.468*	*.266*	*4.7*	*.293*	*-0.7*	*1B -2*	*0.3*

Breakout: 2% Improve: 33% Collapse: 5% Attrition: 19% MLB: 62% *Comparables: Anthony Rizzo, Greg Bird, Jon Singleton*

The Good: "Ball go far, Rowdy go far." Tellez fell right off the assembly line conveyor belt at ACME Brawny First Baseman, Inc. There's obvious—though not easy—plus raw power from his long-and-strong swing. His timing and balance are good enough to get the power into games, even with a big leg kick for some extra oomph. He goes up to the plate with a good idea of what he can drive and what he can't, and overall the approach is solid. He's reasonably athletic for his size and good enough at first he won't have to DH for a while. That sounds more backhanded than it actually is. I've been writing about a lot of first base prospects, man.

The Bad: It's a power hitter's swing for both good and ill. The swing is long with some bat wrap and can be stiff and overly mechanical, and he can already be exploited with offspeed if you can start it in the zone. The power is real, but maybe not this real. The pop is all pull-side and New Hampshire has a very inviting right field porch. Tellez slugged over 100 points better at Northeast Delta Dental Stadium.

The Irrelevant: Rowdy, born Ryan John, actually got his nickname in the womb.

The Risks: First-base-only profile with hit tool/swing questions. You know the drill here. If he doesn't hit, it doesn't work. The Double-A performance may give you a bit more confidence in the profile, but Double-A ain't the majors.

Major league ETA: Late 2017

Ben Carsley's Fantasy Take: I bet you think you know what I'm going to say, what with my endless quest to compare every first base prospect to C.J. Cron. But fear not; I actually like Tellez a lot as a sleeper dynasty prospect. The point above about taking his Double-A line with a grain of salt is well taken, but Tellez is close to the majors, has the type of power fantasy owners crave, and would find himself in a very favorable ballpark. The additions of Kendry Morales and Steve Pearce make his paths to playing time in 2017 a bit murkier, but he's an injury or a great Triple-A performance away from pushing his way to the Majors. I wouldn't rule out a future as a Top-20 first baseman, though that's certainly his max upside.

9. Max Pentecost, C?

DOB: 3/10/1993

Height/Weight: 6'2" 191 lbs

Bats/Throws: R/R

Drafted/Acquired: Drafted 11th overall in the 2014 draft, Kennesaw State University (GA); signed for $2.8883 million

Previous Ranking(s): #6 (Org.)

2016 Stats: .314/.375/.490, 7 HR, 4 SB in 62 games at Low-A Lansing, .245/.288/.469, 3 HR, 1 SB in 12 games at High-A Dunedin

The Role: OFP 55—Everyday major league catcher
Likely 40—If he's not a catcher, it could be the dreaded "right-handed 1B/DH without average power" profile

YEAR	TEAM	LVL	AGE	PA	R	2B	3B	HR	RBI	BB	K	SB	CS	AVG/OBP/SLG	TAv	VORP	BABIP	BRR	FRAA	WARP
2014	BLJ	Rk	21	22	2	2	0	0	3	0	3	0	1	.364/.364/.455	.337	2.0	.421	-0.4		0.2
2014	VAN	A-	21	87	15	2	3	0	9	2	18	2	1	.313/.322/.410	.265	2.6	.388	0.3	C(6): -0.1	0.3
2016	LNS	A	23	267	36	15	3	7	34	21	51	4	2	.314/.375/.490	.318	19.1	.370	1.5		2.1
2016	DUN	A+	23	52	6	2	0	3	7	3	17	1	1	.245/.288/.469	.258	0.3	.310	-0.2		0.0
2017	*TOR*	*MLB*	*24*	*250*	*25*	*11*	*1*	*9*	*31*	*14*	*70*	*1*	*0*	*.232/.281/.400*	*.227*	*-3.6*	*.290*	*-0.3*		*-0.4*
2018	*TOR*	*MLB*	*25*	*242*	*29*	*10*	*1*	*9*	*30*	*15*	*68*	*1*	*0*	*.232/.285/.407*	*.234*	*-2.9*	*.289*	*-0.4*	-	*-0.3*

Breakout: 1% Improve: 3% Collapse: 2% Attrition: 8% MLB: 9% *Comparables: Joey Terdoslavich, Tyler Moore, Ben Paulsen*

The Good: Pentecost's first taste of full-season ball—oh, there will be more on why down below—went about as well as you could expect. He was considered a premium college hitter coming out of the draft in 2014. There were questions about his ultimate power ceiling— and the swing isn't really geared for it— but double-digit bombs in a half-season in tough offensive environments is nice to see. He's athletic for a catcher—more on that down below—and if healthy, could still have an above-average defensive profile as a backstop.

The Bad: Pentecost is a catcher who didn't catch. He spent all of 2016 as a DH as he works his way back from multiple surgeries on his throwing shoulder. In addition to the lost development time—Pentecost will likely start 2017 in the Florida State League as a 23-year-old—we have no idea if he can actually catch yet. If he can't, this just isn't an exciting offensive profile anywhere else, and you could argue (rightfully, I'd say) that he shouldn't even be on this list. If he can catch, well you've got a potential plus hitting catcher with a maybe a bit more pop than expected and a potential average defensive projection. That dude should be higher on this list. He's likely one or the other, but we don't know which, so he gets the prospect list equivalent of ¯_(ツ)_/¯.

The Irrelevant: Given Pentecost's shoulder issues it is ironic he went to school in Kennesaw, GA, which mandates gun possession.

The Risks: About as extreme as you will get for a polished college bat that's had some pro success already. If he can't catch, that means he can't throw, so he's probably limited to first base where the profile isn't all that exciting.

Major league ETA: Late 2018

Ben Carsley's Fantasy Take: If you're going to invest in a Pentecost, don't settle for Partial Pentecost or Minimum Pentecost. Go for the most Pentecost you can get. Max's fantasy future is entirely tied to his ability to catch. If he gets good reviews behind the plate, pick him up immediately. If it looks like he'll need to move from the position, well, let's just say he'd be no C.J. Cron.

10. Bo Bichette, SS

DOB: 3/5/1998

Height/Weight: 6'0" 200 lbs.

Bats/Throws: R/R

Drafted/Acquired: Drafted 66th overall in the 2016 MLB Draft, Lakewood HS (St. Petersburg, FL); signed for $1.1 million

Previous Ranking(s): N/A

2016 Stats: .427/.451/.732, 4 HR, 3 SB in 22 games at the Gulf Coast League

The Role: OFP 55—Above-average regular at third
Likely 40—Power bat off the bench

YEAR	TEAM	LVL	AGE	PA	R	2B	3B	HR	RBI	BB	K	SB	CS	AVG/OBP/SLG	TAv	VORP	BABIP	BRR	FRAA	WARP
2016	BLJ	Rk	18	91	21	9	2	4	36	6	17	3	0	.427/.451/.732	.444	16.9	.484	-0.9	SS(16): 1.7 • 2B(6): 0.3	1.8
2017	*TOR*	*MLB*	*19*	*250*	*22*	*10*	*1*	*7*	*27*	*14*	*81*	*1*	*0*	*.206/.252/.344*	*.199*	*-4.9*	*.279*	*-0.3*	*SS 0 • 2B 0*	*-0.5*
2018	*TOR*	*MLB*	*20*	*314*	*35*	*13*	*2*	*10*	*36*	*19*	*98*	*1*	*0*	*.221/.272/.379*	*.221*	*-2.1*	*.291*	*-0.3*	*SS 0 • 2B 0*	*-0.2*

Breakout: 0% Improve: 5% Collapse: 1% Attrition: 5% MLB: 10% *Comparables: Raul Mondesi, Elvis Andrus, Wilmer Flores*

The Good: Bichette has a lot of things to like: athletic ability, major-league bloodlines, big raw power, and a plus arm. His power was some of the best in his draft class with potentially 70 raw, as he is extremely physical and has plus bat speed with loft. His upper half has room to grow as well, although it could get too stiff. His plus arm plays well and is fairly accurate. Those stats included him missing over a month with a ruptured appendix.

The Bad: To say he's boom or bust is putting it lightly. He hits from an open stance with a really high leg kick and a significant hitch with his hands loading deep in his backside. While this helps him with his power, it can put him off balance against better offerings. His side-to-side range is lacking for a shortstop and while he's an average runner now, he will slow down as he gets older, potentially needing to move to third base.

The Irrelevant: Oh my God!!!!!

The Risks: Bichette is still young, and adjustments need to be made at the plate for better timing and to help cut down the length in his swing. He might lose too much range and become a first baseman sooner rather than later. His in-game power might lag behind given the extreme risk involved in his hit tool. He lacks a ton of remaining physical projection as he is already quite physical.

Major league ETA: 2020 —Steve Givarz

Ben Carsley's Fantasy Take: In very deep dynasty leagues (~200 prospects rostered), you can take a gamble on Bichette thanks to his power. Anything shallower and check back next year, or at least in six months.

OTHERS OF NOTE:

The "throw-ins"

Reese McGuire, C & Harold Ramirez, OF

It's possible both McGuire and Ramirez are now past their prospect sell-by dates as it were. Still, both were Top Ten prospects in a pretty good Pirates system, Top 101 prospects overall, and ended up as thrown-ins to entice the Jays to take on all of Francisco Liriano's contract at the deadline. Both could have made the Jays Top Ten this year. McGuire is still a very good defensive catcher. He still hasn't hit. This was the risk in the profile even as an amateur. He is only 21 and wasn't a complete offensive zero in Double-A, so it's too early to give up on him, But you can reuse my familiar refrain about ranking a catcher you aren't sure will actually hit at all in the Top Ten. We are more sure he is a catcher than Max Pentecost though.

Ramirez has hit. He's hit at every stop in every league. He's been one of the youngest players at every stop in every league. He hasn't hit for much power, however, and that's a bit of a problem since he is going to end up in left field. He's also always had issues staying on the field, and 2016 was no exception. A knee injury knocked him out for the season after he played just one game in New Hampshire post-trade. Ramirez will also show more pop at five o'clock, so you can project some more bombs if you like, but if it hasn't shown up by Double-A, you do start to wonder.

There's post-hype sleeper possibilities for both, but for now they are just noteworthy.

Born down in El Paso, where the tumbleweeds grow

Justin Maese, RHP

Maese, the Blue Jays third round pick in the 2015 draft, is likely destined for the bullpen. It's unfair to throw that tag on a 19-year-old a lot of the time, and he is an athletic kid who committed solely to baseball late in his high school career. So there may be more projection left than I am giving him credit for. It is worth noting though, that in a late-season staff look he didn't throw a breaking ball in the outing. Of course, when you have two fastballs as good as Maese's, you don't need much else to deal with A-ball hitters. His two seamer can get up into the mid-90s and shows good armside life. The cutter is the better present day pitch and sits in the low 90s with late, hard cut. There's a too firm change, as you'd expect from a prep arm with limited aamteur reps, and some command issues to iron out. There's not quite enough here yet past the two fastballs to move him into the Top Ten in this system, but he is definitely worth keeping an eye on in the Midwest League in 2017.

The guy waiting for a 26th roster spot

D.J. Davis, OF

My colleague Jarrett Seidler spent 1000 words opining on the 80 hit tool already. It's not really as difficult to throw an 80 run grade on a player. The Accusplit will tell you what you need to know. And most systems have a guy that can pop sub-4.0 to first. Davis offered a little bit more than that, which is why he was on last year's Jays Top Ten. Toronto had been aggressive with Davis, but he showed signs of life as a Midwest League repeater in 2015. The Florida State League—to be polite—ate him alive in 2016. There's more power than you'd expect from the profile, but he likely won't actually hit enough to make use of it. He probably won't even hit enough to have a real major league career. There's value in leveraging the speed, and Davis could be a Terrance Gore type. But most systems have one of those too.

The finally healthy arm

Ryan Borucki, LHP

Borucki, who has a Tommy John surgery and various other arm maladies blotting his resume, was finally healthy for a full season in 2016. That season started by walking twice as many batters as he struck out in the Florida State League mind you, but he steadied the ship in Lansing and was basically the same pitcher that snuck onto the Jays Top Ten last year. That's a less exciting profile in an improving system though. Borucki's your standard lefty change-up merchant with an averageish fastball and decent command. Still, the Jays thought enough of him to add him to the 40-man roster, even as he looks to start 2017 in the Florida State League again, this time as a 23-year-old.

TOP 10 TALENTS 25 AND UNDER (BORN 4/1/91 OR LATER)

1. Aaron Sanchez	6. Anthony Alford
2. Marcus Stroman	7. Vladimir Guerrero, Jr.
3. Roberto Osuna	8. Conner Greene
4. Sean Reid Foley	9. Jon Harris
5. Dalton Pompey	10. Richard Urena

Can you guess the oldest team in the league last year on average? Well, this is a Blue Jays post, so you probably can. The average Toronto player was just under 30 years old, which is a full year older than the "second place" Giants, Orioles, and Tigers. Normally with a squad like that, you'd expect this list to be mostly populated with prospects. But sitting there, right at the top, you find three major contributors to the club's success. In fact, they would have actually occupied the top four spots, but Devon Travis missed the cutoff by under two months.

It should come as no real surprise that Sanchez is leading off this list. The 24-year-old righty broke out in a big way last year, leading the AL in ERA, throwing 192 innings (100 more than his previous MLB high) and putting up 3.5 WARP. He finished seventh in Cy Young voting, and he really just scratched the surface of his incredible talents. If his command takes another step forward, there's no telling how good he can be. As far as number ones go, this was pretty easy. His good buddy Marcus Stroman wasn't far behind him though.

You may not have known it if you just looked at ERA, but Marcus Stroman was still pretty darn good last year. In his first year back from knee surgery, the diminutive righty put up a 3.43 DRA and 4.5 WARP across 204 innings. Stroman kept the ball on the ground (62 percent groundball rate!) and in the yard, but was occasionally burned by being left in the game too long or simply having softly hit balls find holes. On most lists, Stroman would be an easy number one. The only reason he's not on top here is because Sanchez' ceiling is just too high.

With the big young starters out of the way, Roberto Osuna as the third big leaguer was easy to place. You can argue all you want about the value of relievers, but 21 year old closers with a 2.0 WARP across 143.7 innings are pretty hard to find. I think the Jays would be thrilled if Reid-Foley could give them that right now. Osuna's getting better too; his K/BB increased from 4.7 in 2015 to 5.9 in 2016. The team seems unwilling to move the "Little Cannon" into the rotation where his three pitch mix would probably work just fine, which means it would take one of the other guys leaving for Osuna to move up this list in the future.

Now that the easy ones are out of the way. The tough call here was where to place Dalton Pompey. Just last year, Pompey actually ranked ahead of Sanchez on the Jays top 10 list. Now he is sitting behind a 20 year old who has yet to throw a pitch in double-A and consideration was given to placing behind Anthony Alford and his injury-marred .722 OPS in High-A Dunedin. Reid-Foley's ceiling and polish still kept him above Pompey, who battled multiple injuries and poor performance of his own, but in the end it's hard to get too down on a guy who hit .351/.405/.545 in Double-A in 2015 after hitting .317/.392/.469 across three levels the year before. Because he cracked the big leagues in September 2014, we tend forget that Pompey just turned 24 years old. If he stays healthy next year, the switch-hitting Canadian could rocket up to the top of this list.

The rest of the list is full of hopes and dreams, with a couple of wishes mixed in. Guerrero raked in Bluefield, but he's only 17. And the only players who have even reached double-A are Conner Greene and Richard Urena, both of whom struggled in their first tastes of the advanced level. There's lots of talent there, but the relative youth means we could see a lot of changes to this top 25 next year as certain guys rise up, and others fall flat.

—Joshua Howsam

WASHINGTON NATIONALS

The State of the System: *"The top half of this list stacks up with any organization in baseball, but the lack of overall system depth or close-to-the-majors bats leaves the Nats system as "merely good."*

THE TOP TEN

1. CF Victor Robles	6. OF Andrew Stevenson
2. OF Juan Soto	7. IF Sheldon Neuse
3. RHP Erick Fedde	8. 3B Kelvin Gutierrez
4. SS Carter Kieboom	9. LHP Tyler Watson
5. 3B Anderson Franco	10. RHP Austin Voth

The Big Question: What if Lucas Giolito were a reliever?

[Editor's note: This essay was written prior to when Giolito was traded to the White Sox.]

Since we started filing eyewitness reports at Baseball Prospectus in 2013, our prospect writers have submitted exactly five carrying an OFP 80.

All five were on Lucas Giolito.

Five reports, by four different evaluators, across thirteen months. And a few hundred words from now, we are going to amend those with: "Well, about that…"

There is a school of thought that suggests player evaluation is best approached via *tabula rasa*. One of my predecessors, Jason Parks, used to remark about how he loved trying to identify the best players on the backfields in Spring or instructs, with no identifying information to go on, no idea which skinny teenager got five thousand or five hundred thousand.

Meanwhile, I like to joke that I don't really like doing much amateur coverage, because on the pro side the hard work is already done for me.

But let's say you didn't know anything about Lucas Giolito past the 2016 reports. A fastball that sits in the mid-nineties, a potential hammer curve, but command issues with both that allow better hitters to sit on the heater and be rewarded for it. You wouldn't immediately be moving this prospect to the bullpen of course. The body and delivery looks like a starter, and he's only 22 (you got that from the roster sheet in the press box). It wouldn't be off the table though.

This is reductive, of course, and in addition requires a jaundiced eye. Context matters. Giolito has been better in the past. However, I don't think it is a stretch to say the kid that was hitting 100 in the Area Code Games is not showing up in the majors. I guess you could even reframe the 'big question' as the less clickbaity "How long does prospect pedigree matter?"

It's easier to handle a prospect who has broken out. He is showing you something new, what is now possible. Victor Robles and Juan Soto both have fallen into this category the last two summers. And I think public evaluators are more easily swayed by this kind of novelty. We live for this shit, in fact. It beats writing about Jorge Alfaro and Gary Sanchez for the umpteenth year. And yes I know, *cura te ipsum*.

It's harder to deal with a prospect that is stagnating or regressing. It's easy to default to the assumption of a y = x development path for high-end prospects even though we know that is by far the exception in player development. Giolito is a particularly confounding case because he was both better in the past, but that, even then, there were obvious developmental hurdles still to go.

If you were to imagine the road to a 25th percentile outcome for 2014 80 OFP Lucas Giolito, it wouldn't look all that different from what actually occurred. The velocity never really popped back to where it was pre-Tommy John surgery. The fastball/curve combo which overmatched A-ball bats stagnated a bit in the upper minors. The command profile remained fringy. The change improved, but didn't "jump." Even the best prospects in the minors still have to get better, often a lot better. Consider Archie Bradley. It's not a fair comp, as Bradley had injury issues and lacked Giolitio's "first prep righty to go 1:1" pre-draft profile, but as professional prospects they got similar acclaim and similar "tippy-top-of-the-rotation" projections. This for example could have easily been written by Jason about Lucas Giolito:

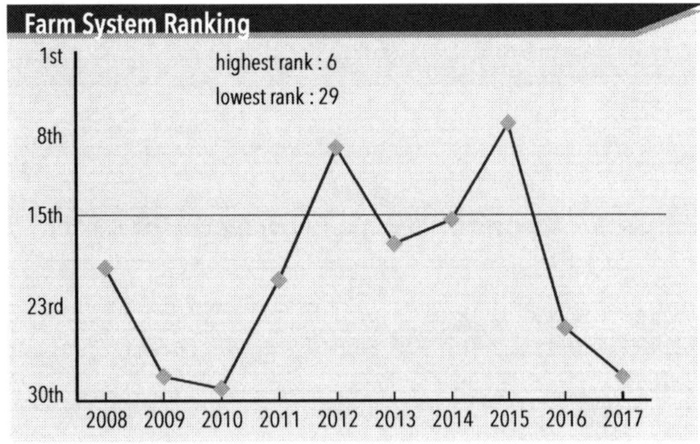

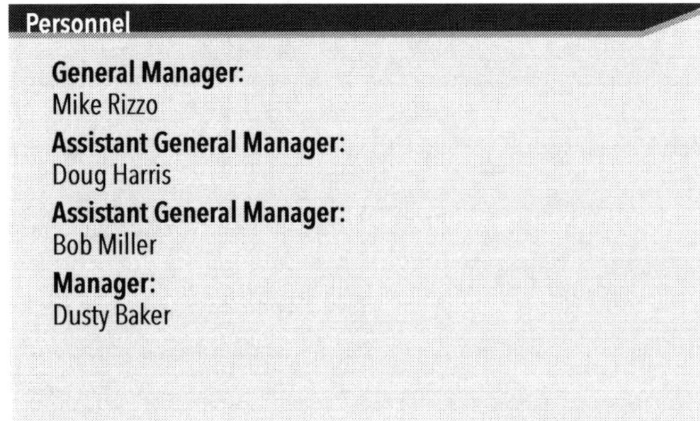
Personnel

General Manager:
Mike Rizzo

Assistant General Manager:
Doug Harris

Assistant General Manager:
Bob Miller

Manager:
Dusty Baker

"Bradley is a true frontline power arm, with size, strength, and a highly intense arsenal that already features two well above-average offerings. The delivery can lack consistency and he struggles to finish his pitches, which can leave the ball up and arm side and cause his power curve to play too high in the zone. If the command continues to refine, a number one starter is a possible outcome; a true top-of-the-rotation starter capable of a heavy innings workload and gaudy strikeout totals."

But Archie Bradley is not Lucas Giolito's destiny. Nor is Giolito necessarily a reliever now. Extrapolating from 2016 is just as dangerous as doing it from 2014. This has not turned into a y = b situation. This is just a snapshot in time. The picture is just a bit fuzzier now.

Lucas Giolitio is still one of the best pitching prospects in the game. That ain't nothing. But you can't have the same OFP forever.

Or put another way:

"Unfortunately the clock is ticking, the hours are going by. The past increases, the future recedes. Possibilities decreasing, regrets mounting."

—Haruki Murakami, Dance, Dance, Dance

1. Victor Robles, CF

DOB: 5/19/1997

Height/Weight: 6'0" 185 lbs

Bats/Throws: R/R

Drafted/Acquired: Signed July 2013 by Washington out of the Dominican Republic for $225,000

Previous Ranking(s): #29 (Top 101), #3 (Org) 2016

2016 Stats: .262/.354/.387, 3 HR, 18 SB in 41 games at High-A Potomac, .305/.405/.459, 5 HR, 19 SB in 64 games at Low-A Hagerstown

The Role: OFP 70—That really good Lorenzo Cain season
Likely 60—Those other Lorenzo Cain seasons

YEAR	TEAM	LVL	AGE	PA	R	2B	3B	HR	RBI	BB	K	SB	CS	AVG/OBP/SLG	TAv	VORP	BABIP	BRR	FRAA	WARP
2014	DWA	Rk	17	213	46	14	4	3	25	16	26	22	9	.313/.408/.484	.314	0.0	.353	0.1		0.0
2015	NAT	Rk	18	94	19	6	1	2	11	10	12	12	1	.370/.484/.562	.359	16.4	.417	3.3	CF(15): 1.5, RF(6): 0.1	1.8
2015	AUB	A-	18	167	29	5	4	2	16	8	21	12	4	.343/.424/.479	.334	18.9	.383	1.1	CF(37): 2.1, RF(1): -0.2	2.2
2016	HAG	A	19	285	48	9	6	5	30	18	38	19	8	.305/.405/.459	.334	33.8	.346	6.2	CF(63): 11.0	4.9
2016	NAT	Rk	19	21	3	0	0	1	1	0	7	0	1	.150/.190/.300	.202	-0.5	.167	0.2	CF(5): 0.2	0.0
2016	POT	A+	19	198	24	8	2	3	11	14	32	18	5	.262/.354/.387	.284	10.3	.304	-1.0	CF(40): 5.1	1.7
2017	*WAS*	*MLB*	*20*	*250*	*34*	*9*	*2*	*7*	*24*	*12*	*59*	*10*	*4*	*.239/.309/.388*	*.241*	*5.5*	*.285*	*0.6*	*CF 6*	*1.3*
2018	*WAS*	*MLB*	*21*	*396*	*48*	*15*	*3*	*12*	*46*	*21*	*92*	*17*	*7*	*.246/.317/.407*	*.264*	*14.7*	*.291*	*1.9*	*CF 10*	*2.6*

Breakout: 6% Improve: 18% Collapse: 0% Attrition: 5% MLB: 20% *Comparables: Byron Buxton, Jose Tabata, Anthony Gose*

The Good: There are very few five-tool, up-the-middle prospects in the minors, and even fewer of them turn into five-tool players in the majors. Robles has a shot. We may be squinting a bit to get the power to average, but we can say with more certainty the he offers three potential 70-grade tools— hit, run and arm— and has made strides with his center field defense (which projects as plus) in his first year of full-season ball. His approach is advanced for a 19-year-old, and he covers all four quadrants of the zone well. The bat speed is outstanding, and the barrel control to match is coming along. And zooming out, he's more polished than you'd expect from the "toolsy 19-year-old center fielder in A-ball" cohort.

The Bad: Robles' game power lags behind his other skills. It may come as he physically matures, but he may "only" creep into double-digit bombs in the majors. The hit tool is still mostly projection until we see him perform against more advanced arms. He could end up as more of a speed/glove 7-hole hitter in the majors.

The Irrelevant: We often harp on minor-league player nutrition, but Robles' potential 2017 home, Harrisburg, PA, is home to Broad Street Market, one of the oldest continuously operating farmers' markets in the U.S.

The Risks: The usual risks for this profile. He hasn't hit in the upper minors yet, and he wasn't quite as spectacular in his first taste of the Carolina League. The offensive tools are far less actualized than the defensive/athletic ones. He may take a bit of time to reach his projection, past just his Major League ETA.

Major league ETA: 2019

Ben Carsley's Fantasy Take: Let's face it, you either already own Robles or you missed the boat on him. Such is life with young, pre-elite fantasy prospects. It's easy to fall in love with Robles and his projection as a future OF1. Take Starling Marte as an example of what a plus-hit tool and plus-plus speed can translate to at the MLB level; a .300-plus average, 40-plus steals and a ranking as the fifth-best fantasy OF in 2016, per ESPN's Player Rater. That's what we could be looking at with Robles, and while the hit tool and power have a ways to go, his floor as a speed-first OF 4/5 makes him mighty attractive. Now that he's in High-A, lead time is becoming less of an issue, too.

2. Juan Soto, OF

DOB: 10/25/1998

Height/Weight: 6'1" 185 lbs

Bats/Throws: L/L

Drafted/Acquired: Signed in July 2015 out of the Dominican Republic for $1.5 million.

Previous Ranking(s): N/A

2016 Stats: .361/.410/.550, 5 HR, 5 SB in 45 games with the GCL Nationals. .429/.500/.571, 0 HR, 0 SB in 6 games with Low-A Auburn

The Role: OFP 60—Your prototypical good everyday right fielder
Likely 50—Solid, but unspectacular corner dude

YEAR	TEAM	LVL	AGE	PA	R	2B	3B	HR	RBI	BB	K	SB	CS	AVG/OBP/SLG	TAv	VORP	BABIP	BRR	FRAA	WARP
2016	NAT	Rk	17	183	25	11	3	5	31	14	25	5	2	.361/.410/.550	.346	16.3	.403	0.5	RF(42): 1.9	1.8
2016	AUB	A-	17	24	3	3	0	0	1	3	4	0	0	.429/.500/.571	.409	4.0	.529	-0.1	RF(6): 0.5, CF(1): -0.1	0.5
2017	*WAS*	*MLB*	*18*	*250*	*22*	*10*	*1*	*7*	*27*	*14*	*77*	*0*	*0*	*.210/.255/.341*	*.206*	*-7.5*	*.279*	*-0.4*	*RF -0, CF -0*	*-0.8*
2018	*WAS*	*MLB*	*19*	*239*	*25*	*9*	*1*	*7*	*25*	*13*	*74*	*0*	*0*	*.212/.255/.351*	*.220*	*-6.1*	*.280*	*-0.5*	*RF 0, CF 0*	*-0.7*

Breakout: 0% Improve: 0% Collapse: 0% Attrition: 0% MLB: 0% *Comparables: Raul Mondesi, Wilmer Flores*

The Good: Cineastes often complain that the sequel is never as good as the original, but the Nats had another teenaged outfielder breakout in the GCL and the NYPL this Summer, and Juan Soto is more The Curse of the Cat People than Honey, I Blew Up The Kid. While the circumstances of his breakout are similar to Victor Robles', they are very different prospects. Soto doesn't have the same loud, up-the-middle tools, but he may have shown an even more advanced bat in the New-York-Penn League. There's a potential plus-hit/plus-power combo here with a good approach for his age.

The Bad: As lovely as the finger lakes are in the Summer, Auburn is a long ways from the majors. The game power is mostly theoretical at this point and Soto is limited to right field. He should be fine there long term as an average runner with enough arm for the position, but he is going to have to hit a lot.

The Irrelevant: Speaking of Auburn, since he was only there a week, we doubt Soto had time to visit the William H. Seward Museum, where Seward negotiated the purchase of Alaska from the Russians as Secretary of State.

The Risks: Soto just turned 18. He hasn't played outside of short-season ball yet. It's a corner outfield profile. There's extreme risk here even accounting for the advanced bat.

Major league ETA: 2020

Ben Carsley's Fantasy Take: If you're going to gamble on players who are younger than the first Harry Potter book, they better have big-time offensive potential. Fortunately Soto does, and this type of hit-tool-first profile is one I prefer to gamble on in fantasy. He's too far away to be a top-100 prospect yet, but now is a very good time to get in on the ground floor.

3. Erick Fedde, RHP

DOB: 2/25/1993

Height/Weight: 6'4" 180 lbs

Bats/Throws: R/R

Drafted/Acquired: Drafted 18th overall in the 2014 draft out of University of Nevada, Las Vegas (NV); signed for $2.5111 million

Previous Ranking(s): #6 (2016) Org

2016 Stats: 3.99 ERA, 4.09 DRA, 29.1 IP, 33 H, 10 BB, 28 K at Double-A Harrisburg, 2.85 ERA, 1.61 DRA, 91.2 IP, 85 H, 19 BB, 95 K at High-A Potomac

The Role: OFP 60—No. 3 starter
Likely 50—No. 4 starter with late-inning relief fallback

YEAR	TEAM	LVL	AGE	W	L	SV	G	GS	IP	H	HR	BB/9	K/9	K	GB%	BABIP	WHIP	ERA	FIP	DRA	VORP	WARP	cFIP	MPH
2015	AUB	A-	22	4	1	0	8	8	35	38	1	2.1	9.3	36	56%	.346	1.31	2.57	2.60	1.57	14.40	1.5	80	
2015	HAG	A	22	1	2	0	6	6	29	24	1	2.5	7.1	23	52%	.274	1.10	4.34	3.48	3.36	6.00	0.6	93	
2016	POT	A+	23	6	4	0	18	17	91^{2}	85	7	1.9	9.3	95	51%	.316	1.13	2.85	3.22	1.27	42.60	4.4	72	
2016	HAR	AA	23	2	1	0	5	5	29^{1}	33	1	3.1	8.6	28	46%	.360	1.47	3.99	3.02	4.09	3.30	0.4	94	
2017	*WAS*	*MLB*	*24*	*6*	*6*	*0*	*19*	*19*	95^{2}	*96*	*13*	*3.3*	*7.2*	*76*	*42%*	*.314*	*1.38*	*4.49*	*4.53*	*5.08*	*5.1*	*0.5*	*121*	
2018	*WAS*	*MLB*	*25*	*8*	*9*	*0*	*27*	*27*	*160*	*152*	*22*	*4.5*	*9.3*	*165*	*42%*	*.326*	*1.44*	*4.49*	*4.83*	*5.08*	*7.2*	*0.7*	*121*	

Breakout: 14% Improve: 18% Collapse: 10% Attrition: 21% MLB: 31% *Comparables: Steven Matz, Sean Manaea, Matt Boyd*

The Good: Fedde found more velocity this year as he got further away from his 2014 Tommy John surgery. He sat in the mid-90s and touched higher, and his slider flashed plus. The fastball has enough life to be a swing-and-miss offering in the majors and the slider has a good chance to get to that point as well. At it's best it features violent late, two-plane break. Fedde also has close to an ideal starting pitcher's build.

The Bad: However, there is enough effort in his delivery to make you wonder if he will have the stamina/command profile to be a 180-inning arm. The changeup is still a work in progress, but can show split-like action at times. The slider is inconsistent and can be more of a chase pitch. He was a little bit old for A-ball for whatever that matters (I don't think all that much).

The Irrelevant: Fedde was also an all-state soccer player in high school, leading Las Vegas High School to a state title his junior season.

The Risks: Fedde has cleared every marker on his TJ recovery, and with his potential plus fastball/slider combo, he should find a major-league role of some sort. However he is still a pitcher (with a Tommy John already on his C.V.)

Major league ETA: Early 2018

Ben Carsley's Fantasy Take: Fedde has flown under the radar a bit for a first-rounder, but he's emerged as a solid, if un-spectacular, dynasty pitching prospect. The lack of front-of-the-rotation stuff means he'll get lumped in with a bunch of other mid-rotation starters in the mid-minors, but that might sell short his upside as a no. 5/6 fantasy SP in the Jerad Eickhoff mold. That might not get your heart racing, but you've started a lot worse. It's a bit early in the process for me to tell exactly, but Fedde should be a back-of-the-top-100 prospect.

4. Carter Kieboom, SS

DOB: 09/03/1997

Height/Weight: 6'2" 190 lbs

Bats/Throws: R/R

Drafted/Acquired: Drafted 28th overall in the 2016 draft, Walton HS (GA), signed for $2 million.

Previous Ranking(s): N/A

2016 Stats: .244/.323/.452, 4 HR, 1 SB in 36 games with the GCL Nationals

The Role: OFP 55—Solid everyday third baseman
Likely 45—Second-division starter or good fifth infielder

YEAR	TEAM	LVL	AGE	PA	R	2B	3B	HR	RBI	BB	K	SB	CS	AVG/OBP/SLG	TAv	VORP	BABIP	BRR	FRAA	WARP
2016	NAT	Rk	18	155	22	8	4	4	25	12	43	1	2	.244/.323/.452	.266	6.5	.319	-0.3	SS(31): 0.8	0.7
2017	*WAS*	*MLB*	*19*	*250*	*24*	*8*	*1*	*6*	*22*	*13*	*92*	*0*	*0*	*.183/.232/.304*	*.187*	*-8.0*	*.266*	*-0.4*	*SS 0*	*-0.8*
2018	*WAS*	*MLB*	*20*	*315*	*33*	*11*	*1*	*9*	*33*	*19*	*111*	*1*	*0*	*.197/.252/.337*	*.214*	*-4.4*	*.279*	*-0.5*	*SS 0*	*-0.4*

Breakout: 0% Improve: 5% Collapse: 2% Attrition: 5% MLB: 10% *Comparables: Raul Mondesi, Nomar Mazara, Elvis Andrus*

The Good: While not quite on the level of Moniak or Rutherford, Kieboom featured one of the best hit tools in the 2016 prep class. Despite a very open stance, long stride, and slight hitch, he always seems to find the ball with the barrel. He has a lean, athletic frame that could add pop as he adds strength in his twenties. His arm will play at either spot on the left-side of the diamond.

The Bad: Kieboom played shortstop in complex ball, but most think his ultimate defensive home is at third base once he fills out. It takes a bit of projection to see him wringing the expected corner infield-power profile out of his swing at present, so he may end up a bit of a tweener or utility type unless he really hits or adds average game power as he ages.

The Irrelevant: Confidential to @70mphfastball: Kieboom's pro future was always going to be at the plate, but he was also a switch-pitcher in high school.

The Risks: High, but about what you'd expect for the profile. A future corner role will put pressure on the power to come, and the developmental time here is significant.

Major league ETA: 2020

Ben Carsley's Fantasy Take: Kieboom isn't one of the premier dynasty prospects from the last draft class, but his bat is decent enough that you might consider him if your league rosters 200-plus prospects. Don't bank on using him at shortstop, but Kieboom has the potential to serve as a low-end starting third basemen or a passable CI who'll do more for your average than he will your power stats, assuming that he's actually a baseball player and not, as his name suggests, an adult movie star.

5.Anderson Franco, 3B

DOB: 8/15/1997

Height/Weight: 6'3" 190 lbs

Bats/Throws: R/R

Drafted/Acquired: Signed August 2013 by Washington out of the Dominican Republic for $900,000

Previous Ranking(s): #7 (2016) Org

2016 Stats: .277/.307/.349, 1 HR, 1 SB in 24 games with the GCL Nationals

The Role: OFP 50—Bat-first regular at third base
Likely 40—Corner bench bat with some pop

YEAR	TEAM	LVL	AGE	PA	R	2B	3B	HR	RBI	BB	K	SB	CS	AVG/OBP/SLG	TAv	VORP	BABIP	BRR	FRAA	WARP
2014	DWA	Rk	16	237	26	8	1	4	35	26	46	4	2	.272/.346/.379	.592	0.5	.323	-0.1		0.1
2015	NAT	Rk	17	170	19	6	1	4	19	14	26	2	3	.281/.347/.412	.280	8.4	.315	-1.0	3B(43): -0.3	0.8
2015	AUB	A-	17	47	0	1	1	0	4	7	2	0	0	.225/.340/.300	.233	-1.4	.237	-1.4	3B(9): 1.7	0.0
2016	NAT	Rk	18	88	9	3	0	1	9	4	11	1	0	.277/.307/.349	.256	2.1	.306	0.0	3B(19): -2.4	0.0
2017	*WAS*	*MLB*	*19*	*250*	*21*	*9*	*1*	*6*	*26*	*13*	*71*	*0*	*0*	*.208/.251/.335*	*.203*	*-7.3*	*.266*	*-0.4*	*3B 1*	*-0.7*
2018	*WAS*	*MLB*	*20*	*338*	*37*	*12*	*1*	*10*	*38*	*20*	*90*	*0*	*0*	*.225/.273/.370*	*.234*	*-1.8*	*.279*	*-0.6*	*3B 1*	*-0.1*

Breakout: 0% Improve: 6% Collapse: 2% Attrition: 6% MLB: 12% *Comparables: Rougned Odor, Raul Mondesi, Wilmer Flores*

The Good: Franco is a strong kid with plus raw power he derives from length and strength. He has the arm and hands to stick at the hot corner.

The Bad: Franco lost significant developmental time this year and was limited to just 24 games in the complex due to a back injury. There are questions about how his approach will fare against higher level arms and in games he can have more of a one gear swing.

The Irrelevant: If Franco does stick at third base, he will only have to beat out Scott Brosius as best third baseman born on August 15th.

The Risks: Extreme. Franco has yet to play in full-season ball and there are already questions about his hit tool. He may end up at first base long term, putting a lot of pressure on the offensive profile. Back injuries are less than ideal and can linger.

Major league ETA: 2021

Ben Carsley's Fantasy Take: You can bury Franco deep on your sleeper list somewhere. Check in on him periodically to see if his offensive tools are starting to translate at higher levels, but there is such a thing as being too early, and you will be if you pick Franco up right now.

6. Andrew Stevenson, OF

DOB: 06/01/1994

Height/Weight: 6'0" 185 lbs

Bats/Throws: L/L

Drafted/Acquired: Drafted in the second round (58th overall) in the 2015 MLB draft, Louisiana State University (LA), signed for $750,000.

Previous Ranking(s): N/A

2016 Stats: .246/.302/.328, 2 HR, 12 SB in 65 games for Double-A Harrisburg, .304/.359/.418, 1 HR, 27 SB in 68 games for High-A Potomac

The Role: OFP 50—Average outfielder
Likely 40—Well, uh, "Probably fourth outfielder"

YEAR	TEAM	LVL	AGE	PA	R	2B	3B	HR	RBI	BB	K	SB	CS	AVG/OBP/SLG	TAv	VORP	BABIP	BRR	FRAA	WARP
2015	AUB	A-	21	80	11	1	2	0	9	7	12	7	3	.361/.413/.431	.294	6.3	.426	1.2	CF(16): 2.8, LF(3): 1.6	1.1
2015	NAT	Rk	21	6	1	0	0	0	0	1	2	0	0	.200/.333/.200	.216	-0.4	.333	-0.3	CF(1): -0.3	-0.1
2015	HAG	A	21	153	28	3	2	1	16	8	16	16	4	.285/.338/.358	.282	10.7	.311	2.7	CF(35): 0.0	1.2
2016	POT	A+	22	300	37	12	8	1	18	24	44	27	9	.304/.359/.418	.287	20.8	.358	3.1	CF(60): 2.4, LF(6): -1.0	2.2
2016	HAR	AA	22	280	38	11	2	2	16	20	51	12	5	.246/.302/.328	.237	-2.3	.299	-2.9	CF(36): 6.6, LF(28): 1.3	0.4
2017	*WAS*	*MLB*	*23*	*250*	*31*	*9*	*2*	*5*	*21*	*15*	*59*	*10*	*4*	*.237/.286/.357*	*.225*	*1.1*	*.292*	*0.8*	*CF 3, LF 1*	*0.6*
2018	*WAS*	*MLB*	*24*	*318*	*34*	*11*	*3*	*6*	*32*	*19*	*72*	*13*	*5*	*.242/.291/.365*	*.242*	*4.3*	*.294*	*1.6*	*CF 4, LF 1*	*1.0*

Breakout: 2% Improve: 7% Collapse: 1% Attrition: 5% MLB: 9% *Comparables: Logan Schafer, Charlie Blackmon, Matt Szczur*

The Good: Stevenson is a gazelle in the outfield. He boasts plus-plus run times and flashes enough leather to entice Chris Berman. His speed and glove will carry the profile, though he shows the potential for a solid-average hit tool thanks to good hands and an ability to control the barrel. Pair that with a steady approach and the ability to recognize spin, and you have the makings of a high-floor player.

The Bad: High-floor players can often translate to "probably fourth outfielder" and that's what Stevenson is. Despite the impact tools above, his game is limited by well below-average raw power that plays down in-game because he doesn't incorporate his lower half into his swing. His value in the field is mitigated by a poor throwing arm and at-times overly aggressive routes.

The Irrelevant: Prior to his participation in the California/Carolina League All-Star Game (held on the west coast this year), Stevenson had never traveled to California.

The Risks: While his glove and legs will carry the profile, the risk in Stevenson is that there's not going to be anything to carry in the upper levels. Upper minors pitchers will attempt to exploit him on the inner half where he has little chance of doing any damage due to his minimal power output. If he becomes an automatic out, he won't see the field, thus losing any chance to accrue value. —Craig Goldstein

Major league ETA: Late 2018

Ben Carsley's Fantasy Take: Stevenson's speed might make him somewhat interesting once he's closer to the Majors, but his lack of other tools and distance from the show conspire to make him a fantasy non-factor for the time being.

7. Sheldon Neuse, IF

DOB: 12/10/1994

Height/Weight: 6'0" 195 lbs

Bats/Throws: R/R

Drafted/Acquired: Drafted in the second round (58th overall) in the 2016 MLB draft, University of Oklahoma (OK), signed for $900,000

Previous Ranking(s): N/A

2016 Stats: .230/.305/.341, 1 HR, 2 SB in 36 games with Low-A Auburn

The Role: OFP 50—Regular third baseman
Likely 40—Quality utility option

YEAR	TEAM	LVL	AGE	PA	R	2B	3B	HR	RBI	BB	K	SB	CS	AVG/OBP/SLG	TAv	VORP	BABIP	BRR	FRAA	WARP
2016	AUB	A-	21	141	16	5	3	1	11	13	26	2	2	.230/.305/.341	.254	2.8	.280	-0.2	3B(26): 1.9, SS(6): 1.1	0.5
2017	*WAS*	*MLB*	*22*	*250*	*22*	*9*	*1*	*6*	*25*	*16*	*74*	*1*	*0*	*.201/.256/.323*	*.202*	*-6.9*	*.264*	*-0.3*	*3B 1, SS 0*	*-0.6*
2018	*WAS*	*MLB*	*23*	*246*	*26*	*8*	*1*	*7*	*25*	*18*	*71*	*1*	*1*	*.203/.267/.337*	*.222*	*-3.9*	*.261*	*-0.4*	*3B 1, SS 0*	*-0.3*

Breakout: 1% Improve: 1% Collapse: 1% Attrition: 4% MLB: 4% *Comparables: Zelous Wheeler, Kaleb Cowart, Steven Souza*

The Good: Neuse was one of the better two-way college players in this year's class, serving both as Oklahoma's starting shortstop and closer. Arm strength is indeed his best asset, playing plus from the left side after delivering fastballs in the 93-95 range off the bump. His smooth right-handed swing is balanced and direct when he's right, with an all-fields approach underlining an ability to turn and lift balls with average power potential. He exhibits an advanced command of the strike zone that bodes well for his on-base skills, and shows no glaring weakness in his game.

The Bad: The approach got too conservative in his pro debut, with a vast majority of his contact heading softly to the opposite field. He can be prone to over-swinging, particularly early in counts, and both the hit and playable power tools may never develop into outright assets. That may be problematic, as his mature body lacks for quickness or a ton of athleticism, and the physicality has already pushed him over to the hot corner. There are big-league tools here, just not much outside of the arm that really stands out, and it's more of a second-division profile.

The Irrelevant: At least some of his signing bonus appears to have been invested immediately and directly in the procurement of a very large truck.

The Risks: Relatively low on account of collegiate polish and breadth of skillset. He didn't exactly hit the ground like Usain Bolt at a level where he may have been expected to excel after signing, but his solid-if-unspectacular projection remains wholly intact. —Wilson Karaman

Major league ETA: Late 2018/Early 2019

Ben Carsley's Fantasy Take: If we ever get a Bat Signal about this guy the sender should immediately have their BP subscription revoked and should in its place receive a one-way ticket directly to the sun.

8. Kelvin Gutierrez, 3B

DOB: 8/28/1994

Height/Weight: 6'3" 185 lbs

Bats/Throws: R/R

Drafted/Acquired: Signed April 2013 out of the Dominican Republic

Previous Ranking(s): N/A

2016 Stats: .237/.326/.342, 1 HR, 2 SB in 10 games at High-A Potomac, .300/.349/.406, 3 HR, 19 SB in 96 games at Low-A Hagerstown, .323/.371/.419, 0 HR, 4 SB in 9 games at short-season Auburn.

The Role: OFP 55—Solid-average third baseman
Likely 45—Contact-first backup at second or third

The Good: Already 22, Gutierrez could be the next in a line of Nationals prospects who took a while to see their skills coalesce before taking off through the system. His leveraged swing and ability to control the barrel pair with a still-developing body to portend future power growth. He's got plus raw power at present. He has the footwork to stick at third base, which is good because his plus arm would be wasted at first.

The Bad: The plus raw power doesn't always make it into games right now, and his swing can get rigid. While he has the footwork and hands to stick at the hot corner, it's just okay and he's inconsistent with both at present.

The Irrelevant: Water freezes at 273.16 Kelvin.

The Risks: Gutierrez is relatively old for his level and still needs to add muscle to take advantage of what is presently pull-side power. If the physical maturation never occurs, his high-contact approach is going to result in a lot more singles and outs than extra-base hits. Any shift down the defensive spectrum will only exacerbate the profile woes that would accompany falling short in the power department.

Major league ETA: 2019

Ben Carsley's Fantasy Take: A good one for your watch list, but that's about it.

9. Tyler Watson, LHP

DOB: 5/22/1997

Height/Weight: 6'5" 200 lbs

Bats/Throws: R/L

Drafted/Acquired: Drafted in the 34th round of the 2015 MLB draft, Perry HS (Gilbert, AZ), signed for $400,000

Previous Ranking(s): N/A

2016 Stats: 4.80 ERA, 4.23 DRA, 15 IP, 16 H, 6 BB, 16 K at Low-A Hagerstown, 1.88 ERA, 1.56 DRA, 30 H, 9 BB, 48 K in short-season Auburn.

The Role: OFP 50—no. 4 starter or setup
Likely 40—Middle reliever

The Good: Watson is your classic tall, projectable lefty. There's low 90s heat here at present—and he hides the ball well—and some projection left in the body. The curveball is potentially above-average as well.

The Bad: Watson's delivery is stiff, upper-body-heavy, and not without effort. The changeup lags behind the the fastball and breaker, which has been a recurring theme with prep arms on these lists, and will continue to be for years to come. The profile might play best in relief long term.

The Irrelevant: The Nationals have never had a 34th round pick make the majors, but the Expos—whose history I begrudgingly include here—had three.

The Risks: Very limited professional resume, more projection required, strong chance he ends up in the bullpen. And of course, he's a pitcher.

Major league ETA: 2020

Ben Carsley's Fantasy Take: Being left-handed only takes you so far ...

10. Austin Voth, RHP

DOB: 6/26/1992

Height/Weight: 6'0" 190 lbs

Bats/Throws: R/R

Drafted/Acquired: Drafted in the fifth round of the 2013 draft, University of Washington (WA); signed for $272,800

Previous Ranking(s): #9 (Org)

2016 Stats: 3.15 ERA, 2.23 DRA, 157 IP, 138 H, 57 BB, 133 K at Triple-A Syracuse.

The Role: OFP 50—no. 4 starter
Likely 45—no. 5 starter

The Good: He's put up really good numbers all the way up the chain, pounding the zone and keeping the ball down. His fastball sometimes gets described as "sneaky" despite marginal velocity. He's got a pretty decent curveball and a usable change. His command is at least above-average. With Lucas Giolito and Reynaldo Lopez gone, there's a lot less standing between Voth and a MLB job than there was at the start of the winter.

The Bad: There isn't an obvious swing-and-miss pitch here. It's just good command of three decent pitches. This is like every 4th/5th starter profile idling in Triple-A you've ever heard, right? The Nationals, in substantial need of pitching help at various points in 2016 and having to add Voth to the 40-man after the season anyway, never did turn to him, so maybe they think ba little less of it than we do? They did, actually, add him to the 40, of course.

The Irrelevant: Voth went to Kentwood High School around the same time as Stefano Langone, contestant on season 10 of American Idol. That's the season where J-Lo replaced Simon Cowell.

The Risks: Outside of getting 2016 Aaron Blair'd, there's very little risk to this profile. He's about as much of a lock to have a substantial career as at least an up-and-down pitcher as you could be, health willing.

I guess it's worth noting that if anything there is some positive risk with this profile, because there's enough in place that any kind of unexpected velocity jump or new plus pitch or it turning out that the command we think is a 55 is actually a 70 does prop Voth up quite a lot. Most of these guys don't pump out, like, Doug Fister's peak, but it does happen from this starting point occasionally.

Major league ETA: 2017

Ben Carsley's Fantasy Take: Shall I compare thee to a midsummer night's spot starter?

TOP 10 TALENTS 25 AND UNDER (BORN 4/1/91 OR LATER)

1. Bryce Harper	6. Erick Fedde
2. Trea Turner	7. Wilmer Difo
3. Victor Robles	8. Carter Kieboom
4. Joe Ross	9. Anderson Franco
5. Juan Soto	10. Andrew Stevenson

The Nationals farm system has graduated much of its best talent lately, and the most promising pieces left are still very young. The 25-and-under list is a weird mish-mash of people who have already won MVP awards at the major-league level and kids who haven't seen tough competition yet. It's a reminder that the organization was supremely lucky to have a consensus no. 1 overall pick at its disposal in 2010, as many of the draft hauls since then have been more challenging. The team did not have first round picks in 2013 or 2015 because of free agent signings. Give credit to the front office for rounding out these slightly leaner years with some excellent trades and international FA signings.

To start things off, have you heard of this guy before? For the sixth year in a row, Bryce Harper makes this list for the Nats. Also, did you hear his 2016 season was a disappointment? Guess that totally-untrue-but-possibly-true rumor of a nagging neck/shoulder injury was maybe/probably true. He'll be just fine. Only a career-ender would jeopardize his spot on the top of this list. By the time he signs with the Yankees for infinite dollars in the 2019 offseason, at least one of the outfielders below will probably be in position to help.

Contrasting Harper's disappointment was the arrival of Trea Turner, whose outstanding overall play came in spite of him playing an unfamiliar position in center field. He's still a shortstop at heart, and GM Mike Rizzo may choose to buy an outfielder to enable the move back. The other big question for next year: will pitchers adjust and exploit the weaker swings on breaking balls?

Actually, you know what would enable Turner to move back to short? The 2019 version of Victor Robles starting in center. Robles has a first-division future with his combination of defensive skills and offensive upside. He doesn't need much power to carry him to higher levels, but as his body matures we'll see for sure if he hits more home runs than triples each year.

Meanwhile, the combination of Joe Ross and Erick Fedde (despite having lost Lucas Giolito and Reynaldo Lopez) is going to win plenty of games for the franchise—although a lot of development is left for Fedde.

Difo is tough to figure. He raced through the minors in 2015 before falling flat in a brief stint in the majors. He flashes major-league tools, including the ability to stay up the middle, and was even included on the Nationals post-season roster, memorably recording the final out of the NLDS against Clayton Kershaw. Still, the rose-colored ceiling is an average regular, and his positional flexibility makes him a prime candidate for the utility man role rather than a second-division regular.

Juan Soto and Carter Kieboom have a combined $3.5 million price tag, and it'll be a few years before we see the returns on investment. Still, the patience has a good chance of being rewarded. Soto, especially, has projection for days and could shoot up prospect lists once there's better proof of concept against professional competition. Kieboom also has a better shot than older brother Spencer at sticking with the big league club.

—Dan Rozenson

The Ones Who Could Jump

by Craig Goldstein

Let's find out, in due time, if a year off has dulled my skills or provided a much needed reset. As ever, this list is culled from the names that do not appear on Bret Sayre and Ben Carsley's Top 101 list, nor were they mentioned honorably. This is an attempt to divine the guys who will go from off list to on, as we know well how deep leaguers and prospect addicts are always on the lookout for the next big thing. This one is for those who fit that description. Cheers.

Magneuris Sierra, CF, St. Louis Cardinals

Sierra, as Andy McCullough would say, got his head kicked in during a 51-game stint at Low-A in 2015, posting a .191/.219/.247 slash line before being demoted to short-season ball where he recovered nicely. Tasked with a second go at Peoria, Sierra proved he was up to the challenge, and at 20 years old, was still on-level for the assignment. Responding to adversity is a great way to earn your organization's trust, and that's exactly what Sierra did last year, slashing .307/.335/.395. You'll note that there's not much in the way of power here, but there is a good baseline for a top-of-the-order table setter, as Sierra swiped 31 bags on the back of his plus-plus wheels. Another steady season in the pitcher-friendly Florida State League should set him up nicely for the back end of next year's Dynasty 101.

Fernando Romero, RHP, Minnesota Twins

A bit of a pop-up prospect, Romero started more games in 2016 than he had from 2012-2014, before he missed 2015 with Tommy John surgery. His fastball can flash double-plus, touching 98 at times with arm-side run. He can miss bats with the pitch and hold his velocity into the later innings. He complements that with a power slider that flashes plus and shows bat-missing potential. The changeup, as it often does, lags, but has a chance to get to average. Add a little consistency to the slider, and some gradual growth to the cambio, and Romero should flourish in the upper minors, health permitting (no small question). If he can do that, he'll land squarely on the 101.

Sixto Sanchez, RHP, Philadelphia Phillies

There's wasn't a chance I was leaving off a diminutive right-hander with a lightning-quick arm and upper-90s velocity. There's a lot of risk present, given the frame and the lack of professional exposure, but the reward is there to balance out the portfolio, as well. He pairs his plus-plus velocity with a curveball that flashes plus and the requisite nascent changeup. Given the height, plus breaker, and big velo, Sanchez will always be dogged by the "future reliever" tag, but that just means there's a chance for discounted value. If he develops as hoped, he has the chance to be a dynamic starter.

Christin Stewart, LF, Detroit Tigers

Name aside, Stewart isn't the most exciting fantasy prospect. He's destined for left field where his potentially plus-plus raw will play just fine. The question will be how much he can get to that power. He has quick hands and above-average bat speed which help compensate for the length in his swing. Stewart has already gotten some time at Double-A, and while he's going to struggle to provide impact in batting average or stolen bases, his penchant for power (and thus, RBI), combined with his proximity to the majors, make him a good bet for next year's list.

Franklin Perez, RHP, Houston Astros

Mowing down the Midwest League as an 18-year-old shouldn't be overlooked, but Perez is a bit as a fantasy asset. He doesn't have a plus-plus fastball or breaker, so it's easy to see why some guys get a little more love, but he brings the potential for three plus pitches to the table, and the cambio has a chance for more than that. Perez is definitely a "feel" guy, but don't mistake that to mean the stuff is lacking. He can run the fastball up to mid-90s, and manipulates the pitch well, and his breaking ball flashes above-average at times. As with most young arms, he'll require some more consistency, but the advanced repertoire and impressive feel means it could all come together quickly for the talented Venezuelan.

Josh Lowe, 3B, Tampa Bay Rays

If you like projectable athletes, you're going to like Josh Lowe. At 6-foot-4, 190 pounds, there's a lot of room for him to add good weight, and coming out of Pope High School, there's a lot of room for Young Pope jokes as well. Impressive bat speed begets impressive raw power, and it covers for some of the length in his swing. How much the bat speed is able to mitigate that length will be crucial to Lowe's development. On the upside, additional good weight could lead to a shorter swing for the same power, as he might benefit from some standard strength rather than loft. Of course that's but one of many viable paths for a teenager with ample swing-and-miss. If it comes to fruition though, you'll have a nice asset on your hands.

Jomar Reyes, 3B, Baltimore Orioles

The odds that Reyes ends up at first are the most damaging thing about the profile. Yes, he suffered through what could charitably be termed as a lackluster season. But he he'll have just turned 20 years old by the time you're reading this and he spent the season in High-A without seeing an increase in his whiff rate nor a significant decrease in his walk rate. The Hot Corner Hulk retains his plus power potential, and a second go at the Carolina League should see improved play. If so, his bat is enough to land him on a future 101.

Taylor Trammell, OF, Cincinnati Reds

Man the Reds are fun. It's not the best system in the world but there's a lot of fantasy potential brewing. Trammell was a supplemental first rounder in 2016 and while he was thought to be more athlete than ballplayer, he should considerable skill in short-season ball. If you're desperate for a comp, Lewis Brinson with softer tools might suffice. The speed is plus-plus, but the power is more average to slightly above down the line. Premium athletes can develop differently than others, and Trammell doesn't lack for athleticism, but it also might be more of a slow burn as he learns to assemble his baseball tools.

Albert Abreu, RHP, New York Yankees

If you like big stuff and you cannot lie, get Abreu in your life. He can pump his fastball up to 96, generally sitting in the low-to-mid 90s, with significant run. There's room in his frame for more weight, and more velocity, too. He'll show a curveball and a slider, both of which flash plus. While many arms that throw both have a tendency to have them run into each other, Abreu's feel for spin allows him to operate with two discrete breaking balls, either of which can miss bats, when he's on. He also throws an average changeup that features hard fade and tumble. His control (and command) has waned more than waxed at present, but refined mechanics could lead to more presence around the strike zone. Given his potent four-pitch mix, Abreu stands to take a big jump if he can just find the zone a little more often. There's ample risk here, but the reward more than justifies an investment.

Dustin May, RHP, Los Angeles Dodgers

This is admittedly a bit aggressive. May is a 2016 third-rounder who hasn't thrown outside of complex-level ball. Still, he's a tall drink of water, standing 6-foot-6, with plenty of room to fill out physically. He sits in the low 90s already with late life and impressive spin rates. That spin transfers over to his breaking ball, too, showing big tilt and plus potential already. There's a ton of growth potential here, and if I was going to pick one arm to take a Triston McKenzie-esque jump in the rankings, it'd be May.

Jose Albertos, RHP, Chicago Cubs

Sometimes, as a writer, you can use the Cubs (or Red Sox/Yankees/Dodgers) hype machine to your advantage. Albertos is forever away, but has obscene talent and if he merely meets expectations going forward, the hype around him could easily push him into the helium-type profile that often occupies a slot in the 85-101 range of our Dynasty 101. He's got the potential double-plus fastball, and an advanced change that could tear up complex ball/the lower minors, which means that even when he succeeds, we won't be finding out much about him. Talent can always go awry, but there's going to be a lot of confirmation bias if Albertos received, and nothing pushes guys up lists faster than a little bias.

Fernando Tatis, Jr., SS, San Diego Padres

Tatito isn't a great bet to stick at short, but he has the projection (and the big-league bloodlines) to fit the bill for second or third. His broad shoulders portend power growth to pair with a potential solid-average hit tool. While he ran a bit in the lower minors, lower-minors catchers (and pitchers) aren't the most adept at holding guys on, and as he fills out he will slow down. Tatis has a very bright future, but it is dulled a bit by the horizon, as he'll take a while to sort out which tools will come to the fore. This might be a year (or even two) early to jump on the bandwagon, but this one is for the deep leaguers who need to be the first ones in.

Shedric Long, 2B, Cincinnati Reds

While he truly would have intrigued if he remained a backstop, there's plenty to like about Long at the keystone, starting with his speed, which borders on elite. He began the year repeating Low-A, but bumped up to High-A and was better almost across the board, despite the higher talent level and pitcher-friendly league. He's not going to sustain a near-.400 BABIP, but the bar to clear for offensive competency at second base isn't extremely high, traditionally. He's got good pop for his size thanks to above-average bat speed, so there's more than just a chance for empty average here. He's a bit of a funky profile and those guys don't always get the love they deserve, but a repeat performance on High-A will put him squarely on the map.

Wander Javier, SS, Minnesota Twins

Javier is more of a concept than a prospect. He's a potential five-tool type who'll be lighter on the power than the rest, but with only nine games stateside, there's more unknown than there is known. Still, he excited evaluators and showed well in that limited debut. For the prospectors who need to know about a name before they're a name, don't wonder; Wander.

Luis Castillo, RHP, Cincinnati Reds

No, not that one. Perhaps not even that other one. This Castillo was traded to the Padres, then sent back to the Marlins because of Colin Rea's injury, then sent to Cincinnati when Miami decided it needed some Dan Straily in its life. He's going to fall on some boards due to age-relative-to level concerns, but that's less of an issue for pitchers with this type of stuff, in my opinion. He's got 80-grade gas, sitting in the upper-90s and touching triple digits. It doesn't have the wiggle you'd like, but at that velo it doesn't always matter. Refining his slider is going to be crucial to his fantasy value as well as avoiding the bullpen. He might well end up there as a power-reliever, but if he can coax some more consistency out of a slider that flashes plus, his ability to retain his velocity could make him an intriguing middle of the rotation arm.

Top 50 Fantasy Prospects

by Mike Gianella

Do you play in redraft leagues but find that nearly every list out there focuses on prospect value for either real life, dynasty leagues, or both? We understand, which is why we have put together this helpful list of the Top 50 prospects for 2017 only. The purpose of this list is to attempt to identify the prospects who will have the greatest impact on your team this year. While some of these prospects will obviously have more (or less) value in keeper leagues, this is simply a straight up ranking of 2017 value.

Andrew Benintendi, OF, Boston Red Sox

With the caveat that there is no such thing as a safe prospect, Benintendi is one of the safest prospects in baseball thanks to his hit tool. A subpar season for Benintendi in his rookie campaign would likely be a boring .270 batting average without a lot of home runs or steals to go with that tepid average. This is damning with faint praise, though, as the upside is a .300 hitter who could flirt with a 20/20 season. Something in the middle of these two outcomes is likely. Benintendi's ceiling isn't nearly as high as some of the studs who typically populate the top of these lists, but his high floor combined with those strong real life tools make his value rock solid, and make him our top prospect for 2017.

Dansby Swanson, SS, Atlanta Braves

Swanson and Benintendi are similar prospects in terms of their 2017 outlook, and given the position difference and Swanson's slightly better overall tools, it was tempting to put Swanson first overall. It is close, but the Red Sox lineup advantage as well as the possibility that Atlanta is going to move Swanson down in the order give Benintendi a slight edge. This is hardly a knock on Swanson, who is one of the most polished prospects in the game and showed no signs of slowing down after the Braves promoted him to the majors in mid-August. As solid as Swanson's overall numbers were, he did most of his damage in his last 23 games, hitting .351/.417/.568. It's a small sample, of course, but Swanson showed why many believe he has a chance to be special.

Manuel Margot, OF, San Diego Padres

If you want fantasy ceiling, Margot is your guy. The stolen bases alone are going to give him value, and he should provide enough batting average to make him relevant in every format. The challenge with Margot is that we still don't know if he will hold his own against major league pitching, and we do know that there isn't much of a ceiling when it comes to power. Think 25-30 steals with a .260 batting average if Margot sticks; everything else above that is gravy. There is risk in the profile, particularly for 2017, but Margot has the best chance of any player on this list to earn $20 or more in fantasy thanks to the stolen bases.

Josh Bell, 1B, Pittsburgh Pirates

The profile is safe but not exciting in fantasy. This creates a quandary as far as a ranking goes. Batting average is Bell's most likely carrying tool, and even in Rotisserie formats unless he is hitting well over .300 every year this won't ever make him an elite player. However, there is something to be said for Bell's reliability, the fact that he is a relatively safe pick in nearly any format in 2017, and the idea his hit tool should keep him in the majors for the entire season. If you are looking for boom/bust players in shallower formats, look elsewhere. But if you need to lock in stats or ensure that you have a reliable backup in leagues with daily lineup changes, Bell is a good choice.

Yulieski Gurriel, 1B, Houston Astros

In a redraft league, it is understandable if you want to walk on by and avoid a 32-year-old hitter who was subpar in 130 major league plate appearances. However, it is common for Cuban imports to struggle in their first go-round in the majors (Jose Abreu is a significant exception to this rule). Gurriel has been pegged as the best Cuban hitter of his generation, and even though he didn't hit for power in 2016 his contact skills are impressive. Assuming the power shows up even somewhat this year, Gurriel could be a .300 hitter with 15-20 home runs.

Hunter Renfroe, OF, San Diego Padres

Here is the precarious risk between crash-and-burn potential oversus the reward of a prospect who can produce big numbers in the here-and-now. No one doubts the power, and now that Petco isn't a hitters' graveyard it is entirely possible that there is a 25-30 home run season lurking in Renfroe, even as a rookie. The downside is that the poor contact profile destroys Renfroe's batting average and he cannot stick in the majors. The guess from this corner is that Renfroe hits enough to stay in the majors but finishes with a low batting average and lots of home runs. That will play in most formats, and Renfroe should be an asset, even if he is never a star.

Yoan Moncada, 2B, Chicago White Sox

The centerpiece in the deal that allowed Chris Sale to cut ties with the White Sox, Moncada ripped through High-A and Double-A before struggling in a brief appearance with the Red Sox. Ignore those struggles. Moncada is going to eventually hit when he does find his way to the majors. The question with Moncada is when does his 2017 debut happen? If we knew for certain that he would be up on Opening Day, Moncada would rank at or near the top of this list. However, even with Brett Lawrie being shipped out of town, he's no lock to debut before June 1. Moncada should steal a bushel of bases and hit for enough power to make him electric when he does debut, but you might only be getting 300-400 plate appearances from him in 2017.

Tom Murphy, C, Colorado Rockies

Murphy is an excellent example of the differences between evaluating prospects in fantasy versus doing so in reality. Questions about his hit tool in general and his swing in particular are legitimate, and Murphy's ceiling in real life is probably as a second-division first stringer. But as a catcher with over-the-fence power who plays half his games at Coors Field, there is serious fantasy potential. Add to this the fact that Tony Wolters is Murphy's primary competition and you could be looking at a Top 15 fantasy catcher in Murphy, even if Murphy only plays 90-100 games.

Tyler Glasnow, P, Pittsburgh Pirates

One of the biggest challenges of putting any composite fantasy ranking together is correctly weighing pitcher value. On ability and ceiling alone, Glasnow should rightfully rank ahead of most of these hitters. But this is a one-and-done ranking for 2017. If rookie hitters are difficult to predict, rookie pitchers are a near impossibility. But Glasnow has a job, is in a very good pitchers' park, and has a very good outfield defense behind him, particularly now that Andrew McCutchen has been moved out of center field. Oh, and Glasnow's stuff is legit. When he is on, major league hitters have trouble squaring up against him. Consistency has been an issue, and while Glasnow could take a big step forward this year, he could also put up an ERA around four and simply be pedestrian.

Mitch Haniger, OF, Seattle Mariners

On the surface, Haniger's advanced age and the fact that he put up his stats in the PCL are two strikes against him. However, this isn't merely the case of an older player feasting on young pitching in the advanced minors. Haniger worked with Bob Tewksbary on a swing adjustment and the former first round pick finally put together the numbers people were expecting from him as a prospect way back in 2012. The power profile is legitimate, and even if everything else is mediocre or worse, the possibility of full-time at bats and a 20-25 home run season catapult Haninger into the Top 10.

Dan Vogelbach, "1B", Seattle Mariners

Dammit, I already used the fantasy/real life example under Murphy. Vogelbach is kind of the same deal, except that he is a first baseman and not a catcher, which doesn't make the reality/fantasy split nearly as extreme. Vogelbach is supposed to start for the Mariners, albeit in a platoon with Danny Valencia, but even with only 450-500 plate appearances, Vogelbach could hit 15 home runs and a .280 batting average. The first base eligibility pushes Vogelbach a little bit higher than he would rank as a DH-only, but since this is a 2017 list only, you don't have to worry yourself about that for now.

Andrew Toles, OF, Los Angeles Dodgers

Toles is the kind of player the prospect guys don't like at all. They'll spend a lot of time knocking his tools and relegate Toles to a "platoon role/fourth outfield" future. While this is certainly possible, Toles is slated to get regular plate appearances for Los Angeles while appearing in a strong lineup. A 10 home run, 20 steal season with a .280 average is a realistic possibility, and while that may sound boring, that will top what most of the hitters on this list will do in 2017. In dynasty, it is fair if you want to steer clear of Toles for some more higher ceiling guys. In redraft leagues, take the value on Toles if your league lets you.

Robert Gsellman, P, New York Mets

The debate about Gsellman revolves around the idea of "pop-up" pitchers, and whether or not he will be able to maintain his gains in 2017. If he has truly mastered the Warthen slider, the answer to that question is "mostly yes", even if the fastball velocity does lose a couple of ticks. Of more pertinent note to fantasy managers is Gsellman's 4.22 DRA and 97 cFIP, which indicate that there was more than a little luck on Gsellman's side last year. This isn't a knock on the overall package. At a minimum, Gsellman should be a middle-of-the-road starter with the opportunity for more.

Jharel Cotton, P, Oakland Athletics

Cotton profiles as a back-end starter in the long-term. This ranking rebels against that profile. Thus far, Cotton has been successful with his repertoire, which means it is possible you could get a 3.50 ERA and a decent WHIP thanks to the first-time-through-the-league-phenomenon combined with the positive park effects. Cotton is always going to be homer prone, but great control and a low walk rate will mitigate the damage. Pitchers like Cotton who aren't highly regarded as prospects are almost always underrated in short-term leagues. Take Cotton in your redraft league over more highly touted pitchers and let others be prouder of their "sleeper" picks who will never see the light of day in the majors this year.

Aaron Judge, OF, New York Yankees

Even in an era when it seems like half of your fantasy lineup has 20 home run potential, Judge's power potential stands out. The batting average makes him risky, and even in the Yankees' rebuilding mode there won't be as much wiggle room as there might be in other organizations. But even with a low batting average profile, the potential for a 30+ home run season with a .240 batting average cannot be ignored. Judge could be a poor man's version of Khris Davis at a much cheaper price.

Charlie Tilson, OF, Chicago White Sox

Tilson doesn't have much of a ceiling, and if you did a straw poll among scouts he would likely be tabbed as a fourth outfielder, at best. What Tilson does have is an opportunity to play full-time for the rebuilding White Sox, as they look to see how things shake out for them with a number of prospects but also with some reclamation projects. Tilson doesn't do much except run, but in traditional Rotisserie formats, 20-30 stolen bases with a .260 batting average would make Tilson viable in every format from 15-team mixed and deeper.

Jose De Leon, P, Tampa Bay Rays

The scouting/stats schism isn't nearly what it once was, but once in a while a player generates healthy debate about his potential versus what he has done thus far. So it is with De Leon, who has breezed through the minors but who also has many questioning how successful he can be without a dominant fastball. The good news for fantasy managers in redraft leagues is that you can mostly avoid these kinds of debates and focus primarily on De Leon's positives. He is a polished pitcher with good command who should be able to step right into Tampa's rotation when called upon and give your team a reliable, fourth starter's level of production with a relatively limited amount of risk.

Lucas Giolito, P, Chicago White Sox

Giolito represents the other side of the short term/long term coin. Ranked 10th overall on Baseball Prospectus' Top 101, Giolito's long-term potential is amazing, but for 2017 alone it is difficult to rank a pitcher who struggled so much in 2016 any higher than this. Yes, Giolito flashed his ace potential at times, but more often than not he struggled to maintain consistency, particularly with his off-speed offerings, and was pounded into submission by more experienced batters in Triple-A and the majors. Perhaps Giolito gets his head on straight this year and tosses 100 great innings for the White Sox, but that ugly PECOTA projection of a 4.75 ERA and a 1.53 WHIP is not out of the realm of possibility. We just don't know which version of Giolito will show up this year.

Luke Weaver, P, St. Louis Cardinals

Yawn. Weaver doesn't excite the prospect watchers all that much, and his limited sample size in the majors didn't inspire much confidence with the fantasy types either. But he will likely have another opportunity in St. Louis, particularly now that Alex Reyes will miss the entire 2017 season. Weaver has a solid fastball with lots of hop, but he plays as a two-pitch pitcher who major league hitters should be able to hit. The Cardinals do have a track record of success with players like this, which gives Weaver more upside than if here were in another organization, but even so what you're paying for here is volume.

Albert Almora, OF, Chicago Cubs

Will Almora play enough to generate fantasy value in anything outside of an NL-only league? Currently, the answer appears to be no. However, Joe Maddon showed last year that he is great at maximizing roster value so it shouldn't surprise anyone if Almora gets most of the starts against left-handers while spelling Kyle Schwarber in left field just enough to get close to full-time at bats. Even then, the problem is that the offensive profile is solid, not sexy. Maybe there will be 15 or so steals to go with a solid batting average and a little bit of pop, but even that is a tad optimistic. Even Almora's pessimistic projection plays out as a superior defensive version of Jon Jay, so it is quite possible that at some point during the season Almora and Jay flip roles.

Matt Strahm, P, Kansas City Royals

With the signings of Jason Hammel and Travis Wood, Strahm is blocked in Kansas City and is likely to start the season in the bullpen, limiting his value. However, Strahm could be on the Danny Duffy path, where he starts the season in the bullpen and then makes his way into the rotation if or when there is a need due to injury. Even if Strahm is only a relief arm, there is still value in deeper formats even if he only pitches 100-120 innings. Don't be surprised if Strahm emerges as a David Phelps/Christopher Devenski type right away.

Reynaldo Lopez, P, Chicago White Sox

Another part of the package that the Nationals shipped to Chicago in exchange for Adam Eaton, Lopez obviously doesn't come anywhere near Giolito's ceiling, but it is possible that he surpasses Giolito's value just in 2017. Lopez throws hard and has a curve that at times is brilliant but his inconsistency at this point in his development speaks to a wide range of outcomes. Giolito and Lopez both rank higher on this list than they would have with the Nationals simply because the short-term opportunity is much better in Chicago than it would have been in Washington.

Lewis Brinson, OF, Milwaukee Brewers

Do you want to play the upside game? If so, Brinson is your guy, even in redraft leagues. He is closer to the majors than you think, and even though he is unlikely to break camp with the big club on Opening Day, a fast start in the minors could put punch Brinson's ticket sooner rather than later. He's also behind Keon Broxton, a boom-or-bust guy in his own right who doesn't nearly have the ceiling that Brinson does. There is a good deal of downside with Brinson, and he could crash and burn. But even if the batting average is a drag, Brinson's power/speed potential plays, especially in the cozy confines of Miller Park.

Roman Quinn, OF, Philadelphia Phillies

Quinn isn't the best Phillies prospect on this list – he barely even cracked the organization's Top 10 – but if you've been reading this list the entire way through and aren't just randomly skipping around you know the deal. Speed plays in fantasy. Quinn is going to steal lots of bases. Whether he does that as a starting outfielder for the Fightins or as a fourth outfielder will have a lot to say about his fantasy value, but Quinn will most definitely have value in 2017. Quinn may not even break camp with the team, but the oft-injured, aged obstacles in front of him are far less intimidating than the young, athletic ones in the minors behind him.

Bradley Zimmer, OF, Cleveland Indians

Had Zimmer continued at the same trajectory he was on entering 2016, he would be at least 10 spots higher on this list, even without assurances of a major league job. Instead, there are questions about his hit tool and whether he can survive in the big leagues. The batting eye gives Zimmer a little more leeway than most prospects who hit .250 in the minors last year, but even with this working for him, Zimmer isn't as much of a "lock" as he once was. All this being said, Lonnie Chisenhall and Tyler Naquin aren't serious obstacles to Zimmer getting an opportunity if Zimmer turns it around and that speed is going to play in fantasy.

Josh Hader, P, Milwaukee Brewers

The numbers in Colorado Springs were bad, but every pitcher in Colorado Springs puts up awful numbers. The larger concern is the inconsistency that dogged Hader and may have put him on a slower track in the short term. On the other hand, the Brewers rotation in front of Hader isn't strong or deep, and Hader's high 90s fastball puts him on the cusp of a promotion at nearly any time. Hader's DRA and cFIP were far more favorable than his bloated Colorado Springs ERA, so don't be surprised if he's up early.

Jacoby Jones, OF, Detroit Tigers

It's more likely than not that Jones flames out, as his tools have still not translated to skills and Jones is hardly a spring chicken. But the opportunity is there for him in Detroit if he can handle center, as both Tyler Collins and Mikie Mahtook won't stand in Jones' way if he does manage to put it all together. The ceiling is 15 home runs and 25 steals, and while that's extremely unlikely to happen, the fact that there is even a slim possibility of it happening is what puts Jones over several superior prospects on this list.

Raimel Tapia, OF, Colorado Rockies

With Carlos Gonzalez, Charlie Blackmon, David Dahl, and Gerardo Parra ahead of him on the depth chart, Tapia is completely blocked at the major league level. He is a Rockies prospect, though, so his immense fantasy potential when he does get the call cannot be ignored. The argument against Tapia is the same argument that was made last winter against Trevor Story. In November, Story's rise to fantasy relevance was as unlikely as Tapia's is right now. Tapia only needs a trade, an injury, or both to find his way to the Rockies. If he does, he gets a big boost thanks to the ridiculous home field advantage that nearly every Rockie gets.

Austin Meadows, OF, Pittsburgh Pirates

Meadows is in the same position as Tapia with the following exceptions. First, he plays in a pitchers' park. Second, he is blocked but the Pirates would trade Andrew McCutcheon if they could find a taker. Meadows hasn't displayed a ton of power yet, but has the kind of bat that should play up in the majors. Even if it doesn't, high batting averages with solid speed are realistic expectations for Meadows. Meadows' value in 2017 is going to be all about the rumor mill, unless there is a serious injury to someone in front of him in Pittsburgh.

J.P. Crawford, SS, Philadelphia Phillies

Crawford was terrible at Triple-A last season, and even accounting for the pitcher-friendly nature of Coca Cola Park, it is next-to-impossible to positively spin a .644 OPS. All that being said, top prospects have a way of quickly figuring things out/turning it around/making the adjustments far more quickly than mere mortals do. Crawford's contact rates remained solid at every level and he's not as far away from righting the ship – or from cracking the Phillies lineup – as his raw stats might make you think. Crawford could quickly find his way to Philadelphia, and if he does, a 5-10 home run, 15-20 steal pace with an OK batting average is a realistic possibility.

Clint Frazier, OF, New York Yankees

The Yankees have little incentive to rush Frazier, but the talented, cocksure prospect may force their hand if he performs well in the early going in the minors. He struggled in brief exposure at Triple-A, but Frazier's power/speed combination make him worth watching, especially since the Yankees are likely to be auditioning many of their future stars sooner rather than later. Frazier's earliest ETA is in the middle of the season, but there is enough potential goodness here to rank him more aggressively than many of the mid-season call-ups listed lower.

Seth Lugo, P, New York Mets

Lugo is not expected to begin the season in the majors, but nearly every arm in the Mets' rotation has injury and/or durability question marks, so expect Lugo to get some starts during the season. The DRA and low strikeout rate screams stay away in large crimson letters, but Lugo's pitching smarts combined with Dan Warthen's strong work in producing yet another major league overachiever cannot be overlooked.

Ozzie Albies, 2B, Atlanta Braves

Albies is the kind of prospect whose minor league numbers won't give you much of an indication of what he'll do in the majors, mostly because he has been very young at every level. The acquisition of Brandon Phillips makes an Opening Day appearance in Atlanta by Albies a near impossibility, but Phillips won't be an obstacle for Albies' eventual arrival. The Braves won't be afraid to promote Albies when they deem he is ready, and that could be as soon as this summer, although an elbow injury does push Albies' timetable back somewhat. The speed will play no matter what Albies does with the bat.

Nick Williams, OF, Philadelphia Phillies

Maybe 2016 was the first we got to see of the real Nick Williams and he'll never amount to anything as a prospect. Just kidding. There is still a great deal of talent, and a very real possibility that he could be a first division regular. It won't happen on Opening Day and it might not even happen in 2017, but the multiple opportunities in Philadelphia combined with Williams's talent make him worth watching and give him a ranking a little bit higher than it would be for a lesser talent.

Jesse Winker, OF, Cincinnati Reds

Winker wasn't exactly disappointing as a hitter, but the power that many were hoping for disappeared almost entirely in 2016, in part due to a wrist injury. Opportunities are there on the rebuilding Reds, and while Winker isn't a high-end prospect he is almost ready and will likely get a chance to show what he can do in Cincinnati at some point during the season.

Brock Stewart, P, Los Angeles Dodgers

The Dodgers rotation is stacked, but they have already discussed the possibility of rotating arms in and out of the rotation to save innings and wear and tear on the staff's arms. This is where Stewart comes in. His major league numbers were terrible, but Stewart has been stellar throughout his professional career and was mostly the victim of a few bad innings last year. He could be a disaster yet again, but it is also possible that he throws 50-100 decent innings for the Dodgers.

Rio Ruiz, 3B, Atlanta Braves

Ruiz isn't all that impressive from a prospecting perspective. But he has already made it to Atlanta (albeit for a brief cup of coffee in September) and the only obstacle standing between Ruiz and a starting job for the Braves is Adonis Garcia. It is possible that Ruiz simply sits in Triple-A all year, but he could win the job early this year if Garcia struggles in any appreciable way.

Sean Newcomb, P, Atlanta Braves

Newcomb has less of a chance to make the majors than nearly every pitcher on this list but more of a chance to do big things because of how good his raw stuff is. Newcomb's command is a work in progress if we're being polite, and very messy if we are not. Pitchers with his ability don't grow on trees (no pitches grow on trees if we're being exact) so if you're looking for upside as opposed to stability, grab Newcomb and hope for the best.

Steven Brault, P, Pittsburgh Pirates

He was bad in Pittsburgh, but the turnaround in Indianapolis combined with the Pirates' good track record with getting the most out of their pitchers cannot be ignored. The park and the possibility that Brault squeezes into a rotation that lacks depth pushes him a few spots ahead of some similar, low ceiling arms on contending teams.

Jeff Hoffman, P, Colorado Rockies

Hoffman has a legitimate opportunity to spend the entire season in a major league rotation. Because that rotation is Colorado's, Hoffman ranks much lower than he would in nearly every other park. This is a high-risk pick and because he doesn't nearly have the ceiling that teammate Jon Gray does it isn't a high reward pick. Hoffman is best left to NL-only owners in 2017. The uptick in whiffs at Triple-A last year is a positive.

Franklin Barreto, SS, Oakland Athletics

My instinct is that Barreto spends all of 2017 in Triple-A, which is why he is ranked so low on this list. But even given is youth, Barreto could move very quickly through his final stop on the minor league ladder and find his way to the majors. His PECOTA projection of six home runs, nine steals, a .249 batting average in 250 plate appearances would be a nice season for a 21-year-old rookie.

Jorge Alfaro, C, Philadelphia Phillies

Rookie catchers who aren't going to start the season in the big leagues typically don't populate lists like this one. But then there is Alfaro, a high end prospect who significantly improved his pitch calling and does enough with the bat that he could be a productive regular right away. He is blocked by Cameron Rupp, but if Alfaro is ready and able he'll find his way to Philadelphia.

Austin Voth, P, Washington Nationals

With Giolito and Lopez off to Chicago, Voth becomes the Nationals in-case-of-emergency-send-a-frantic-text-to-Syracuse guy. The stuff is pedestrian but Voth has more than proven himself in the minors at every step and could be one of those pitchers whose durability and repeatability allows him to have some success in the majors. The added opportunities for wins on a strong team like the Nationals doesn't hurt.

Ty Blach, P, San Francisco Giants

Blach is going to iffy even in mono leagues thanks to that marginal strikeout rate. But he throws strikes, and if he does make it to the Giants will have a very good defense behind him and a great park when he is at home. The ceiling is limited because you're looking at a throwback who pitches to contact, but he is a smart pitcher and maybe he'll fool major league hitters his first time through the league.

Amed Rosario, SS, New York Mets

Rosario is blocked by Neil Walker and Asdrubal Cabrera up the middle, but the Mets infield isn't exactly the epitome of health, so Rosario could get an opportunity in 2017. It's more likely that he doesn't, but the talent is so great that he is worth putting on this list as a hedge, even if he never sees the light of day this year.

Dominic Smith, 1B, New York Mets

As is the case with Rosario, it is likely that Smith spends the entire year at Triple-A, but given that Lucas Duda had a back issue in 2016 and still has not logged significant playing time upon his return, there is a possibility that we see Smith at Citi Field at some point this summer. The fantasy potential is not tremendous, but Smith is a good hitter who should survive in the majors even if he doesn't thrive.

Brent Honeywell, P, Tampa Bay Rays

Most of the ETAs for Honeywell are in 2018, but if there is a pitcher who could fly through the minors quickly and defy the odds it is Honeywell, a fun pitcher who drew a Ginny Baker comp in the Baseball Prospectus annual. Honeywell has the poise that more than makes up for the lack of an overpowering pitch, and he's more fun than some of the vanilla pitchers ranked ahead of him.

Trey Mancini, 1B, Baltimore Orioles

For a little while there, it looked like the Orioles game of chicken with Mark Trumbo might end with Mancini nabbing a starting slot for the Orioles on Opening Day. Instead, Mancini probably will head down to Triple-A and wait for an injury on the big club (there is some chatter that he could be a bench player on Opening Day). The power potential in that park is fun, but it won't do much for you in the minors or on Baltimore's bench.

Jae-gwun Hwang, 3B, San Francisco Giants

When it comes to anticipated production, Korean imports are difficult to predict. But after posting in the winter of 2015/2016 and receiving no interest, Hwang committed to a rigorous strength and conditioning program and saw a significant boost in his KBO stats in 2016. These stats must always be taken with a grain of salt, but the drop in Hwang's strikeout rate was encouraging, and a sign that he could be more than Triple-A insurance. Hwang is likely to be a reserve, but Joe Panik and Eduardo Nunez aren't certainties.

Chance Sisco, C, Baltimore Orioles

Mid-season promotions of catchers are rare, particularly when those catchers are still adjusting to their position, but the hit tool with Sisco is strong enough that it would be remiss not to at least mention him on this list. The fantasy profile doesn't sizzle because of a lack of power, but Sisco is supposed to grow into that, and Baltimore is a great place for a hitter to add more home runs, especially a talented one like Sisco.

Index of Names

Made in the USA
Middletown, DE
28 June 2017